KARL BARTH

Preaching Through the Christian Year

KARL BARTH

Preaching Through the Christian Year

A Selection of Exegetical Passages
from the *Church Dogmatics*

Taken from the English Translation, edited by
G. W. BROMILEY AND T. F. TORRANCE

Selected by

JOHN McTAVISH
Minister of the United Church of Canada,
Bracebridge, Ontario,

and

HAROLD WELLS
Chaplain and Lecturer in Theology,
National University of Lesotho, Roma, Lesotho.

WM. B. EERDMANS PUBLISHING COMPANY
GRAND RAPIDS, MICHIGAN

This selection from the English translation
Copyright © T. & T. Clark Ltd. 1978
This American edition through special arrangement with/
T. & T. Clark by Wm. B. Eerdmans Publishing Co.,
Grand Rapids, Mich. 49503

Library of Congress Cataloging in Publication Data

Barth, Karl, 1886-1968.
    Karl Barth, preaching through the Christian year.

    1. Theology, Doctrinal.   I.   McTavish, John.
II. Wells, Harold.   III. Title.
BT75.B2834   1978   230   77-16275
ISBN 0-8028-1725-4

Second printing, December 1979

PREFACE

KARL BARTH made it absolutely clear at the outset that dogmatic theology is not an end in itself but exists to serve the proclamation of the Church. This selection from his *Church Dogmatics* has been compiled by two ministers whose responsibility it is to proclaim the Word of God weekly in the congregation. In discharging this responsibility we have found the *Dogmatics* a rich source of understanding and wish to commend it to our colleagues. We realise that those thirteen formidable tomes (containing over six million words) understandably intimidate the busy pastor. Yet we are convinced of the indispensability of careful biblical and theological reflection as the only basis for a powerful proclamation of the Gospel. Can we perhaps whet the appetite of others faced with the task of speaking to the contemporary Church a clear and persuasive word well-informed by a rigorous study of the Bible ? To this end we have searched the *Dogmatics* for some of the most significant exegetical passages which occur in the " fine print." In arranging the passages we have kept in mind the Church Year to facilitate sermon preparation. This is not to say that biblical scholars and laypersons will not also find the book of value, particularly as it brings to light the main teaching of Barth as grounded on its biblical basis.

The exegetical counterpart to this volume can be found as " Aids to the Preacher " in T. & T. Clark's recently published English translation of the *Registerband*. We hope that *Karl Barth : Preaching Through the Christian Year* and the new *Index Volume* will guide the reader to greater use of the *Church Dogmatics* work.

v

CONTENTS

CHAPTER I

GOD

1. THE KNOWLEDGE OF GOD IN HIS WORKS

Here again we have pointed to a thread running through the Bible. It is well known what great weight Luther laid upon it. It was for him no less than a principal rule of all knowledge of God. He continually spoke of it with great energy in all possible connexions. When we speak and hear about God we are not concerned with the *nuda essentia* or *natura* of God, but with the *velamen*, the *volucra*, the *certa species*, the *larvae* of His works. We must keep to them according to God's wise and unbreakable ordinance. We must be thankful for them. We must not disregard them, or prefer any direct, non-objective knowledge of God. If we do, we run the risk, not only of losing God, but of making Him hostile to us. We must seek Him where He Himself has sought us—in those veils and under those signs of His Godhead. Elsewhere He is not to be found. There can be no doubt that these affirmations have no little force in the Bible itself, in view of what it indicates and declares to be faith.

It is definitely a mistake to point to the visions and auditions of the prophets and others (in which, apparently, no means or signs enter in), or to the ever-recurring simple formula: " And God spake," as a proof that the Bible allows revelation of God and therefore knowledge of God in His naked, primary objectivity as well, and therefore without the veil of His works and signs.

In opposition to that we have to set first Ex. 33^11-23. We can hardly understand this except as a confirmation of Luther's general rule, and it forms a background for the understanding of all the rest. It says there of Moses that the Lord spake with him face to face, as a man speaks with his friend (v. 11). What does that mean ? We read in what follows that Moses called upon God in consequence of God saying to him : " I know thee by name, and thou hast also found grace in my sight." Thereupon Moses wished to know of God's " ways "—that is, to " know " Him (v. 13) as the One who would " go up with them " in the move from Sinai to Canaan which He had commanded. " If thy presence go not with me, carry us not up hence. For wherein shall it be known here that I and thy people have found grace in thy sight ? is it not in that thou goest with us ? so shall we be separated, I and thy people, from all the people that are upon the face of the earth " (v. 15 f.). God replies that this very thing shall take place. Moses insists that he would see the glory of the Lord (v. 18). And not even this request meets with a blank refusal. No ; God will make to pass before him " all his glory," and he shall hear the name of the Lord : " I will be gracious to whom I will be gracious, and will shew mercy on whom I will shew mercy " (v. 19). But it is precisely in the passing before of God that Moses is to hear His name. " Thou canst not see my face : for there shall no man see me, and live " (v. 20). This " passing before " obviously means that His prayed and awaited going with them had begun, that God actually does go before him and the people. And in this " passing before " God will place him in the cleft of a rock and spread His hand over him so that he can only see Him from the back (and hence in the process of that passing before and going with and going before). It is in this way and not in any other that he can and shall see the glory of God. It is in this way that

God speaks with Moses " face to face, as a man speaketh with his friend." God really speaks with him. Moses hears God's name. He is really encouraged and given directions by God Himself. He knows God, as he has prayed—God in His extremest objectivity. But all this comes to pass in God's passing before and going before, in God's work and action, in which he does not see God's face but in which he can only follow God with his eyes. In this case, more than that would not only be less, but even nothing at all—indeed, something negative. Man cannot see God's face, God's naked objectivity, without exposing himself to the annihilating wrath of God. It would indeed have to be a second God who could see God directly. How could man escape destruction by God ? Hence God shows Moses a two-fold mercy : not only does He actually receive him according to His promise ; but also He does it in a way that is adapted to him as a creature, and speaks to him through the sign of His work. We can hardly presuppose that any of the other scriptural passages and references that should be considered in this context teach anything in opposition to this indirect knowledge of God. Rather we shall have to assume that, even in those passages where means and signs of God's appearance or speaking are not expressly mentioned, they are nevertheless taken for granted by the biblical writers. They always mean the God who is present and revealed to man in His secondary objectivity, in His work.

As far as the prophetic formula : " And God spake " is concerned, we cannot sufficiently keep in mind that the whole of Old Testament prophecy seeks to be, and is, nothing but the proclamation of God in the form of continual explanation of the divine work, of the action of God in the history of Israel, that is to say, in what had happened and what was happening to Israel, beginning with the Exodus as its epitome. It is this God in action, and indeed, this God in His action itself—and hence the God whom they can only follow with their eyes, whom they only know from behind in His secondary objectivity—who speaks to the prophets, and whose words the prophets deliver and whose name they proclaim. How else or whence else could they know Him ? What else could they have to say about Him ? He really stands before them ; He really speaks to them ; they really hear Him. But all this takes place, not in a direct, but in an indirect encounter. What directly confront them are the historical events, forms and relationships which are His work. They see this work, but as followers, as contemporaries of this history, and partly also in expectation of its future continuation. This " Opposite " speaks to them and they hear His voice. Yet not in the same way that we let any sort of event or all events work upon ourselves, and attempt to read out of history in general or out of this or that piece of history what we have first read into it. But they hear Him as prophets of God—and as such, as God's special witnesses and bearers of the divine work—before whose eyes that special event is placed as what it is, the secondary objectivity of God Himself, in which He gives Himself to be known and in which they really know Him.

Moreover, the message of the New Testament is nothing but the proclamation of the name of God on the ground of His gracious " passing before." And it is given in the form of a continual explanation of a definite historical event—of the same historical event that began with the Exodus, even with the call of Abraham, even with the covenant with Noah. But now its concrete aim and its totality become quite clear. The Messiah, the promised Son of Abraham and David, the Servant of Yahweh, the Prophet, Priest and King has appeared ; and not only as sent by God, but Himself God's Son. Yet the Word does not appear in His eternal objectivity as the Son who alone dwells in the bosom of the Father. No ; the Word became flesh. God gives Himself to be known, and is known, in the substance of secondary objectivity, in the sign of all signs, in the work of God which all the other works of God serve to prepare, accompany and continue, in the manhood which He takes to Himself, to which He humbles Himself and which

He raises through Himself. " We saw His glory " now means : we saw this One in His humanity, the humanity of the Son of God, on His way to death, which was the way to His resurrection. Hence, it is again an indirect encounter with God in which the apostles, as the witnesses of the New Testament, find themselves. They, too, stand before a veil, a sign, a work of God. In the crib of Bethlehem and at the cross of Golgotha the event takes place in which God gives Himself to them to be known and in which they know God. The fact that they see this in the light of the resurrection, and that in the forty days they see it as what it really is, God's own presence and action, does not alter the fact that in the forty days they do see this unambiguously secondary objectivity, and in it as such, and attested by it, they know the primary objectivity and hence God Himself. The fact that the God-manhood of the Mediator Jesus Christ is the fulfilment of the revelation and reconciliation proclaimed in the New Testament is equivalent to the fact that the knowledge of faith in the New Testament is indirect (and for that very reason real !) knowledge of God.

And it is precisely this knowledge of faith, attested in the Old and New Testaments as the knowledge of God from His works, which is now the content of knowledge in the message of the Church of Jesus Christ. Since this message is the Gospel of its Lord and therefore of the God-man, the Mediator, it stands in explicit contrast to any message having the pure and naked objectivity of God Himself as its object. It is the Gospel of faith and the summons to faith in that it proclaims God—really God Himself—in His mediability, in the sign of His work, in His clothed objectivity. And it is this just because it does not leave the realm of indirect knowledge of God, but keeps to the fact that in this very realm God Himself—and therefore all things—is to be sought and found, and that this indirect knowledge is the right and true knowledge of God because it is chosen and ordained by God Himself. Letting this be enough for oneself is not resignation but the humility and boldness of the man who really stands before God in faith, and in faith alone. The Gospel of the Church of God is therefore of necessity a defined, circumscribed and limited message. It does not contain and say anything and everything. Its content is not the ἄπειρον, the boundless and groundless that human presumption would like to make God out to be. It does not destroy perception but integrates it. It does not oppose a definite and concrete view but establishes it. It does not teach thought to lose itself in an unthinkable one and all, but forms it to very definite concepts—affirming this and denying that, including this and excluding that. It contains the veritable Gospel, the Gospel of Jesus Christ, the Messiah of Israel, the true God who became also true man in His own time and place. It explains, not an idea of God, but His name revealed in His deeds. And in correspondence with its content it is itself objective in form—visible Church, audible preaching, operative sacrament. These constitute an area of objectivity among and alongside so many other areas of objectivity ; but this is grounded on the witness of the apostles and prophets which must be shown and proved objectively. Nor is it ashamed of this witness : on the contrary, it boasts of it as just one book among many others. Christian faith as knowledge of the true God lets itself be included in this area of objectivity, and allows itself to be kept in this area, which in itself and as such is certainly not identical with the objectivity of God. But in it God's work takes place, and hence God's own objectivity gives itself to be known and is to be known, and this on the strength of the choice and sanctification of His free grace. We shall have to destroy the very roots of the Church of Jesus Christ and annihilate faith itself if we want to deny and put an end to the area of secondary objectivity ; if, to reach a supposedly better knowledge of God, we want to disregard and pass over the veil, the sign, the work in which He gives Himself to be known by man without diminution but rather in manifestation of His glory as the One He is. Faith either lives in this sphere, or it is not faith at all. And just the same thing is also true of the knowledge of God through faith.   [II, 1, pp. 18–21]

__2. THE NAME OF GOD

We are reminded of the clear presentation of this matter in Exodus 3—the meeting of Moses with Yahweh at Horeb. Moses sees the angel of God and therefore Yahweh Himself under this form. But the form is that of a thorn bush which burns without burning away : a devouring fire, which is not consumed ; a creature living and sustained ; and at the heart of it the presence of Him who is its boundary and dissolution ; sacramental reality (v. 2). This incomprehensible event is the revelation of Yahweh. The text emphasises that Moses is at first inclined to regard and understand this event in the way that man will always attempt to regard and understand even the most incomprehensible event in his world of created things (v. 3). In fact, revelation takes place in his place and sphere. But now, from out of the burning bush he is addressed by his human name of Moses by Him who reveals Himself. And the summons is a warning. He cannot and must not approach here in the way that we approach any conceivable or inconceivable being in the creaturely sphere : " Put off thy shoes from off thy feet, for the place whereon thou standest is holy ground " (v. 5). Who is He who is present and speaks here in the form of a burning yet not consuming fire ? What is the significance of this creature which Moses sees, supremely threatened and yet sustained ? Why and to what degree is this holy ground ? Behind the first form there now appears a second. Yahweh speaks. He is the God of his fathers, the God of Abraham, the God of Isaac and the God of Jacob. And now it says of Moses that he hid his face, " for he was afraid to look upon God." The One who acts towards and with the patriarchs, who called and led and delivered them—He is the One who consumes and sustains, who sustains and consumes. Moses now knows that the One whom he would consider and understand comes to him in the way that He came to his fathers. For this reason he knows that he cannot look upon Him. For this reason, he is afraid (v. 6). And the One who comes to him as the God of his fathers does so by now calling and commissioning him also. His action of consuming and sustaining, sustaining and consuming, will continue by his ministry in the future history of Israel. Yahweh is " come down to deliver them out of the hand of the Egyptians, and to bring them up out of the land, unto a land flowing with milk and honey " (v. 8). But Moses still seems not to have fully understood, and asks : "Who am I, that I should go unto Pharaoh, and that I should bring forth the children of Israel out of Egypt ? " (v. 11). And in strict correspondence with this self-defensive question, he asks another : " What is thy name ? " (v. 13)—as if the name " the God of your fathers " were not sufficient. His first question is answered : " I will be with thee," and the second is answered, obviously again in strict correspondence with the former answer : " I am that I am " (v. 14). The translation, " I am He who truly is " has been attempted in the light of the LXX ('Εγώ εἰμι ὁ ὤν) but it is quite impossible in this context. For if the annunciation of this name by God Himself represents, so to speak, a third form of the revelation in which He gives Himself to be known to Moses, the third form definitely has to be understood in the same direction and as an interpretation of the other two. " I am that I am " is none other than the God of the fathers. This is borne out by what follows. If the Israelites ask " who has sent him," then, according to v. 14, he is to say : " I am " has sent me to you. Or, according to v. 15, again expressly : " Yahweh the God of your fathers, the God of Abraham, the God of Isaac, and the God of Jacob, hath sent me unto you : this is my name for ever and this is my memorial unto all generations." Whether we take the verb as present or as future " I am that I am" means : " I am who *I* am (or, who *I* will be)." But that means the One of whom there is no other objective definition but what He gives of Himself by being who He is and by acting as He does. There is therefore no objective definition that we can discover for ourselves. We might say of this revelation of

His name that it consists in the refusal of a name, but even in the form of this substantial refusal it is still really revelation, communication and illumination. For Yahweh means the Lord, the I who gives Himself to be known in that He exists as the I of the Lord and therefore acts only as a He and can be called upon only as a Thou in His action, without making Himself known in His I-ness as if He were a creature. We must now glance at Exodus 33[19], where the same name is expressly paraphrased by the words: " I am gracious to whom I am gracious and shew mercy on whom I shew mercy." God is the One who is called in this way and not another : as He posits and gives Himself in His action. God is the One whose being can be investigated only in the form of a continuous question as to His action. Any other name is not the name of God. Any knowledge of any other name is not the knowledge of God. It is in this way and not another that God stands before man. [II, 1, pp. 60–61]

3. THE UNITY OF GOD

It is worth while recalling first the whole passage, Deut. 4[32-40] : " For ask now of the days that are past, which were before thee, since the day that God created man upon the earth, and from the one end of heaven unto the other, whether there has been any such thing as this great thing is, or hath been heard like it ? Did ever people hear the voice of God speaking out of the midst of the fire, as thou hast heard, and live ? Or hath God assayed to go and take him a nation from the midst of another nation, by temptations, by signs, and by wonders, and by war, and by a mighty hand, and by great terrors, according to all that the Lord your God did for you in Egypt before your eyes ? Unto you it was shewed, that thou mightest know that the Lord he is God : there is none else beside him. Out of heaven he made thee to hear his voice, that he might instruct thee : and upon earth he made thee to see his great fire : and thou heardest his words out of the midst of the fire. And because he loved thy fathers, therefore he chose their seed after them, and brought thee out with his presence, with his great power, out of Egypt ; to drive out nations from before thee greater and mightier than thou, to bring thee in, to give thee their land for an inheritance, as at this day. Know therefore this day, and lay it to thine heart, that the Lord he is God in heaven above and upon the earth beneath : there is none else. And thou shalt keep his statutes, and his commandments, which I command thee this day, that it may go well with thee, and with thy children after thee, and that thou mayest prolong thy days upon the land, which the Lord thy God giveth thee, for ever." And then this recalling of the acts of God's love becomes the basis of the repetition of the Ten Commandments (Deut. 5[1f.]). The first of these : " Thou shalt have no other gods before me " is explicitly based on the words : " I am the Lord thy God that brought thee out of the land of Egypt, out of the house of bondage," and the inculcation of the divine law in Deut. 6 has as its basis the *fundamentum classicum* (so P. v. Mastricht, *Theor. Pract. Theol.*, 1698, II, 8) : " Hear, O Israel : the Lord our God is one Lord : and thou shalt love the Lord thy God with all thine heart, and with all thy soul, and with all thy might " (Deut. 6[4]). If we consult Exodus 20 we see that this is not a mere Deuteronomic construction. There the first commandment has the same decisive basis. And in the context in which they appear the whole ten can have the significance only of the proclamation of the truth which is immediately seen to be valid life-truth for Israel by reason of what Yahweh has actually given Israel, a truth which draws its power, and therefore supreme power, wholly from this actuality. It is not at all the case, then, that we have here first a God who says and does all kinds of things, and then an idea of uniqueness, and that these two have to be brought together in some way, so that this God clothes himself or is even clothed with the characteristic of uniqueness. On the contrary, this God is unique from the very first in the things that He is and says and does. The exhibition of His being and action is the proof of His uniqueness. He has only to place Himself beside the would-be gods of the nations, as He really does in the establishing, upholding and guiding of Israel, and He becomes *ipso facto* manifest as the only God among them. " Thus saith the Lord, the king of Israel, and his redeemer the Lord of hosts : I am the first, and I am the last ; and beside me there is no God. And who, as I, shall call, and shall declare it, and set it in order for me, since I appointed the ancient people ? and the things that are coming and that shall come, let them declare. Fear ye not, neither be afraid : have I not declared unto thee of old, and shewed it ? and ye are my witnesses. Is there a God beside me ? yea, there is no rock : I know not any. They that fashion a graven image are all of them vanity : and their delectable things shall not profit : and their own witnesses see not, nor know ; that they may be ashamed " (Is. 44^{6-9}). Hence the prayer of Hezekiah : " Incline thine ear, O Lord, and hear : open thine eyes, O Lord, and see ; and hear the words of Sennacherib, wherewith he hath sent him to reproach the living God. Of a truth, Lord, the kings of Assyria have laid waste the nations and their lands, and have cast their gods into the fire : for they were no gods, but the work of men's hands, wood and stone : therefore they have destroyed them. Now therefore, O Lord our God, save thou us, I beseech thee, out of his hand, that all the kingdoms of the earth may know that thou art the Lord God, even thou only " (2 Kings 19^{16-19}). Hence, too, the references in Exod. 20^5, 34^{14} and many later passages to the jealousy of God, which is established with painful fulness in the description in Ezek. 23 of the harlotry committed by Judah and Israel, and wonderfully deepened and super-seded by the recollection in Hos. 1-3 of the faithfulness of God which forgives and overcomes the unfaithfulness of His people. It is against this background and this background alone that we can understand the commandment : " Thou shalt have no other gods before me," and with it the " monotheism " of the Old Testament in general. It has absolutely nothing to do with the ambiguous charm of the number " one " or the subjective and objective monism of human self-consciousness and world consciousness, On the contrary, it is in conflict with this monotheism, detecting and passing judgment on its hidden dialectic. It attacks man as a fallen creature who is utterly ignorant of the one and only God and therefore of the true God, a creature who is always looking for the one and never finds it. He finds only what is multiple, because the one is the one person from whom man has fallen away and who is hidden from him and can be revealed to him only by that One Himself. Old Testament monotheism consists in God's disclosing and giving Himself to man as the One who is also the one for which man for his part can only ask in vain. He is not, then, an -ism or a system, which is capable of turning into its opposite. On the contrary, He is the divine reality itself in its uniqueness. For this reason and in this way He possesses power as well. This is not the precarious power of an idea that for a while brings conviction and sets up a school, and later fades again and is replaced by another idea. His is the concrete power that preserves the people of Israel through its long history, which from Israel's standpoint is a continual history of opposition and apostasy. It is the power that preserves it in spite of itself (as depicted in Hosea 1-3) in constant selection and separation at the name of Yahweh as the name of the only true God. It is the power of the divine grace, mercy and patience in which His holiness, righteousness, and wisdom do in fact triumph. It is the power to bind this people in the way in which God Himself, as con-trasted with an idea, binds men, so that it is not always evident how far men glorify Him, but it is always evident that He does glorify Himself among and in these men, and in such a way that His love in its uniqueness never fails or is renounced or becomes equivocal in relation to these men. The God of the Old Testament is not, then, the God to whom uniqueness accrues or is ascribed as a kind of embellishment drawn from the stores of creaturely glory, which He may now wear as the images of the heathen gods wear their embellishments of gold and silver. On the contrary, He is the God who possesses uniqueness in the love that is actively at work on Israel, a uniqueness that is His own, a divine, a unique uniqueness, unique in comparison with all human uniqueness. He is the God who is unique in Himself, quite apart from any corresponding knowledge or service contributed or offered or provided by Israel. Indeed, Israel's knowledge of God and service of God is to be understood as a divine gift subsequent to God's existence and action and to that extent as obedience to God's command. It is drawn always by " the cords of grace," by the " bands of love " (Hos. 11⁴). There is continual resistance from the human side. There is always breaking out to the left hand or the right. This is how Israel comes to the knowledge and service of God, as God opposes to it His own faithfulness.

" Jewish monotheism ? " It was just when something like this had begun to take shape, when apparently all opposition had been broken and apostasy seemed to belong to the past, when polytheism had apparently become a matter of past history and the idols Israel had worshipped were apparently recognised only as the idols of the despised Gentiles or in recollection of the abomination of their disobedient fathers—it was just then, under the sway of this victorious monotheism, that Israel's Messiah was handed over by Israel to the Gentiles and nailed by them to the cross with Israel's approval. Could there be a better proof that this monotheism is not a final achievement and expression of Israel's obedience to the first commandment ? On the contrary, is it not a proof that, like the monotheism of Islam (its later caricature), it is simply the supreme example, the culmination and completion of the disobedience which from the beginning constituted the human side of the dealings of the one and only God with His chosen people ? The conception of the one and only being now actually reached by Israel has as little as that to do with the uniqueness of God. It is—always—the form taken by the supreme and as it were mature contradiction of the one and only God. This does not occur in the remoter ages when Israel worshipped idols, but at the height of its religious development, when it seemed as if the indictments of Moses and the prophets and the threatenings of the Law no longer applied, and the dogma of God's uniqueness had become something that all the parties of the Jewish Church would of course hold in honour. In these very conditions the fulfilment of the whole history of Israel could be and inevitably was misunderstood. The one and only Son of the one and only God, the very incarnate Word of God to which Moses and the prophets had borne witness, could be and inevitably was rejected by Israel, and its whole history could be and was inevitably proved to be the history of human disobedience to the one and only God in a manner both awesome and final. Could there be any better proof that God's uniqueness is really His, God's uniqueness, not a matter of a human idea of God, but of His revelation, of His speaking and acting, of His inmost being, inseparable from His grace and holiness ? Could there be any better proof that it is as little the discovery of a human mind as His grace and holiness and all His other perfections, and that as a divine reality it is dia-metrically opposed to creaturely reality, including even the highest human faculty of construction and foresight, and can become an object of human knowledge only in the way in which God in any of His perfections can become such an object ? In face of the cross of Christ it is monstrous to describe the uniqueness of God as an object of " natural " knowledge. In face of the cross of Christ we are bound to say that knowledge of the one and only God is gained only by the begetting of men anew by the Holy Spirit, an act which is always unmerited and incomprehensible, and consists in man's no longer living unto himself, but in the Word of God and in the knowledge of God which comes by faith in that Word. But faith in that Word means faith in the One whom this very Judaism with its monotheism rejected as a sinner against its monotheism,

a blasphemer against God. This is the gulf which separates Christian monotheism, if we can use the term, from Jewish monotheism and monotheism of
every other kind. It is strange but true that confession of the one and only
God and denial of Him are to be found exactly conjoined but radically separated
in what appears to be the one identical statement that there is only one God.
This one sentence can actually mean what it says, and it can actually not mean
this, but its opposite. What distinguishes these two possibilities, raising the
one to reality and invalidating the other, is the resurrection of Jesus Christ, the
outpouring of the Holy Spirit and faith.

That God is a single unique being is of course stated expressly and in many
forms by the New Testament as well (Mt. 19¹⁷, Gal. 3²⁰, 1 Cor. 8⁴ᶠ·, 1 Tim. 2⁵).
It says this actually and not merely verbally because, like the Old Testament,
it makes the statement in attestation—this time retrospective—of the Word
and work of God.

The passages which speak expressly of the uniqueness of God are only in
a sense the spokesmen for a far more extensive conception of the uniqueness
of the form and content of the event between God and man in which the
being of God as the one and only God has been revealed. They are to be read
and understood against this background, and not by themselves as abstract
statements about God in Himself. The very remarkable fact is to be noted
that (in harmony with the predominant " henotheism " of the Old Testament)
Paul not only did not deny the existence of many that are called (λεγόμενοι)
gods and lords in heaven and on earth (1 Cor. 8⁵), but actually affirmed it :
ὥσπερ εἰσὶν θεοὶ πολλοὶ καὶ κύριοι πολλοί. To such an extent is the New
Testament doctrine of the singleness or uniqueness of God based on the conception of that event, and so little on a preconceived theory. That God is a single
being is clearly reflected, according to the parables of the lost sheep and the
lost coin, in the fact that there is more joy in heaven over one sinner that repents
than over ninety and nine just persons, who need no repentance (Lk. 15⁷⁻¹⁰).
Such is God and such His mercy and righteousness that He is concerned about
the individual man in his need and his redemption. Again God as the One who
is single and unique is reflected in the fact that Martha is wrong to be worried
and anxious about many things. " But one thing is needful : for Mary hath
chosen the good part, which shall not be taken away from her " (Lk. 10⁴¹ᶠ·).
Such is God and such His grace and holiness that there is simply one thing which
He wants from men. Again, in Gal. 5¹⁴ the whole Law is fulfilled in one saying
(the saying : " Thou shalt love thy neighbour as thyself "). For Paul there seem
to have been two objects of what is in the first instance an indirect view of the
singleness and uniqueness of God. First, there is the embracing together of
Jew and Gentile both in sin and in the mercy of God or faith—a decisive mark
of his Gospel : " Or is God the God of Jews only ? is he not the God of Gentiles
also : if so be that God is one, and he shall justify the circumcision by faith and
the uncircumcision through faith ? " (Rom. 3²⁹ᶠ·). " For there is no distinction
between Jew and Greek : for the same Lord is Lord of all, and is rich unto all
that call upon him " (Rom. 10¹²). Or again (and already the connexion with
the direct view of God's uniqueness is present here) : " For he is our peace, who
made both one, and brake down the middle wall of partition, having abolished
in his flesh the enmity, even the law of commandments contained in ordinances ;
that he might create in himself of the twain one new man, so making peace ;
and might reconcile them both in one body unto God through the cross, having
slain the enmity thereby " (Eph. 2¹⁴⁻¹⁶). The saying in Jn. 10¹⁶ belongs to this
context : " And other sheep I have which are not of this fold : them also I
must bring, and they shall hear my voice ; and there shall be one flock, one
shepherd." The second- indirect view of the divine singleness and uniqueness
in Paul—and it is of course directly connected with the first—is that of the
Church as the one body (Rom. 12⁴ᶠ·, 1 Cor. 10¹⁷, 12¹²ᶠ·). " There is one body,

and one Spirit, even as also ye were called in one hope of your calling : one Lord, one faith, one baptism, one God and Father of all, who is over all, and through all, and in all " (Eph. 4⁴ᶠᶠ·). This passage makes it obvious how Paul simply reads off the truth of the singleness and uniqueness of God from the reality of the life of His people created by His Word and work. That this reality represents for him a divine reality is shown by the fact that it is traced back to the reality of the one Holy Spirit both in this very passage (Eph. 4⁴) and in many other places (1 Cor. 12¹¹ᶠ·, 2 Cor. 12¹⁸, Eph. 2¹⁸). For this reason the gift of revelation and reconciliation, visible in the life of the community in all its unity, may and must be described also as a task, and made the object of apostolic exhortation. It is the singleness and uniqueness of God which is proclaimed when in Gal. 3²⁸ (cf. 1 Cor. 12¹³) not only the distinction between the Jews and Greeks but also that between slave and free and male and female is relativised by the statement that " ye are all one in Christ Jesus." And it is the singleness and uniqueness of God which is proclaimed when in Phil. 1²⁷ Christians are called to stand fast in one spirit, " with one soul striving for the faith of the gospel," or in Phil. 2² " to be of the same mind," having the same love, as σύμ-ψυχοι to be of one mind ; or in Rom. 15⁵ᶠ· to glorify the God and Father of our Lord Jesus Christ " with one accord, with one mouth ; " or when it can in fact be said of the community in Jerusalem in Acts 4³² that the multitude of them that believed were " of one heart and soul."

But all this is, after all, only the indirect conception which serves as a basis for confession of the one God. It cannot be understood except against the background of the proper, direct conception which now calls for consideration. But this direct conception, the one with which knowledge of the singleness and uniqueness of God in the New Testament stands or falls, is that of Jesus the Messiah, rejected by monotheistic Judaism. Already in Ephesians 2 and 4 this view is clearly enough visible as the constitutive centre of what is said about the unity of the congregation. It is dominant, however, in the principal passages 1 Cor. 8⁶ and 1 Tim. 2⁵. The first passage says first : εἷς θεὸς ὁ πατήρ and then : εἷς κύριος Ἰησοῦς Χριστός ; the second : εἷς θεός and then : εἷς μεσίτης θεοῦ καὶ ἀνθρώπων, ἄνθρωπος Χριστὸς Ἰησοῦς (" who gave himself a ransom for all "). In neither passage is the connecting καί to be understood as if a second unique being is named alongside a first, but what comes after the καί strengthens, emphasises and interprets what stands in front of it—a common usage. Thus mention of the one Lord or Mediator simply expresses the fact and extent that God the Father is the unique being. He is it in and with the fact that our Lord, the Mediator between God and man, is as such the one unique being. This twofold εἷς does not involve in the least the introduction of a new polytheism, as in the conception of a higher unique being and a lower—analogous to " Allah is great and Mohammed is his prophet." On the contrary, it means the final establishing of the monotheism of Moses and the prophets, the monotheism of the God who is real and revealed, who has His being and makes it known in His Word and work. And it is established by the specific naming of His name. Christian monotheism results from and consists in the fact that Jesus Christ bears witness to Himself and reveals Himself as the Son of His heavenly Father, distinguishing Himself and separating Himself as reigning Lord from the powers and forces of this age, and manifesting Himself as their Conqueror and Master. In the events which not only are caused by God or proceed from Him, but which are identical with His being and action, He reveals Himself and is known in His being as the One who is unique. He is not a unique being in the way in which there are many such. He is *this* unique being. As this unique being He is *the* unique being. Thus everything depends on the revelation and knowledge of this unique being if it is to be a matter of the revelation and knowledge of the uniqueness of God in the New Testament sense.

We must now consider the passages in which the unique God and the unique Christ are not expressly connected, as in 1 Cor. 8 and 1 Tim. 2, but the uniqueness of the divine Word and work as it occurred in Jesus Christ is itself described and emphasised. It is these passages which will be finally decisive for the understanding of New Testament monotheism. For in these passages we go even beyond what has been said above, where the two are set together, and learn the extent to which, in fact. uniqueness—and uniqueness that is divine —is Jesus Christ's by right. According to Mt. 23[8-10], it is His in the sense that He Himself says to His disciples : " But be not ye called Rabbi : for one is your teacher, and all ye are brethren. And call no man your father upon the earth : for one is your Father, which is in heaven. Neither be ye called masters : for one is your Master, even Christ." The passage frankly sounds intolerable if we fail to realise that this is the claim of the one and only God. Yet it should be noted that the very thing which would be completely intolerable if it were a man's testimony to himself—Jesus' witness to Himself as Messiah—is the basis of New Testament monotheism, just as the. basis of Old Testament mono-theism is the witness of Yahweh to Himself as He acts on Israel. We cannot listen to what the New Testament calls " the one God " without listening to His self-testimony. Naturally we may reject this. But in that case we reject not only what is here called " the one God," but this God Himself. This God, the God of the Old and New Testaments, is in His being not only unique, but this unique being. We can react to His self-witness in which He reveals Himself as unique : " I and the Father are one " (Jn. 10[30]), in the same way as the Jews did according to Jn. 10[31] : " They took up stones to stone him." But for all that, it still stands as this self-witness and as such it is the one and only approach to what the Old and New Testaments call " God." For a being which is not the unique being attested by this self-testimony may also be unique in its own way, but it is certainly not this God. This and this alone is the admittedly strait way, the admittedly narrow gate, to the one God of the prophets and apostles. And everything that Paul says in his letters about the unity of the Spirit and the Church has as its background this self-witness. " Keep them in thy name which thou hast given me, that they may be one, even as we are " (Jn. 17[11]). But it is not only through words that this self-witness takes place. For instance, if we read Paul in Rom. 5[12-21] (cf. 1 Cor. 15[21]), there does not seem to be a single word about the uniqueness of God. It is all about the alteration that has taken place in the human situation through Jesus Christ, an alteration from the dominion of sin to the dominion of righteousness, from death as man's destiny to the gift of life. It should be noted, however, on the one hand how utterly un-symmetrical is the relationship of these two sides or possibilities. Grace, righteous-ness and life are absolutely superior, as becomes more and more impressively clear as the end is approached. And it should be noted, on the other hand, how in relation to the power that has been overthrown the victorious power is epi-tomised in the form of the εἷς ἄνθρωπος who has redressed the evil done by another and first εἷς ἄνθρωπος. This latter " one man " was Adam. The other " one man " is Jesus Christ and it is He who is the bringer of the grace and righteous-ness of the life that triumphs over death, a grace and righteousness which shows itself divine by its superiority. This happening is now the Messianic witness of Jesus to Himself. At the same time and as such it is witness to the uniqueness of God. Or, to put it the other way round, here too the witness to the uniqueness of God is simply the Messianic witness of Jesus to Himself. This witness outdoes the testimony to sin and death offered by the human race as embraced in the one man Adam. It does so by a victorious decision which ends and excludes all dispute or competition. This one being has gained His right and lordship over the lives of all—or we may also say, this one being has revealed His dignity as Creator and Lord of all—by dying for them all (2 Cor. 5[14]). And if human priests proved themselves merely witnesses and types by daily sacrifices, which have always to be repeated and " can never take away sins," He, Jesus Christ,

" when he had offered one sacrifice for sins for ever, sat down on the right hand of God ; from henceforth expecting till his enemies be made the footstool of his feet. For by one offering he hath perfected for ever them that are sanctified " (Heb. 10¹¹⁻¹⁴). This, it must be said, is the unique New Testament proof of the uniqueness of God.

We conclude by referring to the fact that this was recognised and acknowledged in the Reformation doctrine of justification with the statement that it is only by faith that man possesses righteousness and holiness. This *sola fide* is simply the reflection of the *soli Deo gloria* with which the fathers of the Protestant Church were equally accustomed to sum up their profession of faith, just as conversely this *soli Deo gloria* is simply the reflection of the *sola fide*. Rightly understood these two *sola* (and the third one, *sola scriptura* too) mean one and the same thing. *Unicus Deus*, because *unicus summus pontifex, patronus et pacificator* (*Conf. Scot.* Art. XI), is the archetype, reflected by both, indeed by all three *sola*. The uniqueness of faith is based on the uniqueness of its object, and therefore *soli Deo gloria*. But the uniqueness of this object requires faith to be unique, because it is only God who is feared, loved and glorified by us, and therefore *sola fide*. But the power of this uniqueness is the power of the name under which God reveals His being and in which faith may believe. The Reformation recovered and brought to light the testimony of the whole of Holy Scripture when it sang : " Ask ye who is this same ? Christ Jesus is His name. The Lord Sabaoth's Son ; He, and no other one, Shall conquer in the battle."

[II, 1, pp. 451–457]

4. ISRAEL AND THE CHURCH :
WITNESSES OF THE JUDGMENT AND MERCY OF GOD

Paul explains in Rom. 9⁶ᵃ that what was said in vv. 1–2 about his sorrow is not in any sense to be taken to mean that he sees cause to lament over a failure of God's Word (with regard to obdurate Judaism). It is " not as though the word of God hath taken none effect," i.e., has been disproved and given the lie by the stiff-necked obstinacy of the Jews. God makes no mistakes, suffers no reverses, and never has to withdraw. His Word is true and always in the right even when man meets it with deceit and puts himself in the wrong. Paul, therefore, (as a true Israelite) cannot lament over Israel without rejoicing (again as a true Israelite)—rejoicing for Israel's sake—in the steadfastness and faithfulness of Israel's God. Paul laments because, at the very moment when in Jesus Christ the perfect form of God's community and therefore Israel's own election is revealed to the whole world, Israel cuts itself off from God's community and goes into the ghetto. He cannot, however, avoid rejoicing that even in this there is effected a confirmation of its election, a fulfilment of the will of the God who elects Israel.

For it is (vv. 6b–7a) not at all the case that according to the Word and will of God all who belong to the race of Abraham, all bearers of the name Israel, were appointed to become members of the Church. They were certainly appointed members of the one elected community of God. This is something that none of this race can be deprived of ; this is something that not one of this race can decline, not even if his name is Caiaphas or indeed Judas Iscariot ; this is what Jews, one and all, are by birth. But they were not all appointed members of the Church hidden in Israel and revealed in Jesus Christ. This was always something different, and until the end of the world—no longer, but until the end of the world—it will be something different. " For they are not all Israel which are of Israel." That is, they are not the true Israel, i.e., the Israel which realises Israel's determination by accepting its proper place in the Church, which realises the mercy of God by joining in the Church's praise. Some of Israel are, of course, Israel. But not all who are " of Israel " are so in the way in which, according to v. 5, this is to be said of Jesus of Nazareth. Strictly speaking, He alone is Israel, and it is only in Him, as His prophets, witnesses, forerunners, that others are as well, those who are specially elected in Him, with Him and for His sake. Not one of them is so by nature ; not one in virtue of his Jewish blood ; not one as a self-evident consequence of his membership of this people : but each only on the ground of a special election in which the election of Israel as such is repeated and established. This special election—and this alone from the very beginning—constitutes the pre-existent Church in Israel, the true, spiritual Israel. " Neither because they are the seed of Abraham, are they all children." It is no small honour to be " Abraham's seed." There is no doubt that as such Abraham's seed is the elected people of God, determined in accordance with its election to be the mirror of the divine judgment, which is, for its part, the veil of the divine mercy. But Abraham's children, the hidden Church in Israel, appointed to announce in advance the one true Israelite coming by God's choice " out of Israel " and thus to show forth the praise of the divine mercy itself, are from the very beginning those of Abraham's seed who (like the coming Messiah Himself) are so by God's special choice. This is God's order in Israel just because Israel is the elected people. Election is its living order from the very beginning. Therefore the phenomenon which occupies Paul, Israel's resistance to the message of the Church, is nothing new according to God's order (revealed in His Word, v. 6a). On the contrary, however serious and painful it may be, it is a fresh occasion for praising the living God who has given Israel this order.

" In Isaac shall thy seed be called " (v. 7b), that is, by the special, sacred name of the children of Abraham, namely, of true Israelites. This saying is a quotation from Gen. 21[12], and thus expressly recalls the exclusion of Ishmael described there. It is in Isaac that there is a repetition and establishment of the election of Abraham, not in Ishmael, although he too is Abraham's son, and although he is not this for nothing. According to v. 8 the purport of this passage from Genesis is : " They which are the children of the flesh, these are not (as such) the children of God, but the children of the promise are counted for the seed." Both Isaac and Ishmael are " children of the flesh," begotten by man and born of woman ; and in the same way later both the elected and the rejected will be equally " children of the flesh." But it is not as such that they are prefigurations of the Son of God and Man coming from Israel, the proclamation of the divine mercy, the children of Abraham in the sense of v. 7b, the bearers of the spiritual name of his seed. It is as " children of the promise " that they are children of God and holy children of Abraham, i.e., as men whose existence (like that of the coming Messiah Himself) is the content and object of the promise given to Abraham with his election irrespective of their " carnal origin." Not the life arising from Abraham's flesh and blood as such but the life arising from the truth and power of the promise given to Abraham is the life of the children of God, the pre-existent Church in Israel. These children of the promise " are counted for seed." In them and them only does the seed receive its sacred name and character, and elected Israel is at the same time true Israel. In the provisional upbuilding of the Church in Israel the main issue in each case as it arises is the freedom of God to " count " as genuine, prefigurative and prophetic the seed which He has specially determined for this purpose (as according to Rom. 4[3] etc. He " counts " the faith of Abraham as righteousness in His sight). It is those who are introduced and have life by the truth and power of the divine promise that are the elect of the God who elected Abraham and who, before Abraham was, elected Jesus Christ ; it is they who are God's children and Abraham's children in the strict and proper sense, they alone and none beside them. Such a one is (v. 9) Isaac. He is so in a way that is made prominent and significant for the whole line after him, for as Paul emphasises in Rom. 4[19] (cf. Gen. 18[11]) he is the child of a miraculous begetting and a miraculous birth. " Isaac " means " one laughs." At the word spoken to Abraham : " I will certainly return unto thee according to the time of life ; and, lo, Sarah thy wife shall have a son " (cf. Gen. 18[10]), man calculating in human terms can only laugh (in sceptical enthusiasm) as in the explicit and extended account in Gen. 18[11f.] It is a divine word of promise corresponding—but in a much purer form—to the word by which, on the ground of his election, Abraham was called and led into the land. It can reach fulfilment either not at all or else only on the ground of its truth and power as a divine word of promise. In this very definite sense Isaac is the child of God and of Abraham. Since he, too, is a " child of the flesh," his existence is purely and simply the fulfilment of the divine word of promise. In this way the election of Abraham is repeated and established in him. In this way the pre-existent Church is built up in him. In this way, then, he is also, although indirectly, a witness to the election of all Israel.

The parallel in Gal. 4[21-31] is to be noted. There, too, we have two sons of the one Abraham, begotten and born, the one " after the flesh " of the bond-woman Hagar, the other on the ground of the promise, of the free woman Sarah. And now the point is expressly stated that in both cases we are concerned with " covenants," but with two covenants (δύο διαθῆκαι, v. 24). Hagar is the representation of the covenant made on Sinai and realised with its limitations in the present earthly Jerusalem. Sarah, " our mother," the one who became a mother miraculously, is the covenant adumbrated by the first, freed from its limitations and realised in the " Jerusalem which is above." " We, brethren, as Isaac was, are children of promise. . . . We are not children of the bondwoman, but of the free " (vv. 28, 31). Observe that it is from the Law itself (v. 21), from Scripture (vv. 22, 27, 30), that Paul derives the point that within what is common to them both (διαθήκη) Israel and the Church are twofold—the Church being distinguished from Israel by the fact that it receives Abraham's promise anew and directly on the ground of special choice.

Attention should also be given to the parallel in Rom. 4[9-25]. Abraham believed before he was circumcised, before he was a " Jew." Circumcision too, the sign of the covenant between God and himself and his seed, he received as a " seal of the righteousness of the faith which he had while he was still a Gentile " in order that he might be simultaneously the father of all who believe, both from the Gentiles and the circumcision (v. 10 f.). That he is to become κληρονόμος κόσμου, i.e., that the world is to become his possession, is something which is not promised either to himself or his descendants διὰ νόμου, i.e., with the establishment of the Israelite Law and with a view to its fulfilment, but διὰ δικαιοσύνης πίστεως, i.e., in virtue of the judgment given by God which has equal validity before the establishment of this Law both in and even outside its sphere, and which Abraham trusted and obeyed (v. 13). Where the promise given to Abraham is assured to man through this judgment given by God, and is accepted accordingly by man in faith, there it is βεβαία, authenticating itself to its recipient, in virtue of the fact that its fulfilment is certain (v. 16). Where it is given and received only in the form of the Israelite Law in itself, where the fulfilment of this Law as such is intended to establish man's claim to this hope, faith loses its point (κεκένωται ἡ πίστις) and the promise itself is made impotent (κατήργηται ἡ ἐπαγγελία, v. 14). For to take one's stand under the Law of Israel means virtually the same thing as to stand in the sphere of the divine wrath. Where there is law there is transgression (discovered, condemned and threatened with punishment). It is only where there is no Law—that is, as a limitation of hope, as a substitute for the living promise—that there is no transgression, that transgression is forgiven (v. 15). But this is the case where the promise is given to man, as it was given to Abraham, through the sovereign judgment of God, and where this is accepted as Abraham accepted it, in faith. This can occur in the realm of circumcision and of the Israelite Law regarded as the sign of the covenant made with

14 *Karl Barth : Preaching Through the Christian Year*

Abraham. But—in the track of this same Abraham's faith—it can also occur outside this realm. Abraham is the " father of us all " (as Sarah, according to Gal. 4²⁶, is in the same sense " our mother "). According to Gen. 17⁵ he is the father of many nations (vv. 16–17), as surely as in his faith in the promise he believes in the God who quickens the dead and calls the non-existent into being (v. 17). That he was strong in this faith contrary to all human calculations was, according to Gen. 15⁶, " counted " as his righteousness—corresponding to the righteous judgment of God (vv. 18–21). In saying this about Abraham, Scripture is obviously speaking not only of him but of us too, of the Church's faith in the One who awakened from the dead Jesus our Lord. As the father of Isaac Abraham is the father not only of Israel but also of the elected Church gathered from Jews and Gentiles.

Thus the Word of God (Rom. 9⁶) is not proved false but established by the phenomenon of the unbelieving Synagogue. According to the testimony of Scripture, God has from the first chosen, differentiated and divided in Israel. He has from the very beginning separated the Church and Israel, Israel and the Church. And in so doing He has confirmed the election of Israel.

This is the insight that is taken up in more acute form in vv. 10–13. It is more acute to the extent that we are now dealing not merely with the two sons of the one father (Isaac—it is he who is now called ὁ πατὴρ ἡμῶν like Abraham in Rom. 4¹, ¹⁶), but with the two sons of one mother as well (Rebecca), indeed with the twin fruits of one and the same begetting (v. 11). In relation to vv. 7–10 we might perhaps ask if Isaac was not after all chosen because of some merits of his own and Ishmael rejected because of some fault of his own. There was much to praise in the later nation Israel (and in Jacob too), and much to blame in Ishmael (and in Esau too). But whatever we may find to praise or blame, the election of the one and the rejection of the other certainly bear no relation to it. The issue is the separation of the Church in Israel. And what can that have to do with what may seem or may actually be praiseworthy or blameworthy in either the one or the other ? In the relationship of Jacob and Esau it becomes wholly clear that every explanation which takes this line can only go astray. For it is palpable there that the decision both ways is made before regard to the good or evil doings of the persons concerned can be considered at all as a ground of decision. " For the children being not yet born, neither having done any good or evil . . . it was (already) said, The elder (that is precisely the one who as firstborn could claim a natural prerogative) shall serve the younger " (vv. 11–12, Gen. 25²³) ; it had already come to pass : " Jacob have I loved, but Esau have I hated " (v. 13, Mal. 1²ᶠ·). The connexion between the determination of both is not to be mistaken in the formulation in v. 12, neither is it to be overlooked in the more trenchant saying of v. 13. The God of Jacob is also the God of Esau. He whose will elected Abraham and his whole race (to which both belong) unites the servant with the master, the hated with the loved one, the rejected with the elected. It is the one (albeit different) blessing of their father Jacob that both will receive. What occurs in both cases occurs within the community. But all the same the emphasis rests on the fact that it is something different which occurs, that the Church and Abraham's race are not identical, that the Church is founded and built by a separation which operates right from the beginning of the history of this race, and has as its principle, not the glory of good works done by man, but, as in the case of the election of the whole race of Abraham, the good-will of God. This separation must happen in order that the predetermination resting on election might stand, not on the ground of (human) works, but on the ground of (the will of) Him who calls (vv. 11–12). It is as the election stands in this elected race, as it continually takes place in this race, or is manifested in it in the form of calling, that the Church is founded and built up and the election of this race is established. But we must not lose sight of the fact that it is in this race that by God's free disposing the Church is founded and built up by the operation of this separation which repeatedly means exclusion. The very fact that the κατ' ἐκλογὴν πρόθεσις τοῦ θεοῦ is continued in this race means that its honour and hope continuingly benefit all its members. Even its rejected members (just because of the separation which excludes them) are not forsaken, but after, as before, share in the special care and guidance of the electing God. When Ishmael was menaced by death on the expulsion of Hagar to the wilderness, " God heard the voice of the lad ; and the angel of the Lord called to Hagar out of heaven, and said unto her, What aileth thee, Hagar ? fear not ; for God hath heard the voice of the lad where he is. Arise, lift up the lad, and hold him in thine hand ; for I will make him a great nation. And God opened her eyes, and she saw a well of water. . . . And God was with the lad ; and he grew, and dwelt in the wilderness, and became an archer " (Gen. 21¹⁷ᶠ·). And in the same way the Esau (Edom) of the Old Testament is not one who is forsaken by God but the ancestor of a covenant people who is recognised in his way by God and the people of Jacob and provided with a genealogy of his own which both in Gen. 36 and 1 Chron. 1 is set forth in great detail alongside that of Israel. This should not be forgotten in arriving at the biblical interpretation of what is to be described as " rejection " in contrast or rather in relation to election. But in the first instance it is the first factor which is decisive. It is the free, divine choice within the elected race which founds and builds up the Church. It is the same choice which constitutes this race as such the elected race. It is the choice of grace which is not bound by any natural or moral presuppositions on the part of the elect but the ground of which is to be sought solely in the will of the electing God, in His revelation, in the fact of His call. It is the special choice of grace which as such is to be accepted and affirmed in faith, which can be accepted and affirmed in faith alone. The free divine choice of some excludes others. According to Scripture there was always an Israel excluded by this free divine choice. Israel as such was never identical with the Church. Thus the phenomenon of the refractory Synagogue is no novelty. The Word of God is not proved false by this phenomenon.

But what is God's purpose with the remainder of Israel which is not appointed for the founding and upbuilding of the Church ? What was His purpose with Ishmael ? or with Esau whom, according to v. 13, He " hated " ? What is His purpose to-day with the refractory Synagogue ? The answer to this question follows in vv. 14–29.

" What shall we then say ? Is there unrighteousness with God ? " (v. 14). The question which Paul here holds out for consideration by Paul is not concerning an abstract righteousness but about the concrete righteousness of the God who elects Israel. Is not this God, the covenant God of Abraham, unjust in a procedure which excludes from this special election so many of Abraham's race without regard to the natural and moral presuppositions that they have to commend them ? In the last resort, is it not His will that disposes in this way an act of arbitrary and unfair preference and prejudice ? We must keep in mind that along with the question raised by the statement of Scripture Paul is at the same time faced with the actual question of the majority of Israel remaining outside the Church. In vv. 6–13 he has explained from the standpoint of Scripture that from the first God has at all times proceeded in the way in which He manifestly still does to-day, so that there can be no doubt about God's constancy. But what if it is in relation to the procedure followed from the first by this constant God, in relation to Ishmael and Esau, that is, from Scripture itself, that the question of the righteousness of this constant God is raised, and extends from there to the consideration of what God is also obviously doing in the present ? In v. 6 f. Scripture was consulted to try to make this consideration of the present easier, but it only seems to have made it harder. Can it be that the " sorrow " which, according to v. 2, Paul endures on account of Israel may ultimately be sorrow that according to His own Word the God of Israel is as wayward to-day as He always was, that in Him there is unrighteousness ?

Paul opposes to this question the horrified μὴ γένοιτο customary with him in such cases (cf. Rom. 3⁴, ⁶, 6², ¹⁵, 7⁷, 11¹, ¹¹). In the consideration of Scripture as of present-day life he therefore holds fast to the confession of God's righteousness. And this can only mean in the context that it is clear to him that in the procedure described in vv. 6–13 the God of Israel is not acting in defiance of but in accordance with the order established by Himself, that is to say, not arbitrarily but in profoundest harmony with Himself and in a manner supremely worthy of Himself and therefore in the most objective sense righteously. According to v. 15 the proof of this is the divine name which is revealed to Moses and which characterises the nature of God. According to Ex. 33¹⁹ it runs : " I will have mercy on whom I have mercy, yea, I will have compassion on whom I have compassion." This is obviously a paraphrase of the simpler formula of Ex. 3¹⁴ : " I will be he that I am." According to this revealed name of His, God's nature consists in the fact that He renews, establishes and glorifies Himself by His own future ; or materially, that He renews, establishes and glorifies His being by His future being, or even more materially, His mercy by His future mercy, His compassion by His future compassion. It is because Paul has clearly in view this nature of God that to the question whether in this procedure there is not present some unrighteousness on the part of God he opposes the horrified μὴ γένοιτο, rejecting the question as absurd. This procedure—and this procedure alone—corresponds to the revealed name and the nature of God characterised by this name. It is this nature of God which is His righteousness and therefore the measure and sum of all righteousness. God's nature is that the One He now is in freedom He will be again in the same unconditioned, unassailable freedom to posit and affirm Himself by Himself. In that God will be He who He is, He is in no way unrighteous, arbitrary or wayward. On the contrary, His righteousness consists precisely in the fact that He renews, establishes and glorifies His present by His own future, that as the One He is, but as such positing and affirming Himself afresh, He advances from each to-day posited in His freedom into a to-morrow which in its turn will be posited in His freedom. It is in this way that the eternal God lives in His relationship to time, in His relationship and covenant with the man loved and created by Him. It is in this way that He lives in the election of Jesus Christ and in the election of the community. But what Ex. 33¹⁹ says here has a still richer content. God's nature consists in the fact that as He freely shows mercy, so He will again show mercy. By doing this and thus maintaining the continuity between His present and His future God does not give man any occasion to complain of an injustice inflicted on him. His righteousness indeed consists in the fact that He not only is but always becomes again the merciful One, that He does not cease to show mercy, but by what He will do in His mercy establishes the truth of what He does and already has done in His mercy. This is how God lives in covenant with man in the election of Jesus Christ and in the election of the community. This is how He renews, establishes and glorifies this covenant. But it is just this nature of God which is the secret of the divine procedure described in vv. 6–13. As God elects Abraham, so among his sons He elects Isaac, and among Isaac's sons Jacob. So, too, He elects Moses. As yesterday He showed mercy, so He does to-day and so He will do to-morrow. All renewal, establishment and glorification of His present (His mercy already shown) by His own future (His mercy yet to be shown), and therefore the life corresponding to His nature in the realm of His creation and in covenant with man, are finally effective and visible in their perfect and at the same time original form, and the day of His future dawns, in the fact that He has mercy on the man Jesus and in Him on all men by becoming man Himself, by taking up and taking away man's burden in order to clothe man with His own glory. In view of the day of this one man in whom God will renew, establish and glorify His righteousness (the righteousness of His mercy) by suffering Himself the judgment which overtakes man, the Israel from which this One will be taken is subject to the order : " I will be he that I am," and the Church is continually separated within Israel. Is there any appropriate stand-point from which we can legitimately complain of this order and accuse it as unrighteous ? God is righteous in the fact that when He shows mercy to Israel—for the sake of all men and all Israel as well—He is concerned with His future act of mercy and therefore with this one man and with His Church. God is righteous in the fact that He causes this electing mercy towards His Church in Israel to follow upon His special electing mercy shown to Abraham and all his race. This sequel, indeed, only renews, establishes and glorifies that beginning. Even in loving Jacob and hating Esau (v. 13), God is supremely righteous—and supremely righteous in the disregard (vv. 10–13) thereby shown with respect to all natural and moral presuppositions of the persons affected. " So then it is not of him that willeth, nor of him that runneth, but of God that sheweth mercy " (v. 16), if (in addition to the fact that as a member of Abraham's race he has a share in the mercy of God) this special mercy falls on anyone, if he is called to the Church. This is true of Moses, true of Isaac and Jacob. If it were of anyone's willing and running, then God would be unrighteous, He would not be consistent with Himself, because He would be letting another attitude, one conditioned by the willing and running of man, follow upon the free mercy in which He elects Abraham. God is righteous when He elects Isaac and Jacob and Moses with the very same disregard of all prior considerations, in the very same free mercy, in which He had already elected Abraham.

But the answer has not yet been given to the question : What is it that God wills and does with Ishmael, with Esau, with all Israel that is not called to the Church ? What is the meaning of : " Esau have I hated " (v. 13) ? Does what was said in vv. 15–16 about the righteousness of the divine mercy apply to him too, and to all the rest as well ? This is, in fact, what Paul is trying to say in the following section. While vv. 15–16 speak of Moses and, retrospectively, of Isaac and Jacob, they form at the same time the major premise for what is to be said in v. 17 f. in relation to Ishmael, Esau and all others rejected within elected Israel. In relation to them, too, the righteousness of God's conduct is exalted far above all doubt because God's name is : " I will be he that I am," or, " I will have mercy on whom I have mercy," and because His conduct with regard to them also accords with this name or with the nature expressed by this name.

The word of God to Pharaoh quoted in v. 17 is not, as one might expect, opposed to that given to Moses by the use of δέ, but set alongside it by the use of a confirmatory γάρ. What follows confirms the insight expressed in vv. 15–16. The figure now used as an example is none other than the mighty opposite of Moses, the Pharaoh of the Exodus. What has he to do with the Israel who is the theme of the whole passage ? Obviously it is only that as its worst enemy and persecutor he is a proper prefiguration of what Paul, as Saul the persecutor of Christians, had himself once been, and what the Synagogue of the present time still is in relation to the apostolic community. But it is this indirectness which makes so very impressive his appearance on this scene as a representative of reprobate and rebellious Israel. In the place where Pharaoh once stood the remainder of Israel now stands. But the context says that Israel necessarily stands there without regard to its running and willing, its purpose and achieve-ment. The God who is righteous in the spirit of v. 15 has placed it there. And what God wills and does by this is to be interpreted with reference to the Pharoah of the Exodus. Not every act of God's mercy is necessarily followed by a further one—for in that case how would it be mercy, how would it be the mercy of God ? That one act of mercy should follow another is a matter for the free decision of Him who is merciful, which might equally well cause a failure in this sequence.

This is the negative side of the truth of v. 15. And it is on its negative side that it affects Ishmael, Esau and Pharaoh. But in the first place this has the following positive significance. In the relation of his history to that of Israel, there is an original act of God's mercy towards Pharaoh also. This is how it is represented by the Old Testament itself. The context of the words quoted in v. 17 is indeed : " I could by now have stretched forth my hand and smitten thee and thy people with pestilence ; and thou wouldst have been cut off from the earth ; but in very deed for this cause have I upheld thee (Paul read in his Greek text —I have ' raised thee up ') that thou mightest know my power (LXX and Paul : 'that I might show my power in thee ') and that my name might be declared throughout all the earth " (Ex. $9^{15f.}$). God lets one warning miracle after another take place before his eyes. Pharaoh does not fail to acknowledge on occasion his sin and guilt (Ex. 9^{27}, 10^{16}). Neither does he fail to appeal to Moses to intercede on his behalf ($8^{8, 28}$, 9^{28}, 10^{17}). And Moses does in fact repeatedly pray for him ($8^{12, 30}$, 9^{33}, 10^{18}) ; repeatedly his punishment is, in fact, stopped before it gets the length of his annihilation. In the last resort all this is hardly less than what appears in Israel's own history in the shape of manifest traces of the original divine mercy. What does not befall Pharaoh (unlike Isaac, Jacob and Moses), corresponding to the negative side of the truth of v. 15, is the renewal, establishment and glorification of this original act of mercy by the event of a further one. God makes use of His freedom to refuse him this future. But, of course, even in this use it is the freedom of His mercy. Even while he is refused what is given to Moses, because both acts occur in the same freedom, Pharaoh is still in the same sphere as Moses. The original mercy of God is not turned in vain even towards him, but with a very definite and positive purpose. He, too, has a function in the service of the God who bears this name, and he, too, participates in the honour and hope associated with it. God " upholds," " raises him up," in order to make him a witness to His power, in order by his destiny to proclaim His name over all the earth. It is to be considered that even this dark prototype of all the rejected in Israel serves to show forth the δύναμις τοῦ θεοῦ which in Rom. 1^{16} is identified with the Gospel, in 1 Cor. 1^{18} with the Word of the cross, in 1 Cor. 1^{24} with Christ Himself—and to proclaim the ὄνομα τοῦ θεοῦ, i.e., the self-manifestation, self-interpretation and self-affirmation of God that is achieved in God's revelation. God's purpose in the election of His community is executed through Pharaoh too, and not through Moses only. In the way marked by His deeds, which leads on to the day of His future, to the day of Jesus Christ, God finds and uses even him, and not Moses only. He stands fittingly beside Moses because he makes it clear that in respect of its fulfilment God's purpose in the election of His community is not bound up with (v. 16) the willing and running of any man (not even with that of Moses), that in one way or another it has to be carried out by the person concerned. He stands fittingly beside Moses because in his own very different way he bears witness to the righteousness of God and indeed to the righteousness of His mercy. In the same sense, too, Ishmael stands fittingly beside Isaac, Esau beside Jacob, and to-day the refractory Synagogue beside the Church.

" Therefore hath he mercy on whom he will have mercy, and whom he will he hardeneth " (v. 18). The saying obviously looks back on the one hand to Isaac, Jacob and Moses, and on the other to Ishmael, Esau and Pharaoh. Before expounding it in the sense of the classical doctrine of predestination attention should have been paid to the fact that here the twofold θέλει cannot possibly be regarded neutrally, i.e., as an indeterminately free willing which now takes the one direction and now the other. To be sure, this willing of God is free. But it is not for that reason indeterminate. It is determined in the sense given by God's name (v. 15). And it is determined in this sense that it has this twofold direction. On both sides, although in different forms, God wills one and the same thing. The contradiction of ἐλεεῖ and σκληρύνει is bracketed by this θέλει, the one purpose of God in the election of His community. As will be stated in Rom. 11[32] with complete unambiguity, this purpose is the purpose of His mercy. It is just this purpose which, according to vv. 15–17, both Moses and also Pharaoh must carry out. They do so in different ways and to this extent the single will of God has a differentiated form. He chooses Moses as a witness of His mercy and Pharaoh as a witness of the judgment that in and with this mercy becomes necessary and is executed. Thus He determines Moses as the voluntary, Pharaoh as the involuntary servant of His power and His name. He renews His mercy with regard to Moses. He refuses this renewal to Pharaoh. If it is self-evident that for the men concerned it means personally something very different to be dealt with and used by God in these different ways, there is no mention of that here. It was perhaps the decisive exegetical error of the classical doctrine of predestination that—being more concerned about the things of men (although not to their advantage) than the things of God—it thought to see the scope of Rom. 9[18] in the personal situation and destiny of Moses and Pharaoh (as of Rom. 9[6f.] in that of the different sons of Abraham and Isaac). But the point at issue here is precisely how the diversity of the personal situation and destiny of Israelite man, which, conditioned by the divine predetermination, is so characteristic of the history and life of the chosen people Israel, does not contradict but corresponds to the election of Israel and the righteousness of the mercy of its God. We are told that there must repeatedly be this division in the sphere of Israel's history and life because its history is in fact the history of the expectation of its crucified Messiah and at the same time the pre-history of the Church of the risen Lord, because it is in this sphere that God intends to justify both Himself and man, and will, in fact, do so. Ἐλεεῖν describes in v. 18 the special act of mercy, the renewal of mercy, in which God's purpose with Israel is revealed and becomes effective in its positive aspect, the founding in its midst of the Church and the mercy shown to it, the prefiguration of the mercy in which God will take man's part on the day of His future, in the resurrection of Jesus Christ from the dead. Σκληρύνειν means to stiffen, harden, make obdurate, petrify (Vulg.: *indurare*), and describes the isolation of the original and the withholding of the special new act of mercy as a result of which the same purpose of God with Israel takes effect in its negative aspect, in the constitution of Israel for itself and as such, the prefiguration of the judgment which God, on the same day of His future— in the course of showing mercy—will send forth upon man, to which He will on this day submit Himself on man's behalf. V. 18 is, therefore, to be paraphrased as follows: Whomsoever God's merciful purpose in the election of His community determines for the prefiguration and reflection of His mercy, for the unveiling of the goodness of His sovereign dealing, of the grace of His freedom, to him He reveals and gives Himself as He who has and executes this purpose, so that he may serve His will like Moses, as God's friend, voluntarily, in thankfulness and therefore in obedience and under God's blessing. Whomsoever God's merciful purpose in the election of the community determines for the prefiguration and reflection of His judgment, for the unveiling of the impotence, unworthiness and hopelessness of all man's will and achievement as opposed to God's, for the unveiling of the severity of His sovereign dealing, of the freedom of His grace, to him He refuses fellowship and denies Himself, so that like Pharaoh he must serve Him as God's enemy, involuntarily, with an unthankful heart and therefore through the medium of his sin and guilt and under the curse and punishment of God.

The question which Paul voices in v. 19 and which he answers in vv. 20–22 is a challenge. " Thou wilt say then unto me, Why doth he yet find fault ? For who hath resisted his will ? " In order to interpret this we must also quote the formulation which it is taken up again in v. 20 : " Why hast thou made me thus ? " It is such an obvious question that it is superfluous to settle whether it was actually put to Paul and by whom, or whether he discusses it here just because he reckons that it might be raised at this point. Clearly it records the defence of a man who, according to the exposition in vv. 17–18, when he looks at his willing and running (v. 16), sees himself put by God Himself among His enemies, indeed determined as one of these enemies, without regard to what he can advance in favour of the right, the worth and the usefulness of his efforts What, then, can God have against him, if all his willing and running receive no consideration at all, if he is made a Pharaoh by God's will and work whatever course his willing and running may take ? How can he still be responsible, chargeable, punishable ? What occasion is there for him to repent, to make use of God's offer of His grace ? Is he expected, even with his best efforts, to be able to offer resistance to the will and work of God ? And if this is beyond him, what is wrong about being Pharaoh ? There would be some point in this question if in v. 18, as the classical doctrine of predestination will have it, Paul had been speaking of an absolute power of disposal belonging to God. It was not for nothing that on the basis of this presupposition all the arguments in answer to this question and in refutation of this defence were so feeble that about 1700, after 150 years of discussion, it was still or again possible to introduce this *scrupulus de praedestinatione hominis irregeniti* (S. Werenfels, *Opusc.* II, p. 135 f.) with the same lachyrmose assurance as formerly the opponents of Calvin and earlier still those of Augustine and Gottschalk had done. If it is the *decretum absolutum* that Paul proclaims in v. 18, even his own answer to this question in v. 20 is no real answer. But in v. 18 Paul does not proclaim the *decretum absolutum*. On the contrary, he speaks of the merciful will of the free God. In view of this, the challenge in v. 19 is irrelevant. It is irrevelant because if the God who is free in the exercise of His mercy determines man to be the witness of His judgment no man can be in a position to oppose Him with the question why He finds fault, or why He has made him thus. " O man, who art thou that repliest against God ? " (v. 20a). The tenor of the answer which Paul has in mind with this counter-question is not as has so often been assumed : " After all you are only a creature with which God as its Creator has power to deal as seems good to Him." Of course, God " has power " to do this. Of course, man is therefore a being with whom God " has power " to deal in this way. But it is not in respect of an indeterminate power of God that Paul's counter-question puts man in his place. This would only give fresh vigour and a new pretext for the question of v. 19. On the contrary, the " power " of God in His dealing with man, in face of which it becomes man to be humble, is something wholly determinate ; it is settled by the determined purpose on which God has decided with respect to man in Jesus Christ. The tenor of the answer hidden in the counter-question of v. 20 is : " In any case, whether you are a friend of God like Moses or an enemy like Pharaoh, whether your name is Isaac or Ishmael, Jacob or Esau, you are the man on account of whose sin and for whose sin Jesus Christ has died on the cross for the justification of God, and for whose salvation and bliss, and for whose justification, He has been raised from the dead " (Rom. 4²⁵). This man—the man who is concerned in this twofold justification achieved in Jesus Christ, who is confronted with this twofold justification—cannot possibly make the challenge of v. 19. The defence of the man appointed as a witness to the divine judgment will surely wither away on his lips, if he can ever conceive of it at all. Not only the friend but also the enemy of God, not only His voluntary but also His involuntary servant, must be told : " You are this man, and as this man you cannot possibly wish to dispute with God. As this man, whoever and whatever else you may be, you are who you are and what you are by the merciful will of the free God. In every case you have occasion for thankfulness, in every case occasion to recognise your ingratitude, in every case occasion to be aware of your responsibility for it, in every case occasion to repent, in every case occasion to put your hope in God and God alone. Whatever God makes of you, whether you stand in the light or the shadow of His merciful purpose, whether you have to witness to God's goodness as such or to the weakness and unworthiness of man in relation to Him and therefore to the seriousness of the divine judgment—this is what you have occasion for, and therefore you have no occasion to make this challenge." Paul meets it—the sequel will show that this is how he wants to be understood—by preaching and urging the claim of the Gospel of the justification of God and man achieved in Jesus Christ. Man justified in Jesus Christ cannot oppose this challenge to the God justified in Jesus Christ. He accepts this divine reproof. He does not will to resist God. For whatever purpose he may be determined and created he glorifies the hand of God that is upon him. (The *scrupulus de praedestinatione* was the punishment for the way in which the classical doctrine of predestination opposed an indeterminate God and an indeterminate man. Paul did not do that. Therefore he did not need to fear this *scrupulus*.)

The parable of the potter follows in vv. 20–21. This is the focal point of the whole exposition as we can see if we keep in mind the evangelical spirit of the preceding rejection of the question of v. 19, if we interpret the parable itself as it is used in its Old Testament prototypes, especially Jer. 18¹⁻¹⁰, and finally if we pay attention to the interpretation of it which is given afterwards in vv. 22–24 and introduced by an in no sense unimportant δέ. The parable of the potter is, in the first place, a repetition and confirmation of v. 18. God is in His mercy free to disclose Himself here and withhold Himself there. He is free to let His power and His name be shown forth and proclaimed in one way by Moses and in another by Pharaoh. He who in Jesus Christ will have mercy upon sinners uses for the revelation of His way to this goal witnesses to His merciful purpose as such, His Church in Israel, " vessels of honour "—and also witnesses to His judgment (as the operation of His mercy), Israel in itself and as such, " vessels of dishonour." He uses them both as witnesses to Jesus Christ, each in its own way. This is how the potter, the God of Israel, deals in and with His people—not according to the caprices of His omnipotence but in the determinate purpose, corresponding to His name and nature, of His own justification in the death and man's justification in the resurrection of Christ, in the revelation of the way taken by Him in His advance towards the day of His future. Two things are necessarily revealed on this way, that Israel is the place of His glory, and that this glory is His own and not Israel's. But already in Paul's Old Testament sources the twofold action of the potter does not by any means take place along parallel lines, in symmetry and equilibrium, so that proceeding from a centre of indifference (on the principle of the see-saw), with the same seriousness and the same meaning, indeed with the same finality—with an eternity before Him to the right and to the left—God will now accept and now reject, now disclose and now withhold Himself, now show mercy and now harden. Rather—while both operations are His—His operation εἰς τιμήν is one thing and His operation εἰς ἀτιμίαν is another, and they stand in an irreversible sequence and order. If to the right He says Yes, He does this for His own sake, expressing His ultimate purpose, declaring what He wills to do among and to men in His mercy operative and revealed in Jesus Christ. If to the left He says No, He does this for the sake of the Yes that is to be spoken to the right, on the way to the execution of His ultimate purpose, declaring that which the operation and revelation of His mercy make necessary because they happen among and to men. Without prejudice to the seriousness of the divine purpose on both sides, the relationship between the two sides of the one divine action is one of supreme incongruity, supreme a-symmetry, supreme disequilibrium. The light of the divine willing and the shadow of the powerful divine non-willing are indeed related at this point, but they are necessarily governed by an irreversible sequence and order. " For his anger endureth but a moment ; his favour a lifetime " (Ps. 30⁵). " For a small moment have I forsaken thee ; but with great mercies will I gather thee. In a little wrath I hid my face from thee for a moment, but with everlasting kindness will I have mercy on thee " (Is. 54[7f.]). " For as the heaven is high above the earth, so great is his mercy toward them that fear him. . . . As for man, his days are as grass ; as a flower of the field, so he flourisheth. For the wind passeth over it, and it is gone ; and the place thereof shall know it no more. But the mercy of the Lord is from everlasting to everlasting . . . and his righteousness unto children's children " (Ps. 103[11f.]). This is the relationship between the two courses of action followed by the potter, the God of Israel. A failure to recognise this relationship is the error of the question of v. 20a. The thing that is fashioned cannot with Is. 29[16] say to Him who fashioned it : " He made me not " ; nor can it ask : " Why hast thou made me thus ? " This is forbidden, not by the power, but by the meaning, the tendency, the right of the power of its fashioner. If the " vessels of dishonour " are appointed to demonstrate the impotence and unworthiness of man, of the " lump " out of which they and the " vessels of honour " are taken, " the vessels of honour," shaped by the same hand, stand in relation to them as a demonstration of what God's will and purpose are with this man. How can man, instead of praising God's work with him, deduce from his impotence and unworthiness attested by the " vessels of wrath " a right and a necessity to absolutise them, to play off the divine No against the divine Yes, when the former is, in fact, spoken only for the sake of the Yes ? What option has the man who is determined as a " vessel of dishonour " except by his witness to the impotence and unworthiness of man—which he must give involuntarily in any case—voluntarily to corroborate the witness of the one who is determined as a " vessel of honour," as he sees God Himself, not cancelling His Yes by His No, but corroborating it ? To provide this corroboration is Israel's appointed task in the elected community of God. Israel in itself and as such is the " vessel of dishonour." It is the witness to the divine judgment. It embodies human impotence and unworthiness. For by Israel its own Messiah is delivered up to be crucified. In its midst, however, there stands in relation to it from the very first the Church with its comprehensive and final commission to proclaim to this man the work of God—the Church which in virtue of its Head, the risen Lord, is the " vessel of honour," the witness to the divine mercy, the embodiment of the divine goodness which has taken the part of this man. Can Israel ask : " Why hast thou made me thus ? Why hast thou not made me an Israel which as such and in itself is already the Church ? " It cannot raise questions like this because as Israel, as a vessel of wrath, as a witness to the divine judgment, it has the Church within it from the very first ; because it is with its proclamation of the divine No that it has been determined for and is called to entrance into the Church—called to serve voluntarily where it must in any case serve involuntarily. This calling which it has to be subordinate to the proclamation of the greater divine Yes is God's prior justification in relation to it and its own prior justification in relation to God. It is this which with a factuality that Israel cannot contest makes this question as impossible as that of v. 19. Ishmael is called by Isaac, Esau by Jacob, Pharaoh by Moses—the Synagogue of the present by Paul. In view of this call, in view of the Gospel so clearly addressed to them, can they dare to repeat this question, the challenge of v. 19 ?

That this interpretation of vv. 19–21 is the only possible one is shown by the exposition of the parable of the potter given in vv. 22–24. It consists of an interrogative sentence in the form of an anacoluthon which stylistically fits vv. 19–21 very well in so far as there no less than five questions in all, not directly answered by Paul, form the content of his exposition. The parable of the potter seems to have set a riddle. " But what if (this is taken to mean that) God, willing to show his wrath, and to make his power known, endured with much long-suffering the vessels of wrath fitted to destruction," in order (namely) " that he might make known the riches of his glory on the vessels of mercy, which he had afore prepared unto glory—as which he hath called even us, not of the Jews only, but also of the Gentiles ? " The whole statement is articulated and the relation between God's action to left and right brought into clear view by the καὶ ἵνα of v. 23 (which is to be understood in both a consecutive and a final sense). The sequence of the ἐλεεῖ and σκληρύνει of v. 18 and the εἰς τιμήν and εἰς ἀτιμίαν of v. 21b, conceived in view of the goal, is now reversed in a genetic development, and the apparently unrelated proximity of the two is clarified. In vv. 22-24 it is quite unambiguous that Paul is not speaking of a content of God's will which is to be interpreted as an abstract duality, but of God's way on which in execution of His one purpose He wills and executes in a determined sequence and order this twofold operation. The harsh appearance that can descend on the preceding passage if vv. 22-24 are not taken into account in advance—as if God's mercy and hardening, the existence of " vessels of honour " and of " dishonour," were the two goals of two different ways of God—is now finally dispelled. The principal verb of the decisive second half of the sentence (v. 23) is γνωρίσῃ. Not that there are " vessels of mercy," but that God reveals in them the riches of His glory, is the goal of the divine way, and it is only for this revelation that the " vessels of mercy " are also needed. Similarly the principal statement of the first half of the sentence (v. 22) does not consist in establishing the fact that there are " vessels of wrath," that God has prepared them as such and therefore for destruction, nor even that He has done so in order to show forth His wrath and reveal His power, but in the fact that God has " endured these vessels of wrath with much long-suffering." This is the principal statement of v. 22, not merely because ἤνεγκεν is the principal verb, but above all because it is with this ἤνεγκεν that the statement of v. 23 is connected. God endured these vessels in order to reveal the riches of His mercy through the others. This is the Pauline interpretation of the parable of the potter. According to v. 22 the one will of God has indeed the form both of the manifestation of wrath and of the revelation of power. In showing mercy God is indeed also wrathful—He has " brought forth the weapons of His indignation," says the passage in Jer. 50[25] to which Paul alludes. That is, He is wrathful against the perversity that encounters Him from the side of man. And in showing mercy He is also free in His omnipotence, in contrast to the impotence of man. That which He in His mercy on Israel will execute in Jesus Christ will also be an act of judgment and rejection. He will (Rom. 1[18f.]) pronounce a devastating No upon all the willing and running of man by the very fact that He takes his affairs out of his hands into His own. He will in every way disinherit man and dispossess him. But hidden in this very operation of wrath He will be gracious to him. By the very means of this judgment—the shame and distress of which He will bear Himself—He will save him. The history of Israel leading up to this goal can be nothing but an increasingly close succession of intimations of this judgment. That is why there are " vessels of wrath " throughout the whole course of its history. In them is shown and revealed the divine No, veiled in which the divine Yes to man will be spoken in the suffering and death of Israel's Messiah. For the sake of its election and its hope, Israel—otherwise it would not be Israel—must always have in it as well these " vessels of wrath fitted to destruction." Indeed it must finally become a single " vessel of wrath." In delivering up its Messiah to be put to death, it must become in its totality a witness to the divine judgment. But even according to v. 22 the negation of man has no independent or final significance in the will of God, nor has its demonstration and revelation therefore in God's will and dealing with Israel. Paul has clearly in view that at the goal of Israel's history God will not say No to man but that veiled under the No He will say Yes ; that He will not leave Jesus in the grave after being put to death but will raise Him from the dead. Seen in the light of this goal the decisive statement about these " vessels of wrath " is necessarily to the effect that God has endured them with much long-suffering. He has not only left them their time, and in that time life. He has not only waited, although in vain, for their repentance and conversion. He has indeed done that. But He has done more. In willing and using them as " vessels of wrath " He has, in fact, sustained them, carried them with Him, taken them up into the teleology of His merciful willing and running. He has not endured them in vain. The long-suffering in which He left them time, in which He waited in vain for repentance, was not an empty, meaningless tolerance ending at last in disillusionment, but an act of the divine patience, and as such an act of the divine wisdom. Because He bore in His own Son the rejection which falls on mankind, the fact of Ishmael's rejection, of Esau's, of Pharaoh's, of all Israel's also, is in the end superseded and limited ; it is characterised as a rejection borne by God. " To bear " in this context means more accurately to bear forward, to bear to an expected end. It is for the sake of Him who is to come, for the sake of the Lamb of God who will bear away the sin of the world (Jn. 1²⁹), that the sustaining, long-suffering of God (cf. Rom. 3²⁵ᶠ.) which befalls the " vessels of wrath " is possible and necessary. This bearing to an expected end is the secret of the history of Israel—and therefore also the secret of the continuing existence of the Synagogue alongside the Church. God not only bears with it. He not only waits for its repentance. But in so doing He wills it as a sign of His wrath and freedom which is also the abiding sign of God's mercy. " No power in the world will be able to extirpate Judaism. Indeed, not even the Jews themselves will be able to extirpate themselves so long as God's long-suffering endures this year also (Lk. 13⁸) the vessels of wrath." (E. Peterson, *Die Kirche aus Juden und Heiden*, 1933, p. 34.) It may be asked whether after all the Church does not actually need the intrinsically so incomprehensible counterpart of this Israel which after the fulfilment of its hopes repeats its old obduracy and even in so doing is carried towards its hope. It has in any case repeatedly to learn from the existence of the Synagogue, as a living commentary on the Old Testament, from what sort of " lump " (v. 21) it has itself been taken, how it is with man who is found by God's grace, and in the reflection of this knowledge how it is with the grace of God itself, how deeply God has humiliated Himself on man's behalf in order to exalt him so highly.

The goal of this enduring the " vessels of wrath " is indeed, according to v. 23, the revelation of the riches of the glory of God in the " vessels of mercy " prepared for glory, which are then in v. 24 expressly identified with the Church gathered from Jews and Gentiles. We cannot pay too much attention to the consecutive-final connexion of vv. 22 and 23 if we are to understand properly these two verses and with them the whole context of vv. 13–29 as an answer to the question of the righteousness of God in the election of the community. The *telos* of this election is now expressly indicated. God is wrathful and judges and punishes as He shows mercy, and indeed for His mercy's sake, because without this He would not be really and effectively merciful. We now learn explicitly that God's mercy is His glory (His self-confirming and self-demonstrating essence). In His mercy (and therefore not without the justification of man) God justifies Himself, as in the revelation of His wrath. The revelation of His wrath is therefore followed by that of His mercy. The latter must be preceded by the former because this will also be the order in the fulfilment of Israel's hope, in the confirmation of its election by God's self-humiliation for the purpose of exalting man in Jesus Christ, because Jesus Christ Himself will be this " way." But just because of the fact that Jesus Christ will be this irreversible " way," He is already the secret of Israel's history, which has its goal in Him. For this very reason the bearing with the " vessels of wrath " must be interpreted as a " bearing to an expected end." The meaning of its history cannot, then, be perceived in a juxtaposition of two different purposes of God. The existence of the " vessels of wrath," the existence of Israel standing at last before us as a single " vessel of wrath " embodied in the " traitor" Judas Iscariot, has no end in itself. God's sentence of rejection on Israel is not a final word, not the whole Word of God, but only the foreword to God's promise of His glory later to be revealed on this shadow-Israel. The witnesses of this final and whole Word of God, of the glory of God in its revelation speaking irrefutably for itself, are called in v. 23 the " vessels of mercy " in the same special sense in which in v. 15 and v. 18 Moses was designated an object of the divine mercy. " Vessels unto honour " they are called in v. 21. But we are not told there that the " vessels unto dishonour " proceeding from the hand of the God of Israel have not also in their special position and function to serve the coming glory of God and therefore His mercy. On the contrary, from the connexion between v. 22 and v. 23 we have to conclude that in their way they actually do this. Indirectly the real witnesses of the wrath of God are necessarily also witnesses of His mercy. But they are not its special, proper and direct witnesses—the witnesses of the resurrection and ascension of Christ, the witnesses of the Holy Spirit of whom He is conceived in the Virgin Mary, and whom He communicates to His own, by whom He is the Son of God and by whom men are called and may become sons of God. These witnesses are the " vessels of mercy " after and alongside them, taken from the same "lump " (v. 21), the Israelites who are " of Israel " in the sense that Jesus of Nazareth is, who in and with this One may positively and voluntarily confirm Israel's election. The sign of grace in their existence is also set up in Israel, and under this sign of grace Israel is not only the pre-figuration of the Synagogue " prepared for destruction " but is also the pre-figuration of the Church prepared for the vision and witness of the glory of God, for the praise of His mercy. Although the Israel determined for this service is reduced at the culmination of its mission to the prototype of the one person of the Son of David prepared beforehand, it already exists before Him (since this prototype proceeds from the midst of Israel itself) in many others, in all the children of Abraham and sons of David, in all the prophets and servants of God, in all the poor and as such righteous who form the steadily diminishing " remnant " of those who not only have Israel's calling and hope, but bear it in their hearts. In these " vessels of mercy " there pre-exists along with the Son of David, Jesus of Nazareth, the Church of those called and gathered by Him, of those who believe in Him. The One who creates in Him the Church is therefore no other than the potter, the God of Israel, who wills and produces not only " vessels of wrath " but also " vessels of mercy "—and even the " vessels of wrath " only in order that among the " vessels of mercy " every mouth may be stopped that would glory in man at the expense of God, in order that among them and by them the glory of God alone may be exalted. It is as Isaac has at his side an Ishmael, Jacob an Esau, Moses a Pharaoh, the Church a Synagogue, that they are the genuine children of the promise and faith of their father Abraham. Thus the Church founded by the elected apostles, even though there is a Judas Iscariot among them too, is the unveiled secret of the election—and of the twofold realisation of the election of Israel.

This, however, is not expressly stated until v. 24. The vessel of mercy (pre-figured in the patriarchs, in Moses, in David and in the prophets) is primarily the Lord Jesus Christ risen from the dead, and secondarily the apostolic Church called and gathered by Him through the Gospel, " . . . even us whom he hath called not only of the Jews but also of the Gentiles "—so runs the conclusion of the great anacoluthon of v. 22 f. It is this finding, so unexpected to any who might have interpreted too narrowly the vocabulary between v. 6 and v. 23, which (explained by quotations from Hosea, vv. 25–26, and from Isaiah, vv. 27–29) forms the final and culminating point of the Pauline exposition on the subject of the divine dealing with the elected people Israel. Its pregnant wording obviously says that in God's dealing with the Church too, as the goal towards which His dealing with Israel, as a unique prototype, was directed, and in close correspondence to this dealing, we are concerned with two things. There are called and gathered into the Church not just a few " vessels of mercy," a few

Jews who as children of Abraham, as heirs of Israel's distinction and endowment described in vv. 4–5, seem to have the exclusive claim to this and to justify this claim by their faith. No, called and gathered with them and justified by the same faith there is a whole abundance of manifest " vessels of wrath," a horde from among the Gentiles, from the realm of Moab and Ammon, of Egypt and Assyria—the very realm into which the whole of that hardened Israel (beginning with Ishmael and ending with the kings and people of Samaria but ultimately also with the Davidic kings and Jerusalem itself) seems to be thrust out by God's harsh dealing with His elected people. On the ground of the divine calling, says v. 24, the former and the latter together form the Church, vessels of mercy at the end and goal of the history of Israel, witnesses to the resurrection of Jesus Christ, recipients and instruments of the Holy Spirit, possessors of the " riches of the glory " of God (v. 23). The miracle of the Church consists not only in the fact that now when the history of Israel comes to its conclusion with the betrayal of its Messiah and the destruction of Jerusalem a few of this Israel subsequently repent and believe ; that Abraham may again beget an Isaac from the now lifeless womb of Sarah (Rom. 4^{19}) ; that Jacob and his people, wakened in these few from the dead, receive a new life. The miracle of the Church does consist in this too. Paul himself, as is well known, has with particular, proud thanksgiving made the most of his membership of this Israel (of the lost and yet preserved tribe of the Benjamin who was dear to Jacob above his brethren, Rom. 11^1, Phil. 3^5) plucked like a brand from the burning. The existence of Christian Jews as a sign of the indestructible continuity of the divine way, as an immediate reminder of the awakening of Lazarus, or rather of the awakening of the man Jesus from the dead, will always remain a special sign of grace. And only a cheerless, unspiritual way of thinking can occasion a Christian Jew to be ashamed of his origin from Israel or a Gentile Christian to hold it against him. It is a mark of supreme and indelible honour to be a Christian Jew. But the miracle of the Church does not consist only in the fact that there were and are Jews who finally come to believe, i.e., to know the God of Israel who has taken away from it all its sins. Over and above this it consists also in the fact that Gentiles, many Gentiles, were and are called to the same faith in the God of Israel, an abundance of men from the nations beside and around Israel, from the nations who as such are not elected, who as such have no part in its promise, distinction and endowment, to whom its Messiah is a complete stranger. They, too, were certainly men living on God's earth, His creation, and in the sphere of His rule. As their history impinged upon Israel's, they had stepped repeatedly into the light of the divine work and at times also of the divine promise. Yet they had, as a rule, served only as the dark foil to Israel's history. Israel's sanctification was always its separation from them. Israel's grace was always its preservation from their might and hostility. Israel's distinction was always its discrimination from them. That God loved Israel always seemed to mean that He did not love the nations as such, but let them go their own ways, let them share in His work for the most part only as instruments of His wrath against Israel. Every exception only confirmed the rule that Israel was elected, the nations were not. They did not seem to have either a positive or negative share in God's mercy even in the shape of that " hardening " (v. 18) as " vessels of dishonour " (v. 21) or of " wrath "—and they certainly did not seem to have any claim to a share in the glory of God. Or must this picture be radically corrected ? Did the juxtaposition of Israel and the nations in the sphere of the Old Testament always have a different meaning ? Had the exceptions signalised the true rule ? Is it not rather the case that God did not really concern Himself incidentally with the nations only for the sake of Israel, but that He concerned Himself in such a special way with Israel for the sake of the nations ? Is it not that the special calling of Israel was only the veiling of the divine calling of man and this veiling only the preparation for its unveiling to all peoples as the calling of God's community affecting the whole cosmos ? Is it not that the promise given to Israel was the promise for every man who believes ? From the standpoint of the end and goal of Israel's history the relationship can obviously be seen and understood in no other way. For here in the Church the few from the elected people are accompanied by the many from the non-elected peoples, called along with the former, and children of Abraham like them by faith in Abraham's promise. How does this come about ? What have the Gentiles to do with Israel's Messiah ? Fundamentally and in complete objectivity only what is revealed in the figure of Pontius Pilate. To them He is delivered up by Israel itself to be put to death and after their miscarriage of justice and by their hands He is, in fact, put to death. They thus execute at one and the same time the decisions both of the evil will of Israel and of the gracious will of God with Israel. It is in this way and this way alone that at the eleventh hour they participate concretely in the fulfilment of Israel's hope. But for all that it is soon enough for one of them to be able to utter immediately after Jesus' death the first unambiguous confession of faith and sin : Ἀληθῶς οὗτος ὁ ἄνθρωπος υἱὸς θεοῦ ἦν (Mk. 15³⁹). The Gentiles have taken the last step on the long road of Israel's history, and with the confession of the Gentiles it now begins anew even before the apostles are awakened to the life of the new and true Israel by the resurrection of Jesus Christ and the outpouring of the Holy Spirit. Thus the death of Jesus unites what was divided, the elected and the rejected. Immediately before this it is said (Mk. 15³⁸) that the veil between the holy of holies and the forecourt of the temple " was rent in twain from the top to the bottom." As Israel's hope is annihilated it is reinstated ; the Church, the secret substance of Israel, is already born ; and what happened on Easter morning can only establish the birth of the Church in the blood of Israel's Messiah, in whom the Gentiles once " without Christ, aliens from the commonwealth of Israel, and strangers from the covenants of promise, having no hope, and without God in the world," (Eph. 2¹²) are " fellow-heirs " and members " of the same body " and " partakers with them " of the promise (Eph. 3⁶). " For he is our peace, who hath made both one, and hath broken down the middle wall of partition, the enmity in his flesh . . . for to make in himself of twain one new man . . . and that he might reconcile both unto God in one body by the cross, having slain the enmity thereby " (Eph. 2¹⁴ᶠ·). " Through him we both— not only from the Jews but also from the Gentiles—have access by one Spirit unto the Father " (Eph. 2¹⁸). That this is so is (Eph. 3¹⁰) the work of the mystery of the πολυποίκιλος σοφία τοῦ θεοῦ which even the angels have to learn only in view of the Christian Church and which forms the central content of the apostolic, the New Testament message, of the Word of God's mercy realised in judgment.

What is the point of the surprising assertion in v. 24 that the Church is called from both Jews and Gentiles ? The opinion of Peterson (*op. cit.*, p. 36 f.) cannot be sustained, that there lies hidden " behind this insignificant copula the whole tragedy and pathos of the unbelieving Synagogue," and that the Scripture quotations following in v. 25 breathe " something of the divine bitterness." For what does this tell us ? The question at issue in the whole context is surely that of the righteousness of God's mysterious guidance of Israel from the very first and in the present, and therefore of the meaning of the divine bitterness which Israel had and still has to experience, the meaning, too, of the " tragedy and pathos " in which the Synagogue confronts the Church. And this question was answered in vv. 22–24 with the insight that all the wrath of God upon the one Israel is always co-ordinated with His mercy upon another Israel which He was preparing within the first to cause it finally to arise from it in the form of the Church. If according to v. 24 the Church is now called from both Jews *and* Gentiles, this casts over the past and present of Israel, not new shadow, but a new, surpassing light. The sin of Israel, which in past and present stands under the wrath of God, will be discussed separately in 9³⁰ to 10²¹, but only after the question of God's righteousness with respect to Israel has been (independently) met. The answer of 9[14] is that God's righteousness in the history of Israel consists in the fact that He willed to manifest and has actually manifested in this people His mercy (not without His judgment). It is precisely this which is revealed in the miracle of the existence of the Church gathered from Jews and Gentiles as it is asserted in v. 24. Thus the assertion of v. 24, in its connexion with vv. 22–23, is intended to assist the decisive insight that every accusation to be made in the manner of vv. 14, 19, 20 against the God who deals with Israel as the potter with the clay is irrelevant because even in the course of His wrath the God of Israel does not cease to show mercy, because He shows wrath in order all the more fully and decisively to show mercy. Who, then, can dispute with God ? But to what extent does this particular assertion serve this insight ? According to the Old Testament explanation which now follows in vv. 25–29, it does so in a twofold way.

In so far as it speaks of the calling of the Gentiles, v. 24 proves, according to vv. 25–26, the absolute superiority and triumphant power of the mercy towards men revealed in Jesus Christ at the goal and end of Israel's history. The sayings in Hos. 2[25] and 2[1] which Paul quotes here speak of a people which once was " not my people " (because it was addressed in this way, because it was, therefore, expressly rejected by God), but was then called " my people " by the same God. They speak of an unloved one whom He calls His beloved. At the very place where the judgment, " Ye are not my people " was declared, they are called " the sons of the living God." In both the Hosea passages the people to which this prophecy refers is the people Israel, and particularly the people of Northern Israel characterised and designated in Hos. 1[8-9] as *Lo' Ruḥama, Lo' 'Ammi*, in contrast to Judah as Jezreel. Of this rejected, major part of Israel it is said in Hos. 1[10]–2[1] : " Yet the number of the children of Israel shall be as the sand of the sea, which cannot be measured nor numbered ; and it shall come to pass in the place where it was said unto them, Ye are not my people, there it shall be said unto them, Ye are the sons of the living God. Then shall the children of Judah and the children of Israel be gathered together, and appoint themselves one head, and they shall come up out of the land ; for great is the day of Jezreel. Say ye unto your brethren, *'Ammi* ; and to your sisters, *Ruḥama.*" And similarly in Hos. 2[21-33] : " And it shall come to pass in that day I will hear, saith the Lord, I will hear the heavens, and they shall hear the earth ; and the earth shall hear the corn, and the wine and the oil ; and they shall hear Jezreel. And I will sow her unto me in the earth ; and I will have mercy upon *Lo' Ruḥama* ; and I will say to *Lo' 'Ammi, 'Ammi-atha*! and they shall say, thou art my God." It is to be noted what Paul does when he quotes these passages. It is undoubtedly in the calling of the Gentiles to the Church that he sees the fulfilment of this prophecy of salvation for rejected Northern Israel, the dawn of the great day of Jezreel. The Gentiles, the believers from the nations, from the great darkness surrounding the people of Yahweh, were *Lo' Ruḥama* and *Lo' 'Ammi* in quite a different way from the rejected Northern tribes, and now even these Gentiles have heard the appeal and summons that makes all things new : My people, the sons of the living God. So wide is the sweep of prophecy ! So supreme, so triumphant at the goal and end of Israel's history, is the deed of God's mercy announced by Hosea ! So great is the miracle of the revelation of glory towards which all things there were striving ! But we must not apply negatively against Israel Paul's indication of this overflowing fulfilment of prophecy in the calling of the Gentiles to the Church, as if the Hosea quotations were meant to say : " What was there prophesied for rejected Israel has now passed into fulfilment, not for it, but in its stead for the believing Gentiles. It no longer applies to them." On the contrary, the tenor of the statement is positive. To it, to rejected Israel there was given there the prophecy of God's repentance fulfilled in the calling of the Gentiles, of His mercy that surpasses His wrath, of His Yes that follows His No. It is the *Lo' Ruḥama* which is one day to be addressed as *Ruḥama*, the *Lo' 'Ammi* which is one day to be addressed, and has already been addressed, as *'Ammi*. When Paul states that he sees the prophecy concerning Northern Israel fulfilled in the calling of the Gentiles we have to do with a conclusion *a maiori ad minus*. If God's mercy is so rich and powerful even upon Gentiles who were standing wholly under His curse and sentence of rejection, how much more so upon those to whom He has already promised it! Indeed we must even read and understand the Hosea quotations quite simply as a repetition of the prophecy originally—and as established by its comprehensive fulfilment, definitively—addressed to *Israel*, namely to that other, *rejected* Israel. In the course of speaking of the calling of the Gentiles they speak—and now that this has become event, they speak no less but all the more strictly—of the future of this rejected Israel. Admittedly they too, like the passages from Genesis and Exodus quoted earlier, speak of the vessels of wrath and dishonour in which the history of Israel is uncannily rich. Of the twelve tribes, ten are in Hosea already assigned quite summarily to this side. So they, too, speak of the riddle of the Synagogue, of the elected people which can only be called *Lo' Ruḥama, Lo' 'Ammi*. They speak of it, however, in such a way as to keep before it as such the word of grace which applies to it, too, and in it to promise a future that will not be the work of God's wrath but of His mercy which applies to Israel also. This future of the lost people *Israel* already become present in the calling of the Gentiles justifies the God of Israel even as the God of Ishmael and Esau, even as the God of Pharaoh. The God who has given this promise precisely to the rejected among His elected people, and who has fulfilled this promise in the ten times rejected who had never been His elected people, cannot possibly be accused, but in view of the miracle of His mercy can only be praised, for His faithfulness and wisdom. Israel has only to recognise this miracle and hold to it as the consolation given to it, as the picture of its own future, and it will have no more occasion for complaints about the unrighteousness of God.

But the assertion of v. 24 serves the apprehension of the righteousness of God in His mercy in still another way. V. 24 does indeed speak also of the calling of the Jews and thus proves, according to vv. 27–29, that what has been revealed in Jesus Christ at the goal and end of Israel's history is divine mercy and not human merit, grace and not nature, freedom and not necessity. How otherwise can it be the righteousness of God, or any kind of righteousness at all? How otherwise can we take heart from what has been revealed here? The quotations from Is. 10²²f. and 1⁹ are meant to prove this aspect of the matter. It is to be noted that these passages also speak of God's steadfastly continuing grace towards Israel. The first passage in its context runs : " And it shall come to pass in that day that the remnant of Israel, and such as are escaped of the house of Jacob, shall no more again stay upon him that smote them ; but shall stay upon the Lord, the Holy One of Israel, in truth. The remnant shall return, even the remnant of Jacob, unto the mighty God. For though thy people Israel be as the sand of the sea, yet a remnant of them shall return : the consumption decreed shall overflow with righteousness. For the Lord God of hosts shall make a consumption, even determined, in the midst of the land. Therefore thus saith the Lord God of hosts, O my people that dwellest in Zion, be not afraid of the Assyrian : he shall smite thee with a rod, and shall lift up his staff against thee, after the manner of Egypt. For yet a very little while, and the indignation shall cease, and mine anger in their destruction " (Is. 10²⁰⁻²⁵). And the second passage forms a reassuring conclusion to the opening complaint and accusation of the book against a people which in spite of every punishment and distress continues in apostasy : " The daughter of Zion is left as a cottage in a vineyard, as a lodge in a garden of cucumbers, as a besieged city. Except the Lord of hosts had left unto us a very small remnant, we should have been as Sodom, and we should have been like unto Gomorrah " (Is. 1^{8-9}). The special point given to this promise of grace is clear. It has less regard than that of Hosea to the future of all Israel and more to its present in individuals. It speaks of the remnant of Israel that remains, of its preservation and its future as such. It is just this remnant as such that Paul has before his eyes in the Jews of whose calling to the Church v. 24 speaks. In them as in the believing Gentiles prophecy has come to its fulfilment. Isaiah has " foretold " (v. 29) their existence as the existence of a " remnant." That it is only a remnant is stressed in neither of the Isaiah passages nor is it to be stressed according to what Paul has in mind. The decisive thing here, too, is the positive aspect. The matter at issue is Israel, which in spite of its apostasy is saved from merited ruin and brought by a miracle to conversion ; which is, in fact, being converted. It is not because it is Israel that it may live on as Israel, but because as Israel it is saved by its God, preserved amid the rising tide of consumption and decision. Otherwise it would almost have become like Sodom and Gomorrah. It was entirely due to God, to His gracious reversal of His purpose, that it did not become like Sodom and Gomorrah, but that, like Lot, it was delivered from destruction, that it was given a place of repentance. Thus the calling of the Jews to the Church is also to be understood as the plucking of a brand from the burning (Amos 4^{11}, Zech. 3^{2})—how much more so, then, the calling of the Gentiles ! It is obvious that in their case above all it is a case of sheer divine deliverance. Over the whole face of the earth there flows the tide of the divine consumption and decision. The conclusion this time is *a minori ad maius*. If even for the rich Jews, according to the prophecy fulfilled in them, absolutely everything depends on God's wonderful mercy, how much more so for the poor Gentiles ! Even the Jews as they rely on the profoundest consolation promised to them as Jews can recognise in their calling only mercy and not merit, only God's grace and not human nature, only creative freedom and not creaturely necessity. It is their mission in the Church—that of believing Jews—to keep this insight clear. But the juxtaposition of converted and unconverted Jews, the splitting up of Israel into Church and Synagogue, can only underline and deepen the insight to the extent that in this very juxtaposition it is actual and visible that the end and aim of all God's ways, His ways with Jews as with Gentiles, is the act of His free mercy. And retrospectively from this point we have to say that Israel's mission as a preparation for the Church and its prefiguration consists in the fact that it has always to exist as this remnant which is saved and to be saved again, as the spared σπέρμα, as the LXX translated Is. 1^{9}, and as it was undoubtedly understood by Paul with concrete reference to the " seed " of Abraham who is also the " root of David " (Rev. 22^{16}). Israel lives by the grace of God, and living in this way it is identical with the offspring for whose sake it was chosen, and in turn identical with all who believe in this offspring, with the totality of those who will be called to faith in this offspring. In this mission of Israel, and ultimately in this its identity with Jesus Christ and His Church, lies the justification of God with respect to what He has willed and done, and still wills and does, with this people.

[II, 2, pp. 213–233]

5. THE RICH YOUNG RULER AND THE COMMAND OF GOD

It will serve to stress this final and decisive christological determination of the form of the divine command if we conclude with a consideration of the story of the rich young man in Mk. 10^{17-31} and par.

The narrative describes very fully the form of the divine claim. It shows that the demand of the living divine command made in the person of Jesus aims at the genuine, joyous and sustained decision of man for this person and therefore at the fulfilment of the one entire will of God. It shows this negatively in the figure of the rich man who was unequal to this demand, and positively in the disciples of Jesus who have become obedient to it.

Both the rich man and the disciples, the disobedient and the obedient, are within the sphere of the judicial authority and power, the *regnum Jesu Christi*, being subject to the living command of God embodied and established in Him. Even the rich man, the disobedient ! That this is the case, he himself shows in a particularly ostentatious way. " He ran up and fell on his knees before him " (Mk. 10[17]). We cannot say why or for what reason or with what mind and intention, but the fact remains that he does it. And in so doing he adjusts himself to the order which is still order even where we are disobedient to it. He ranges himself with the disciples. He bears testimony to what the command is which has force for him as well as them. He cannot and will not reverse or nullify this testimony by his later withdrawal (Mk. 10[22]). No one can withdraw from the kingdom of Christ. It embraces even the kingdoms of disobedience and all their inhabitants. " He went away sorrowful." By his sorrow in disobedience, he again testifies what the command of God is which has force even for him ; he again testifies that even he, even in his disobedience, is in the kingdom of Christ and not elsewhere. It is quite possible to leave or be expelled from a society, but never from the kingdom of Christ, from the community in which that order is established and obtains. This does not imply any mitigation of the sin and guilt of his disobedience. On the contrary, it makes it manifest. It clearly points again to the hope of which he is not deprived even in and with his disobedience. Even as one who is disobedient he is still at the place where another time he can obey, although he has failed to do so this time. " Good teacher, what shall I do that I may inherit eternal life ? " This is the question which he had put to Jesus as we have it in Mk. 10[17]. He was sure, therefore, that beyond the insecure possession and enjoyment of the present temporal and therefore fleeting life it is necessary for man to attain eternal life, the true life that persists in contrast to the problematical character of this present life as it is revealed in death. He was also sure that in this present fleeting life man has to be and do something definite in order to attain this eternal life. Who can secure the inheritance if he is not the heir ? What must I do to act and prove myself as such ?—is what he asks, therefore. And, finally, he was sure that it was to Jesus that he had to come with this question. He could not answer it himself, and he did not expect anyone but Jesus to answer it. All this confirms at once the witness which he has already borne by his running to Jesus and kneeling before Him. With all this he confirms the validity of the order under which he, too, stands. It is in Jesus that man has this future, and therefore this present task. And it is Jesus who has to tell him about this task. For it is in Jesus that there has been concluded between God and man the covenant which forms the beginning of all the ways and works of God, and therefore the objective law under which the existence of all living creatures runs its course. But what will be the relationship to Jesus into which he enters as one upon whom and for whom all this is necessarily valid and binding objectively ? Will that which is objectively valid for him become true or not true in this relationship ? Will it be realised as obedience or as disobedience ? Will he conduct himself as one to whom eternal life is so necessary that, to obtain it, he will do what is necessary, i.e., exactly what Jesus commands him ? This is the judicial question to which he exposed himself when with his question he testified to his objective membership of the kingdom of Christ.

That this question is now a burning one emerges in Jesus' first answer in Mk. 10[18] : " Why callest thou me good ? None is good except the one God." Calvin's interpretation (*Comm. ad loc.*, C.R. 45, 537) is probably right : *Tu me falso bonum vocas magistrum, nisi a Deo profectum agnoscis. . . . Iam quidem aliquo obediendi affectu imbutus erat, sed eum vult Christus altius conscendere, ut Deum loquentem audiat.* The man who desires His, Jesus', judgment upon his life asks for nothing other or less than *God's* judgment. Is he conscious of this ? Is he prepared to listen to this judgment ? Has he come to Him for it ? Is he willing and ready to listen not to the instruction of a good human teacher, but to that of the divine Teacher Himself ? It is possible to listen to the instruction of a human teacher—even the best—and still find it possible and necessary to test whether the case is as he says, and only to make up our mind and act after this test, and therefore ultimately on the basis of our own judgment (even if it is stimulated and enriched by that of the teacher). But this cannot be done with Jesus. Jesus is not a " good teacher " of this kind. And although the man has certainly come to the right person, he has not come in the right way to this right person if his question is meant only as it can be directed to a human teacher, perhaps the best imaginable. The Word that he will hear from Jesus will be the Word that closes all further questioning and excludes all scrutiny, and it is by his obedience or disobedience to it that he will stand or fall. This is the way in which Jesus Christ is Lord in His kingdom, i.e., in the whole sphere of the man with whom God has made His covenant in Him. When He calls, God calls, and when man encounters Him, he encounters God—the one God, outside and alongside whom there is no other. Therefore the question put to man in this, His kingdom, the decisive question which is secret, but from time to time suddenly revealed, is whether he will or will not meet Him with the obedience which the one God demands and which he owes the one God. That this decisive question has been revealed for him is proved by the fact that this man honours the objective order under which he stands, and comes to Jesus with his question. How will it fare with him and how will he stand in the light into which he has stepped and in which he now actually stands ?

According to Mt. 19[16], his question was somewhat different : " Teacher, what good thing must I do that I may inherit eternal life ? " The presupposed objective certainty of the questioner in regard to the aim, the way and right information about this way, is clearly the same as according to the Markan account. The only difference is that here the idea of good is not connected with the addressed " teacher " but with the action concerning the right form of which he would like the latter to instruct him. Jesus' answer is (Mt. 19[17]) correspondingly different : " Why do you ask me concerning that which is good ? One there is who is good." But the point of the answer is the same : If you ask me about what is good, then you must know that you are asking about what is good in the sight of God—in the sight of the One who is the good. When you ask me about the good, you step before the seat of the Judge from whose verdict there is no appeal to a higher court. And when I give you an answer to this question, you are answered in such a way that there can be no further question either to yourself or to others about the good that you ought to do. Will you listen to this verdict ? Are you prepared to listen to that which, once it is uttered and heard by you, means that you cannot possibly shelter behind any test or scrutiny or decision of your own ? Do you know that with your question about the good you have demanded this Word, and therefore decided in advance your righteousness or unrighteousness before God ?

What follows next, the reference to the commandments and the rich man's answer that he had observed them all from his youth, is at once a preparation and postponement of the communication of the inexorable Word which—in the light into which he has now entered—he must now accept. It is a preparation in so far as the reference to the commandments does in fact make the communication, and the rich man's reaction to the reference is a proof that he is actually in a position of disobedience, and therefore through this reference is condemned by Jesus and therefore by God. It is a postponement in so far as the communication of this Word occurs only in a concealed form in this reference, as does also the actual disobedience of the rich man in his reaction to it. Jesus does not appear to have said anything new to him with this reference, and he for his part does not see any reason, on the basis of this reference, to confess his disobedience and go away, as he did later. The divine judgment already made is still hidden under the form of a continuing conversation between the rich man and Jesus—continuing apparently to his advantage. Now that he has stated that he has done, and does, everything that Jesus with His reference to the commandments has described as the action in question, what is to prevent his being told : You will obtain eternal life ; for you are on the right road to it ; you are living as one must live who has the prospect, claim and hope of it ? Why can he not be told this ? Why is the apparently so promising conversation about the commandments nothing more than a preparation for the disclosing of the divine judgment, to the proclamation of which the rich man has exposed himself, and which secretly already—and very much to his disadvantage—has been pronounced over him ?

According to Mk. 10[19], Jesus strengthened the warning as to the Judge before whom he stands with the statement : " You know the commandments "—therefore you know the Law by which the Judge to whom you have appealed will judge you, according as your actions correspond or do not correspond to it. According to Mt. 19[17], this part of the answer of Jesus runs: " If you would enter into life, keep the commandments." The point is the same, for the man who has to do with God, as we have seen, has only to be reminded of what God wills of him—the God of Israel, the God of grace and pity, the God in whose sphere he has shown himself to be with his question. He is to do what this God wills of him according to His commandments. When he does this, and does not do what they forbid, he is on the road to life, eternal life. The reference, therefore, establishes a twofold fact. First, the questioner is within hearing of the command of God. When he comes to Jesus with his question, he has actually heard already what he asks. And, second, this range of the hearing of God's command is the sphere of the authority and power of the One whom he questions. The One who is questioned and the One God who is so well known to the questioner are not two but One. Therefore when He answers the questioner, in principle and substance He can only repeat what He has already said to him. That is just what He does when He refers him to the commands. He has already told him what he should do to inherit eternal life. Therefore the questioner knows very well what should be the form of life of one who has this prospect, claim and hope. It is not for nothing that he was in the kingdom of Jesus Christ even before he came to Him.

In Mt. 19[18] the rich man interposes a question : " Which (commandments) ? " This draws attention to the fact that the command of God is an ordered quantity. The Law has both an external and an internal side, a μορφή and a τέλος (Rom. 10[4]). In the different commandments, i.e., in the different proclamations of the one command of God, it may sometimes be the one and sometimes the other which is more or less visible, or even hidden. It is not the Decalogue in its entirety, nor is it even the comprehensive double command of love to God and one's neighbour (Mk. 12[29f.]), which is adduced by Jesus when He refers the rich man to " the commandments." What Mk. 10[19] enumerates are the commandments of the so-called " second table," somewhat rearranged, reduced and enlarged : Do not commit adultery ; Do not kill ; Do not steal ; Do not bear false witness ; Do not rob ; Honour your father and mother. And Mt. 19[19] adds from Lev. 19[18] : " Love your neighbour as yourself." The selection and combination is clear. The well-known command of God is set before the rich man in its external aspect—the aspect from which it can be seen that it involves a concrete doing or not doing. It is not as if there were not included in these forms the command to love and fear God above all things, the prohibition of making or worshipping images of God, the command to keep holy His name and His sabbath—just as the commandments of the " first table " do not exclude but include the concrete forms of the God of the " second." In the New Testament sense it is not possible either to love one's neighbour without first loving God, or to love God without then loving one's neighbour. We can and must say, indeed, that in this unity of the command of God there is reflected the mystery of the person of Jesus Christ—the unity of the eternal Word with our flesh, of the Son of God with the Son of David and the Son of Mary. At any rate the genuineness with which the command is heard and kept on the one side is always a test whether it is also done on the other, and therefore as a whole. We have a test of this kind in the present passage. How this man is related to God, whether he loves and fears God above all things, is what decides—and has already decided—whether or not he is on the road to eternal life. And the concrete form of the test to which he has exposed himself is whether he will hear in the voice of the human teacher, Jesus of Nazareth, the voice of the one God and obey it accordingly ? That is what he must do to inherit eternal life. But it is for this very reason that he is presented with the commandments of the second table, the external side of the divine command, the side that relates to life with one's neighbour. " You know the commandments "—how they are given you in the sphere of the most con-crete doing or not doing, in dealings with your fellow-man. It is in this sphere that you meet them again, now that you confront your neighbour in Me and in My person. Be and do now what you must be and do in accordance with them, and you will prove that you give God the glory and that you will therefore be an heir of eternal life. The answer of the rich man in v. 20, that he has observed all these things from his youth, naturally implies : I expect and am willing to observe them in the same way in the future as well. If Jesus has no more to say than merely to repeat these commandments, the questioner's answer means that he is fortified and confirmed in the way which he has always gone and intends to continue. He will now tread it to the end in the certainty that this is the way to eternal life.

According to the sequel, this is undoubtedly a misunderstanding of the answer which Jesus gives. But again according to the sequel, the mistake which trips him is not to be sought in the fact that he has subjectively deceived himself and Jesus with that assertion of v. 20, hypocritically or foolishly making himself out to be a saint when in fact he is a transgressor of all these commandments.. This may well have been the case. It will in fact turn out to be so. But Jesus Him-self is not interested in it according to the text. That he has observed everything that he had to do according to these commandments, that he has not been guilty of adultery, murder, stealing, robbery, calumny or disrespect to his parents, and that he will not be guilty of them in the future, is at once accepted without ques-tion, as in the case of the servant in Lk. 17[10]. He has had the commandments of God before him. To the best of his knowledge and conscience he has done what they command, and not done what they forbid. Regarded from his own point of view and with respect to the external form of the command, his relation to the command of God is in order. He meets his neighbour as required by the command of God. No accusation can fairly be brought against him either by himself or others. He has good cause indeed to ask (Mt. 19[21]) : " What lack I yet ? " If it is a matter of keeping the commandments, what more can be required of me, what more can be done by me ? Has he not put his confident answer to the final and supreme test by coming to Jesus Himself and throwing himself down on his knees before Him ? Yet this is all a misunderstanding and delusion. Indeed, it is a demonstration of the disobedience in which he stands, in which he has come to Jesus, and in which he will also leave Him. The com-mandments which he knows—he does not really know. Observing them, he has not really observed them. And coming to Jesus, he has really passed Him by. He lives in His kingdom. He knows its order and the respect he owes this order. He has no choice but to observe this respect. He has done this from his youth, and formally and at the decisive point face to face with Jesus he has now done so again. So far nothing can be said against him. He can have the clearest conscience—but only the clearest conscience of the disobedient man who, although he stands objectively under God's order, and necessarily and willingly acknowledges this subjectively, is still a rebel, determined to go his own way even under this order, allowing the command of God to determine his action but not himself, not subjecting himself to it. For it is himself that all the commandments demand —even the external commandments of the second table with all their reference to his life with his neighbour. Binding him externally, they aim to do it internally. Directing him to his neighbour, they aim to send him to God. That he should *be* something—the covenant-partner of God—is what all the commandments demand when they claim both what he does and what he does not do. That he should *love* his neighbour is what God wills when He tests him with all these directions regarding his relationship with his neighbour. That he should *belong* to Jesus— as King of the kingdom in which he lives—is the necessary meaning and truth of the obedience which he is now so willing and ready to give to Jesus. That he is very far from this being, loving and belonging will emerge later. And since he is so far from it, it is clear that even his action in fulfilling the commandments, of which he can justifiably boast from his own point of view and in respect of the external form, is not what he takes it to be—the action which God demands of an heir of eternal life. His mistake is that he looks at the external form of the command. And he does this from his own point of view, so that judging himself along these lines he naturally acquits and justifies himself. He thinks that the external form of the command is the whole command, the command itself. He thinks that when he has heard the whole command, the command itself, he has a position from which he can judge and acquit and justify himself. According to the best of his knowledge and conscience, he clings to its external form, to what it tells him either to do or not do. But in so doing, he alienates himself from the imperious will of God in the commandments of the second table. He does not encounter this imperious will of God in Jesus' solemn repetition of the commandments. This is the mistake which is still hidden—but secretly unveiled— in the intervening conversation about the commandments in vv. 19–20. And it is this mistake which will now emerge.

What follows in v. 21 is certainly astonishing. For it does not bring the expected unmasking of the fallacy of which the questioner was guilty when he regarded himself as a doer of the Law. On the contrary, there is the unexpected statement : " Jesus looked upon him and loved him." At this point, we cannot agree with Calvin (*Comm. ad loc., l.c.*, p. 540 f.), who softens the important ἠγάπησεν αὐτόν to mean that Jesus loved him as God loved Aristides and Fabricius on account of their civil virtues and therefore on account of the *commune bonum* of the world : *quia illi grata est humani generis conservatio, quae iustitia, aequitate, moderatione, prudentia, fide, temperantia constat.* Nor can we agree with the exposition of C. Starke (*Syn. Bibl. Ex. in N.T.*, Vol. I, 1733, p. 912) : " At least there was this in him to love and praise, that he had not defiled his youth with gross vices, but had led an honourable life, and displayed a zeal to learn how to attain blessedness." There is more to be said for the conjecture of the same author : " And it may be, too, that Jesus saw many things in him which would be revealed later, as we read of Nicodemus." But why should ἀγαπᾶν have a special meaning in this case ? In relation to the disobedient man, Jesus does the very thing which, for all his so-called keeping of the commandments, this man does not do in relation to Jesus : He loves him, i.e., He reckons him as His ; He does not will to be without him ; He wills to be there just for him. For whom else is Jesus there but for the disobedient ? Whom else has God loved from eternity ? Necessarily He will pronounce the divine judgment by which he is declared disobedient, and on the basis of which he must prove that this is the case by going away from Jesus. But He does not do this because He hates him. He does not do it because He is indifferent to him. He does it because He loves him. In this ἠγάπησεν αὐτόν, which is to be followed by a no less emphatic unmasking of the sinner, the Law is obviously the form of the Gospel ; the judgment declared by the Law is the shape taken by the grace of God. When Jesus now goes on to tell him what he lacks, He loves him and wills him for Himself. But the very thing that the questioner lacks is that he will not see this. He will not lay hold of it. He respects and measures himself by a law, the reference and concern of which is only for what he does and does not do, and not for himself in what he does and does not do. This law is not the Law of God, the living Law established and confronting him in the person of Jesus, the reference and concern of which is for himself, because the Lawgiver, the one God Himself, with whom he has to do, does not will to be without him, because He has made His covenant with him, because He has made him His covenant-partner and therefore demands that he should live as such. It is required that he should let himself be loved. This is the demand to which he is not equal, to which he is disobedient, of which he will be unmasked as a transgressor. But even so, the demand does not cease to be the form of the good tidings addressed to him that his Judge is his Friend and Helper. He can certainly reject what Jesus wills of him. He can certainly go away, as he later did. But he cannot overthrow or leave the kingdom of Jesus Christ. And, similarly, he cannot destroy the inalienable, decisive element in the light into which he has now entered—the fact that Jesus loved him, loved him the obdurate and evasive rebel, who would later return to the darkness without the Gospels having any reason to tell us how far Jesus did perhaps see " many things " in him. The fact that Jesus loved him is the one thing to which we can cling in his favour— quite apart from what he does or does not do. But who, strictly, can cling to anything better in his own or anyone else's favour ?

Yet the form of the love of Jesus is the command, the declaration of what he lacks, of what he has not done in and with all that he has done : " There is one thing you lack " (v. 21b). What follows is the long-expected sentence upon the questioner. Having failed to do this one thing, and not being willing to do it, he characterises himself as unrighteous before the judgment seat of God, as one who goes another way than that which leads to eternal life. For he has not penetrated to the τέλος of the Law as it is brought out in Mt. 19²¹. Yet this accusation, too, must in the first instance be understood positively. The Word of God which is now uttered condemns the man who resists it, but it is also the justification of the man who accepts it. It is the command, but at the same time it is also the divine offer, and it is still this even for the man who will not obey it. What the questioner lacks is the fulness of what Jesus has, and has for him, the fulness with which Jesus loves him and is therefore willing to be responsible for him. And if he is, as it were, invited to remedy this lack, the remedying consists only in a readiness to let the fulness of Jesus, and therefore the fulness of God which is ready even for him, stream over him and benefit him. His sin is that he is not ready for that which is ready for him in Jesus. But more is to be gained from noting the opportunity offered than how badly he let it slip.

What he lacks is now revealed (v. 21c). He is not the covenant-partner of God. He does not love his neighbour. He does not belong to Jesus. This is what he lacks. But it is not described in an abstract and academic way. It is aimed concretely at his specific existence and condition. We see it as that which he personally lacks. It is only now that we learn—indirectly—that the man is rich. And this is not stated explicitly until v. 22b : " He had great possessions." " Go, sell all you have and give it to the poor—so you will have a treasure in heaven—and come, follow me." This is the sentence. This is what the man lacks for the life of an heir of eternal life. This is the substance and the aim of all the commandments which he has not recognised as such, and to which he has not done justice with all his so-called observance of the commandments. This is what he has not done even in his coming to Jesus and falling on his knees before

Him. Woe to him, the transgressor of the Law! But we do not overlook the fact that the sentence has the form of an invitation and direction. Formulating what the man lacks, it opens for him the door to the fulness which is there even for him: Go! Sell! Give! Follow Me! This is all an opportunity and possibility. It is not only offered, but it will remain open even when it has been let slip. It will follow him even when he is disobedient to all these imperatives. He can never complain that the saving Word—even in the form of the command of God, interpreted, revealed in its substance and its aim, and therefore unmasking and annihilating him—is not near him, that it is (Rom. 10[8]) not laid on his heart and lips. Grace has met him as he is placed under God's judgment. Above all, therefore, let us not forget that it is as Jesus loved him that He uttered this judgment on him and gave him finally this saving direction on the way. He does not condemn him without seeking him, without willing to have him for Himself; and He does this by interposing Himself and making Himself responsible for him. And for the man who ought to be living but is not living as an heir of eternal life, the direction which He also gives is saving, and genuinely consoling, because as a direction it is always the indication according to which what God has already done for him belongs to him and will accrue to his benefit if he will only make use of it. The essential content of this Word of Jesus is obviously threefold : Sell what you have! Give to the poor! Follow Me! The three Evangelists all agree on these three elements. In Lk. 18[22] the first is accentuated by the addition of πάντα, but this only expresses the undoubted meaning contained in the wording of Mark and Matthew. None of the three elements must be overlooked, or allowed to slip into the background in favour of the other two. But each of them must be understood as a characterisation of that one thing, that whole, which Jesus has said to the man in answer to his question.

That he should sell what he has, that he should therefore part with what belongs to him, indicates what he lacks as the freedom in which he could and should live as the covenant-partner of God. What the commandments of the second table, which he thinks that he knows and has kept, require of him from this first standpoint is, therefore, the total obligation to the gracious and compassionate God who has chosen and called him into covenant with Himself, an obligation which has to be implemented in the sphere of his relationship to his neighbour. What he lacks is, therefore, obedience in the special sense of the commandments of the first table. The commandments of the second table require that he should confront his neighbour as one who is utterly bound to this God and who lives by nothing but His grace and compassion—if he lives in this way he will not kill, or commit adultery, or steal. They require that he should be wholly and genuinely free in relation to his neighbour : freed by his absolute obligation to God ; freed from all other divine or quasi-divine masters ; and therefore freed for an action which will really do justice to his neighbour. If he does not stand in this freedom, he will strive in vain to keep these commandments. He knows them quite well, but he does not know them at all. He does what belongs to their fulfilment, but how can he fulfil them when he neglects what they really require of him, when he is captive and bound by a regard for other lords and powers besides God ? The man who is a captive in this way is a murderer even if he does not harm a fly, an adulterer even if he never looks on a woman, a thief even if he never appropriates a straw that does not belong to him. The man who is a captive in this way is impure even if he is never so pure. Demanding that he should sell what he has, Jesus wills that he should be bound to God and therefore freed from all other lords. He is not this. He is a captive of his " great possessions." What he has really has him—in the very way in which God would have him, and alone should have him. He is ruled by the life proper to his great possessions with their immanent urge to preservation, exploitation and augmentation. The grip of mammon—of the life proper to what he has, to what really has him—makes him inaccessible and useless as far as the command of God is concerned. It does this in a very simple way. It, too, instils into him fear and love, and trust and hope. It, too, demands obedience, because it, too, is his lord. And if the commands of all other gods might tolerate man's subjection to the commands of mammon or similar lords as well as to themselves, the command of the gracious and compassionate God who has chosen and called man to covenant with Himself does not tolerate a division of this kind. For this God is not prepared to be a lord alongside other lords. The reason for this is that He is not a lord alongside other lords, but the Lord of all lords, the only Lord. We can live by His grace and compassion, in covenant with Him, only completely or not at all. His commands are kept only by the man who does not accept any command but His, because apart from Him he has, in fact, no lord whom he must honour and respect. The man who honours and respects another lord apart from Him transgresses all His commands, as a captive of this other lord, even if he does every thing that belongs to their fulfilment. The aim of Jesus' requirement that the rich man should divest himself of his wealth is plain to see. In accordance with the truth, he may and must be free from his other lord, from mammon, from the life proper to his great possessions, in order that, freed in this way, he may fulfil God's commands. As long as he has great possessions, they have him, and as long as they have him, God cannot and will not have him. He can only transgress His commands. He can never be an heir of eternal life. He must die—as the rich man he is, he must really die and pass—he must become poor if he is to tread the way of life. Because he is not willing to do this, it is in vain that he asks about this way even when he comes with his question to Jesus. Or is it in vain ? He is certainly told what he wants to know. He now knows what is involved. He has only to act. Even if he is still a prisoner, he is no longer a helpless prisoner. The door of his prison is wide open. Jesus loved him when He put to him the absolute demand : Sell what you have. He would not have loved him if He had spared him this demand. He proclaimed great joy to him when He did not spare his hearing this demand, when He did not withhold from him the saving Word of God.

The second element is that the proceeds of the sale should be given to the poor. This tells us positively that what he lacks is that love to the neighbour which is the meaning of the commandments of the second table. What they require of him is that he should not only not do what they forbid, but do something definite. That is, as a covenant-partner of the gracious and compassionate God and therefore as a free man, he should meet his neighbour as God meets him. But God meets him as the infinitely rich—what are his own " great possessions " compared with the possessions in God's house ?—and in His covenant with him this God has really given him what He has, placing it at the disposal of him, the poor man. This is how God acts in contrast to all the other so-called lords of man, in contrast particularly to mammon, whose dazzling gifts are distributed only to make man more and more subservient to himself. God is rich in the sense that He gives away what belongs to Him without return, without making man subservient, but free. And it is in this that man may and should become His imitator in relation to his neighbour. What has he to give his neighbour in proportion to what God has given him and still gives him ? But let him give this little as a small acknowledgment of what he has himself received. Anything less than all this little will be totally inadequate. What is the love which man can show to his neighbour in comparison with the love with which he is himself loved ? But let him give this little love to his neighbour and let him give it all. More is not possible, therefore more is not demanded—but all this little cannot be too much. It is when he gives what he has—not more, but also not less—that he fulfils God's commands. The aim of all of them is that, as the man who has been freed from strange lords, within the modest limits of his existence but within these limits unlimitedly, man should be free to be for his neighbour what God is for him—to be there for him, to be at his disposal, as God is there for him and stands at his disposal. " Give it to the poor." And in that way prove that you really have it, that it does not have you. In that way prove your freedom. Prove that God is your Liberator and that you are a witness to this Liberator. Note the addition : " So you will have a treasure in heaven." The dying of the rich man is not, then, a futile and meaningless dying ; his becoming poor does not mean his destitution, but his true and genuine enrichment. At bottom, therefore, it is not required of him that he should not have what he now has. On the contrary, he is shown that he may really have it, and how he may really have it. Giving it away, and so proving that freedom, he will change it into a possession which—in contrast to the false show with which mammon deceives—he may really have as his own. If with the little that is his he does what God does with the infinite wealth of His goodness, he enters into fellowship with this God. He receives the confirmation that his inheritance is sure, that eternal life already belongs to him even as he waits for it. He is not only the possessor, but the genuine owner of what he has. When he gives it to the poor—it cannot be taken from him. But to become its owner, he must subject it to this transformation. He must give it away. He must not hesitate to die as a rich man, to become poor. And it is because he is not ready to do this that he is disobedient and therefore off the way to eternal life, and it is in vain that he asks about it or even brings his question to Jesus. Not being willing to give what he has, he is not the child of God. But there is now displayed to him the invitation to give—to give not only something but all that he has to the poor. And in this invitation he sees the substance and the aim of all the commandments. If he has not known and not observed the commandments and therefore the saving Word of God, there can be no doubt that that Word now confronts him so plainly and has attacked him so sharply that his question is answered. He has been instructed. He has only to look at his life with his neighbour, and the goods which lie freely in his own hand, to know at once what he has to do to inherit eternal life. And Jesus loved him when He gave him this instruction. He did not want to take from him what belonged to him. On the contrary, what He wanted was to give to him what did not belong to him, and yet did belong to him as the child of God. He wanted him really to have this. He wanted him to have treasure in heaven. He wanted to help him to his rights against all strange lords. It was to this end that He demanded so sternly that he should sell all he had and give to the poor. He would not have loved him if He had pressed him less sternly. He brought him good tidings even as He pressed him so sternly.

The third demand of Jesus, or the third form of the one demand, is that he should come and follow Him. It is only in this third form that the two first, although they do not lose their own inherent force, are brought clearly into focus. What is required of this man if he is to inherit eternal life ? It is required that he should belong to Jesus. He has run to Him and fallen on his knees before Him. But he has obviously not come near enough. He has not really come close. He must come to Him—this is what the third form of the demand says— in order that he may stay with Him, not going away any more but directing his future course in accordance with that of Jesus. In place of his self-movement he may and must enter this new movement : Follow Me. This is again, and decisively, the interpretation of the commandments of the second table as they are supposed to be known to the questioner and fulfilled by him. The freedom for God which they demand from man is freedom for Jesus. And the freedom for one's neighbour which they demand is again freedom for Jesus. They aim at the true God and true man when they aim at God and man. And here in the person of Jesus the true God and true man stand face to face with the addressee and hearer of the commandments of God. With God, and as the Son of God, Jesus waits for our acknowledgment that He alone is the Lord, and as the Brother of the poor who are our neighbours He waits for our attestation that this Lord is so kind. The two obligations—that this man should sell what he has and therefore become free for God, and that he should give it to the poor and therefore become free for his neighbour—both derive their meaning and force from this final demand, that he should come and follow Jesus. To follow Jesus is the practice of this twofold freedom to the extent that life in the following of Jesus is the life of that covenant-partner of God who as such is so completely bound to his neighbour. To follow Jesus is to acknowledge the justice of the command of God in both these aspects. And to acknowledge the justice of the command of God in both these aspects is necessarily to follow Jesus. It is precisely at this point that the man comes short. Captivated by the claims of his great possessions, occupied with the maintenance, exploitation and augmentation which they demand of him, and kept back by these claims from the attestation of freedom with which he would have to meet his neighbour, he wants to continue in his own way. He does not see or realise that in this self-movement he is not free on either side. He does not want even Jesus to disturb him in the unfreedom which he regards as freedom. When the Word of Jesus discloses this state of affairs, it shows him that he is excluded from eternal life. It is a Word of judgment. But it is a Word of judgment which—decisively in this third form—reveals the direction in which eternal life is present and is to be sought and found by him. In this third form especially it is a command which is also an offer. When Jesus summons the man to follow Him, He offers him nothing less than Himself. He offers him nothing less than that he should belong to those at whose head and in whose place He has set Himself. He offers him nothing less than that He Himself assumes responsibility for his temporal and eternal future. He offers him nothing less, therefore, than participation in His own freedom.

But in v. 22 we are told that the rich man was horrified by this saying, this explanation of the commandments, and went away sorrowful. This definitely confirms the fact that what was said to him was the communication of his condemnation from the throne of God. He was not equal to the command of God in the form in which it was now completely and unequivocally revealed and authentically interpreted. He did not even dare to contemplate doing what was required. Much less did he proceed to do it. And so he stood confronting it, unworthy, impotent and lost. What was required was incommensurably too much, too great for him. He could not sell what he had—he could not free himself from the lordship and the commands of mammon. He could not give his possessions to the poor—he could not make himself a witness to the goodness of the eternally rich God. He could not follow Jesus—he could not stop the self-movement of his life, turning it into the movement of thankfulness. He was not the man for this. He could not do it. He was disobedient. How could he obey or even want to obey ? He was not free for the freedom commanded and proffered. And so the opportunity with which he was presented to become an heir of eternal life could, in fact, only be the opportunity by which it was revealed that this was something which he could not become, since he lacked the being which was the presupposition of this becoming. He could only be horrified at this. He could only go away by the same road as he had come—a different road from that which leads to eternal life. And he could only go away sorrowful : sorrowful at the unattainable remoteness and strangeness of the glory of God which he had encountered, and sorrowful at his own incompetence and insufficiency in relation to it ; sorrowful in face of the contrast between God's will and his own. And all the sadness which he might feel and express could only be a shadow of the real and infinite sadness of this contrast. What opened up at his feet was the abyss of the absolute impossibility of the relationship between God and the man who has committed sin and who as sinner sets himself in opposition to God.

But although that is the last that we are told about the man, it would again be a mistake to see and understand the incident only negatively. We recall what was stated at the very outset : that it is within the sphere of the kingdom of Jesus Christ that the incident is enacted. The sovereignty and majesty of Jesus are no less attested by the fact that the rich man sorrowfully goes away than by the fact that he came with his question. It is with Him that he has still to deal even in the state of disobedience out of which he came and to which we now see him returning. It was on Him and therefore on the command of God that he was shattered. It was His fulness that he lacked, and to the lack of which he had now to confess. Jesus is the man who is free from all other forces and lords because He is completely bound to God. Jesus is the man who stands at the disposal of the poor with all that He is and has, as a witness to the goodness of the rich God. It is only in and through Jesus Himself that another man can and will become and be a follower of Jesus. It is in relation to Jesus that he is the poor rich man—the man who is determined and ruled from elsewhere, the man who has great possessions. He has all possessions except the one—the fulness of Jesus. And this is what condemns him. This is what excludes him from eternal life. This is the abyss of the inner impossibility at his feet. This is what makes him disobedient to God's command, and there-fore sorrowful. God's command is : " Rejoice." It is the one that has the fulness of Jesus who fulfils God's command, who may and must rejoice. But how can this be done by one who does not have the fulness of Jesus even if he has ever so great possessions ? What else can they mean for him but the confirmation of what he lacks and therefore the confirmation of his disobedience and therefore an intensification of his sorrow ? But just because he has this lack, the fact that he is now unmasked as disobedient, and can only go away sorrowful, cannot in any sense mean that he is abandoned. We do not know what happened to him later. But we do know that what he lacked, the fulness of Jesus, was still there even for him, even for poor rich like himself—and for them especially. We remember that Jesus loved him as He proclaimed that sentence. What else does this mean but that even as He condemned him He willed always to be totally there for him, the condemned, that even as his Judge, He willed always to be his Friend and Helper ? His kingdom—the kingdom of this One who loves—embraces the evil contrast between the will of God and human will, between God and sinners, between God's glory and the unworthiness, impotence and lostness in which man confronts Him. His kingdom embraces the abyss of the inner impossibility of human existence, in which His fulness—the fulness of the love with which God loved the world before it was—is misunderstood, derided and resisted. Where else but in the depths of this abyss has He established His kingdom ? Sinking into this abyss man will continually encounter Him and in Him will continually find and have One who does not desire his loss in this abyss and who, in spite of all the power of his impotence, will not tolerate or accept it.

The unmasking of human disobedience in the story of the rich man, the sorrow with which he went away, show that, in virtue of the totality in which it confronts man in the person of Jesus, the command of God kills. But the continuation in v. 23 f., in which Jesus confronts His disciples as the Commander of those who are obedient to His commands, shows that, in virtue of the same totality, even as it kills, it does not cease to make alive. The saying of Peter in v. 28 is not contradicted. They have indeed left all and followed Him. They have therefore done what the rich man was incapable of doing. They have satisfied the total demand by whose proclamation he was unmasked and con-demned as disobedient. They are, therefore, on the way to eternal life, as they are assured in v. 30. Twice (in v. 23 and v. 27) it is stated emphatically that Jesus " looked on " them. He is looking at His own. It is the look of the One who knows that they are His own, and also how and why they are. But for this very reason it is not an exclusive look. He does not turn away his eyes from the one who has gone away sorrowful. On the contrary, according to all that follows, He looks right past and through them after or towards the one who has gone away. If the one Word of God has made a separation between the obedient and the disobedient, it is not that the Word of God itself has disintegrated into two parts. It remains a Word of judgment even to the obedient, and a Word of promise even to the disobedient. And it is in this indivisible totality that it is now imparted and presented by Jesus to His own. What Jesus has to say to His disciples after what has taken place between Himself and the rich man is certainly not that a man like this with his great possessions is as such excluded from the kingdom of God—that he cannot possibly enter this kingdom. But what they are twice emphatically given to consider in Mk. $10^{23\text{-}25}$ is that it is " hard " for men like this to do so—harder than for a camel to go through the eye of a needle. A veritable hill of difficulty stands in the way of what they have admittedly done—the keeping of the commands. It is on this hill that the rich man has been broken before them. According to his own decision and according to the confirmatory word of Jesus, he was not the man to conquer or remove it. Were they then, the disciples, the men to do it ? It is remarkable that this obvious conclusion is drawn neither by Jesus nor by the disciples themselves, and that the statement of Jesus does not create for them the joy and satisfaction of having left this hill behind by doing what the man did not do. Why is it that they, too, are " amazed " (v. 24) and " more astounded than ever " (v. 26) ? Where is that peace of a good conscience which they can surely enjoy if in the words of v. 26 they even have to ask : " Who then can be saved ? " They surely know that everyone can be saved, and how. They have surely done what is necessary, and therefore can do it. To be sure, it is a hard and thankless matter. To be sure, it needs a very radical resolve and a very free will to do what was required of the rich man and what they themselves in their way have done. But where is the so terribly difficult thing, the downright impossibility, which seems to loom before their eyes, and in face of which, although they are in fact obedient, they are so astounded, so full of questions, and even compelled to accept solidarity with the disobedient in a concern for salvation ? There can be no doubt that even according to the view of the Evangelist their astonishment and question are strictly appropriate. It is quite right that, even though they have fulfilled the commands of God, they should be surprised by the demand addressed to the rich man, his refusal and the statement of Jesus about the great difficulty of this fulfilment—just as if they had heard all this for the first time, just as if all that they had left to follow Jesus still towered before them in all its value and necessity, and could still hold and hinder them from being obedient to Him. As the Evangelist saw it, what took place between Jesus and the rich man had obviously shown them—the obedient—in a completely new and surprising way what obedience is, how great a step obedience involves, and that even when this step has been taken once, it has to be taken again and again in all its difficulty. Standing as the obedient alongside the disobedient, they are made to realise plainly that even the obedient are always standing on the edge of the abyss of disobedience, and that this abyss yawns even at their feet. And this is the significance of the story according to vv. 23–31. The disciples themselves have been made to realise it. In face of the command of God they have had to confess their solidarity with the disobedient. That is why they ask : " Who then can be saved ? " That they have done what this man did not do cannot prevent the revelation of this fact and must not prevent them confessing it. In relation to Jesus, in relation to the command of God, they are in exactly the same position as this man. Even their own entry into the kingdom of God seems to be harder to them than the passage of a camel through the eye of a needle. According to the saying of Jesus in v. 27, even that they—the obedient—should be saved is impossible with men. And their only hope is the same as that of the disobedient —the fact that with God all things are possible, and therefore even their salvation, and, as the way to their salvation, their obedience. This saying in v. 27 is obviously the hinge on which the whole narrative turns. The saving of anyone is something which is not in the power of man, but only of God. No one can be saved—in virtue of what he can do. Everyone can be saved—in virtue of what God can do. The divine claim takes the form that it puts both the obedient and the disobedient together and compels them to realise this, to recognise their common status in face of the commanding God. What it requires, and what it invariably achieves when it is proclaimed, is that we come to stand on the spot where—whether we are obedient or disobedient—we cannot be helped at all by ourselves, but only by the power of God, the power of His pity. The claim is as radical as that, and it grips and binds us as radically as that. According to the text we are studying, it demands of the rich man something that is quite impossible on the strength of what he can do. We have seen that what he lacks in the matter of the fulfilment of the substance of the commands is life in the fulness of Jesus, His freedom for God and for His neighbour. It is only in this freedom that he can be obedient. But it is just this freedom which he lacks. He is not Jesus. He is only the man with great possessions and as such not capable of this freedom. He can only be disobedient to the commands of God. He cannot even enter the way to eternal life, much less travel it. To do this he would have to be another man than he is. As the man he is, he is excluded from it. And who can make himself to be another than he is ? With men, in virtue of human capacity, it is impossible. Human capacity does not include within it this ability. It is easier for a camel to pass through the eye of a needle than for a man to do what is necessary for entry into the kingdom of God—to make himself another man than he actually is. But this is also true of the disciples of Jesus who inconceivably confront this rich man as those who have done what he has not done, what he could not do, and who are to be blessed as those who are on the way to eternal life. From the point of view of their own ability, they, too, lack everything that he lacked. They, too, do not possess the fulness of Jesus, His freedom for God and for His neighbour. They, too, have no organ, no aptitude, no power to apprehend this. They, too, are not Jesus. They, too, being what they are, can only be disobedient to the command of God, and miss the way to eternal life. They, too, are unable to make themselves into other men than they are. The hill of difficulty which confronts him also confronts them. This is the discovery with which they are faced according to our text. Who can be saved ? Nobody can. Even they cannot. The judgment upon the rich man, the affirmation of the one thing which he lacks, has a direct reference to them too. Without the omnipotence of the pity of God they, too, could only give themselves up for lost. But we do not fully describe what God's command requires of man if we characterise it as what is impossible with man. On the strength of what God, not man, can do, what is impossible with men is possible with God. In this way, therefore, it is really possible with man too, not in virtue of his own, but in virtue of divine power. And what distinguishes the disciples of Jesus from the rich man, and gives them the advantage over him, what differentiates the obedient from the disobedient, is the fact that they may be witnesses to this divine possibility. They have actually left all and followed Jesus. How did this happen ? It happened as they made use of that which they possessed as little as he, but which was at their disposal as the gift and present of God. It happened as they recognised, claimed and appropriated that which they lacked no less than he, but which was available for them in Jesus. It happened as—without regard to their own inability to apprehend, which was no less than that of the rich man—they accepted the fulness of Jesus as their own. It happened as they let His freedom—which was not theirs—count as theirs. It happened as they put it into effect. It happened as at the Word of Jesus they held to Jesus without being Jesus. It happened, therefore, as they accepted Jesus' different existence as determinate for themselves and therefore lived as other men without actually being other men. In this humility or boldness—or, rather, in virtue of the grace which allowed and commanded this

humility or boldness—the impossible became possible to them. To them ?
No, it was never possible to them. It was still possible only to God. But in
the knowledge that what is possible only to God has become possible *for* them,
in this confidence, in this humility or boldness—we can now say simply in
faith—they became obedient. They accepted it as true that Jesus was obedient
for them. They became obedient with Him, as those who on the strength of
their own ability can be only the disobedient—obedient in following His obedience. They believed, i.e., they were pleased to have His ability attributed to
them, to have their own inability covered over by His ability. They undertook
to live in the shade and shelter of His ability. This life in the shade and
shelter of His ability was their obedience—their willingness and readiness
to leave all and follow Him. It is just because they are in this way obedient
and on the way to eternal life that the judgment upon the disobedient must
obviously fall upon them too. In this humility or boldness they have grasped
at the freedom of Jesus attributed to them. They have placed themselves
in the shade and shelter of His ability. But this being the case, how can
they help being frightened when—in the light of the disobedience of another
—they again see how they themselves would be situated without this freedom,
without this shade and shelter. How impossible it would then be even for
them to be obedient ! How disobedient they themselves would be outside this
shade and shelter ! How could they possibly imagine that they had turned
themselves into other men, that of themselves and by their own efforts they were
other men than their true selves, and therefore, on the strength of their ability
and accomplishment, secure in face of the judgment that falls on him ? If
they do not lack the one thing that is needful for the fulfilment of the divine
command, it is certainly not because they themselves possess it and achieve it.
It is only because it is there for them in Jesus. It is only because they are pleased
to accept it by faith in Him. And it is just because they are in this way—and
only in this way—obedient and on the way to eternal life that they must obviously
not apply only to themselves the acquittal which they have received in contrast
to the rich man, the disobedient, and the hope and confidence in which they
are permitted to live in contrast to him ; not keeping these things to themselves
in face of him. If they stand with him under the judgment which is passed upon
all that is possible with men, he on his side is united with them under the promise
of that which is possible with God. To what is possible with God there obviously
belong both their present obedience and also the future obedience of the rich
man, both their own prospect of eternal life and his also. If they really live
by the fact that the fulness of Jesus is there for them, the disobedient, they can
only view and address this other disobedient on the basis of the fact that the same
fulness is there for him too. If their own fulfilment of the command consists
simply in the fact that they live as those who make use of the freedom of Jesus
attributed to them, and therefore of the ability of God which is greater than their
ability, how else can they judge this or any other transgressor of this command
except as one for whom also this freedom is there, but who has not yet made
of it the use which he may ? If there was and is grace for them—the grace of
the divine ability that covers their own inability—how can there fail to be
grace for this man or for any others who like themselves lack the ability ? No
disobedient man can evade the all-prevailing authority and validity of the divine
command which demands that man should be committed to the compassion of
God. And no obedient man can conceal this fact from others, or use it for his
own advantage to the disadvantage of others. On the contrary, those who
know it must attest and tell it to those who do not yet know it. It is for this
end and only for this end that they are better off than they, and distinguished from
them. As it emerges in the incident of which they were witnesses, the significance
of what marks off the disciples, the significance of their differentiation from the
rich man, is simply that these disciples, who are what they are and are permitted

to do what they do by the grace of God, become apostles, i.e., men who proclaim what is impossible with men, but possible with God. (There is unmistakeably reflected and repeated in the relationship between the disciples and the rich man of this story the relationship between the Church and Israel, and not only this, but the relationship between the whole community of God and the surrounding world.) Made obedient and set on the way to eternal life, in relation to all other men they are witnesses to the fact that what they are permitted to be and do is the will of God for them too, and that the possibility by which they themselves live is given to them too, and may be used by them. Saved by faith alone, they may and must say to all who are not yet distinguished in this way, that this distinction is their determination too, and that even in the deepest depth of their disobedience they cannot cease to be determined for it. To that extent, when Jesus looks on the disciples as His own, as the obedient, He also looks after and towards the rich man, the disobedient, and all those like him, as those who are within the range of the divine command and cannot possibly be removed from it.

The interchange between Jesus and Peter in Mk. 10^{28-31}, which brings the whole story to a conclusion, ends in v. 31 with the significant saying : " Many that are first shall be last, and the last first." These final words seem to make it unmistakeable that everything that has taken place between Jesus and the rich man on the one side and the disciples on the other involves a threat of judgment even for the disciples and a promise even for the rich man. It is to be noted that the basic presupposition is again predominant that the kingdom of Christ is the sphere in which the whole action is played out and to which it all bears witness. We do not hear of the saved and the lost, or of those who are within and those who are without, or of participants and non-participants, but of a serious, and yet for all its seriousness not an absolute, difference within the same sphere. We hear of the first and the last, and this means of the possibility of a very radical change within this sphere in the status and estimation of different people, the obedient and the disobedient, who are its citizens and inhabitants. The disciples with their obedience, which they do not owe to themselves, but to the divine ability bestowed on them, are now first, and the rich man, in virtue of his human inability, is one of the last. The former are distinguished, and the latter is disdained. Yet both participate in both presuppositions. The relationship between the former and the latter is reversible in virtue of the presuppositions that are true for both. The rich man, who is now the last, could become a first on the strength of the divine ability, which is not withdrawn even from him, but available even for his use. And the disciples, who are now the first, could become the last in virtue of their own human inability which resists the divine ability. We remember Rom. $11^{14f.}$ The visible situation which has developed between these men and that man is not fixed or absolute. Only the command of God is fixed. Only Jesus is absolute as King of the sphere in which both exist, as the rule of the divine pity to which both are accountable, and before which both stand in need of help.

The interchange between Jesus and Peter in vv. 28–30, to which this final statement belongs, reveals at once both the high distinction and also the great peril of the disciples themselves. It shows that their position is first, but it also shows that from being first they may actually become last. " We have left all and have followed thee," is what Peter said in v. 28 in reply to the saying about what is not possible with men but is possible with God. His words are appropriate in one sense. For on the strength of what is possible with God, the disciples had, in fact, done what is impossible with men. But they are also highly inappropriate, for—as Matthew has rightly understood it—the announcement expresses a jarring concern : " What becomes of us ? " This concern does not derive from faith in what is possible with God and therefore from the obedience which distinguishes the disciples from the rich man, but, if at all, only from what they unfortunately have in common with the rich man—the disobedience which was theirs too, and which was unmasked and condemned with that of the rich man. To judge by this concern, the obedience in which they had left all and followed Jesus had not been a joyous obedience. To judge by this concern, they had no doubt looked forwards in faith, but they had also looked back at all they had left behind to follow Jesus. But how, then, had they really left it ? How, then, had they—in contrast to the rich man—really followed Jesus and really done justice to the substance of the divine commands ? Was it not inevitable that, in spite of what they had done, they must see themselves seriously and totally called in question along with the rich man ? How, then, could they fail to be threatened by the possibility which he now realised—the possibility of being last instead of first ? He had gone away sorrowful. But what had they done when, to judge by the concern in their question, they had come sorrowful ? In this question, what is possible and impossible with men in regard to the command of God emerges no less evidently in the case of the disciples than it had done in the case of the rich man, and, along with it, the danger in which they, too, stood. Jesus tells them consolingly in v. 29 f.—to some extent quietening and dissipating their concern—that there is no man that has left house, brothers, sisters, mother, father, children or lands for His and the Gospel's sake who will not receive a hundredfold for what has been surrendered, even now in this world in the midst of persecution, and in the world to come eternal life (and, according to Mt. 19[28], He strengthened this promise by a reference to their apostolic office, in virtue of which they are destined to be judges of the twelve tribes of the people of God). But while this is true, we must not overlook the inherent reference to the danger that faces them, the threat of judgment that is addressed against them too. Those who, following Him, have for His sake left everything, are those who are not only certain of eternal life in the world to come, but have not really lost anything in this world, since they will receive again all that they have lost, not merely as they lost it, but a hundredfold, what they had never had before and could never have attained. They are those who already in this world proceed to the richest and truest reward. They will have to the full everything that man can have or desire in human and material values and goods. They are the meek who, according to Mt. 11[29], will find rest for their souls, and, according to Mt. 5[5], will inherit not only eternal life but also the earth. But is this really the case ? That is the very critical question which lurks in the promise. Are they those who have this promise and live with it ? When they leave all and follow Him, have they heard and accepted the Gospel as good news for life and death, body and soul ? When they choose obedience to God's command instead of disobedience, have they really chosen the better, the best, which is what this obedience surely is ? If they have done this, how then can they put the plaintive question : " What becomes of us ? " How then can they look back ruefully, as it were, at what they have given up ? How can the man who is capable of looking back be obedient, if obedience means to gain by surrendering, to lose a little and be given infinitely more ? If they are capable of this backward look, are they even a single step in advance of the rich man who went away sorrowful ? Do they not stand with him already among the last in the kingdom of Christ ? Is it not possible that they may have at any moment the experience of being outstripped by him and seeing him in their place among the first ? But, of course, it is not by accident that this question, and with it the threat of judgment addressed to the disciples and revealing their serious peril, is so completely covered and clothed by the dazzling promise which Jesus gives them. And the seriousness and weight of the threat lie in the fact that it meets them in this concealment—indirectly. Between the word of Peter in v. 28 and the answer of Jesus in v. 29 f. there is a supremely indirect relationship. A great gulf obviously opens up between the being which the disciples (within the limits of what is possible and impossible with men) have represented as theirs, and that other being, based on what is possible in God's free compassion, which is ascribed to them by Jesus as their new and proper life; the being which He sees in them and does not cease to see in spite of their representation of themselves. When Peter and the other disciples look back in concern and half-regret at what they have lost they are obviously not the same as those whom Jesus—as if nothing had happened—addresses as men who have left all for His sake and the Gospel's, and who as such are worthy and certain not only of this hundredfold temporal but also of the eternal requital and reward. Does Jesus not know that, as the saying of Peter shows, they are still these others, and that by this same saying they have unmistakeably denied what they are through Him? He obviously knows it well. The saying determines His answer. But in His answer He steps, as it were, over that abyss for them and with them—again making them, from what they are by themselves, into what they are permitted to be by and with Him. This silent action is a repetition of the act of creative goodness, in which He called, indeed " made," them out of nothing to be apostles (Mk. 3¹⁴, ¹⁶). And on the strength of this act they are now addressed as what they are not according to that anxious question. They have now ascribed to them an existence which is so contradictory of the presuppositions of the question. They are now described as those who are sure of all these temporal and eternal benefits just because they have lost all and followed Him, and can therefore be certain, and cannot therefore be anxious. It is to be noted that this is how they are comforted. In face of their scarcely concealed defection, Jesus becomes and is again, and this time truly, Jesus the Saviour. He steps in again with His freedom to supply their deficiency. And in so doing He assuages and dissipates their concern. This would obviously not be possible in any other way. For in any other way they would be left standing on the other side of that abyss. Now that they had lost all, their concern would not only be natural, but necessarily it would be limitless and invincible. And how could they ever move away from this position? They are relieved of their concern by the fact that Jesus takes it on Himself. And it is as He intervenes for them that the promise He gives them becomes powerful and decisive. It shines out for them and over them, because it is the reflection of His own glory, of His hidden but real kingship. As He Himself lays down His life in His great freedom for God and men, in order by this very means—risen from the dead, sitting at the right hand of God—to win it again in incomparable divine splendour, they will have the same experience, for all that He does is done for them. And as He Himself is already, here and now, in the secrecy of His existence in the flesh, really in possession of all the rights and joys of His kingdom, the same is true of them, i.e., in and with Him, through the fact that all that is His belongs also to them. If it meant anything else but this, the promise of v. 29 f. could hardly be more than a strange *fata morgana* not very appropriate to the existence of the Church " in the midst of persecutions " (v. 30). It is because what Jesus says to His disciples is filled with the dynamic of what He Himself is and does—is and does for His own— that His promise is full of reality, clarity and truth, and is therefore a consoling promise, not only contradicting concern, but destroying it. But as such, it is obviously directed not only to the disciples, but also to the rich man who went away sorrowful. From the Markan (and Lukan) account it is quite clear that this is the meaning of the text. To the saying of Peter: " *We* have left all and have followed thee," the answer of Jesus stands only in an indirect relationship with its general declaration: " *No one* that has left house, brothers, sisters . . . who shall not receive again a hundredfold." This is the general answer which holds for all the anxious, all who are not free, all who still stand on the other side of that abyss, all who are bound by what is possible and impossible with men. The decisive element in this answer is what Jesus is and does for those bound people. But this being the case, it is obviously true for the rich man who went away no less than for the disciples. No matter what attitude he assumes, even if he runs to the very depths of hell, he cannot evade either the command of God or the divine promise which is its meaning. What has been said and done in their favour by Jesus, the disciples cannot refrain from repeating in favour of him and those like him, and with the same indefatigability as Jesus devoted to them.

There remains for the rich man the explicitly stated hope : " The last shall be first." But we now understand the fact and extent that what Jesus said must really affect the disciples, too, as a Word of judgment—not in spite of the fact, but just because of the fact that it is so completely covered and clothed with the promise. If they were not still at the place where they were, according to the saying of Peter, how could they be accessible to God's accusation, or be held responsible as transgressors of His command ? If it is not possible with men to be other than they are, is there not justification and even excuse for their anxieties ? But they are accused and condemned because they are addressed on the basis of their new existence, as those who benefit by what is possible with God ; because, indeed, this new existence is again and rightly adjudged and assigned to them. This, the grace of Christ, is the attack upon the old being to which, according to that anxious saying, they again wished to return or had already returned. It is this that makes them responsible, guilty, inexcusable and, of course—for otherwise the story would not be in the Gospels— ready to confess their guilt and repent. This is the demand—that they should turn and draw back, regretting their regret. They are told who they are, and at the same time who they cannot be ; where they belong, and at the same time where it is impossible for them to belong. Thus the story of the rich young man shows us in all its aspects the constancy of the divine faithfulness in the divine command, so far as its substance consists in the fact that it binds the man who hears it (protesting against his unfaithfulness, but also victorious over the evil into which that unfaithfulness plunges him) to the person of Jesus.

[II, 2, pp. 613–630]

CHAPTER II

CREATION

1. CREATION OUT OF NOTHING

Among the words used by the Bible to describe the divine creation (cf. for what follows the Art. κτίζειν by W. Foerster, *TWzNT*, III), the Old Testament *bara'* is lexicographically unequivocal to the extent that in the strict sense—as in its immediate appearance in Gen. 1¹—it can denote only the divine creation in contrast to all other : the creation which does not work on an existing object or material which can be made by the Creator into something else ; the *creatio ex nihilo* whose Subject can only be God and no one apart from Him—no creature. B. Jacob (*op. cit.*, p. 22) calls the statement in Gen. 1¹, with reference to this *bara'*, " the first great act of the Torah, of the religious genius of Israel." But this of all statements surely cannot be understood when we think that we can say this of it, turning the glory of the God which this *bara'* proclaims and to which it obviously redounds into a glorification of Israel and its religious genius. Where is this genius in the LXX rendering of *bara'* as ἐποίησεν ? But be that as it may, the miracle of the will and act of God on the one side, and of the existence and essence of heaven and earth on the other, is not bound to this untranslateable word by which it is denoted. Both the Old and New Testaments are sparing in their use of ultimate and decisive words and more prodigal with penultimate terms. There is no reason for surprise, therefore, if in addition to the unique *bara'* other verbs are used to describe the creative activity of God—verbs which in themselves and apart from their context may not have the force of this *bara'*, but which stand in the light of it and may be interpreted by it : *qanah* (or κτίζειν), to acquire or procure or prepare for oneself ; *yatsar* (or πλάσσειν), to fashion or form or shape in some way ; *'asah* (or ποιεῖν), to manufacture or to make ; and *yasad* (or θεμελιοῦν) to establish. When these terms are applied to the creative act of God, there can be no real doubt that they too denote that wonderful relationship between God and the object of His act—the incomprehensible, indeducible and contingent transition from the potentiality which has its basis only in God Himself to the actuality of another reality by the execution of His divine will and decree. The God of the Old Testament is the Creator in this sense, and everything that is not God is opposed to Him in this sense as creature. It is significant that without a single exception the LXX carefully avoided the familiar Greek verb δημιουργεῖν as a rendering of the Hebrew words used to denote the creative activity of God to the Greeks. A δημιουργός is really one who performs a definite work for the public, i.e., the seer, or doctor, or builder, or herald, or singer. More commonly, he is the artisan, and even more commonly the expert in contrast to the layman —the man who unlike others can make something out of a given material. When δημιουργός is used of God in Greek literature it is to describe Him as the One who has transformed the world from ἀταξία into κόσμος. The God of the Old Testament does, of course, fashion the world, but He does so as the Creator. In evident awareness of this, the LXX does not wish to equate Him with the demiurge of Greek philosophy and mythology. It was left to Christian Gnosticism to obliterate this distinction. Apart from this restraint, the positive fact is equally impressive that the LXX preferred κτίζειν to ποιεῖν, πλάσσειν and θεμελιοῦν, so that this has become the true technical term for the divine creation. According to Foerster, κτίζειν signifies " the decisive act of will which underlies the erection, institution or foundation (e.g., of a city, theatre, temple, baths, etc.) and which is then followed by the actual execution (δημιουργεῖν). Since the days of Alexander the Great, κτίζειν in the Hellenistic sense has had particular reference to the autocratic ruler with aspiration to divinity, who irrespective of what was there before causes a πόλις to arise by his word or command or will (backed by his power), thus acquiring divine honour in this city, since it owes its very existence wholly to him as its κτίστης. The word bara' is not consistently translated κτίζειν. The first variation occurred as early as the creation story. On the other hand, it is true to say that this Greek word, like the Hebrew, indicates the direction of biblical thinking in this matter. In both cases we are pointed to the transcendent and therefore unique character, to the mystery, of the divine action described as creation. We cannot lay too strong an emphasis on this mystery. According to Heb. 11³ creation is coming into being which no φαινόμενα either precede or underlie. According to Rom. 4¹⁷ it is an act of God which can be linked only with the resurrection of the dead—creation and resurrection being distinctive marks of the God to whom Abraham yielded the faith which was imputed to him for righteousness. A number of passages in the New Testament deal with the καταβολὴ κόσμου beyond which nothing exists or is even conceivable (according to Eph. 1⁴) apart from our election in Jesus Christ as the eternal decree of the will of God, and therefore apart from God Himself. And if more is needed, we are taught by the declaration of Ps. 73²⁵ : " Whom have I in heaven but thee ? and there is none upon the earth that I desire beside thee " ; by Mk. 13³¹, that heaven and earth will pass away, but the words of Jesus will not pass away ; and by the definite expectation of a new heaven and a new earth in Rev. 21¹ and 2 Pet. 3¹³, how immeasurably transcendent in the sense of the biblical witness is the act denoted when we say that God created the present heaven and earth. How can this act, and the relationship based upon it, be really known except in Jesus Christ, and therefore in the faith of the New Testament witnesses ? And how can it be confessed, therefore, except in the form of an article of the Christian creed ?

The particular nature of heaven and earth, their inter-relationship and their unity in man, require many exegetical and terminological elucidations for which we have no space in the present context.

The following points are, however, incontestable and of great significance for our purpose. The Old and New Testament Scriptures, when they speak of God's creation, actually do so in such a way that they repeatedly and most emphatically describe it as twofold, and then just as emphatically comprehend the two elements in a single totality, and understand this totality as the creation willed and created by God. Rather significantly, the Old Testament has no word for this uniform conception of the " world." It occasionally uses (Ps. 8⁶, Is. 44²⁴) the expression " the whole " (hak-kol), but as a rule it can only enumerate the various elements. To some extent " heaven and earth " form the backbone of this enumeration, although the order may be reversed according to the standpoint of the passage concerned, and sometimes (as in Ex. 20¹¹ and Neh. 9⁶) the sea may be added (to which there is a special relationship !). Everything that goes by the name of and is occasionally referred to as creature (in great detail in passages like Job 38 f.)—the sun and moon and stars in the one case and earthly creatures in the other—is what is " therein " (Ex. 20¹¹), comprehended in heaven and earth, the inhabitants of heaven and earth. The same usage persists for the most part in the New Testament. According to the solemn exposition of Ex. 20¹¹ in Rev. 10⁶, God is He " who created the heaven καὶ τὰ ἐν αὐτῷ, and the earth καὶ τὰ ἐν αὐτῇ, and the sea καὶ τὰ ἐν αὐτῇ " (cf. also Rev. 5¹³, Ac. 4²⁴, 14¹⁵). According to Col. 1¹⁶, He created τὰ πάντα ἐν τοῖς οὐρανοῖς καὶ ἐπὶ τῆς γῆς, τὰ ὁρατὰ καὶ τὰ ἀόρατα, and according to Hebrews (1³, 11³) the αἰῶνες. In Jn. 1¹⁰, Rom. 1²⁰ and Ac. 17²⁴, and in connexion with the concept of the καταβολή, there is mention of the κόσμος as the object of creation.

This double kingdom is the totality (τὰ πάντα in Col. 1¹⁶, Eph. 3⁹ and Rev. 4¹¹) of that which is created. In order to understand the biblical witness we must bear in mind the threefold content of the statement. That this kingdom is double characterises it—more precise elucidation will be required—as one in which there is an upper and a lower, and therefore an orientation even within creaturely life, i.e., the possibility and necessity of a definite, irreversible direction. Augustine's interpretation may be quoted in this connexion (*Conf.* XII, 7, 7): *De nihilo fecisti coelum et terram, magnum quiddam et parvum quiddam . . . unum prope te, alterum prope nihil, unum quo superior tu esses, alterum quo inferius nihil esset.* And Col. 1¹⁶ gives us the direction for further thinking on this matter. There is in this sphere of creation both a lower, smaller and visible and also an upper, larger and invisible reality. The two spheres have been repeatedly understood in this sense since the time of Irenaeus (*Adv. o. h.* II, 30, 9), especially by Augustine, but also in the later confession of the Church since the *Nicaenum.* This double sphere is, however, the totality of creation, which as such is homogeneous and united, and in this homogeneity and unity the only creature. This is true even though, according to the witness of both Testaments, it is as such immensely rich and varied, deep and incomprehensible. No matter what God has created, it is to be found in this double sphere of reality. It may take thousands of forms unknown to us. It may be infinite in itself. But there is no reality outside this sphere apart from that of God Himself. In heaven and earth and man as their unity, we have to do with the work of the whole, undivided love of God. As the creature in whom these two are one, we are the object of His whole, undivided attention. And the fact that this double sphere is created as a totality by God—ἐξ οὗ τὰ πάντα (1 Cor. 8⁶, Rom. 11³⁶) and: *ex omnibus nihil subtractum est* (Irenaeus, *Adv. o. h.* I, 22, 1)—means that there may be pretended but no genuine gods and lords, either here below on earth in the sphere of our observation of accessible natural elements and forces, or up above in heaven in the higher, hidden regions of the spirit and spirits. There can be no greater secularisation of that which on its highest as on its lowest rung belongs to *saeculum* than the recognition that God really created heaven as well as earth. For according to this insight even the most powerful dominion in the former sphere is no less really in His hand than the most obvious impotence. That the totality has been created by God also means that there can be many pretended but no genuine things that are not within this totality; nothing wholly contemptible either in heaven or on earth, either in the realm of the spirit or in that of matter. And there can be no greater honour for the secular reality of that which is not God than the recognition that God really created earth as well as heaven. For according to this insight even that which is most miserable in the sphere of earth is no less really in His hand than that which most obviously is glorious in the courts of heaven. [III, 1, pp. 16–17; 19–20]

2. CHRIST AND CREATION

We have had in mind, of course, the well-known series of New Testament texts which speak of the ontological connexion between Christ and creation; and we have been attempting an exegesis of these passages. In Col. 1¹⁷ it is said of the Son of God: αὐτός ἐστιν πρὸ πάντων; in Jn. 1¹ of the Word of God: ἐν ἀρχῇ ἦν ὁ λόγος; in 1 Jn. 1¹ (without any direct description) of the object of the Christian proclamation: ὁ ἦν ἀπ᾽ ἀρχῆς; and in 1 Jn. 2¹³ᶠ·: ἐγνώκατε τὸν ἀπ᾽ ἀρχῆς (an indisputable masculine). To the same group there also belongs Col. 1¹⁵ which tells us that the Son of God is the πρωτότοκος πάσης κτίσεως (not as the first of creatures but as the image of the invisible God, as the One " through " whom all was created). The meaning of all these passages can only be that Christ stands as God and with God before and above the beginning of all things brought into being at the creation ; He is the beginning as God Himself is the beginning. Jn. 1¹ adds expressly that the Word was with God and was God. It is also said of God's Son in Col. 1¹⁷ : τὰ πάντα ἐν αὐτῷ συνέστηκεν ; again of the Son in Heb. 1³ : φέρων τε τὰ πάντα τῷ ῥήματι τῆς δυνάμεως αὐτοῦ ; of the Word of God in Jn. 1¹¹ : εἰς τὰ ἴδια ἦλθεν ; of Christ in Col. 2¹⁰ : ὅς ἐστιν ἡ κεφαλὴ πάσης ἀρχῆς καὶ ἐξουσίας ; and of Christ again in 1 Cor. 8⁶ : δι' οὗ τὰ πάντα. Mt. 28¹⁸ records Christ's own words : ἐδόθη μοι πᾶσα ἐξουσία ἐν οὐρανῷ καὶ ἐπὶ γῆς ; and so too does Jn. 5¹⁷ : πατήρ μου ἕως ἄρτι ἐργάζεται, κἀγὼ ἐργάζομαι. In Jn. 5¹⁹ we read : ἃ γὰρ ἂν ἐκεῖνος ποιῇ, ταῦτα καὶ ὁ υἱὸς ὁμοίως ποιεῖ ; in Jn. 16¹⁵ : πάντα ὅσα ἔχει ὁ πατὴρ ἐμά ἐστιν ; and in Jn. 17² : ἔδωκας αὐτῷ ἐξουσίαν πάσης σαρκός. It should not be over-looked that in all these passages the position, dignity and power of the Creator—the exercise of unlimited lordship over against His creatures—are unquestion-ably ascribed to Christ. But we read distinctly in Rev. 3¹⁴ that He is Himself : ἡ ἀρχὴ τῆς κτίσεως τοῦ θεοῦ ; in Heb. 1² : δι' οὗ καὶ ἐποίησεν τοὺς αἰῶνας ; and in Heb. 1¹⁰ : σὺ κατ' ἀρχάς, κύριε, τὴν γῆν ἐθεμελίωσας καὶ ἔργα τῶν χειρῶν σού εἰσιν οἱ οὐρανοί. In Jn. 1³ we read of the Word of God : πάντα δι' αὐτοῦ ἐγένετο, and καὶ χωρὶς αὐτοῦ ἐγένετο οὐδὲ ἕν ὅ γέγονεν, a negative expression which confirms the positive. Of the same Word we read in Jn. 1¹⁰ : ὁ κόσμος δι' αὐτοῦ ἐγένετο ; and Col. 1¹⁶ tells us of the Son of God : ἐν αὐτῷ ἐκτίσθη τὰ πάντα ἐν τοῖς οὐρανοῖς καὶ ἐπὶ γῆς, τὰ ὁρατὰ καὶ τὰ ἀόρατα . . . τὰ πάντα δι' αὐτοῦ καὶ εἰς αὐτὸν ἔκτισται. The above passages make it clear that the Son or Word of God, or concretely Jesus Christ, does not just become but is Lord of all things, for He is as God and with God, instituted as such by God, and Himself in full divine dignity and power the Creator of all things. *Omnia per ipsum fecit Pater* (Irenaeus, *Adv. o. h.* I, 22, 1). Polanus (*Synt. Theol. chr.*, 1609, *col.* 1653) rightly interpreted not only Irenaeus but also the διά and the ἐν of the New Testament when he paraphrased this sentence : *ipsius propria vi et efficacia et potentia omnia esse creata*, thus desiring the Son or the Word to be understood not merely as *causa instrumentalis seu administra*, but as *causa αὐτουργός*, as *causa efficiens, socia Patris in creando*. It should be observed in this connexion that even the διά, which seems to be particularly well brought out by the thought of a *causa instrumentalis*, is applied also to the activities of the Father (Rom. 6⁴, 1 Cor. 1⁹, Eph. 2⁴).

It is now known that in this respect the writers of the New Testament found themselves on prepared ground inasmuch as the notion of a second divine being assisting in the work of creation had become general in their day. What they ascribe to Jesus Christ in all the above passages was not only ascribed by Philo to the Logos but also by the syncretistic theosophy and cosmology of the time to Hermes, to death, to Athene, to the Wohu-Manu, to the Mithra of Zoro-astrianism and to the Mandæan Hibil-Ziva. The bearer of revelation who was to bring the low, dark world into contact with the exalted, pure God was gener-ally thought of as the one by whom the relation between God and the world is established, i.e., by whom creation is accomplished. So great is God, and so great is the riddle of the universe, that a mediator of this kind is required. And so great is the bearer of revelation that he is the instrument of the original mediation which lays the foundation. There can be no doubt that in the passages under consideration the New Testament writers were referring to this element in the religious world of their day. The shattering of the consciousness of God and the world was revealed in the invention of this intermediate being, in the pro-clamation of all kinds of bearers of revelation and finally in the identification of the bearers of revelation previously recognised with this intermediate being. But to say that the apostles were referring to this element in the religious inherit-ance of their environment does not mean that what they said was borrowed from it. This was not the case. They had no need to take over from their con-

temporaries even the form of their statements about Jesus Christ. They could
be quite content merely to refer to what they heard their contemporaries say.
For, quite apart from questions of substance, the third part of the Old Testament
Canon offered them an older literary model in Prov. 2 and 8 and Job 28 with
their portrayal of the " wisdom " which is inaccessible to man, or accessible only
by its self-revelation—a wisdom which is nothing other than God's holiness
and righteousness addressing and instructing and directing and sustaining man
for the sake of His patience, and the beginning of which must always be for us
men the fear of the Lord. Of this wisdom they read in Prov. 8²²ᶠ· that God had
possessed it from eternity, before the beginning or origin of the world ; that it
was present with Him as His favourite (or as His overseer) when He made the
heavens and laid the foundations of the earth, after the separation of the waters
below and above the firmament. They read quite expressly in Ps. 136⁵ and
Prov. 3¹⁹ that God had created the heavens and the earth by this "wisdom."
If the foregoing New Testament quotations are to be traced to any literary
source it is certainly this one, which even later Judaism had pertinently utilised
and diligently exploited. But in this "wisdom" of the Old Testament which
had participated in creation—and this brings us to the material difference—we
do not have (1) any metaphysical principle to unite the God-concept with the
riddle of the universe. We have to realise that these passages do not in any
sense deal with the problems of the doctrine of God and an understanding of the
world ; that this " wisdom" is in reality very simply and profoundly the divine
revelation addressing and directing the man covenanted with God as practical
wisdom ; and that it is undoubtedly understood in this sense in the one New
Testament passage which deals with it expressly, i.e., 1 Cor. 1 and 2 (and also
in Mt. 11¹⁶⁻¹⁹ ; Col. 1⁹, ²⁵ᶠ·, 4⁵ ; Eph. 1⁷ᶠ·, ¹⁷ᶠ·, 5¹⁵ ; and Jas. 1⁵ᶠ· and 3¹³ᶠ·).
There is thus no trace in any of the New Testament passages quoted of the
suggestion that the participation of Jesus Christ in creation is significant for these
writers because they too had been affected by the general shattering of the
consciousness of God and the world, or because they had been seeking an intermediate principle and had given to this postulate the name of Jesus Christ.
Not they but their contemporaries had been shaken and were therefore looking
for such principles. They, the apostles, on the other hand, were the bearers of
the objective, shattering message of the kingdom of God drawn near, and the
consequent end of all mediating philosophy, theosophy and cosmology. As
against the views of their contemporaries, which seemed to be so similar, they
could not have spoken more critically than they did when they described Jesus
Christ as the One " through whom " or " in whom " God had created all things.
In so doing they were actually extending to every doctrine of God and view of
the world an invitation to faith, i.e., to practical participation in God's covenant
of grace and its history. And so the " wisdom " of the Old Testament is not
in any sense (2) an intermediate being—a kind of third existence—between God
and the world. It had certainly become something of this kind in the interpretation of later Judaism. But in the canonical passages it is never more than
God's revelation to man ; it has no third aspect but only that of God and man—
of the One who gives it and the one who receives it. It is only in this way, and
not as a " hypostasis," that according to these verses it is in the beginning,
and is indeed itself the beginning, the Creator of all things. What these passages
say is that this divine activity with man had already begun in and with creation
as its meaning and basis. But this is also the case when the New Testament
passages speak of Christ in the same connexion. It is clear (1 Tim. 2⁵) that He
is for them " the Mediator between God and man," but that He is not for this
reason an intermediate being, a third between the two. Between God and man
there is the world of angels. But even angels are not " intermediate beings " ;
they belong by nature to the creaturely sphere. The New Testament does not
ascribe this function to any angel. The passage cited from Heb. 1¹⁰ stands in a

context whose point is precisely to distinguish Christ from the angels, as is also done expressly in 1 Cor. 8[6] and Col. 1[16]. He to whom the New Testament ascribes participation in creation has only divine and human form, like the " wisdom " of the Old Testament. He is not an " intermediate being." He is the divine person who acts, suffers and triumphs as man ; the Humiliated and Exalted, the Crucified and Resurrected. And in this way, and just because He is not a " hypostasis," He is the Mediator between God and man, like the " wisdom " of the Old Testament. What interest would the writers of the New Testament have had in interpreting Him as a " hypostasis," and from what standpoint could they have done so ? He meant something much more and far better to them than that. And again, they could not have been more critical of the views of their contemporaries than when with undoubted reference to them they said of this person—that God had created all things by Him. In so doing they summoned man to faith in God. And in this way they did not add another to the plethora of supposed " intermediate beings."

Far more important than the question of religious history is the factual question how the writers of the New Testament for their part understood the important δι' αὐτοῦ or ἐν αὐτῷ ; what they meant by associating with God the Father His Son or Word or Jesus Christ in creation. It is clear from all the passages quoted—we have only to think of the most important, Jn. 1[3f.], Heb. 1[2f.] and Col. 1[15f.]—that we are dealing with a special emphasising and distinction of the person of Jesus Christ. It is not God or the world and their relation which is the problem of these passages but the lordship of Jesus Christ. The starting point is not that deity is so exalted and holy or that the world is so dark ; nor is it the affirmation that there is something like a mediation between the two which bears the name of Jesus Christ. What they have in view is the kingdom of God drawn near ; the turning point of the times, revealed in the name of Jesus Christ, as the fulfilment of all the promises of the covenant of grace. To give to the Bearer of this name the honour due to Him, or rather to bear witness to the honour which He has, they venture the tremendous assertion that the world was created through Him and in Him as through God, and in God, in God's eternal will and purpose. And so we have to see first the simple fact that in so doing they thought concretely of the ineffable and inclusive reality of Jesus Christ as the κύριος ; that their aim was to give a comprehensive description of His κυριότης ; and that they therefore found it necessary to describe it in this way, setting it at the beginning of all things.

But now we may and must ask further whether it was the eternal Son (or eternal Word) of God as such in His pure deity that they had in mind ; or whether, more inclusively and more concretely, it was the Son of God as the Son of Man, the Word made flesh. If it was only the former, the λόγος ἄσαρκος, the " second person " in the Trinity in itself and as such, to whom they referred with their δι' αὐτοῦ and ἐν αὐτῷ, one can only be astonished at the force with which these expressions so unmistakeably point to a specific creative causality. It is certainly true that the wisdom and power of the Creator are also those of the eternal Son or Word of God. But this would not explain the particularity of the divine causality of which these expressions appear to speak. As we have seen, the only possible connexion between the eternal Son or Word of God on the one hand and creation on the other is that it is commensurate with and worthy of the Father of the eternal Son, the Speaker of the eternal Word as such, that He should be the Creator in His dealings *ad extra*. Perhaps the writers of the New Testament wished to say this too. Indeed, there can be no doubt that they did. But was this all they wished to say ? If so, they could not have described Jesus Christ as the actual divine ground of creation, as the peculiar creative causality, to which those expressions seem to point. It has to be kept in mind that the whole conception of the λόγος ἄσαρκος, the " second person " of the Trinity as such, is an abstraction. It is true that it has shown itself necessary to the christological and trinitarian reflections of the Church. Even to-day it is indispensable for dogmatic enquiry and presentation, and it is often touched upon in the New Testament, though nowhere expounded directly. The New Testament speaks plainly enough about the Jesus Christ who existed before the world was, but always was with a view to the concrete content of the eternal divine will and decree. For this reason it does not speak expressly of the eternal Son or Word as such, but of the Mediator, the One who in the eternal sight of God has already taken upon Himself our human nature, i.e., not of a formless Christ who might well be a Christ-principle or something of that kind, but of Jesus the Christ. The One who according to Heb. 1³ upholds all things by the Word of His power is also the One who according to the following verse, when He had purged our sins, sat down on the right hand of majesty on high. According to Col. 1¹⁵, He is " the firstborn of every creature," and, according to v. 14, the One in whom we have ἀπολύτρωσις, i.e., the forgiveness of sins. According to verse 18, He is the " firstborn from the dead ; that in all things he might have the preeminence." How could this be said of the λόγος ἄσαρκος ? We shall misunderstand the whole Johannine Prologue if we fail to see that the sentence οὗτος ἦν ἐν ἀρχῇ πρὸς τὸν θεόν (Jn. 1²)—which would otherwise be a wholly unnecessary repetition—points to the person who is the theme of the whole ensuing Gospel, and of whom it is said in v. 14 : " the Word became flesh and tabernacled among us." And in just the same way in this event it became historical reality, as the Word incarnate—how else ?—this Word was in the beginning, i.e., in the divinely determined counsel with God before the world was. The real basis of creation, permitted and even demanded by the unprecedented continuation in v. 3, that " all things were made by him, and without him was not anything made that was made," is that the Word was with God, existing before the world was, and that from all eternity God wanted to see and know and love His only begotten Son as the Mediator—His Word incarnate. It is not difficult to prove that no other meaning can be read into the passages adduced than that they refer to Jesus the Christ, who is certainly very God, but who is also very man. Irenaeus has correctly assessed the meaning of the New Testament (in this respect no other assessment is really possible) : *Mundi factor vere verbum Dei est : hic autem est Dominus noster, qui in novissimis temporibus homo factus est, in hoc mundo existens, et secundum invisibilitatem continet quae facta sunt omnia et in universa conditione infixus, quoniam verbum Dei gubernans et disponens omnia ; et propter hoc in sua venit (Adv. o. h. V, 18, 3).* Coccejus, too, has rightly assessed the meaning of the New Testament : *Fundatio mundi subordinatur decreto electionis et ad id respectum habet (S. Theol., 1669, 37, 29). Ille qui ab initio coelum terramque condidit, est is, qui Deus Israelis nuncupari voluit, et quum ea creavit, iam tum vidit se facere mundum theatrum gloriae gratiae suae* (note the quiet but very definite improvement of the expression of Calvin) *qua velut praecipua laude triumpharet (ib., 33, 1).* So, too, has H. Witsius : *Ipsa terrae fundatio sine intuitu mortis Christi facta non est. Nam quum manifestatio gloriosae suae gratiae in homine per Christum summus Dei hominem creantis finis fuerit, fundatio terrae, ut bonis habitaculum esset, medii ad finem istum rationem obtinet. Neque conveniens Deo fuisset terram condere in habitaculum hominis peccatoris, nisi eadem illa terra lustranda aliquando fuisset sanguine Christi, sanctificantis et glorificantis electos suos. Propter omnes has rationes mactatio Christi* (Rev. 13⁸) *et fundatio mundi non incommode iunguntur (Oecon. foed.,* 1693, III, 4, 16). Also J. Wichelhaus (*Die Lehre d. hl. Schrift,* ³ 1892, p. 349 f.) : " How could God call into existence what is not-God . . . what is in itself dead, obscure and transitory ? He could not have done so had there not been something in God which in His eternal love He posited outside and before Himself, had there not existed in Him an eternal decree (on p. 352 a divine counsel and covenant of peace which had been formed between Father and Son before the foundation of the world) in which all His perfections were to be revealed (Eph. 1¹⁰, Col. 1¹⁵ᶠ.). God could not have created a world which He could have loved for its own sake and which could have had life in itself. . . . What God had in view at creation was His Son, the Son of His love, and a Church elected in Him by eternal decree. . . . What God has created in Christ Jesus is a dark world which He willed to enlighten and to fructify, and a poor son of man whom He willed to save." Or on p. 351 : " It was the will and good-pleasure of inexplicable kindness and mercy, the free movement of grace and love, that in His Son, in Christ, God willed to impart His glory to a creature which in itself is dust and ashes ; that He willed to exalt the most needy and most helpless creature above all the works of His hands (Ps. 8, Heb. 2). And it was thus that His eternal love willed to create for itself an object of its compassion and kindness." " The glorification of God's name in Jesus Christ is accordingly the final goal of creation, so that everything is ordered for this purpose, and everything, be it light or darkness, good or evil, must serve this purpose " (p. 355).

To sum up, the New Testament passages in question say that the creative wisdom and power of God were in the beginning specifically the wisdom and power of Jesus Christ. For in the first place He was the eternal Son and the Word of God, the whole of divine being revealed and active in creation being His own eternal being. Second, His existence as the Son of God the Father was in some sense the inner divine analogy and justification of creation. Finally and supremely, He was already in the eternal decree of God the Mediator ; the Bearer of our human nature ; the Humiliated and Exalted as the Bearer of our flesh ; a creature and precisely as such loved by God ; and in this way the motivating basis of creation. If God willed to give His eternal Son this form and function, and if the Son of God willed to obey His Father in this form and function, this meant that God had to begin to act as Creator, for there could be no restraining His will. Hence, as these passages of the New Testament declare, it is not only God the Father, but in particular the Son Jesus Christ, who is *propria vi et efficacia et potentia* the Creator of all things.   [III, 1, pp. 51–56]

3. THE HOLY SPIRIT AND CREATION

We possess no series of direct New Testament attestations of the relationship between the Holy Spirit and creation similar to those which occupied us in connexion with the Son or Word of God. When the *Symb. Nic.-Const.* calls the Holy Spirit τὸ ζωοποιοῦν, it is, of course, quoting directly from Jn. 6[63] : τὸ πνεῦμά ἐστιν τὸ ζωοποιοῦν ; and there is also an allusion to 1 Cor. 15[45] : ὁ ἔσχατος 'Αδὰμ εἰς πνεῦμα ζωοποιοῦν, and to 2 Cor. 3[6] : τὸ δὲ πνεῦμα ζωοποιεῖ. But we have to remember that in all these references ζωοποιεῖν is primarily a soterio-eschatological term, describing the quickening and animation effected by the work of Jesus Christ, or by faith in Him, in those who without Him are the victims of death, and that it was certainly adopted in this sense in the *Nic.-Const.* All the same this deliverance effected by the Holy Spirit is itself the confirmation of creation when God first gave to man the life which he then lost. That the New Testament writers had this connexion in mind is obvious from the fact that in the three references (and particularly 1 Cor. 15[45]) there is a clear allusion to Gen. 2[7], where through God's inbreathing of the " breath of life " (πνοὴ ζωῆς) man becomes a " living soul " (ψυχὴ ζῶσα). And this certainly means that it is by the communication and impartation of that in which God exists as God that it comes about that man can exist as man. Gen. 7[15] describes not only the human but also the animal world as ἄρσεν καὶ θῆλυ ἀπὸ πάσης σαρκός, ἐν ᾧ ἐστι πνεῦμα ζωῆς. Ps. 33[6] says that even the host of heaven is made by the breath of God's mouth (πνεύματι τοῦ στόματος αὐτοῦ). Ps. 139[7] asks even more inclusively : ποῦ πορευθῶ ἀπὸ τοῦ πνεύματός σου. And finally in Ps. 104[29f.] we have the remarkable antithesis : " Thou takest away their breath (τὸ πνεῦμα αὐτῶν), they die, and return to their dust. Thou sendest forth thy spirit (τὸ πνεῦμά σου) they are created : and thou renewest the face of the earth." We are thus confronted with the remarkable fact that the Old Testament statement under consideration undoubtedly refers to the first creation and the preservation of the world and of man. It does not say anything concerning the breath or Spirit of God corresponding to what is said of " wisdom " in Prov. 3 and 8. That is, it does not say (nor is this the meaning of Ps. 33[6]) that the world was created " by " the Spirit. But it describes Him (this is especially clear in Ps. 104[29f.]) as the divine *conditio sine qua non* of the creation and preservation of the creature. It says that it is only through Him that the creature has its indispensable life ; only through Him that it has continued enjoyment and exercise of the existence loaned to it in creation ; and that without Him it cannot possibly be what on the basis of its creation it was destined to be. But this very statement, which was no doubt intended cosmologically, is the one which in those New Testament passages is suddenly adopted and understood soterio-eschatologically. We are told in Jn. 6[63] how in a final allusion to His return to the Father Jesus adds to the " hard saying " about the eating and drinking of His flesh and blood as the true meat and the true drink the explanation : " It is the spirit that quickeneth ; the flesh profiteth nothing : the words which I speak to you, they are spirit and they are life." In 1 Cor. 15[45] the distinction and sequence of the present existence of the creature and its future spiritual existence to be realised in the resurrection is emphasised by an antithesis which expressly points back to Gen. 2[7] : " The first man, Adam, was made a living soul ; the last Adam was made a quickening spirit." And in 2 Cor. 3[6] the " new covenant " of Jer. 31[31], which is not of the letter but of the Spirit, is explained by the statement : " For the letter killeth, but the spirit giveth life." Thus the Spirit of Jesus (His words spoken to His disciples which, as such, carry the Spirit and bring life) makes His flesh and blood—impotent in themselves for this purpose—the true meat and the true drink. The last Adam (in virtue of His resurrection from the dead) is Spirit, and therefore that which makes the first a " living soul " ; and again, it is the Spirit who is the distinctive essence of the apostolic ministry. What does this mean ? It surely means that the writers of the New Testament look into a dimension which is still hidden in the Old Testament sayings about the " breath of God." But it also means that they too, looking into this new dimension, describe the Spirit as the *conditio sine qua non* of creaturely existence, i.e., of its glorification, its hope, its adaptability for its appointed existence and activity. Like the Old Testament, they are answering the question : How exactly can the creature as creature not only become but be ? The answer is necessarily indirect. For them there is no ζωή and therefore no ζωοποίησις of the creature apart from that already initiated in the resurrection of Jesus Christ and to be expected from Him. And it is in this ζωοποιεῖν that they see the work of the Spirit. In this indirect way, by expecting life—life in the new æon which is true life for them—from the work of the Spirit, and from Him alone, they also bear witness that there could be no creature, nor any creation, if God were not also the Holy Spirit and active as such, just as He is also the Father and the Son and active as such.

This being so, we obviously cannot say that theological tradition moved along unscriptural lines when it referred the ζωοποιοῦν of the *Nic.-Const.* to the presence and the activity of the Holy Spirit in the first creation. The lines of the Whitsun hymn *Veni creator Spiritus* :

> *Imple superna gratia*
> *Quae tu creasti pectora,*

show that in so doing it followed much the same line of exegesis as that which we have just propounded. Among the Reformers Calvin especially took up the position that the Holy Spirit is to be understood as the divine *virtus* poured out on all things and supporting, sustaining and quickening all things (*Cat. Gen.*, 1542, *qu.* 19; *Instit.* I, 13, 14), although unfortunately he did not give any more detailed explanation of the relationship. This should not be too difficult if we keep in mind that the Holy Spirit is in some sense the necessary divine justification and sanctification of the creature as such, and therefore, if not the ground, at least the fundamental condition of its existence. The ground of creation and of the creature is, as we have seen, the incarnate Word of God as the content and object of the eternal divine decree of grace—the pre-existent Jesus Christ. It is for His sake that God wills the creature and accomplishes creation. But this decree of grace, and the creative will of God founded on it, has its necessary inner presupposition in the fact that the unity, love and peace between God the Father and Son are not unsettled or disturbed but transcendently glorified by the fact that the Word of God becomes flesh, that in His Son God takes to Himself man's misery and undertakes his redemption, thus addressing His love to another than Himself, i.e., the creature, and willing and bringing about the existence of another than Himself, i.e., that of the creature. That in His very humility and exaltation in human nature, in Jesus Christ crucified and risen and for His sake in the existence of the creature, the being of God should radiate and triumph—bigger and stronger than if He had kept His glory to Himself—is obviously the inner presupposition of the divine decree of grace and of the divine creative will founded upon it. In some sense it is a matter of the self-justification and self-sanctification of God without which He could not have loved the creature nor willed or actualised its existence. The fulfilment of this presupposition, the eternal accomplishment of this divine self-justification and self-sanctification, is the Holy Spirit of the Father and the Son *qui procedit ex Patre Filioque*, who in His common origin in the Father and the Son not only does not hinder their fellowship but glorifies it; in whom God does not restrict His deity but causes it to overflow even in the decree of grace and His creative will. In this way the Holy Spirit is the inner divine guarantee of the creature. If its existence were intolerable to God, how could it be loved and willed and made by Him? How could it emerge and be? That its existence should not be intolerable to God but destined to serve His greater glory—the creation of this essential condition of its existence is the peculiar work of the Holy Spirit in creation. In view of this work of His, He can indeed be called with Calvin God's *vertu et puissance, laquelle est espandue sur toutes créatures : et neantmoins reside tousiours en luy.* If, then, in the New Testament especially His activity in the historical execution of the covenant of grace is described as the ζωοποίησις of the creature subjected to death, as the divine power of the work and witness of Jesus Christ, and therefore as the power of the new birth and faith, of salvation and hope, we do not find it difficult to recognise in this activity the character which is already peculiar to Him in that first work of His.   [III, 1, pp. 57–59]

4. HISTORY, MYTH AND SAGA

Hearing history such as that which is an event in the revelation attested in the Bible obviously cannot mean regarding such an event as possible, probable, or even actual on the basis of a general concept of historical (*geschichtlich*) truth. Even histories enacted between God and man do, of course, come under this general concept of history on their human side and therefore in relation to the statements on its temporal form which are so assiduously emphasised in the Bible. But they do not fall under this general concept on their divine side. Hence the " historical " (*historisch*) judgment which presupposes this general concept can in principle relate only to the temporal side. It can neither claim nor deny that at this point or that God has acted on men. To be able to claim or deny this it would have to abandon its presupposition, that general concept, and become a confession of faith or unbelief *vis-à-vis* the biblical witness. No genuinely " historical " verdict can be passed on the singular historicity of the history recorded in the biblical witness. But again—and this is less obvious—hearing a history such as that enacted in the revelation attested in the Bible cannot be dependent on the " historical " assessment of its temporal form. The judgment in virtue of which a biblical story may be regarded with some probability as history in the sense of the general concept of historical truth is not necessarily the judgment of faith *vis-à-vis* the biblical witness. For the judgment may be passed without any understanding of the story in its particularity, i.e., as history between God and man. Again, the opposite judgment need not be that of unbelief, for it may involve an understanding of the story in its particularity, i.e., as history between God and man. The question which decides hearing or non-hearing of the biblical history cannot be the question of its general historicity ; it can only be that of its special historicity.

Thus the judgment that a biblical story is to be regarded either as a whole or in part as saga or legend does not have to be an attack on the substance of the biblical witness. All that might be said is that according to the standards by which " historical " truth is usually measured elsewhere or generally, this story is one that to some degree eludes any sure declaration that it happened as the narrative says. Saga or legend can only denote the more or less intrusive part of the story-teller or story-tellers in the story told. There is no story in which we do not have to reckon with this aspect, and therefore with elements of saga or legend according to the general concept of " historical " truth. This applies also to the stories told in the Bible. Otherwise they would have to be without temporal form. Yet this fundamental uncertainty in general historicity, and therefore the positive judgment that here and there saga or legend is actually present, does not have to be an attack on the substance of the biblical testimony. For (1) this judgment can in any case concern and contest only the general historicity of a biblical record, (2) even in the clearest instance it is by nature only a judgment of probability, and (3) even saga or legend is in any case meant to be history and can thus be heard as a communication of history irrespective of the " historical " judgment. So long as this is so, the question of the particular historicity of the story at issue is at least not answered negatively.

The situation changes when the category of myth is introduced. The verdict that a biblical story is to be understood as a myth is necessarily an attack on the substance of the biblical witness. This is because " myth " does not intend to be history but only pretends to be such. Myth uses narrative form to expound what purports to be always and everywhere true. It is an exposition of certain basic relationships of human existence, found in every time and place, in their connexions to their own origins and conditions in the natural and historical cosmos, or in the deity. These are given narrative form on the assumption that man knows all these things and can present them thus or thus, that he controls them, that in the last resort they are his things. Myth (cf. for what follows Eduard Thurneysen, " Christus und die Kirche," *Z.d.Z.*, 1930, esp. p. 189 f.) does not impute any exclusive character to the event narrated by it—in other words : " What myth narrates as a fact may happen in any time or place. It is not a unique event but one that can be repeated. . . . But what can be repeated and can happen over and over again, even though it may be surprising, is a general possibility akin to natural occurrence. What happens in this way rests on nothing other than the assumption that the man to whom the revelation narrated in myth is imparted stands ultimately in an original and natural relation and connexion, hidden, of course, but present potentially at least everywhere, to the final ground of his existence, to his God. In the events narrated in myth this latent possibility becomes, so to speak, active. In ever new theophanies man experiences the ground of the world as present and himself as connected to it. But this means that there is here an ultimate identity between God and man. There is no thought of a profound and final distinction. What myth, then, recounts as a unique happening is not unique at all ; it is the unchanging, final, basic relation which, evoked by all kinds of wizardry and magic, is again lived through and experienced and will be continually lived through and experienced."

> Joyous was it years ago—
> So eagerly the spirit strives
> To seek and come to know
> How nature, in creating, lives.
> And 'tis the eternally One
> That is manifold revealed.
> Small the great and great the small,
> Each according to its kind ;
> Ever changing, standing fast,
> Near and far and far and near,
> Forming thus and then transforming—
> To marvel am I here.
> (Goethe, *Parabase*, Jub. Edn., Vol. II, p. 246).

This is the birth of myth. (The only distinction between myth and speculation proper is that in speculation the narrative is stripped off again like a garment that has become too tight, so that what is presented as fact in myth is now elevated to the sphere of pure idea or concept, and the present and acknowledged wealth of the origins and relations of human existence is thus expressed in its " in and for itself." Myth is the preparatory form of speculation and speculation is the revealed essence of myth.) To be sure, one cannot prevent a historian from applying the category of myth to some of the events recorded in the Bible. One might ask, of course, whether the supposed myths have really been found in the text of the Bible and not somewhere behind the text, whether the context in which the passage concerned finds its point has not been dissolved, whether what it says in the context has not been ignored on the assumption that so-called " sources " of a special character and independent content underlie the biblical text, and whether certain parts of the biblical text have not been combined with parts of non-biblical texts which might perhaps be claimed as mythical. In a word, one might ask whether the verdict " myth " as applied to the biblical texts is not even from the purely " historical " standpoint a mistaken verdict because it can perhaps be made only when there is a failure to hear what the real biblical texts are trying to say and do say if we read them as we actually have them, in their narrower and broader context, as biblical texts. But even if this objection does not seem to make sense, the historian who resolves on this verdict must realise at least that if this verdict is possible for him he has as it were read the Bible outside the Christian Church, that he is not asking about revelation but about something else, perhaps myth or speculation, that perhaps he himself is quite unaware or forgetful of the fact that there is such a thing as revelation, that perhaps he himself is aware, or at this moment aware, of no more than man's general ability to control the origins and relations of his existence by fable or thought or some other means, because these are in fact his own things. It is really quite natural that an age whose thought, feeling and action are so

highly mythical as the so-called modern period that culminates in the Enlightenment (including Idealism and Romanticism) should seek myth in the Bible too—
and find it. Historicism is " the self-understanding of the spirit in so far as its
own achievements in history are concerned " (E. Troeltsch, *Ges. Schriften*,
Vol. III, 1922, p. 104). Good ! For the person who does not ask about revelation
there is nothing left, of course, but to ask about myth, and the man who asks
about myth because he must, because myth is his own last word, will not be
restrained by the objection that even a historian might feel from seeking myth in
the Bible too, and really finding it there, and perhaps, strictly speaking, finding
a little of it in every part of the Bible. We can only declare that the interpretation
of the Bible as the witness to revelation and the interpretation of the Bible as
the witness to myth are mutually exclusive. The category of saga, the questioning of the general historicity of the biblical narratives, is not an attack on the
substance of the Bible as witness, but the category of myth is, for myth does not
just question but fundamentally denies the history as such, and therefore the
special historicity of the biblical records, and revelation regarded as myth
would not be a historical event but a supposed non-spatial and timeless truth,
i.e., a creation of man.

The history of creation is " non-historical " or, to be more precise, pre-historical
history. We must be careful not to fall back into the equally impossible exegetical
and dogmatic proposition that it is not history but the disguise of an unhistorical
and timeless reality. But again we have to insist on dogmatic and exegetical
grounds that it is not a " historical " history. Not all history is "historical."
We repeat that in its immediacy to God every history is in fact " non-historical,"
i.e., it cannot be deduced and compared and therefore perceived and comprehended. But this does not mean that it ceases to be genuine history. In its
decisive elements or dimensions, in the direction in which alone it is ultimately
important and interesting, all history—as genuine history—is " non-historical."
And this the more so, and the more palpably, the more this element predominates,
the more this dimension—the immediacy of history to God—emerges. The history
of creation has *only* this element. In it Creator and creature confront each other
only in immediacy. In this supreme sense it is genuine history, but also in this
supreme sense it is " non-historical," pre-historical history. And for this very
reason it can be the object only of a " non-historical," pre-historical depiction and
narration.

We must dismiss and resist to the very last any idea of the inferiority or
untrustworthiness or even worthlessness of a " non-historical " depiction and narration of history. This is in fact only a ridiculous and middle-class habit of the
modern Western mind which is supremely phantastic in its chronic lack of imaginative phantasy, and hopes to rid itself of its complexes through suppression. This
habit has really no claim to the dignity and validity which it pretends. It acts
as if only " historical " history were genuine history, and " non-historical "
false. The obvious result is to banish from the portrayal and understanding of
history all immediacy of history to God on the pretext of its non-historicity,
dissolving it into a bare idea ! When this is done, the horizon of history necessarily becomes what it is desired to be—a highly unreal history, a more or less
explicit myth, in the poor light of which the historical, what is supposed to be
the only genuine history, can only seem to be an ocean of tedious inconse-
quence and therefore demoniac chaos. We must not on any account take this
course. In no way is it necessary or obligatory to maintain this rigid attitude
to the " non-historical " reality, conception and description of history. On
the contrary, it is necessary and obligatory to realise the fact and manner that
in genuine history the " historical " and " non-historical " accompany each
other and belong together.

In addition to the "historical" there has always been a legitimate "non-historical" and pre-historical view of history, and its "non-historical" and pre-historical depiction in the form of saga.

As far as I can see and understand (cf. the competent articles in *RGG*[2] by H. Gunkel, W. Baumgartner, O. Rühle, P. Tillich and R. Bultmann), modern ethnology and religious science cannot give us any illuminating and acknowledged clarification, distinction and co-ordination of the terms myth, saga, fable, legend and anecdote, let alone any useful definition of their relationship to history and historical scholarship. The non-specialist must try to find his own bearings in this sphere.

In what follows I am using saga in the sense of an intuitive and poetic picture of a pre-historical reality of history which is enacted once and for all within the confines of time and space. Legend and anecdote are to be regarded as a degenerate form of saga : legend as the depiction in saga form of a concrete individual personality ; and anecdote as the sudden illumination in saga form either of a personality of this kind or of a concretely historical situation.

If the concept of myth proves inadequate—as is still to be shown—it is obvious that the only concept to describe the biblical history of creation is that of saga.

This comes out very clearly when we compare the biblical creation saga with the genuinely mythical texts of the Babylonian epic *Enuma elish* (*c.* 2000 B.C.) which calls at once for historical consideration in this context ; and also with the cosmogony of Berosus (3rd century B.C.), etc. (H. Gressmann, *Altorientalische Texte zum A.T.*[2], 1926, p. 108 f.). The researches of experts appear to agree (cf. F. Delitzsch, *Genesis*, 1887, p. 40 f., and Gunkel, *op. cit.*, p. 119 f.), that there can be no question of a direct dependent relationship between these passages and Gen. 1 and 2, but only of a common relationship to still older traditions from which Gen. 1 and 2 and these Babylonian texts may perhaps derive. But it also seems to be generally accepted that the material agreement of Gen. 1 and 2 is only in " certain parts " (Gunkel, p. 129) or "isolated relics " (p. 128) ; and that the mythical tradition in Gen. 1–2 has been " very much deflated " (p. 122), or " muffled," or even " reduced to a mere fragment " (p. 130), having been " amalgamated " (p. 129) with the religion of Israel. In relation to the other biblical passages which touch on creation, it has been said that in Israel myth has been " historicised " and rendered " impotent " as myth ; that it has no autonomy but remains only in individual cases as a " poetic ornament " (W. Eichrodt, *Theol. d. A.T.*[1], Vol. II, 1935, p. 56). But " historicised " myth is not myth but a saga which, although it may work with mythical materials, differs sharply from myth in the fact that it does seriously and without any after-thought try to say how things actually were. In these circumstances, it is hard to see why there has been no agreement that the kind of saga which is found in the biblical creation narratives of creation is as such different from myth, and that the theme of the Babylonian myth—irrespective of textual relationships—is different from that of the biblical saga, so that the latter cannot be called myth in virtue of its theme.

The epic *Enuma elish* is not a history of creation, nor " pre-history," but a portrayal of the constantly recurrent change of relationships which is exactly the same in pre-historical time as any other within the cosmos as it has come into being and now exists. The unity, totality and singularity of the cosmos are not altered by the fact that there are in it the dreadful contradictions, changes and convulsions, bases and emanations, causes and consequences, births and deaths, conflicts, victories and defeats, divisions, reconciliations and fresh divisions, which are the theme of myth. But all this is merely the inner rhythm of the cosmos and has nothing to do with its creation. Tiamat, the mother of the gods, the gods who originate in her, and her youngest and most successful scion, the hero and later demiurge Marduk, who by his final victory over the original power which is both friendly and hostile comes to the aid of the other more or less impotent divinities—all these are of one species and kind. And if heaven and earth arise because Marduk (who according to Berosus is identical with Bel and the Greek Zeus) literally attacks the arch-mother of all the gods and all beings, cleaving and dismembering her and turning her into heaven and earth, this decides the fact that everything outwith the Godhead is in fact only a transformed but genuine element of the divine being, and that conversely we have to recognise in this the original form of all being. In these forms and events we nowhere see a genuine horizon of this One and All as it is found in the concept of creation. There is no qualitative difference between divine and every other reality. What kind of a deity is it in whose very bosom there is so much darkness and such a dialectic of good and evil, in whom conflict, victory and defeat, life and death, reign side by side ? It cannot possibly be the Creator of the cosmos but only its first cause, partly struggling and partly suffering, dividing itself in a dreadful self-contradiction, in an unnatural but necessary tumult. It is no modern supposition that in all this we have an allegorical presentation of natural processes, but one which was declared as a self-evident truth by Berosus, a priest of Marduk's temple. The same relationship is to be found as between the Godhead and man. This is prefigured already in Marduk hastening to the aid of the older gods as a champion against Tiamat, and it is fulfilled in the event which follows. The gods themselves need completion ; indeed, according to tablet 6 of the epic, they need a redemption which must be accomplished in the form of service rendered to them. For this purpose man, i.e., Babylonian man, is necessary, and therefore the city of Babylon is necessary as the seat of the gods who would otherwise be homeless. And so according to the supremely laudable decree of Marduk one of the other gods is sacrificed, and from his blood there is formed the man who will build Babylon and there render true service to the gods. But it is obvious that this cannot and obviously will not be understood as true creation and a true history of creation. The *Enuma elish* also formed the textbook of an annual dramatic liturgy enacted on New Year's day (at the close of the rainy season) when the reigning monarch had to act the role of Marduk. We may ask whether it is possible to imagine a similar application of Gen. 1 and 2 and the personification of the Creator God of Israel by a David in Jerusalem. But it corresponds only too well to the nature of myth. Marduk's role, the person of the mythical " creator," can indeed be acted by the creature, for properly and originally it is his own role and person. Nor is mythical " creation " anything but the timelessly valid connexion, confirmed in constant repetition, between emergence and existence, dissolution and rebirth, in the world of created things. Nor has mythical creation anything to do with a pre-historical positing of the world of created things. The fact that it is accomplished in the actions of gods and god-like figures does not in any sense make them real founders and lords of this world, either individually or collectively. It is not they who have produced the world. On the contrary, they have emerged from the same basic cause and are to that extent of the same nature. They, too, are in their way weak and helpless. They, too, are condemned to suffer. They, too, are an embodiment of its dualism. They are not this out of free and superior participation and compassion, but because they have no option, because the same destiny that rules the world rules them, because they themselves are the first who must endure the dualism, the schism and the need which are evidently distinctive of that basic cause. And if the creaturely world is nothing but the sum of the transformed and fashioned members of their own half-friendly and half-hostile arch-mother, it is clear that they are not really over the world. They do not really control it. They have in their relation to it no claim to a greater or indeed to any real honour. On the contrary, they are bound and under obligation to it. And finally and supremely they depend no less on man, who is himself formed of divine blood, than he depends on them. The position of man is that he has to exist, that he has to be created, that Babylon has to come into being, for the sake of the gods, because the gods need the worship of a human shrine. And man is made out of divine blood which is given under compulsion. Thus he is surely as much the lord of the gods as the gods lords over him. We may calmly ask indeed if there is any true or final distinction between him and these gods ; between these gods and gigantic but shadowy projections of human experiences and needs, struggles and sufferings, hopes and possibilities ; between the Babylonian deity and the Babylonian king and Babylonian man. In the figure of Marduk the three are in fact indistinguishable. There can be no question in this epic of any pre-history, of any genuine history of creation. On the contrary, we have only the transparent apparel of a deep insight into the already existing reality of the world and of man. This reality and its inner problem have here no boundary, no beginning and no end, no given determination enabling it to escape the caprice or fate of its own movement.

What we read in Gen. 1 and 2 are genuine histories of creation. If there is a connexion with the Babylonian myth or its older sources, it is a critical connexion. Everything is so different that the only choice is either to see in the Jewish rendering a complete caricature of the Babylonian, or in the Babylonian a complete caricature of the Jewish, according to the standpoint adopted. In Gen. 1 and 2 no less than everything obviously depends on the uniqueness and sovereignty of the Creator and the creative act—so much so that a reciprocity of creaturely speech or activity is not even mentioned in the first account, and only incidentally at the end of the second (in the naming of the animals and the saying about the woman brought to man). Gunkel is not wrong when, with reference to the " development of the action " in Gen. 1, he almost complains that " there is no real plot and no opponent. The whole narration consists of related words and acts of God " (p. 117). What the two accounts of Genesis offer is cosmogony in the strict and exclusive sense of the term. This means in the first instance that they really visualise the emergence of the world by the Word and work of God to the exclusion of the notion of a world-basis presupposed in this act. And it means secondly that they are not in any sense a theogony : they visualise the origin of the world to the exclusion of the notion of a preceding or simultaneous genesis of the Deity. For this reason there can be no question in either account of a monistic or dualistic speculation and systematisation. A monistic is excluded because God the Creator is always different in essence from His work ; because there is no transition and mediation between Him and the creature ; and because no secret identity between God and the world is possible. And a dualistic is excluded because the possibility and reality of a world contradicting the will and the act of God are excluded in and with the act of creation and can come into consideration only in this exclusion, while in the world as it is willed and actually created by God there is as little duality and schism as there is in God Himself. Creation, according to Gen. 1 and 2, is not in any sense a proper predicate of the creature, or identical with the self-propelled " wheel of emergence " (τροχὸς τῆς γενέσεως, Jas. 3⁶). Creation includes this motion of the creature in itself only in so far as it first gives rise to it, and indeed gives to the propelling and propelled creature its existence and nature. Creation, then, does not aim at the kingdom, the power and the glory of man. It does not aim at the government, the building of cities, the wars and lion hunting of any hero or potentate. Its aim is the history of the acts of God in the world created and controlled by Him and in relation to the man created and guided by Him. In this way it is an original and typical reflection of the purpose and plan and triumph of God, and not of the ambiguities of man's experiences and possibilities of the advent of his kingdom, of the glorification of his name, and of the successes and adventures to which he looks forward when the storms subside. Here, then, we have a record of genuine history, unique of its kind ;

and not just a textbook which can be consulted with the same zest as each New Year day comes with its retrospect and prospect. Here the concept of pre-history is fulfilled, as is also the concept of pure saga. The reference is not to a timeless primal state but to a genuine primal time and its events as the hidden beginning of our time and its events. And it is this historical source of actual history which here forms the object of divination and poetry. This may also be seen in the fact that there is here no necessity to people the pre-historical era, as is done particularly in the cosmogony of Berosus, with all kinds of obviously meaningless and artificial mythological creatures (like two or four-winged, two-headed and bi-sexual men, or crosses between men and animals, or fishes and dogs or horses, and other monstrosities), but that the world and its inhabitants emerge in the state in which they will later exist as the theatre and bearer of the historicity which follows creation. No particular events or figures need here be invented to depict pre-time. These are needed only in play or acting, where the narrative is used only under the proviso of esoteric interpreta-tion and at bottom there is only timeless speculation. They are not needed in these histories because God the Creator is quite enough on the one hand and the actual creature as it always has been and will be on the other. And as the con-tent of these histories, as the event which takes place between these two, the speech and operation of God is quite enough on the one hand and the emergence of the creature on the other. For this reason there can be full and clear con-tinuity between primal time and that which follows, primal history and the " historical " history which succeeds it. This is the originality of the biblical creation saga. This is its relationship to myth. And even though we recognise material elements, this may be rightly assessed only as a critico-polemical relationship. [I, 1, pp. 326–329; III, 1, pp. 80–81; 87–90]

5. THE GOODNESS OF CREATION

It is now said of light that God saw that it was good. This is followed at once by a reference to the existence of darkness. But just as it does not say that God created darkness, so it does not say that He saw that it was good. This can be said of light and of light alone—of the light which according to what follows was separated from darkness. And if the same will later be said of God's other works, they will all be characterised by this first work as works of light and not of darkness, of the day and not of the night ; their goodness neces-sarily corresponding to the goodness which God found and saw in this first work. But what does it mean when it says that God " saw the light, that it was good " ? Gunkel gives the following exposition of this expression and its later parallels : " Like an artificer who critically passes in review his work when the bustle of activity has passed, so God subsequently proves each created thing and sees what has come of it, and He finds each to be good and beautiful. His work has succeeded. . . . The verdict of the narrator is naturally the same as God's verdict on the world : the world is good. In this Song of Triumph the ancient Israelites celebrate the wisdom and goodness of the Creator of the world. The thought of later Judaism is altogether different ; to it the world was in the hands of the evil one." With all due respect we can only say that this exposition is at every point quite inapposite. It is obviously foolish to speak of a coming and passing hustle and bustle of activity in a process which consisted solely in God's *way-yo'mer*. And surely the fact that God saw it does not imply that He passed it critically in review. What it does say is rather that " God saw the light, that it was good," i.e. (as B. Jacob correctly paraphrases it) how good it was. That it was good because it was created by the Word of God is self-evident. But it is not at all self-evident that God should see and accept as good this good thing which is so different from His own goodness ; that He should recognise as good this good thing outside His own goodness ; that it could be the object of His good-pleasure. Nothing outside God Himself, and nothing that He Himself has created and created good, has any claim and right in and by itself to His good-pleasure and therefore to be called good with genuine and final truth. " Why callest thou me good ; there is none good but God alone " (Mk. 10[18]). Except, of course, when someone or something is found to be good by God Himself ! But when this is the case it is always God's discovery, and His freedom is not surrendered or lessened because He has created the thing in question good. That it was good when He created it does not mean the impartation and appro-priation of an inherent goodness which no longer needs the divine discovery. As its becoming good is a matter of divine creation, so its being good is a matter of divine seeing. But this seeing is grace. There is no need of created light for God to see at all. Again, it is not as He sees it in its own goodness and in the power of its truth that He sees how good it is. It is in the freedom of undeserved and unmerited favour that God grants to it—and later grants to all His other works—His good-pleasure ; that in its distinction from Himself He finds in it a correspondence to the goodness of His creative will and acts. In this connexion only that can be called " good " which corresponds to God's will and act as Creator, and for this reason and in this way in a positive relation to Himself. The recognition of this correspondence is the grace of the Creator, His seeing of the goodness of the creature. This divine " seeing," and what the biblical author desires to attest by this expression, has nothing to do with a divine optimism, or an ancient Hebrew optimism whose triumphant song could later give way to pessimism (like that of the followers of Leibnitz after the Lisbon earthquake). For " good " does not just mean " good and beautiful," but is obviously related to the separation of light from darkness which is mentioned immediately after-wards. In finding light worthy of this separation—and this is not self-evident, for it is only a created thing and not God—God sees how the light is good, i.e., that it is good for something, to wit, to be His witness and sign. The other qualities and advantages of light, e.g., that it enables us to see, that it is usually accompanied by heat, that it is one of the necessities of animal life, have all claimed the attention of various exegetes, but they do not seem to be of any interest to the biblical author. The good thing about light as it is graciously seen by God is that according to the phrase which follows He plans to establish it as a landmark against darkness, and therefore against chaos.

The fact that the divine fiat is : " Let there be light," and not : " Let there be darkness," means that the possibility of the latter creation and creature is rejected by God. In this way He supersedes the sphere of Gen. 1[2] and reveals His wisdom and the sum of all wisdom, His righteousness and the sum of all righteousness, and His truth and the sum of all truth in contrast to all folly, unrighteousness, and falsehood, whose negativity was decided by the fact that He created light and not darkness, and saw how and why light was good and not darkness. Here and in the second act of creation, and clearly enough even in the first part of the third, to create is to separate. What is entailed by this separation emerges clearly in vv. 3–5. It is not merely that light is the appointed boundary of two spheres like the firmament of vv. 6–8, or that there are two spheres in their variety as in vv. 9–10, but that as the boundary light is also itself that which bounds or is bounded. Between light and darkness there is no third element like the firmament between the waters above and below (vv. 6–8). Nor are light and darkness peacefully co-existent like the terrestrial ocean and the mainland (vv. 9, 10). They are mutually exclusive. The one confronts the other ; light darkness, and darkness light. Nor is there any question here of symmetry or equilibrium between the two. They confront one another in such a way that God separates the light, which He acknowledges to be good, from the darkness. " In darkness and night remnants of that primal state intrude into the ordered world " (Zimmerli). The reference can be only to the darkness mentioned in v. 2 as the predicate of chaos, for otherwise it would mean that darkness was also created by God and found good in its own way. Since this is not the case, it is obvious that the antithesis to light, and therefore to the good creation of God, is chaos. And it belongs necessarily and integrally to the creation which begins with the creation of light that God rejects chaos, that He has for it no creative will or act or grace, but has these for light and light alone. Commencing in this way, creation is also a clear revelation of His will and way. Whatever may become a reality from and for chaos, by the commence-ment of the divine creation it is separated as darkness from light, as that which God did not will from that which He did, as the sphere of non-grace from that of His grace. Only from the majesty and supreme lordship of God is it not separated. Since darkness cannot offer any resistance to the emergence of light ; since it has to acquiesce in the fact that light is separated from it ; since it is later given a name as well as light, and has assigned to it a somewhat anonymous place in the domain of day, it is clear enough that it is not exempt from the sway of God, but has to serve Him in its own way, so that there can be no ques-tion of an absolute dualism. Here, then, and at root in the processes depicted in v. 6 f. and v. 9 f., to " divide " does not mean only to " distinguish " and " separate " but to " create order." At the same time it is to set up an impass-able barrier. Whatever else may take place between light and darkness, light will never be darkness and darkness will never be light. It is also to establish an inviolable hierarchy. However small and weak it may be, light will always be the power which banishes darkness ; and however great and mighty it may be, darkness will always be the impotence which yields before light. It is light that *is*. Of darkness it can be said only that, as long as light is, it is also, but separated from it, marked and condemned by it as darkness, in opposition to it, as its antithesis, and at the same time serving light as its background. Dark-ness has no reality in itself ; it is a by-product. It would like to be something in itself. Again and again it claims to be this. But it cannot make good its claim. It necessarily serves that which it tries to oppose. It is obviously in view of the place and role assigned to them in the hierarchy of creation that the existence of light and darkness are described in Job 38[19] as the secret of God, and that Is. 45[7] can and must say of darkness that God has " created " it. In this striking application of the verb *bara'* there is revealed the reverse side, the negative power, of the divine activity, which we cannot, of course, deny to the divine will. The best analogy to the relationship between light and darkness is that which exists between the elect and the rejected in the history of the Bible : between Jacob and Esau ; between David and Saul ; between Judas and the other apostles. But even this analogy is improper and defective. For even the rejected, even Satan and the demons, are the creation of God— not, of course, in their corruption, but in the true and original essence which has been corrupted. But darkness and the chaos which it represents are not the creation of God any more than the corruption of the corrupt and the sin of the rejected. Thus a true and strict analogy to the relationship between light and darkness is to be found only in the relationship between the divine election and rejection, in the eternal Yes and No spoken by God Himself when, instead of remaining in and by Himself, He marches on to the *opus ad extra* of His free love. When God fulfils what we recognise in Jesus Christ to be His original and basic will, the beginning of all His ways and works in Himself, He also accomplishes this separation, draws this boundary and inaugurates this hierarchy. This is what is attested by the story of creation in its account of the work of the first three days, and particularly in its account of the work of the first day.

[III, 1, pp. 121–124]

6. MOZART AND THE NEGATIVE SIDE OF THE GOOD CREATION

I must again revert to Wolfgang Amadeus Mozart. Why is it that this man is so incomparable ? Why is it that for the receptive, he has produced in almost every bar he conceived and composed a type of music for which " beautiful " is not a fitting epithet : music which for the true Christian is not mere entertainment, enjoyment or edification but food and drink ; music full of comfort and counsel for his needs ; music which is never a slave to its technique nor sentimental but always " moving," free and liberating because wise, strong and sovereign ? Why is it possible to hold that Mozart has a place in theology, especially in the doctrine of creation and also in eschatology, although he was not a father of the Church, does not seem to have been a particularly active Christian, and was a Roman Catholic, apparently leading what might appear to us a rather frivolous existence when not occupied in his work ? It is possible to give him this position because he knew something about creation in its total goodness that neither the real fathers of the Church nor our Reformers, neither the orthodox nor Liberals, neither the exponents of natural theology nor those heavily armed with the " Word of God," and certainly not the Existentialists, nor indeed any other great musicians before and after him, either know or can express and maintain as he did. In this respect he was pure in heart, far transcending both optimists and pessimists. 1756–1791 ! This was the time when God was under attack for the Lisbon earthquake, and theologians and other well-meaning folk were hard put to it to defend Him. In face of the problem of theodicy, Mozart had the peace of God which far transcends all the critical or speculative reason that praises and reproves. This problem lay behind him. Why then concern himself with it ? He had heard, and causes those who have ears to hear, even to-day, what we shall not see until the end of time—the whole context of providence. As though in the light of this end, he heard the harmony of creation to which the shadow also belongs but in which the shadow is not darkness, deficiency is not defeat, sadness cannot become despair, trouble cannot degenerate into tragedy and infinite melancholy is not ultimately forced to claim undisputed sway. Thus the cheerfulness in this harmony is not without its limits. But the light shines all the more brightly because it breaks forth from the shadow. The sweetness is also bitter and cannot therefore cloy. Life does not fear death but knows it well. *Et lux perpetua lucet* (sic !) *eis*—even the dead of Lisbon. Mozart saw this light no more than we do, but he heard the whole world of creation enveloped by this light. Hence it was fundamentally in order that he should not hear a middle or neutral note, but the positive far more strongly than the negative. He heard the negative only in and with the positive. Yet in their inequality he heard them both together, as, for example, in the Symphony in G-minor of 1788. He never heard only the one in abstraction. He heard concretely, and therefore his compositions were and are total music. Hearing creation unresentfully and impartially, he did not produce merely his own music but that of creation, its twofold and yet harmonious praise of God. He neither needed nor desired to express or represent himself, his vitality, sorrow, piety, or any programme. He was remarkably free from the mania for self-expression. He simply offered himself as the agent by which little bits of horn, metal and catgut could serve as the voices of creation, sometimes leading, sometimes accompanying and sometimes in harmony. He made use of instruments ranging from the piano and violin, through the horn and the clarinet, down to the venerable bassoon, with the human voice somewhere among them, having no special claim to distinction yet distinguished for this very reason. He drew music from them all, expressing even human emotions in the service of this music, and not *vice versa*. He himself was only an ear for this music, and its mediator to other ears. He died when according to the worldly wise his life-work was only ripening to its true fulfilment. But who shall say that after the " Magic Flute," the Clarinet Concerto of October 1791 and the Requiem, it was not already fulfilled ? Was not the whole of his achievement implicit in his works at the age of 16 or 18 ? Is it not heard in what has come down to us from the very young Mozart ? He died in misery like an " unknown soldier," and in company with Calvin, and Moses in the Bible, he has no known grave. But what does this matter ? What does a grave matter when a life is permitted simply and unpretentiously, and therefore serenely, authentically and impressively, to express the good creation of God, which also includes the limitation and end of man.

I make this interposition here, before turning to chaos, because in the music of Mozart—and I wonder whether the same can be said of any other works before or after—we have clear and convincing proof that it is a slander on creation to charge it with a share in chaos because it includes a Yes and a No, as though orientated to God on the one side and nothingness on the other. Mozart causes us to hear that even on the latter side, and therefore in its totality, creation praises its Master and is therefore perfect. Here on the threshhold of our problem— and it is no small achievement—Mozart has created order for those who have ears to hear, and he has done it better than any scientific deduction could. This is the point which I wish to make. [III, 3, pp. 297–299]

7. NOTHINGNESS

The first and most impressive mention of nothingness in the Bible is to be found at the very beginning in Gen. 1² (cf. *C.D.*, III, 1, p. 101 f.), in which there is a reference to the chaos which the Creator has already rejected, negated, passed over and abandoned even before He utters His first creative Word, which He has already consigned to the past and to oblivion even before the beginning of time at His command. Chaos is the unwilled and uncreated reality which constitutes as it were the periphery of His creation and creature. It is that which, later depicted in very suitable mythological terms and conceptions, is antithetical both to God Himself and to the world of heaven and earth which He selected, willed and created. It is a mere travesty of the universe. It is the horrible perversion which opposes God and tempts and threatens His creature. It is that which, though it is succeeded and overcome by light, can never itself be light but must always remain darkness. Note that the first creative work (Gen. 1³ᶠ·) is simply separation—the separation of light from darkness, of the waters on the earth from the threatening waters above the firmament, of the dry land from the seas. Note also that with this separation there arises even within the good creation of God a side which is as it were the neighbour and frontier of chaos. But chaos is not night, or the waters above the firmament, or the earthly sea. It still remains not merely distinct from the works of God, but excluded by the operation of God, a fleeting shadow and a receding frontier. Only in this way can we say that it " is." But in this way it undoubtedly " is," and is thus subject to the divine sovereignty. In this way it is present from the very outset with God and His creature. In this way it is involved from the very outset in the history of the relationship between God and His creature, and therefore from the very outset the biblical witness to this history takes its existence into account. The sin of man as depicted in Gen. 3 confirms the accuracy of our definition. It is purely and simply what God did not, does not and cannot will. It has the essence only of non-essence, and only as such can it exist. Yet the sin of man also confirms the real existence of nothingness. Nothingness is a factor so real that the creature of God, and among His creatures man especially in whom the purpose of creation is revealed, is not only confronted by it and becomes its victim, but makes himself its agent. And all the subsequent history of the relationship between God and His creature is marked by the fact that man is the sinner who has submitted and fallen a victim to chaos. The issue in this whole history is the repulse and final removal of the threat thus actualised. And God Himself is always the One who first takes this threat seriously, who faces and throws Himself against it, who strives with chaos, who persists in His attitude, who continues and completes the action which He has already undertaken as Creator in this respect, negating and rejecting it. As He affirms and elects and works His *opus proprium*, the work of His grace, God is always active in His *opus alienum* as well. And He is always holy. Therefore He always wills that His creature should be holy. He wills to take part in its conflict. Since it is really His own cause, He wills to place Himself alongside it in this conflict.

[III, 3, pp. 352-353]

8. THE IMAGE OF GOD AND THE TRINITY

What are we to make of the divine plural in v. 26 ? The question is important because it not only says " Let us make man," but then goes on to say expressly : " in our image, after our likeness," so that what we mean by this " image " depends on our decision concerning the subject envisaged by the saga. Expositors are unanimous that the use of this striking plural is connected with the peculiar significance of the creation of man now under discussion : *magnum se quiddam et singulare aggredi testatur. . . . Est homo eximium quoddam inter alias creaturas divinae sapientiae, iustitiae et bonitatis specimen* (Calvin). " This supreme creature could be created only by the common activity of the whole divine council " (Gunkel). " A special self-determination of God indicates the extraordinary event which is to follow " (G. von Rad, *TWzNT*, II, 388). Expositors are also unanimous that it cannot be interpreted merely as a formal expression of dignity. We are reminded of the so-called *Plur. maiestat.*, which is usually traced back to a Persian origin, but this is quite foreign to the linguistic usage of the Old Testament. We cannot escape the conclusion that the saga thought in terms of a genuine plurality in the divine essence, and that the priestly redaction within which it is presented in Gen. 1 did not see fit to expunge this element. " Behold, the man is become as one of us, to know good and evil," is a parallel in Gen. 3[22] (based on the J source). And again in Gen. 11[7] (in the story of the Tower of Babel) we find : " Go to, let us go down, and there confound their language." We may also refer to Is. 6[8] : " Whom shall I send, and who will go for us ? " And dramatic pictures of God's celestial entourage are given in such passages as Ps. 89[5, 7], 1 K. 22[19], Job 1[6], Dan. 4[14], 7[10] and particularly in relation to creation in Job 38[7]. But Gen. 1[26] does not speak of a mere entourage, of a divine court or council which later disappears behind the king who alone acts. Those addressed here are not merely consulted by the one who speaks but are summoned to an act (like the " going down " of Gen. 11[7]), i.e., an act of creation, the creation of man, in concert with the One who speaks. There is no reason why we should assume with F. Delitzsch and B. Jacob that they did not actually participate in the work in question but were merely present as interested spectators. The truth is rather that the saga wishes the creation of man to be understood in the true sense as a concerted act on the part of the speaker and those addressed by Him. Further, it is to be noted that in the " Let us make man " we have to do with a concert of mind and act and action in the divine being itself and not merely between God and non-divine beings. How could non-divine beings even assist in an advisory capacity in an act of creation, let alone have an active part in the creation of man, as we are expressly told ? And the image which in v. 26 is called " our " image is immediately afterwards (v. 27) expressly described as " His," God's image. The explanation of F. Delitzsch, that man was created "in the image of angels as well as God," has no support in the text, is alien to the purpose of the saga, and can hardly be regarded as biblical in view of Ps. 8[5] (" Thou hast made him a little lower than the angels "). If we take the passage as it stands, there are indeed serious difficulties against the view of F. Delitzsch and B. Jacob that we can at once refer the " we " with whom God associates Himself to a heavenly council or court of angels, spirits and Elohim in the improper sense. For if we wish to speak of a plurality of Elohim in this connexion, we cannot dispute the fact that in ascribing to them an active part in creation, and calling their image the image of God, we give to the term its most proper sense, and thus endow them with the attribute of true deity. The well-known decision of early exegesis was that we have in Gen. 1[26] a reference to the divine triunity. It may be objected that this statement is rather too explicit. The saga undoubtedly speaks of a genuine plurality in the divine being, but it does not actually say that it is a Trinity. On the other hand, it may be stated that an approximation to the Christian doctrine of the Trinity—the picture of a God who is the one and only God, yet who is not for that reason solitary, but includes in Himself the differentiation and relationship of I and Thou—is both nearer to the text and does it more justice than the alternative suggested by modern exegesis in its arrogant rejection of the exegesis of the Early Church (cf. for instance, Gunkel). If we think that what is here said about the Creator can finally and properly be understood only against the background of the Christian doctrine of the Trinity, we have at least the advantage of being able to accept everything that is said quite literally and without attenuation in this or that respect. We can take seriously not only plurality in the being of God, but also the " Let us " as a summons to a real divine act of creation, and the " our " image as the true image of God as in the equivalent in v. 27. Those who are not prepared to think of God's triunity must ask themselves whether they can really do the same.

If we agree that we must keep close to the wording and context of the passage if we are to understand the divine likeness of man as expressed in vv. 26–27, then—not without genuine astonishment at the diversity of man's inventive genius—we shall have to reject a good deal that has been said in supposed exposition, and decide for a path which is more direct.

We certainly come closer to the text, and decisively so at the most important point, if with W. Vischer (*Das Christuszeugnis des A.T.*, Vol. I, 1934, p. 59 f.) we take Gen. 1[26f.] to mean that in man God created the real counterpart to whom He could reveal Himself ; " that man is the eye of the whole body of creation which God will cause to see His glory ; that all creation aims at the confrontation of God and man and the inconvertible I-Thou relationship between Creator and creature, . . . which is the true and sole motive of the cosmic process." It cannot be contested that the wider literary context, of which the biblical creation history is the first part, is not interested in man *in abstracto*, in his soul or spirituality, in his body or even in the superiority which he certainly enjoys over all other creatures, but in the future partner of the covenant, the kingdom and the glory of God, in the true counterpart of God, in the earthly subject, addressed and treated by God as a " Thou," of a history which begins with the creation and continues right up to the end of time. In what other sense than this is man in the Bible an *eximium divinae iustitiae et bonitatis specimen* ? Can it be otherwise at this point ? Is there any justification for the extraordinary apparatus set in motion for the creation of man : " Let us make man in our image, after our likeness," if, in harmony with all that follows, the aim is not already this confrontation, this differentiation and relationship in a particular historical relation between God and man, if the point at issue is not the making possible of this relation ? If we are to get to the root of the primary interest of the passage, we shall have to think further along the lines already indicated by W. Vischer.

Dietrich Bonhoeffer (*Schöpfung und Fall*, 1933, p. 29 f.) offers us important help in this respect. He asks how God can see, recognise and discover Himself in His work. Obviously only if and to the extent that the thing created by Him resembles Him and is therefore free : not free in itself ; not possessing a freedom which (as in a vacuum) is its own quality, activity, disposition and nature ; but free for Him who as the Creator willed and always does will to be free for His creature. That God makes man free in this sense, and causes him to be free, is expressed in the fact that He created him as an earthly image of Himself. " Man is distinguished from other creatures by the fact that God Himself is in him, that he is the image of God in which the free Creator sees Himself reflected. . . . It is in the free creature that the Holy Spirit calls upon the Creator ; uncreated freedom is worshipped by created freedom." But this created freedom finds expression in the fact " that that which is created is related to something else created ; that man is free for man." It is expressed in a confrontation, conjunction and inter-relatedness of man as male and female which cannot be defined as an existing quality or intrinsic capacity, possibility or structure of his being, but which simply occur. In this relationship which is absolutely given and posited there is revealed freedom and therefore the divine likeness. As God is free for man, so man is free for man ; but only inasmuch as God is for him, so that the *analogia relationis* as the meaning of the divine likeness cannot be equated with an *analogia entis*.

Bonhoeffer comes closer to the text than Vischer, for obviously he not only takes seriously and exploits the concept, inseparable from the idea of a prototype and copy, of a counterpart realised in free differentiation and relationship, but also emphasises the content of v. 27, where (with the threefold application of *bara'*) it is stated in a way that cannot be overlooked: " And God created man in his image, in the image of God created he him ; male and female created he them." Is it not astonishing that again and again expositors have ignored the definitive explanation given by the text itself, and instead of reflecting on it pursued all kinds of arbitrarily invented interpretations of the *imago Dei* ?—the more so when we remember that there is a detailed repetition of the biblical explanation in Gen. 5[1] : " In the day that God created man, in the likeness of God made he him ; male and female created he them." Could anything be more obvious than to conclude from this clear indication that the image and likeness of the being created by God signifies existence in confrontation, i.e., in this confrontation, in the juxtaposition and conjunction of man and man which is that of male and female, and then to go on to ask against this background in what the original and prototype of the divine existence of the Creator consists ? " These two, male and female, are to Him ' man ' because they are one before Him. Both are created in this divine image, so that the enjoyment of the divine felicity— to the extent that a creature was made capable of receiving it—was communicated to man as a married couple, filled by God and in God with mutual divine love, from which we may understand and conclude the high dignity of marriage " (H. F. Kohlbrügge, *Schriftauslegungen*, Vol. I, p. 14). Is it that expositors were too tied to an anthropology which expected the description of a being in the divine likeness to take the form of a full description of the being of man, its structure, disposition, capacities, etc., and found it impossible to think that it could consist only in this differentiation and relationship ? But the text itself says that it consists in a differentiation and relationship between man and man, and they ought to have kept to this point. Or did they perhaps find it too paltry, too banal, too simple, or even morally suspect, that the divine likeness of man should consist merely in his existence as man and woman ? But when it is twice there in almost definitive form, why did they not let themselves be constrained to consider it instead of speculating at large, and especially to make sure that the differentiation and relationship between man and woman is really so unimportant or even disreputable as they were obviously inclined to accept ?

Why did they not allow such passages as Hos. 1²ᶠ·, 2²ᶠ· ¹⁶, 3¹ᶠ· ; Is. 54⁵ᶠ·, 62⁵ ; Jer. 3¹ᶠ· ⁶, 4³⁰, etc. ; Ezek. 16¹, 23¹ ; 2 Cor. 11² ; Eph. 5²³ᶠ· ; Rev. 12¹, 21² to put to them the question whether this differentiation and relationship, as distinct from whatever may be said about man's spirituality and corporeality, might not actually have the constitutive meaning for the being of biblical man here ascribed to it (and even more expressly in the second creation saga) ? There is indeed no good reason why we should continue to neglect this aspect of the matter, loitering at the distance where one explanation may indeed be more attractive but is also more arbitrary than another.

But if we proceed on the assumption that the saga really finds the being and therefore the divine image and likeness of man in the confrontation and conjunction of man and woman, and if it is against this background that we enquire concerning the original and prototype in the being of God, we are not driven to a pragmatical construction like exegetes who jump from the *dominium terrae* to the *imago Dei*. In this way we can also emphasise, with the text itself, a fact which has not been taken into account either by Vischer or by Bonhoeffer, i.e., the " Let us " as the distinctive form of the creative fiat in v. 26, and therefore the plurality in the divine being plainly attested in this passage, the differentiation and relationship, the loving co-existence and co-operation, the I and Thou, which first take place in God Himself. Is there no significance in the fact that this matter is expressed in this connexion ? It is not palpable that we have to do with a clear and simple correspondence, an *analogia relationis*, between this mark of the divine being, namely, that it includes an I and a Thou, and the being of man, male and female. The relationship between the summoning I in God's being and the summoned divine Thou is reflected both in the relationship of God to the man whom He has created, and also in the relationship between the I and the Thou, between male and female, in human existence itself. There can be no question of anything more than an analogy. The differentiation and relationship between the I and the Thou in the divine being, in the sphere of the *Elohim*, are not identical with the differentiation and relationship between male and female. That it takes this form in man, corresponding to the bisexuality of animals too, belongs to the creatureliness of man rather than the divine likeness. It also belongs to his creatureliness that the relationship between the I and the Thou in man takes place only in the form of the differentiation and relationship between two different individuals, whereas in the case of God they are included in the one individual. Analogy, even as the analogy of relation, does not entail likeness but the correspondence of the unlike. This correspondence of the unlike is what takes place in the fact that the being of man represents, in the form of the co-existence of the different individuals of male and female, a creaturely and therefore a dissimilar repetition of the fact that the one God is in Himself not only I but also I and Thou, i.e., I only in relation to Himself who is also Thou, and Thou only in relation to Himself who is also I. This is the God who as Creator is free for man, and the corresponding being is the man who as a creature is free for God. This God can see, recognise and discover Himself in man ; and for his part the man who corresponds to Him can know God and be the seeing eye at which all creation aims and which is " the true and sole motive of the cosmic process." This God can and will say to man " Thou," and the man who corresponds to Him can also be responsible before Him as an " I." But between this God and the man who thus corresponds to Him there exists—and we have to emphasise this point by way of supplement to Vischer and Bonhoeffer—a unique relationship in organic creation to the extent that among plants and the different animals of land, air and water, as is continually underlined, there are different groups and species, but that this is not the case among men, so that in relation to other organic creatures man is an *ens sui generis*, and the distinction of sexes found in man too is the only genuine distinction between man and man, in correspondence to the fact that the I-Thou relationship is the only genuine distinction in the one divine being. Hence it may be seen that the distinction has not only a special but a unique connexion with the divine likeness, and from this standpoint it may be appreciated that the dominion of man over the beasts already has its inner basis in his divine likeness, but that there is no compulsion pragmatically to deduce the one from the other. Supplemented and focused in this way, the thesis of Vischer and Bonhoeffer is surely the explanation of Gen. $1^{26f.}$ which comes closest to the actual text of the narrative.

The main point may be briefly recapitulated. In Gen. 2 (like Gen. 1), the account of the creation of man as male and female is the climax of the whole history of creation. In both cases it is solemnly emphasised and introduced by the mention of special reflection on the part of the Creator. In this case, the reference is as follows : " It is not good that the man should be alone ; I will make him an help meet for him." In this saying there is a radical rejection of the picture of man in isolation. And the point of the whole text is to say and tell—for it has the form of a story—who and what is the man who is created good by God—good as the partner of God in the history which is the meaning and purpose of creation. This man created good by God must have a partner like himself, and must therefore be a partner to a being like himself ; to a being in which he can recognise himself, and yet not himself but another, seeing it is not only like him but also different from him ; in other words, a " help meet." This helpmeet is woman. With her he is the man created good by God, the complete human creature. He would not be this alone. That he is not alone, but complete in this duality, he owes to the grace of his Creator. But the intention of this grace is as revealed in this completion. And according to the fine declaration of the text its intention is not merely that he should acquire this duality, woman, but, acquiring her from God, recognise and confess her by his own choice and decision as a helpmeet. God the Creator knows and ordains, but He leaves it to man to discover, that only woman and not animals can be this helpmeet. Thus the climax of the history of creation coincides with this first act of human freedom. Man sees all kinds of animals. He exercises his superiority over them by giving them names. But he does not find in them a being like himself, a helpmeet. He is thus alone with them (even in his superiority), and therefore not good, not yet complete as man. In the first instance, then, he exercises his human freedom, his humanity, negatively. He remains free for the being which the Creator will give him as a partner. He waits for woman, and can do so. He must not grasp after a false completion. But who and what is woman ? That man obviously waits for her does not mean that he knows her in advance. She is not his postulate, or ideal, let alone his creation. Like himself, she is the thought and work of God. " And (he) brought her unto the man." She is not merely there to be arbitrarily and accidentally discovered and accepted by man. As God creates both man and woman, He also creates their relationship, and brings them together. But this divinely created relationship—which is not just any kind of relationship, but the distinctive human relationship—has to be recognised and affirmed by man himself. This takes place when he cries triumphantly : " This is now bone of my bones, and flesh of my flesh." Here we have the second and positive step in the act of freedom, in the venture of free thought and speech, of man exercising his humanity in this freedom. At the heart of his humanity he is free in and for the fact that he may recognise and accept the woman whom he himself has not imagined and conjured up by his desire, but whom God has created and brought. With this choice he confirms who and what he is within creation, his own election, the particularity of his creation. He is man in this negative and positive relationship. Human being becomes the being in encounter in which alone it can be good. His last objective assertion concerning another being becomes his subjective confession (as a male) of this other being, this fellow-man, the woman who has her own equal but proper and independent honour and dignity in the fact that she can be his helpmeet, without whose participation in his life he could not be a man, and without whose honour and dignity it would be all up with his own. " Therefore shall a man leave his father and his mother, and shall cleave unto his wife " means that because woman is so utterly from man he must be utterly to her ; because she is so utterly for him he must be utterly for her ; because she can only follow him in order that he should not be alone he must also follow her not to be alone ; because he the first and stronger can only be one and strong in relationship to her he must accept and treat her, the second and weaker, as his first and stronger. It is in this inversion that the possibility of the human, the natural supremacy of the I over the Thou, is developed in reality. It is in this way that the genuinely human declares its possibility. It is in this form that there exists the possibility of man in isolation, but also of all androcracy and gynocracy. " And they were both naked, the man and his wife, and were not ashamed." The human is the male and female in its differentiation but also its connexion. Hence there is no humiliation or shame. The human cannot be a burden or reproach. It is not an occasion for unrest or embarrassment. It does not need to be concealed and hidden. There can be no shame in respect of the human. In the work of God—which is what the human is—there is nothing offensive and therefore no *pudendum*. The work of God is without spot, pure, holy and innocent. Hence man does not need to be ashamed of his humanity, the male of his masculinity or the female of her femininity. There is no need of justification. To be the creature of God is self-justification. Only sin, the fall from God, can shame the human, i.e., the masculine and the feminine, and thus make it an object of shame. And the awful genius of sin is nowhere more plainly revealed than in the fact that it shames man at this centre of his humanity, so that he is necessarily ashamed of his humanity, his masculinity and femininity, before God and men, and every attempt to escape this shame, every self-justification, or concretely every denial and suppression of sexuality can only confirm and increase the shame. It is to be noted carefully that this is the climax of this text, and therefore of the whole biblical history of creation.   [III, 1, pp. 191–192; 194–197; 291–292]

9. MAN AND WOMAN : " ONE FLESH "

To this we must first add an exegetical note. In both 1 Cor. 6[16] and Eph. 5[31] we have a quotation from Gen. 2[24] : " They two shall be one flesh " (εἰς σάρκα μίαν). In both cases, we are undoubtedly to think of physical sexual union, Eph. 5[31] referring to that which takes place in marriage and 1 Cor. 6[16] referring to union with a harlot. In the Corinthian text, indeed, Paul expressly uses the other phrase : " He which is joined to a harlot is one body " (ἐν σῶμα). And of course Eph. 5[28] also alludes to " being one body " in marriage : " So ought men to love their wives as their own bodies " (ὡς τὰ ἑαυτῶν σώματα), i.e., as those who have become one body with them. Yet both σάρξ and σῶμα denote more than the physical body. Therefore the expressions about the two being one flesh and body do not merely imply their physical union in itself and as such. While " flesh " and " body" incontestably include the physical, they go much further and denote the whole man as a psycho-physical being which is established, animated and sustained by the spirit. And if two human beings become one flesh or body, while this does also express their physical union, beyond this it denotes the union of their total being to total and indissoluble fellowship. Not something in the man and something in the woman, but the man himself and the woman herself become one. This means that anything in the nature of a physical sexual union in itself and for itself, as a purely bodily act apart from the other aspects of man's being, does not exist. But in the apparently partial nature of this event man and woman are totally engaged and also become totally what they formerly were not : one, μία σάρξ, ἐν σῶμα. Thus the continuation in Eph. 5[29f.] can run : " He that loveth his wife loveth himself. For no man ever yet hated his own flesh ; but nourisheth and cherisheth it, even as the Lord the church : for we are members of his body." Notice that as he loves his wife he does not love something in himself, but himself. Notice further the use of the Christian word ἀγαπᾶν (and not ἐρᾶν, which does not appear in the New Testament). And notice especially the analogy of the supreme mystery of the Christian faith under which this event, the love of husband and wife, is classified. All this is understandable if in the physical consummation of marriage it is a question of the whole man and the whole woman and of the total union of both. Then and only then can it be said of the man that as he loves his wife he loves himself, and his love can be described as an ἀγαπᾶν and compared with the love of Christ for His Church. All this would not be understandable if the text had regarded this consummation as a partial event in a particular and lower plane. The same view is implicit in 1 Cor. 6[16] where it is again a question of sexual union, not this time in marriage, but in fornication. Again the whole understanding of the situation and of the Pauline argument depends upon the realisation that a merely bodily or physical and therefore partial and transient relationship of man and woman, such as fornication essentially is, is here represented as utterly impossible. There were obviously in the Christian community of Corinth (undisciplined in other respects too) people who were of a different opinion, who wanted to regard physical sex relations as something morally neutral and sexual intercourse with harlots as something quite simple, on a par with the satisfaction of other bodily needs : " Meats for the belly, and the belly for meats " (v. 13). Paul sees the matter in a different light. In other connexions, indeed, he refuses to allow that eating and drinking are morally indifferent matters. And in any case he here disallows any false conclusion from his comparison. In the relation between man and woman more is at issue than the χοιλία. It is a question of the σῶμα. Thus for the Christian it is a question of the man himself in his psycho-physical totality. Not a part or a special function of his being, but the man himself and as a whole belongs to the Lord (v. 13), looking for his own resurrection because of that of Christ, and in the unity of his existence being one of His members (v. 15) and a temple of His Holy Spirit. He does not belong to himself ; he is bought with a price and thus in the totality of his existence He must praise God (vv. 19–20). This would not preclude intercourse with a harlot, if the σῶμα of which all this is said were one thing and sex and its needs something different ; if the Christian life described could be lived out in one sphere and sexual life, following its own law, in another. But this is not the case. Just as certainly as he that is joined to the Lord is one Spirit with Him, so he that is joined to a harlot becomes one body with her. The one excludes the other, because in the one as in the other it is a question of man himself, the whole man. For the Christian the fact that he is joined to the Lord in one Spirit excludes the possibility of his becoming one body with the harlot. Put in positive terms, just as he himself wholly and as a whole is in communion with the Lord, only he himself and as a whole can have intercourse with woman. Hence he can only flee fornication (v. 18), because in such contacts he cannot be wholly himself. To attempt them leads to mutual deception and lying. This is just what he who is one Spirit with the Lord cannot do. His sexual needs and their satisfaction (even within marriage, as the context shows us) cannot be sundered from the other aspects of his being and from the total responsibility of his relationship with woman. He cannot regard the sexual sphere either as being specially unclean or as being specially clean. In this sphere, too, he must and will be wholly himself, and allow the woman to be wholly herself. He will realise that he can enter into such a relationship with her only if each is concerned for the whole being of the other, so that for both of them it is not a question of something partial or furtive, as in whoredom, but, as the terms indicate, of something total : μία σάρξ, ἓν σῶμα.

We are to-day in the pleasant situation of being able to point to the fact that even from the standpoint of medical psychology thinkers are increasingly inclined to accept and emphasise this view of the matter. Only thirty or forty years ago, in the age of Sigmund Freud, it would have been otherwise. That was the time in which a strong movement in the literary genre of the novel began to take up a not unreasonable struggle against the usual repression, concealment and discrimination of the sexual problem which characterised the later years of the Victorian era of bourgeois respectability. The movement was headed by the sensational D. H. Lawrence, whose books not only left nothing to be desired but definitely went much too far in mentioning the unmentionable, and in emphasising and over-emphasising, to the exclusion of all else, what was not customarily emphasised. In the field of medical psychology, there corresponded to this literary tendency the discipline of so-called psycho-analysis which attempted the diagnosis and therapy of the sick soul through the discovery and removal of complexes repressed and effectually operating in the unconscious. Among these, as the research of the period saw it, the sexual libido played a decisive if not an exclusive role. Not only was it to be recognised as more powerful than had previously been supposed, but practically all the impulses and tendencies of the life of the soul were to be understood in terms of its manifestation. In certain forms of the teaching, at any rate, it seemed that the human element as such was to be brought under the denominator of the specifically sexual. We withhold all the comments and criticisms to which we are not entitled as those unable to co-operate in this sphere of enquiry. We simply take note that this phase in the interpretation of the matter now seems to have been left behind even in medical psychology, so that we should be tilting against windmills if we were to make our relevant theological affirmations in opposition to the received standpoint in the medical sphere. Indeed, it is worth consulting some of the things which have recently been said in this field, since they excellently illustrate the insight that we have been compelled to acknowledge from our own special angle—that of the divine command. The opposition to Victorianism in the widest sense had its season and its justification. But even in the medical sphere it has been clarified, in the development characterised especially by the names of Alfred Adler and C. G. Jung, into the general opinion that while the specifically sexual is to be estimated very differently from previous views, it must now be understood in relation to the psycho-physical existence of the whole man and not *vice versa*.

We shall make only a brief reference to *Sexualität und Persönlichkeit* by Oswald Schwarz. Its only historical interest, if I am not mistaken, is that it reveals the transitional stage through which clinical psychology passes from the era of Freud to the ideas which are current to-day. This is shown in the fact that the consequences of the progressive insights already noticeable in the introduction are not really drawn in his depiction of the stages of development through which normal sexuality passes. To a considerable extent, Schwarz concedes to sexuality its own specific laws which compel the author for example to describe onanism as an " obligatory," and fornication, characterised in 1 Cor. 6 as impossible, as an " indispensable " stage in this development, followed by " relationship " as the next higher, and finally—and in a direct line of evolution— marriage. But I must not fail to quote certain thoughts (from the introduction) in which this book seems to point beyond itself and to promise better things. The impulses on which everything in our life is based can work themselves out only according to a certain structure which is determined by the Spirit. Thus the sexual drive gains its characteristic power only in so far as it is assimilated by the whole personality and grows into indissoluble unity with love and with the spiritual element of moral purposes. In this union the force of sexuality as a mere biological urge becomes truly human. Bodily sexuality is no more and no less than the stamp set upon the apprehension and finding of the Thou and even of the I, from which the path leads into the world of the objective and the realm of spirit.

Thus T. Bovet is not expressing a peculiarly Christian view when he emphasises (p. 17 f.) that the human *eros* is distinguished from the animal by the fact that, although as a sexual tinge it characterises the whole life of man, it does not make sexual indulgence inevitable, but is free to bring the biological impulses as such into conjunction with the other aspects of life, i.e., to control them instead of being controlled by them. These impulses are capable in man of transposition and transformation. Their energy can be used up in creative artistic or other activities and can be lived out on the intellectual instead of the physical plane. Erotically those who know only the immediate biological urges and succumb to them in bitter earnest are poorly endowed. We might well call them " brutish." The truly erotic man is whole and free even in the sexual act ; he thus seeks and discovers in it the free and total person of the other. He attains *eo ipso* to an atmosphere common to both and to its continuance, to the most varied and enduring fellowship with the beloved, to the fullest possible inward penetration of their personalities to a common erotic world. This world is called marriage, which represents for man the only perfect form of *eros* and the sexual impulse. Against the same background and in the same direction the Roman Catholic doctor Ernst Michel (*Ehe : Eine Anthropologie der Geschlechtsgemeinschaft*, 1948, p. 88 f.) has given us a statement which is more penetrating and comprehensive, less theologically vulnerable, and surprisingly free in relation to the attitude and accepted doctrine of his Church. Recalling the New Testament passages, he tells us that " communion of the body " is not to be equated with sexual intercourse. No doubt the latter has central significance for the former, but only on condition that it is embedded in a communion—and this is the true communion of the body—which brings into play and seeks its satisfaction in the mutual self-disclosure and total embrace of the individual lives concerned. It is a question of an " almost scrupulous psycho-physical feeling for each other " for which sexual union must not only prepare the way, but which to some extent, and without causing any disturbance, can effectively operate in its place. It is a question of a love which includes sexual intercourse in freedom, but which does not expect every benefit from it, and which therefore need not constantly circle around this problem. If anything is all-embracing at this point, it is the sense of full partnership which must not be distorted either by the urge of the male for power and possession or by the maternal impulse of the female. If it is true that the " communion of the body," rightly understood in the sense of this partnership, culminates in sexual union, it is not true that sex in the narrower sense should rule in the choice of love and sexual intercourse, asserting itself in disruptive independence. In itself it is not a fundamental natural impulse which man has in common with animals and which has then to be morally controlled and directed. By nature it is a human sexuality, primarily and inwardly stamped and moulded by man's specific nature and by the mental and spiritual structure of human life, and only on this basis capable of being understood biologically. Where sex assumes the mastery, and thus gives rise to the question of its moral control, it is clear that itself and its desires are no longer in accordance with man's original nature ; that they no longer flow from the rational unity of love and physical communion ; that they are no longer aimed at this particular individual human being of the opposite sex, but at something in him of hetero-sexual value which he has to give. Such a fatal outburst of sexuality is not the product of a strong biological impulse but of a strong self-centredness and bondage to self which merely exploits that natural impulse, detaching it from the psycho-physical unity of natural love and using it in the service of self-preoccupation or a flight from the self. Used in this way, it is not bestial but demonic, i.e., human in a negative determination and in conflict with man's ineradicable relationship to the Thou, as a relapse into self-exaltation or an evasion of the self. Without self-giving to a Thou the sexual act becomes the magical practice of a demonised sex ; the attempt by a sort of conjuration, by fusion with the sexual polar opposite (masculine or feminine), to secure that which is to be had only in mutual individual and personal self-surrender. Not what is called fleshly lust, or animal impulses, but this attempt, this violation of the human, is what is really evil in this sphere, i.e., apostasy from the authentic human conception of sexuality. Deliverance from such non-human sexuality can be effected only by a reintegration from the heart's core by love and fellowship. It is not true, therefore, that every experience of sexual intercourse, whether rooted in genuine love or flowing from impulsive desire, is the same in character. On the contrary, experiences arising from self-absorbed, self-enslaved sexuality, even at maximum intensity, are only deceptive experiences of the moment, ending in sterility and depression, in open or hidden feelings of shame, and this not on ethical grounds but because of the metaphysical distortion of nature. Such experiences have no place in the " biography of the common life." They have the fascination only of a supposed but in reality refused and denied encounter sought only in purely sexual relations. Don Juan is not really a great eroticist, but a type of the man who is incapable of true love and sexually weak, restlessly seeking in woman after woman his sexual counterpart and inevitably hastening from one disappointment to the next. But we have to realise that all this is no less true, both positively and negatively, of bodily union in marriage. Even under the protection of this sacred institution, and on the assumption of individual moral restraint, the sexual act is not the real thing, nor is it natural and right, apart from this presupposition. And the reason for the frailty of modern marriage is not the lack of moral restraint, nor the disappearance of the binding power of the institution, but the surrender of this presupposition. To-day more than ever marriages are contracted from " love," and thus a greater demand is made on the enduring and creative power of love than was formerly the case. A fresh enquiry is thus demanded into the character of love and its foundation in faith. The natural affirmation of the sexual which characteristises our age is to be whole-heartedly accepted, but in itself it is not enough. It may also entail a naturalising or neutralising of the sexual ; indeed, this is the stage which we seem to have reached to-day. If we no longer have the bad conscience of former times in regard to the sexual, we do not have the new and good conscience which springs from the power of love and its development, and which leads on to the assimilation of the sexual into a properly integrated life. It is in this forward direction, and not backwards as attempted by moralists and pastors (Michel means by preaching the usual desperate solutions of resignation, adjustment, heroism or endurance from religious motives), that the solution of the present-day crisis is to be sought. There has still to be a sanctification of sexual life not only in Roman Catholic but also, in spite of the theoretical proclamation of the freedom of a Christian man, in Protestant ethics. Indeed, one hardly knows whether to be pleased or ashamed to see a theme which is so eminently Evangelical defended so stoutly by a Catholic layman.

As far as concerns the famous book of T. van der Velde—*Die vollkommene Ehe*, which went through more than fifty editions—it is to be noted that the relationship between its title and its contents can be very misleading. For the work deals only with the physiology and techniques of sexual intercourse, and while perfection in this sphere is desirable it does not constitute perfect marriage. Nor is this van de Velde's opinion. It must be realised the book represents only the first volume of a trilogy. Precisely in order to make plain the limits of sexual life in the narrower sense, some one had to be bold enough to give honest, sober and instructive information, with a due sense of its relativity, about what is usually discussed only vaguely and allusively. We must be grateful to van de Velde for daring to do this, even though we may suspect that in indiscreet hands his book may not accomplish the reasonable purpose intended. We can be sure that it would have helped many if they had come to this book in time as serious-minded readers.

We may conclude this short survey by referring to the contribution of Charlot Strasser, " Seelische Gleichgewichtsstörungen im geschlechtlichen Eheleben," in the symposium published in Zurich in 1948 under the title *Die lebendige Ehe* (p. 203 ff.). We cannot attempt a summary of what is in my opinion its essential substance, but can only indicate some of the characteristic ideas which again illustrate the apparent agreement or material parallelism between what we have presented on a theological basis with the findings of modern clinical psychology. Indeed, the ideas expressed in this essay are so sound that it would be a pity not to include them in our discussion. We do violence to nature, writes Strasser, if we measure the nature of man by that of the animal. Human nature has a physical but also a psychical structure. Hence it is erroneous to suppose that human nature is frustrated if in the time of physical sexual maturity it cannot be sexually active, but it must await a suitable opportunity for this activity. Nobody has yet been made ill or destroyed through sexual discipline. What is always natural and right in this matter is the exclusion of caprice, i.e., discipline. This is completed in the lasting and exclusive psycho-physical relationship between two partners in marriage, while everything which as free sexual activity deviates in any way from this principle (speaking strictly in basic principles and with no Pharisaic allusion to individual cases) is indiscipline. The co-operation of body and mind in love does not permit of the frivolity and the loose disposing of self found in undisciplined and capricious sexual activity. Therefore we must not try to justify this frivolity. " The humbug of the absolute necessity of sexual satisfaction in some way or other must be finally defeated " (213). There is a sexual need in adolescence when it is sexually mature but hindered from sexual activity by external causes. " How is this difficulty to be overcome ? By a policy of waiting. By training for right decisions about marriage. By stressing the educational necessity of developing further all the other bodily and mental capacities, which at puberty have by no means reached even their normal term of development, let alone their perfection. By trying to avoid placing sexuality in the centre of interest, and thus neglecting on its account the training of the other faculties " (p. 215). And then further, it is claimed that the source of error operative at this point consists in a failure to recognise the indissoluble co-operation of mind and body. " Sexuality is no affair of the inferior bodily impulses alone. Only the mistaken, specialised treat-ment of sexuality could make fashionable the expression ' sex appeal.' The only kind of sex appeal which is salutary is that which does not satisfy the needs of the body at the expense of those of the mind. Sexual impulses and love are indissolubly united ; love without mental control is impossible. But every love relationship which is entered into between two partners without the sense of mutual obligations, which is not inspired by the realisation of its exclusiveness and the consciousness of responsibility in common action, thus involving the self-evident permanence of the relationship, is to be repudiated as no less danger-ous to the individual mind than to the partnership. All men and woman who in entering into sex relations are not ready to bear all the consequences, who from the start fail to look upon their life together as a truly binding union whether legalised or free, who do not regard themselves as freely and permanently bound to each other by the mutual surrender of their whole psycho-physical ego, commit an injustice to each other and therefore to society. The sexual impulse is through and through spiritualised in man. Beyond the biological need there stands spiritual decision. Love means much more than bodily satiety in sexual intercourse. Love is something beyond an organically conditioned disturbance of our ego below the navel " (p. 216 f.). And the concluding words of this essay of Strasser, which discusses these false emphases with an understanding that is

both wise and human, generous and uncompromising, may be regarded as a
positive antidote to the errors : " Love means active goodness leading to surrender
and self-sacrifice, to religious sentiment in the truest sense ; it means being a
man among men ; it means being tested and experienced in the duplication of
the ego between two partners in love who are mutually related in a permanent
and exclusive union for the enjoyment of the higher values, the communication
of the power and security thus attained to the family and finally to human society
as a whole, and the promotion of the free development of each individual personality in voluntary fellowship with all " (p. 270 ff.).   As a theologian, one could
and would have to say these things very differently, and much else besides.   But
there is every reason to rejoice that a modern doctor can say what he has to say
in such parallelism to Christian truth, almost as though he had taken his bearings
from Eph. 5 and 1 Cor. 6, as may well be the case with Charlot Strasser by way
of Jeremias Gotthelf and Dostoievski.   [III, 4, pp. 134–139]

CHAPTER III

ADVENT

1. THE ELECTION OF ISRAEL

For a third illustration of the differentiating election of God, we turn to an investigation of the self-contained chapter, 1 K. 13—the story of the man of God from Judah, and the old prophet of Bethel, in the days of Jeroboam I. The passage appears to be drawn from another source than its context. This can hardly be the same, but it is perhaps similar to the Elisha-cycle at the beginning of 2 Kings. It certainly reflects thought and judgment about the connexion between the authentic man of God and the professional prophets, and the parallels to the Book of Amos are so remarkable and distinctive that it is not impossible that what we have here—not in form, but in substance—is a fragment of ancient tradition concerning the nature of the Israelite prophet and the relationship between the two Israelite kingdoms. And the content of the passage, from whatever period it may have originated, is so meaningful and so instructive for our particular question that it is well worth considering. The story is that of the highly dramatic and complex confrontation between a nameless man of God from Judah (the land of the city of David and Solomon's temple, and the worship established there in accordance with the divine will) and a prophet in Bethel, where Jeroboam, the first leader of the larger Israel, divided from the house of David, had just instituted a national pseudo-cult which he was about to inaugurate. The peculiar theme of the chapter is the manner in which the man of God and the prophet belong together, do not belong together, and eventually and finally do belong together; and how the same is true of Judah and Israel.

The first section (vv. 1–5) describes how the man of God from Judah, who like Amos (7^{14}) is not a member of the prophetic guild, visits the sanctuary at Bethel by the command of God (cf. Amos 7^{15}), in order to announce his prophecy of judgment against the cult. The Word of God is laid upon him in the form of an address to the altar erected by Jeroboam. A son of David's house, Josiah, will one day publicly and definitively profane and dishonour this altar by slaying its priests and then burning human bones upon it. It is inconceivable that there could be a harsher denial of the legality of the worship practised at Bethel, a harsher threat regarding its future, a harsher expression of the irreconcilability of what takes place there with the cult at Jerusalem, a harsher emphasis on the fact that cleansing and vengeance will come from Jerusalem because God is there and not here, and says Yes there and No here, a more complete exclusiveness in favour of David's kingdom as opposed to the separated North, than are expressed in this divine utterance. A directly imminent divine sign will confirm the truth of this word; the altar will be reft and the ashes lying upon it will be scattered. But King Jeroboam himself is standing at the altar addressed in this way, at the head of his unlawful priesthood, in the presence of the people of Israel, whom he has summoned to a festival planned by himself ($12^{32f.}$). He stretches forth his hand from the altar against the man of God : Seize him ! Then his hand stiffens so that he cannot draw it back, and instantly the sign announced actually takes place ; the altar cracks, and the ashes are scattered.

Up to this point, we could almost think that we are dealing with a rather more circumstantial variant of the encounter which took place at the same place between Amos and Amaziah, the priest of Jeroboam II (Am. 7[10]).

But in 1 K. 13 the encounter between the bearer of this divine utterance and the Cæsaro-papism of Northern Israel is only the material and presupposition for the real subject. In a second section we hear of a temporary softening of the contrast, although this does not actually alter the harshness with which it was previously revealed, except that now it seems to be momentarily veiled. Jeroboam, that is, shows that he is shocked by what has happened, and begs the man of God to intercede for his paralysed hand: " Entreat now the face of the Lord thy God, and pray for me, that my hand may be restored me again." This duly takes place, and the miraculous punishment of his hand is in fact cancelled. The result is a friendly invitation by the king to the man of God. He calls him to his house. He wants to offer him food and drink. He wants to send him away with a gift. Has he forgotten the threat against the altar, the radical questioning of the whole Bethel cult, and therefore of the legality of his whole monarchy and kingdom, by the word of the man of God, and the confirmatory sign of the rent altar ? Or can he think that this sign of the patience of God is accompanied by a cancellation of the threat of judgment that had been pronounced, that the crack in the altar will close itself again, and the even worse future never come to pass ? The invitation to share food and drink seems, as a matter of fact, to suggest this. What Jeroboam would like is reconciliation, tolerance, amicable compromise between himself and the divinely commissioned bearer of the word from Judah. For his own part he sees no reason why they could not shake hands, or why Jerusalem and Bethel could not settle down alongside one another. It is precisely that which the man of God refuses to concede by refusing the invitation. It is precisely that which God has forbidden him to do, and to which he could not agree even were Jeroboam to offer him the half of his royal possessions. He is commissioned to lodge that protest at Bethel, and is therefore debarred from accepting even a crust of bread in Bethel, or even the smallest gesture of fellowship between Bethel and Jerusalem. On the contrary, he is to return home by a different route from that by which he had come. He is evidently not to tarry anywhere in this realm except in passing, nor is he to set foot again on any portion of it, as though he had any other interest than to lodge this protest. Even his intercession for the king was clearly not a sign of this kind of fellowship, but was simply to show the king that what had happened to him was actually a miracle of punishment, just as the miracle itself was only to prevent him from seizing the man of God. The contrast was veiled by this mitigating incident. But the attitude which the man of God had still to adopt shows that it was not cancelled.

But the real subject of the passage does not emerge even at this turning-point in the episode. Jeroboam is no more than an introductory figure in the conflict which is to be depicted. The conflict itself emerges in the third section (vv. 11-19). A new figure is now introduced. This is an old prophet, dwelling in Bethel. Unlike the man of God from Judah, he is one of the professional prophets. The existence of these prophets is one of the self-evident presuppositions of the older history of Israel. It is vindicated but at the same time threatened by the existence of these men of God, authentically and directly called, to whom their name was later transferred. It is vindicated because on occasion they could become bearers and announcers of authentic divine oracles. It is threatened because this did not happen necessarily, nor was their function and calling as prophets constituted by the commissioning of such divine oracles. Often enough they might have nothing at all to say ; indeed, they might even be false prophets. One such prophet, about the rest of whose life we are not informed, now intervenes in the story of the man of God from Judah, the bearer and announcer of the divine oracle. He now takes the place of the king in relation to the stranger's word. He himself did not take part in the scene at the altar ; he was only informed about it by his sons. But we are now told that he inquires about the route which the other had taken to return to his homeland, that he saddles his ass and rides after him, that he finds him sitting under a terebinth and urges him to return and eat and drink with him under his own roof. This obviously means neither more nor less than that he has perceived the importance of the refusal given to Jeroboam in vv. 6–10, and that he is determined to reverse it at any price. He has grasped the fact that for the greater Israel everything depends upon ending this emphatic refusal by Judah in the name of God, and upon bringing about the fellowship between Jerusalem and Bethel, the toleration and compromise, which had been the goal of Jeroboam's invitation. He for his part cannot accept the refusal that has been given to the king. At any cost he must and will help him. The man of God from Judah must still eat and drink in Bethel. And in this way he must still demonstrate that the matter is no more ended by the crack in the altar, by the threat of judgment upon it and upon the whole northern kingdom, than it was ended by the king's paralysed hand. This is the reason for his hurried departure and his urgent invitation : " Come home with me and eat bread." And we are now told that the other answers him as he had previously answered the king : " I cannot." He cannot, because he is not permitted to do so : " For it was said to me by the word of the Lord, Thou shalt eat no bread nor drink water there, nor turn again to go by the way that thou camest." At first the prophet of Bethel is also faced by the same insurmountable argument as was Jeroboam. And he would fail in his purpose, like the latter, if it were not that he is a prophet. He may not have much personal experience of divine oracles, but all the same he is a specialist in such questions. Theoretically, at least, he is aware of the possibility of countering this argument with an argument of equal authority and power. His desire to avert the threatened danger to his king and people, and therefore to arrange this meal, prevails —and so he ventures the ambiguous statement : " I am a prophet also as thou art." The ambiguity of his existence as a professional prophet permits him to make this ambiguous statement. There then follows the lie (" he lied unto him ") : " An angel spake unto me by the word of the Lord, saying, Bring him back with thee into thine house, that he may eat bread and drink water." The first crisis in the story is thus reached. The whole issue now rests on a razor's edge. One Word of the Lord asseverated by its recipient is balanced against the other, a later against an earlier. The man of God from Judah has to decide whether what he has received has to be revised and corrected by what the prophet asserts that he has received. Was the threat against the altar, and therefore against the whole of greater Israel, and therefore the sole sovereignty of the God of David and his house, only a provisional truth and revelation ? When God heard his prayer for the king's paralysed hand, had He also had in mind the separation of the two realms which was really at issue? Were grace and judgment, after all, not so apportioned to the two that a friendly agreement between them must be excluded ? Was not the God of David, after all, more tolerant, in reality, than He had at first appeared or shown Himself to be ? Was it not, then, quite in order to give that sign of fellowship ? A " word of the Lord " from the mouth of the prophet of Bethel gave clear support to this view—and the man of God from Judah accepted it as such : " He went back with him, and did eat bread in his house, and drank water." Notice that no moral is drawn. Even the old prophet's lie appears in the text to be culpable only because it was integral to the rejection of Jeroboam, Bethel and the whole northern state that the prophet's intervention on their behalf was possible only by means of a lie. The decision of God had already been taken against this whole kingdom, and even with the best of human intentions it could be denied only in empty words. Nor does the prophet from Judah succumb to a defect in his own character, but to the curious fact that there really were prophets in this rejected kingdom as well. The possibility that a new divine oracle would meet him there was a very real one and could not be *a priori* excluded. It was not to a strange god, but—even under a restoration of the ancient bull-worship—to the God of Israel that sacrifice was made on that altar. In this obscurity between election and rejection the man of God from Judah wavers and falls.

But now the fourth section (vv. 20–26) brings a tremendous surprise, and then the second crisis of the story. For the truth suddenly emerges from the lie : " As they sat at the table, the word of the Lord came unto the prophet that brought him back." The possibility latent in his strange calling is realised. God can use him, too, in the delivery of His Word. He can do so regardless of the fact that of himself this prophet would rather say and represent something totally different. He can do so regardless of the fact that by his lie he had, as it were, slandered the possibility of his speaking the Word of God and forfeited from the very outset his role as a divinely commissioned messenger. On the contrary, it is now as if he is to be nailed down to his lie, to the empty claim with which he had previously spoken. The roles are reversed. He who had previously spoken the truth must now hear the Word of the Lord from the mouth of the liar. He must hear that he has disobeyed the command of the Lord, that in so doing he has incurred punishment, that the judgment of God prophesied by him against Jeroboam and his altar remains in force and is now directed against himself, that the next stroke of divine wrath will fall upon him, the previously faithful but now unfaithful messenger of God : " Thy carcase shall not come unto the sepulchre of thy fathers." The other, the liar, now speaks the truth. He now cries out against the man of God the commandment of the Lord which he had earlier tried to deny and disown. He himself, therefore, undoes the peace-making in whose interest he had thought he should do it. He denies expressly that the gesture of fellowship fraudulently secured by the meal has any significance. How can it have any significance when it has taken place contrary to the will of God ? The advocate of the compromise must himself tear it to pieces, and denounce the one whom he had just convinced of its necessity and legitimacy. And it is along the lines of his prophecy that the incident now develops. The man of God from Judah starts a second time on his homeward journey. A lion meets him and kills him, and " his carcase was cast in the way, ard the ass stood by it, the lion also stood by the carcase." A singular scene ! Why did the lion kill him but leave him unmauled beside the ass ? Then the old prophet learns that this strange sight has been seen by travellers, and he knows immediately whom and what it concerns : " It is the man of God, who was disobedient unto the word of the Lord ; therefore the Lord hath delivered him unto the lion, which hath torn him, and slain him, according to the word of the Lord, which he spake unto him." He who speaks in this way is the very one who led the dead man into his error, and who, by a wicked abuse of his calling, caused his disobedience ! But that again is of no importance for the record. In it he exists at this moment solely as the witness who knows and who must confirm that the affair with the lion was no accident. Because this man actually did resist the decision of God, he is actually implicated in this same decision—His decision against Jeroboam, against Bethel and its altar, against the whole of Northern Israel, being incidentally struck down like someone touching a high-voltage transmission cable. He is put to death because he made a peace which God did not will and had not made. The disavowal which this signified for the prophet of Bethel himself, for his king, and for the whole cause which he represented, did not require expression. There lay the corpse and there stood the lion which had killed the man. It had all turned out as the man of God had originally said, and as the prophet had been forced to confirm against him and against his own wish and intention. God did not intend peace between Jerusalem and Bethel. The man from Judah had gone against this will, and therefore against his own election and calling ; and so he could only die in the foreign land where he had done that which was not his commission and which was opposed to his commission. Nor is it without significance in the light of Gen. 49[9], or Am. 1[2] and 3[8], that it was a lion which had to execute the judgment upon him.

The story does not end here, however, but hastens towards a third crisis in the fifth section (vv. 27–32). The prophetic expert of Bethel who has now become an authentic prophet, the liar who has now spoken the Word of God against the true man of God, and therefore against himself and the cause which he represents, does not let the matter rest with this reversal of roles. He, too, sets out a second time, and hurries to the scene of the calamity. He finds everything as it had been described to him, and brings the body back with him to Bethel to mourn and bury the man of God. " He laid his carcase in his own grave ; and they mourned over him, saying, Alas, my brother." He then arranges that he himself should eventually be buried next to the dead man. " Bury me in the sepulchre wherein the man of God is buried : lay my bones beside his bones : for the saying which he cried by the word of the Lord against the altar in Bethel, and against all the houses of the high places which are in the cities of Samaria, shall surely come to pass." Evidently the roles are exchanged once more. Just as the sin and punishment of the man of God from Judah have in no way altered his mission, so they have not altered his value or his superiority over the prophet of Bethel. For it is not merely to honour him that the latter conveys him to his own grave, and buries him. It is in order in this way to create a refuge for himself. It is in order that he may actually be secure in his own grave when the threat which has only been reinforced by the sin and punishment of the dead man, and which the prophet of Bethel now solemnly expresses in his own name, is actually fulfilled.

The provisional epilogue (vv. 33–34) which again links the record to the story of Jeroboam tells us that this experience does not cause him to desist from " his evil way " : " This thing became sin unto the house of Jeroboam, even to cut it off, and to destroy it from off the face of the earth." But the real epilogue to the story is only found in 2 K. 23[15-20]. There we read how Josiah carries out the threat of the defamation of the Bethel altar and the other Samarian sanctuaries. He has a burial-ground opened up in order to find the human bones required for this act. In so doing he comes across the grave of the man of God of Jeroboam's time, and when his story is related to him he orders that the grave is to be left undisturbed : " So they let his bones alone, with the bones of the prophet that came out of Samaria."

When we consider the complex nature of this story we may well ask, but cannot decide, what the real problem is. Is it the contrast between the real man of God and the man of the prophetic guild, or is it that between the realms of Judah and Israel ?—for both problems are so interwoven in the story that we obviously have to consider both in order to understand it. Unmistakeably, the prophetic problem is in the foreground. But the problem of the two kingdoms is undeniably more than merely accessory to it. In view of the context of 1 K. 13, we are almost tempted to say the opposite, that the prophetic problem is raised only in order to illustrate the problem of the kingdoms, and therefore that it is only a background to that problem. And if we postpone a decision on this question, it is also difficult to decide which of the figures, representing the two sides, stands, as it were, in the centre as the victorious hero of the story : the man of Judah or the man of Bethel ; or behind them the royal sinner Jeroboam, or the prophesied royal reformer and avenger Josiah, who appeared later. For if neither of the two kings can be left out of the picture, each presupposing and completing the other, even more so the ways of the two prophets who occupy the foreground are so involved in their manifold intersections that they are unmistakeably meant to be taken together. If in spite of this we try to understand the whole, while keeping the intertwined threads apart, two double-pictures emerge at once ; one on the right hand and one on the left.

The double-picture on the right is that of the man of Judah, with the figure of Josiah at a distance behind him : authentic, divinely commissioned prophecy, as a representative of the authentic Davidic monarchy and kingdom ; or, conversely, the Davidic monarchy and kingdom as the abode and bearer of authentic divine prophecy.

We see the positive aspect in the first drastic approach of the man of God from Judah to the altar of Jeroboam, and in the confession with which he subsequently refuses the king's invitation, and which he later repeats and maintains in the presence of the prophet of Bethel. What we have here is obviously the divine commission, the divine legitimacy and authority, the divine grace, which elected David and Jerusalem, and called them to the execution of His will. And concretely (as the reverse side of the gracious will) it is the judgment of God, according to which He does not will the worship paid Him in Bethel, or the whole nation which is assembled with its king about that altar, even although this people is called (with particular emphasis) " Israel," even although its king did not reach his throne apart from God and the call of a prophet of God. For their apostasy from the house of David is simply a concealed or flagrant apostasy from Himself. His people have ceased here to be His people. The man of God from Judah is the herald of this divine displeasure. So, too, is the whole being of Judah in its contrast to that of Israel. And so, too, at a later date is the reformer and avenger, Josiah. It is for this reason that the hand of Jeroboam must stiffen in the moment when it is threateningly raised against the man of God. It is for this reason that the altar at Bethel cracks, as a sign of the even worse fate which one day will befall it. It is for this reason that there ultimately follows this worse fate itself. The progress of the cause which the man of God from Judah represents is irresistible. Like the cause of David before it, it is the cause of God Himself. The strict obedience with which the man of Judah at first follows his commission, and the intransigence with which he refuses any compromise, testify to this majestic irresistibility. So, too, does the fact that scarcely has the commission of God been betrayed by its legitimate bearer than it straightway finds a new representative in its opponent, the prophet of Bethel. So, too, does the fact that the lion of Judah immediately appears and strikes when the man of Judah ceases to will to be that which he still is, and shall be, and cannot possibly cease to be. One thing does not happen. He is killed but he is not devoured by the lion. His body is preserved, and also buried. Admittedly, it is buried in a foreign grave. But it is buried properly, securely and with honour. And even later, when judgment breaks on Bethel, the remains of this man of Judah are providentially spared—only his bones, but still his genuine remains. The consistency of the cause which he represented has stood the test, not only of his sin but also of his punishment, and even of his death and what followed. His remains are preserved. The grace of God towards Jerusalem, the faithfulness of the God of Israel, constant to itself, does not finally abandon even this representative of His cause who has proved unworthy. His bones at least are preserved from destruction. No genuine man of God, however serious his trespass, stands finally under any other sign. Neither Jerusalem, nor Judah—in spite of all their sins ! His remains are preserved. The stock of David, hewn down to the ground, is preserved. For the grace of God cannot weaken, the covenant of peace cannot fail. That grave in Bethel is the powerful sign of this grace and this covenant.

The negative aspect of this picture on the right naturally consists in the fact that the representative of the cause of God, who is its subject, does at a fateful moment prove unworthy, actually betraying the cause by his mistaken decision about the invitation of the prophet of Bethel. The secret of this mistaken decision is not lack of character, but an astonishing deafness to the Word of God which he has himself already loudly proclaimed and confessed. Is it really possible that he can hear the Word of God and himself obediently execute it, and fail to do that which he ought to be expressing by deeds as well as words, by intransigent opposition to the compromise ? Is it really possible that he can take the Word of God, which he himself has heard and uttered, and balance it against a contradictory, supposed word of God from the lips of another ? Is it really possible that this second word should tip the scales ? According to the story, it is not merely possible but true. The same man of God who executed his commission before the altar at Bethel, who made his good confession before the king and then before the prophet—this same man now denies and betrays the whole cause by what he does, as though nothing had happened. He ? Yes, he shows the abyss on whose edge, as is clear from this passage, every man of God and every genuine prophet walks. The Word of God may be denied and betrayed in this way by the very man who is called to bear it. And it is not only the genuine prophet who here becomes a traitor and denier, but in him and like him Jerusalem, the city of David and of God ; in him and like him the kingdom in whose midst stands the house which Solomon built for God, and within which the true God has not disdained to dwell. All Jerusalem and all Judah will do as this man of Judah has done. They will weigh the commission entrusted to them, and heard and clearly proclaimed by them, against the alleged commission of another. They will listen to supposed angelic voices from far and near. And their decision, too, will be false. They will become tolerant and then disobedient. They will eventually fall into every form of apostasy. They will become almost or altogether indistinguishable from the northern kingdom, at least in that which they desire and do. Has not all this begun already, under Rehoboam—yes, under Solomon himself, and even further back, in David's time ? And in spite of every attempt to check it, in spite of Josiah and his reformation, it will work itself out to the letter. True, Jerusalem and Judah will continue to be what they are. Their commission is not withdrawn, whether they execute it well or badly or not at all. It is not in any sense taken from them. But in the person of so many of their kings, and finally and decisively in the person of the last king, they will do that which displeases the Lord in monstrous contradiction of their commission, just as this man of God did in a first and hardly noticeable step. And the inevitable result is that the lion of Judah turns upon Judah itself, that the voice of judgment that roars from Zion shakes the house of God itself, and finally shatters it. The man of God himself must die for the truth of the Word which he has heard and executed. And Jerusalem itself, even the kingdom of David, must perish because of the power of the truth which its prophets—Isaiah, Micah and Jeremiah— have now to proclaim as judgment upon it. And all that remains in this kingdom is graves—honourable graves, graves of kings and graves of prophets, but graves. It is a city proud with memories such as Samaria never had, but it is still a ruined city which can never again be that which once it was. And the grave of the last descendant of David will not be the burial-ground of his forefathers, but a grave in a foreign land. That is the negative aspect of the picture to the right.

The double-picture on the left naturally displays quite different features. In this case the negative side must be studied first because it is dominant. Jeroboam first occupies the centre of the stage. He is the king who as such also wants to be a priest, the *summus episcopus*, and who obviously has the makings and stature of the author of a new political and religious creation. And we see him on the day proclaimed by him as a festival of the national cult which he has inaugurated, not lacking a genuine dæmonism as he bears the first censer before the altar. Here we have the State-Church and the Church-State in one person. Here the sin of Israel, rejected by God, is unmasked in all its nakedness —the image of the bull is not necessary and is not specifically mentioned in the text. In Jeroboam it is immediately apparent why God says No to this altar and this throne, to this religion and this politics. Jeroboam is *Saul redivivus*, and the people who adhere to him are by this very fact the people who have rejected God as their king—and therefore the house of David. But in the story it is the prophet of Bethel, and not the king, who is the real representative of this dark kingdom ; the prophetic profession in contrast to the prophetic confession of the man from Judah. It is naturally no accident that the roles are allotted exactly as in Amos : on the one hand the institution, the bare possibility ; and on the other the reality of prophecy rooted in the freedom of God. The legitimacy of the institution is not itself denied by this contrast. Prophets of this type were also found in Judah, and conversely there were real men of God in Israel. But confession is shown to be characteristic of the south, and profession of the north, and the light naturally falls upon the former, and the shadow upon the latter. The shadow which lies upon the professional *Nabi*-ism is that which it has in common with the national kingdom of the north. Like it—if we disregard the divine election which is also possible in this kingdom, but immediately signifies its judgment—it is in itself and as such a representative of the Israelite form of the Canaanite vitalism, the religion of blood and soil, which, according to the will of the God of Sinai and Jerusalem, is the very opposite of the life and worship demanded of His people Israel. It is thus no accident that this prophetic order has to the northern kingdom—and later, of course, to the corresponding kings of Judah as well—the affinity which is proper to it in the story. The prophet simply reiterates to the man of God the desire of his king that he should eat and drink in Bethel and thus offer a gesture of fellowship between Jerusalem and Bethel, between Judah and Israel. This kingdom, the Israel separated from David's house, does not wish to stand outside but inside the divine covenant. Jeroboam aims in a special way to be the king of the divinely elected nation Israel, and it is the one God of Israel who is to be worshipped in Bethel. This is also the aim of the *nabi* of our story. It was inevitable that this monarchy and this prophetic order should degenerate openly into undisguised Canaanitism, as happened in the case of King Ahab and the " priests of Baal " who stood at his side. But that was merely its degenerate form. Here we have its purer form, in which, as in our passage, it claims nothing except tolerance for this Israelite, Yahweh-believing variety of Canaanite vitalism, of a religiously determined nationalism. It is because this man is a prophet that he is more aware than the king of the need for a theological justification of the North-Israelite kingdom and cult which are challenged at the altar by the word of the man of God from Judah, and which would be rehabilitated by his eating and drinking at Bethel. Again, it is because he is a prophet that he knows a better method of reaching this objective than the simple man-to-man talk by which the king had sought it—the divine communication which is to be expected of him because of his profession, and which he is now actually able to introduce in virtue of the authority of his profession. Thus the professional prophet becomes that which was impossible for the king of Israel— the true and successful tempter and destroyer of the man of God. That is why he is the real and the worse representative of the kingdom of darkness in this story. That is why what Jeroboam does looks only grey compared with what this professional does. For worse than the fact that Israel is Israel, and as such hastens to meet the judgment which inevitably comes and has been clearly enough announced by Jerusalem, and worse even than the abomination of Jeroboam and all his successors, is the fact that Jerusalem and Judah are led into temptation by Samaria. At first it is only the desire for mutual forbearance and friendship, for such a loyal relationship as later existed between Ahab and Jehoshaphat, for example. But in and with this desire there is the wholly devilish temptation to accept the Israelite form of Canaanitism (" I am a prophet also as thou art ") as the Israelite way of life, as a possible and legitimate form— within the divine covenant—of the life of the one people of God. In agreement with his king, but more effectively, the *nabi* of Bethel takes up this cause and carries it through to victory. He dares to use a divine oracle of his own free invention, suggesting that fellowship between the two is not merely permissible but is commanded by God. And this divine oracle—for, after all, he is the legitimate representative of the legitimate agency dealing with divine oracles—smacks of truth although it is definitely a lie, so that the man of God yields to him (as Jerusalem and Judah were later to succumb to the temptation to tolerance, and eventually to end as Samaria ended). In view of this, there can be no doubt the professional is the real Satan of our story. The peculiar sinful element in the sins of Jeroboam and of the northern Israelites as a whole is not that they question the divine judgment and render themselves liable to it, but that in so doing they compromise the house of David, and his people, and the temple in Jerusalem and therefore the promise and hope of Israel. In this way they attack the very substance of all life in covenant with God. Formally, the attack seems harmless enough to begin with, but in fact it is fatal from the very outset. And according to 1 K. 13 the instrument of this attack is the prophet of Bethel, the very experienced and therefore all the more dangerous representative of the evil cause of Samaria. That is why the prophet is the main character on this negative side of the picture to the left.

But this, too, is a double-picture ; and as that on the right has a negative aspect, so this on the left has also a positive. For one thing, we must observe the patience of God, which is not lacking even in the severe word of judgment against the altar at Bethel. For this judgment has still a future reference so that time is given to Jeroboam and his people. This is still the case even in its subsequent repetition in the mouth of the prophet of Bethel, when it is accentuated by what has happened in the meantime. It is another question that according to the epilogue in vv. 33–34 it was not understood as a warning, and therefore the time afforded elapsed without being used. The time itself is still given. Jeroboam and his kingdom have time. In the first instance God judges only in the form of the word which the man of Judah has to utter against the altar, and in the form of the sign which befalls the altar. The Word of God can still be heard and obeyed. Here, too, there is a divine repentance like that which benefited the people of Nineveh according to the book of Jonah. Bethel, and later Samaria, also stand under this sign of God's patience. It is for this reason that while there are no good kings there, there are genuine men of God, like Elijah and Hosea, and also authentic witnesses to Yahweh in the prophetic guilds or communities as they appear in the time of Ahab and Jezebel, enduring persecution and martyrdom. It is also for this reason that the Old Testament history does not omit to record the events which transpired in this realm right up to the fatal year 722 B.C., as well as the events which took place in the realm of Zion, even ascribing to the figures of Elijah and Elisha a grandeur and a significance unparalleled by the royal and prophetic figures of the Davidic kingdom. It is as if God Himself willed to wait patiently from century to century. The healing of the king's paralysed hand is also relevant in this connexion. Certainly he had to be prevented from using violence against the man of God. But he can be forgiven for trying to do so if only he will hear what is so impressively said to him in the accompanying miracle of punishment. But what happens in the case of the prophet of Bethel is again far more important. For this old sinner, the real Satan of the story, is the very one who from being a theologian of the worst type later becomes the bearer of the real Word of God. After he has lied, he must and may give himself the lie. He can now see that the one whom he had sought to persuade, and had in fact persuaded with fatal consequences, was in the right. What did it matter if this was against himself ? He was in the right. And he can now act on behalf of the right which the other no longer represents. He, the mere professional, now takes over the office of the genuine man of God. He, the Israelite, now answers for the affairs of Judah and Jerusalem. He is a forerunner of Elijah and Hosea ; and, like them, he is now clearly opposed to his king and nation and country. For how can he utter the Word of God without having to stand in this opposition, without dissolving the affinity between *Nabi*-ism and national-monarchism, without putting to the flames that which formerly he worshipped ? But the very fact that this is possible and actual, even in the form of a contradiction which is all that it can have, is not just a sign but a concrete part of the reality of the grace of Israel's God, which has not destroyed him but now claims and uses him, which is not simply lost and forfeited by the whole realm of Bethel and Samaria, for all the tremendous sins of that realm and the menacing approach of the year 722 (and the day of Josiah). The God of David has neither forgotten nor abandoned the lost sheep of the house of Israel. There is no occasion for the men of Jerusalem to disdain Israel ; and for Israel itself there is no reason for despair. There is an election and calling of the ungodly also. Is there any other ? Was not the faith of Abraham faith in Him who justifies the ungodly ? Was not the elect king David himself, according to the story of his sin, a brand snatched from the burning ? Was there in Jerusalem or in Judah another or better consolation than that of the God who so freely and so wondrously receives a lost people to Himself ? It is the consolation of this God which now overflows and falls to the share of the wretched *nabi* of Bethel ; and in such abundance that perhaps in that hour there was no such confident, no such genuine prophet even in Jerusalem and Judah, as this old sinner of a professional, who now, because he must place the man of God and his own king and people, and above all his own self, under the judgment of God's Word, becomes the mouthpiece of that grace of David which cannot be shaken or annulled by any human folly or wickedness. If we have noted everything which is against him, we must also seriously recognise who and what is far more emphatically for him in this situation which God has so radically altered : for him, and therefore implicitly for Jeroboam and all his sinful kingdom hastening to its downfall ; for him, and therefore for Israel, in spite of its impenitence, in spite of its neglect of the time afforded, in spite of the judgment whose execution will not tarry nor delay for ever. One thing at least is made perfectly clear in the figure of this prophet : that the one true God of Israel, even if He is completely misunderstood and even if He is revered in a way which is quite false and illegitimate, has not ceased to be its God ; that His Law and also His promise continue to stand even in relation to Israel. He, God, is the substance of the covenant of grace between Himself and His people. Therefore this substance is indestructible, however much it may be attacked by seducers and seduced, by Israel and then by Judah itself. Finally and above all there belongs to this positive aspect of the picture on the left the conclusion. For if the necessary punishment of the human trespass in this story does not fall on Jeroboam, in whom the sin of Israel found its true representative and who sought to seduce the man of God from Judah, neither does it fall on the prophet as the theologian who justified Jeroboam's sin and successfully carried this seduction to its goal. But it falls on the one who in fact participates in the guilt of this sin only to the extent that—contrary to the will of God—he does not finally refuse the fellowship of food and drink requested by the sinners. It falls on the one who is here only the seduced. It is this alien figure, and he alone, who is struck by the lightning of divine wrath. The lion slays the man of God from Judah, while Jeroboam survives with his healed hand, and the prophet is at least able to meet his end in peace. He, the most guilty, goes free. He is even preserved beyond his death ; for together with the bones of the man of God from Judah, his bones are spared and preserved on the day of judgment. That is the strange light which falls on the picture to the left, the positive aspect which it obviously does not lack.

If we begin again with the picture on the right, whose chief character is the man of God from Judah, his mission to Israel already attests that the true Israel in the south has no right to an existence which is tranquil and settled in itself. It cannot possibly rejoice or boast in its election to the derogation of the false Israel in the north. Nor can it come to terms with it and accept it without at once addressing itself afresh to this Israel. There is, therefore, no possibility of self-sufficiently leaving this false Israel to its error and destruction. On the contrary, it is under obligation to Israel. It has the commission of the divine Word in respect of Israel. The desire for tolerance and fellowship, by which the man of God from Judah is ensnared in Bethel, is therefore misdirected from the very outset. The disruption did not mean that the north was released and expelled from the sphere of the Word of God, and therefore from the scope of His grace. The disruption was hardly completed before salvation began to appear more than ever in the place where grace had been repudiated—and from that place where it had been received as grace, from the Jews. And the right to existence of these Jews was their message, the Word of God given them for themselves—yet not for themselves alone, but for all Israel. It is only by going to the north with this Word that the man of the south can confirm and justify his own election. Thus the cause of Jeroboam and his prophet was vindicated even before it was expressed and executed in its folly. Long before and in a very different way God Himself had provided a common table for His whole people. Nothing could come, therefore, from that arbitrary table fellowship. Genuine fellowship between the true and the false Israel cannot and will not consist in the conclusion of any peace between them, but in the addressing of the Word of God by the former, as the messenger of God, to the latter. Speech and hearing are the mode of the real love which is to rule and conquer here. What is necessary and redemptive is that there should be an utterance and hearing of the Word of God. Certainly this involves disruption. The only thing that matters is that it must be said and heard. But it is also the grace of God in the disruption that His Word is present, that the utterance and the hearing of His Word are not ended but now have a new beginning. The true Israel must converse with the false Israel just because it is not a stranger to the latter's guilt, because everything that separates Israel as a whole from God has simply been made explicit in the northern people, sundered from the house of David and the temple in Jerusalem. It is not from a secure elevation, but from the depths of the same distress, sustained by the unmerited grace of God alone, that Judah addresses and necessarily must address Israel by the mouth of its prophets, and must speak to it the one Word, i.e., the Word of God, which is its own support. From this point of view, the fellowship sought in Bethel has existed long before in a very different way from that imagined. It is just because this other and better fellowship, which is based upon the Word of God and continues in their common guilt, is already present, that the existence of the false Israel now means the serious jeopardising of the true Israel. Everything now depends upon the realisation of this fellowship between the two and not another : not any other ; not one in which the Word of God is stifled and the common need denied. The Word of God must be spoken and heard. There must be no tacit agreement by which both sides quietly come to terms with one another. And the common need must remain exposed. Here, again, there must be no tacit agreement on the basis of which both sides try to reach a mutual understanding, rather than maintaining their relation of speaker and hearer. The false Israel creates for the true Israel the acute danger of an invitation to yield to this suppression and denial which not only allow the false Israel to continue to be what it is but cause the true Israel automatically to become false. The special right to existence of the true Israel consists solely in the fact that it is given and that it assumes the responsibility and initiative with respect to the false Israel. If it does not use them, it immediately surrenders fellowship with the other and with itself also. It has repulsed the grace which made it an elect and called people in preference to the other. Its only remaining option is the guilt which certainly binds it to the other, the sin of David which of itself has no power to unite all Israel—this power belongs to the Word of God alone—but which can only tear David apart. Persisting in their guilt and repelling the grace of God, both sides cannot and do not come together, but of necessity can only fall apart. Only the love commanded by God has unifying power. If this fails, then enmity alone remains. The existence of the false Israel means for the true Israel the danger that it can fall away from this love. And now our story shows that this is more than a danger, that the false Israel is, in fact, the tempter and destroyer of the true. It tells us how the man of God from Judah actually accepts the invitation, and thus becomes unworthy of the service ordained for him and the blessing bestowed upon him—so unworthy that he can only be put to death. He does the very thing which distinguishes the false Israel from the true. He, too, repels the grace of God. And because he does this, he has to reveal in his own person that which was not yet revealed to the false Israel—that where there is only guilt without grace, there is nothing left but death, and Israel returns to the nothingness from which it was created. And the guilt of the false Israel avenges itself upon the true Israel because the guilt is that of the true Israel as well. Only the grace of God holds it above the abyss of this common guilt. And the grace of God is the only hope of the false Israel. The true Israel ought to have lifted high this one hope which it has now surrendered. Much is required of him to whom much is given. Much was given to the man of Judah, infinitely more than to Jeroboam or the prophet of Bethel. Therefore nothing less than his life can now be required of him. He staked everything, and he must now forfeit everything. But this fact—the fact that the false Israel becomes the tempter and destroyer of the true—is still far from being the end of the story. On the contrary, the story now moves on to its sequel, that the very tempter and destroyer must now take up the flag which the other had let fall. The fact that the false Israel as such had not ceased to be the Israel of God is now revealed, to the terrible shame but also to the supreme consolation, of the true Israel. For the Word of God cannot be silenced, nor can the common need be denied, even though Israel as a whole now seems to have chosen the false possibility, the rejection of the grace of God. That which cannot be executed by the true Israel, to its shame and destruction, is now executed by the false, and against the true, but obviously on behalf of all Israel. The professional, the false prophet of Bethel, may and must now stand up against the true prophet, and in this way maintain their mutual cause and Judah's commission as well, in order that the destroyed fellowship, and the love commanded by God, may be re-established between the two sides, and that—in a very different way from what he had intended or desired —the sign of hope may be raised again for the false Israel. So the prophet of Bethel now stands alongside the man of God from Judah. He is his judge, but he is also and supremely his saviour. For if the lion must and does kill him, he is also saved by the fact that the Word of God is not actually silenced, nor the common guilt denied. It is not by his service but by the grace of God that that which makes a people of God out of all Israel, and therefore out of Judah, is actually maintained and revived even in the midst of Judah's treachery. This was and still is—in spite of the lion—the grace of David, the promise made to Judah and Jerusalem. This is the faithfulness of God to which Judah owes its distinction. To be sure, it does not live by its distinction, but by the ongoing work of God, the power of the divine preservation and vivification which it ought to serve in accordance with its distinction. But if it now proves unworthy of this distinction, if it has now to die and pass, the fact that the work of God does actually continue confirms and saves its life in the midst of death. If the saying of the prophet of Bethel : " I am a prophet also as thou art," was at first only a presumption and a lie, and if this saying, whose falsehood the man of Judah could not discern, echoed mockingly in his ears upon the fatal road which he now had to travel, yet the same word was filled with consolation and promise in view of the grace of God that triumphed in his weakness. I am a prophet also as thou art. That which upholds both thee and me is independent of thy standing or falling. It is not whether thou and I are prophets that saves us, but this—that God does not cease to give prophets to His people. And if the cry of mourning uttered in Bethel over the man from Judah : " Alas, my brother ! ", could only be a cry of mourning, yet it did express an objective truth. Even in the false Israel he did have one who called him brother. And this one was his brother. And in his word and activity—because it was the Word and work of God—his own lived on, and therefore he himself lived on. To be sure, this brother had nothing more than a grave to offer him. Both here and in the whole sphere of the Old Testament history of kings and prophets there can be no visible consummation of the restored fellowship other than this common grave. It is Israel's grave into which Judah itself is first laid, and then Israel. The historical conclusion brings a reversal in the actual sequence of events. But either way, it is in this grave that the reunion of the separated brothers is completed. And this grave as such, and the remains of each united within it, will outlast the judgment— the remains of Israel for the sake of those of Judah. An undestroyed element of both is to be the provisional evidence of the faithfulness of God towards His whole people Israel. It should be noted in this conclusion of the story that the superiority of the one side over the other is never abolished, and that there is no retraction of the qualification that the one is the false and the other the true Israel. The man of Judah has not ceased to be the elect, nor has the prophet of Bethel ceased to be the rejected. But in their union as elect and rejected they form together the whole Israel from which the grace of God is not turned away. For the rejected acts on behalf of the elect when he takes over the latter's mission. And the elect acts on behalf of the rejected when he suffers the latter's punish- ment. Similarly, at the end, the rejected acts for the elect by making his own grave a resting-place for the latter. While again the elect acts for the rejected in that the bones of the latter are kept and preserved for his sake, and together with his own bones. It is exactly the same with the distinction and mission of the true Israel. It is betrayed in this way by itself, and yet also honoured in this way by God. What better thing can overtake the true Israel than this humiliation and this exaltation ?

And now, as in a mirror, we see it all again in the very different picture to the left, whose chief character is the prophet of Bethel. From the very outset now we are in the sphere of rejection. Here dwells the Israel which has forfeited that name and its very right to existence, which is already, so to speak, cast out among the heathen and to be reckoned among them. The guilt of all Israel has erupted here, and as lepers expelled from the congregation must form a wretched community for themselves, so does this Samarian Israel exist, cut off from the throne of David and the temple of God, without right or claim—it has itself flung them away—to membership in the covenant of God, without a share in its promise : an object of horror and a source of danger for the real people of God, as it is an object of wrath and a source of offence to God Himself. What can a king of Israel in Samaria be other than a usurper, a miserable and blas- phemous imitation of the promised son of David ? And what can a prophet be in this realm but a mere functionary, a presumptuous liar and a false prophet ? All that can be seen from here, as we look towards Jerusalem, is that which is lost : the lost status of grace from which they have fallen ; the lost home to which they have become strangers. And all that can be expected from that point forward is the confirmation of the judgment under which they have fallen and to which they must now be subject. The beginning of the story corresponds to this. That which the king and people of Israel have to hear through the man of God from Judah is their own rejection *a limine* in and with the threat against the Bethel altar. And the rejection is underlined by the strict refusal of the requested table fellowship ; the most absolute intolerance. Yet even this event itself has its other side. We have already seen that precisely in this harsh form there is a resumption of contact between Jerusalem and sinful, separated Northern Israel, almost before the latter is aware of its separation. It is not indifference at all events, that encounters Israel from this quarter. At least in the form of judgment the grace of God is not removed from Israel the moment it sins. On the contrary, it has hardly left this kingdom before it returns. The guilt which lies upon it is the common guilt of all Israel. But the Word of God which Judah has and Israel does not have is addressed to all Israel, and is, therefore, to be directed by hearing Judah to unhearing Israel. This twofold solidarity is the secret of the beginning of the story, which does not possess for nothing the character of a revelation of the patience of God even in His wrath, which already at the very outset—even though it is a dark and unsatisfactory, tragic beginning —does not speak of an ending, but, on the contrary, of a genuine new beginning of God with this lost people. God chastises, certainly, but He does not destroy; He chastises with the severity of a rod, not of a sword. He chastises with fatherly severity, as was promised to David concerning his son in 2 Sam. 7^{14}. God is always God; the God who on His side does not abandon the covenant, not even in face of the covenant-breakers. He is always the God even of the lepers. It is even the case that at this moment He is favourably disposed to the pure only in order that they may be at His disposal for service to the lepers. The true nature of the sin of Israel—that it is not rejected unjustly, but with justice— is certainly disclosed at once by the fact that it does not respond to the mission of the man of Judah with repentance, but seeks to evade his summons by the sentimental trick of that invitation. It will not continue in the salutary distance at which it was placed to hear the Word of God from that distance, but it tries to bridge the distance as fast as possible, to conclude an arbitrary peace, when all the time God is really the enemy with whom it must wrestle like Jacob to be blessed anew by Him. Because it does not do this, it confirms that it is not the true but the false Israel. And because its effort at first succeeds, its sin is blood-red, and it does not merely thrust away the blessing itself which the strong hand of God obviously willed to hold out to it, but it becomes a successful tempter and destroyer both of Judah and its mission. The point now seems to have been reached when all Israel must sink into the abyss of its common guilt; an abyss into which the grace of Judah also falls, and with it every hope for the whole. But it is in this very situation that the miracle happens to Israel itself and its lying prophet. The evil and ungrateful man, addressed by the Word of God, becomes himself its bearer and messenger. This is not, of course, because he has any merit or worth. It is apart from and even against his own intention. It is simply because God is always God, because He has not cast away His people, His whole people Israel. Now, in the person of the lying prophet of Bethel, the sinful kingdom and people of Samaria, which so flagrantly discloses the guilt of all Israel, both may and must appear in the saving service of this God, whom His elect have denied. In the very moment when the wrath of God does actually break forth (as it did not before), when the lion of Judah slays and kills—this whole dark kingdom can let itself be represented by the elect of God in the bearing of the punishment of the sin which is indeed the common sin, but *in concreto* is primarily its own, the seducer's sin. It is he who now lies prone upon the road. It is he who must now be buried in a foreign grave. But they go free. And in the case of the prophet of Bethel his own ambiguous word is fulfilled : " I am a prophet also as thou art." He, the unworthy, can now represent the worthy in the proclamation of the Word of God. Is he no longer unworthy ? Obviously he still is. He is this primarily in relation to God. No worth is imparted to him by this commission. But God has put forth His own worth, and to this end He has used his voice, the voice of the unworthy. He is also unworthy in relation to the man of Judah, whom he well knows to be, in spite of his trespass, a true and righteous man of God in distinction from himself, and over whose death he cannot rejoice as one rejoices over the downfall of a godless man, but for whom he mourns—" Alas, my brother ! "—as David mourned the death of Saul and Jonathan, with the deepest sincerity. The fact that the word entrusted to him was fulfilled against this righteous one, and that he is no longer alive, does not mean any gain for himself now that, in all his unworthiness, he has become a messenger of the Word of God like the other. Nor does it mean a confirmation of his own mission. On the contrary, it means the loss of the most necessary guarantee of the office which has now fallen to him, the unworthy. For what is a prophet in Bethel to do, even though he bears on his lips the most authentic Word of God, apart from the man of God from Judah, who himself is the original and genuine bearer and proclaimer of the Word of God ? What is Israel, apart from Judah ? Samaria, apart from Jerusalem ? The election, the covenant and the promise are in the latter, not the former. What is the former if there is no latter ? What happens to the strangers in a city if the citizens are exterminated ? If in spite of his rejection the rejected is elected by the incomprehensible grace of God, to what is he to cling if the sight of the elect is taken from him because, in spite of his election, the elect stands as rejected in the judgment of God ? To what is he to cling if the herald of the patience and grace of God is snatched away because he has dishonoured the worth of God by his unworthiness ? There can be no question, then, of a victory for the prophet of Bethel, or of any kind of vindication either before God or man. On the contrary, he must make a refuge for himself in his own grave (Mt. 27[59, 60]), first laying the dead man of God from Judah in it, in order that he may later rest beside him—bones beside bones, remains beside remains. But here, too, in the appointed order : the remains of the rejected are to be laid alongside the remains of the elect, Israel alongside Judah, and not the reverse ; just as, when judgment falls, the remains of Israel are to be preserved and protected for the sake of the remains of Judah, and not the reverse.

We shall not develop again in detail the two questions of the reality and the unity of what is attested in this passage, but must be content with a very brief indication. The two questions are both raised, of course, and they are both, if anything, even more difficult to answer if we keep to the confines of Old Testament history. The grave stands only too eloquently at the end of the story of these prophets. And it is not an empty grave, but a grave " which indeed appears beautiful outward, but is within full of dead men's bones, and all uncleanness " (Mt. 23[27]). Certainly it is a grave of prophets, which as such could be built and garnished (Mt. 23[29]), and which obviously was built and garnished, so that much later it was recognised for what it was by Josiah and his people. Yet it is only a grave. And in it the elect and the rejected, the worthy and the unworthy, the confessional and the professional prophet, Judah and Israel, Jerusalem and Samaria, in all their unity, diversity and relatedness, lie finally together in that corruption and decay which is our last human possibility and expectation ; buried, and on the third day—forgotten, finished, because our time is over. It is surely remarkable that this story, perhaps the most expressive and at any rate the richest and most comprehensive prophetic story in the Old Testament, should end with this grave, and that the only positive thing which is finally unambiguous in both the double-pictures of the story is merely the preservation of their common grave in the judgment which does not spare even the gravedigger. This does not mean, of course, that they are any less dead and done with than any other buried people. Is it not as true of them as of all others that " all flesh is grass," and that " the grass fadeth " ? When our story lays both prophets eventually in the same grave, there can be no doubt that it is saying that this is true of them also. But it obviously means to say something in addition when it speaks of the preservation of the grave and therefore of the remains of the two prophets. According to Is. 40[8], this addition can only be : " But the word of our God endureth for ever." It may well be said that this is in fact the beginning and end, the sum and substance of 1 K. 13—that the Word of God endures through every human standing and falling, falling and standing on the left hand and on the right. But the story itself cannot tell what happens beyond this to the men who have to hear and proclaim this Word, to receive its grace and endure its judgment, on the right hand and on the left. Nor can it tell whether or how far they share in this permanence of the Word of God. The story as such, as an account of Old Testament prophets, cannot tell this within its own Old Testament sphere. Or it can do so only by speaking of the preservation of that grave and therefore of the enduring remains of the two prophets. The eternal duration of the Word of God, and the lengthened but still temporal duration of these remains, are obviously two very different things, just as the remains themselves lie side by side, but are two different things ; the remains of these two so utterly different prophets, and of the two so utterly different Israelite kingdoms they represented. But since they do not continue for ever, it is clear that the question of the eternal duration of the Word of God is raised and—left open. In the same way, the problem of the reality and unity of what is attested by the story is also raised and unresolved. But this story, too, does point to one real subject if Jesus Christ is also seen in it, if at the exact point where this story of the prophets breaks off a continuation is found in the Easter story. The Word of God, which abides for ever, in our flesh ; the man from Bethlehem in Judah who was also the prophet of Nazareth ; the Son of David who was also the king of the lost and lawless people of the north ; the Elect of God who is also the bearer of the divine rejection ; the One who was slain for the sins of others, which He took upon Himself, yet to whom there arose a witness, many witnesses, from the midst of sinners ; the One lifted up in whose death all was lost, but who in His death was the consolation and refuge of all the lost—this One truly died and was buried, yet He was not forgotten and finished on the third day, but was raised from the dead by the power of God. In this one prophet the two prophets obviously live. And so, too, do the two Israels—the Israels which in our story can finally only die, only be buried, only persist for a time in their bones. They live in the reality and unity in which they never lived in the Old Testament, but could only be attested. They remain in Him, and in Him the Word of God proclaimed by them remains to all eternity.

Where else do they remain ? What else is chapter 1 K. 13 if it is not prophecy ? Where else is its fulfilment to be found if not in Jesus Christ ? These are the questions which must be answered by those for whom the suggested result of our investigation may for any reason be unacceptable.   [II, 2, pp. 393–408]

2. THE WORD MADE FLESH

We shall elucidate these statements by a short exegesis of the passage Jn. 1$^{1-2}$: Ἐν ἀρχῇ ἦν ὁ λόγος, καὶ ὁ λόγος ἦν πρὸς τὸν θεόν, καὶ θεὸς ἦν ὁ λόγος. οὗτος ἦν ἐν ἀρχῇ πρὸς τὸν θεόν.

" *In the beginning* was the Word "—this is the emphasis according to the order of the sentence. The sentence does tell us, of course, what was in the beginning. But it does so in the form of a declaration about the Word. The Word was in the beginning. It did not arise later. It did not enter in as one moment with others in the totality of the world created by God and differentiated from Him. Again, it was not merely the first and original link in the development of this totality. It was not merely (as Philo said of his Logos): πρεσβύτατος τῶν γένεσιν εἰληφότων. And we certainly must not understand in this sense what Prov. 8^{22} says concerning wisdom : " The Lord possessed me in the beginning of his way, before his works of old ; " for the continuation in v. 23 tells us : " I was set up from everlasting, from the beginning, or ever the earth was." Again we cannot understand in this sense the statement in Col.

1¹⁵, πρωτότοκος τῆς κτίσεως, for it continues : ὅτι ἐν αὐτῷ ἐκτίσθη τὰ πάντα. The First-begotten is thus clearly removed from the series of created realities. What is said in these passages, and in the Johannine ἐν ἀρχῇ (or ἀπ' ἀρχῆς, 1 Jn. 1¹) is this. The Word as such is before and above all created realities. It stands completely outside the series of created things. It precedes all being and all time. It is like God Himself. As was rightly said concerning it in the exposi-tions of the 4th century : " There was no time when it was not." And this Word was in the beginning and at the beginning of all that which, being created by Him, is distinct from God. Within the sphere of this creation there is, then, no time which is not enclosed by the eternity of this Word, no space which does not have its origin in its omnipresence and which is not for this reason condi-tioned by it. There is, in fact, no possibility of escaping or avoiding this Word. But the question arises, where, except in or with God, can there be any being which is " in the beginning " in this sense.

The answer to this question is given in the second statement. " And the Word was *with God*." Here the emphasis falls beyond all doubt upon the two final words. This statement too, then, constitutes an assertion concerning the Word. It declares that there was, in fact, no being " in the beginning " in this sense except in and with God. But the Word itself was in and with God. Πρὸς θεόν does not mean " for God," as in the famous saying of Augustine : *Ad te me creasti* ; nor does it mean " in communication with God " (T. Zahn). These statements could both be made of a being which was not " in the beginning " in this sense. Strictly speaking, they could be made only of such a being. If the second assertion is to elucidate and not to contradict the first, then the πρός must be understood quite plainly and simply to mean this : That He could be " in the beginning " who was with God, who is beyond all created reality, because He belongs to God, because His being is as the being of God Himself. It was because the Word was " with God " in this sense that it could also be " in the beginning." But how could it be " with God " in this sense ? What do we mean when we say that it belongs to God, or that its being is as the being of God Himself ?

The answer to this question is given in the third statement ; and as in the first two, we must again find our subject in " the Word " : " And the Word was *God*." The sentence tells us, then, that the Word was itself God ; it partici-pated absolutely in the divine mode of being, in the divine being itself. The fact that there is no article before " God " does not mean that deity is not ascribed to the Word in the strictest and most proper sense. What is done is simply this. The mode of being, and being, of a second " He," the Logos, is identified with the mode of being and being of the first " He," God. Thus the deity of ὁ θεός is also ascribed to ὁ λόγος. In saying this, we are at once pre-supposing that in view of the definite article " the Word " ought to be character-ised as a " He " in exactly the same way as " the God." That this presupposition is correct is forcibly demonstrated by what follows. And if it is correct, then here, too, the exegesis of the 4th century must have been on the right track with its doctrine of the *homoousion*, or unity of substance of the three distinctive divine persons, prosopa or hypostases. The step taken in the third sentence is this—that the Word can be with God, and it can be " in the beginning," because as person (that of the Son) it participates in its own way with the person of " God " (the Father) in the same dignity and perfection of the one divine being. It must be conceded that read in this way, after the manner of so-called " orthodoxy," the verse is at any rate meaningful within itself, each word being intelligible in its own place.

But who or what is the Word whose predicates are declared in Jn. 1¹ ? As is well known, in the Johannine Prologue the concept recurs only once (v. 14), and in the rest of the Gospel it does not recur at all in this sense. In the presenta-tion as a whole its character is obviously that of a stop-gap. It is a preliminary indication of the place where later something or someone quite different will be disclosed. The same is true of the only other place in the whole of the New Testament where the concept is unequivocally used in the same sense as in Jn. 1[1]. In Rev. 19[13] it is said of the Rider on the white horse that one of the diadems on His head bears a name which no one knows (i.e., understands) but He Himself. And this name, which can be read but which only He can understand, this ideogram which only He can decipher, is as follows: ὁ λόγος τοῦ θεοῦ. Here, too, the concept is used as a stop-gap. It is a preliminary and veiling concept for that other and true concept which the Rider on the white horse has of Himself, which, as it were, consists and is expressed in His very existence. In Jn. 1[1] the reference is very clear: ὁ λόγος is unmistakably substituted for Jesus. His is the place which the predicates attributed to the Logos are meant at once to mark off, to clear and to reserve. It is He, Jesus, who is in the beginning with God. It is He who by nature is God. This is what is guaranteed in Jn. 1[1]. But why specifically by means of this concept? If we ask this as a question in historical genetics, we are faced by a whole host of possibilities, ranging from the Logos of Philo to the personal, semi-personal and impersonal essences of Mandaistic theory. Within this medley it will probably always be a waste of time to look for that unknown quantity, the source used by the writer of the Fourth Gospel; for we do not know in what form the author took over this widespread and variously used concept, nor do we know in what way he transformed this concept, nor finally can we be absolutely certain of the fact that he did take over the concept from some other source. What is certain is that he had no intention of honouring Jesus by investing Him with the title of Logos, but rather that he honoured the title itself by applying it a few lines later as a predicate of Jesus. He offered no other exegesis of the concept apart from that in which he made this predication. We can only say that by offering this exegesis he rejects all other possible interpretations of the concept in this context, interpretations which would define it primarily and essentially as the principle of an epistemology or of a metaphysical explanation of the universe. There is no doubt that in Jn. 1[3] (and 1[10]) a cosmogenic function is ascribed to the Logos. But there is also no doubt that the Evangelist did not adopt the concept for the sake of this interpretation of it. It is rather that in vv. 3 and 10 he recalls this interpretation in order to emphasise and elucidate what he has said in vv. 1 and 2. And he leaves it at once without construing anything more out of it. Having touched lightly on this aspect of the concept he moves forward quickly to his own conclusion: the Word was the bearer of life (v. 4), the life which was the light of men in their age-long battle with darkness (vv. 5, 9); the Word became flesh; the Word is the μονογενὴς θεός, which was in the bosom of the Father; and as such the Word has made known to us the unknown God (v. 18). Such is the Johannine Logos so far as we can define it at all apart from the recognition that the Logos is Jesus. It is the principle, the intrinsically divine basis of God's revelation, God's supernatural communication to man. And this was what the author of the Fourth Gospel found in Jesus. Jesus was the life which was light, the revelation of God, the saying, or address, or communication in which God declares Himself to us. But as this revelation He was not something other outside and alongside God. He was God Himself within the revelation. He was not revelation alone, then, but in the revelation He was the principle, the intrinsically divine basis of revelation. He was revelation in its complete and absolute form. It was to show this that the Evangelist—no matter where he derived the concept, or what else it conveyed to him—made use of the term Logos. We can be satisfied with the translation " Word." In German the word *Spruch* (saying) might be better, since it would proclaim the contents of v. 2 in the masculine as is done in the Greek. As is well known, Goethe's *Faust* found it difficult to rate the concept "word" so highly, and he thought that the term should be translated differently. " Suddenly I see the way and boldly write : In the beginning was the deed." But the moment he had boldly written it, the devil appeared ! " Word " or " saying " is the simple but genuine form in which person communicates with person. It is by the Word that God communicates with man. Because it is God's Word it is not called " a " word but " the " Word, the Word of all words. There is no need to import into this Word reason, signification, power, etc., for it contains all these within itself in virtue of the fact that it is Word, the divine self-communication proceeding from person to person and uniting God and man. It may be noticed that the Evangelist presupposes that the Word is there, that it has been given or spoken. This is not something which must be proved, or inferred from anything else. The force of the threefold $\mathring{\eta}\nu$ in Jn. 1^1 is more than axiomatic. It points to an eternal happening and to a temporal : to an eternal in the form of time, and to a temporal with the content of eternity. For this reason no stress is laid upon the threefold $\dot{o}$ $\lambda\dot{o}\gamma o\varsigma$, and there can be no point in attaching oneself to this or that signification of the concept as authenticated elsewhere. It is there as an ideogram, like the inscription on the diadem of the Rider of the Apocalypse. It is something which we can read but not comprehend. It is the x in an equation whose value we can know only when the equation has been solved. Of this solution Jn. 1^{19} is the beginning. But the Prologue states the equation, giving the unknown factor its place in relation to those which are known, God, the universe, man, the testimony (of John the Baptist) and the believer. The beginning of this presentation is Jn. 1^1: Where God is, that is, in the beginning, there is the Word. It must, therefore, belong to God, and by nature it must itself be God. If the Word of God is to be there in the beginning, then God Himself is required, no more and no less. But the Word is there, and therefore God Himself must be there with it. Thus far v. 1.

The Prologue continues : " The same was in the beginning with God." The supposition that these words are a recapitulation of v. 1 is quite unconvincing. For one thing, v. 1 does not stand in need of any such recapitulation. For another, there is no clear reason why it should be given in v. 2. And since the third assertion in v. 1 is itself the elucidation of the first two, we can hardly hold (with T. Zahn) that the repetition of the first two in v. 2 is meant, for its part, to be an elucidation of the third. We ought rather to follow A. Schlatter on this point : that the $o\mathring{v}\tau o\varsigma$ must be understood as a reference forward and not backward. The expression $o\mathring{v}\tau o\varsigma$ $\mathring{\eta}\nu$ occurs again in the Prologue, at the climax of the most important record of the witness of the Baptist (v. 15 f.) : " This was he of whom I said, He that cometh after me is preferred before me : for he was before me. And of his fulness have all we received, and grace for grace." The remaining contents of the Prologue all show clearly enough that the Evangelist has appropriated this attestation of the Baptist, and that he has identified himself with the testimony which he bore. This first becomes apparent in the significant anticipation in v. 2. The Evangelist himself (also a " John ") points to $o\mathring{v}\tau o\varsigma$ $\mathring{\eta}\nu$. And this reference in v. 2 shows us that v. 1 is meant as the marking off or reservation of a place, for it points us to that which fills the place indicated by the concept Logos. The statement tells us, then, that " the same," the One who no more needs to be made known as a person than the One described as $\dot{o}$ $\theta\epsilon\dot{o}\varsigma$, the One whom we all know because He has come forth to all of us, " the same " was in the beginning with God, and " the same " was Jesus. For this reason, when we think of the Word which was in the beginning with God and which belongs to God, we may count upon the fact that it has been spoken with a certitude which is far more than axiomatic. And for this reason, too, we have no need to project anything into eternity, for at this point eternity is time, i.e., the eternal name has become a temporal name, and the divine name a human. It is of this name that we speak. V. 2 is, then, a part of the third assertion of v. 1, but it is not a repetition of it. What v. 2 does tell us, with backward reference to v. 1, is that " the same," Jesus, is the Word which partakes of the divine essence. What it tells us is that "the same," Jesus, was in the beginning because as this same divine Word he belongs legitimately to God. Thus this witness of the Evangelist, this οὗτος ἦν, answers two of our questions at the same time : Who was in the beginning with God, sharing His divine nature ? and : Is it true that there was anyone in the beginning with God, sharing the divine essence ? The answer to both questions is that it was He, Jesus. The naming of this name (and for the moment it is only indicated) is at once a thesis and a proof in relation to that which was in the beginning with God. And as v. 2 is to be understood in this way, as a reference to the name and person of Jesus, we are forced to the following exposition of the third statement in v. 1, with its identification of two distinctive persons in respect of their divine essence : that side by side with the One described as ὁ θεός, and itself partaker of the same θεότης, there has entered in the Word (that Word which is "the same," οὗτος).

It is to Him, then, "the same," that the αὐτοῦ refers in vv. 3 and 10, where we are told that τὰ πάντα, the κόσμος, was made by Him, and that without Him was not anything made that was made. And here the unique statement of Jn. 1¹·² issues in a reflection which is quite familiar in the witness of the New Testament. Thus in Col. 1¹⁷ we read that the Son of God—the Son *in concreto* and not *in abstracto*, Jesus Christ, who is the Head of His body, the Church— this Son is "before all things," and "in Him all things consist." It was, in fact, "the good pleasure of the fulness of the Godhead" (and here the concept of election is quite clear) to take form, or to take up residence in Him (κατοικῆσαι . . . σωματικῶς, Col. 1¹⁹, 2⁹). For this reason we must understand the passages 2 Cor. 4⁴, Col. 1¹⁵ and Hebrews 1³ exclusively : He is the one "image of God," "the effulgence of his glory," "the image of his substance," and therefore "before all things" He is "the mystery of God . . . in whom are hid all the treasures of wisdom and knowledge," "the mystery which from the beginning of the world hath been hid in God, who created all things" (Eph. 3⁹). For this reason He Himself is categorical and exclusive : He is "the first-born of every creature" (Col. 1¹⁶), and in order "that in all things he might have the pre-eminence" He is affirmed to be such by the fact that "he is the beginning, the first-born from the dead" (1 Cor. 15²⁰, Col. 1¹⁸). For this reason He is the κεφαλή of all principality and power (Col. 2¹⁰), so that in the revelation and reconciliation which He has accomplished there can be only an ἀνακεφαλαιοῦσθαι of all things, "both which are in heavens, and which are on the earth" (Eph. 1¹⁰). For this reason He is "the fulness of him that filleth all in all" (Eph. 1²³), so that His temporal manifestation and work must necessarily be called "the fulness of time(s)" (Gal. 4⁴, Eph. 1¹⁰). It is, then, only by way of explanation of His being as the God who is conceived of in this primal, original and basic movement towards man that Heb. 1² (like Jn. 1³·¹⁰) says concerning Him that He whom God "appointed heir of all things" is the one "by whom also he made the worlds," and Heb. 1³ that He "upholds all things (φέρων) by the word of his power," and Col. 1¹⁶ that "by him were all things created, that are in heavens, and that are in earth, visible and invisible . . . all things were created by him and for him."

If that is true, then in the name and person of Jesus Christ we are called upon to recognise the Word of God, the decree of God and the election of God at the beginning of all things, at the beginning of our own being and thinking, at the basis of our faith in the ways and works of God. Or, to put it the other way, in this person we are called upon to recognise the beginning of the Word and decree and election of God, the conclusive and absolute authority in respect of the aim and origin of all things. And this authority we must acknowledge not merely as something which is like God, but as God Himself, since God Himself in all His ways and works willed wholly and utterly to bear this name, and actually does bear it : the Father of our Lord Jesus Christ, the Son of the Father, the Holy Spirit of the Father and the Son. There is given to man under heaven no ἕτερον ὄνομα . . . ἐν ᾧ δεῖ σωθῆναι ἡμᾶς (Ac. 4¹²), and if this is the case, it is decided even more comprehensively that " at the name of Jesus every knee should bow, of things in heaven, and things in earth, and things under the earth " (Phil. 2¹⁰). If this is so, then there is no higher place at which our thinking and speaking of the works of God can begin than this name. We are not thinking or speaking rightly of God Himself if we do not take as our starting-point the fact which should be both " first and last " : that from all eternity God elected to bear this name. Over against all that is really outside God, Jesus Christ is the eternal will of God, the eternal decree of God and the eternal beginning of God.   [II, 2, pp. 95–99]

3. THE DEITY OF CHRIST

First, the New Testament statement about Christ's deity can be taken individualistically as the apotheosis of a man, a great man, who as such, through the mystery of his personality and work, had such an effect on those around Him that there inevitably arose the impression and idea that He was a God. Such a man was Jesus of Nazareth, the author and preacher of a life-style unheard of in His own time and more or less in later times—a life-style of childlikeness, freedom, obedience, love and faithfulness even to death, so that He became the more or less willing or unwilling Founder of the Christian religion and the Christian Church. From the inspired and inspiring country Rabbi He was, and as whom His disciples originally respected Him, He rose in their eyes to the stature of an Elijah. From the political Messiah He originally was for them as well, He rose to the stature of the Son of David who as such could also be called the Son of God, of a heavenly being who attests His presence in visions even after death, who lives on in His " spirit," and is thus pre-existent, until, gaining in fervour in inverse ratio to its remoteness from the historical object, the claim transcends itself and equation between Jesus and God is no longer impossible. The idea now is that at some specific point, at His birth or baptism or transfiguration on the mount or resurrection from the dead, God appointed the man Jesus to this dignity and adopted Him as His Son. This could be a good symbol for what men themselves had done in the zeal of their Christ-enthusiasm. To the " eye of faith " a remarkable man who had once been known as such, and who strictly was always kept in view, was idealised upwards as God, as could happen and actually had happened to other heroes. This is Ebionite Christology, or Christology historically reconstructed along the lines of Ebionitism.

Secondly, the New Testament statement about Christ's deity could also be taken in just the opposite sense, collectively. In Him, the theory runs, we have the personification of a familiar idea or general truth, e.g., the truth of the communion of deity and humanity, or the truth of the creation of the world by God's word and wisdom, or the truth of redemption by the way of " Die and Become," or the truth of the juxtaposition of truth and goodness or forgiveness and claim. The fact that the manifestation of this idea was seen in Jesus of Nazareth was more or less accidental and indifferent, so indifferent that the concrete humanity of His earthly existence, or finally even its historical reality, could be queried. He was believed in as theophany or myth, as the embodiment of a general truth, as the familiar Son of Man of Daniel or the familiar pre-existent Logos or the familiar world-deliverer of whom all Hellenism thought it had some knowledge, or as an analogue of the divine hypostases taught by the Rabbis when they spoke of *Memra* (the Word), *Shechinah* (the glory) and

Metatron (the supreme archangel of God). As and to the degree that the symbol of this idea was seen and venerated in Jesus of.Nazareth, He was called Kyrios, Son of God, and finally, in full awareness of the implied dialectic, God Himself. The power of the Christ-enthusiasm which had both the ability and the need to make this equation was the power of the idea, the power of the concept of the condescending and self-manifesting God, which simply found in its connexion with Jesus of Nazareth its specific crystallisation, just as then and in other ages it has demonstrably found similar crystallisations. The general " eye of faith " had now also and specifically fallen on Him. But what was in view was the idea, not the Rabbi of Nazareth, who might be known or not known as such with no great gain or loss either way, whom there was at any rate a desire to know only for the sake of the idea. This is Docetic Christology, or Christology historically reconstructed along the lines of Docetism.

These two conceptions or explanations of the statement about the deity of Christ seem to be in greater self-contradiction than is actually the case. The former understands Jesus as the peak or a peak of history soaring into super-history. The latter understands Him as the sucker of super-history reaching down into history. According to the former He is the supreme manifestation of human life, while according to the latter He is the most perfect symbol of divine presence. Obviously it should not be very hard to relate these two conceptions to one another dialectically or to reconcile them with each other. Common to both is the notion that strictly speaking the New Testament statement about Christ's deity is a form of expression that is meant very loosely and is to be interpreted accordingly.

As early as the 2nd century the Church rejected both Ebionitism and Docetism and in so doing it also ruled out in advance the corresponding modern explanation. And the New Testament statement about Christ's deity can in fact be understood only on the assumption that it has nothing whatever to do either with the apotheosis of a man or with the personification of an idea of God or divine idea. It avoids these alternatives. But this takes place, of course, on a line in which the plane on which the Ebionite and Docetic lines intersect is itself cut by another plane, and therefore in a third dimension, perpendicular to it and to the two lines. If one thinks persistently on this plane with its two dimensions one can never escape the dialectic of history and super-history or super-history and history, the conception of a Christ-enthusiasm in which a heavenly essence arises out of a historical form or a historical form out of a heavenly essence. In this case one will persistently speak, not of the Christ of the New Testament, but of idealising and mythologising man, and of Jesus as the object of the thought of this man. But if so one is not speaking of God's revelation. The New Testament statement about Christ's deity makes sense only as witness to God's revelation. Any other exegesis is blatantly opposed to the opinion of the authors and in conflict with them. Ebionitism and Docetism are misunderstandings of a dialectic that is inevitably at work in the thought and utterance of the New Testament authors, for it is indisputable that men—because it has pleased God to assume humanity—are thinking and speaking here, and that the first plane with its two dimensions is the sphere in which they think and speak. (We shall return to the dialectic present in the New Testament itself in connexion with the doctrine of the incarnation of the Word.) Even on this plane, however, what they think and say has a different meaning from that it seems to have when seen from the standpoint of Ebionite and Docetic thinking. This other meaning is given by the fact that while the thought and utterance of the New Testament witnesses takes place on the first plane like all human thought, it is related to the second plane which falls upon it .perpendicularly and which is identical with

God's revelation. It is thus true that even in what the New Testament witnesses think and say one may plainly see and distinguish a kind of opposite movement. It is true that especially in the Synoptists we are presented on the whole with a christological thinking which finds *God* in Jesus and that especially in the Fourth Gospel we are presented on the whole with another christological thinking which finds God in *Jesus*. But the first does not mean that the Synoptists found God in a mere man, in the figure of a great man, in an impressive personality, in a hero. And the second does not mean that John found an idea, a general truth of an intellectual, moral or religious kind, personified specifically in Jesus. One will search the New Testament documents in vain for the fatal starting-point of Ebionite Christology, i.e., personality, or the fatal starting-point of Docetic Christology, i.e., idea. These can never be anything but an arbitrary construction behind the documents and in contradiction with them. The starting-point of Synoptic thought, which finds *God* in Jesus, is the fact, manifest to certain men, of the divine envoy as such. It is the unambiguous fact of the man who was among them teaching and healing, dying and rising again, as a reality which did not first have to be disclosed and interpreted and asserted, but which directly called to their lips the confession : Thou art the Christ, the Son of the living God (Mt. 16¹⁶), not as a synthetic but as an analytic statement. And the starting-point of Johannine thought, which finds God in *Jesus*, was the fact, manifest to certain men, of the divine mission, message and revelation which they found in Jesus, the enactment of " grace and truth," " resurrection and life," the actual event of their being fed with the bread of life (Jn. 6³⁵), their actual drinking of the living water (Jn. 4¹⁰). " We beheld—his glory." And this led again, though now in the reverse direction, as a synthetic and not as an analytic statement, to Peter's confession, which must be here : Κύριε, πρὸς τίνα ἀπελευσόμεθα; ῥήματα ζωῆς αἰωνίου ἔχεις· καὶ ἡμεῖς πεπιστεύκαμεν καὶ ἐγνώκαμεν ὅτι σὺ εἶ ὁ ἅγιος τοῦ θεοῦ (Jn. 6⁶⁸). In the light of these real starting-points of New Testament thought, and already with these starting-points, the common goal, the statement about Christ's deity, is easy to understand. It was not that a historical figure had first to be changed into a heavenly being or a heavenly being into a historical figure, and that either way knowledge had to be transformed into faith. The New Testament witnesses tell us how their unbelief, not their knowledge, was changed into faith, and the opposed movement of their thought then takes place within faith. This has in fact nothing whatever to do with the dialectic of Ebionitism and Docetism. For what is meant by the first step on a way at whose end a man is equated with God, and what is meant by the first step on another way at whose end God is a man ? Can this be the end of a way if it was not already its beginning ? Can the decisive assertion in the corresponding statements, or the corresponding statement which is to the same effect in both instances, be understood as a result of thought won in ascending or descending reflection or interpretation ? Can this assertion be anything but an explanation of the presupposition taken directly from the presupposition, a *petitio principii*, as a logician would unquestionably have to say here ? The material point in the New Testament texts is that *God* is found in Jesus because in fact Jesus Himself cannot be found as any other than God. And God is found in *Jesus* because in fact He is not found anywhere else but in Jesus, yet He is in fact found in Him. This factual element at the start of the two ways of New Testament thought is revelation, the point of reference which lies in another dimension and which distinguishes this thinking from that of the Ebionites and Docetics and their modern successors. Against the background of this factual material which is simply there in the New Testament texts one may certainly advance the following considerations too. When the Ebionite and Docetic Christologies presuppose that at the end of ascending or descending reflection—reflection on the man Jesus as such and reflection on deity in special relation to the man Jesus—we simply have a small or even a big exaggeration with whose help the statement about Christ's deity arises or is explained, they ascribe to the thought of the biblical witnesses an achievement which the latter themselves would have regarded as the blasphemy of which Jesus was accused, but falsely so, according to their records. If Jesus had called Himself, or the primitive Church had called Him the Son of God in the sense presupposed by these two conceptions, then He and His Church would have been rightly expelled from the Old Testament community. For what could the idealising of a man or the mythologising of an idea be but characteristically the very thing that the Old Testament understood by the setting up and worship of an idol, of an unworthy and empty rival of Yahweh ? Those who think, or hyperbolically allege that they think, that a man can really become God or that the real God could have a copy in a man have very little understanding of the word " God " in the Old Testament sense. If we can claim that the first generation of the witnesses of Jesus are in any degree true Israelites or Palestinian Jews ; if we can be confident that they understand the difference between God and man, not as a quantitative one that could be easily bridged, but as a qualitative one, then we can describe it as an *a priori* impossibility that they should have thought in the way they would have to have thought if they understood the statement about Christ's deity along the lines of those two conceptions. If they could make this statement at all as Palestinian Jews ; if they believed that they could not only reject the charge of blasphemy against Jesus as a frightful misunderstanding but also proclaim it as the end of the Old Testament, as the event in which Israel, by rejecting no more and no less than Yahweh Himself, finally renounced its own birthright, then on their lips the statement could not be the product of ascending or descending speculation but in its twofold movement it could be only the expression of an axiomatic presupposition, an explanatory statement about the absolute beginning of their thought which is posited in advance for their thought. The explanation of their statement that Jesus is Lord is to be sought only in the fact that for them He was the Lord, and was so in the same factual and self-evident and indisputable way as Yahweh was of old Israel's God. The utter embarrassment of a historical approach which on the one hand cannot conceal the fact that the statement " is already essentially present in the most ancient literary testimonies, the epistles of Paul," and yet on the other hand will not take this presupposition into account, may be seen in the words of Johannes Weiss : ' " The fusion of hitherto unrelated conceptual elements at this centre presupposes a power of attraction which we cannot overestimate. How strong the indirect or direct effect of the personality of Jesus must have been on the souls of His followers if they were ready to believe this of Him and to die for this belief ! " (RGG[1], Art. " Christologie," I). What is the meaning of " power of attraction, of indirect or direct effect," in this case, in relation to this effect ? One may well ask whether apart from all else, the early Church did not perhaps have more sense of historical reality and possibility when it left it to heretics to wander to and fro along the beaten tracks of apotheosis and hypostasis Christology and thought it more natural to seek the meaning of the New Testament statement about Christ's deity in the corresponding factual presupposition as this is presented to us in the New Testament itself.   [I, 1, pp. 402–406]

4. THE VIRGIN BIRTH

In the Creeds the assertion of the Virgin Birth is plainly enough characterised as a first statement about the One who was and is and will be the Son of God. It is not a statement about how He became this, a statement concerning the basis and condition of His divine Sonship. It is a description of the way in which the Son of God became man. The New Testament and the Early Church never understood the relationship between the Holy Spirit and the Virgin Mary in mythical fashion as a ἱερὸς γάμος. The Holy Spirit has never been regarded or described by any serious Christian theologian as the divine Father even of the man Jesus. In the exposition of this dogma—and thoroughly in the sense of its New Testament presuppositions—it has been frequently and energetically explained that it might have pleased God to let His Son become man in some quite different way than in the event of the miracle attested as the Virgin Birth. It did in fact please Him to let Him become man in this way, but this event is not the basis of the fact that the One who there became man was the Son of God. It is the sign which accompanies and indicates the mystery of the incarnation of the Son, marking it off as a mystery from all the beginnings of other human existences. It consists in a creative act of divine omnipotence, in which the will and work of man in the form of a human father is completely excluded from the basis and beginning of the human existence of the Son of God, being replaced by a divine act which is supremely unlike any human action which might arise in that connexion, and in that way characterised as an inconceivable act of grace. " Conceived by the Holy Ghost " does not, therefore, mean " begotten by the Holy Ghost." It means that God Himself—acting directly in His own and not in human fashion—stands at the beginning of his human existence and is its direct author. It is He who gives to man in the person of Mary the capacity which man does not have of himself, which she does not have and which no man could give her. It is He who sanctifies and ordains her the human mother of His Son. It is He who makes His Son hers, and in that way shares with humanity in her person nothing less than His own existence. He gives to her what she could not procure for herself and no other creature could procure for her. This is the miracle of the Virgin Birth as it indicates the mystery of the incarnation, the first attestation of the divine Sonship of the man Jesus of Nazareth, comparable with the miracle of the empty tomb at His exodus from temporal existence. The question is pertinent whether His divine Sonship and the mystery of His incarnation are known in any real seriousness and depth when these attestations of it are unrecognised or overlooked or denied or explained away. But in any case these attestations are based on His divine Sonship, not His divine Sonship on these attestations. They have a great deal to do with it noetically, but nothing at all ontically.

Among those who dispute the sign we must first discover the man concerning whom we can at the same time unhesitatingly admit that he shows a reliable acquaintance with the thing signified by this sign. Is it chance that in all of them recognition of the mystery of Christmas is menaced and weakened by being related to some form of natural theology ? Is it the case that denial of the Virgin birth involves the assertion of a point of contact ? Or does the assertion of this point of contact produce blindness to the miracle of the Virgin birth ? A fatal connexion does actually exist here. It is particularly instructive to re-read Schleiermacher's (*The Christian Faith*, Eng. tr., p. 404 ff.), disquisitions on this point. At first sight Schleiermacher appears to know exactly what is at issue in the Virgin birth. In his phraseology he calls it the " supernatural " element in the person of the Redeemer, and says regarding it : " The reproductive power of the species cannot be adequate to produce an individual through whom something is to be introduced, for the first time, into the species, which was never in it before. For that it is necessary to postulate, in addition to this reproductive power, a creative activity combined with human activity. . . . In this sense everyone who assumes in the Redeemer a natural sinlessness and a new creation through the union of the divine with the human, postulates a supernatural conception as well. . . . The general idea of a supernatural conception remains, therefore, essential and necessary, if the specific pre-eminence of the Redeemer is to remain undiminished. But the more precise definition of this supernatural conception as one in which there is no male activity has no connexion of any kind with the essential elements in the peculiar dignity of the Redeemer ; and hence in and by itself is no constituent part of Christian doctrine. . . . And everyone has to reach a decision about it by the proper application of those principles of criticism and interpretation which approve themselves to him." We simply comment : " The general concept of a supernatural genera- tion " is quite enough to denote what Schleiermacher means by the mystery of Christmas as he sees it, namely, the miraculous manifestation of a creative activity united to the activity of the human species to produce the peculiar being Jesus Christ. In other words, this thing signified needs no sign at all. What Schleier- macher calls " a new creation " is really the completion of the creation of the human species, a completion the necessity of which we may know *a priori*, and the achievement of which may therefore be postulated in the union of the divine with the human in Christ as " a supernatural generation." Of this we are not forced to say that it is new, and so it does not require a sign. In this connexion the view of P. Althaus (*Grundriss d. Dogm.* II, 1932, p. 98 f.) is also instructive. He attributes to the *natus ex virgine*, so to speak, a contingent significance, depending upon the decision as to the age and source-value of the Matthaean and Lukan passages. If a positive decision can be reached here, then it is true that " the God who could let His Son become Man and make the new man by natural generation, here takes a different road, in order also (!) to prove by it that in reality the new Man has been born and God has become Man." But for those who decide the historical question in the negative, who thus see in the passages in question an untenable postulate derived from docetic ways of thinking, Christ's birth must be a "creative miracle of God," consisting in the fact " that He suffers the Son to become Man in the context of human life, creating the Man who ' without father, without mother, without descent ' (Heb. 7³) breaks through the context of sinful humanity as the new Man of God, the First-born of the new creation." To this we must reply : If this " creative miracle " is actually attested otherwise than by the sign of the *natus ex virgine*, if this sign is therefore unimportant and may be abandoned to the mercy of historical judgment, then does not this " creative miracle " belong to the presupposition of Althaus' Christology ? I refer to what he himself calls the " prime revelation " which, though it is admittedly insufficient and points beyond itself, he regards as present to all men in every age in and through their own reality in the world. According to Althaus, it is in virtue of this " prime revelation " that Christology is at once the recognition and the conquest of the offence (*op. cit.* p. 10, 13 f., 83 f.) ? Where the sign can be dispensed with, any conquest of the offence seems to be superfluous and recollection as such leads to the goal. Possibly (if it is so in the historian's view) God did take this road to attest the " creative miracle," but we are still aware of this " miracle " even if it is not the case. Does not then this " miracle "—and this makes everything plain—mean something else, something different from what we have described as the mystery of the *vere Deus vere homo* ? In this connexion we may reply briefly to the question of popular theology, whether in order to believe in a really Christian way " one " would have to believe fully in the Virgin birth. We must answer that there is certainly nothing to prevent anyone, without affirming the doctrine of the Virgin birth, from recognising the mystery of the person of Jesus Christ or from believing in a perfectly Christian way. It is within God's counsel and will to make this possible, just as it cannot be at all impossible for Him to bring anyone to the knowledge of Himself even beyond the sphere of the Church visible to us. But this does not imply that the Church is at liberty to convert the doctrine of the Virgin birth into an option for specially strong or for specially weak souls. The Church knew well what it was doing when it posted this doctrine on guard, as it were, at the door of the mystery of Christmas. It can never be in favour of anyone thinking he can hurry past this guard. It will remind him that he is walking along a private road at his own cost and risk. It will warn him against doing so. It will proclaim as a church ordinance that to affirm the doctrine of the Virgin birth is a part of real Christian faith. It will at least require of its servants, even if there are some who personally cannot understand this ordinance, that they treat their private road as a private road and do not make it an object of their proclamation, that if they personally cannot affirm it and so (unfortunately) withhold it from their congregations, they must at least pay the dogma the respect of keeping silence about it.

At this point we must recall the extraordinary section in E. Brunner's book, *The Mediator*, in which he deals with our theme. Beyond everything that has been said since Schleiermacher, Brunner develops the queer objection that the doctrine of the Virgin birth means a " biological interpretation of the miracle " (meaning the miracle of the incarnation), and is in fact an expression of " biological inquisitiveness." The divine miracle, he contends, is supposed to be explained here in its How, whereas we should be content in faith with the That. The Virgin birth is an event in space and time, a fact of observation, of the reality of which we may be aware without having faith in it. For that reason we ought to declare our indifference toward it. In reply to this we must first of all make an exegetical statement (cf. recently and particularly M. Dibelius) : neither in the New Testament nor in the creed is the doctrine of the Virgin birth a " biological " explanation. There is not a single word in which it takes anything to do with the biological happening as such—even on the analogy of the Easter story. It is content to indicate the fact prospectively and retrospectively. This fact is, of course, of such a kind as to belong to the area of biological enquiry. But on this point it must first of all be said that what happens here in the field of biology is in itself, as Irenaeus (see above) has already said, only the *signum*, or sign, of that inexpressible reality of revelation which lies on the borderland of every field of human study, the *vere Deus vere homo*. If we cannot separate the sign from the thing signified, as, with so many others, even Brunner unfortunately wishes to do, the sign is still not the thing signified. It is certainly true that up to the date of canonical and credal formulation assuredly no one who acknowledged the Virgin birth as its sign even remotely thought of anything like legitimate or illegitimate inquisitiveness in this connexion. The sign itself was always left as free of explanation as possible. More important still is the fact that the sign did not in the least explain the thing signified. Rather it brought to light essentially and purposefully its very inexplicability, its character of mystery. That Brunner should object to the sign undeniably taking place in the sphere of biological enquiry is very strange. How and where could there be signs if not in this field and in other fields of human enquiry, in the " sphere of space and time occurrence " ? Might not Brunner's annoyance at it also be voiced against the appearances of the risen Jesus, against the empty tomb and against all Jesus' miracles ? Of course one could and can be " aware apart from faith " of a sign of revelation. In relation to the Easter miracle this awareness without faith will take the form of a hypothesis of vision or deception or apparent death, and in relation to the Christmas miracle it will take the form of one of those arbitrary Jewish legends, through which awareness of the fact was thought to be actually possible without faith. It may even be thought that a naive cosmological supernaturalism made it possible in earlier times (although certainly not to the universal extent usually assumed) to talk oneself into an awareness of facts of this kind which does not require faith. The awareness which either explains the miracle away or is a mere awareness of *portenta stupenda* must be described from the standpoint of faith as an erroneous or false awareness. As signs of revelation, in their descriptive function and so in their only real nature, these miracles cannot be known in either of these ways. What does the possibility of this " awareness without faith " avail against the reality and gravity of its object ? Brunner's denial of the Virgin birth is a bad business. As is also the case with Althaus, it throws an ambiguous light over the whole of his Christology. The sigh of N. Berdyaev is mine too : " I read Brunner's book with tremendous interest, because I felt in him tenseness and acuity of thought, religious sensibility. But when I reached the passage in which Brunner confesses that he does not believe in Jesus Christ's birth of the Virgin, or at least confronts it with indifference, my mood became sad and the matter grew tedious. For it seemed to me as though everything had now been cancelled, as though everything else was now pointless " (*Orient u. Occident, Heft* 1, 1929, p. 19). Brunner's contribution to this matter in his more recent book, *Man in Revolt*, is so bad that my only possible attitude to it is silence.

[IV, 1, p. 207; I, 2, pp. 180–181; 183–184]

5. THE HUMILITY OF GOD

The hymn on the humiliated and therefore the exalted Jesus Christ quoted by Paul in Phil. 2⁶ᶠ· is obviously set in the context of an exhortation to concord, in which the final lesson is that in lowliness of mind (τῇ ταπεινοφροσύνῃ) the readers should each esteem other better than themselves, not looking every man on his own things, but every man also on things of others. They are to have the mind (τοῦτο φρονεῖτε) in them (ἐν ὑμῖν) which was also in Christ Jesus (ἐν Χριστῷ Ἰησοῦ), who having the form of God. . . . As we have seen, the law of ταπεινοφροσύνη applies in the first instance to Christ Jesus. He entered under this law, and because He went His way under it He was exalted to be the Lord. They are to model themselves on His bowing beneath this law. In this way they are to live with one another and to be at peace. We have to do with the one binding law for both the Head and the members, for Jesus and His people, and because for Jesus therefore also for His people. Why is it this law ? Why is it in ταπεινοφροσύνη that Christians are to unite themselves with Christ ?

The same thought occurs elsewhere in Paul. With a remarkable similarity to this passage in Phil. 2 he says in 2 Cor. 11⁷ : " I abase myself that ye might be exalted." According to 2 Cor. 10¹ he had been κατὰ πρόσωπον base among the Corinthians. According to 2 Cor. 7⁶ His God is the God " that comforteth them that are cast down." In Phil. 4¹² Paul boasts that he knows how to abase and how to abound. The exhortation in Rom. 12¹⁶ is to the same purport : " Mind not ὑψηλά but condescend to that which is lowly." Hence the summons in Gal. 6² to bear one another's burdens and so fulfil the law of Christ. Hence ὑποταγή as the basic concept in the Christian attitude to the civil powers (Rom. 13¹ᶠ·), but also in the attitude of wives to their husbands (Col. 3¹⁸), and also according to Eph. 5²⁰ in the attitude of all Christians one toward another. Hence the ὑπακοή of children to their parents (Col. 3²⁰) and servants to their masters (Col. 3²²). Hence the τιμή, the respect in which, according to Rom. 12¹⁰, all Christians are to prefer one another, and which, according to 1 Pet. 2¹⁷, they all owe one another. Hence the description of ταπεινοφροσύνη in 1 Pet. 5⁵ as the " girdle " with which all Christians are to be girdled in their relationship one to another, setting themselves in the appropriate place. And to the same category there obviously belongs 1 Cor. 1²⁶ᶠ·, the well-known passage on the external aspect of the Christian community : " For ye see your calling, brethren, how that not many wise men after the flesh, not many mighty, not many noble are called ; but God hath chosen the foolish things of the world to confound the wise ; and God hath chosen the weak things of the world to confound the things which are mighty ; and base things of the world, and things which are despised, hath God chosen, yea, and things which are not, to bring to nought things that are : that no flesh should glory in his presence." Why is this necessarily the case ? Why is there this radical downward trend ? Why do the authors of the First Epistle to Peter (5[5]) and the Epistle of James (4[6]) love that saying from the Proverbs (3[34]) : " God resisteth the proud, but giveth grace to the humble " ? Why can Paul (necessarily) write in 1 Cor. 15[31] : " I die daily," and in 2 Cor. 12[9f.] : " Most gladly therefore will I rather glory in my weakness, that the power of Christ may rest upon me," and : " I take pleasure ($\epsilon\dot{v}\delta o\kappa\hat{\omega}$) in infirmities, in reproaches, in necessities ($\dot{\epsilon}v\ \dot{a}v\dot{a}\gamma\kappa a\iota s$), in persecutions, in distresses for Christ's sake : for when I am weak, then am I strong " ? And what is the Word of the Lord addressed to him and heard by him : " My grace is sufficient for thee : for my strength is made perfect ($\tau\epsilon\lambda\epsilon\hat{\iota}\tau a\iota$) in weakness " ? We see that it is a matter of fellowship with Christ, with His life and finally with His suffering : " Always bearing about in the body the dying (in Gal. 6[17] the marks, $\sigma\tau\dot{\iota}\gamma\mu a\tau a$) of the Lord Jesus . . . always in our mortal flesh delivered unto death for Jesus' sake " (2 Cor. 4[10f.]). The necessity to follow in His steps rests on a looking to Christ and His way as an example ($\dot{v}\pi o\gamma\rho a\mu\mu\dot{o}s$), just as in the First Epistle of Peter (2[21] and *passim*) we are in the same context compellingly summoned to patience in suffering. Even in 1 Cor. 1[26f.] it is a matter of the connexion of the communion of the lowly with the crucified Jesus. But what is the authority and force of the law that necessarily leads into this community with Christ ?

At this point we are taken beyond the indications which point in this direction in the New Testament Epistles to the (if possible) even more radical and comprehensive sayings of the Gospels. The kind of thing that we already find in Lk. 1[51] in the Song of Mary even before the birth of Christ : " He hath put down the mighty from their seats, and exalted them of low degree." Why does it say this ? Or the saying that we must humble ourselves like a child placed in the midst of adults if we are to be the greatest in the kingdom of heaven (Mt. 18[4]). Or the saying in Lk. 14[11] : " For whosoever exalteth himself shall be abased, and (the second part is remarkably like Phil. 2) he that humbleth himself shall be exalted." Or the similar inversion in Mk. 10[31] : " But many that are first shall be last and the last first." Or even more sharply in Mk. 8[35], the saying about trying to save one's life and losing it, and saving it in losing it for the sake of Jesus and the Gospel. Or in Mk. 8[34] the saying about the necessity to deny one's self and take up one's cross. Or at the beginning of the Sermon on the Mount (Mt. 5[3f.]) the blessing of the poor in spirit—taken simply as praise of the poor in Luke's Gospel and the Epistle of James—of those that mourn, of the meek, of those that hunger and thirst after righteousness, of the merciful, of those who are persecuted and reviled and slandered for righteousness' sake. Or (in Mt. 5[39f.]) the command not to resist evil, to allow oneself to be smitten on both cheeks, to give one's coat and one's cloak also, and above all, in Mt. 5[43f.], the injunction to love one's enemies and to pray for one's persecutors. Why is it that here too—and especially here—this is the tenor of New Testament exhortation ?

The very strange and yet in some way remarkably illuminating content and the unconditional form of these demands have often been rather idly admired and valued as exemplary, while their manifest impracticability has been indolently affirmed and deplored. As against that, men like Francis of Assissi and Tolstoy and others have called us to take it all quite literally and to put it into practice, and that was obviously the original idea of monasticism in a Church which was being rapidly secularised. Again, it was this which so dreadfully affected the nerves of Nietzsche as the perverse philosophy of the small man triumphing at the time of the decadence of antiquity. Our simple question is : What underlies this conception of human life ? What is it that gives to New Testament ethics this direction, this tendency, this dynamic, this pull which in experience has again and again been found to be dominant and exclusive and irresistible, setting aside all pretexts and excuses, the pull from the heights to the depths, from riches to poverty, from victory to defeat, from triumph to suffering, from life to death ? This pull is obviously connected with the way and example of Jesus Christ. It is nothing other than the call accepted by the New Testament witnesses, the compulsion which they felt, to enter into and to remain in fellowship with the Crucified. This is clearly enough emphasised in many passages in the New Testament. Col. 1²⁴ is a culminating statement with a genuine Pauline flavour. Here the apostle describes his sufferings as a filling up in the place of Christ, an ἀνταναπληροῦν τὰ ὑστερήματα, " of the afflictions of Christ for his body's sake, which is the church." To understand this properly, we must disperse any remaining appearance of chance or arbitrariness with which the whole phenomenon might be enshrouded.

As we have seen, in its ethics the New Testament is speaking in terms of necessity, not of chance or arbitrariness, if in all these sayings—as in those concerning the lowly existence of the man Jesus as the Son of God—we have to do with a reflection of the New Testament concept of God. If in fellowship with Christ Christians have to be μιμηταὶ θεοῦ (Eph. 5¹), if the τελειότης, the fulfilment of the being and essence, of their heavenly Father is the measure and norm of their own τελειότης (Mt. 5⁴⁸), then in its original and final authority and compulsion the demand addressed to them is necessarily this and no other. The περισσόν, the special thing which is commanded of and has to be done by them as distinct from the publicans and Gentiles, is that which marks them out as the children of the Father in heaven, the περισσόν of God Himself which cannot be lacking in His children. God does not love only those who love Him, or greet only His brethren : " He maketh his sun to rise on the evil and on the good, and sendeth rain on the just and on the unjust " (Mt. 5⁴⁵). He obviously does not have to be exalted ; He can also be lowly. He does not have to be alone or among friends ; He can also be abroad among enemies. He does not have to judge only ; He can also forgive. And in being lowly He is exalted. Among His enemies as their God He is supremely exalted. In forgiving He judges in righteousness. As this God, in this divine nature, as the " Father of mercies " (2 Cor. 1³), as the " God that comforteth those that are cast down " (2 Cor. 7⁶), He is the Father of Jesus Christ, the One who in Him reconciles the world to Himself. And as this God He is the Law-giver and Himself the law for those who know Him in Jesus Christ, who can rejoice in their own atonement made in Jesus Christ : those who can recognise themselves as the children of God in Jesus Christ (exalted in Him and by Him). From this point their way leads into the depths, and ταπεινοφροσύνη is not to them something strange or remarkable, an ideal which is quite impracticable in its strict sense. It is necessarily that which is natural to them. From this point they cannot choose whether they will exalt or abase themselves, whether they will save their life or lose it and in that way save it, whether they will leave or take up their cross, whether they will be offended by the beatitudes or put themselves under the light of them, whether they will hate their enemies or love them, whether they will accept or not accept the exhortation to ὑποταγή, to ὑπακοή, to τιμή, to the bearing of the burdens of others, to suffering in the discipleship of Christ. This could and would be a matter of choice, and the choice would not be in accordance with the directions of the New Testament, if the God in whose name and authority it is demanded were like the scribes and Pharisees of whom it is said in Mt. 23⁴ : " For they bind heavy burdens grievous to be borne, and lay them on men's shoulders ; but they themselves will not move them with one of their fingers," or if He were like the doctors who take good care not to take the medicine they prescribe for others, if He had no part in the ταπεινοφροσύνη He demands of others, if He were the wholly other God, absolute, high and exalted, far removed from any lowliness and quite alien to it. To achieve the obedience demanded in the New Testament no less than everything depends upon the fact that He is not this God. If He were, then that strange basic feature in New Testament ethics might be regarded as accidental and arbitrary, as facultative and non-obligatory. There would then be good reason to turn this ethics into a moral system, with high praise for its idealism or impatience at its unworldliness and unpractical nature, or perhaps in the form of doubtful experiments, filling it out from the goodly store of practical wisdom and so reducing it *ad absurdum*. According to the New Testament this obviously cannot happen because God does not stand in the far distance high above this ethics, but it is His divine nature to exist in the sense of this ethics, this ethics being only the reflection of His own being. It does not call man under a yoke that He must bear in the name of God because God wills it. It calls him into the freedom of the children of God, into a following of the freedom and the work in which God Himself is God.

Although it has seldom been appealed to in this way, New Testament ethics is an indirect and additional attestation of the true Godhead of Christ. True Godhead in the New Testament is being in the absolute freedom of love, and therefore the being of the Most High who is high and almighty and eternal and righteous and glorious not also but precisely in His lowliness. The direct New Testament attestation of this Godhead of Christ is the attestation of the man Jesus Himself as the Son of God become flesh and suffering and crucified and dying for us, the message of Christ crucified (1 Cor. 1²³, 2²). It is clear that in the sense of the New Testament this and this alone is decisive and basic. There is no lowliness which is divine in itself and as such. There is therefore no general principle of the cross in which we have to do with God (in principle). The cross in the New Testament is not a kind of symbol of an outlook which is negatively orientated, which speculates *à la baisse*. The limits of humanity are one thing, but God's visitation of us in the limits of humanity, in our creatureliness, in our humanness, in our sinfulness and mortality, in the incarnation of His Word and the crucifixion of His Son, that is quite another. Salvation is not in those limits, but in the concrete event of this visitation, in what took place in the man Jesus. And the Godhead revealed and active in this event is His Godhead. But the Godhead which the New Testament attests directly as His alone it attests indirectly in the form of the commandment under which it sees His people placed with Him, which it applies to the men of this people. The existential factor in the Christian claim which calls men from the heights to the depths, and therefore to suffering and dying with Christ, is not the first thing in the New Testament but the second, not the *a priori* of the *kerygma* but the *a posteriori*. The content of the New Testament *kerygma* is in substance the way of Jesus Christ and only in accident the way of the believer in Him. The second stands or falls with the first. First of all Jesus Christ is the Son of God and as such, in conformity with the divine nature, the Most High who humbles Himself and in that way is exalted and very high. Only then are Christians " in Christ," delivered by God " from the power of darkness, and translated into the kingdom of the Son of his love " (Col. 1¹³). It is only because He is the Son of God in this sense that they are called and empowered in fellowship with Him to choose the ταπεινοφροσύνη which is natural to the children of God. Always this second and existential aspect follows and confirms the first. That it should follow and confirm it is necessary, just as it is necessary that there should be this fellowship of man with the God who is in being and essence this God, just as it is necessary that this fellowship should be a fellowship with Christ in whom He has made His being and essence open and accessible to men, just as it is necessary that this fellowship grounded in Him should be lived out by men and put into effect in their existence. The true deity of Christ is to be known and understood and believed and confessed in both the first and the second, the direct and the indirect form, but in this irreversible order and sequence. It is the deity of the true God revealed in the humility of Christ which as such can and must find its confirmation in our own humiliation. But the confirmation is of something which so far as I know Gregory of Nyssa (*Or. Cat.* 24) was the only one of the Church fathers expressly to mention : that the descent to humility which took place in the incarnation of the Word is not only not excluded by the divine nature but signifies its greatest glory : περιουσία τίς ἐστιν τῆς δυνάμεως. [IV, 1, pp. 188–192]

6. THE CALLING OF THE WITNESSES OF REVELATION

According to the simplest meaning of the terms, a prophet is one who has to declare something and an apostle one who has to deliver a message. According to this simplest and most general meaning of both terms, which meet in that of witness, all those who are called in the Bible are thus both prophets and apostles. There is disparity in respect of what the prophets of the Old Testament have to attest as compared with the apostles of the New, and *vice versa*. On the one side it is a matter of the acts of God in the history of Israel as it moves forward to Jesus Christ, whereas on the other it is a matter of His acts in the history of Jesus Christ which is the goal of the former history. These are two different things. Yet there is parity in respect of their function as witnesses. In both spheres, of course, they are all different from one another. For all the common features, the biblical accounts of vocation and the commissions disclosed in them are all specific and are not therefore interchangeable. This is of a piece with the fact that the work of God, the Word of which the called have to hear and attest to others, is an ongoing and at all points differentiated history in the course of which God continually wills and does particular things and therefore has always something particular to say, even though He always speaks of His present, past and future rule and action. It is for this reason that He calls so many different witnesses at specific times and in specific situations. It is for this reason, too, that the form and content of their witness are so rich and varied.

According to Gen. 12¹ (and cf. 20⁷ where he is also called a prophet) Abraham is a witness of God, i.e., of His action as it moves towards its far distant and therefore totally hidden goal, not only to the men of his home town and kindred and to the inhabitants of Canaan, but also to the estranged Sarah, to the unsuspecting Isaac and to all those implicated in his particular history. He is this quite simply by doing what he is told to do in strict obedience and blind trust. He emerges as one who is called by God to represent and reveal by way of anticipation what God wills to do and will do, even though He begins to do it in great concealment. This is his " righteousness " (15⁶), the exemplary character of which for Christians is emphasised by both Paul (Gal. 3⁶, Rom. 4³) and James (2²³). As God gives him this task, his name becomes a term of blessing (12²) for all the nations of the earth (12³). And as he takes up this task, he cannot be worsted and does not need to fear, since Yahweh is His shield and he lives with the promise of the richest reward (15¹).

When we turn to the call of Moses (Ex. 3¹⁻¹⁴), we find that Yahweh comes in strange, mysterious and terrifying form to a man who unsuspectingly stumbles upon Him, i.e., upon the portent of the burning bush which is not consumed. This man is one who has already committed an abortive act of violence on behalf of his people oppressed and tortured in Egypt. He has been the adopted son of the king's daughter. He is now the shepherd of his Midianitish father-in-law, and has no fixed programme for the rest of his life. What does this encounter mean for him ? Lo, it is the God of Abraham, Isaac and Jacob—the work begun in their time is being carried a stage further—who as such, as the God of the people descended from these patriarchs, has seen their sufferings and heard their cry in Egypt, and has come down to save them and to lead them into the land promised to their fathers. His concern is wholly and utterly with this people and His further plans for it, and only for this reason is He also concerned with Moses, who by divine commission is first to go to Pharaoh and then to lead out the Israelites to the place appointed. " Who am I," asks Moses, that I should undertake and execute such a task ? The question is futile. He is the one ordained to do this by Yahweh. " I will be with thee "—this can and should be enough. And if the Israelites ask who has sent him, he must make the bold answer : " The God of your fathers hath sent me unto you." And if they ask the name of this One who has sent him, and therefore of the God of their fathers, he must tell them that He is called and is " I am, who I was as the God of your fathers and will be as your God." The second period in the life of Moses, which begins with this encounter on the mountain of God, is absolutely filled and claimed by active attestation of the work of this God as expressed in its fulfilment and as it points both to the past and present. Moses has heard its expression. He must now attest and re-attest it in difficult circumstances to Pharaoh and in even more difficult circumstances to the people of God. This task and its execution are the goal of his vocation. And the personal reward which will certainly not be lacking (Ex. 33[11]) is that God will speak with him, with the man who is bound and committed to him, " face to face, as a man speaketh unto his friend." Can a man demand more ? Has any mystic, Pietist or Romantic experienced anything higher ? It was in the fulfilment of his *ministerium Verbi divini*, however, that he had this supreme experience.

According to the Deuteronomically conceived Book of Joshua (1[1-11]), the calling of Moses was followed by the special but related calling of Joshua. The work of God still goes forward. The land is wide open before the people and is already given them. " Every place that the sole of your foot shall tread upon, that have I given unto you, as I said unto Moses." Joshua has to lead the people in, and therefore across Jordan. The occupation—a term which is meaningful only if it is understood as supremely active acceptance—is now to commence. Its execution is the task and active witness of Joshua. Is it not greater than that required of his more illustrious predecessor ? But rivalry is expressly negated : " As I was with Moses, so I will be with thee (in all thy ways, as is said later) : I will not fail thee, nor forsake thee." Joshua has thus nothing to fear, for no one can withstand him. " Only be thou strong and very courageous (this is said three times), that thou mayest observe to do all the law, which Moses my servant commanded thee : turn not from it to the right hand or to the left, that thou mayest prosper whithersoever thou goest." He is to speak of this law and meditate in it day and night. No doubt this precise statement can be attributed to a later stratum of the tradition. But Israel's self-understanding in respect of its origins is here rightly in substance explaining that calling as active calling to witness—it is the Lord of the whole history of Israel who calls— takes place in a continuity even though it is new in each case, and that in this continuity the work and Word of God yesterday cannot be separated from His work and Word to-day, but the two belong together and form a single whole for all the differentiation in detail. The particular task of Joshua in continu- ation and completion of that of Moses is the motive which according to the Deuteronomic presentation controls his particular existence.

Gideon is called in the same way according to Jud. 6[11-24]. He, too, is summoned, and after initial hesitation impelled, to the specific active witness of repulsing the desert tribes which constantly threaten Israel : " Thou shalt save Israel from the hand of the Midianites : have not I sent thee ? " It is to this mission that he must devote his life, and he does so. Again, Samuel is called in the same way according to 1 Sam. 3[1-21]. The task given him in early youth is specifically that of proclaiming the divine judgment on Eli and his house, but this is obviously extended as he grows up : " The Lord was with him, and did let none of his words fall to the ground. And all Israel from Dan even to Beersheba knew that Samuel was established to be a prophet of the Lord." According to the tradition, he then exercised this prophecy supremely in connexion with the rise and fall of Saul, the first king of Israel, and then the elevation of David and his house in place of Saul.   Again, David's unexpected anointing by Samuel (I Sam. 16$^{1-13}$) is to be understood as a calling, and his assumption and discharge of the royal office are thus to be regarded as his own specific witness to the fulfilment of the will of Yahweh for His people, and indeed for all peoples, as distantly revealed already in the great extension of his dominion.   It is surely no accidental coincidence that the greatest record of the confession, not lacking even in the Old Testament, of the individual and collective experience of salvation, the Book of Psalms, has been brought into such close relationship with the name of this hero and ruler who was the most forceful of all the active witnesses to the Word of God's action in the history of Israel and therefore in the world, and that in certain detailed passages it is perhaps to be understood as an effective parergon of the historical mission of David.   In the very Psalms devoted to the active praise of the divine action in the sphere of creation, it could and should also be stated *expressis verbis* what it meant personally for all God's witnesses that their human activity as such was accompanied by the repeated promise : " I will be with thee."   We must not read the Psalms, as Christians unfortunately so often do, in abstraction from their Messianic setting, and therefore from the witness to God's kingdom so powerfully given in the life and acts of David. Otherwise we may well misinterpret the unforgettable things which they say concerning the existence of the called in all its dimensions, misapplying them in the sense of an individual and collective egoism of salvation.

Again, we have to think of the calling of the prophets in the narrower sense. Except in the cases of Moses and Samuel, it is only with them that word, speech and writing, i.e., declaration in the more literal sense, may be said to stand in the forefront of their task and sending.   Of course, their witness, too, consists decisively in their existence as those who are called by God.   But their spoken word now becomes the typical expression of their existence and form of their witness. God speaks to them as to all their predecessors.   He tells them what His will and act were and were not, are and are not, will be and will not be, in world-occurrence and particularly in events within the sphere of Israel and Judah. Hence the formula : " Thus saith the Lord "—their acceptance of what God says being the basis, authorisation and power of their own human preaching, teaching, proclamation and (in the appropriate place) writing in the service of the divine Word.   What they do in this service usually has symbolic significance, not merely in representation of what they say, but in depiction of the fact that they do not refer to timeless truths but to the past, present and future occurrence in which the will and action of God are declared to them.   They are certainly called to declaration in the literal sense.   But it is seldom that this is not presented in their writings. or in later accounts, as an event in their lives which is in many cases dated.   The Word of the Lord came to them.   It imperiously entered their lives like an unexpected guest.   Even where there is no such reference, it may be naturally assumed.   In effect, the Old Testament gives us actual accounts of calling only in the cases of Isaiah, Jeremiah and Ezekiel.   All of these have distinctive characteristics.   Yet for an understanding of what is meant by vocation they all point in the same direction.

The calling of Isaiah, like that of Moses, begins with a divine theophany (Is. 6$^{1-13}$).   In this case, however, it is on a much grander scale than the appearance in the bush, and it is immediately recognised for what it is by the one who is called.   He sees a King so high and lifted up that his train fills the great expanse of the temple in Jerusalem.   Above Him and around Him, representing the heavenly cosmos within the earthly, are the seraphim with their threefold *Sanctus*. At the continuation of this hymn or ascription, the posts of the door are moved and the whole house is filled and enveloped by the smoke of what is clearly an invisibly threatening fire.   The words of the continuation should be noted, for they constitute a historical declaration which goes beyond anything previously said to the called. They are to the effect that " the whole earth is full of his glory." It is not merely that the temple, which can hardly accommodate His train, is full of His glory, nor indeed Jerusalem, nor Judah, but the whole earth. It is thus that He is the thrice holy. This is what is sung and said by the seraphim. This is something which is resolved and settled in relation to King Yahweh whom Isaiah sees majestically enthroned. This is what is proclaimed by the stroke of the historical hour of this prophet. Isaiah is the man who sees King Yahweh in this way, who hears the *Sanctus* with this addition, continuation and extension. But we misread the situation as he himself saw it if we expect that a word along these lines, the proclamation of the universal rule of Yahweh as such, will be his task and the purpose of his mission. So far there has been no mention of any commission. What shatters and seizes Isaiah in face of the exalted King and as a hearer of the hymn or ascription of the seraphim is a recognition, which pierces asunder to the very joints and marrow, of the total disparity and discrepancy between the being and rule of Yahweh, as disclosed to him by the declaration articulated in the saying of the seraphim, and himself as a member of the temple community and the people of Jerusalem and Judah. The contrast is a mortal blow : " Woe is me ! for I am undone ; because I am a man of unclean lips, and I dwell in the midst of a people of unclean lips." It is to be noted that he does not speak of the unclean heart, but of the unclean lips of himself and his people. It is thus clear to him from the very first that what he has seen and heard demands to be expressed and proclaimed. It must go out as a human word on human lips, to be sounded forth and heard in its immeasurable positive and negative significance among all men throughout the earth. But he knows of no human mouth which is able and worthy to form and express that which corresponds to the matter. He must confess that he is a member of the community and people in which there are only unclean lips which contradict rather than correspond to the matter. He thus knows that what he has seen and heard must be expressed and yet cannot be expressed by a human mouth. It is in view of this dilemma that he cries : " Woe is me ! for I am undone." And the distinctiveness of his calling is to be found in the fact that his own commissioning is thus delayed and he himself must first be made able and worthy. There thus follows at the hands of one of the seraphim the touching of his mouth with a live coal taken with tongs from off the altar : " Lo, this hath touched thy lips ; and thine iniquity is taken away, and thy sin purged." There must be no mistaking the fact that the remission and purging which he is granted—whatever personal or private significance they might have—relates strictly to his enabling, to his being made worthy, for a service of his lips which is not yet but obviously will be required. Its purpose is strictly to make him free to render this service in distinction from the other members of his community and people. It is a further surprise that this is not followed at once by his commissioning and sending as such but by a kind of general promulgation of the task as though it might be accepted by others : " Whom shall I send, and who will go for us ? " There then follows the further unique feature of the free offer of Isaiah. Being freed for the purpose, he is free to attempt the task without presumption : " Here am I ; send me." There then comes a final and truly confusing and astounding surprise. Isaiah is commissioned, but for what ? He is sent, but to whom ? It might have been supposed that like Paul he would have been sent to the nations to tell them that the whole earth is full of the glory of thrice holy King Yahweh. But like all his predecessors, apart from Moses' commission to Pharaoh, he is sent only to Israel, and indeed with even greater restriction to this people of Jerusalem and Judah. And if we might have been expected that he would be sent to them to speak to them the wonderful Word of Yahweh and His royal dominion, and to call and direct them to a joyful acceptance of the special mission among and to

all peoples, we are again disillusioned, for the dreadful task of Isaiah is as follows :
" Go, and tell this people, Hear ye indeed, but understand not ; and see ye
indeed, but perceive not. Make the heart of this people fat, and make their
ears heavy, and shut their eyes, lest they see with their eyes, and hear with their
ears, and understand with their heart, and convert, and be healed." This is a
dreadful message for the hearers, but even more dreadful for the speaker who
has nothing to impart to the people of God among all the peoples but that it is
too late to receive any other word, and that it cannot and will and shall not
understand any other. " Lord, how long ? " is the startled cry of the man who
is given this task. How long will this Word apply ? How long will the appearance of the enthroned King and the saying of the seraphim mean this and this
alone for the people chosen and beloved by Him ? How long is it to be told only
that God passes it by and has no more to say to it ? The answer is given : " Until
the cities be wasted without inhabitant, and the houses without man, and the
land be utterly desolate " ; until even the tenth of the people which is yet spared
is destroyed ; until only a stump remains of the felled terebinths and oaks ;
until the judgment of the King of whose glory the earth is full has been executed
to the bitter end on this people. It belongs to another chapter that the stump
will still be a holy seed, and that the history of the acts of God among and to
this people will not come to an end with this judgment. The clock has now struck
twelve. The axe is laid to the root of the tree. Isaiah, the witness of the will
and act of Yahweh in this hour, has to attest this and this alone to his people.
It is for this that Yahweh has appeared to him. It is for this that he has heard
the seraphim magnify Him as the King of the whole earth. It is for this that his
lips are purged. It is for this service that he has freely and readily offered even
though he did not suspect its nature. It is in order that he may discharge it
that he is separated from the community of the temple and from the people,
and set over against them as the messenger of Yahweh.

The hour of the calling of Jeremiah as described in Jer. 1⁴⁻¹⁹ is different
again. The universality of the lordship of Yahweh over His people and the
other nations has taken very concrete form in the history of his time, and so,
too, has its recognition as this is granted to Jeremiah. The judgment intimated
by Isaiah now stands at the very doors in the form of the overwhelming Babylonian threat. This is the meaning of the visions of the almond tree and the
seething pot. " I will hasten my word to perform it," and : " Out of the north
an evil shall break forth upon all the inhabitants of the land." This is not just
a political situation which can be remedied by diplomatic or military means.
Yahweh is about to make irresistible use of His power as the Ruler of the world.
There can be no averting the fall of Jerusalem, of the temple and of the house
of David. This is what Jeremiah has to tell the people of Jerusalem, the political
and ecclesiastical leaders, and all members of the people, through all the changing
circumstances of the reigns of Josiah, Jekoiakim and Zedekiah, in flat opposition
to all optimistic prognoses, constantly swimming against the stream, suspected
of defeatism and even treason, and constantly provoking irritation and hostility.
His account of his calling to deliver this message reflects the irresistibility of
the happening but also the dreadful nature of the task of proclaiming it as the
will and act of Yahweh. Yahweh had chosen him for it before he received it,
indeed, before he existed, before Yahweh formed him in his mother's womb.
He had sanctified and ordained him, before he came forth from the womb, to
be a " prophet unto the nations " in this strict sense and as the unwelcome
bearer of this message. He would have to abandon himself to abandon this
task and therefore to cease to be a prophet in this sense. In other parts of the
Book (20⁷⁻¹⁸) we find his complaints and accusations in respect of the impasse
to which Yahweh has brought him. Yahweh has deceived him, and he has let
himself be deceived. Yahweh has overwhelmed and subjugated him. In terms
even sharper than the sharpest words of Job, he curses the day of his birth and

the man who announced it to his father. It would have been better if he had not been born to tread this unavoidable path. For the Word of the Lord has become to him a daily reproach and derision. He admits, of course, that he cannot actually be untrue to his election and ordination : " Then I said, I will not make mention of him, nor speak any more in his name. But his word was in mine heart as a burning fire shut up in my bones, and I was weary with forbearing, and I could not stay." In his vocation this outer and inner conflict is still before him. The account gives us only the sigh : " Ah, Lord God ! behold, I cannot speak: for I am a child." But this is dismissed. The answer is made : " Say not, I am a child : for thou shalt go to all that I shall send thee, and whatsoever I command thee thou shalt speak." Thou shalt go ! Thou shalt speak ! He can only do as he is told. For in his case too, though no detailed description is given, there is a touching of the mouth which constitutes the decisive moment in the act of calling : " Behold, I have put my words in thy mouth. See, I have set thee this day over the nations and over the kingdoms, to root out, and to pull down, and to destroy, and to throw down, and to build, and to plant." Finally, in relation to the power granted with this ordination, like so many of his predecessors he is given the promise : " Be not afraid of their faces : for I am with thee to deliver thee," and then even more explicitly : " Be not dismayed at their faces, lest I confound thee before them. For, behold, I have made thee this day a defenced city, and an iron pillar, and brazen walls against the whole land, against the kings of Judah, against the princes thereof, against the priests thereof, and against the people of the land. And they shall fight against thee ; but they shall not prevail against thee ; for I am with thee, saith the Lord, to deliver thee." In accordance with this Jeremiah can confess even in the sombre retrospect of that later passage : " The Lord is with me as a mighty terrible one : therefore my persecutors shall stumble, and they shall not prevail." It is noteworthy that this promise, which is lacking in Is. 6, should be present in the case of Jeremiah, who later treads such a desolate and afflicted path, so that even on this path there gleams through a final personal assurance, security and triumph which he particularly is granted. At the same time it is even more obvious that this promise is absolutely bound up with his task and mission, that it is co-ordinated with the difficult action of his witness, and that it is not in any sense the theme of his history.

The most explicit and bizarre of all the biblical accounts of vocation is that recorded of Ezekiel in the first chapter of his Book (vv. 3–27). Our attention will not be directed to the features which it shares with earlier callings, but rather to that which gives it its own colouring and has perhaps a useful and important contribution to make to the total picture. A strange circumstance in this case is that the true act of calling consists in the fact that, when Yahweh appears to him in a splendid vision, Ezekiel is given to eat a roll which is written on both sides (2⁹f.). This obviously emphasises the precision with which he must simply accept and pass on that which is most objectively given him by God. Nor should we overlook the fact that this extraordinary food is said to be as sweet as honey when he puts it in his mouth (3³). Concerning the content of the writing, and therefore the message which Ezekiel has to deliver, we are given only three words. These are " lamentations," " mourning " and " woe " (2¹⁰). While Jerusalem moves forward to its destruction, and the work of Jeremiah to its critical point, the younger Ezekiel must join hands with the latter and with Isaiah before him in proclaiming the accusation and judgment of Yahweh to the exilic community in Babylon which has not yet been instructed by the catastrophe which has already engulfed it. The whole house of Israel (3⁷), whether Samarian or Judean, whether in exile or in the homeland, presents a hard forehead and a stony heart to God and His Word : " They will not hearken unto thee ; for they will not hearken unto me " (3⁷). Hence the divine equipment of the prophet (3⁸f.) can only consist in making his face as hard as theirs and his forehead as adamant : " As an adamant, harder than flint, have I made thy forehead." His task thus seems to be simply to embody God's defiance of the defiance of man and to stand like a sharp and impregnable rock among them. He must spring to his feet and cry " Thus saith the Lord " among these impudent and stiffhearted children (2^{2-4}). But what does the Lord say ? One of the strange features of these chapters is that the mission of the prophet seems to consist simply in attestation of the fact that Yahweh speaks. The question of the practical goal and effect of his witness is thus left completely open. As is continually impressed upon him with increasing sharpness, he has simply to give it, to represent the Word of Yahweh among them " whether they will hear, or whether they will forbear " ($2^{5, 7}$, 3^{11}). The purpose of his mission is simply that they should " know that there hath been a prophet among them " (2^{5}). In Ezekiel we have obviously reached a final point which also seems to indicate a critical point in the history of Old Testament prophecy. Even the witness of Isaiah, Jeremiah and the other prophets cannot really be understood pragmatically, i.e., from the standpoint of a practical, moral or even religious goal obvious to the prophets themselves and to the hearers and readers of their histories. And basically are we not forced to say the same of the call of Abraham, Moses and the rest, even though we may discern in detail certain subsidiary aims such as the formation and existence of the people, its liberation and direction, its entry into and security in the land, and the reference to ways in which it must walk in virtue of its election ? What is the real purpose of the whole history of Israel ? What is the real purpose of the Word of Yahweh spoken in and with it and attested by the called ? It becomes increasingly improbable that either the history or the Word can have any inherent meaning or purpose as more and more they assume the pronouncedly negative character of a history and Word of pure judgment which emerges unmistakeably from at least the time of Amos and Isaiah. In the sphere of the Old Testament there is no answer to the question of the goal of the history of Israel or the final purpose of prophecy. This is what seems to be confirmed and sealed in the calling of Ezekiel. What is made clear in this is simply the naked fact that the history of Israel is the interconnected work of Yahweh, who is not dumb but speaks in its occurrence and therefore in His action. What is made clear, then, is simply the necessity and consistency of what is said and done in the sphere of the Old Testament. What is made clear in the inscrutability of its goal and purpose is the fact that what is said and done here points beyond itself.

When we turn to the New Testament we must begin by stating that there neither is nor can be any history of the calling of Jesus. As is particularly emphasised in John's Gospel, but occasionally in Matthew and Luke as well, He is sent. As the Son of God, He is sent by the Father to the world, to earth and among men. He has come as One who is sent. In at least one passage He can thus be explicitly called an " apostle " (Heb. 3^{1}). But He is also a " prophet," charged with an incomparable task, and expressly described as such in several places in Matthew, Luke and John. Yet there is no becoming of Jesus which underlies and precedes this being and can be narrated as such. There is thus no account of the coming into being of His prophecy and apostolate. There is a voice from heaven in the story of His baptism and again in that of His transfiguration on the mount, but this is not a calling in virtue of which He becomes what He was not before after the pattern of those commissioned by Yahweh in the Old Testament. It is His proclamation as the One who as the Son of God is the Prophet and Apostle *per se*, and is to be heard as such. It describes and confirms Him as the One who needs no calling because He is called essentially. But in saying this we say rather more than the New Testament, which does not apply the concept of vocation to Jesus at all. Of Him it can only be said and told that He Himself calls. He is the foundation of the apostles and prophets (Eph. 2^{20}), and only as such is He Himself to be called Apostle and Prophet.

He stands at the point where in the Old Testament Yahweh confronts those who are to be called and are actually called by Him. This is the new starting-point with which we have to reckon in the New Testament stories of calling. The Subject who calls with the authority and efficacy of the Old Testament Yahweh is a man, this man, who as such encounters other men, calls them to Himself and His service, and constitutes, equips and sends them forth as His witnesses. The existence of the man who may and must do this, and actually does it, is the new factor which is the origin and theme of the New Testament. This is the act of God at the goal and end of the history of Israel and its prophecy. " As thou hast sent me into the world, even so have I also sent them into the world " (Jn. 17¹⁸). " As my Father hath sent me, even so send I you " (Jn. 20²¹). This καθώς includes the fact that the historical work of God and the spoken Word of God are no longer two things but one, the former as the transparency which is illumined by the light of the latter. Hence the work of God, i.e., the fulfilment of His action in the history of Israel by the existence of the man Jesus sent forth by Him, no longer stands in need of any special Word to reveal it as the work of God, since it speaks and is itself the Word of God as such. The Word spoken by this man, as distinct from that of all the Old Testament prophets, can and must, therefore, consist simply in the self-revelation of this man and the proclamation of His own existence as the Son of God. He Himself is the work of God in the fulfilment now attained and effected. Through Him, the Son, God " who at sundry times and in divers manners spake in time past unto the fathers by the prophets," has now spoken at the end and goal of all times (Heb. 1¹ᶠ.). But can the Son, as Witness of the work of God now accomplished in His own existence, bear testimony to anything other or higher than Himself ? And if He for His part, unlike any of the Old Testament prophets, calls and sends out others, what charge can He give them, or to what can He commission them, except to be witnesses of the work of God accomplished in Him, and therefore His witnesses, i.e., witnesses of His existence, proclaimers of the Word of God spoken in His existence ? In correspondence and accordance with (καθώς) His own sending, He sends them. Neither together nor individually could the Old Testament prophets be witnesses of the fulfilment of the work of God " when the fulness of time was come " (Gal. 4⁴), namely, of the fulfilment in which this work, having reached its goal in the existence of the man Jesus, is both a fact and a saying, in which it is also the Word of God as such. Hence their genuine witness concerning the work and Word of God in the history of Israel could only be incomplete. It could not finally be perspicuous in itself. It could only point beyond itself. But in so far as the work of God attested by them moved in fact to this completion ; in so far as the history of Israel moved in fact to that of Jesus Christ ; in so far as it was the indispensable presupposition, preparation and intimation of it, their witness, too, had reference to the One who was to come and did come, and therefore the witnesses of this One who came, the apostles sent by Him, were not mistaken when even in the provisional word of the prophets of the One who had not yet come they found genuine witness to Christ, and even placed it as such before their own direct witness, basing their own witness on that of the fathers and respectfully taking their place behind them.

If we are to understand and estimate the New Testament accounts of calling as such, our best plan is to start with the account of the calling of the disciples in the Fourth Gospel (Jn. 1³⁵⁻⁵¹). A first point to catch our attention is that the distinctive call of Jesus in the Synoptic stories : " Follow me," while it is addressed to Philip in v. 43, is now exceptional and almost occasional. It is, of course, known to the Fourth Evangelist (cf. 8¹², 12²⁶, 21²²). But in the reciprocal relationship of Jesus and the disciples it seems to have more of the character of a deduction from the presupposition which really underlies this relationship and not to be itself the underlying presupposition. When we turn to the others mentioned in this account, we find that Andrew comes first, so that with reference to this passage, and not without rivalry against Peter and Rome, he is celebrated as the πρωτόκλητος in the Eastern Church. Together with Andrew is an unknown disciple, who is surely identical with the unknown disciple who appears frequently in this Gospel. Then comes Andrew's brother Peter, then Philip and then Nathanael, who is brought by Philip after some resistance and who cannot be identified for certain with any of those mentioned by the Synoptists. None of these, however, is called verbally ; we are told of one after the other that as soon as they saw Jesus, in some cases brought by the others, they spontaneously followed him. The two first (v. 35 f.) seem originally to have been disciples of John the Baptist who met Jesus in company with John and attached themselves to Him when they heard the Baptist's cry : " Behold, the Lamb of God ! " Simon came when he was told by Andrew : " We have found the Messias " (v. 41), and Nathanael was similarly brought by Philip (v. 45 f.). Whether with or without this mediation, they all seem to take the decisive step of themselves with an astonishing freedom and necessity. In the case of none of them do we have express reference to any task or mission. Is this really an account of calling at all ? In the intention of the Gospel, it undoubtedly is, and exactly as it is narrated. The basic importance which this Evangelist ascribed to the coming of the disciples may be seen already from the exact statement in v. 39 that it began at the tenth hour of the third day of the fellowship of the Baptist with Jesus. Again, on a closer examination there can be no mistaking the fact that in this coming of the disciples to Jesus the decisive acting Subject both in His own sight and theirs is Jesus Himself. For this Evangelist, too, Jesus is thus the One who calls. The only point is that, except in the case of Philip, the calling is not verbal according to this presentation. It is rather the underlying presupposition of verbal calling. This is the concern of the Fourth Evangelist. There can be no ignoring the difficulty and indeed the impossibility of harmonising his account with that of the Synoptists from the standpoint of the historical pragmatics of the process. But even if we prefer to follow the Synoptists for this reason or in this respect, we have to allow that from the purely material standpoint the Johannine account constitutes a strangely original statement which is needed alongside that of the Synoptists to point to their background. It tells us that it needed only the initial impulse of the saying of the Baptist, and certain men had to follow Him, and did follow Him, and were thus called, commissioned and sent by Him, without any verbal summons on the part of Jesus and with supreme objective necessity. According to the view of the Fourth Evangelist there existed between Him and them a kind of predestinarian, and as such highly efficacious, bond which was simply disclosed, confirmed and actualised in their encounter. Thus Simon was immediately addressed by Jesus (v. 42) not only with his full name but also with the surname Cephas, which according to the Synoptists was given him only at the climax at Caesarea Philippi, and which denotes his future function. Again, Nathanael is at once described as " an Israelite indeed, in whom there is no guile." Again, one after the other is simply found (v. 41, 43, 45), and they for their part declare : " We have found the Messias " (v. 41), or : " We have found him of whom Moses in the law, and the prophets did write, Jesus of Nazareth, the son of Joseph " (v. 45). Again, Jesus saw Nathanael under the fig tree even before Philip called him (v. 50). And the mere declaration : " I saw thee," together with the recognition that Jesus knew him, was enough to evoke from Nathanael the confession : " Rabbi, thou art the Son of God ; thou art the King of Israel " (v. 49). What the Johannine account obviously intends to say is that the encounter of these men with the man Jesus is in itself and as such strong enough to bring into effect their relationship of discipleship to Him as something already resolved concerning them. He calls them as they become aware of His existence and of the determination of their own existence for discipleship. He speaks, calls and summons by His presence. And what they are called to—there is no mention of personal salvation or perdition in this story—is highly practical recognition of His existence and commitment to it. The confessions of Andrew, Philip and Nathanael show that with their actual calling to this recognition—the concept of believing occurs in v. 50—they also acquire and have taken up their task and are already engaged in discharging it. What is still ahead according to the concluding verse of the story is simply the fulfilment of the confession already made and the task already accepted and undertaken : " Ye shall see heaven open, and the angels of God ascending and descending upon the Son of man." It is certainly tempting and possible to regard this Johannine account as a theological commentary on the Synoptic records which are so much shorter and more explicit. In any case, it is legitimate and indeed necessary to see in it an indication and description of the basic process enacted between Jesus and the disciples when He came to them and they to Him, and to derive from the Synoptic accounts the explication of this basic process, in which the man Jesus did not in the first instance need to call other men verbally because in His being as the One He was, as the completed work of God, He was also the Word of God which as such had both the content and the power of calling.

When we come to the Synoptists, we shall take first the story of the calling of Levi (Mk. 2¹³⁻¹⁷ and *par*.), who is called Matthew in the First Gospel, because this gives us the explication of the basic process in its simplest and therefore its most eloquent form. For all that it is so astonishing, the decisive event in the story is as simple as possible and is described in a single verse in all three versions. All emphasise the apparently casual nature of the occasion. Jesus is passing through Capernaum on His way to the lake-side, and in passing (παράγων) He sees Levi the son of Alphaeus sitting in his tax-office, which is apparently open to the street. Whether Levi sees Jesus is irrelevant. Jesus sees Levi. According to the context Levi is a rich man. But he is more than suspect to the strict Jews of the city on account of his calling, the collection of taxes being a lucrative business farmed out by the alien rulers to large-scale operators who then committed it to lesser middlemen like Levi at a lesser profit, and also probably on account of the harshness and trickery which were almost inseparably bound up with the operation of the system and to which Levi probably owed his wealth, like the more highly placed Zacchaeus in Jericho (Lk. 19⁸). In any case, Levi belonged to those who in exercising this calling excluded themselves *ipso facto* from the national and religious society of the Jews, and could only be reckoned as transgressors before the Law and in the eyes of its commissioned expositors and representatives. This is the man whom Jesus sees in passing. He says to him : " Follow me." And he arises, and leaves everything (Lk. 5²⁸), and follows Him. On the side both of the One who calls and of the one who is called, it is all quite unequivocal, totally unprepared, and highly improbable, and yet the records tell us with great sobriety that it happens. How does Jesus come to call this man ? He does so. How does this man come to obey Jesus ? He does so. In this simple event which is so astonishing on both sides and yet which happens, there arises the mastership of Jesus on the one hand and the discipleship of this man on the other. And the context gives the happening a specific note which is most significant. For in the continuation Levi invites Jesus and the disciples who are already following Him to a feast in his house, to which he also invites a great company of worthy or less worthy associates in his unhappy calling and reputation, " many publicans and sinners " who " sat together with Jesus and his disciples." This table fellowship of Jesus with " publicans and sinners " arouses the serious displeasure of the Pharisees, and in relation to them Jesus introduces the comparison of the doctor in his dealings with the sick and the well, and says : " I came not to call the righteous, but sinners to repentance." What does this mean ? The fact that in all three versions it is related to the earlier incident, and that Jesus speaks expressly of καλεῖν, makes it plain that in the light of the calling of Levi Jesus is here saying something decisive and well

worth pondering concerning the meaning and purpose of His calling generally.
" I came not to call the righteous." The righteous are those who in their own
judgment and that of other righteous people, who are never lacking in the world
even without the intervention of Jesus, are standing in the right place as distinct
from others, namely, at the side of God. Apart from their reconciliation to
God effected in Jesus, and therefore apart from His prophecy, there is a relatively large minority of men who see in themselves and one another those who
are already placed at the side of God, who are already called, who seem in some
sense to form God's party in the world, and who can advance many good reasons
for claiming to do so, in contrast to the majority of the godless with whom as
such they are in conflict. The Pharisees belong to this party of those who are
already righteous and called. The publicans and sinners obviously do not, but
belong to the party of the godless assailed by them. And now Jesus comes to
the scene of battle and finds the righteous on the one side and the ungodly on
the other. To whom does He belong ? To whom does He issue His call ? The
righteous seem not unwilling at first to hail Him as one of them. Does not He
call men out of the *massa perditionis* to set them at God's side within the world ?
Surely this implies a welcome confirming and strengthening of the already
flourishing and militant divine party of the warriors of light against darkness.
Surely it holds out the prospect of their overwhelming and definitive victory
against all opponents. But there now comes the great disappointment and
alienation. It is astonishing enough that Jesus calls a notorious publican to be
His disciple. But this may be condoned on the natural assumption that He is
calling him out of the great company of worldlings and ungodly and leading him
into their camp. To make proselytes has always been a fine occupation for the
righteous. Yet this is not what happens. What happens is that Jesus seems
to follow the one who is called by Him rather than *vice versa*. He accepts his
invitation, goes to his house, sits down at table not only with him and the
existing disciples but with a highly dubious company of worldlings, eats and
drinks with them, and in this way openly and publicly dissociates Himself from
the righteous and associates with the ungodly. Is this what it means to call and
set Levi at the side of God ? Can a righteous man, one who is himself at the side
of God, do a thing like this ? " A man is known by his company." Who, then,
is Jesus if this is His company ? Can a man who does this be righteous and call
to righteousness ? The astonishing answer of the three Evangelists is that this
righteous man, this man who calls to righteousness, the man Jesus, actually
has to do this. He does not stand in the camp of those who are already righteous.
He does not take their righteousness seriously. He has no intention of leading
the one who is called by Him into that camp or integrating him into the phalanx
of the party of God in opposition to the godless. He goes before him, and
His existing and future disciples, by first following him into his house, sitting
at table quite unreservedly with a great company of publicans and sinners, and
very peacefully and non-heroically holding a celebration with them. He has
not come to call the righteous, those who in their own judgment and that of those
likeminded are already righteous and stand at the side of God. Why should He ?
In regarding themselves as such, and conducting their party politics as such,
they obviously do not need to be called by Him, any more than the physician
by those who are well. Nor has He come to strengthen them in their righteousness or to give validity and new thrust to their party politics. Nor can He use
them in His discipleship for what He has in mind for those who are called by
Him. They are the very last who can become and be His witnesses. As those
who are already righteous, they can never be this. As His disciples, as Christians,
they could only cause confusion and offence by understanding and representing
His Gospel as a new and higher kind of Pharisaism. He, Jesus, is not against
publicans and sinners at the side of God. He is for them. He is for the worldlings
and ungodly. He conducts their case at and from the side of God. This is His

righteousness which He calls and sends out His own to proclaim. Those whom He calls to Himself He calls to the side of God where they, too, cannot be against but only for the children of the world. Those who are already righteous, and thus contend against the ungodly, He can only pass by. He can only wait until perhaps one day they step down from their lofty pulpit or platform and abandon their righteousness and therefore their contest. He has not come to call them, but to call sinners. Levi is a notorious sinner and nothing more. As such he is usable as a witness of Jesus. As such He calls him. And in confirmation and proclamation of the full seriousness of the calling, commissioning and sending of this sinner, he sits down with him and all his fellow-publicans and fellow-sinners, eating and drinking with them in celebration of his calling, the meaning and goal of which, since it is the act and Word of the free grace of God, can consist only in the attestation and proclamation of this free grace. To know, to receive and therefore to attest and proclaim this grace, a man must be a sinner, and know himself as such, and allow himself to be known by others as such. In no sense and in no circumstances, then, can he regard himself as already righteous, or conduct himself accordingly. This is clear enough in the case of Levi. It is for this reason that his calling can and must be an event which is as unexpected and improbable as appears at the beginning of the account. Nor should we miss the basic significance of the passage. In this respect the calling of Levi is not exceptional but typical. The calling of Jesus is never a calling of those who are already righteous. All those who are already righteous, and remain such, are *per se* the uncalled from whom He can only dissociate and whom He can only pass by, turning instead, and most surprisingly, to the sinner in the tax-office. His calling is always a calling of sinners, because, as calling to Him and to His discipleship, it is always calling to the proclamation of the free grace of God which as such can take place authentically, credibly and acceptably only in the mouth of sinners, of those who are wholly directed to it.

The calling of the four fishermen, Simon, Andrew, James and John, comes at the beginning or immediately after the beginning of the whole Gospel narrative in the three Synoptists. The Synoptic tradition agrees with the Johannine in a presentation which first presupposes a Jesus who exists alone, e.g., in his baptism, in the temptation in the wilderness and in the assumption of His teaching office, but which is then rapidly broadened by the calling of the disciples, in this case of these four as the first, before the idea of a Jesus without disciples can harden and establish itself. Other callings must have followed these first, as may be seen from the lists of apostles adduced later ; though only that of Levi is narrated, unless we refer to the incident in Lk. 9[59], where Jesus called an anonymous figure to be His disciple, but he wanted first to go and bury his father, and was told in reply : " Let the dead bury their dead : but go thou and preach the kingdom of God." When we turn to the calling of the four, one thing stands out plainly in the essentially similar accounts in Mk. 1[16-20] and Mt. 4[18-22] and also in the Lucan version in 5[1-11] which obviously follows a special tradition and purpose. This is that this first calling, which is the most important to the community on account of the persons involved, stands in direct connexion with the beginning of the public proclamation by Jesus of the fulfilled time and the imminent kingdom of God, and of His call to be converted and believe in view of this good news. Throughout the Gospel narrative which follows, this prophetic action will always be His, and will consist in words personally spoken and deeds personally performed by Him. It is only in Acts that we shall be concerned with the words and deeds of the disciples. But according to the presentation in all the Gospels this prophetic action always has as its aim that it should be taken up and continued by His disciples. From the very outset it demands their presence as witnesses who see and hear. They are to go along with Him on His way through Galilee and later to Jerusalem. They are to accompany Him, whether they understand or not. According to Mk. 6[7f.] and *par.* they will indeed be sent out a first time in distinctive anticipation of their later execution of their commission, and although we are given no details they will thus go into action both in word and deed. But almost from the very first, when Jesus Himself makes His debut as Prophet, His call to discipleship implies commissioning to their own future speech and action. Hardly has His own Word gone forth concerning the fulfilled time, the kingdom, conversion and faith, before they must attach themselves to Him and in some sense tread on His heels. In Mark and Matthew we are introduced to a group consisting of two pairs of fishermen who are obviously engaged in very different tasks. The first two, Simon and Andrew, are casting their nets ; the others, James and John, assistants of their father Zebedee, are mending theirs. In this case, too, the text emphasises the casual nature of the encounter. It is as Jesus is walking ($\pi\epsilon\rho\iota\pi\alpha\tau\hat{\omega}\nu$) by the sea that He meets the first two, and as He goes a little farther ($\pi\rho o\beta\dot{\alpha}s$) that He finds the second. He might well have overlooked either the first, the second, or both. But He sees them as He later saw Levi, and this differentiating and electing seeing decides their fate according to the Evangelists, being followed at once by a call which can hardly be translated in its dramatic intensity : $\delta\epsilon\hat{\upsilon}\tau\epsilon\ \dot{o}\pi\dot{\iota}\sigma\omega\ \mu o\upsilon$, and in the power of which they cease to be what they were and become what they were not. Why should they come and follow Him ? In contrast to the story of Levi we are here given an explanation which is formulated rather clumsily in Greek : " I will cause that you become fishers of men " (Mk. 1^{17}). Jesus will make them fishers of men instead of ordinary fishers. " He made twelve, that they should be with him, and that he might send them forth " (Mk. 3^{14}). They will have to give up any further exercise of their previous calling, but their previous calling is made a similitude of the goal of their vocation. It may well be that their own salvation, the saving of their souls etc., are part of this goal. But there is no mention of these things in this important passage. No, the concern is supremely and finally with the men themselves, and with others near and distant. It is a matter of seeking them out, of reaching them, of encircling them, of gathering and fetching and winning them, not for any selfish end, but for the sphere of lordship and light of the One whom they have now to follow as He goes before them in Word and deed. It is to do this, as once they did it in the careful casting, the wider and bolder throwing and the steady drawing in of their fishing nets, that they are now called and have to follow Jesus, i.e., to become His disciples. Now, at once, is intended, and now, at once, they do what they are told as Levi was to do later : " And straightway they forsook their nets (and their father in the case of the second pair), and followed him." It is to be noted that there is no discrediting of their previous honest, modest and very useful work. Indeed, even the prior occupation of Levi is not disparaged. The fishermen might well have continued quite confidently in their job for the rest of their lives. But their material service is now transformed into service in and to the broader world of men. Their gaze and concern are to be with people. For the gaze and concern of Jesus are not directed on things, though these are not despised nor rejected, but on people. He is the Saviour of people, of $\dot{\alpha}\nu\theta\rho\omega\pi o\iota$. The whole effort of those who are called to His discipleship must be concentrated, therefore, on the winning of people, not to themselves, but to Him. This does not mean that their previous calling is devalued. Their calling to a material ministry is made a parable of their new activity and thus given a new and higher value.

We now turn from Mark and Matthew to Luke, who is obviously seeing, understanding and depicting the same incident in his own way. The prior history of Jesus without His disciples is much more extended in his case. Did He wish to emphasise the special, peculiar and gracious character of the first and of every event of vocation by postponing its description and first recording at some length the visit and sermon of Jesus in his own city of Nazareth, the story of an exorcism, a case of healing, and a summary account of many such incidents ? The idea that Jesus needed His disciples in the sense that He had to turn to them and their discipleship is certainly very effectively excluded by the Lucan account. And in the depiction of the actual event of their calling he treads a distinctive path which makes it a waste of time to attempt harmonisation with Mark and Matthew. According to Luke, it is the pressure of the crowd in its eagerness for the Word of God preached by Jesus which brings Him to the lake-side and therefore to the two ships, one of which belongs to Simon, no mention being made of Andrew in this account. Simon and his two partners in the other ship are washing their nets after an unsuccessful night outing. It is worth noting that we are not actually told that Jesus " saw " the two ships, and that His first interest seemed to be in Simon as the owner and pilot of one of the vessels. At the request of Jesus, Simon places the boat at His disposal, in order that He may address the crowd on the shore from a suitable distance. It might appear as though another person could just as well have given Him this minor technical assistance. But Jesus now gives him in return comparatively much greater technical assistance by telling the surprised and hesitant fisherman to launch out again and causing him to experience the miracle of the enormous draught of fishes. This means—and everything points to the fact that this is Luke's intention—that the boat of Simon becomes in quick succession the scene (1) of an action of the Word of Jesus, and (2) of a σημεῖον accompanying His Word. It means, therefore, that Jesus enters the sphere of this man's life and work, that He requisitions him, that He draws him into His sphere of action, though not without twice demanding that Simon should have a part. But what is to become of Simon ? As Luke obviously sees it, it is the σημεῖον of the miraculous draught of fishes which opens his eyes to what has happened, namely, that with the ship as his sphere of life and work he himself is requisitioned, that he is claimed by Jesus for Himself, that he is drawn into His sphere of action, and therefore—for how else are we to express it ?—that he is called by Jesus. He is obviously called to participate in that which Jesus has enacted there before his eyes and ears, in the proclamation, fulfilled and to be fulfilled in speech and action, of the work and Word of God, the Word of His kingdom drawn near and of all the consequences of its approach. Jesus calls him by invading his own sphere and speaking and acting in it. How can he fail to understand that this implies a call to act with Him ? If we understand the incident in this way, then, and only then, are we able to understand the distinctive expression with which Simon, like Moses, Isaiah and Jeremiah, first tries to escape his calling : ἔξελθε ἀπ' ἐμοῦ, i.e., depart from this sphere of mine. Why does he want Him to depart ? Because he does not feel worthy for what is assigned to him with this entry of Jesus, nor does he regard himself as capable of it, " for I am a sinful man, an ἀνὴρ ἁμαρτωλός, and not one of the rigl.teous who might perhaps be considered for co-operation with Jesus in His work. His partners, too, undoubtedly understood the miraculous catch, which they helped Simon to bring in, as an entry of Jesus into their sphere which directly included in itself their calling, and Luke records that they were gripped by a similar astonishment (θάμβος). They, too, are called like Simon and Levi. The saying of Jesus at the conclusion of the incident is addressed to them as well as to him : " Fear not." Once the call of Jesus has gone forth, it is too late and unnecessary to fear it as flagrant sinners or to try to evade it by confession of sin. As we learn from the story of Levi, Jesus has come to call sinners and not the righteous. The fate of the sinful man is decided, and he must act accordingly. As Jesus says in exercise of supreme sovereignty : " From henceforth (ἀπὸ τοῦ νῦν, now that I have come to thee) thou shalt catch men." Thou shalt, as Jeremiah was once told when he pleaded that he was too young. Now that I have come to thee, thou sinful man art made worthy and able to be my witness. Thou art given thy commission in association with My own speech and action and in its service. Thou hast no option but to accept and discharge it. It was in the sense of this ἀπὸ τοῦ νῦν that Simon and his partners, who are now identified as James and John (with no mention of Andrew), experienced and understood the incident: " When they had brought their ships to land, they forsook all, and followed him." This is the result in which the Lukan account agrees again with those of Mark and Matthew. This is the outcome which according to all three Evangelists constitutes that of the story of Levi too. From the standpoint of historical pragmatics, it is no more possible to harmonise Luke with Mark and Matthew than it is the Johannine version of the calling of the disciples with that of all the Synoptists. Yet the New Testament picture of the event of the calling of the disciples is so enriched materially by this distinctive account, and the material agreement with the others is so significant, that discrepancy from the standpoint of historical pragmatics is a trivial price to pay.

To conclude the series of typical biblical accounts of calling we must naturally consider that of Paul. There can be little doubt that it towers above all those recorded in the four Gospels, not only in respect of the person of the one called, but also in respect of the uniqueness of the story and *telos* of his calling. In this story we are not dealing with a man who belongs to the disciples of Jesus in the narrower sense. He himself acknowledges this. As he says, he entered the group " as one born out of due time " (1 Cor. 15[8]). And yet he became the chief of all, who impressed himself upon the later Church—if only it had listened to his witness more carefully !—as the apostle *par excellence*. Nor is there any story which brings out more plainly than his the sharpness of the transition and the basic and dominating purpose of the event of vocation in which a non-Christian becomes a Christian. We shall not attempt any detailed analysis of the story because it has already claimed our attention in an earlier context on p. 198 f. of this volume. Repetition of this analysis could only confirm the main features, and underline the typical significance, of the picture which has already emerged of what is meant by vocation in the Bible, and particularly of what constitutes the goal of vocation. We may simply recall how Paul himself understood the purpose of his existence as a man personally called by Jesus Christ. It pleased the One who separated him from his mother's womb, like Jeremiah, to call him by His grace by causing His Son to be revealed to him and in him (ἐν ἐμοί, Gal. 1[15]). Why ? In order to endow him personally with temporal and eternal blessings ? This was included, for otherwise where would have been the grace which he experienced in his calling ? Yet he does not mention this. By the revelation of His Son God has called him to proclaim this Son of His, and therefore the Gospel, the good and indeed the best news, among the Gentiles. Hence in the parallel passage in 1 Cor. 15[9f.] : " By the grace of God I am what I am "—I, the least of the apostles, who am not worthy to be called an apostle, because I persecuted the Church of God. What were Simon Peter and the publican Levi compared with a sinner of this nature ? Yet the fact remains that " his grace upon me was not in vain." In what respect was it not in vain and therefore effective ? Because he was saved, justified and sanctified by it ? Of course ; yet this is not what Paul says, but rather that by the grace of God " he laboured more abundantly than they all " (i.e., the other apostles), and therefore became in fact the most active of the apostles. To be κλητός means for him (Rom. 1[1]) quite self-evidently and naturally to be κλητὸς ἀπόστολος, to be separated for service to the Gospel of God promised by the prophets in Holy Scripture, and as such to be a debtor (ὀφειλέτης) both to the Greeks and the barbarians, the learned and the unlearned, indeed, the whole human race (Rom. 1[15]). " Grace and apostleship, the address of Jesus Christ to him and his own sending to fashion " obedience of faith " to His name among the Gentiles, are one and the same thing (Rom. 1[5]) rather than two different determinations of his existence. God has committed to him the λόγος καταλλαγῆς, preparing for it an abode in his person (θέμενος ἐν ἡμῖν), so that he is the ambassador of Christ and exists in order to plead with men in His stead that they should be reconciled to God in correspondence with the reconciliation of the whole cosmos in Him (2 Cor. 5$^{19f.}$). He does not gain anything, any καύχημα, nor does he make any claim for himself, in preaching the Gospel. He has no option. Necessity (ἀνάγκη) is laid upon him to do so. "Woe is unto me, if I preach not the gospel " (1 Cor. 9^{16}). In Phm. 9 and Eph. 3^1 he describes himself as the δέσμιος Χριστοῦ 'Ιησοῦ, and in both passages he surely means not only that he is a prisoner for Christ's sake in Rome but also that he exists as one who is held captive by Jesus Christ. His personal salvation was no doubt very dear to him, but it was only secondary, as we see from the almost frightening passage in Rom. 9^3, in which he says bluntly that he would be ready to be personally accursed (ἀνάθεμα) from Christ if he could thus benefit his brethren in Israel, to whom he knows that he is continually bound even as an apostle to the Gentiles. And in this true ministry of his to the Gentiles he regards himself not only as a λειτουργὸς Χριστοῦ 'Ιησοῦ who as to such is ordained to "celebrate " (ἱερουργεῖν) the Gospel in order to present the Gentiles as a worthy offering to God (Rom. 15^{16}), but he also regards his own life with joy as a drink-offering to be poured out with the offering of the faith of his congregations (Phil. 2^{17}). This is the kind of man he has become with his conversion from Saul to Paul. All the three accounts of this event in Acts agree with his self-understanding and self-testimony in this respect. It was for this that he was called or converted before Damascus. His conversion meant his calling, commissioning and sending. Its purpose was that Jesus meant to have this enemy as His friend and apostle. Without asking him, He made him this, just as He made those men in Galilee His disciples according to the accounts in the Gospels.

[IV, 3, pp. 577–592]

CHAPTER IV

EPIPHANY

1. THE FULNESS OF TIME

We may now turn our attention to the important New Testament concept of "the fulness of time."

We naturally begin with Gal. 4¹ᶠ. In this passage Paul suggests that there was a time when the heir, i.e., man elected and created by God to be His son, was still in the position of a minor. Although the rightful "Lord of all," he was subjected to "tutors and governors," i.e., the apparently autonomous and omnipotent powers of created being (the στοιχεῖα τοῦ κόσμου). Man would thus seem to be no more than a slave among other slaves. "But when the πλήρωμα τοῦ χρόνου was come, God sent forth his Son, made of a woman, born under the law, to redeem them that were under the law, that we might receive the adoption of sons." The Son of God "came"; He was sent from God, sent to men. Therefore He was Himself "born of a woman, born under the law." He entered the temporality which is that of each and every man. With Him came the "fulness of time." Note the emphasis laid on the final phrase, at first sight almost as if an independent event had made the mission of the Son possible, as if the time were now ripe, the historical situation favourable, for the mission of the Son. But this is not what Paul meant. The mission of the Son actually brings the fulness of time with it, and not *vice versa*. With the mission of the Son, with His entry into the time process, a new era of time has dawned, so far-reaching in its consequences that it may be justly called the fulness of all time. Man has now reached maturity. He has become God's son and heir, the "Lord of all." He has become a free man. This is the event which gives time its fulness. But the term πλήρωμα τοῦ χρόνου has a further meaning. This event does not merely make this particular time fulfilled time. This fulfilled time is before or after all other time. Hence it makes all time, χρόνος as such, in the sequence and succession of which this fulfilment was achieved, fulfilled time. The *raison d'être* of all time, both past and future, is that there should be this fulfilment at this particular time. Time may seem to move into the void but it is actually moving towards this event; just as it may seem to move out of the void, but it is actually moving from this event. The fulfilment of time has now "come," epitomising all the coming and going of time. Henceforth all time can be regarded only as time fulfilled in this particular time.

Now let us turn to Eph. 1⁹ᶠ., where we read that "before the foundation of the world" it was the good-pleasure (εὐδοκία) of God to achieve a purpose which He had decided and resolved to execute. This purpose was once a mystery, but now it is no longer so, for it has been revealed and executed in the Gospel. The content of this purpose is ἀνακεφαλαιώσασθαι τὰ πάντα ἐν τῷ Χριστῷ. That is to say, Christ is to become the Head of all creation. He is to rule it and give it meaning. This is God's plan for the world, and it is the execution of this plan which involves the οἰκονομία τοῦ πληρώματος τῶν καιρῶν. Its execution will coincide with the inauguration of the "fulness of time." This is what has happened and has been revealed by the Gospel. For God's plan to sum up all things under Christ as their Head, and therefore the "fulness of time," has actually taken place and may therefore be known by us in terms of this event. Note again how the one depends on the other. The One who wills and accomplishes and reveals the ἀνακεφαλαίωσις also wills and accomplishes and reveals the "fulfilment of the times." It is with the summing up of all created being in Christ as its Head that the καιροί—the individual times of individual created things—are not cancelled or destroyed but fulfilled. None of these times moved into the void. They all moved towards this goal, this event, and therefore this particular time.

These two Pauline texts will help us to understand Mk. 1¹⁴ᶠ·, which is so important in this connexion. It gives us first a comprehensive summary of the activity of Jesus. He had been baptised by John and confirmed by the voice from heaven as the beloved Son of God, the object here too of His εὐδοκία. Then He had been tempted by the devil forty days in the wilderness among the wild beasts, after which angels came and ministered to Him. And now, we are told, He "came" into Galilee, the intermediate territory between Jew and Gentile. He "came," bringing the "glad tidings" of God, saying : "The time is fulfilled, and the kingdom of God is at hand : repent ye, and believe the gospel." We may accept the translation "is at hand," or, "has drawn nigh," for this is the message of John the Baptist in Mt. 3², and the disciples are entrusted with the same declaration in Lk. 10⁹, ¹¹. It implies that the irruption of the kingdom into history is imminent. On the other hand, if we adopt the suggestion that ἤγγικεν is simply a restrained expression for "has come," the use of this term is quite in accordance with the esoteric character of the pre-Easter history of the man Jesus, being wholly in line, for instance, with His command to the disciples to tell no one that He is the Messiah (Mt. 17⁹). Jesus' Messiahship is His secret, and can be published only when it has been disclosed from within. Similarly, the kingdom of God can be said to have come only when God has revealed it. Until then men must pray for its coming (Mt. 6¹⁰). Indeed, they will still have to pray for its coming even after it has been revealed. Until then the restrained ἤγγικεν must be used. Yet all the time there is a secretly implied ἐλήλυθεν. This is brought out plainly in the Beelzebub controversy (see Kümmel, op. cit., p. 63 f.). "If I by the Spirit of God cast out devils, then is the kingdom of God come upon you" (ἔφθασεν ἐφ᾿ ὑμᾶς, Mt. 12²⁸). The strong man has already been bound, and his house can now be plundered (Mt. 12²⁹). And Jesus' reference to His deeds in the reply to John the Baptist (" the blind receive their sight, and the lame walk . . ." Mt. 11²ᶠ·) implies that the eschatological salvation is no longer just a future expectation, but a present reality. Lk. 17²¹ puts it beyond all doubt : "The kingdom of God is in your midst." So, too, does the saying : "But blessed are your eyes, for they see : and your ears, for they hear. For verily I say unto you, That many prophets and righteous men have desired to see those things that ye see, and have not seen them ; and to hear those things that ye hear, and have not heard them" (Mt. 13¹⁶ᶠ·)—a saying which is in remarkable contrast with Lk. 17²² : "The days will come, when ye shall desire to see one of the days of the son of man, and ye shall not see it (any longer)." We should also notice the reason Jesus gives for the power which even the disciples have over demons : "I beheld Satan as lightning fall from heaven" (Lk. 10¹⁸). How could the kingdom be stormed by violent men (Mt. 11¹²) if it were not already present ? And how could a dividing line be drawn between the time before John the Baptist and the time after him, as is done in the continuation of the saying : "For all the prophets and the law prophesied until John. And if ye are willing to receive it, this is Elijah, which is to come. He that hath ears to hear, let him hear" (Mt. 11¹³ᶠ·), if the kingdom had not come after the coming and delivering up of this "Elijah"? And how could Jesus say that He had come to fulfil the law if the kingdom had not already come

(Mt. 5^{17}) ? It is not, therefore, surprising to find Mark 1^{15} prefacing the statement that the kingdom had drawn nigh with the observation that " the time is fulfilled." There is an undoubted tension between the two phrases. The latter is not esoteric or restrained in this context. It is tolerable and intelligible only if ἤγγικεν is given an esoteric sense, if it encloses the mystery of an ἐλήλυθεν. For the phrase πεπλήρωται ὁ καιρός is undoubtedly meant to describe an absolutely unique event marking an end and a new beginning in time. An event of the present gives meaning to the time before it and therefore also to the time after it. " The time is fulfilled " is so emphatic a statement that the one which follows would be quite flat and banal if it really meant no more than that the kingdom had drawn nigh, i.e., if in the ἤγγικεν we did not read the concealed ἐλήλυθεν. Indeed, in Gal. 4^4 the parallel to the " fulness of time " is the solemn assertion that God sent His Son into the world, while in Eph. 1^{10} the parallel is the ἀνακεφαλαίωσις of all things in Christ. Moreover, Mk. 1^{15} speaks expressly of a coming in a very real sense : ἦλθεν ὁ Ἰησοῦς εἰς τὴν Γαλιλαίαν κηρύσσων τὸ εὐαγγέλιον τοῦ θεοῦ. This is certainly more than a mere announcement. It is an actual irruption rather than mere imminence. If the kingdom could only be announced prior to its manifestation with the coming of Jesus as the Bearer of God's good news, in and with Him there also came, in hidden but very real form, the kingdom and therefore the fulness of time, just as with the coming of Jesus the Law was fulfilled and its whole meaning disclosed. When Jesus came, all the promises and prophecies of the Old Testament were fulfilled. No more was now needed than that this coming should run its course in time. The " year of grace," the " great and glorious day of the Lord," the true Sabbath of which the weekly Sabbath was only a sign, the Sabbath kept by God and man together, was not only at the doors but had actually dawned. If the good news of God was that the time was fulfilled, nothing less could have happened. Anything less would be inadequate to explain the tremendous cæsura indicated by the expression " fulness of time," whether we think of the conclusion of the time " until John " on the one hand or the dawning on the other of the new time obviously granted solely for the purpose of enabling men to receive the good news of God, to accept God's immediate presence and rule in time, and therefore to repent and believe, clearly in the form of concrete acts in time. Μετάνοια means a complete re-orientation, both inward and outward, of the whole man to the God who in a very real sense has turned to him in time. Πίστις means the unquestioning trust in this God which is the positive side of this re-orientation ; the new life which is the only possible life after this event in the time which follows it. In the language of Gal. 4$^{1f.}$, it means turning right about and acquiring the confidence of a son who becomes " lord of all " on his coming of age ; or, in the language of Eph. 1$^{9f.}$, it means a complete re-appraisal of the human situation in the light of the ἀνακεφαλαίωσις which has already been achieved. The difference between Mk. 1 and these other passages is that it explicitly calls attention to the consequence of all this for the time which follows. This is of a piece with the fact that it does not speak abstractly about πλήρωμα, but concretely about an event, the event of πληροῦσθαι, the reference being concretely to the coming of Jesus into Galilee, which, unless we are completely mistaken, is identical with His advent, and therefore with the advent of the kingdom. It also explains why the μετανοεῖτε καὶ πιστεύετε has so imperatively concrete a reference to the future, and therefore why the beginning of the new time is explicitly indicated with the ending of the old. Mk. 1 makes it clear beyond all doubt that in the life of Jesus we have to do with a real event in time, but with a particular event and therefore a particular time, the time of the centre which dominates all other times. The fact that in His life all time comes to fruition means that all time before it moved towards it and all time after it moved away from it. In the last resort the only real reason why men had time at all was that—although they did not realise it, apart from the prophets who prophesied " until John "—this day was to come. And the men after Christ have time only in order to orientate their lives in the light of this day which in the series of days has now appeared ἅπαξ and ἐφάπαξ and is proclaimed with an explicit imperative. A similar idea is expressed in Paul's speech on the Areopagus (Ac. 17³⁰f.) : " The times of this ignorance (χρόνοι τῆς ἀγνοίας) God winked at ; but now commandeth all men every where to repent : because he hath appointed a day (ἔστησεν ἡμέραν), in the which he will judge the world in righteousness by that man whom he hath ordained ; whereof he hath given assurance unto all men, in that he hath raised him from the dead."

But behind the application of the concept of the fulfilment to that of time in Gal. 4, Eph. 1 and Mk. 1 there lies a definite view of time. It is pictured as an empty vessel, not yet filled, but waiting to be filled up at a particular time. As all the commandments, promises and prophecies of the prophets and righteous men of the Old Testament, as all its sayings and types, are without content, apart from the coming of the kingdom in the man Jesus, and therefore defective in themselves, yet, being related to this event, and destined all along for this content, they are not for nothing, so too it is with time in itself and as such. It, too, is empty in both the negative and positive sense : empty of this content and empty for this content. It has both the defect and the advantage of being time which is hastening toward the time of Jesus and is then destined to move away from His time. Standing as it does in this relation to His time, it is in an indirect, though very real sense, His time. Its fulness resides in His time, in the πληροῦσθαι, the πλήρωμα, of the event of His life. In Him, the Son and Head of all things, in the kingdom of God which came to Galilee and was proclaimed in Galilee, all time is brought to an end and begins afresh as full and proper time.

It is important to remember how concrete all this is. The fulfilment of time itself had this particular time which is datable in relation to other times. There is no fulfilment of time without the time of fulfilment. That is why 1 Pet. 1²⁰, speaking of the time of the revelation of the Lamb chosen before the foundation of the world, calls it the " last " time, the ἔσχατος τῶν χρόνων. It is linked with a whole sequence of prevailing times. It forms the term of this sequence, but also marks the beginning of a new sequence of times. It was on the " last " of these days that God, having at sundry times and in divers manners spoken in those days unto the fathers by the prophets, spoke in His Son, whom He had made the heir of all things, and by whom also He created the times (æons, Heb. 1¹f..). " But last of all (when He had sent one servant after another) he sent unto them his son " (Mt. 21³⁷). And it is obviously significant that it was on the last and great day of the feast (Jn. 7³⁷) that " Jesus stood and cried, saying, If any man thirst, let him come unto me, and drink." This fulfilment proceeds even during this great day of His until it is completed and lies behind. The day of Jesus lasts, and as long as it lasts He must work the works of Him that sent Him, standing and issuing His summons and invitation. " As long as I am in the world, I am the light of the world " (Jn. 9⁴f.). This text clearly envisages a real day, with a morning and evening ; a real time with beginning, duration and end. For it says explicitly : " While it is day," and then continues : " The night cometh when no man can work." Thus the fulfilment of time is itself an event which fulfils time, an event which begins, continues and ends. It is for this reason that Jesus justifies His delay at the marriage of Cana of Galilee with the words : " Mine hour is not yet come " (Jn. 2⁴), and His initial absence from the feast at Jerusalem with the words : " My time is not yet fulfilled " (Jn. 7⁸). The assault of His enemies gathers weight before it reaches its climax and contributes to the fulfilment of time, and it must be held in check until the right moment (Lk. 20¹⁹, 22⁵²f.). Even the climax is marked by development. First we read : " The hour is at hand, and the Son of man is

betrayed into the hands of sinners " (Mt. 26⁴⁵), and only then : " The hour is
come " (Jn. 17¹) ; " This is your hour and the power of darkness " (Lk. 22⁵³) ;
" Father, save me from this hour " (Jn. 12²⁷). Only then can the clock of Good
Friday begin to strike until we reach the τετέλεσται which Jesus can say only
as He dies on the cross, and which according to Jn. 19³⁰ is His very last word.
It is for this reason, too, that when Heb. 5⁷ᶠ· comes to speak of what He did " in
the days of his flesh," and of the way in which He brought in the fulness of
time, it sums it all up in a reference to the last of His days, the day of the passion.
It is as Jesus travels this road to the bitter end that there takes place what the
New Testament calls the " fulfilment of time," and His time becomes fulfilled
time, and is revealed as such to His disciples in the Easter time.

[III, 2, pp. 458–462]

2. BAPTISM AND TRANSFIGURATION OF JESUS

Thus far we have not referred to one element in the preaching of John and
consequently in the meaning of his baptism. According to all the Evangelists
this is obviously the most important element which in their view includes all the
rest within itself. This element is that John the Baptist worked in prospect of a
very concrete form of the imminent act of God which would change all things.
He worked in prospect of a human person who was to come after him, from whom
and from whose baptism he and his baptism were totally because qualitatively
distinct, but with reference to whom he wished that he himself, his preaching,
and specifically his baptism should be understood. He announced this Man,
this Other, when he announced the coming kingdom, the coming judgment, and
the coming remission of sins. The imminent new act of God would consist in the
history of this Man. What was he, John, in relation to Him ? Certainly not the
light, but the one whose business it was to bear witness to the light (Jn. 1⁸). In
the Benedictus (Lk. 1⁷⁶) John is described as the prophet of the Highest who is
to go before, but only to go before, the coming One, the Kurios. He is regularly
called the forerunner or precursor described in Is. 40³ and Mal. 3¹. In keeping
is the sharp contrast (Mk. 1⁷ᶠ· par.) which he himself draws between himself and
the One who comes after him, though in so doing he associates himself with Him.
This is the " mightier " than he (ἰσχυρότερος) whose shoes' latchets he is not
worthy to unloose. For while he baptises men with water, that One will baptise
them with the Holy Ghost (and with fire, Lk. 3¹⁶). He is the One—this element
is to the fore in Mt. 3¹² ; Lk. 3¹⁷—who executes that penetrating judgment. In
the Synoptists the arrangement of the different·sayings of the Baptist which have
been preserved shows that this explicitly Messianic proclamation is regarded as
the true burden of his preaching and baptism, of his whole history. The whole
account of his word and work is as such the ἀρχὴ τοῦ εὐαγγελίου Ἰησοῦ Χριστοῦ
(Mk. 1¹). Then in the Fourth Gospel, in keeping with the striving of the author
for concentration, abbreviation and precision, everything is focused on the one
point that John simply witnesses to Him (περὶ αὐτοῦ, v. 15), to Him as the true
light (v. 7). John is simply the man with the outstretched finger who only points
to Him (οὗτος, v. 2, 15, 30, 34) who comes after him but who was in truth before
him (v. 15, 30). Almost unmistakably implied in John is a polemic against over-
estimation of the person and mission of the Baptist, or of water baptism as such.
John is the man who in relation to Jesus, while he is not outdated or set aside,
must still decrease (ἐλαττοῦσθαι) in order that Jesus may increase (3³⁰). He is
not the Bridegroom, but only (though still) the friend of the Bridegroom who is
glad to hear His voice (3²⁹). The reason (the only, but still, the reason) why he
baptises with water, the purpose (the only, but still, the purpose) of his existence,
which according to his answers to all those sênt from Jerusalem (1¹⁹⁻²⁷) was

obviously felt or suspected to be in some way Messianic : ἵνα φανερωθῇ τῷ Ἰσραήλ (v. 31), is that His coming should be declared and made known to the people, and that they should adopt the right attitude to this event. He, John, who did not know about Him before (v. 31, 33), saw the Spirit alight and rest on Him (v. 32f.), and thus recognised Him as the One He was, the Baptiser with the Holy Ghost (v. 33), the Son of God (v. 34), the Lamb of God which taketh away the sin of the world (v. 30, 36). On the basis of this recognition he bore witness to Him (v. 34). He did this by baptising with water. The impressiveness of the distinctive concentration of the Fourth Gospel on the Messianic declaration of John is enhanced by fact that, though this refers, as in the Synoptists, to Him who is still to come (v. 15), it then refers (from v. 26 onwards) to Him who, unrecognised by the questioners, is already in their midst, and finally, in v. 29f., 35f., there is direct reference (hence the urgent οὗτος) to the incarnate Word (v. 14), to Jesus, with whom he and his disciples are confronted a second and a third time. One cannot deny that the way is already prepared for this concentration in the Synoptic presentation. For them, too, John was first and finally the prophet of Him whom he had already dramatically encountered while still in his mother's womb (Lk. 1[41]). Hence the conversion which he demanded in view of the act of God which was impending and already in process of fulfilment did not have a character which might be described in the categories of impersonal morality or religion. It consisted simply in conversion to the Messiah Jesus, in faith in the kingdom which had drawn nigh in Him, in the judgment which was to be executed by Him, in the remission of sins which He should pronounce. Furthermore, the water baptism which John required and gave, and which was received from him, could be only the concrete and binding form of this conversion, of faith in Jesus. A saying which Ac. 19[4f.] attributes to Paul when he was talking to the disciples of John found at Ephesus is perhaps typical of the view of John's baptism which obviously came to be held quite generally—and it is interesting that the saying is traced back or attributed to Paul. It runs as follows : " John verily baptised with the baptism of repentance (ἐβάπτισεν βάπτισμα μετανοίας), saying unto the people that they should believe on him which should come after him, that is, on Christ Jesus. When they (not John's disciples, but the people at the Jordan) heard this, they were baptised in the name of the Lord Jesus." What needs to be said authoritatively to these disciples of John (v. 6f.) by the laying on of Paul's hands is simply that in being baptised by John they did in fact accomplish the conversion to Jesus which was the point of his baptism, they did in fact meet the requirement that they should believe in Him, and therefore, baptised in His name, they already belong to His people and are Christians. That this is so is confirmed at once by the fact that their earlier disturbed confession to Paul : " We have not so much as heard whether there be any Holy Ghost " (v. 2), is rendered pointless, since there at once comes on them that which on the Day of Pentecost had come on the disciples, who had probably been baptised by John too : " The Holy Ghost came on them ; and they spake with tongues, and prophesied." Those baptised by John in the Jordan were as such truly called, invited and summoned to faith in Jesus Christ. Accepting John's baptism, they made in fact a genuine confession of Jesus Christ.

Our question, however, is as follows : At this focal point, in its Messianic character, explicitly as a reference to the coming and already present Jesus, what is the meaning of John's preaching and baptism for Jesus Himself, for Him as the Hearer of this preaching and decisively for Him as the Recipient of the baptism of John ? It will perhaps sound rather strange—though this does not exhaust what must be said on the point—if the first answer that is unquestionably to be given in relation to this supreme and comprehensive aspect of John's preaching, which is also as such the decisive point of his baptism, is simply that Jesus, when He had Himself baptised by John, confessed Himself, sought baptism into His own name, i.e., into His mission, into the work laid upon Him, accepted the fact that He was claimed and committed to the execution of this work, and committed Himself to it. When with all the rest He listened to God's Word through John in this supreme Messianic form, this Word, as the Word of God's coming rule, judgment and forgiveness, applied to Him in a different way from all the rest to the degree that He did not merely recognise, experience and suffer it as God's act, but that even as He had to recognise, experience and suffer it, He also sought to execute it. As God's act He willed that it should be done by Him personally, by Him as the one Israelite who was elected, ordained and born and who lived to do this, as the Israelite who was also Israel's Judge and Deliverer, its Messiah, the eschatological Son of David, the goal of its whole history, in His own person the fulfilled purpose of the mission of Israel to the nations. He lived for this. This was the name which only He could and did bear. In fulfilment of the covenant made by Yahweh with Abraham and his descendants He was to prosecute victoriously the cause of God among men and the cause of men before God. He, the Man of Galilee, who came to the Jordan with thousands of others, was the One appointed to exercise this ministry in God's place and in the place of all men, the ministry of the reconciliation of the world of God. The discharge of this ministry was to be His future, the content of His life-history. This meant μετάνοια and βάπτισμα μετάνοιας for Him. He had to sacrifice Himself for this ministry, this future. He had to put Himself wholly at the disposal of God and men. He had to subordinate Himself unconditionally, to give Himself, not to save His life but to lose it for the sake of God and men.

According to Mt. 3¹⁴ the Baptist opposed His readiness for this, for His μετάνοια, by seeking to restrain Him from baptism : διεκώλυεν αὐτόν. Did the Judge, Deliverer and Messiah of Israel, who was to come and who had already come, need in baptism to commit Himself unconditionally to God, to confess Himself a sinner before God in solidarity with all the people, to give Himself up to God's judgment, to be referred solely to His promise of the coming forgiveness of sins ? What John was *not* in contrast to Jesus is more clearly reflected in this objection than in the saying, recorded in all the Gospels, about his unworthiness to unloose the shoes' latchets of this One. We read later that John had doubts about Jesus (Mt. 11²ᶠ· ; Lk. 7¹⁸ᶠ·) : " Art thou he that should come, or do we look for another ? " Here the same uncertainty takes a different form : Is he not blaspheming by letting Jesus receive the βάπτισμα μετάνοιας with all the rest ? Could his water baptism be any affair of this Man ? " I have need to be baptised of thee, and comest thou to me ? " One is naturally reminded of Peter's saying in Mt. 16²² : " Be it far from thee, Lord." But the horror of John, like that of Peter (ἐπιτιμᾶν), was no small error. It was the greatest conceivable error. In both instances not just something but everything was at stake : all righteousness (πᾶσα δικαιοσύνη), the doing of the holy and gracious will of God which was to be fulfilled personally by Jesus in His history, His whole readiness for the hazarding and sacrifice of His life in the service of God and men, the μετάνοια which was necessarily demanded of Him specifically in this form, His obedience to the command which He specifically had been given to confess Himself, His election and calling, His own true name, in this particular way. It was not accidentally or arbitrarily, but from the very first with the set intention of being baptised by John, that Jesus came from Galilee to the Jordan (Mt. 3¹³). It " became " Him to fulfil all righteousness. He came to do it. Accepting this ministry and office of His, He had to be baptised. This was very much His affair. Hence He could not be stopped. He gave the command (as the One He was and in relation to what He had to be and do, He could give an imperious command at this point, and had to do so) : ἄφες ἄρτι : " Let it be done at once." And so, οὕτως, in this way which befitted the fulfilment of the whole righteousness of God which now commenced, it was done.

To draw together our previous deliberations in the light of what has just been said, the baptism of Jesus is quite plainly the act of obedience in which he entered upon His ministry and way of life in a manner typical and decisive for all that was to follow. The Evangelists, however, were not content merely to portray this as His act of obedience, as the concrete form of His subjection to God, as the concrete achievement of solidarity with the men of His people, or finally as His concrete confession of Himself and His election and calling. They continued and concluded the account of this event with the story of a contrapuntal and crowning event from the other side, of something which was done directly by God Himself, of a happening which by its very nature could be described only " mythologically," but which, described thus, is the more impressive in its unique bearing on what was told before. We read that when Jesus had been baptised and came up out of the water, then (immediately, as stressed by Mark and Matthew) heaven opened and Jesus (the Baptist according to Jn. 1³²ᶠ·) saw the Holy Ghost (ὡς περιστεράν, or more precisely in Lk. 3²² : ἐν σωματικῷ εἴδει ὡς περιστεράν) descending upon Him (and abiding upon Him according to Jn. 1³²ᶠ·). And then (only the Synoptists recount this) a voice was heard from heaven : " Thou art (Matthew : This is) my beloved Son, in whom (or him) I am well pleased " (in Luke some MSS follow the royal Ps. 2⁷ : " Thou art my Son, this day have I begotten thee "). The variations in the four accounts do not affect the substance of the common statement. Even the surprising σήμερον γεγέννηκά σε in Lk. 3²² does not say that (in Adoptionist fashion) Jesus only became God's Son at that moment. As in Ps. 2⁷ the " this day " is the day of God which cannot be fixed chronologically, the *νῦν aeternitatis* of His election which is now proclaimed. What is the common statement made here ? First it is plain that reference is here made to a word and act which are immediately divine—immediately as compared with the ῥῆμα θεοῦ laid on John (Lk. 3²). In addition to all that has already taken place between John and Israel, John and Jesus, heaven now takes a hand. The Gospels are none too lavish with such accounts of direct interventions from above. Parallels which suggest themselves are the appearance and address of the " angel of the Lord " to the shepherds of Bethlehem, the multitude of the heavenly host which followed the angel (Lk. 2⁹ᶠ·, ¹³ᶠ·), the story of the transfiguration (Mk. 9²ᶠ· par.), the voice from heaven heard in the temple after the entry of Jesus into Jerusalem (Jn. 12²⁸ᶠ·), and the angel which appeared to Jesus in Gethsemane to strengthen Him (Lk. 22⁴³). As in the present context, the function of all these events is to confirm and display the divinity of the mission of Jesus at certain turning-points. One might write across them all the text in Jn. 16³² : " I am not alone, because the Father is with me." They furnish the turning-points with more than life-size exclamation marks which call attention thereto. The event which is appended to the baptism of Jesus, and which may be called at once " supranatural," is a decisive reference of this kind. To the ἀναβαίνειν of Jesus out of the water there now corresponds the καταβαίνειν of the Spirit which is visible to Him (also to the Baptist according to the Fourth Gospel), and the sounding forth of the voice from above. That which in a decisive hour took place and was said and done on earth at the Jordan is here, as in similar incidents, answered, confirmed and approved from heaven.

In this interrelation the difference between the two actions is also plain.

In no sense does the text suggest that the heavenly action is to be regarded as a kind of interpretation of the earthly action, that the καταβαίνειν is projected into the ἀναβαίνειν, the baptism of the Spirit into water baptism, the dispensing of grace and the revealing Word of the Father into the work done on earth, that along the lines of speculation only too well known elsewhere there may be ascribed to the performing of the work as such the character of the direct divine work and word of which the end of the story of Jesus' baptism speaks. This story follows the beginning, is set in juxtaposition to it, stands in relation to it, but it is related to it precisely in its character as a human work, the pure act of obedience there done by Jesus. It is true that with this act of obedience Jesus entered upon and began His ministry as the Mediator of God's grace and revelation to men. But He performed the act as the incarnate Son of God who, as Man taking the place of all other men, lived, acted and suffered for them. If we are to understand His ministry as Mediator of the covenant of grace it is thus decisively important to perceive that He did not enter upon it and begin it in an act in whose performance He *ex opere operato* became, and has ever since been, the Lord, Owner and Worker of God's grace and revelation. He entered upon and began this ministry in a pure act of obedience in which there could be no question of disposing of God's grace and revelation, in which, conversely, He placed Himself at the disposal of God and men, in which He was able and willing to find a place only for His divine election and calling as Man. The baptism of Jesus was the act of One who is lowly in heart (Mt. 11²⁹). It raised no claim. In it His hands were not divinely filled. προσευχόμενος (Lk. 3²¹), He stretched them out to God as empty hands, not trusting in a power secretly native to this act, and certainly not glancing at the inner goodness and meritoriousness of the act as a reason why they should be filled, but in simple reverence before the God who ordered the act. In the act there was thus no getting, grasping or receiving of the grace and revelation of God needed for the discharge of His ministry. There was only—one is continually reminded of Gethsemane—His practical, concrete Yes to the ministry corresponding to His election and calling, and therewith also to the freedom towards Him, of the God by whom He was elected and called, and to His own utter need in relation to God. How else could He fulfil all righteousness ? How could He be the true Son of Man as Son of God, how could He act for God among men and for men towards God, if He discharged His ministry, if He sought to enter upon it and to begin it, in any other way than by accepting His election as election, His calling as calling, grace and revelation for Him too, and precisely for Him, as free grace and revelation, God's sovereign gift to Him ? This is how the Man chosen and called by God stands in relation to His God. He shows Himself to be the true Son of God and Son of Man by accepting water baptism in obedience to the direction of His Father, and by acting *gratis* therein, not having or seeking anything, not receiving anything as a possession, giving God alone the glory. This and this alone, not appropriation, not seizure of God's grace and revelation, but His own appropriation to the will of God, is what He does when He has Himself baptised by John. Thus, and thus alone, does John serve Him when he admits Him to his water baptism. Thus, and thus alone, does the water with which He is baptised serve Him—for it is in no sense an instrument of grace and revelation. This is what is made clear in the Gospel account of His baptism when it contrasts what Jesus and John do with the work and word of God, when it tells of the opening of heaven over what took place on earth.

For the obvious meaning of the event from opened heaven, which is not to be equated or confused with what took place on earth, is that it is the divine response to what took place on earth, namely, the divine appreciation, acknowledgment, approval and affirmation. It is the proclamation, the making visible and audible, of the divine *de iure* to the entry into service which Jesus effected *de facto* in His baptism. This entry into service neither rested on an illusion nor consisted in an usurpation. He who here began to act did so neither by His own whim nor in His own strength. He neither contrived nor seized anything. He did not deck out His own caprice as obedience. His subjection to God was not a refined attempt at divine dominion, nor His solidarity with men a fraternising with a view to His own ends. His entry into service was not a pretension to office. What could He seek or attain by letting Himself be summoned to conversion and baptised by the desert preacher along with thousands of others ? What was there great in this ? What could it establish for Himself, for Israel, even for God ? The answer to this, as later to the enigma of the passion, could only be the free and sovereign answer of God Himself. God's answer was His full appreciation, acknowledgment, approval and affirmation of what Jesus undertook and began, His divine Yes to the Yes spoken by His Son who became man and who thought, willed and acted as such, His Amen to the human work and word of His Son. It would not have been His human work and word if it had not needed this divine affirmation. Even in its fulfilment in the crucifixion it needed divine affirmation, justification and glorification by the fact that the Father raised Him from the dead. Its divine affirmation, justification and glorification is at issue here at the beginning. The account thereof is the continuation and conclusion of the story of the baptism of Jesus. The Evangelists did not have to reflect or speculate whether there was a divine affirmation of the baptism of Jesus as His human work, how this might come about, how it would have to be understood. They were acquainted with it as a fixed element in the story handed down by them. They had to bear witness to it, to narrate it, as the beginning of His history. They had to do this no less definitely and concretely than they had to record the human Yes of Jesus uttered in and with His baptism in the Jordan. They could not tell it in any other way than they did—even though it might seem to come under the rubric of the " mythological " account of a " vision " and " audition." Heaven opened, the Spirit came visibly on Jesus. The Word of God which described Jesus as the Son was spoken. Described thus with material clarity, Jesus did not submit in vain to μετάνοια and water baptism. Not for nothing did He subject Himself totally to God, or accept absolute solidarity with men, or set Himself thus in the service of God and men. He did this—this was visibly and audibly proclaimed in His justification and vindication—as the Man on whom the Holy Ghost descended, who received Him, who was baptised with Him, who was thus equipped to baptise with the Holy Ghost, but who was also ordained and pledged to enter on and to tread that way into the depths, the way of the Servant of the Lord of Is. 53. Furthermore, it was not in vain that in all this Jesus acted with humility of heart, without claim, *gratis*, like Job (1⁹) *chinnam*, in free and absolutely generous obedience. Only He who was freely elected and called by the free God, only His beloved Son, would and could act thus, and had to do so, and was now addressed by God Himself as this Son of Man on whom God's good-pleasure rested as on the first among ἄνθρωποι εὐδοκίας (Lk. 2¹⁴). Finally, it was not in vain that Jesus, when He had Himself baptised by John, confessed Himself, His commission and ministry. It was not in vain that He irrevocably identified Himself therewith. He did this—and this was now made visible and audible from heaven—as He whom God had confessed from of old, as He to whom God had entrusted His work and word from of old, as He to whom He had assigned His grace and revelation from of old. What was manifested in this anticipation of His resurrection was that Jesus needed the almighty mercy of God like any other man, but that, without controlling it, speculating on it, or meriting it, He was sure of it, so that He could be free to take up His task without murmuring or complaint, to enter on His ministry with complete unselfishness, to fulfil it again and again in the future, and thus to confess God, men and Himself. If, then, in describing what Jesus did when He had Himself baptised by John we use the rather strange expression, not found in the New Testament, that He had Himself baptised " into His own name," we have to add by way of explanation that in that which took place from opened heaven it was made visible and audible that His own most proper name, which He confessed when He had Himself baptised, was the name given to Him by God, the name which is above every name (Phil. 2⁹) and alongside which there is under heaven none other from which salvation may be expected (Ac. 4¹²).

This, then, is what the Evangelists had to attest and narrate, in a way which is decisive and definitive for all else, when along with the story of what Jesus Himself did at the beginning of His history they spoke of the disclosure of the mystery, not of the Baptist and His baptism, and least of all of the water which he used, but of the One who in obedience had Himself baptised with water there.

The transfiguration as recorded in Mk. 9²⁻⁸ and *par.* is a good example of how the apostles regarded the pre-Easter life of Jesus from the present to their own time. It might almost be said to anticipate the Easter-history as the latter does the return of the Lord. At a first glance it looks like any other miracle story. But it is really unique, for this time the miracle happens to Jesus Himself, and is not something performed by Him. It comes wholly from outside. He does not say or do anything to bring it about. Perhaps it is meant to be taken as a preliminary key to all the other miracles. " He was transfigured before them." Moses and Elijah appear, talking with Jesus (according to Lk. 9³¹, it was about " his decease which he should accomplish at Jerusalem "). A cloud, the symbol both of concealment and revelation, overshadows them. A voice speaks from the cloud : " This is my beloved Son : hear him." Everything suggests a theophany. Hence the note in Mk. 9² and Mt. 17¹ : " after six days " (Lk. 9²⁸ says it was eight days), is not to be dismissed as an irrelevant detail. Immediately before the transfiguration comes the famous saying : "Verily I say unto you, that there be some of them that stand here, which shall not taste of death, till they have seen the kingdom of God come with power." The Markan and Matthaean versions are to be read in the light of Luke's express statement that the transfiguration took place eight (six) days " after these sayings." In other words, the transfiguration, for the Evangelists at least, was a first and provisional fulfilment of the promise contained in that saying. But the six (eight) day interval between promise and fulfilment is no doubt intended to suggest that the transfiguration with its fulfilment of the saying marks the dawn of a special Sabbath. We are obviously in close material proximity to the resurrection story. This is further suggested by the location of the episode on a high mountain ; by the statement in Mt. 17⁶ : " (They) were sore afraid" ; by Lk. 9³² (cf. Jn. 1¹⁴) : " They saw his glory " ; and by Peter's curious proposal, recorded in all the versions, to erect three tents (again cf. Jn. 1¹⁴). Evidently Peter wanted the vision to stay, if only for a short time. Mark's comment on this is : " He wist not what to say " (9⁶), which implies that he did not really understand what he was saying. But the vision did not stay, as Peter hoped it would. It vanished as quickly as it had come. Jesus is again seen alone, and no longer transfigured before them. He tells them (Mk. 9⁹) to say nothing about it to anyone until He is risen from the dead. This obviously suggests that the transfiguration is the supreme prefigurement of the resurrection, and that its real meaning will not be perceived until the resurrection has taken place. It is surprising that 2 Pet. 1¹⁶ᶠ·, speaking of the apostles as eyewitnesses and preachers of the " power and coming of our Lord Jesus Christ," says nothing about the resurrection itself, but seems to regard the preceding transfiguration as more important. The obvious post-Easter parallel to the transfiguration is the conversion of Saul. And its purpose in the pre-Easter period is obviously to demonstrate that even in this time, although in concealment, He was actually and properly the One He was revealed to be in His resurrection. And even this time was not without transitory indications of His true and proper being. In Jn. 2[11] the account of the miracle of Cana and Galilee closes with the words : " This beginning of miracles did Jesus . . . and manifested forth his glory." This would seem to imply that the miracles of Jesus are to be taken as " signs " in the sense that they point to what He already was, to the hidden presence of the kingdom of God which would later be unveiled during the forty days in an abiding manifestation, in a σκηνοῦν of the Lord in the midst of His disciples—a disclosure which will become definitive and universal at the end of all time in His coming again. That there are such signs, and that in the transfiguration, as in no other miracle, this sign is performed on Himself, shows that the mystery of His being revealed at the resurrection has not been acquired in the meantime but had been present all along and was in fact *revealed* at this later point.

[IV, 4, pp. 61–67; III, 2, pp. 478–479]

3. THE SINLESSNESS OF JESUS

In becoming the same as we are, the Son of God is the same in quite a different way from us ; in other words, in our human being what we do is omitted, and what we omit is done. This Man would not be God's revelation to us, God's reconciliation with us, if He were not, as true Man, the true, unchangeable, perfect God Himself. He is the true God because and so far as it has pleased the true God to adopt the true being of man. But this is the expression of a claim upon this being, a sanctification and blessing of this being, which excludes sin. In it God Himself is the Subject. How can God sin, deny Himself to Himself, be against Himself as God, want to be a god and so fall away from Himself in the way in which our sin is against Him, in which it happens from the very first and continually in the event of our existence ? True, the Word assumes our human existence, assumes flesh, i.e., He exists in the state and position, amid the conditions, under the curse and punishment of sinful man. He exists in the place where we are, in all the remoteness not merely of the creature from the Creator, but of the sinful creature from the Holy Creator. Otherwise His action would not be a revealing, a reconciling action. He would always be for us an alien word. He would not find us or touch us. For we live in that remoteness. But it is He, the Word of God, who assumes our human existence, assumes our flesh, exists in the place where we exist. Otherwise His action would again not be a revealing, a reconciling action. Otherwise He would bring us nothing new. He would not help us. He would leave us in the remoteness. Therefore in our state and condition He does not do what underlies and produces that state and condition, or what we in that state and condition continually do. Our unholy human existence, assumed and adopted by the Word of God, is a hallowed and therefore a sinless human existence ; in our unholy human existence the eternal Word draws near to us. In the hallowing of our unholy human existence He draws supremely and helpfully near to us.

That God sent His own Son ἐν ὁμοιώματι σαρκὸς ἁμαρτίας is at once explained in Rom. 8[3] by περὶ ἁμαρτίας, i.e., for sin, in matters of sin and so not in order to do sin Himself ; and then the main clause unambiguously declares that κατέκρινεν (ὁ θεὸς) τὴν ἁμαρτίαν ἐν τῇ σαρκί. That is, in the likeness of flesh (unholy flesh, marked by sin), there happens the unlike, the new and helpful thing, that sin is condemned by not being committed, by being omitted, by full obedience now being found in the very place where otherwise sin necessarily and irresistibly takes place. The meaning of the incarnation is that now in the flesh that is not done which all flesh does. "He hath made him to be sin for us" (2 Cor. 5²¹) does not mean that He made Him a man who also sins again —what could that signify "for us"?—but that He put Him in the position of a sinner by way of exchange (καταλλάσσων, in the sense of the Old Testament sin-offering). But whom did He put in that position? τὸν μὴ γνόντα ἁμαρτίαν. Because this man who knew no sin is "made to be sin," this "making" signifies the act of a divine offering περὶ ἁμαρτίας, ὑπὲρ ἡμῶν, judgment upon sin, its removal. *Ipse ergo peccatum, ut nos iustitia, nec nostra sed Dei, nec in nobis sed in ipso, sicut ipse peccatum, non suum, sed nostrum* (Augustine, *Enchir.* 41). This is the obvious definition of *vere homo* on this side—but its definition, not its limitation, not its secret sublimation. The commission of sin as such is not an attribute of true human existence as such, whether from the standpoint of its creation by God or from that of the fact that it is flesh on account of the Fall. And that is why it says that He was tempted in all things like as we are χωρὶς ἁμαρτίας (Heb. 4¹⁵). He is the suitable Highpriest for us because He is holy, harmless, undefiled, κεχωρισμένος ἀπὸ τῶν ἁμαρτωλῶν (Heb. 7²⁶). The Lamb of God which taketh away the sin of the world is "a lamb without blemish and without spot" (1 Pet. 1¹⁹); ἁμαρτίαν οὐκ ἐποίησεν (1 Pet. 2²²). He was manifested (ἐφανερώθη) to take away sins, καὶ ἁμαρτία ἐν αὐτῷ οὐκ ἔστιν (1 Jn. 3⁵). The prince of this world cometh—καὶ ἐν ἐμοὶ οὐκ ἔχει οὐδέν (Jn. 14³⁰). And "which of you convinceth me of sin?" (Jn. 8⁴⁶). It was on just these lines that the Early Church developed its thought and teaching: *Confirmamus eam fuisse carnem in Christo, cuius natura est in homine peccatrix, et sic in illa peccatum evacuatum, quod in Christo sine peccato habeatur, quae in homine sine peccato non habebatur* (Tertullian, *De carne Christi*, 16).

But if we ask where the sinlessness, or (positively) the obedience of Christ, is to be seen, it is not enough to look for it in this man's excellences of character, virtues or good works. For we can only repeat that the New Testament certainly did not present Jesus Christ as the moral ideal, and if we apply the canons usually applied to the construction of a moral ideal, we may easily fall into certain difficulties not easy of solution, whether with the Jesus of the Synoptics or with the Jesus of John's Gospel. Jesus Christ's obedience consists in the fact that He willed to be and was only this one thing with all its consequences, God in the flesh, the divine bearer of the burden which man as a sinner must bear.

According to Phil. 2⁸ this was found in His human form: "He humbled himself, by becoming obedient unto death, even the death of the cross." He learned obedience ἀφ ὧν ἔπαθεν (Heb. 5⁸) "For the joy that was set before him he endured the cross, despising the shame" (Heb. 12²). "Therefore doth my Father love me, because I lay down my life" (Jn. 10¹⁷). We learn from the story of Gethsemane what its opposite would be, the sin which Jesus does not do. It would have consisted in His willing against God's will that "this cup" should pass from Him (Mt. 26³⁹). And positively, from the temptation story, it would have consisted in His exercise (and consequent denial) of His Sonship to God in the manner and style of a human hero for His own advantage and glory, i.e., in worshipping the devil (Mt. 4¹ᶠ·). That is why Peter, wishing to restrain Him from going up to Jerusalem, receives the answer: "Thou thinkest not of the ordinance of God but of the ordinance of men" (Mt. 16²³). And that is why the rich young man is rejected with his greeting, "Good master." "Why callest thou me good? There is none good but God alone" (Mk. 10¹⁷ᶠ·). "The Son of man came not to be ministered unto, but to minister, and to give his life a ransom for many" (Mk. 10⁴⁵). That this should be the rule of His life and that it should be kept is the sanctification, the obedience of the Man Jesus.

Jesus' sinlessness obviously consists in His direct admission of the meaning of the incarnation. Unlike Adam, as the "second Adam" He does not wish to be as God, but in Adam's nature acknowledges before God an Adamic being, the state and position of fallen man, and bears the wrath of God which must fall upon this man, not as a fate but as a righteous necessary wrath. He does not avoid the burden of this state and position but takes the conditions and consequences upon Himself.

It is just this that we continually refuse to do. In this consists the rebellion of sin, in which daily and hourly man repeats the ancient rebellion of Adam. For as Adam refused to preserve the order of Paradise, i.e., the limits of his creatureliness, man as Adam's child refuses to fit into the order of restoration. He will not understand and admit that he is flesh, stands under judgment, and can only live by grace. He will not admit that God is right in His verdict upon him, and then cling entirely to this God's mercy. At the very least he insists upon still standing and walking on his own feet. He wants, at least in co-operation with what God does, to " save his life " ($\sigma\hat{\omega}\sigma\alpha\iota$ $\tau\dot{\eta}\nu$ $\psi\upsilon\chi\dot{\eta}\nu$ $\alpha\dot{\upsilon}\tauο\hat{\upsilon}$, Mk. 8[35]). By that very process he loses his life. On that very rock he suffers shipwreck. For by that very process sin in the flesh is not judged, but rather is committed afresh. By that very process man does afresh what Adam did. It is otherwise with Jesus. He made good what Adam perverted. He judged sin in the flesh by recognising the order of reconciliation, i.e., put in a sinner's position He bowed to the divine verdict and commended Himself solely to the grace of God. That is His hallowing, His obedience, His sinlessness. Thus it does not consist in an ethical heroism, but precisely in a renunciation of any heroism, including the ethical. He is sinless not in spite of, but just because of His being the friend of publicans and sinners and His dying between the malefactors. In this sinlessness He is according to Paul the " second Adam " (1 Cor. 15[45f.]), the One who by His obedience sets the many before God as righteous, whose righteous act confronts in reconciliation the transgressions of the many who by following Adam are involved in hopeless death. In this righteous act there is achieved a justification for all, a justification that brings life ($\delta\iota\kappa\alpha\dot{\iota}\omega\sigma\iota\varsigma$ $\zeta\omega\hat{\eta}\varsigma$, Rom. 5[12f.] ; 1 Cor. 15[22]). By the Word of God becoming Adam the continuity of this Adamic existence is broken and the continuity of a new Adamic existence is opened up. But the continuity of the old Adamic existence is broken, just because unshielded by illusions, circumvented by no artifices, its truth is simply recognised, its needs are borne openly and readily.

This is the revelation of God in Christ. For where man admits his lost state and lives entirely by God's mercy—which no man did, but only the God-Man Jesus Christ has done—God Himself is manifest. And by that God reconciled the world to Himself. For where man claims no right for himself, but concedes all rights to God alone—which no man did, but only the God-Man Jesus Christ has done—the world is drawn out of its enmity towards God and reconciled to God.

Upon the actual basis of the New Testament understanding of the statement as to the sinlessness of Jesus we cannot describe the questions involved as altogether opaque, even though we cannot and will not try to solve the mystery to which they point. On the one hand the New Testament has treated the *vere homo* so seriously that it has portrayed the obedience of Jesus throughout as a genuine struggle to obey, as a seeking and finding. In Lk. 2[40] it speaks. of a " growing and waxing strong," and in Lk. 2[52] it speaks of a $\pi\rho\omicron\kappa\dot{ο}\pi\tau\epsilon\iota\nu$ (strictly speaking, an extension by blows, as a smith stretches metal with hammers, *Griech. H.W.B.* by Pape-Sengebusch, *s.v.*) of Jesus in wisdom, in stature and in favour with God and men. Moreover the temptation narrative (Mt. 4[1ff.]) obviously describes the very opposite of a mock battle, and it would be wrong to conceive of it as a merely " external molestation by Satan," to reject it as an " inward temptation and trial " of Jesus. To the *vere homo* there also belongs what we call man's inner nature. (Opposing B. Bartmann, *Lehrb. d. Dogm.*[7] vol. I, 1928, p. 360.) Equally vital is the saying $\pi\epsilon\rho\dot{\iota}\lambda\upsilon\pi\dot{ο}\varsigma$ $\dot{\epsilon}\sigma\tau\iota\nu$ $\dot{\eta}$ $\psi\upsilon\chi\dot{\eta}$ $\mu\omicron\upsilon$ (Mk. 14[34]), and " My God, my God, why hast thou forsaken me ? " (Mk. 15[34]).

Jesus " in the days of his flesh, when he had offered up prayers and supplications with strong crying and tears unto him that was able to save him from death, καίπερ ὢν υἱός yet learned obedience by the things which he suffered " (Heb. 5⁷ˡ·). The New Testament has nowhere attempted to describe this " learning," and it is always an impertinence on our part to attempt to imitate it. The New Testament simply points to the facts of the case. But from the facts of the case no deductions can be made without obscuring the point at issue in the assertion of sinlessness. The point is that, faced with God, Jesus did not run away from the state and situation of fallen man, but took it upon Himself, lived it and bore it Himself as the eternal Son of God. How could He have done so, if in His human existence He had not been exposed to real inward temptation and trial, if like other men He had not trodden an inner path, if He had not cried to God and wrestled with God in real inward need ? It was in this wrestling, in which He was in solidarity with us to the uttermost, that there was done that which is not done by us, the will of God. " In that he himself hath suffered, being tempted, he is able to succour them that are tempted " (Heb. 2¹⁸)—not otherwise. From this may be seen how right was the attitude of those who in the so-called monothelite controversy of the 7th century upheld and eventually led to victory the doctrine that along with the true human nature of the God-Man there must likewise not be denied His true, human will, different from the will of God although never independent of it.

Of course, the meaning of the New Testament is that Jesus cannot sin, that the eternal Word of God is immune from temptation even in the flesh, that Jesus is bound to win in this struggle. But that this is the case is the mystery of revelation which it attests. It is the truth of the event of the reality of Jesus Christ. It can be understood only as this truth breaking forth in event. The sinlessness of Jesus thus does not admit of a systematic connexion with the fact that here a true man had a serious struggle, but only of establishment and acknowledgment in its historical connexion with that fact. He who struggled here and won is He who was bound to win, He who when He entered the contest had already won. He really had no awareness of sin. That is the truth of the *vere Deus*. The New Testament makes this assertion because it is aware of His resurrection. The resurrection was the revelation of the *vere Deus*, the revelation of the fact that the Word was made *flesh*. But this revelation is in contrast to its background that the Word was made flesh. To understand, we shall have to travel together, here as everywhere, the way indicated from the cross to the resurrection of Christ. [I, 2, pp. 155–159]

4. FAITH AND MIRACLES

In Mk. 11²³ the saying about the faith which can move mountains is introduced in relation to the cursing of the fig-tree. In Mt. 17²⁰, however, its connexion is with the failure of the disciples to cure the epileptic boy, and in Lk. 17⁶ (where it is a tree that is moved) it is Jesus' answer to the request : " Increase our faith." In the two latter versions a new feature as compared with Mark is the comparison with the grain of mustard seed, which obviously implies that what is needed is not a great or massive or heroic or striking faith, easily recognisable as such, but that even a minimum faith is enough for the performance of what is impossible (a miracle) to men. This faith as a grain of mustard seed, to which the promise is given, obviously has nothing whatever to do with the little faith which is so common in Matthew, which always has the form of direct speech (ὀλιγόπιστοι), and which is used always as a term of reproach, indicating a faith which is doubtful and vacillating, as in Mt. 14³¹. What is meant is clearly a faith which is minimal and insignificant from the quantitative standpoint (in respect of its physical intensity or power of external manifestation), but distinguished by a definite quality even in this supreme littleness. Those who have this faith are promised that their word will have the power to reduce even a mountain to this unaccustomed " obedience " (Lk. 17[6]). " And nothing shall be impossible unto you " (Mt. 17[20]). In all three versions the saying has to do with the faith to which the disciples are called for the fulfilment of their commission in the world. They, too, are to preach the kingdom of God which has drawn near, not only in words but, as we are told with a startling definiteness in Mt. 10[8], by healing the sick, raising the dead, cleansing the lepers, driving out demons. We will return to this commission, and thus to the saying about this faith as a grain of mustard seed, at a much later stage, when we have to speak of the sending out of the community into the world. But the saying is important in our present context because, in general terms, it describes the faith which stands in a positive relationship to miracles as one which is definitely qualified— so qualified that even where it is present only in the minutest quantity it is the faith which has the promise of the performance of miracles.

This particular faith is obviously meant when Jesus reproves His disciples after the calming of the storm, asking : " Why are ye so fearful ? how is it that ye have no faith ? " (Mk. 4[40]) ; or when He encourages the ruler of the synagogue : " Be not afraid, only believe " (Mk. 5[36]) ; or when He asks the two blind men : " Believe ye that I am able to do this ? ", and when they reply that they do, says to them : " According to your faith be it unto you " (Mt. 9[28f.]) ; or when He says to the hesitating father of the epileptic boy : " All things are possible to him that believeth " (Mk. 9[23]) ; or when it is said that He saw the faith of those who uncovered the roof where He was and let down the bed on which the sick of the palsy lay (Mk. 2[4f.]) ; or when He says to the woman of Canaan : " O woman, great is thy faith : be it unto thee even as thou wilt " (Mt. 15[28]) ; or when He says of the centurion of Capernaum : " I have not found so great faith, no, not in Israel " (Mt. 8[10]) ; or when finally the short stereotyped formula occurs twice in Matthew and four times in Luke : " Thy faith hath saved thee " (ἡ πίστις σου σέσωκέ σε). With only one exception (Lk. 7[50]), this always stands in relation to the occurrence of a miracle, and in almost every instance it is clearly brought into direct connexion with the actual moment or event of its occurrence, which it seems to describe and explain ; whereas the other sayings that we have quoted (apart from the rebuke of the disciples) look forward to a moment of occurrence which has still to come. In every case it is obvious that in the twofold sense of that saying we have to do with the faith which it calls faith as a grain of mustard seed. That is to say, it is a faith which (a) is insignificant as regards its external appearance, and usually has to be the subject either of enquiry or even a definite demand. In many cases it is the faith of Gentiles, and never of those who habitually stand in faith or can point to it in any recognisable form. But it is also (b) a faith which for all its insignificance has a specific nature or quality in relation to which there is the prospect of a miracle, and in the light of which (according to that formula) it can, if it has it, be explained as that which brings about the miracle. And it is quite obvious from the Gospel records that Jesus definitely expected to find this faith as a grain of mustard seed in His actions, and that He did in fact meet with it.

What is this quality of the faith which has a share in the working of miracles and which Jesus expects or misses or sometimes welcomes in men ? What is it that makes it a faith which, even though it is no greater than a grain of mustard seed, can move mountains—a faith for which all things are possible ? What is this πίστις of which that formula can even say that it saves men ? This first question is decided by our explanation of the saying in Mt. 9[28], which is the only concrete indication in the Synoptics of the actual content of faith : " Believe ye that I am able to do this ? " (ὅτι δύναμαι τοῦτο ποιῆσαι). This might be taken to mean : Do you really accept the fact, are you convinced, that beyond and above the natural and human possibilities which you know there may be a higher possibility which you do not know, perhaps an absolute and unconditional possibility, which is so great and wonderful that it can, for example, make the blind to see ? Are you really persuaded that I control this higher possibility, and that if I will I can do this for you, giving you sight ? " Believe ye that I am able to do this ? " would then mean : " Do you believe in miracles, and that I can work miracles ? " But it is plain that a " faith " of this kind would be faith in Jesus only in so far as the two blind men accepted Him as a bearer and agent of this higher power who could of course be replaced by any other human person similarly gifted and equipped. It is plain that it would be faith in God, if at all, only in so far as they might (but did not necessarily) regard this power as the power of God or a God—a name which could easily be replaced by any other, e.g., by "higher nature" or even "super-nature." It is plain, finally, that it would as such be a strong philosophical conviction to this effect, fashioned as such convictions are usually fashioned and now finding this necessary and willing *ad hoc* expression. But was this really the faith for which Jesus asked, which they confessed with their : " Yea, Lord," and which He then had in mind when He answered (v. 29) : " According to your faith be it unto you " ? Again, was this really the faith which He missed in His disciples during the storm, or which He found in the centurion and the woman of Canaan and those who bore the sick of the palsy ; the faith to which He summoned the ruler of the synagogue ; the faith which has the promise that all things are possible to it, even the moving of a mountain ; the faith of which He can say again and again that it hath saved thee ? It is surely evident that if this explanation of the question is correct, the way in which the word " faith " is here (and in other passages) used by Jesus according to the tradition is very different from the use of πίστις and πιστεύειν in the rest of the New Testament, and is at variance even with the literal sense of the terms. It is not with a philosophical possibility and its supposed realisation that faith is concerned in the New Testament, nor is it from anything of this sort that it receives its nature and form. Is there any reason, then, why the present instances should be an exception ?

It is to be noted, however, that the cry of the two blind men is actually : " Thou Son of David, have mercy on us." They do not turn to a wonderworker who, if he had not been Jesus of Nazareth, might well have been someone else. They turn to Jesus as the King of Israel, beside whom there can be no other. They do not ask concerning the operation of an anonymous higher power or omnipotence, nature or super-nature. They ask concerning the act of the God of Israel fulfilling His promise in the existence of the Son of David. Their cry is not inspired by any conviction (even a supernaturalistic), nor is it uttered with the corresponding expectation. It is a cry for mercy wrung out of their misery. Above all, it is a cry in which they recognise and confess the Son of David and therefore the God of Israel and His fulfilled promise, taking Him seriously and claiming Him for their own need. Therefore what they are asked is whether they did really believe this (τοῦτο) as their cry seemed to suggest. Did they really believe that the Son of David and therefore the God of Israel had come, and that He would have mercy on them, and could take their misery from them and dismiss it from the world ? Did they really believe that He, Jesus, had the power to do this ? And it is as they confessed this faith that Jesus touched their eyes and Himself confessed their faith : " According to (this) your faith be it unto you." And what took place was not at all unusual or strange—except that it had the strangeness, the newness, of the kingdom of God which had drawn near. " Their eyes were opened."

We may now consider the other passages to see if the faith demanded or missed or found by Jesus did not always have this nature and form in which it corresponds, although with a peculiar intensity, to the meaning of the term and its use in the rest of the New Testament. Generally speaking, is it not always the privileged and characteristic act of sufferers afflicted with a vital physical need in their relationship to the faithful God of Israel fulfilling His promise, which means, concretely, in their relationship to Jesus the Deliverer, in whom the hope of Israel has found its fulfilment ? When we are told in these passages that men believed, this means that they were in this relationship, which is only secondarily a matter of mind or will or disposition and primarily a matter of being. They belonged already to Jesus the Deliverer because they were already found by Him before they knew Him, because they were recognised by Him. They thus responded with their own recognition of Him as Lord. They had the freedom—this is the climax reached in these passages—to throw themselves and their vital physical need at His feet as it were, and in His person at the feet of the faithful God of Israel. They had the freedom to recognise and confess and claim Him as the One who could save them totally and therefore in this affliction, thus healing them physically, making them whole, restoring to them a normal life, rescuing them from the threatening power of death. He was under no compulsion to do this. But He could do it. For the fact that He had come from God as Israel's Saviour, that He was present with them as such and present in this way, that they belonged to Him as sufferers, and could count themselves His, and throw themselves at His feet and beseech Him—all this was God's free and absolutely unmerited grace, His sheer pity, to His people, to the world, to each individual, and therefore to them. They were thus confronted with the fact that, as an overflowing of this mercy, their Saviour saw also their particular physical need and could avert and remove and take it from them. There was no question, of course, of His having to do this, of their having a right to demand it, for in relation to Him they had no right to assert, no claim to anything. But they had the freedom to trust Him for this overflow of His mercy, to be absolutely certain that in the power of His free grace He could also do this. The freedom of this confidence was the faith to which He called some, which He missed in others, and sometimes found. The distinctive feature of the New Testament faith in miracles is that it was faith in Jesus and therefore in God as the faithful and merciful God of the covenant with Israel ; and that in this way and as such it was this confidence in His power.

Alongside Mt. 9²⁷ᶠ· we should set the story of the man born blind in Jn. 9¹ᶠ· As a commentary on the " Believe ye that I am able to do this " it is all the more instructive because the decisive question is now explicitly raised (v. 35) : " Dost thou believe on the Son of man ? "—and the whole story takes place in reverse as it were, thus reflecting as in a mirror the answer to our problem. This time the miracle takes place right at the beginning. We are given an active demonstration of the free grace of God in the specific form of the removal of the blindness of this man. In the first instance no question is raised either as to the sin of the man or his parents or as to the faith of the man, who has not even expressed a desire for healing. He is simply given his sight, almost, as it were, over his head, and quite irrespective of what he was or was not in relation to Jesus. " The works of God were to be made manifest in him " (v. 3). When Jesus had anointed his eyes, he had only to obey, to wash in the pool of Siloam, and he could see, and those around realised that he could see. In the long interrogation to which he was subjected he could only say that it was " a man that is called Jesus " (v. 11) who had done this, and given him this command, so that he could now see. When he was pressed, he admitted that he regarded Jesus as a prophet (v. 17). He gave no judgment whether or not He was a sinner (v. 25), but then argued, rather more loudly, that He could hardly have this power from God if He was a sinner. " But if any man be a worshipper of God (θεοσεβής), and doeth his will, him he heareth " (v. 31). And : " If this man were not of God, he could do nothing " (v. 33). When he said this he was cast out by the Pharisees with the explanation that he, too, was a sinner, and if anything even more so than Jesus (" altogether born in sins," v. 34). But this again obviously took place over his head as the text sees it, for he did not realise the true meaning and significance of what he said. His role is only that of object and not subject in the whole occurrence and the disturbance which it caused. But Jesus now meets him a second time (v. 35 f.), and He asks him directly, without any preparation or explanation : " Dost thou believe on the Son of man ? " He replies with a counter-question which clearly betrays his ignorance : " Who is he, Lord, that I might believe on him ? And Jesus said unto him, Thou hast both seen him, and it is he that talketh with thee. And he said, Lord, I believe. And he worshipped him " (προσεκύνησεν αὐτῷ).

In the first instance, therefore, we have simply the presence of Jesus in face of this little piece of human misery. In the first instance the sufferer experiences the mighty action of His pity and is enabled to see. For a long time there neither is nor can be any talk of his faith, but only of its object, only of the One in whom He was ultimately able and forced to confess that he believed, and before whom he then prostrated himself as before the presence and revelation of God Himself. And in the first instance it is only as through a veil that we even see this object of his faith. He does not reveal Himself as such to this blind man who could later see. The reference is only to the " man that is called Jesus," whom the Pharisees, unable to deny what had so obviously taken place, described as a sinner, and in respect of whom the healed man himself could only appeal again and again to what had happened, to the fact that he could now see. More under pressure than of himself, he is ready to go to the length of saying that he does not regard Jesus as a sinner, but as One who fears God. But that is all. Yet it is not quite all, for there is another side to the matter which emerges even under this veil. This is that the blind man obeyed Jesus and, in contrast to his more cautious parents (v. 18 f.), steadfastly confessed both the favour which he had received and the One who had conferred it—and whom he knew only by name. He finally allowed even the very dangerous saying to be wrested from him that He was necessarily from God. Are we not forced to see and say that he obviously belonged factually, objectively and ontologically to the Unknown who had done this. " Thou art his disciple " was the accusation of the Pharisees (v. 28), and they at once understood and condemned his final saying as a definite confession, casting him out as a sinner, making him as it were from the very first a witness who suffered with Him. This factual, objective, ontological reality—that Jesus was with Him and therefore, although he did not know it, he was with Jesus—was brought to light by Jesus' question concerning his faith. We are not speaking about a concealed faith of the man himself, but about its real presupposition—who and what Jesus was for him, and who and what he himself was for Jesus, even before he believed. For Jesus was for him the One who brought the free grace of God in its overflow as physical healing. And he was for Jesus the one who received this overflow, and was therefore confronted with Jesus as the One who brought this free grace. The two stood in this relationship the one to the other. They were genuinely bound together in this way. Without desiring it, without even understanding it, blind in this respect too, he had actually experienced what the Son of Man could do. This was the real presupposition of his faith. It had now only to be brought to light, as took place in the final conversation. The One whose capacity, whose power, the blind man had experienced, who had given him his sight, and could therefore bless him, was far more than a mere prophet or a man who feared God. He was the Son of Man whom all the prophets and those that feared God in Israel had hoped for and expected. He was the merciful God of Israel in the act of fulfilling His promises. It was only natural that as an Israelite he should be ready to believe in the God of Israel and therefore in the Son of Man. But what was the value of this readiness when he did not see the One in whom he was prepared to believe, when he did not recognise the One who fulfilled the divine promises ? " Who is he, Lord, that I might believe on him ? " He really did not see or know Him, although He was not merely able to be seen and known, but corporally present as the neighbour who had shown this mercy on him and was already believed in virtue of this demonstrated power. But this door could not be opened from outside. It could be opened only from inside, by Jesus Himself. As the Son of Man made Himself known to him—" it is he that talketh with thee "—He opened the eyes of faith as well as the physical eyes. With irresistible power, it took place that he was awakened and called to faith. He was hurled into that *proskynesis* as though he had been struck by lightning. All the different elements were necessary for this to happen : the factual, objective, ontological relationship between Jesus and Himself ; in this relationship the miracle of free grace in its overflow ; the physical encounter with Jesus as the actualisation of this relationship ; and again, and supremely, the decisive fact that Jesus Himself spoke of Himself, that of Himself He gave Himself to be known by him through His Word, that as the object of his faith, which He was already, He made Himself also the Creator of his faith.

The remarkable lesson of Jn. 9[1f.] is that man starts at the very point (the miracle of Jesus and therefore Jesus Himself and therefore God) to which we see him moving in Mt. 9[27]. Faith is not merely his entrance into the kingdom of God revealed in the miracle, but also his exit from it. It is not merely the root, but the fruit. To sum up, it is faith qualified in this twofold sense—man's turning to Jesus and His power upon the basis of the fact that Jesus has turned to man in His power. When all this is borne in mind, faith in miracles as the New Testament sees it cannot possibly be confused with the monstrosity of an acceptance of the possibility and actuality of all kinds of miracles of omnipotence.

And now we must address ourselves to another problem which forces itself upon us in this matter. This is the question of the connexion which links faith to miracle on the one hand, and miracle to faith on the other.

Let us take the second aspect of the question first. What is the way which leads from miracle to faith ? In the light of the story in Jn. 9[1f.] it can hardly be contested that the connexion does also have this direction, that it does also include in itself this way. And this finds theoretical and rather harsh formulation in Jn. 10[37f.] : " If I do not the works of my Father, believe me not. But if I do, though ye believe not me, believe the works : that ye may know, and believe, that the Father is in me, and I in him." It is likely enough that Jn. 4[48] is also to be understood in this positive sense : " Except ye see signs and wonders, ye will not believe." And in the first ending of the Fourth Gospel in 20[31] we again have the categorical statement that the signs which Jesus did in the presence of His disciples are written in this book " that ye might believe that Jesus is the Christ, the Son of God ; and that believing ye might have life through his name." It is unmistakeable that in the context of the life-act of Jesus as it calls to faith and awakens faith miracles have an important and, rightly understood, indispensable function. He would not have been the One He was if He had not also done these acts. And since, as the One He was, He was one long summons to faith in the action of God as it took place in Him, the power of His summons was also the power of His acts. But some clarifications are needed at this point. It is a matter of His acts in their specific character as the omnipotent acts of the mercy of the God of Israel acting and revealing Himself in faithfulness to His promise ; in their character as signs, as manifestations of the kingdom of God drawn near. They led to faith where they were seen and understood in this character, i.e., where Jesus Himself revealed Himself in them as the Bringer of the free grace of God addressed to men, and where He Himself was recognised as such by men. Their occurrence in itself and as such did not lead anyone to faith : " Though he had done so many miracles before them, yet they believed not on him " (Jn. 12[37])—but only to that θαυμάζειν. The only practical result could be the *cul de sac* which is described in Mt. 11[20f.] in relation to the unrepentant cities of Galilee. Indeed, there might even be a heightening and explosion of the offence already taken at Him, as we see from John's presentation. At the conclusion of the story of Lazarus (Jn. 11⁴⁷ᶠ·) it was the acts of Jesus which led the council to resolve on His destruction because of the fear that the people might be influenced. It was not at all the case that in themselves and as such the acts led to faith—merely as the unusual phenomena as which they immediately presented themselves to everyone's notice. They were not mechanically effective instruments to produce faith. They were not what they are presupposed to be in the question of Jn. 6³⁰ : " What sign shewest thou then, that we may see, and believe thee ? " If they were demanded from Jesus as necessary conditions of the faith which He expected, as " miraculous credentials," —" He sighed deeply in his spirit " (Mk. 8¹¹ᶠ· and par.) and refused to do them. His concrete aim in acting—and all His acts have a definite individual end—was to help, to do good, in His conflict for man against the power of chaos and death which oppresses him. And in this concrete form His action was that of the Bringer and Revealer of the kingdom. Those who did not ask for His mercy, and therefore for the Son of David, the Son of Man, for the faithfulness and omnipotence of the God of Israel, asked in vain for the acts of Jesus, and, even if they saw them, saw them in vain. They might well see an act of power, but they did not see the sign of the coming kingdom. They could not come to faith in this way. The Word of Jesus was needed to expound His acts, to light them up from within, as the acts of the mercy of God, the warlike acts of the Deliverer, the promised King of Israel who had now appeared, and therefore as the signs of the kingdom of God which had now drawn near. And it needed obedience to the Word of Jesus to accept this exposition, to receive the light which shone in His acts, and to awaken to faith in so doing. The mere fact that His acts took place was not then an infallible means to this result, any more than the mere fact that His words were spoken. It was only Jesus Himself, acting in His words and works, who infallibly led men to faith. He did so as He was " mighty in deed and word before God and all the people " (Lk. 24¹⁹). But it was He Himself who did so in and through both His deeds and words. Thus the faith awakened by both, by the totality of His life-act, was faith in Himself, in the One who had sent Him and was in Him, in God's free grace. It was a faith in miracles, but it was a concrete and not an abstract faith in miracles, a faith which was directed by the miracles to the One who did them, to His purpose, to the revelation which took place in Him, to the mercy of God active in Him. Both in the Synoptics and in John, therefore, faith (even though it may be faith in miracles in the concrete sense that it has its origin in a miracle) is not at all faith in the miracles, or the inconceivability of their happening, or, generally, in their possibility or actuality. On the contrary, it is a recognition—in the light of the miracle which has happened, inspired and instructed and awakened and evoked by its happening, by its specific inconceivability—of the One who has acted in this inconceivable way, of the will and purpose and lordship of the One who has spoken through these acts of power and mercy, giving Himself to be known by them as the Son of David, the Son of Man, the King in the kingdom of free grace. It is to Him and not to the miracle that the believer gives his attention and interest. It is to Him and not to the miracle that he gives the glory. In all the majestic incomprehensibility of the miracle He Himself is the true and decisive factor which makes it incomprehensible. It is a miracle which He does, but what counts is He Himself and not the miracle. What is learned from the miracle is who and what He is—the Lord. It might just as well have been learned from His Word. Sometimes it has already been learned from His Word. That is why there is no strict pragmatics in the New Testament. There is no rule that must always derive in practice from the experience of miracle. Even the Word of Jesus is an incomprehensible act. It has the dimension of miracle. It has the character of an act of divine mercy and power. That is why the two blind men in Mt. 9²⁷ᶠ· (as distinct from the man born blind in Jn. 9¹ᶠ·), and many others in the New Testament, do not derive their faith from a miracle which they have already experienced, but go forward to the miracle which they are to experience with hands which seem to be empty. It is decisive, however, for the true hearing of the Word of Jesus that it, too, should belong to this dimension, that the faith which is based on a hearing of His Word should have this dimension, that it should therefore be faith in the One who in the mercy and power of God can also work miracles. To the extent that Jesus Himself is the One who is "mighty in deed and word," to the extent that He is not only light but as such life, there is no faith that does not have its origin also in miracle, that does not in some way rest on the miracles of Jesus, or, more precisely, on Jesus Himself as the great Wonderworker. If Jesus had not been this, how could He have been the Bringer of the kingdom of God, and therefore recognisable as the Saviour of man from the power of the devil and death ? How could His Word have been distinguished from purely moral teaching and religious instruction, such as could be and was actually given by the scribes ? How could it have proved itself to be a Word of power, the proclamation of the dawn of a new age ? Jn. 10³⁷ is relevant in this connexion : "If I do not the works of my Father, believe me not." And if in faith in Him it could have been overlooked and concealed that He was the great Wonderworker, how could faith really have as its theme and content Himself as the herald of the kingdom of God, and not just a deserving benefactor and individual and social reformer ? Jn. 4⁴⁸ may well have a lesson for us at this point : "Except ye see signs and wonders, ye will not believe." The necessity of the way from miracle to faith is ultimately grounded in the fact that a total faith, i.e., a faith which grasps the total liberation and renewal of man in Jesus, can derive only from the totality in which Jesus is really the Saviour of men and manifest as such.

But there is also a way which leads from faith to miracle. We will tackle the question at its most difficult point and ask point-blank what is really meant by the formula : "Thy faith hath saved thee " ? And our explanation will be decisive for an understanding of the function assigned to faith in other passages where sufferers are asked to believe in relation to acts of power for which they ask or which they simply need. It makes matters easier (in spite of appearances to the contrary) that the formula is not as Luther translated it : "Thy faith hath helped thee." The word "help" is weaker, but it so easily suggests something that Luther himself obviously did not intend—that there is a partial co-operation of man in the occurrence of the miracle which happens to him. But the original σέσωκέν σε ("hath saved thee") does not refer merely to a part of the process. It refers to the whole. I maintain that this eases the exegetical situation because it does at least exclude the idea of a co-operation in the working of the miracle. "Saving" is an action in which there is a saviour and a saved, but not a co-operation of the two. The general reference of the formula is to man's salvation generally from the power of darkness, but also and concretely from the specific physical ailments which afflict him, the curing of his eyes or ears or limbs, his preservation from the lordship of φθορά which threatens and torments him. Of this salvation the formula seems to say that it is altogether the act and work of man, of his faith. The contradiction to which this gives rise seems unavoidable and intolerable. For is it not Jesus, and in what He says and does God, who saves man in both the general and the concrete sense ? "Jesus Christ maketh thee whole" (Ac. 9³⁴), says Peter to Aeneas. How is it, then, that in this formula man's faith can be called the saviour ? The obvious difficulty is sharply brought out by the puzzling relationship between two other sayings of Jesus. For in Mk. 10²⁷ we read : "With God all things are possible," but in Mk. 9²³ : "All things are possible to him that believeth." The problem would be vexatiously insoluble if we did not remember that in the miracle stories and throughout the New Testament faith is only secondarily described as a disposition or attitude or act of man. It is this, but the decisive thing is that it also reaches behind this whole sphere to a primary thing from which it proceeds as a human action when man is awakened and called to it. In the New Testament sense the word " faith " does not only describe the believing thought and knowledge and confession and activity of man. It also embraces the presupposition of all these things, which as such does not belong to the mental sphere, but the sphere of reality. We have called it the factual, objective, ontological standing of man—not all men, but certain men—in a concrete relationship with Jesus Christ and the God who is active and revealed in Him. Those who believe do so in this status—because, as Paul says, they are " in Christ," they belong to Him, they are set at His side. It is in virtue of this that they believe. The act or work of their faith derives from their being, just as a shoot does from a root. Who can say where the root ends and the shoot begins ? What is a shoot if it no longer grows from the root (as on a tree-trunk which has been cut down) ? Is not the only sure distinction between the two the fact that the one is visible and the other is not ? Those who believe in the New Testament sense do so, as their own free act, because they have the freedom to do so from the One in whom they believe. And in the exercise of this freedom they reach back to that which is before their faith and independent of it. They cling to Jesus, to the God active and revealed in Him. And they are sustained by this ontological reality both behind and before. Or rather, they are drawn and set in motion by it like an iron bar by a magnet, and in such a way, again, that it is futile to try to differentiate between the attraction and their own movement. The secret of faith is that as the work of man it has this origin and this goal. That is why Heb. 11^1 can call it the ὑπόστασις or actuality of that which is hoped for and the ἔλεγχος or demonstration of that which is not seen. That is why Paul can make the important statement in Rom. $3^{21f.}$ that a man is not justified in the verdict of God, and therefore in truth, by any work that is demanded by the Law, but διὰ πίστεως, ἐκ πίστεως, πίστει, as πιστεύων. He is justified in truth because in faith he has both his origin and goal in this One who is in truth, in Jesus Christ. It is obviously in this sense that we can and may and must say that a man is saved, healthy, whole, preserved from death, by his faith ; that the experience of the divine act of mercy even in the physical sphere is not merely promised to his faith, but that faith itself is that which accomplishes it, the saviour ; that faith is that which redeems the believer from his own particular need, but also, as is presupposed in the charge to the disciples in Mt. 10^8, that which by the ministry of the believer can and should redeem others from their specific needs. " All things are possible to him that believeth " (Mk. 9^{23}). " Said I not unto thee, that, if thou wouldest believe, thou shouldest see the glory of God ? " (Jn. 11^{40}). And again : " Verily, verily, I say unto you, He that believeth on me, the works that I do shall he do also ; and greater works than these shall he do " (Jn. 14^{12}). Also : " He that believeth on me . . . out of his belly shall flow rivers of living water " (Jn. 7^{38}). We can accept these sayings because they are said to men about their faith by the One (Jesus Himself) whose sovereignty is not rivalled or diminished by what He ascribes to their faith (their πιστεύειν εἰς ἐμέ), but revealed in its full compass. When He says this about their faith He does not do despite to the glory of God, but gives it the greater praise. Everything would, of course, be obscured and falsified if we abstracted from the fact that in what is said about faith it is a matter of what He Himself ascribes to faith in Him, or if, in a further abstraction, we looked at the secondary means, at the human action of faith as such, at its mental fulfilment, thus regarding and admiring and broadcasting this aspect of faith, the believer himself, as the one who accomplishes the divine act, as his own saviour, and as the saviour of others in his ministry to them. The declaration of Heb. 11^1 and the Pauline doctrine of justification can only be obscured and falsified by these abstractions. If we are guilty of these abstractions, we need not be surprised if the way from faith to miracle seems both theoretically and practically to be one long absurdity which it is better to recognise and abandon as such, making a fresh start before the disillusionments and errors become too great. We understand all these sayings with the clarity and truth which they have as said by Jesus if we accept the fact that in the New Testament sense of the word the human action of faith can only represent the transition from this origin to this goal, from the free election of man to his free calling, or, to reduce it to its simplest and most concrete terms, from Jesus to Jesus : and if we then recognise that as this transition it has a real part in the being and power of this origin and goal, in Jesus Himself, from whom and to whom we can believe. When we look to the place from and to which faith goes we see in truth and clarity that it is indeed " the substance of things hoped for, the evidence of things not seen " ; that it does really justify the sinner ; that it does really save the sufferer and through him other sufferers ; that nothing is in fact impossible to it ; that the way from faith to miracle is indeed open and can be traversed. So great is the sovereignty of Jesus, and the glory of the God active and revealed in Him, that for faith in Him this way is actually open and can be traversed. These sayings do not claim too much if we let them say only what they do say, and let it be said by the One who said it. As faith in Him faith is actually that which saves man, and all things are actually possible for it. The inner delimitation of what is promised is self-evident. Because the reference is not to the human action of faith as such, but to it only in relation to its origin and goal, it does not ascribe to faith any possibilities or capacities that man might imagine or desire for himself or in the service of others, or that he might even try to assume in a burst (or better perhaps a spasm) of self-inspired credulity. It ascribes to it the true force in which Jesus Himself acted : the force of the kingdom of God drawn near ; of the faithfulness and mercy of the God of Israel ; of that spirit which is not a random spirit but the Holy Spirit. The way from faith to miracle would close at once—indeed, it would never be open—if the power of faith were desired and claimed as a power in which man had the capacity to do just as his desire or fancy led him. The promise is that as faith in Jesus and the God active and revealed in Him faith has the force which is proper to it under the discipline and in the concretion of this origin and goal, and in the exercise of which it is wholly and utterly this faith. But with this determination and limitation there is actually ascribed to it an unconditional force. We may well realise how very different is our own situation from that of the men of the New Testament at this point. But this need not prevent us from stating that the faith proclaimed in the New Testament and lived by men according to its witness was of such a kind that this unconditional force was ascribed and promised to it, and it could experience and exercise it. It had the freedom to do this. [IV, 2, pp. 233–242]

5. JESUS AND THE NATURAL ORDERS

Attention should first be paid to what we might call the passive conservatism of Jesus. Rather curiously, Jesus accepts and allows many things which we imagine He ought to have attacked and set aside both in principle and practice, and which the community in which the Gospels arose had to a very large extent outgrown. It did not—and obviously could not—find it a source of vexation to have to maintain this aspect of the traditional picture.

He accepted the temple as quite self-evidently the house of His Father (Lk. 2⁴⁹). Even the astonishing act of cleansing it of the traders and moneychangers presupposes (Mk. 11¹⁷) that it is for Him the house of God. As we see from Mt. 23¹⁶ᶠ·, He does not take it, or the altar in it, less seriously but more seriously than the scribes and Pharisees. He assumes that the pious Israelite will still go up to it to bring his sacrifices (Mt. 5²³ᶠ·). When He Himself comes to Jerusalem, He does not teach in the streets and market-places, but daily in its forecourt (Mk. 12³⁵, 14⁴⁹). It is there that the Pharisee and publican make their prayers in the parable which brings out so strongly the difference between Himself and those around Him (Lk. 18[9f.]). We may also note the description of the conduct of His disciples in the closing verse of St. Luke's Gospel : " And they were continually in the temple, praising and blessing God." We may also recall that after His crucifixion, resurrection and ascension they still continued " daily with one accord in the temple."

But respect may also be seen for the order of the family, for according to Lk. 2[51] Jesus was at first subject to His parents in Nazareth. And in Mk. 7[11f.] He insisted that the duty of caring for father and mother must take precedence of all cultic obligations. We may also remember, with reservations, the provision which He made for His mother even on the cross, according to the saying handed down in Jn. 19[26].

Again, at least at the beginning of His teaching activity, He did not separate Himself from the Galilean synagogues (Mk. 1[21], 3[1]). Indeed, in Lk. 4[17f.] we have an obvious description of the way in which He adapted Himself to current synagogue practice. As concerns the Law, He not only protests (Mt. 5[17f.]) that He has not come to destroy it and the prophets, but He maintains that He has come to fulfil it, that not one jot or tittle shall pass from it until heaven and earth pass away, and that only those can be great in the kingdom of heaven who practise and teach even its most minute regulations. In Mt. 23[1f.] He concedes (even if ironically) that the scribes and Pharisees who expound the Law sit in Moses' seat, so that if the people and His disciples have to be warned against their example, they are also enjoined : " All therefore whatsoever they bid you observe, that observe and do." And if in Mt. 23[23f.] He accused them of hypocritically tithing mint and anise and cummin and omitting the weightier matters of the Law, judgment, mercy and faith, He added as something self-evident : " These ought ye to have done, and not to leave the other undone." In Mt. 13[52] again, He recognised the possibility of the scribe " instructed unto the kingdom of heaven " who " is like unto a householder, which bringeth forth out of his treasure things new and old "—the old as well as the new. The antithesis in Mt. 5[21f.] (" Ye have heard that it was said by them of old time. . . . But I say unto you . . .") certainly implies a more radical understanding of the Ten Commandments, but this in turn involves a recognition. And the same is true of the more precise exposition of the three traditional exercises of almsgiving, prayer and fasting in Mt. 6[1f.]. Even to the sayings on the cross, the tradition likes to see Jesus speaking in direct or indirect quotations from the Old Testament, and it sets Him generally in the confines, not merely of the world of religion, but of the special religious promise given to His own people. In Jn. 4[22] we even have the express saying that " salvation is of the Jews." The point is made so emphatically that it can be reported without any inhibitions that some of His more kindly-disposed contemporaries regarded Him merely as " a prophet, or as one of the prophets " (Mk. 6[15]), or perhaps a particularly " great " prophet (Lk. 7[16]). Similarly, in the later search for the so-called " historical Jesus " the suggestion could be made that He might be reduced to the figure of a (very outstanding) representative of a reformed and deepened Judaism.

It is also to be noted that we never see Him in direct conflict with the economic relationships and obligations of His time and background. We have only to think of the uncritical equanimity with which He accepted in the parables of the kingdom the existence of free employers of labour and employees dependent on their good will, of masters and servants and capital and interest, as though all these things were part of the legitimate *status quo*. In Lk. 16[1f.] unqualified praise was given to the οἰκονόμος, not as a deceiver, but at least as one who knew how to act wisely within the current arrangement in relation to rents. To the man who asks Him to see that his brother divides the inheritance fairly He replies in Lk. 12[13f.] that it is not His office to judge and divide in such matters. In this request, at any rate in the context in which Luke reports it, He sees only the cry of covetousness and not at all a cry for justice. " Ye have the poor with you always " (Mk. 14⁷), is His answer to the disciples who would have preferred a corresponding almsgiving to the woman's lavish devotion. He thus takes it as almost axiomatic that there must always be poor people—a thought which has given an illusory comfort to many in subsequent periods. And then in Lk. 16⁹, ¹¹ we are told to make friends with mammon (even the unrighteous mammon), and that the true riches (τὸ ἀληθινόν) will not be entrusted to those who are not " faithful " in relation to it. This was certainly not an invitation to maintain and augment our financial possessions as cleverly as possible—a process which later came to be regarded almost as a specific Christian virtue in certain parts of the Calvinistic world—but it is obviously not a summons to socialism.

Traces of the same attitude may finally be discerned in respect of political relationships and orders and disorders. It is freely presupposed in Mt. 5²⁵ᶠ· and elsewhere that there are judges and officers and prisons. That there are those who " think to rule over the nations " (the qualifying δοκοῦντες is to be noted), and do in fact exercise dominion and authority over them, is certainly described in Mk. 10⁴²ᶠ· as a procedure which is not to have any place in the community, but there is no direct criticism of it as such. The God who does not allow His elect to cry to Him in vain (Lk. 18¹ᶠ·) can appear in the guise of a notoriously unjust judge who neither fears God nor has any respect for man. It is expressly recognised by Jesus in Jn. 19¹¹ that Pilate has an authority even in relation to Himself, and that this is given him from above. In Mt. 26⁵² He did not allow Peter to offer any resistance to the Sanhedrin guard, but ordered him to put up his sword into its sheath. We do not find in the Gospels the slightest trace either of a radical repudiation of the dominion of Rome or Herod, or, for that matter, of any basic anti-imperialism or anti-militarism.

It is quite evident, however, and we must not ignore this aspect, that there is also no trace of any consistent recognition in principle. We can describe the attitude of Jesus as that of a passive conservatism in the further sense that it never amounted to more than a provisional and qualified respect (we might almost say toleration) in face of existing and accepted orders. Jesus acknowledged them and reckoned with them and subjected Himself to them and advised His disciples to do the same ; but He was always superior to them. And it was inevitable—we will now turn to this aspect—that this superiority, the freedom of the kingdom of God, should occasionally find concrete expression in His words and actions, that an occasional creaking should be unmistakeably heard in the timbers.

As regards the temple, He made it plain to the Pharisees in Mt. 12⁶ that there is something greater than the temple. When He paid the temple tax for Peter and Himself in Mt. 17²⁴ᶠ·, He did not do so on the basis of an unqualified recognition which the disciple was to regard as binding, but " lest we should offend them." For : " What thinkest thou, Simon ? of whom do the kings of the earth take custom or tribute ? of their own children, or of strangers ? " And when Peter answered : " Of strangers. Jesus saith unto him, Then are the children free."

Again, it was an unmistakeable assault on the order of the family, which is so firmly stabilised by nature and custom, when in Mk. 3³¹ᶠ He gave to His mother and brethren, who had " sent unto him, calling him," the following answer : " Who is my mother, or my brethren ? " and then, " looking round about on them that sat about him " : " Behold, my mother and my brethren." And we need hardly refer to the even harsher saying in the story of the wedding at Cana : τί ἐμοὶ καὶ σοί, " What have we in common ? " (Jn. 2⁴). It also has a most destructive sound in this respect when He replied to the man who wanted to be His disciple, but only after he had buried his father : " Let the dead bury their dead : but go thou and preach the kingdom of God " (Lk. 9⁵⁹ᶠ·), and to the other who asked if he might first make his farewells to those at home : " No man, having put his hand to the plough, and looking back, is fit for the kingdom of God " (Lk. 9⁶¹ᶠ·).

Again, there are breaches of the prevailing religious or cultic order. The accusation was made in Mk. 2¹⁸ᶠ· that His disciples did not fast like those of the Pharisees or even the Baptist. To those who raised this point He gave the puzzling answer : " Can the children of the bridechamber fast, while the bride-groom is with them ? " There was also the complaint in Mk. 7¹ᶠ· that His disciples neglected the purifications prescribed for meals : " Why walk not thy disciples according to the tradition of the elders ? " In reply, Jesus explains that it is not what is without but what is within that really defiles a man—the evil' thoughts and acts which come from the heart (Mk. 7¹⁴ᶠ·). Above all, there is His attitude to the sabbath, which allowed His disciples to satisfy their hunger by plucking ears of corn (Mk. 2²³ᶠ·) and Himself to heal on the sabbath (Mk. 3¹ᶠ· ; Jn. 5¹ᶠ·, 9¹ᶠ·). The offence which He gave and the reproaches which He incurred at this point were particularly severe. His answers were as follows : " Is it lawful to do good on the sabbath days, or to do evil ? to save life, or to kill ? But they held their peace " (Mk. 3⁴). " If a man on the sabbath day receive circumcision, that the law of Moses should not be broken ; are ye angry at me, because I have made a man every whit whole on the sabbath day ? " (Jn. 7²³). And above all : " The sabbath was made for man, and not man for the sabbath : therefore the Son of man is Lord also of the sabbath " (Mk. 2²⁷ᶠ·). As appears in Mk. 3⁶ and elsewhere, this breach was one of the most concrete things which made His destruction necessary in the eyes of His opponents.

Again, there are some striking breaches of the contemporary (and not only the contemporary) industrial and commercial and economic order. We may mention certain features in the parables which are definitely not taken from real life but are quite foreign to customary practice in these spheres. As Goethe pointed out, no sensible husbandman would ever sow as did the man in Mt. 13³ᶠ·, scattering his seed irrespectively over the path and stony ground and among thorns as well as on good ground. And what servants will ever be pre-pared to say that they are unprofitable when they have done all that they are required to do (Lk. 17¹⁰) ? What king will ever be so magnanimous as to pro-nounce unconditional freedom from punishment or guilt on the steward who has so obviously misappropriated that which was entrusted to him (Mt. 18²³ᶠ·) ? What owner of a vineyard will ever pay his workmen as did the owner in Mt. 20¹ᶠ· ? And what sense does it make that the man whose land has been fruitful and who therefore plans (in good and sensible fashion) to pull down his barns and build greater, hoping to enjoy a future in which he can take his ease and eat and drink and be merry, is described by God as a fool—simply because he has the unavoidable misfortune to die before his enterprise can be completed, and he can no longer call all these goods his own (Lk. 12¹⁶ᶠ·) ? Nor does Jesus seem to have a proper understanding of trade and commerce when we consider the story, recorded in all four Gospels, of the expulsion from the temple of those who changed money and sold doves. " A den of thieves " (Mk. 11¹⁷) is rather a harsh description for the honest, small-scale financial and commercial activities which had established themselves there. These detailed signals only give warning of the real threat and revolution which the kingdom of God and the man Jesus signify and involve in relation to this sphere, but they are signals which we ought not to overlook.

There are similar signals in the political sphere as well. Can we adduce in this respect the not very respectful way in which Jesus describes His own particular ruler, Herod, as a " fox " (Lk. 13³²) ? However that may be, the question and answer in Mk. 12¹³ᶠ· are certainly relevant. Ought tribute to be paid to Cæsar or not ? Well, the coin bears the image of Cæsar, and there can be no doubt that authority rests in his hands, so : " Render to Cæsar the things that are Cæsar's—precisely those things and no more, is the obvious meaning—and to

God the things that are God's." There is not a second kingdom of God outside and alongside the first. There is a human kingdom which is authoritative and can demand obedience only as such. And this kingdom is sharply delimited by the one kingdom of God. According to Jn. 19[10] Pilate's power over Jesus is only the power to release Him or to crucify Him. When He asked : " Art thou the king of the Jews ? " Jesus did not owe him a defence which He never made— for although Pilate, like the high-priests, made a case against Him, Jesus did not conduct any case—but only the confession : " Thou sayest it." Even the more explicit statement recorded in Jn. 18[33f.] is only a paraphrase of this confession, this καλὴ ὁμολογία as it is called in 1 Tim. 6[13]. With this confession as the one thing that He had to set against it He both honoured the imperial kingdom and yet at the same time drew unmistakeable attention to its limitations, setting it under a cloud and calling it in question. " Behold, I cast out devils, and I do cures to day and to morrow, and the third day I shall be perfected," was His answer when Herod threatened Him (Lk. 13[32]). To the extent that it is another form of the same confession this saying is also relevant in this context.

But the crisis which broke on all human order in the man Jesus is more radical and comprehensive than may be gathered from all these individual indications. Our best starting-point for this deeper consideration is the comparison recorded by all the Synoptics in connexion with the question of fasting : " No man also seweth a piece of new cloth on an old garment : else the new piece that filled it up taketh away from the old, and the rent is made worse. And no man putteth new wine into old bottles : else the new wine doth burst the bottles, and the wine is spilled, and the bottles will be marred : but new wine must be put into new bottles " (Mk. 2[21f.]). For Jesus, and as seen in the light of Jesus, there can be no doubt that all human orders are this old garment or old bottles, which are in the last resort quite incompatible with the new cloth and the new wine of the kingdom of God. The new cloth can only destroy the old garment, and the old bottles can only burst when the new wine of the kingdom of God is poured into them. All true and serious conservatism, and all true and serious belief in progress, presupposes that there is a certain compatibility between the new and the old, and that they can stand in a certain neutrality the one to the other. But the new thing of Jesus is the invading kingdom of God revealed in its alienating antithesis to the world and all its orders. And in this respect, too, the dictum is true : *neutralitas non valet in regno Dei.* There is thus concealed and revealed, both in what we called the passive conservatism of Jesus and the individual signs and penetrations which question the world of human orders as such, the radical and indissoluble antithesis of the kingdom of God to all human kingdoms, the unanswerable question, the irremediable unsettlement introduced by the kingdom of God into all human kingdoms.

In Mk. 13[1f.], when His disciples were admiring the temple, Jesus answered them : " Seest thou these great buildings ? there shall not be left one stone upon another "—a saying that was brought against Him in Mk. 14[58] (and again on the cross in Mk. 15[29]) as implying that He Himself would destroy the temple made with hands and replace it in three days by another not made with hands. Mark and Matthew ascribed this version of the saying to false witnesses. But according to the version preserved in Jn. 2[19], although He did not speak of Himself destroying the temple, He certainly spoke of its rebuilding in three days. The comment of John is that He spoke of the temple of His body (Jn. 2[21]). Either way, while He honoured the temple as the house of God and was even jealous for its sanctity, He could not ascribe to it any permanent place or significance in the light of what He Himself brought and was. Unlike the Law in Mt. 5[17f.], it was not to continue until heaven and earth passed away. The saying to the Samaritan woman is relevant in this connexion : " Woman, believe me, the hour cometh, when ye shall neither in this mountain, nor yet at Jerusalem, worship the Father " (Jn. 4[21]). And what is said about the heavenly Jerusalem in Rev. 21[22] is like an echo of all these sayings : " And I saw no temple therein : for the Lord God Almighty and the Lamb are the temple thereof."

Everything else that we have to say concerning the radical antithesis of the new thing which was actualised and appeared in Jesus to the totality of the old order can be said only in relation to its complete ignoring and transcending of this order. We can merely attempt to see with what profundity He attacked it by this ignoring and transcending. He attacked it—in a way from which it can never recover—merely by the alien presence with which He confronted it in its own sphere. What was, in fact, this way in which He confronted it ?

In the first place, He Himself remained unmarried—no one has ever yet explained with what self-evident necessity. And in Mt. 19[12] He reckoned with the fact that there might be others who would remain unmarried for the sake of the kingdom of heaven. In this way He set against the whole sphere of the family (in addition to the sayings already adduced) the basic question of its right and permanence to which there could be given only a provisional and relative answer. " For when they shall rise from the dead, they neither marry, nor are given in marriage " (Mk. 12[25]).

But above all we must take up again the question of His relationship to the economic order. It, too, was simply but radically called in question by the fact that neither He Himself nor His disciples accepted its basic presupposition by taking any part in the acquisition or holding of any possessions. It is as if the declaration and irruption of the kingdom of God had swept away the ground from under us in this respect. We have already mentioned the passage in the commissioning of the disciples in Mt. 10[9] which refers to the total insecurity to which He abandons His disciples. Those who followed Him had left everything (Mt. 19[27]), their nets and boats (Mk. 1[18f.]), their families and houses and lands (Mt. 19[29]). " Lacked ye anything ? " He asks them, and their answer is : " Nothing " (Lk. 22[35]). But this is not due to acquisition or possession. Those who came to Him, those who went through the narrow gate, were told : " Sell whatsoever thou hast, and give to the poor, and thou shalt have treasure in heaven " (Mk. 10[21]). Those who were sad and went away grieved when they came to this narrow gate (v. 22) did not come to Him. A dangerous alternative for all the economic attitudes and practices conceivable or serviceable to man ! As is well-known, in Ac. 2[44] we read of a bold attempt by the most primitive post-Pentecostal community to take up this basic challenge. " And all that believed were together, and had all things common ; and sold their possessions and goods, and parted them to all men, as every man had need." There is only one other direct mention of this attempt, in Ac. 5[1f.] It has often been taken up since in different forms. But in whatever form can it ever have more than the significance of an attempt ? It is worth pondering that the venture was at least made. And it will always be inevitable that there should be impulses in this direction wherever the Gospel of Jesus is proclaimed and heard. But it has never happened—least of all in the modern system called " Communism "—that even in smaller circles the way which leads in this direction has been trodden to the end. And the proclamation in Mt. 6[19] is even more dangerous : " Lay not up for yourselves treasures upon earth, where moth and rust doth corrupt, and where thieves break through and steal," and especially in Mt. 6[25f.] : " Take no thought for your life, what ye shall eat, or what ye shall drink ; not yet for your body, what ye shall put on. . . . Take therefore no thought for the morrow : for the morrow shall take thought for the things of itself." Surely there could be no sound or solid economy, either private or public, without this laying up and taking thought ? But this is what Jesus says in words which are strangely illuminating and pregnant and penetrating—who can escape their truth and comfort and inspiration ?—even though they obviously do not give to the community in which the Gospels arose any directions as to their practical realisation, and have a final validity even though they are exposed from the very outset to the accusation that they are incapable of practical realisation. And how dangerous it is when this laying up and taking thought are scorned as " Gentile " and there is opposed to them the freedom of the fowls of the air and the lilies of the field which neither worry nor work ! How dangerous it is that the concept of mammon, which seems to denote only the idea of material possession, is used as a comprehensive term for the whole of that dominion which is opposed to the kingdom of God, the antithesis of the rich and the poor being adopted as a basic *schema* for all the blessedness or otherwise of man ! Obviously this is to shake the basic pillars of all normal human activity in relation to the clearest necessities of life—and in the irritating form, not of the proclamation of a better social order, but of the free and simple call to freedom. This is indeed a new piece which cannot be sewn on the old garment, new wine which cannot be put into old bottles. Its relation to the old is that of something which is unmistakeably different and opposed, the strident proclamation of its end and of a new beginning beyond this end, a question and challenge and invitation and demand which cannot as such be silenced. It was the new thing—we must be content, for the moment, with the simple affirmation—of the royal man Jesus penetrating to the very foundations of economic life in defiance of every reasonable and to that extent honourable objection.

It is exactly the same in relation to the juridical and political sphere. Here, too, we have a questioning of the very presuppositions which is all the more powerful in its lack of any direct aggressiveness. What are all the attempts at reform or revelation in which Jesus might have taken part or which He might have instigated or directed compared with the revolution which He did actually accomplish in this sphere ? He did not oppose the evil which He came to root out. He was the Judge and He did not judge : except, perhaps, those who thought that they could be the judges ; except by causing Himself to be judged for these usurpers of judgment. His injunction to His followers, not as a law, but as a free call to freedom, is of a piece with this. They are not to resist evil (Mt. 5[38f.]). They are to let themselves be smitten on the left cheek as well as the right. They are to give away their cloak if their coat is taken from them. They are to go two miles with those who compel them to go one. More than that, if they do not want to be judged, they are not to judge (Mt. 7[1f.]). More still, they are to love their enemies (Mt. 5[43f.]) and pray for their persecutors, as children of their Father in heaven who causes His sun to shine on the good and the bad and His rain to fall on the just and the unjust, and obviously as brothers of Jesus, who, when His enemies (really the enemies of God) did their worst against Him, prayed for them (Lk. 23[34]) : " Father, forgive them ; for they know not what they do." It is again clear—for what political thinking can do justice or satisfaction to this injunction and to the One who gives it ?—that this involves a shaking of every human foundation ; that the right of God is in irreconcilable conflict with every human right ; that the divine state is quite incompatible not merely with the wicked totalitarian state but with every conceivable human regime ; that the new thing cannot be used to patch or fill the old. It is evident that human order is here betrayed into the proximity of a final and supreme menace. The community has again and again stifled and denied and even forgotten this, so that it could also be forgotten by the world around. But in this dimension too it has never been able to free itself completely from the unsettlement which it has within itself—whether it accepts the fact or not—as the community of this royal man. Nor has it been able completely to hide it from the world around. For in so far as it has been present as the community of this man, it has been present as such for the world, and the confrontation of the old order with the incommensurable factor of the new has been inescapable in this respect too. From the very outset and continually—cost what it may—the presence of this man has meant always that the world must wrestle with this incommensurable factor.

In all these dimensions the world is concretely violated by God Himself in the fact that the man Jesus came into it and is now within it.

[IV, 2, pp. 173-179]

6. THE GOOD SAMARITAN

It is the context of the Lucan version of our text, the pericope of the Good Samaritan (Lk. 10²⁵⁻²⁷), which is calculated to help us most in this respect. What first strikes us in this account is that the twofold commandment of love is not introduced as a saying of Jesus, but as a saying of the lawyer (νομικός), who is trying to " tempt " Jesus. To his question: What shall I do to inherit eternal life ? Jesus answered with a counter-question: " What is written in the law ? How readest thou ? " (v. 26). And it is by way of answer to this counter-question that the lawyer recites the twofold commandment (v. 27). Purposely in his mouth, the unit, of the two commandments seems to be more strongly emphasised, by omitting the distinction into a first and second, than is the case in Matthew and Mark, where the twofold commandment is introduced as a formulation of Jesus Himself. There is, therefore, in the third evangelist an awareness of the fact that a twofold love is demanded of the one man who as the rest of the account makes clear is neither ready for nor capable of it. Of course, it is not by nature or of himself that the lawyer knows what he recites. He is in fact a doctor of the Law in Israel. Therefore outwardly and in appearance, by his very calling, he belongs to the community of Yahweh. In an important function he lives in the sphere and by the tradition of this community, claiming to be a member and in fact a prominent member of it, with a special claim to participate in the associated promises. The word of faith is nigh him, as it says in Rom. 10⁸, in his mouth and in his heart. It is false exegesis to assume that he is necessarily guilty of subjective insincerity. But whatever his subjective sincerity, he betrays the fact that he does not really know the near word, the two commandments, which he can recite so faithfully. Jesus praised him for his good knowledge and faithful recitation: ὀρθῶς ἀπεκρίθης. But he then challenges him to do the very thing which he knows and can express so well, and in that way (for this was his original question) to inherit eternal life. Why does he not go and do it ? Why does he ask what he should do when he obviously knows so well ? Indeed, why ? The reason is evident, for he goes on to ask: " And who is my neighbour ? " (v. 29). He had answered rightly, very rightly, in respect of love to God. But he does not ask: And who is God ? That is something which he seems to know and thinks he knows. He asks only in regard to the unperspicuous latter part of the doctrine which he has so weightily advanced. He asks only in regard to a single concept in the second of the commandments advanced by him, the concept neighbour. It is only this concept which he wants clarified. But from the very fact that he can ask this question the physician Luke regards him as mortally ill. He thinks that the question reveals that this doctor of the Law does not actually know the second commandment at all, and therefore not the first. Luke does not, of course, express it in this way. He goes further back. He finds the real reason for the question in the fact that the man " wished to justify himself " (v. 29). The lawyer does not know that only by mercy can he live and inherit eternal life. He does not want to live by mercy. He does not even know what it is. He actually lives by something quite different from mercy, by his own intention and ability to present himself as a righteous man before God. Or he thinks that he can live in that way. He wished to justify himself. That this is the case is revealed by the question: And who is my neighbout ? If a man does not know who his neighbour is, if he does not or will not know what mercy is, if he does not live by mercy, then obviously his intention and effort is to justify himself. But how can he understand the second commandment if this is his relation with his neighbour ? And how can he understand the first apart from the second ? Why does he not go on to ask : Who is God ? what is loving ? above all—the most obvious question in the light of what Jesus had just said : what is the " doing " which these commandments require ? But, of course, if he had asked all the things which have to be asked he would have known the two commandments and stopped asking. But by asking " only " about his neighbour, he shows that he does not really know either of them, even though he can recite them : and that is why he wants to justify himself. The converse must also be stated : that because he wishes to justify himself, he does not really know the two commandments at all, although he can recite them. If he had no wish to justify himself, he would know the commandments in that case, and he would then know who is his neighbour, and everything else that has to be known at this point. Again, if he had known who is his neighbour, he would know the commandments, and would not wish to justify himself. Which is the first and basic element in his perversion ? His self-righteousness, or his lack of knowledge of revelation ? Who is to decide ? The one certain thing is that in this man the two go hand in hand and confirm each other. So then, to the question : And who is my neighbour ? and the background that " he wished to justify himself," Jesus answers in the Lucan version (vv. 30–35) with the story or parable of the good Samaritan : the man who fell among thieves, who lay wounded and half-dead by the roadside, whom the priest and Levite saw and passed by on the other side, until at last the Samaritan appeared, who took charge of him without hesitation and with unsparing energy. What is the meaning of this story as an answer to the question ? We might expect— and current exegesis of the text is in accordance with this obvious expectation— that Jesus would have said to the teacher of the Law: This Samaritan did not ask questions like you. He found his neighbour in the man that had fallen among thieves. He treated him accordingly. Go and do thou likewise. But the assumption on which (v. 37b) this final challenge is reached, according to the statements of the text, which in themselves are quite clear, although obstinately surrounded by traditional exposition, is really quite a different one. The question with which Jesus concludes the story is which then of the three (i.e., priest, Levite and Samaritan) proved to be a neighbour to the man who fell among thieves ? And the teacher of the Law himself had to reply: " he that showed mercy on him," i.e., the Samaritan. This man as such, as the one who showed mercy, is the neighbour about whom the lawyer was asking. And that is the only point of the story, unequivocally stated by the text. For the lawyer, who wants to justify himself and therefore does not know who is his neighbour, is confronted not by the poor wounded man with his claim for help, but by the anything but poor Samaritan who makes no claim at all but is simply helpful. It is the Samaritan who embodies what he wanted to know. This is the neighbour he did not know. All very unexpected : for the lawyer had first to see that he himself is the man fallen among thieves and lying helpless by the wayside ; then he has to note that the others who pass by, the priest and the Levite, the familiar representatives of the dealings of Israel with God, all one after the other do according to the saying of the text: " He saw him and passed by on the other side ; " and third, and above all, he has to see that he must be found and treated with compassion by the Samaritan, the foreigner, whom he believes he should hate, as one who hates and is hated by God. He will then know who is his neighbour, and will not ask concerning him as though it were only a matter of the casual clarification of a concept. He will then know the second commandment, and consequently the first as well. He will then not wish to justify himself, but will simply love the neighbour, who shows him mercy. He will then love God, and loving God will inherit eternal life. But now the text takes a last surprising turn. In fact, the lawyer does not see his own helplessness. He does not see that the priest and the Levite bring him no help and the Samaritan does. He does not really know his neighbour. Therefore he does not know either the second commandment or the first, although he can recite them so well. Therefore he does not love, he does not do what he must do to inherit eternal life. What advice or help can be given to him ? The section closes with the again quite unexpected challenge flung out at him by Jesus, v. 37b : " Go and do thou likewise " (ὁμοίως). From what precedes, we might have thought that He would summon him to that threefold knowledge. But that is not the case. He is merely summoned to do what the Samaritan did. He is summoned to be the neighbour who must bring comfort, help, the Gospel to someone else. Once he is, he will no longer want or need to ask : And who is my neighbour ? He who is merciful—at this point we can and should remember Mt. 5⁷—will receive mercy. We see and have a neighbour when we show mercy on him and he therefore owes us love. We see and have a neighbour when we are wholly the givers and he can only receive. We see and have him when he cannot repay us and especially when he is an enemy, someone who hates us and injures us and persecutes us (Mt. 5⁴³ᶠ·). The Samaritan also receives : he receives from the man who fell among thieves, by giving to him. The fact that he becomes a good neighbour to him is merely a witness that he himself has found a compassionate neighbour in the man who is half-dead. And those who do likewise, as neighbours who exercise mercy—and who therefore themselves see and have a neighbour— really know both the second and the first commandments. They know them because they keep them. Their intention and attempt to try to justify themselves is smashed. They can only respond to the mercy which has met them. They can only love. They praise God. And in so doing they know what they must do to inherit eternal life. At this point we might ask whether and how it was possible to summon the lawyer—who obviously does not see or have a compassionate neighbour, who lacks all the necessary presuppositions—to go and do likewise and in that way to praise God. Well, it is Jesus Christ who gives the summons, and we cannot abstract Jesus Himself from the summons which He gives. On His lips the " Go and do thou likewise " is only Law because it is first Gospel. The good Samaritan, the neighbour who is a helper and will make him a helper, is not far from the lawyer. The primitive exegesis of the text was fundamentally right. He stands before him incarnate, although hidden under the form of one whom the lawyer believed he should hate, as the Jews hated the Samaritans. Jesus does not accuse the man, although judgment obviously hangs over him. Judgment is preceded by grace. Before this neighbour makes His claim He makes His offer. Go and do likewise means : Follow thou Me. There the story ends. We do not hear what becomes of the lawyer, whether he finally learns to know the Law in doing it or whether he only continues to recite it. But his question : Who is the neighbour, his neighbour ? has been unmistakably answered.

[I, 2, pp. 417–419]

7. THE PRODIGAL SON

It would be a strained interpretation to try to give to it a direct christological reference, as has been attempted. In what it says directly, i.e., with its parabolic reference according to the context (in concretion of the parables of the Lost Sheep and the Lost Coin) it speaks of the sin of man and the mortal threat which comes to him in consequence, of his repentance and return to God, and of the overwhelming grace with which this one who turned away and then turned back to God is received by Him. According to vv. 1–2 this is all with a view to the " publicans and sinners " who come to Jesus and hear Him, whom He receives (προσδέχεται), and with whom He eats—in contrast to the scribes and Pharisees, who seem to shun Him for this reason. In the parable the latter correspond to the elder son, who will not rejoice at the return of the younger, but (v. 28) is angry, and will not take part in the feast prepared by the father. But the elder son is only the—indispensable—contrast, just as the scribe or Pharisee, the righteous who needs no repentance, has only the significance of contrast in relation to the main statement of the passage. The real message is to be found in the story of the son who left his father but then returned and was received by him with joy and honour. And in this story it tells of the turning away and turning back of man in his relationship to God, in which there is not only no diminution but a supreme heightening and deepening of the fatherly mind and attitude of God towards him. We cannot say that more than this is said directly in the passage, nor can we extract more than this from it in direct exegesis.

But if there is the danger of a strained interpretation, it is also possible not to do full justice to the passage, to miss what is not expressly stated but implied in what is stated, and therefore necessary to what is stated, as that which is said indirectly. To this category there belongs that which was emphasised by Augustine (*Quaest. ev.*, 2, 23), very cautiously by C. Starke (in his *Syn. Bibl. exeg. in N.T.*, 1741) and on a more scientific basis by F. C. Baur and his school : the relationship between the lost and re-found younger son, the sinful but penitent *'am ha'aretz* of publicans and sinners, and the election, calling and redemption of the Gentile world as it turns to the Gospel—in contrast to the Israel as revealed in the elder brother, which (v. 29) has served God for so many years, and thinks and claims that it has never transgressed His commandment, and in so doing excludes itself from the Messianic feast. There is no explicit mention of this relationship to the Gentiles in the text. But is it not there, as everywhere where the New Testament deals with this *'am ha'aretz* ? Was it not definitely in the mind of the third Evangelist with his very pronounced universalistic interest ? Is it really read into the text ? Is it not the case that we cannot really expound the text without taking it into consideration—not in direct exegesis, because it is not there—but in and with and under what is said directly ? Do we not fail to do full justice to the passage if we ignore this relationship ?

But the question also arises whether we have not to take from the text, in the same indirect way, a christological content, because it does actually contain this—although not explicitly. It has often been maintained, and in recent years triumphantly emphasised, that in the act of penitence to which this parable refers (as in the parable of the Pharisee and the Publican in Lk. 18[9f.], or the discourse on the Last Judgment by the Son of Man in Mt. 25[31f.]) there is no mention at all of the person and work of Jesus Christ. From this it is hastily concluded (as in Harnack's *Essence of Christianity*, Lect. 8) that not the Son and the atonement accomplished in Him but only the Father and His goodness belong to the Gospel preached by Jesus Himself, and that according to this Gospel of His nothing extraneous can interpose itself between God and the soul, the soul and its God. And, indeed, there is not a single word in the parable about Jesus Christ and the atonement accomplished in Him.

But does this mean that a discussion of what is not said but definitely implied along these lines like that of Helmut Gollwitzer in his *Die Freude Gottes* (1941, II, p. 91 f.), is illegitimate, or even avoidable ? As he sees it, the scribes and Pharisees did not understand that the Messianic work of salvation does not consist in the coronation of righteous Israel but the blessing of sinful Israel. Jesus' eating with the publicans and sinners is a fulfilment of this blessing. Not the theory of a Father-God who self-evidently and consistently pardons, but the miraculous actuality of this act of God, is the non-explicit but indispensable presupposition of the happening between God and man which is envisaged in the relations between father and son described in the parable. In the parable, then, Jesus is " the running out of the father to meet his son." Jesus is " hidden in the kiss which the father gives his son." Jesus is the power of the son's recollection of his father and home, and his father's fatherliness and readiness to forgive. This is the indirect exegesis. And it is not allegorical but legitimate if there is to be an exposition of the parable in the context of the whole of the Third Gospel, and the whole New Testament message. It does justice to what is there in the light of its background, i.e., it expounds it from its context. Yet although there can be no objection to it on grounds of method, it is not altogether satisfactory. For, throwing all the emphasis upon the action of the father, and deriving the reference to Jesus Christ from this, it destroys the essential balance of the parable, and cannot therefore offset more recent Protestant exegesis—which is guilty of exactly the same error—as effectively as is required. For this reason, although not opposing it in content, I prefer to replace or rather to complete it by a different exposition.

For after all the main figure in the story is the younger son who leaves his father and is lost, but returns and is found again. And what we have to demonstrate in face of more recent Protestant exegesis is the presence and action of the Son of God, and therefore of the atonement accomplished in Him, in what takes place between God and man as indicated in the parable. Directly, this cannot be demonstrated from the text. That would be a strained interpretation. There can be no simple equation of Jesus Christ with the lost son of the parable—and even less, of course, with the flesh of the fatted calf which was killed for his reception, as Ambrose once suggested. But again we do not do justice to the story if we do not see and say that in the going out and coming in of the lost son in his relationship with the father we have a most illuminating parallel to the way trodden by Jesus Christ in the work of atonement, to His humiliation and exaltation. Or better, the going out and coming in of the lost son. and therefore the fall and blessing of man, takes place on the horizon of the humiliation and exaltation of Jesus Christ and therefore of the atonement made in Him. It has in this its higher law. It is illuminated by it. In this, and therefore in itself, it is clear and significant and important.

In the parable the son comes with his greedy and arbitrary demand, takes his inheritance from the hands of his father, makes his way into a far country, wastes his substance in riotous living—with harlots, as we are later told (v. 30)—and then suffers want in the famine which comes on that land, being glad at last to feed on the husks which do not belong to him, but to the swine which he is charged to keep. This is the way of man in his breaking of the covenant with God—the way of lost Israel, of the lost " publicans and sinners," of the lost Gentile world. It is certainly not in any direct sense the way of the Son of God who is obedient to the Father, the way of Jesus Christ. And yet it cannot be denied that the way of the latter is in fact the way into the far country of a lost human existence—the way in which He accepts identity and solidarity with this lost son, unreservedly taking his place, taking to Himself his sin and shame, his transgression, as though He Himself had committed it, making his misery His own as though He Himself had deserved it, and all this in such a way that the frightfulness of this far country, the evil of the human situation, is revealed in its full depths only as it becomes His situation, that of the holy and righteous Son of God. What is the fatal journey of the lost son as seen from this standpoint ? Surely it is only a sorry caricature of the going out of the one Son of God into the world as it took place in Jesus Christ, of the humiliation in which, without ceasing to be who He is, but in the supreme exercise and expression of His Sonship and deity, He became poor for our sakes (2 Cor. 8⁹). But it is obviously its caricature. As away from the heights to the depths, from home to a far country, it is analogous to it. It is similar for all its dissimilarity, like the being of Adam in relation to that of Jesus Christ : τύπος τοῦ μέλλοντος (Rom. 5¹⁴).

But then in the parable the lost son comes to himself among the unclean beasts with whom he associates, remembering the well-being in his father's house which he has exchanged for this imminent death by hunger. He resolves, therefore, to return to his father with a confession of his fault and a request to be received at least as a hired servant. In execution of this resolve, he sets off on his way. But the father sees him afar off, and has pity on him, and runs to meet him, and falls on his neck and kisses him—and all this before he has even uttered his confession and request, let alone proved them by corresponding actions of amendment. And beyond all this the father gives the order to clothe the one who has returned with the best robe and a ring and shoes, to bring and slay the fatted calf, and there is a great feast with music (lit. "symphonies," v. 25) and dancing, which annoys the elder son so terribly as he comes home from his conscientious labours. This is the "way back" of man, the way of man as he turns again to God in repentance and sorrow, sincerely and therefore without claim, eagerly and therefore resolutely, and as he is received and accepted again by Him without hesitation or reservation, simply because he belongs to Him, and with even greater joy than He had in him before he left. Again, there can be no simple equation of this way with that of the exaltation of Jesus Christ, of the Son of Man as He goes to His heavenly Father and is crowned by Him. Yet again—and this cannot be denied—the way of Jesus Christ is primarily and properly the way to that home of man which is not lost but remains, not closed but open ; the way to his fellowship with God ; the way on which He precedes all men as a King who draws them after Him to share His destiny ; the way to the end of which He Himself has already come, so that this home of theirs is already visible and palpable to the men who still tread it. What is the redemptive return of the lost son as seen from this standpoint ? Surely it is only a feeble reflection of the entry of the one Son of Man into fellowship with God as it took place in Jesus Christ, of the exaltation in which, without ceasing to be true man, without being divinised, but in our nature and flesh, He is at the side of the Father in heaven, participating as man in His power and glory, in the exercise of His grace and mercy. More than a copy, an analogy, a type of this entry, the way of the refound son in the parable, and therefore of the man reconciled with God, cannot possibly be. But, on the other hand, it cannot possibly be less. It cannot be more because what he himself is and does and experiences on this way back can only be a very little thing in relation to that of the one Son of Man, and even this very little does not lie within the range of his own possibilities, as though even temporarily he could set himself even in the most imperfect fellowship with God. But it is also not less because the little that he is and does and experiences is carried and therefore capacitated by the great and original and proper being and action and experience of the one Son of Man, being empowered by the fact that in Him it is a wonderfully complete reality. It is not the original. It is only a copy. But it is the copy of this original, and therefore to be understood only in its relationship to it.

But the elder brother, the scribe and Pharisee, who forms a contrast in the parable, failed to understand, not only the going out and coming in again of the younger, but also and primarily the love of their common father, as it was not diminished but increased by this twofold movement. He failed to understand, therefore, the fact that in His grace God is the God precisely and exclusively of the man who makes this twofold movement. Primarily, originally and properly, the scribe and Pharisee does not reject merely a distasteful doctrine of sin and forgiveness, but the God who is the God of this man, the man who is the man of this God, the actuality of the Son of God and His humiliation, and of the Son of Man and His exaltation, the atonement which takes place in this One. He rejects Jesus Christ. This elder brother will finally bring Him to the cross, not merely because He said about God and the sinner what is said in this parable, but because He is the man in whom what is said in this parable (beyond anything that is merely said) is actuality. What puts this figure in the parable so terrifyingly into the shadows is that it is a personification of the conflict against the actuality of the God-man. But it is better to keep before us the final saying of the father to this elder son which forms the conclusion of the parable. In v. 28 f. he had summoned his servants to prepare the feast with the words : "Let us eat, and be merry : For this my son was dead, and is alive again ; he was lost (had gone off, disappeared), and is found." And now he woos the disgruntled brother with the pressing words : " Son, thou art ever with me, and all that I have is thine. It was meet that we should make merry, and be glad : for this thy brother was dead, and is alive again ; and was lost, and is found." Yes, this is also in the text. And if there is any point where we can ask whether there is not finally a direct as well as an indirect christological reference, and therefore need of a christological exposition, it is in face of these two verses, of this " my son " and " thy brother," of this dead man who was alive again, of this lost man who was found, of the rejoicing which rings out in these words. For to whom does all this refer ? Are not the expressions almost too strong to be applied, or applicable, to the lost son of the parable and what is represented in him ? I will not press the point, but will say only that in these two verses we are invited by the text itself to the indirect, not allegorical but typological, or *in concreto* christological exposition here attempted. So much we may say, and it will have to be taken into account in even the most cautious exegesis of the parable. [IV, 2, pp. 21–25]

8. JESUS AND THE ADULTEROUS WOMAN

The woman referred to in Jn. 8³⁻¹¹ was caught in the very act of adultery (v. 4). There can be no doubt that she had transgressed the command in the most literal sense. And the Pharisees were right in the sense that according to the literal tenor of the Law of Moses (Deut. 22²²⁻²⁴) a person who was guilty in this respect was to be put to death. They wanted Jesus to disclose His attitude in such a situation : " What sayest thou ? " (v. 5). The narrator adds the comment : " This they said, tempting him, that they might have whereof to accuse him " (v. 6). If He forbade them to carry out this direction of the Law, He became indictable because of His contravention of the Law of Moses. If He told them to carry out the command, He could be accused before the Roman authorities which reserved to themselves such supreme acts in the administration of justice. It is clear that the Pharisees were concerned neither about the Law of God nor the sin of the woman. Their concern was simply to oppose Jesus. But was Jesus concerned in all earnestness with the Law of God and the sin of this woman ? Yes, with hers, but not only with hers. We are told that " he stooped down, and with his finger wrote on the ground " (v. 6). The most obvious explanation of this striking action is that He thus indicates what God did on Sinai (Ex. 34¹, Deut. 4¹³ etc.). He writes the Law (His finger and the ground must suffice for the gesture), thus proclaiming Himself to be the Author and therefore the competent Expositor of the command which arraigns and condemns to death this adulteress. But the Pharisees refuse to recognise both the Lawgiver and His laws. Disputing the authority of both, they press their question : " What sayest thou ? " (v. 7). And now Jesus looks up, and as the Author and therefore the competent Expositor of the Law He gives the crystal clear but for them supremely captious direction : " He that is without sin among you, let him first cast a stone at her " (v. 7). In other words, let the one who is guiltless in this respect take action as her judge and executioner. And having said this, He again makes the eloquent gesture of stooping down and writing on the ground (v. 8). We are reminded of Jer. 17¹ᶠ· : " The sin of Judah is written with a pen of iron, and with the point of a diamond : it is graven upon the table of their hearts, and upon the horns of your altars, and upon their Asherim, upon every green tree, upon the high hills, and upon all the mountains in the fields." Why does no one obey the direction given ? Why do they all go away ? (v. 9). What has happened ? One thing at least is clear. The intended prosecution of Jesus in the two seemingly unavoidable eventualities has now become impossible. He is justified before God and man. But what else ? The Law of God and the sin of men are together revealed as terribly earnest realities, and in such a way that those who took seriously neither the one nor the other, but wanted to accuse Jesus, must confess themselves in the wrong by their own attitude. With His direction the Author and Expositor of the Law has obviously caught them all redhanded. The radical and universal character of His command has clearly shown its effectiveness. He has obviously compelled them to include themselves in one category with the adulteress, and to own that they are no less guilty and worthy of death. As accusers of the adulteress they are thus extinguished. What else takes place ? " He was left alone, and the woman standing in the midst" (v. 9)—there, where as the one rightly accused she had expected the merited sentence of death and its execution. But now she is alone with Jesus, alone in His judgment. " Woman, where are those thine accusers ? hath no man condemned thee ? (v. 10). She said : " No man, Lord." But it is not yet decided whether Jesus will pronounce judgment against her, and deliver her up to the death she deserves. Why should He not do so ? He is without sin. He does not belong to those who in so doing must be afraid of condemning themselves. He is the legitimate and competent Judge of this woman. Will He allow justice to take its course ? Listen : " Neither do I condemn thee " (v. 11). And notice that in this very way He allows justice to take its course. In this very way, as the Author and Expositor of the Law, He takes up a concrete attitude to the sin of which she is undoubtedly guilty. His judgment is : Pardon the adulteress. It is equivalent to the judgment which her accusers involuntarily pronounced in leaving the place. The very Law whose Author and Expositor He is obviously requires this pardon. What does this Law imply ? Certainly not that this woman has not sinned and is not guilty and culpable. But obviously in accordance with this pardon that the merited death sentence has already been pronounced and executed, that it has fallen on another in her place and has thus been fulfilled. Hence it would not merely be useless but unjust to allow her to bear it over again. She is thus delivered. How could Jesus condemn her ? According to the Law of the grace of the one true God, established, proclaimed and applied by Him, it is He, the sinless One, the Lawgiver and Judge, who is condemned in her place, and she, the sinner, who there, the victim of His sentence, remains alone with Him and is pardoned. He takes in all seriousness both the Law of God and the sin of this woman by substituting Himself for the transgressor and exculpating her. Why have the Pharisees departed ? Their fault was not that they were not without sin, but that they were just as guilty and culpable as the adulteress. It was that they were unwilling to recognise the Lawgiver who stood before them with His Law, that they refused to hear and accept the judgment of the gracious God upon the adulteress and upon themselves. Their fault was that their solemn and basically unsuccessful attack upon the adulteress, upon their sister in adultery, was in truth directed against Jesus and the free grace manifested in Him, and therefore against God and His Law. Their fault was that they persisted in this attitude. Obviously, along with the woman, they might have been pronounced free and righteous by Jesus (just as they were guilty and accused with her), and therefore for their salvation they might have stood again and very differently alongside this woman. Their fault was that they failed to do this. And failing to do it, they did not keep the command.

But we must again go further and say that a man keeps the law of God, and is free and righteous before God, when he permits himself to be raised up and directed by the wonderful judgment of grace to a sincere willing of that which even as transgressor he can will, and a resolute performance of that which even as transgressor he can perform, according to the direction of the command.

Hence the conclusion of the message of Jesus to the adulteress is : " Go, and sin no more " (Jn. 8[11]). The meaning of this summons cannot be that now (ἀπὸ τοῦ νῦν), after her encounter with Jesus, the Lawgiver and Judge, and after the acceptance of His judgment, she both must and can undo what is done, cancelling its inner and outer consequences, emerging from the condition of the sinner and redeeming her life from ruin.   For her birth to newness of life in virtue of the Law which confronted her with this challenge has already taken place in the person of the Lawgiver and Judge, and nothing can be added to this her total justification and liberation by the One before whom she stood alone in the midst.   But the summons is that from now on she may and must live as a transgressor who is raised up and directed by the judgment of the gracious God, who even in her condition as a sinner stands under the powerful impulsion of her translation in Jesus into the condition of eternal righteousness, innocence and blessedness, who even in the irreparable disorder of her life is already orientated towards the order of the divine kingdom, who even within the limits of what is beyond her power to alter is already willing and doing what she in fact can and must will and do in virtue of the promise made to her.   Because of this counter-action, there had to be for her a henceforth.   It necessarily meant a change that she had stood alone with Jesus in that circle, that she was subject to His judgment and that she was pardoned by it.   " Henceforth to sin no more " means that now, when the verdict of Jesus has been pronounced and heard, one must not live as though it had not been pronounced and heard, or, more positively, one must live as one who in all his uncleanness is sanctified by the preaching and hearing of this verdict.   [III, 4, pp. 234–236]

CHAPTER V

LENT AND EASTER

1. THE TEMPTATION OF THE SERPENT

When Adam and Eve made that move to self-help in paradise, and ate the fruit of the tree, what did they do to themselves and one another? They had been incited to do this. They had allowed their peace with God to be broken. They had allowed the serpent successfully to approach them when he ought not to have approached them. And was not the only result that they ceased to be independent? and that deceiving and deceived they were strangely separated from one another? They had helped themselves so well that they suddenly became aware of their nakedness (v. 7) and were ashamed of it. And then, confirming the isolation and separation from one another which had come with their alienation from God, they made their second and this time open attempt at self-help and brought in the first fashion, that of the fig leaf. And this was followed (v. 8) by the lamentable necessity of being ashamed before God and trying to hide from Him, as though He had not created them good in their nakedness. *Naturalia* have become *turpia*. And then the pitiable excuse of the man: "The woman whom thou gavest to be with me, she gave me of the tree, and I did eat" (v. 12). Just like Aaron on Sinai: "There came out this calf." And then the pitiable excuse of the woman: "The serpent beguiled me, and I did eat" (v. 13). These texts are well worth pondering. They make it plain that man's attempt to help himself is a complete failure. He has tried to help himself and he has become catastrophically helpless. Such is the human subject when he tries to live out his subjectivity otherwise than in the framework of the free grace of God and therefore in the obedience of thankfulness.

The speech of the serpent in Gen. 3 smacks throughout of true human development. It circles around the theme of the necessity open to and indeed laid upon man to judge and then to act in respect of that which is worthy of him and proper to him. First of all there is the general question which obviously creates the atmosphere with its tone of sincere sympathy (and it is worth noting that as opening the way to autonomous action it is addressed to the wife): whether God has really said that they are not to eat of any of the trees of the garden? (v. 1) whether poor man has actually to be content to live in paradise and to be deprived of its fruits? No, is the correct and orthodox answer of the one addressed. God has not said that. It is not so bad as that. "We may eat of the fruit of the trees of the garden: But of the fruit of the tree which is in the midst of the garden, God hath said, Ye shall not eat of it, neither shall ye touch it, lest ye die" (v. 2 f.). A right understanding of the text shows that the very beginning of the conversation was the decisive point. The serpentine possibility of the thought had emerged that God had perhaps commanded something which was not worthy of man, or not proper, or, at any rate, less proper to him, with the result that man would have to take matters into his own hand in relation to God. He knows and confesses that the one is not true and the other not necessary. But the limit which God has set him (in respect of the fruit of one of the trees in the garden) has been brought to consciousness and under the scrutiny of the question whether God is not perhaps in some way a hard and unkind Lord in view of this limit, whether His grace is quite enough, whether this prohibition, even if he has nothing else to complain of, does not mean that man is being deprived of something very precious, the most precious thing of all ? The reflection whether it is not perhaps advisable to test his subordination to the will of God has already been introduced in spite of, and, we might say, in, with and under the orthodox answer. It would have been better not to give the serpent an orthodox answer. For in conversation with the serpent no orthodox answer is so sure that it cannot be demolished by the serpent. Was not this beast of chaos not only more subtle than any beast of the field that the Lord God had made (v. 1), but far cleverer than the man created by God—dangerously so from the moment that man allowed himself to converse with and answer it ? There are some men that we ought not even to greet (2 Jn. 10 f.), for " he that biddeth him God speed is partaker of his evil deeds." The serpent in paradise is the essence of all those that we ought not to greet. But the greeting took place, and it was followed at once by the demolition of man's orthodox answer. In effect the good lady comes to know that behind this limit which is set to man there lies the most precious thing of all, which man cannot do without but must have whatever else he may lack : " Ye shall not surely die : For God doth know that in the day ye eat thereof, then your eyes shall be opened, and ye shall be as gods " (v. 4). Therefore the grace of God does suffice up to a point, but it is not enough. God is in some sense a hard and unkind Lord. He will grant man all kinds of things, but not the best of all. He has led him by the nose in relation to this supreme good. He has indeed directed him falsely, pronouncing a threat where a supreme promise awaited him. In effect, this state of affairs cannot go on. In effect—the serpent does not need to say it but man can and will deduce it for himself—it is time for man to be enlightened and to come of age. It is time for him to appeal from a *Deus male informatus* to a *Deus melius informandus*, to do a little demythologising, to pass from the decision of obedience to God to that of his own choice, from service in the garden to rule. And what if his own perception supports and confirms the exegesis of the serpent ? what if the woman sees that the supposed tree of death is, in fact, " pleasant to the eyes and a tree to be desired " ? Then it follows at once : " She took of the fruit thereof, and did eat, and gave also unto her husband with her ; and he did eat " (v. 6). Man makes himself lord, or acts as such. And what is the evil ? Is it not a legitimate development, a necessary movement from dependence to independence, from heteronomy to autonomy, a required progress from childhood to maturity ? Is it not man's true development : " the education of the human race " ? Why should not the woman speak with the serpent and learn how unsatisfying is the orthodox answer and be convinced of the correctness of the serpent's teaching and with the man act accordingly ? Why not ? Of course, when we ask this, we have to ignore the fact that the serpent is the beast of chaos. But we can do this. Or we can interpret chaos in such a way that it is only in encounter and conversation and agreement and covenant with it that we attain our true manhood.

We are again confronted by the wisdom of the serpent on Gen. 3, whose most powerful argument we have not so far considered. There is a definite content to the promise : *Eritis sicut Deus*, and to the concealed invitation to man to become the master of his own destiny. What the serpent has in mind is the establishment of ethics. Its teaching is that, far from there being any real menace in the warning in respect of the tree in the midst of the garden, the eating of the tree will mean that men's eyes are opened, that they will be as God, and that they will therefore be given to know good and evil (v. 5). God knows good and evil, and it is His glory as God and Lord and Creator that He does so. Is it not by this knowledge that He has done His creative work, and therefore distinguished and chosen and judged between cosmos and chaos, light and darkness, order and disorder ? Has He not placed on the right hand and the left, affirming and accepting here, denying and rejecting there ? Do not heaven and earth, the very existence of man—and in another way even that of the serpent—rest on this knowledge and activity ? Is man, therefore, to be prevented from doing the same, from taking his place at the side of God, from himself recognising the first and basic thing, and then doing it, from judging, therefore ? Does this really mean a fall into immorality ? On the contrary, is it not a rise to genuine morality, to the freedom of a knowledge which distinguishes and an activity which elects, and therefore to the freedom of genuine commitment, of a final and true unity with God ? From this point of view there seems to be nothing base or evil in the analysis of the prohibition laid upon man. From this point of view everything in this analysis seems to be concerned with things which are right, the most right of all. The only trouble is that it is an analysis, i.e., a dissolving or unravelling, of the divine commandment, and that it is the serpent, the beast of chaos that God has rejected and judged and originally and definitively set at His left hand, who conducts the analysis and leaves man to draw the practical consequences of it. And who, then, is to guard against all the possible misinterpretations ? In the last resoιι why should not this beast be the true illuminator and liberator of man, and his wisdom the beginning of all wisdom ? Why not ?

For the last time we will consult the wisdom of the serpent in Gen. 3. The poor men in paradise are not as God. They are not lords of paradise. They are not even their own lords. They do not know good and evil, and they are forbidden to judge between them. There are so many conditions and limitations in paradise. Of course, there are also so many reminders of the covenant which God has made with them, so mnay reminders that He is for them the Judge who knows and is responsible, that He is the Lord of paradise and their Lord, that in His grace He is theirs, their God and helper, that He cares for them in the best and most sufficient and perfect way, that they are in His house where they do not need to help themselves. But also, of course, so many reminders of their own helplessness in face of these limitations, the helplessness in which they are only and can only be helped by God. What has the clever serpent to say to all this ? The central point is obviously as follows : that this helplessness (1) is not happy or sensible or necessary but painful and irrational and restrictive and imposed only by an obscure divine caprice ; and (2) that it is not obligatory or definitive but can be overcome and removed by a bold act ; they have only to cross the boundaries set, and in so doing they will experience that man is in a position to help himself and is not, therefore, thrown back upon the help of God. We have to remember that the subtle serpent is speaking only in theory. It is left for man to draw the conclusion and to will and do that which corresponds to it. The serpent does not sin. It is only the serpent. In its animal person it is only the impossible possibility of human sin.` If man listens to the theory, and moves on to the corresponding practice, if by his listening and action he affirms the impossible possibility and therefore sins, the act is exclusively his own. And the character of his act as the self-help which is forbidden is disguised by all kinds of fine or useful results, or best of all it is hidden behind a possible appearance of necessity, of a justifiable desire for knowledge, of a proper pride, a joyfully grasped autonomy. The only trouble is that it is not analogous to the act of God the Creator and the life of creation, but to the dark movement of the beast of chaos and therefore of that which is not. The result is that—by the action of the good creatures of God—chaos in all its nothingness is brought into creation, and creation itself is given the character of the chaotic and that which is not. But who is to see and decide that this is the case : whether the supposed evil of this first act of self-help is not the first good, the prototype of everything that we have to call good and not evil in the sphere of humanity, as man's self-help. Why should not that which happened be the prototype of all true human development, and therefore not chaos but cosmos ? Why not ?

[IV, 1, pp. 466; 434–436; 488; 463]

2. THE GOLDEN CALF

We will now turn to the decisive statement concerning the setting up and worshipping of the golden calf. Its description as a calf is a derogatory judgment on the part of the narrator, not merely in relation to the form of presentation of that which is meant, but in relation to the thing itself : a stupid and helpless and ridiculous calf is set up and worshipped as god : a *vitulum, in quo nihil consentaneum vel affine erat Dei gloriae* (Calvin). The matter is treated lightly, but what is meant—whether on the model of Egyptian or Canaanitish religion or not is a question we need not decide—is the bull as a symbol of virility and fertility, signifying the essence of the people's power as a people, of the mystery of its existence and continuance, of the demonstration of its being as deriving from the tribes themselves, of joy in its own present and of the ideal of its future. The bull is for Israel " a god who understands it and in whom it understands itself " (W. Vischer). Israel itself was this bull, defiantly standing on its short thick thighs and feet, tossing its horns and threshing its tail. But Israel in a divine eschatological form as felt and experienced and seen by itself. Israel transcending and hypostasising itself, and therefore its god. And Israel, too, in the divine form constructed and manufactured by itself—not without the joyful sacrificial offering of golden ear-rings. The god, therefore, which is its possession, which lives by its own imagination and art, by its riches, by the generous offering of its goods ; the god which belongs to it and is pledged to it, as it is brought forth by it. *Volunt esse Dei creatores* (Calvin). Creators of a new and alien god ? Not by a long way, however much the ideas of other peoples may have been imitated : " These be thy gods, O Israel, which brought thee up out of the land of Egypt " (v. 4). It is not a matter *novo et insolito ritu quidquam redemptori suo detrahere, sed potius hoc modo amplificari eius honorem* (Calvin). With the invention and construction and manufacture of the bull they think they can see and understand in themselves, in the mystery of the power of their own existence, their *redemptor*, Yahweh the Liberator, Helper and Lord, and the hope of their future. They do not plan and purpose any apostasy from their relationship with Him, but the deepest and most faithful and fitting interpretation of it, its actualisation in all its particularity. It is not to an idol that the altar to the bull is set up and offerings are brought, burnt offerings as the representation of unconditional worship, of complete and undivided sacrifice, and peace offerings as a witness to the freedom and joy of the sacrifice, culminating in a communion feast in which those who sacrifice enter into enjoyment of that which is sacrificed. What is described is not, therefore, an idol-feast : " And the people sat down to eat and drink, and rose up to play." No : what Aaron called them to, and what, as we learn later (v. 17), was celebrated with a noisy song like a noise of war, was a " feast to the Lord," as Aaron put it in his proclamation, a feast to Yahweh as now at last he was known and made present and existentially perceptible in his true form, to Yahweh as the champion and work and possession of Israel, to Yahweh the bull, and therefore in this image of the bull. This was the breach of the covenant, and Israel regarded it as the supreme fulfilment of the covenant, an act of concrete religion.

The role of Aaron in all this is worth noting. According to Ex. 6[20], he was the elder brother of Moses. According to 4[16] he was to speak for him to the people (and, according to 7[1], to Pharaoh), Moses himself being to him in the place of God. According to 17[10] he was one of the two who held up the arms of Moses in prayer during the battle with the Amalekites. According to 19[24] he went with Moses to the mount when the Ten Commandments were received. According to 24[9f.] he was at the head of the seventy elders who saw God, or, at any rate, the clear work under His feet. Are we to understand from chapters 28–29 that his investiture as high-priest had already taken place ? What is quite clear is that this elder brother is not, like Moses, a prophet. He is called a prophet in 7¹, but only as the one who speaks for Moses. He is not a charismatic, but the type of the institutional priesthood, the keeper of the tent of meeting and its possessions, the supreme official in the ministry of sacrifice. In his own way he is an indispensable figure. Yet he does not stand with Moses but with the people, mediating between him and the people (and to that extent between God and the people), over against Moses and under Moses, without any independent relationship with God and therefore without any independent mission to the people. The one who receives and mediates the divine revelation, the friend who speaks with God as an equal, is Moses himself. Aaron and all the others are only witnesses. For Aaron, too, Moses stands "in the place of God." "*L'institution et l'évenement*" (J. L. Leuba, 1950) are not two factors of equal but of different rank, the one being subordinate to the other. What this means from the point of view of the institutional priesthood and its activity is something which was revealed by Old Testament prophecy from the days of Amos onwards, and it is brought out very plainly in Ex. 32. Aaron the priest as such had not risen above the development and power of the sin of the people. On the contrary, he both takes part in it and he is the exponent of it. He is the man of the national Church, the established Church. He listens to the voice of the soul of the people and obeys it. He is the direct executor of its wishes and demands. He shows the people how to proceed and he takes the initiative. He orders the offering of the golden rings and he himself receives them. He pours the gold into a mould. He himself "fashions" the bull before which they see themselves and cry : "These be thy gods, O Israel." His later excuses are not without a certain humour. The people gave him their gold, he cast it into the fire, and there came out a calf (Luther : it became a calf)—entirely of its own accord, or by means of a little miracle. If the institution does not achieve the event of revelation and faith, it does not prevent the very different event of sin. The institution can always support and execute it. At any moment the calf can self-evidently proceed from it. Priestly wisdom as such can be effective in the form of supreme priestly folly. The priestly art as such—building altars and celebrating liturgies and ordering and executing sacrifices and proclaiming feasts of the Lord—is a neutral activity which can turn into the very opposite of all that is intended by it. The priest as such can always be a deluded and deluding pope. This is the role assigned to Aaron in the breach of the covenant—in this respect it is unmistakably influenced by prophecy. He is not above but under and actively in the activity of which Israel is guilty. There is no support in the text for a sharp personal judgment, such as we often find in commentaries and sermons. The rebuke which Moses addresses to him in v. 21 is remarkably gentle : "What did this people unto thee, that thou hast brought so great sin upon them ? " The people are called stiff-necked and indisciplined, but not Aaron, of whom the narrator simply says (v. 25) that "he had made them naked unto their shame among their enemies." As far as he is concerned the only offence is that of connivance. For that reason, although he might appear to be the chief offender before God, he is not one of the victims of the mass-execution carried out by the Levites (his own men). And there is no question of any personal punishment or expiation being laid upon him. His office does not seem to be compromised by what he has done. He has simply accepted the *vox populi* as the *vox Dei* and acted accordingly. According to the text the guilty party is the people and only the people. Aaron himself belongs neither to the side of light nor to that of darkness in this story. He is in the shadows, significant and great neither for good nor evil. What appears from his role is that he is not Moses, not a prophet, but only Aaron, only a priest, a man of religion, and that as such he cannot arrest but only acquiesce in the fall of Israel, which is itself a great religious occasion.

The key to the story is to be found in what is, if we come to it from chapter

31, its very surprising beginning. How does the people suddenly come to the point of gathering together unto Aaron and asking him to " make " a god to go before it ? The text points to a concealed development of which this is the culmination. The long delay of Moses has given rise to considerations which have led to this appeal to Aaron. The breach of the covenant, of the relationship between the people and Yahweh, arose out of the relationship of the people to Moses, or concretely out of the breach of that relationship.

We have to remember that Moses was what Aaron was not. He was the prophet, the charismatic leader of Israel. God spoke to him, calling him by his name. He was the man who heard and mediated the Word of God, advising and leading and, in fact, ruling the people, not in his own power, but in that of the Word of God which he heard and mediated. And we know, too, that he was the man who prayed for Israel in his solitariness with God, in a sense forcing himself upon God, keeping Him to His promises and earlier work as the covenant Lord of Israel, and being approved and heard by God. He was the man who anticipated in his relationship to Israel the mission ordained for it in its relationship with the nations as the meaning and scope of the covenant which God had concluded with it. He steadfastly represented the people before God even at the risk of his own person and his own relationship with Yahweh. In the Old Testament (with Jeremiah and the Servant of the Lord in Is. 53) he was the most concrete type of the One who represented all men before God and therefore God before all men. Because of this he was the prophet and leader and regent and ruler of the people. The mystery of the grace of God is the mystery of this man, and of the connexion between him and that One. The elevation of Israel stands or falls with his election. This mystery lies behind the claim with which he came to give direction and instruction to the people. By the word and act of this man Yahweh had led the people out of Egypt and brought them to the land of their fathers, showing them by him that the deliverance from Egypt which had come to it was the work of His electing goodness, proclaiming by him the covenant and the Law of the covenant. To look to God meant to Israel to look to this man, to hear God to hear the word of this man, to obey God to follow his direction, to trust God to trust his insight.

And now this man had disappeared and for a long time they had not been able to see and hear him. Had they really known him as the one that he was among them and for them ? Had they known themselves in him ? That is to say, had they known Yahweh as present in their midst, represented by him as His witness and servant : His grace, His holiness, His commandment, and therefore their own election, their own existence as the people of the covenant, their own responsibility before Him, their own mission, their own way with Him from the past to the future ? If they had known Moses, and by him God and themselves, the God who had condescended and given Himself to be their God, and themselves as the people sanctified by His grace, then even if they had not been able to see and hear Moses (for a long or short time) they would have had no option but to abide by what they had received from him ; to live just as though they could still see and hear him ; to be of themselves what they ought to be according to his witness and ministry, this people of their God ; to think and act of themselves in the freedom of the obedience and trust in which they had been placed by his witness and ministry ; in fact, to be those who were called by him—to a thankful actualisation of their election, i.e., to faith—just as though he were still in their midst.

But because—for a while—he was no longer in their midst, it was revealed that they were not, in fact, those who were called to faith, that they had received but not accepted his witness and ministry. They had understood him and allowed him to take control. They had respected him. They had even believed in him as the strong and clever and pious man who had, as they could see, brought them out of Egypt and led them thus far. On his authority they had even said a fairly convincing Yes to the God whom he had proclaimed to them as their God. They had rejoiced in His works and given their approval to His will and commandments. But on Moses' authority. They themselves, their hearts, were quite obviously not in it. They had made reservations in respect of the God proclaimed by Moses, and therefore in respect of Moses as His witness and servant. This was revealed when they could no longer see and hear Moses. All that remained now was they themselves, with the reservation which they had had for a long time in respect of Moses and His God; they themselves as a race of men, including Aaron the priest and his priestly wisdom and craft, listening and looking in the void with empty ears and empty eyes; they themselves with their historical existence, their past and their future, their needs and necessities and hopes, the greatness and the problematical nature of their being. Nothing more.

Is it not obvious that in these empty hearts, in the place which was left empty and was now shown to be empty, there had to rise up this snorting and stamping and tail-threshing bull, the picture of their own vital and creative power as a people when left to themselves and controlling their own life? Those who at very best had listened to and trusted Moses and not God, who had subjected themselves to the authority of Moses and not to that of God, had of necessity, if their further life was to be possible at all now that Moses was no longer accessible, to fall back on something of their own which they had always reserved to themselves, on the confidence which they had obviously never given up but stored away under the impress of the authority of Moses : " God helps those who help themselves." What of it if this confidence had only the name Yahweh in common with the God whom Moses proclaimed, and His grace and covenant and will and commandment? Why should they not know the true Yahweh in this confidence, in the idea, the symbol, the image of the bull created out of their own hearts? Now that Moses had gone, why should they not trust in this Yahweh and therefore in themselves and their divinity? Why should they not believe in themselves and therefore in the true God? Why should they not satisfy themselves and therefore the true divine will? Why not? " Up, make us gods, which shall go before us; for as for this Moses, the man that brought us up out of the land of Egypt, we wot not what is become of him." Aaron is there, and as a priest he is on their side, he is one of them, he is pledged *ex officio* to listen to their request. No opposition is to be feared from him. On the contrary, his priestly wisdom will find the correct theological interpretation of their request, the right symbol for the true Yahweh who has only just been discovered. And his priestly craft will not hesitate to show them how this can be achieved technically and cultically.

We must not misunderstand this appeal to Aaron. There is in it nothing of resignation. The zero hour of abandonment and doubt and uncertainty—if there ever was one—has already passed when the appeal is made. Nor is it in any sense the expression of a demand to hear further what the Word of God is. They know what they want. And what they want is not what they could have expected of Moses. The *horror vacui* has already had its effect. The void into which they may have looked for a moment has already been filled. The appeal is full of reforming zeal. The true Yahweh who has been discovered is already at work. He needs only revelation and a cultus. Therefore the sad reflection on the fate of Moses is equivocal. There is in it an admixture of genuine human regret at his probable and tragic death and at the, in its way, great period which Israel had experienced under his leadership—which involved, of course, his peculiar proclamation of Yahweh. He would certainly not have been denied a state burial. But there is obviously no desire to have him back. He and his authority are no longer indispensable. The bull-god and therefore Israel's own knowledge and power will now continue and improve what he has done. Above all, his proclamation of Yahweh, his exposition of the grace and holiness and

covenant and commandments of God, the whole mystery about His person are
no longer indispensable, indeed they have become antiquated and redundant
and even destructive. It was now necessary that the whole mystery about
His person should be explained clearly and simply as the mystery of the Israelite
himself, that the consciousness of God should become a healthy self-consciousness,
that the expectation of help from God should be transformed into a resolution
boldly to help oneself, that the holiness of God should be understood as the
dignity of Israel's humanity, the grace of God as the joy of thinking and acting
in its own fulness of power, the covenant of God as its own understanding of its
historical destiny, of its national nature and mission and the future development
of it, the commandment of God as the cheerful will to live out its singular life.
The time had come to move over from mediacy, and the regime of mediation in
the form of a charismatic praying alone and hearing and authoritatively proclaiming only the Word of God, to the immediacy of the people as such, and man
as such, to God, the regime of their own mediation and therefore of their own
divinity. The time had come to take seriously the immanence of God, a
concession being made to His undeniable transcendence by the setting up of an
image which would inspire confidence from the very first because it was its own
creation, the reflection of Israel and the Israelite. Moses with his Yahweh who
stood so high above Israel and stooped down to it did not need to return, and
would be better not to return. Moses was *passé*. The age of the bull, a new
epoch in the religious and political history of Israel, had now dawned, and for this
epoch Moses had no message. The true Yahweh, understood by and enlighten-
ing all, palpably glorious and serviceable, had both the word and the power to
bring everything to a successful issue, and would increasingly do so. It was only
right and proper to celebrate a feast to Him, to bring burnt offerings and peace
offerings, to keep communion, to eat and drink before Him with joy, to make
the greatest possible noise and to seek the greatest possible enjoyment. And
no thought that perhaps the replaced Moses . . . and perhaps with him the
replaced Yahweh . . . ? When things have gone so far men do not think of this
perhaps, or of the absurdity of that which they think is their true god—the calf
which is themselves—or of the danger into which they plunge themselves with
this game.

Such was the breach of the covenant in Ex. 32—man as the *creator Dei*,
self-controlling and self-sufficient and self-deifying man, the man of sin in this
first form of his pride, and as exposed by the revelation of the God whose name
is unchangeable: " I will be gracious to whom I will be gracious, and I will
have mercy on whom I will have mercy." [IV, 1, pp. 427–432]

3. DAVID AND BATHSHEBA

We will again turn to the Old Testament for an illustration, and this time
to the strange story of David and Bathsheba in 2 Sam. $11^{1-12, 25}$. It is a story
which is strange even in relation to its context. It is set at the very heart of an
account of the exploits of David after he was instituted king. It therefore forms
an intrusive element, and the painful impression which it makes is not removed,
although it is perhaps mitigated, by the tragic and yet conciliatory and even
hopeful conclusion. If we note how the story of the Ammonite war which was
begun in 2 Sam. 10 is taken up again at once in $12^{26f.}$, we may indeed suspect
that the incident was supplied by another source in the redaction of the Book
of Samuel, especially as it is not to be found in the corresponding passage in
1 Chron. 19^1–20^3. Is it just a matter of introducing the person of Bathsheba,
who according to 12^{24} is the mother of Solomon, and therefore the ancestress
of the whole later house of David, reappearing in the New Testament with three
other curious women (Thamar, Rahab and Ruth) as one of the ancestresses of

Jesus (Mt. 1³ᶠ·) ? If this is really one of the reasons why the story is inserted, it is only with the very different one of the demonstration of David's sin, in the shadow of which this personage is introduced who is so important for the establishment of the house of David. It is to be noted in this respect that the figure of Bathsheba remains rather a colourless one throughout the narrative. In supreme antithesis to Abigail, she seems to be only an object in the whole occurrence. She never has the initiative, and she does nothing to shape the progress of events. The transgression of David is the background which dominates the story of her introduction. And it is this that makes it so strange. In all the previous narratives of the Books of Samuel we have never been told that David sinned, but that he always refrained, or, as in the encounter with Nabal and Abigail, was restrained from doing so. But now, in remarkable contrast to that earlier story, he does not refrain in the very slightest, and there is no one to restrain him. He now does what he could not possibly do earlier as the bearer of the promise. And he does it without any shred of justification, but in a sudden act of wicked arrogance. He can only accept the accusation of the prophet Nathan (who is also introduced for the first time in this story) : " Thus saith the Lord God of Israel, I anointed thee king over Israel, and I delivered thee out of the hand of Saul ; and I gave thee thy master's house, and thy master's wives into thy bosom, and gave thee the house of Israel and of Judah ; and if that had been too little, I would moreover have given unto thee such and such things. Wherefore hast thou despised the commandment of the Lord, to do evil in his sight ? " (12⁷ᶠ·). Note the sharp contrast between the divine I and David, who now occupies the place which normally belongs to all Israel in the message of the prophets ; the place of the one who has received nothing but good at the hand of Yahweh and has repaid it with evil. To be sure, in and with this evil he has not ceased to be David, the one whom God has elected and called. He proves this at once by the fact that when he is accused by Nathan he freely admits : " I have sinned against the Lord " (12¹³). It is also proved by the fact that, unlike Saul (1 Sam. 15³⁰), he is given the answer : " The Lord also hath put away thy sin ; thou shalt not die." His sin is forgiven. But it has taken place with all its consequences. If the attitude of David on the death of the child of Bathsheba reveals a greatness which is wholly worthy of himself, this cannot alter the fact that the child conceived in the act of his sin had to die. And it is surely intentional that the whole story, embedded in the ultimately victorious war against the Ammonites, constitutes a sombre crisis in what had hitherto been the continually mounting way of David, beyond which he plunges at once into the great catastrophe of the revolt of Absalom. From this point onwards David no longer stands out in contrast to Saul as a figure of unambiguous light. We might almost say—although it would be a consideration which is quite foreign to the account itself—that he becomes a more human character. The whole point of the story, except in so far as it serves as an introduction of Bathsheba, is simply to prove that David too shares in the unfaithfulness of Israel to Yahweh, and thus stands with Israel (although not destroying His faithfulness) under the judgment of Yahweh.

The decisive content of the story is given with startling swiftness. In the affair in which David becomes a transgressor there is no element of human greatness even in the tragic sense. It is primitive and undignified and brutal, especially in the stratagem by which David tries to maintain his honour. How else can we describe it except as an act of dissipation ? When we turn to it from the first Book of Samuel, it surely strikes us that the same cannot be said of the sin of rejected Saul. The offence of Saul was to want to be a *melek* like the kings of other nations. In this perversion he ceased to be a charismatic and was possessed by an evil spirit. But Saul was a whole man even in his transgression (which was so slight from the moral standpoint). He was great even in his demon-possession and tragic end. On the other hand, the elect David who is called and set up in his place is painfully mean and undignified when he transgresses, despising the commandment of the Lord (12^9). Indeed, he is contemptible even to himself. If only he had been caught up in an evil principle and programme ! If only he had gone astray and shown his fallibility in a significant entanglement ! But as far as he is concerned it is only a trivial intrigue, however savage and evil in its outcome. It amounts only to an almost casual departure from the order which he knows and basically recognises, although one for which he himself is fully responsible. It is a side-step, as it were, in which he takes on a character foreign to himself, and in consequence of which he does that which is equally foreign, almost mechanically involving the greater transgression which is obviously inevitable once he has departed from that order. At every point, both at the outset and in the sequel, it is all below his usual level and petty and repulsive.

The manhood of Israel (with the ark of Yahweh, 11^{11}) is encamped under Joab in the open fields. The king has remained behind in Jerusalem, and has just awakened from a siesta (11^2). He is there on the flat roof of his palace. It is not an evil situation, but it is not a very promising one. He gazes indolently at the courtyards of the lower neighbouring houses. " Thou shalt not covet thy neighbour's wife " (Ex. 20^{17}). The gaping David covets the woman—Bathsheba, the wife of Uriah the Hittite, as he is told—whom he there sees washing herself. " Thou shalt not commit adultery " (Ex. 20^{14}). David wills to commit adultery with this woman. He has only to command her as the king, and he does so. Has he not already committed it in his heart (Mt. 5^{28}) as he looks on her and lusts after her—the wife of another ? But he does commit that which has already been committed. The woman becomes pregnant. Will he stand by what he has done, not only in her sight, but in that of her husband, of all Jerusalem, perhaps of the child who is yet unborn ? The king of Israel an adulterer ? The consequences are incalculable. He is afraid of them, not unreasonably, but unjustly. Already, however, he is his own prisoner. It is only by further wrong that he can avert the consequences of the wrong which he has already done. First, he tries to practise a clumsy deception. Uriah is recalled. The ostensible reason is that he should report to David on the progress of the campaign. The real purpose is to restore him to his own house and therefore to Bathsheba. He will therefore think, and even at worst cannot prove a contrary opinion, that the expected child is his own. But this plan is defeated by an unexpected obstacle : " And Uriah said unto David, The ark, and Israel, and Judah, abide in tents ; and my lord Joab, and the servants of my lord, are encamped in the open fields ; shall I then go into mine house, to eat and to drink, and to lie with my wife ? as thou livest, and as thy soul liveth, I will not do this thing " (11^{11}). He will not do it even when he is pressed to do so, and invited to the royal table and made drunk, but sleeps two nights at the entrance to the palace with David's bodyguard. He " went not down to his own house " (11^{13}). David has come up against a man—and it is almost a final appeal to himself—who knows what is right, and who keeps to it even in his cups. His only option therefore—if he is not to retreat, as he is obviously unable to do—is to cause this man to disappear, to die, in order that he may marry Bathsheba and conceal the adultery which he has committed. As king, he has the power to do this. " Thou shalt not kill " (Ex. 20^{13}). Well, he has the power to kill without having to admit it even to himself. And he does it by sending his famous directive to Joab, carried by the returning husband himself, to place him in the fiercest part of the battle against the besieged city of the Ammonites, and then to leave him in the lurch, so that he is killed by the enemies of Israel. His orders were obeyed, involving an unnecessary, imprudent and costly attack which in itself David could only have censured. But he was quite unable to do so. For the report sent by Joab concluded with the news which he desired : " Thy servant, Uriah the Hittite, is dead also." This makes up for everything

—even the death of the others who had lost their lives in this futile enterprise. " Then David said unto the messenger, Thus shalt thou say unto Joab, Let not this thing displease thee, for the sword devoureth one as well as another : make thy battle more strong against the city, and overthrow it : and encourage thou him " (11²⁵). He has no real interest now in Joab or the army or the city of Rabbah. The true encouragement is for himself. He can now enjoy the peace which he desires, and which is created by the death of Uriah that he has so skilfully arranged. Bathsheba mourns for her husband. " And when the mourning was past, David sent and fetched her to his house, and she became his wife, and bare him a son " (11²⁷). He could now be born without any scandal. It all belonged to the past. It had all been covered over.

" But the thing that David had done displeased the Lord." This was the message that the prophet Nathan had to give him. He had done what he should not and could not do as the elect of Yahweh. He had contradicted at every point himself, his election and calling, and therefore Yahweh. He had allowed himself to stray and fall into lust and adultery and intrigue and murderous treachery—the one following the other by an iron law—and therefore into the sphere of the wrath and judgment of God. " As the Lord liveth, the man that hath done this thing shall surely die," is his own confession when his act is held up before him in the mirror of Nathan's parable. And it invites the crushing retort : " Thou art the man " (12⁵ᶠ·). He is the one who has been involved in this incident. No, he is the one who has willed and done it even to its bitter end. He, the bearer of the promise, is also a man of this kind. This is what is revealed with such remarkable frankness in the story of 2 Sam. 11–12. David is now playing the role and aping the style and falling to the level of the petty *melek*, or sultan, or despot of other peoples. David is like all other men. He cannot be relieved of this charge. On the contrary, this is a charge and burden which rests on all Israel and every man. And this has to be brought home by David's very human, yet not on that account excusable, but supremely guilty slip ; by what is revealed to be at bottom the normal manner and action even of the heart and life of those who are elected and called.   [IV, 2, pp. 464–467]

4. STUPIDITY

When the Bible speaks of the *nabal* or *kesil*, as, for example, of those who say in their hearts that there is no God (Ps. 14¹), there can be no question of any lack of intellectual endowment, or of powers of thought and comprehension, or of the erudition which we both need and desire. The biblical dolt or fool may be just as carefully taught and instructed as the average man at any particular cultural level. He may be below the average, but he may also be above it, and even high above it. What makes him a fool has nothing whatever to do with a feebler mind or a less perfectly attained culture or scholarship. It is not in any sense a fate. Those who have only weak intellectual gifts and a rudimentary scholastic equipment—the " uneducated "—are not necessarily fools as the Bible uses the word. We have only to think of the νήπιοι of Mt. 11²⁵ to realise that they may very well be wise. In the biblical sense a man is a fool or simpleton when (whatever may be his talents or attainments) he thinks that he has no need of enlightenment by the revelation and Word of God ; that he ought, indeed, to oppose it ; and that he can live his life on the basis of the resultant vacuum, and therefore by the norm of maxims and motives which are perverted from the very outset—on a false presupposition and therefore by a false method.

Anselm of Canterbury was quite right when, introducing the denier of God's existence of Ps. 14¹ at the beginning of his proof of the existence of God (*Prosl.* 2), he did not describe him as *ignorans* but as *insipiens* (=*insapiens*). His objection, which Anselm discusses, is that God is not a real object, but only one

which we think or can think ; that He is not a *res*, and therefore does not exist :
non est Deus. He does not think and speak in this way because he is limited or
uneducated. He does so because of a fundamental lack which consists in the fact
that he is not an *intelligens id quod Deus est* (*Prosl.* 4). · He does so because of
his lack of understanding, grounded in his unbelief, of the revealed name of
God, in virtue of which God is *quo maius cogitari nequit.* Anselm opened his own
argument with a confession of his faith in God as the One who bears this name
(the name of the Creator above which no legitimate thinking can exalt itself,
but from which it can only derive). His enquiry and demonstration have reference to the knowledge of this faith, which necessarily includes the knowledge of
the existence of God. They are evoked and stimulated by the objection of the
denier, but it is obvious that the latter can have no part in the ensuing discussion.
For he thinks and speaks as *insipiens*, and therefore from the point where he
does not know, and as an unbeliever cannot know, the One whose existence he
questions. This is his folly in which he excludes himself from the outset from
the knowledge of God's existence. And it is in answer to his folly that Anselm
deliberately proves that, presupposing the understanding of His revealed name,
God's existence *cannot* be questioned. What a misapprehension it was that the
good Gaunilo found it necessary to rush to the help of the atheist with the defence,
Pro insipiente : as though his denial, deriving as it does from his folly, and
denying what he does not know and understand, could still be championed and
discussed ; as though, proceeding from stupidity, it could be anything else but
stupid.

The stupidity of man consists and expresses itself in the fact that when he
is of the opinion that he achieves his true nature and essence apart from the
knowledge of God, without hearing and obeying His Word, in this independence
and autonomy, he always misses his true nature and essence. He is always either
too soon or too late. He is asleep when he should be awake, and awake when he
should be asleep. He is silent when he should speak, and he speaks when it is
better to be silent. He laughs when he should weep, and he weeps when he
should be comforted and laugh. He always makes an exception where the rule
should be kept, and subjects himself to a law when he should choose in freedom.
He always toils when he should pray, and prays when only work is of any avail.
He always devotes himself to historical and psychological investigation when
decisions are demanded, and rushes into decision when historical and psychological investigation is really required. He is always contentious where it is
unnecessary and harmful, and he speaks of love and peace where he may confidently attack. He is always speaking of faith and the Gospel where what is
needed is a little sound commonsense, and he reasons where he can and should
commit himself and others quietly into the hands of God. In Eccl. 3 we are
given a list of different things for which there is a proper time—in accordance
with the fact that God Himself does everything in its own time. The genius of
stupidity is to think everything at the wrong time, to say everything to the wrong
people, to do everything in the wrong direction, to lose no opportunity of misunderstanding and being misunderstood, always to omit the one simple and
necessary thing which is demanded, and to have a sure instinct for choosing and
willing and doing the complicated and superfluous thing which can only disrupt
and obstruct.

Again we have to realise that stupidity is sin if we are to estimate the
dangerous nature of its power. Its very character betrays how dangerous it is to
life and society, to state and Church. Like the demons, and as one of the most
remarkable forms of the demonic, stupidity has an astonishingly autonomous life
against whose expansions and evolutions there is no adequate safeguard. It has
rightly been said that even the gods are powerless in face of it. And it is in vain
that we appeal to many gods to counter it. We may meet it in righteous anger,

or with ironical contempt. We may play the schoolmaster. We may try to overcome it by approximation or advances. We may try to use it, to harness it for better ends. But even when we are trying to overcome it in ourselves, to liberate ourselves from it, we must always be on the watch lest we merely augment stupidity with stupidity, either secretly or openly giving it place and nourishment, and being only the more completely overrun by it as we seek to encounter it.

It is particularly and supremely dangerous because it has an uncanny quality of being able to attract, to magnetise and thus to increase. The folly of one seems irresistibly to awaken that of another or others : whether in the form of mutual boasting or sinister collusion, of cold or hot warfare or the formation of massive collectives and majorities which trample down all opposition like a herd of elephants ; or even more dangerously by an inward process, in the form of winning others, of begetting children, and of acquiring fresh vitality in them. It is also dangerous in the fact that we do not usually recognise it (or only when it is too late) as the beam in our own eye, our own stupidity, so that in our unconcerned and self-conscious pandering to it we only help it to gain a greater hold on others. It is also dangerous because it is only very seldom, and probably never, that we see it unmasked and undisguised and unadorned. It normally takes, as we shall see later, the form of its opposite, of a superior cleverness and correctness, or even of an excess of noble feeling. For how sure and quick and persistent it is in finding and building up reasons for what it thinks and maintains and does and impels to do ! With what assurance it always presupposes that it is right, and has always known better (" What did I tell you ? ") ! How it loves to make itself out to be either the pillar of society or the sacred force of revolutionary renewal ! How powerfully (in contradiction or agreement with the form in which it encounters one in others) it can strengthen and deepen and advance itself by itself, continually preparing for, and embarking upon, fresh adventures of basic inactivity ! It is also dangerous because at a first glance it is so innocuous, so kindly disposed, so familiar, knowing how to awaken tolerance or a pardoning sympathy or even a certain recognition, but concealing somewhere, and probably behind its probity and gentleness (like the claws of the feline species behind their soft pads), the supreme malice and aggressiveness and violence which will pounce on a victim and tear it to pieces before it is even aware of them.   [IV, 2, pp. 411–412 ; 413–414]

5. THE JUDGE JUDGED IN OUR PLACE

We are now at the end of the important section dealing with the general question (closely linked with that of the previous section) which was asked by Anselm : *Cur Deus homo?* and with the particular question what Jesus Christ was and did *pro nobis*, for us and for the world. To this question we have given four related answers. He took our place as Judge. He took our place as the judged. He was judged in our place. And He acted justly in our place. It is important to see that we cannot add anything to this—unless it is an Amen to indicate that what we say further has this fourfold but single answer as a pre-supposition. Whatever we say further depends upon the fact that in the sense we have noted He was the Judge judged in our place. All theology, both that which follows and indeed that which precedes the doctrine of reconciliation, depends upon this *theologia crucis*. And it depends upon it under the particular aspect under which we have had to develop it in this first part of the doctrine of reconciliation as the doctrine of substitution. Everything depends upon the fact that the Lord who became a servant, the Son of God who went into the far country, and came to us, was and did all this for us ; that He fulfilled, and fulfilled in this way, the divine judgment laid upon Him. There is no avoiding this strait gate. There is no other way but this narrow way. If the nail of this fourfold " for us " does not hold, everything else will be left in the void as an anthropological or psychological or sociological myth, and sooner or later it will break and fall to the ground. If it is to be meaningful and true, and with it all those doctrines of man's plight and redemption, of his death and life, of his perdition and salvation, which seem to be so sure in themselves, then it must first be demythologised in the light of this " for us." For that reason this is the place for a full-stop. Many further statements may follow, but the stop indicates that this first statement is complete in itself, that it comprehends all that follows, and that it can stand alone.

To make this point, we will not proceed any further for the moment, but test the statement by asking whether it still holds good even in the variations forced upon us by the different ways in which the New Testament speaks of this *pro nobis* and in which the Church too will always speak of it. If we fail to notice these variations, there will be a formal if not a substantial lacuna in our presentation, and we shall also miss certain definite insights. A long, retrospective note is therefore required.

When we spoke of Jesus Christ as Judge and judged, and of His judgment and justice, we were adopting a definite standpoint and terminology as the framework in which to present our view of the *pro nobis*. In order to speak with dogmatic clarity and distinctness we had to decide on a framework of this kind. And the actual importance of this way of thinking and its particularly good basis in the Bible were a sufficient reason for choosing this one. But exegesis reminds us that in the New Testament there are other standpoints and terminologies which might equally be considered as guiding principles for dogmatics. The fact that in the New Testament more than one starting-point is proposed for our systematic reflection on the *pro nobis* ought to be a salutary reminder that in dogmatics we cannot speak down from heaven in the language of God but only on earth as strictly and exactly as we can in a human language, as the New Testament writers themselves did—the variety of the standpoints and concepts which they adopted being the attestation. In all its contexts theology can speak only approximately. It is a matter of finding and keeping to those lines of approximation which are relatively the best, which correspond best to what we want to express. That is what we have tried to do in this matter of the *pro nobis* with the selection and exposition of four concepts taken from the sphere of law. But we have to recognise that in the New Testament there are other similar spheres, and therefore that other lines of approximation are possible in principle.

For example, in addition to the forensic imagery which we have chosen there is also, strangely enough, a financial in which the being and activity and even the self-offering of Jesus Christ for us and in our place are described as the payment of a ransom (λύτρον, Mk. 10⁴⁵), and therefore as a λυτροῦν (1 Pet. 1¹⁸, Tit. 2¹⁴), an ἀπολύτρωσις (Rom. 3²⁴), an ἐξαγοράζειν (Gal. 3¹³, 4⁵). In the majority of these passages, although not all, the important concept ἀπολύτρωσις does, of course, speak of an event which will take place only in and with the appearance of Jesus Christ. This strand is relatively slender. Not infrequently (as in Rom. 3²⁴) it crosses the one of which we have been particularly thinking. And it would be difficult and not very profitable to try to think out the whole event within the framework of this imagery. Fundamentally, no doubt, that is possible. But it is surely enough if we are ready to use the particular force of these categories in an occasional and subsidiary manner to clarify the matter to ourselves and others.

There is perhaps also a military view of the work of Jesus Christ behind passages like Mk. 3²⁷ (the invasion of the house of the strong man and his binding), or Col. 1¹³ (our snatching away from the power of darkness and removal to the kingdom of God's Son), or even the πανοπλία θεοῦ of Eph. 6¹¹ᶠ· The Eastern Church especially, but also Luther, loved to regard and describe this work as a victorious overcoming of the devil and death which took place on our behalf. But it may again be asked whether it is advisable to try to work out systematically our thinking in this direction. What is clear is that a place should be found for this group of images and the particular truth which it presents.

There is, however, one group of New Testament views and concepts and terms which stands apart both from those we have just mentioned, and from the forensic group we have preferred, with sufficient distinctness and importance to merit a special appraisal. We can give it the general title of cultic. One important New Testament writing, the Epistle to the Hebrews, is almost completely dominated by it. But it is obviously presupposed and expressly used in Paul and the Johannine writings. May it not be that the most primitive Christianity, because of its great nearness to the Old Testament, partly in agreement with it and partly in opposition to it, did in fact think and speak far more in the images and categories of this group than we can detect from the New Testament ? It occurs again and again in unmistakable allusions. For example, the Jesus Christ who gives Himself for us is called the " Lamb of God," and the giving of His life is referred to as "His blood." When this happens, we are clearly using cultic language. Of course in the New Testament the different groups of terms cut across each other very frequently. It is therefore inevitable that we should have occasionally met expressions from this group in our previous discussion. And of itself it would be quite possible to put our whole presentation within the framework of this standpoint. The older Protestant dogmatics did in fact give to the doctrine of the work of Jesus Christ the title *munus Christi sacerdotale* when they treated it under the aspect of the *pro nobis* as we have done in this section. The only trouble was that their expositions under this title did at their heart slip into forensic notions (which were more or less foreign, or were applied in a way that was more or less foreign to the Bible itself). At any rate, they did not bring out the specific features in the cultic standpoint and terminology. If we ourselves have refrained from presenting the whole in this framework it is for two reasons. First, and quite simply, material which is already difficult would have been made even more difficult by trying to understand it in a form which is now rather remote from us. Second, and above all, we are able to see the matter better and more distinctly and more comprehensively under the four selected concepts taken from the forensic area of biblical thinking than would have been possible even at the very best if we had committed ourselves radically to a cultic view. But this need not prevent us from now trying briefly to see and test from this different standpoint, which is so very important in New Testament thinking, the knowledge which we have gained in the framework of this other outlook. In this respect we may remember Zinzendorf, whose theology of blood I have not really been trying to avoid. What we have tried to say in another way, if it is said correctly, cannot be anything other than that which could and can be said in the images and categories of cultic language. It would therefore bode ill for our results if we could not recognise them in the mirror of this other language in which it was so important to the men of the New Testament to think and speak. For the moment, then, we will not continue our thinking, but re-state and verify it in another direction.

1. Jesus Christ took our place as Judge. We can say the same thing in this way. He is the Priest who represented us. He represented a people oppressed by its sins, threatened because of them, and in need of propitiation, a people from which the will of Yahweh is concealed, which will not be instructed properly concerning His rights and law, which cannot really sacrifice or pray for itself. The priest is the mediator and representative who by virtue of his office (originally, perhaps, understood in charismatic terms) actually makes possible the access of the people to its god. We must not be vexed when we see that the close

parallel between this image and the work of Jesus lies in the very characteristics of the concept of priest which make it quite impossible for us to use the term to describe any order of men in the Church. According to the definition of Thomas Aquinas (*S. th.* III, 22, 1) a priest is a *mediator inter Deum et populum in quantum scilicet divina populo tradit, unde dicitur sacerdos, quasi sacra dans*. In relation to the work of Jesus Christ for us this is not only not too strong, but not strong enough. The exclusiveness with which the priest acts alone, not only in His function of imparting the *divina* or *sacra* to the people, but also in that of representing the people before God, is, of course, the *tertium comparationis*. Jesus Christ is *the* Priest, between God and man, the one μεσίτης (1 Tim. 2⁵). The image indicates the fact. But the fact is greater and more powerful than the image. It necessarily transcends it.

The exclusiveness of all other priests is limited by the fact that all other priests, even the high priests of the Old Testament in their representative capacity, need to do for themselves what they do for others. " He shall make atonement for himself, and for his household, and for all the congregation of Israel " (Lev. 16⁶, Heb. 9⁷). This reservation makes his position and function understandable and tolerable from the human standpoint but it also compromises it. He acts as a *primus inter pares*. But only symbolically, or representatively, is he a *sacra dans*. He himself must receive the *sacra* no less than others. There is no such reservation in the case of Jesus Christ. As the Son of God He acts exclusively on behalf of the people and not for Himself.

For this reason He is the true, and essential and original Priest, the " great high-priest " (Heb. 4¹⁴), " not after the law of a carnal commandment, but after the power of an endless life " (Heb. 7¹⁶), not " after the order of Aaron, for even as man He did not belong to the tribe of Levi, but to that of Judah " (Heb. 7¹¹f·), but as Hebrews constantly repeats from Ps. 110⁴ " after the order of Melchisedec, King of Salem " (Gen. 14¹⁸f·), who met Abraham and blessed him, to whom Abraham (and in his loins Levi) paid tithes and therefore recognised his precedence, who was a king of righteousness and peace, " without father, without mother, without descent, having neither beginning of days, nor end of life ; but made like unto the Son of God " (Heb. 7¹f·). What the priest after the order of Aaron does must be authorised by the Law, which is before him and after him and therefore over him and those like him. And the dignity and force of his offering consists in the fact that it is brought according to this Law, that the bringing of it is a single case under this Law. That is why it has to be repeated. That is why—and this is the great limitation of all other priestly work—it is not the thing itself, the reconciliation of man with God, but only the " type and shadow " of it (Heb. 8⁵), an indication only, a powerful symbolising and attesting of the atonement which will be made by God Himself. If in Jesus Christ we had to do with a high-priest of this kind, with another symbolical representation of the atonement, then we have to ask under what law He stands, what He represents, what general necessity there is for the " satisfaction " He makes, what higher truth is revealed in the reality of His cross. There is always a strong temptation to look for Him on this level and therefore to put questions like this. But He is a Priest after the order of Melchisedec. That is, He is an instance of priestly action for which there is no parallel, which cannot be deduced from anything else, which stands under no law but that established and revealed in the fact that there was this instance. And this is the instance of effectively priestly action because in it the action is complete. It is not the symbol for a general truth which lies above it. It is the instance in which satisfaction—that which suffices for the reconciliation of the world with God—has been made (*satis fecit*) and can be grasped only as something which has in fact happened, and not as something which had to happen by reason of some upper half of the event ; not, then, in any theory of satisfaction, but only as we see and grasp the *satis-facere* which has, in fact, been achieved.

From this it follows that in His ministry, unlike other priests and high priests, He cannot and need not be replaced by any other priestly person. He does not have and exercise this office within the framework of an institution, as one of its many representatives, but on the basis of an oath which God swore by Himself, and therefore as a Priest for ever (Heb. 7^{20-24}), not with daily or annual repetitions, but ἐφάπαξ (Heb. 7^{27}, $9^{12, 26}$, 10^{10}), in a single action accomplished and effective once and for all, by a θυσία, by a προσφορά (Heb. $10^{12, 14}$) accomplished, not in the forecourt or the outer court, but with His entry into the innermost tabernacle, the Holiest of Holies of God Himself (Heb. $9^{1f.}$). In this way the work of Jesus Christ is at once the essence and fulfilment of all other priestly work but also that which replaces it and makes it superfluous. At the point to which the existence of the Old Testament priest, the human priest called by God, points and can only point, there now stands and acts Jesus Christ in a way which is different from that of every other human priest, even the priest and high priest of the Old Testament. And from this point He has now crowded out and replaced from the very outset every other human priest. He is the Mediator, the Representative of His people before God. He is that which every other priest can only signify in his work—and signifying it in this way can only do that which—as the Epistle to the Hebrews emphasises again and again—is completely insufficient: insufficient to create a genuine correspondence of man to God in the divine covenant; insufficient to make man capable of acting in relation to God; insufficient for the reconciliation of the world with God. In the work of Jesus Christ and in that work alone there takes place the real and sufficient priestly work, the *sacra dare*. In Him we have the One we need as a Priest to act for us (Heb. 4^{14}, 8^1, 10^{21}): ἔχομεν. And by Him we obviously have that which we also have as those justified by Him as Judge (to revert to our earlier terminology), that is, peace with God, access to Him, and hope in Him (cf. Heb. $10^{19f.}$ with Rom. $5^{1f.}$).

In fact we can equally well describe the work of Jesus Christ as His high-priestly work as His judicial work, and we shall mean and say exactly the same thing. In both cases He takes the place of man, and takes from man an office which has to be filled but which man himself cannot fill. In both cases a new order comes into force to establish a new covenant, which is really the genuine fulfilment of the old. It does so in this very different man who in both cases as the Son of God made man takes the matter into His own hands to execute it according to its true meaning and purpose. In both cases this involves the deposing and therefore the serious discrediting and humiliating of man. And in both cases this and this alone means the liberation and hope of man.

2. We will combine the second and third points of our main discussion. Jesus Christ is the One who was accused, condemned and judged in the place of us sinners. But we can say the same thing in this way: He gave Himself to be offered up as a sacrifice to take away our sins. It is perfectly plain that whichever view we take or expression we use it is with reference to the same thing, the passion of Jesus Christ. We have not yet mentioned that which according to the Epistle to the Hebrews constitutes the decisive difference between Himself and all other priests and high priests. The supreme and distinctive function of the priest is to offer sacrifice. But this Priest—and here the image breaks down completely and the parallel with Melchisedec is abandoned—is not only the One who offers sacrifice but also the sacrifice which is offered ; just as He is also the Judge and the judged. He does not offer anything else—not even the greatest thing—He simply offers Himself. He does not pour out the blood of others, of bulls and calves, to go into the Holiest with this offering (Heb. $9^{12, 25}$). It is a matter of His own blood, of the giving of His own life to death. " Through the eternal Spirit He offered himself without spot to God " (Heb. $9^{14, 23, 26}$; cf. 7^{27}, $10^{12, 14}$)—Himself as προσφορά καὶ θυσία Eph. 5^2). He Himself is the Lamb of God which taketh away the sin of the world (Jn. 1^{29})—a

lamb without spot or blemish, i.e., the lamb most suitable for this offering, as is emphasised in 1 Pet. 1[19]. He Himself was offered as our Passover (1 Cor. 5[7]). Similarly the expression " my blood of the covenant " in the saying at the giving of the cup at the Last Supper (Mk. 14[24]) undoubtedly involves a similar comparison of His own self-giving with the blood of sacrifice which, according to Ex. 24[8], was sprinkled over the people on the conclusion of the covenant at Sinai. Or, again, His blood is for those who believe in Him that which the *kapporeth* sprinkled with the blood of the animal sacrifice, the ἱλαστήριον of the covenant, could only signify for the people of the old covenant : the demonstration, the revelation, the event, the ἔνδειξις τῆς δικαιοσύνης θεοῦ on earth (Rom. 3[25]). Because it is this Priest, the Son of God, who makes this offering, which is Himself, therefore in contrast to all others His sacrifice is effective and complete, making an " eternal " redemption (Heb. 9[12]). It is the one true sacrifice, just as He who makes it is the one true Priest : the fulfilment of what is meant by all sacrifices, and at the same time the end of all sacrifices, just as He who makes it fulfils the concept priest and at the same time makes the existence of any further priests superfluous and impossible.

For what does the term sacrifice mean ? There is no doubt that like the term priest it stands in relation to that of sin, to that of the discord in which man finds himself with God and himself. Sacrifice is an attempt to deal with this discord. This is something which can perhaps be shown even from most or perhaps all the views of sacrifice that we find in non-biblical religions. But there is no doubt that in the system of sacrifice which was normative for the New Testament, that of the covenant with Israel in its completed form, its purpose is to order the encounter of a sinful people with God in the way which God Himself has instituted. It is the possibility and actuality of a communication and communion of Israel and the individual Israelite with God which, if they do not do away with that gulf, do at least temporarily bridge it. The member of the covenant people still belongs to Yahweh even though he has a part in the rebellion and transgression in which this people is caught up. He cannot forget Him. He cannot escape his guilt and responsibility in relation to Him, his commitment to Him. He can and must make an offering (this is where the mediatorial ministry of the priest is so important). Offerings are substitutes for what he really ought to render to God, but never does do, and never will. They are gifts from the sphere of his most cherished possessions which represent or express his will to obey, which symbolise the life which has not in fact been offered to God. He can bring these gifts. He ought to do so. He acknowledges Yahweh and the fact that he belongs to Him by bringing them. He recognises his guilt and obligation. He confesses that he is a member of the people which, in spite of everything, is His elect people. It is not, therefore, a fact that in his sacrifices the man of the Old Testament merely gave proof of a longing for reconciliation, that he only expressed and tried to mitigate the unrest which filled him by reason of his situation in conflict with God and himself. The sacrifices of the Old Testament do belong to the human history of religion, but there is more to them than that. They are also a provisional and relative fulfilment of the will and commandment of God. They are a genuine element in the history of the covenant and the history of redemption. In sacrifice Israel —fallible, sinful and unfaithful Israel—is summoned to bow beneath the divine judgment, but also to hold fast to the divine grace. Of course, this living meaning of sacrifice can sometimes fade. It may become a mere religious observance. It may be understood as a *do ut des*. It may become an attempt on the part of the people to acquire power over God, to assure oneself before Him, to hide one's sin instead of acknowledging it. Instead of a terror-stricken flight to God it may become a sinful flight from Him to a sacred work. When this happens, but only when this happens and as an attack upon it, the prophets (Amos 5[21f.], Is. 1[10f.], Jer. 7[21f.]) and many of the Psalms (like 40[7f.], 50[13f.], 51[18f.]) take up their well-known inflexible attitude against it.

The real problem of sacrifice is not the imminent misuse to which like any cult it can be put, but the fact that in face of the sin of man, while it can mean an impressive summons to repent and convert, a cheerful encouragement to do the best we can, and even a serious encouragement, and while its fulfilment does call us to remember the presence and will and commandment of the holy and merciful God, it does not in any way alter either sin itself or the situation of conflict and contradiction brought about by sin. As Paul has put it in Rom. 3²⁵, we have to do with a πάρεσις τῶν προγεγονότων ἁμαρτημάτων ἐν τῇ ἀνοχῇ τοῦ θεοῦ which has to be sought and attained again and again. Sacrifice in the Old Testament cannot bring to an end the state of things between God and His people, replacing it by a new state. It can only restore a temporary order (so far as this is possible without more savage penalties). It can only leave open and in the air the disturbed and broken relationship between the two, making a common existence at least bearable and possible. But the alteration which it brings about is only temporary and incidental. Things are made easier and better until the next time. There is promise, but no fulfilment. There is truth, but no actuality. That is why in the bitter terms of Heb. 10³ it is ultimately only an ἀνάμνησις ἁμαρτιῶν. It does shed a certain light, but in so doing it can only make man all the more bitterly conscious of the dark background to his existence, which is still unchanged. It aims at atonement, but it only represents it; it only symbolises it, it does not make it. It is permitted. It is commanded. At its best, it is offered with obedience and thankfulness and a readiness to serve. But it is still only a substitute for what has to happen, for an offering which is made to God in true faithfulness. It is only a substitute for what has to happen when the people and individuals who are disobedient to God are set aside, in order to make way for the new individual and the new people. Sacrifice does not do this. An animal is brought and slain, and its blood is shed. But this animal is not the old man which has to be made to disappear. And the showing of it is not that ἔνδειξις τῆς δικαιοσύνης θεοῦ (Rom. 3²⁵, ²⁶). It is not the establishment of that radical and effective and definitive new order in which a man who is righteous before God can encounter the righteous God. It does not accomplish any τελειῶσαι of those who bring the animal. The offering of it is only a "shadow of things to come" (Heb. 10¹). *Significat ?* Yes. *Est ?* No. That is the limitation and problem of sacrifice in the Old Testament.

Of course alongside this we can and must set the fact that the history of Israel attested in the Old Testament is one great series of dark and heavy judgments on the part of God, and that Israel is a people which is constantly judged by God in the severity of His faithfulness. The forbearance of God revealed in His institution and acceptance of sacrifices is not without its limits. There are some sins of individuals which cannot be atoned by any sacrifices but when they are committed can be met only by the extirpation of the guilty from the community. Similarly, sacrifices do not exclude the punishments of God for the inconstancy and obstinacy of the people as a whole. The history of the dealings of God in and with this people is one which gives many proofs of His goodness and help, but it is also a history of the great and greatest retributions and excisions which come upon it. These, too, are full of the secret grace of God. They are signs of the election of this people. They are never without promise. But nowhere is it apparent that any one of them (not even the destruction of Jerusalem and the temple) could really or basically alter the perverted situation between God and this people, the disharmony in its existence as the unfaithful people of its faithful God. At his own time and place and in his own way, does not each of the prophets who have to announce these judgments have to begin at the beginning like his predecessors, as though nothing had happened ? They all attest the judgment, the day of the Lord, which will be accompanied and followed by salvation. But the day itself remains obstinately on the horizon of the history of Israel. It is not any of the days in that history. None of the events in that history is this judgment. None of them brings in an Israel which has been really and finally judged by its God, that is, put finally in the right, effectively and definitively subjected to His will and therefore well-pleasing to Him. It is judged again and again, just as it must offer sacrifice again and again. But in all the frightful events of this history there is as little of the ἔνδειξις τῆς δικαιοσύνης θεοῦ as in the offerings of its sacrifices. This people is always the same and fundamentally untrustworthy partner in relation to God. On its side the covenant of God with it is always the covenant which has not been kept but broken. The punishments which come upon it from God, like the sacrifices which are commanded by God and made according to His institution, can be described only as "shadows of things to come." Israel signifies man judged by God and judged therefore to his salvation, man brought to actual conversion by the judgment of God, man passing through death to life. But Israel is not that man.

This is where the one sacrifice of Jesus Christ intervenes : the real sacrifice for sin, the sacrifice which sets it aside, which effects and proclaims its effective and complete forgiveness, which brings before God the just man which Israel could signify in its sacrifices as well as in the judgments it had to undergo, but which it could only signify, which it could introduce only in substitute, in a kind of *Quidproquo.* The sacrifice of Jesus Christ, the offering of which is taken out of the hands of all priests, is entirely His own affair, and it is no longer a shadow and figure, but a fulfilment of the reconciliation of man with God. That ἔνδειξις of the righteousness of God is no longer an episode on the way, but the goal of the history of the covenant and redemption determined by God from all eternity and initiated with the election of Israel. To what extent ? To the extent that in it we no longer have to do with a human and therefore a merely human, an improper and provisional fulfilment of the divine will. It is, of course, a human action—but in and with the human action it is also a divine action, in which there takes place that which all human offerings can only attest, in which the reservation under which all human offering takes place, and its character as merely representative, symbolical and significative are done away, in which the concept of sacrifice is fulfilled and the true and effective sacrifice is made. Our whole understanding depends upon our recognising that God's own activity and being, His presence and activity in the One who is His own Son, very and eternal God with the Father and the Holy Spirit, is the truth and power of that which takes place here as a history of human sacrificing and sacrifice.

God wills and demands—what ? Further substitutes in a further ἀνοχή for the purpose of further πάρεσις ? Further attestations of the covenant which He has established between Himself and man ? Further temporary communications and communions of man with Himself ? The further and more serious and perfect offerings of all kinds of *Quidproquo* ? A further and perhaps final history of priests and sacrifices ? No : all the things which are temporary and on this level are done away and superseded. God Himself has intervened in His own person. His great day has come. He now wills and demands the fulfilment of the covenant, the new man who not only knows and recognises and actively gives it to be understood, but lives wholly and utterly by the fact that He belongs to God, that He is His man. He wills and demands not merely the bridging and lessening of the conflict between Himself and us, but its removal, not only light in darkness, but as on the first day of creation the dispersal of darkness by light. He wills and demands the sacrifice of the old man (who can never be this man, who can only die). He wills and demands the setting aside of this man, his giving up to death, which is not fulfilled merely by giving up this or that, even the best he has. God wills and demands the man himself, to make an end of him, so that the new man may have air and space for a new life. He wills and demands that he should go through death to life. He wills and demands that as the man of sin he should abandon his life, that his blood as this man should finally be shed and fall to the ground and be lost, that as this man he should go up in flames and smoke. That is the meaning and end of sacrifice. And that is the judgment which is not fulfilled in any other sacrifices. It is fulfilled in the sacrifice of Jesus Christ, in the shedding of His " precious blood " (1 Pet. 1[19]). It has the power of a real offering and taking away of the sinful man, the power to bring about his end and death as such, and therefore to create a new situation in which God no longer has to do with this man, in which His own faithfulness will meet a faithful people and a faithful man. In the sacrifice of Jesus Christ the will of God is fulfilled in this turning, in this radical conversion of man to Himself which posits an end and therefore a new beginning.

But it is fulfilled in this sacrifice because now it is God Himself who not only demands but makes the offering. He makes it in that He the Lord willed to become a servant, in that His Son willed to go into the far country, to become one with us and to take our place as sinners, to die for us the death of the old man which was necessary for the doing of the will of God, to shed our wicked blood in His own precious blood, to kill our sin in His own death. In Israel's sacrifices in obedience to the command of God this could only be intended and willed and attested and represented—because they were made within and under the presupposition of a constant rebellion against God, and in the sign of the constant provocation of His wrath. But now it has actually taken place—taken place because and to the extent that in Jesus Christ God Himself has acted in place of the human race, Himself making the real sacrifice which radically alters the situation between Himself and man. In Him God not only demands but He gives what He demands. In Him He does that which has to take place to set aside sin and remove the conflict. He shows Himself to be pure and holy and sinless by not refusing in Him to become the greatest of all sinners, achieving the penitence and conversion which is demanded of sinners, undertaking the bitter reality of being the accused and condemned and judged and executed man of sin, in order that when He Himself has been this man no other man can or need be, in order that in place of this man another man who is pleasing to God, the man of obedience, may have space and air and be able to live. He who gives Himself up to this is the same eternal God who wills and demands it. Christ *certo respectu sibi ipsi satisfecit* (Hollaz, Ex. *Theol. acroam.*, 1707, III, 3, *qu.* 77). Both the demanding and the giving are a single related decision in God Himself. For that reason real satisfaction has been done, i.e., that which suffices has been done, that setting aside and repudiation has been utterly and basically accomplished.

3. We have seen that Jesus Christ was just in our place. In cultic terms this is equivalent to saying that in our place He has made a perfect sacrifice. He who as the perfect Priest took the place of all human priests, by offering Himself, has substituted a perfect sacrifice for all the sacrifices offered by men.

That He has made a perfect sacrifice means primarily and comprehensively and decisively that He has fulfilled the will of God the doing of which the action of all human priests and all the sacrifices made by men could only proclaim and attest. With His sacrifice He has left the sphere of that which is improper and provisional and done that which is proper and definitive. His offering was that which God affirmed, which was acceptable and pleasing to Him, which He accepted. His sacrifice meant the closing of the time of the divine ἀνοχή, the time of the mere πάρεσις of human sins endlessly repeating themselves, the time of the alternation of divine grace and divine judgment, in which human priests had their function and the offerings made by men had a meaning. His sacrifice means that the time of being has dawned in place of that of signifying—of the being of man as a faithful partner in covenant with God, and therefore of his being at peace with God and therefore of the being of the man reconciled with Him and converted to Him. We are told in Jn. 19[28] concerning the crucified

Jesus that He knew ὅτι ἤδη πάντα τετέλεσται. And His last word when He died was τετέλεσται (Jn. 19³⁰). Jesus knew what God knew in the taking place of His sacrifice. And Jesus said what God said : that what took place was not something provisional, but that which suffices to fulfil the divine will, that which is entire and perfect, that which cannot and need not be continued or repeated or added to or superseded, the new thing which was the end of the old but which will itself never become old, which can only be there and continue and shine out and have force and power as that which is new and eternal. Notice the exposition of Ps. 40⁷ in Heb. 10⁸ᶠ· : " Above when he said, Sacrifice and offering and burnt offerings and offering for sin thou wouldest not, neither hadst pleasure therein ; which are offered by the law ; Then said he, Lo, I come to do thy will, O God. He taketh away the first, that he may establish the second. By the which will we are sanctified through the offering of the body of Christ once for all." In this respect we can and must think of the positive intention and meaning of the Old Testament opposition to the sacrifices which Israel misused and therefore God rejected, and even to the institution of sacrifice itself. For in and with this one perfect sacrifice it comes about that " judgment runs down as waters, and righteousness as a mighty stream " (Amos 5²⁴). The evil deeds of men are removed from the sight of God. The doing of evil ceases. It is now learned how to do good. Regard is now had for right. The violent are now restrained, the orphans are helped to their right and the cause of the widow is taken up (Is. 1¹⁶ᶠ·). Thanks is brought to God, and in this way vows are paid to the Most High. In the day of need He is now called upon, that He may redeem man and that man may praise Him (Ps. 50¹⁴ᶠ·). There is now offered to God the sacrifice which pleases Him and which He will not despise, that of a broken spirit and a contrite heart (Ps. 51¹⁹). Ears are open to Him ; there is a desire to do His will ; His Law is in the hearts of men (Ps. 40⁷ᶠ·). All these things have now taken place : " by the which will (the taking place of the sacrificial action of Jesus Christ) we are sanctified." There has been brought about that radically altered human situation to which all human priests and all the offerings brought by men could only look forward, the reconciliation which lit up their whole activity only as a promise on the horizon, warning and comforting, but only as an indication, not as presence and actuality. Now that Jesus Christ has done sacrifice as a priest and sacrificed Himself, all these things have come, for in Him that which God demanded has taken place ; it has been given and accomplished by God Himself. In the person of His Son there has taken place the event towards which the history of the old covenant was only moving, which it only indicated from afar—the rendering of obedience, humility and penitence, and in this way the conversion of man to God, and in this conversion the setting aside, the death, of the old rebellious man and the birth of a new man whose will is one with His. In Jesus Christ there has come the Priest who feels with the ignorant and errant, who is Himself compassed with infirmity (Heb. 5²), who as a Son " learned obedience by the things which he suffered " (Heb. 5⁸), and in this way proved Himself to be " holy, harmless, undefiled, separate from sinners " (Heb. 7²⁶), " in all points tempted like as we are, yet without sin " (Heb. 4¹⁵)—in fact, the only Priest who is qualified to act. And in that He has offered Himself there has been done by this Priest the acceptable work, indeed the work which was already accepted and approved by God even as it was performed, the work which was necessary on man's side for the making of atonement. In His sacrifice God has affirmed Himself and the man Jesus as His Son. This is, therefore, the true and perfect sacrifice.

We do not add to the completeness of this exposition, but simply describe it once more, when we say that this perfect sacrifice which fulfils the will of God took place in our stead and for us. For what other reason was there ? God did not need to act as a priest and to suffer as a sacrifice in the person of His Son. But we need this Mediator and His mediation. The will of God towards us is the purpose of this sacrifice, and His good pleasure towards us is its end. In Him there takes place that which we need but which we cannot do or bring about for ourselves. It is a matter of our reconciliation, our peace with God, our access to Him, our freedom for Him, and therefore the basic alteration of our human situation, the taking away of that which separates us from Him and involves His separation from us, our death as sinful men and our living as obedient men. The perfection of the sacrifice of Jesus Christ, the whole divine height and depth of the turning made in Him, is therefore the perfection of the love with which God has loved us. In the making of this sacrifice He loved us in perfect love ; He Himself and by Himself doing and bringing about all that is necessary for us ; without any merit of ours, indeed against all our merits ; without any assistance from us, indeed in face of our resistance. As we close it is as well to look at this perfection again in contrast with us whom it favours. There can be no question of a love with which we loved Him in the fact that this happened, that He sent His Son as ἱλασμός for our sins (1 Jn. 4¹⁰ ; cf. 2²). For who are we ? We are defiant sinners, the obstinately godless, the open enemies of God, who cannot contribute anything to this happening, who if it were in our power would only interrupt and prevent it. The only good thing that can be reported of us is that this perfect sacrifice was made in our place and for us—a superior act of divine defiance meeting our defiance ; that it is the perfect action of God in this turning to us (which we cannot interrupt or prevent). All that can be said of us is that without this perfect action of God we would be lost ; that apart from it we can have no refuge or counsel or consolation or help. But of God we have to say that this perfect action which He Himself did not need has in His merciful good pleasure taken place for us ; that He willed to make it and did make it a need of His, a matter of His own glory, to do this for us, that is, to accept the perfect sacrifice, the righteousness of Jesus Christ as our righteousness, our sacrifice, and therefore as the finished work of our reconciliation. Not only as though we had brought this sacrifice, but as the sacrifice which we have brought. Not only as though the righteousness of Jesus Christ were ours, but as the righteousness which we have achieved. Not only as though the work of re-conciliation finished in Him were our work, but really as the work which we have done. We remember that in the sacrifice of Jesus Christ we no longer have a substitute for that which we cannot do. It is no longer a question of a *Quidproquo*, an " as if," beyond which we still need something more perfect, a real reconcilia-tion which has still to come. In the doctrine of the justification of man, of the reach of that which has taken place in Jesus Christ, we have to see that we are saying far too little when we use a favourite expression of the Reformers and call it an imputation of the alien righteousness of Jesus Christ. It cannot in any sense be an improper justification of man which has its basis in this happen-ing. Otherwise how could it be a perfect happening, and how could the love of God for man realised in it be a perfect love ? Rather, the alien righteousness which has been effected not in and by us but in the sacrifice of Jesus Christ does become and is always ours, so that in Him we are no longer unrighteous but righteous before God, we are the children of God, we have the forgiveness of our sins, peace with God, access to Him and freedom for Him. That this is the case is the righteousness which Jesus Christ has accomplished for us, the perfection of His sacrifice which cannot be added to by anyone or anything. He has sacrificed in our name with a validity which cannot be limited and a force which cannot be diminished. What He has done He has done in order that being done by Him it may be done by us ; not only acceptable to God, but already accepted ; our work which is pleasing to Him ; our own being as those who are dead to sin and can live to righteousness. He alone has done this, but because He has done it, in a decision which cannot be reversed, with a truth which is absolute, He has done it for us.   [IV, 1, pp. 273 ; 273–283]

6. JUSTIFICATION BY FAITH ALONE

The combination of the words δικαιοσύνη and πίστις is obviously a special element in the theology of Paul. He spoke of δικαιοσύνη πίστεως (Rom. 4¹³), or τῆς πίστεως (Rom. 4¹¹), of δικ. ἐκ πίστεως (Rom. 9³⁰, 10⁶), and in Phil. 3⁹ of δικ. διὰ πίστεως and ἐπὶ τῇ πίστει. In Paul all these combinations indicate the place where and the manner in which man's relationship to the redemptive activity accomplished in the judgment and sentence of God, His δικαιοῦν, the δικαιοσύνη θεοῦ in its actuality, is known and accepted and apprehended, is in fact " realised " on the part of man. There is no instance of the combination δικ. διὰ τὴν πίστιν. This means that from the standpoint of biblical theology the root is cut of all the later conceptions which tried to attribute to the faith of man a merit for the attainment of justification or co-operation in its fulfilment, or to identify faith, its rise and continuance and inward and outward work with justification. The pardon of sinful man in the judgment is God's work, His δικαιοῦν, His δικαιοσύνη. Paul has not marked this off so sharply from any supposed or ostensible δικ. ἐκ νόμου or ἐν νόμῳ or ἐξ ἔργων, from any ἰδία δικ. (Rom. 10³) or ἐμὴ δικ. (Phil. 3⁹), from any justification of man by his own attitude and action, merely in order to accept this other human attitude and action, the work of faith, as the true means to create the right of man. As a human attitude and action faith stands over against the divine attitude and action described as δικαιοῦν, without competing with it, or preparing it, or anticipating it, or co-operating with it, let alone being identical with it. As far as I can see—the passage in 1 Cor. 12⁹ where πίστις is called one of the gifts of the Holy Spirit is not relevant—Paul nowhere says explicitly that there can be faith only on the basis of a divine work and gift. But if this is so, it is merely because it was for him the most self-evident presupposition. Yet even as grounded in the work and gift of God the work of faith is still a human work. And its part in the justification of man is that it alone is the human work—we can say this quite definitely in the sense of Paul—which is adapted, which corresponds on the human side, to his divine justification. Not because of its intrinsic value. Not because of its particular virtue, or any particular power of its own. But because God accepts it as the human work which corresponds to His work. Because, according to the phrase adapted from Gen. 15⁶ (Gal. 3⁶, Rom. 4³ᶠ·) it is " reckoned " (ἐλογίσθη) to man by God as δικαιοσύνη, as a righteous human work, i.e., a work which corresponds to His righteousness. God recognises, not that by this action man fulfils a condition or attains something which makes him worthy of the divine pardon, but that in this action of man, and this action alone, His pardon actually comes fully into its own. God recognises that in this way, and only in this way, but in this way seriously and fully, His work and Word will be accepted, " realised " by man, that in this action of man to which He awakens and calls him, His own action has its counterpart and analogy—in Rom. 3³ the one word πίστις can denote both the action of God and the analogous human action. God recognises that in the man who is caught up in this action He meets the man who makes a faithful and authentic and adequate response to His own faithfulness ; that He finds the man who does this, who believes, adapted to be the hearer and witness of His pardon. It is the good pleasure of God which singles out from all others this particular human action. But by that good pleasure it is, of course, radically singled out from all others. The election and calling of Abraham are manifested in the fact that he believes, and that his faith is imputed to him for righteousness. Thus far Paul.

As the doctrine of " justification by faith " (alone) this conception of Paul was rediscovered in the century of the Reformation, and as such it was both attacked and defended. It was understood and misunderstood on both sides and in the centre in the most diverse ways. And it finally became one of the most important (the most important of all in Lutheranism) of the basic doctrines of

Evangelical Christendom.   In our discussions up to this point we have concentrated all our attention upon the " objective " content of the doctrine of justification.   The time has now come when we must turn to what has become this very
important " subjective " side.

Of the Reformers Calvin made this distinction with particular sharpness.
Faith as such cannot contribute anything to our justification : *nihil afferens
nostrum ad conciliandum Dei gratiam (Inst.* III, 13, 5).   It is not a *habitus.*   It
is not a quality of grace which is infused into man (on *Gal.* 3⁶ ; *C.R.* 50, 205).
La foi ne justifie pas entant que c'est une oeuvre que nous faisons.   If we believe,
we come to God quite empty (*vuides*), *non pas en apportant aucune dignité ni
mérite à Dieu.*   God has to close His eyes to the feebleness of our faith, as indeed
He does.   He does not justify us *pour quelque excellence qu'elle ait en soy,* but
tellement que d'autant qu'elle défaut ; only in virtue of what it lacks as a human
work does He justify man (Serm. on *Gen.* 15 ; *C.R.* 23, 722 f.).   For that reason
there is no point in inquiring as to the completeness of our faith.   Exegetes who
understand the ἐλογίσθη of Gen. 15⁶ as follows : *Abram a esté reputé preud'homme
et que c'a esté une vertu à luy de croire à Dieu* are condemned by Calvin quite freely
and frankly : *ces chiens-là nous doivent bien estre abominables.   Car voilà les
blasphèmes les plus énormes que Satan puisse dégorger* (*ib.* 688).   As if there were
nothing worse than this confusion !   And, indeed, according to the fresh Reformation understanding of the Pauline justification by faith there could not be anything worse than this confusion.   It is clear that if faith was to be a virtue, a
power and an achievement of man, and if as such it was to be called a way of
salvation, then the way was opened up for the antinomian and libertarian misunderstanding, the belief that a dispensation from all other works was both
permitted and commanded.   And the objection of Roman critics was only too
easy, that in the Reformation *sola fide* this one human virtue, power and achievement was wildly overestimated at the expense of all others.   Even at the present
day there is still cause most definitely to repudiate this misinterpretation, for
which the Pauline text is not in any sense responsible.

In this context Paul obviously meant by ἔργα the works which the Old Testament demanded of the members of God's chosen people Israel to mark their
distinction from other peoples or positively to attest the fact that they belonged
to the covenant which He had made with them.   He did not reject or under-
estimate these works of the Law as such.   According to accounts in the Acts of
the Apostles, which it is better not to reject, he did himself, as a Christian and
an apostle, occasionally perform such works.   But—as he saw it, not in contradiction to, but in agreement with this Law, as a legitimate interpretation of it—
he unconditionally rejected the idea that the doing of any of the works demanded
by the Law either is or includes the justification of any sinner.   And if, as the
Galatian errorists taught, the fulfilment of the works of the Law is placed side
by side with faith, as something which will justify a man, if it is commanded
as a necessary completion of the work of faith, if it is to be laid and enforced
upon Gentile believers as necessary, then this is judged to be an apostasy from
faith and its radical denial.   Faith is relentlessly opposed to the works of this
Law, and Gentile believers are in practice forbidden to allow themselves to be
won over to the doing of this Law, the introduction of circumcision, the keeping
of the Sabbath, purifications, etc.   This was an antithesis which could not come
easily to a man who was not a stranger to the world of these works but quite
at home in it if not bound by it.   It is a complete misunderstanding to think that
in Galatians and Romans and Philippians, and Colossians too, he is involved
in a wilful movement of emancipation and liberation, as do the Jews who hate
him for it and the Liberals of all times who cannot sufficiently praise him.   But,
as contained in these Epistles, the message of this conservative and not at all
revolutionary Jew of the dispersion was bound to have that ring once faith as
the place at which man comes to justification was exposed to the rivalry of works,

the works of that Law which to him was still and indeed only now genuinely holy. As he saw it, the Law was not at all given for this purpose. The justification of man cannot be accomplished or revealed by the fulfilment of its works. When this question arose, Paul could see only an Either-Or between faith and the works of the Law. And faced with this alternative he could see only one outcome—the rejection of all its works in favour of faith, and for Gentile Christians only faith and the works of faith, which cannot as such be considered as justifying works. The *sola fide* does not actually occur in the Pauline texts. Yet it was not an importation into the texts, but a genuine interpretation of what Paul himself said without using the word *sola*, when Luther translated Rom. 3²⁸ : " Therefore we conclude that a man is justified by faith alone without the deeds of the law." Say what we will about the possibility and the freedom and the right and the compulsion and the practical necessity of the doing of works—the works of the Law or the works of faith—according to Paul a man is not justified by the fact that he does these works, and therefore to that extent he is justified χωρὶς ἔργων νόμου, without them. And the faith by which a man is justified stands alone against this " without," even though it is not without works, even though it is a faith which " worketh by love " (Gal. 5⁶). But if he is not justified by the works of the holy Law of God, but by faith, then obviously he is justified only by faith, by faith alone, *sola fide*. The Reformers dared to see the situation in their own time in the light of the situation of Galatians, and therefore indirectly (and often very directly) to equate the Law of Israel with the cultic and general order of the late mediæval Roman Church, the doing of its works with the achievements of the ostensible or actual piety of their contemporaries in correspondence with that order, the Galatian errorists with the exponents of the ecclesiastical doctrine of justification current in their day, and finally the apostle as the preacher of the faith which alone justifies—with themselves. We have only to read Luther's exposition of the Romans in 1516, and especially his commentary on Galatians in the definitive form of 1535, to see to what extent exposition and application—this exposition—intermingle with one another almost from the very first verses of the New Testament text to the very last. And fundamentally the same is true of the commentaries of Calvin, who was a much more careful exegete, and who occasionally at least did bring out the difference between the two ages. The risk involved in this kind of *explicatio* and *applicatio* was a very big one. The strength of Reformation theology is the directness with which it tried to place itself under Scripture and listen to it and allow it to speak, the power with which it dug out its buried centre, allowing it to illuminate the tangle of corruptions and new beginnings, the dissolution of old and the development of new ties in its own day, the courage in that light to decide with God and to call for decisions in the name of God. But this very strength was perhaps its weakness—a too hasty identification of the biblical situation with its own, and therefore as a result of its own impetuous understanding of the present a failure to see many of the nuances, and the other aspects and parts of the biblical texts, or conversely, because of its impetuous exposition of the texts, a lack of many of the necessary nuances and differentiations in its judgment of the present. Only those who have tried to understand and expound the Bible, and especially Paul as a man of his own day, only those who have happily escaped the dangers which threaten us on these two sides (exposition and application), are entitled to cast the first stone. Certainly in Galatians (not to speak of other parts of Paul's writings and of Scripture generally) there were and are many more things to be discovered than what Luther discovered then. Certainly there was and is much more to be said of the Roman Church and Roman theology both then and since than what the Reformers said then within the *schema* of Galatians. We do not need to consider ourselves bound either in the one respect or in the other by their attitude.

But in the relationship between the original and Reformation Paulinism there is one very important thing which is unaffected by any doubts we may have about Reformation exegesis. For it cannot well be denied that it was only at the time of the 16th century Reformation that, if not the whole of the New Testament or the whole of Paul, at least Paul in his conflict with Judaism in the Church, was again understood at all adequately and sympathetically. From its very beginnings in the 2nd century the Catholic Church did not understand this Paul (with the exception of Marcion who misunderstood him). At a later date even Augustine, the only name we can consider, did not understand him as the Reformers did. He did not understand the principle underlying the Pauline distinction of faith and works. He did not understand the passion of the antithesis, of the mutual exclusiveness with which he viewed the two. He did not understand the bearing of the antithesis on the exposition either of faith or works or especially of justification itself. How could Augustine—and in his wake all Catholic exegesis and dogmatics—possibly have understood justification as a process which is fulfilled in the human subject, allowing it simply to begin with faith and to be completed with the infused grace of love, if he had had before him the contrast of Galatians as it revealed itself afresh to Luther ? The most primitive post-apostolic Church had moved too far away from the world of the Old Testament, and conversely it had too quickly become a doublet of the community and order of the Old Testament, to be able to adopt the Pauline view of the Law as the order of life which is revealed and holy but of no value at all for the justification of man. A detour was necessary to rediscover what the Law did and did not mean for Paul. The Reformers—and in the first instance Luther—had to be confronted by the problem of another order of life, the order of life and the redemptive system of the Roman Church, which was there and was administered and imposed on mediæval man with a claim to justifying power, which introduced man to the outworking of that process. These are exegetical points—I am mentioning only the most important in our narrower context— the illumination of which by Reformation theology we cannot very well deny, no matter how arbitrary that theology may have been in matters of detail.

Even in its application of the Pauline insights to the contemporary scene, we have to note that it cost Luther in particular no less than it did Paul to win through to his understanding of the " Law " as we find it in his writings—to the most radical departure from the view that man can and must attain his justification as a sinner by the fulfilment of the works prescribed by the Law. The Law was for him primarily and concretely the demand of the monkish regulations which had become obligatory by reason of his oath. He had expected his justification by the observance of these regulations no less seriously than Paul had once expected his by the observance of the Law of Moses. And by Law in its wider sense he meant the whole structure of duties with which the Church had surrounded the way to the sacraments and their reception and therefore access to the grace of God, the life which is well-pleasing to God within the framework of the *corpus christianum*. With Luther, too, it was not a repudiation of this Law as such, nor was it a demand for freedom in opposition to it, which led him to his doctrine of justification by faith alone. By nature Luther was even more conservative than Paul. And the situation was even more complicated for him than it was for Paul to the extent that what the Law meant for him was normative as the Law of the Church of Christ and therefore as the Law of faith, e.g., the monkish oaths were an exposition of the evangelical sayings, the system of indulgences, which brought about an open breach was an exposition of the evangelical summons to repentance, and the ecclesiastical and especially the papal authority which guaranteed the whole was the authority of the Lord and His apostles which it was never his intention to repudiate. It is common knowledge with what hesitancy he won through to the perception that all this was not the Law of Christ and the Gospel, that it was not the holy and just and good Law of God as Paul had seen it in the Law of Israel. It is common knowledge with what reluctance he first stood out against this supposed Law of God except in so far as it was a matter of remedying palpable abuses, and with what anxious and, to those near and rather more distant from him, almost painful reserve he time and again confessed that he had no interest in, indeed that he was opposed to, the contesting of this Law as such. To the Law and its works he did not really oppose freedom but (even in his proclamation of the *libertas christiana*) faith. It is wrong to censure him, and a grotesque misunderstanding to applaud him, as a Liberal. And in this respect Zwingli and Calvin, too, were fundamentally in agreement. They did not come as he did from the cloister, but from a pious humanism. By nature they were much less conservatively inclined. They were never so attached as Luther to the whole idea of the *corpus christianum*. But in attitude, doctrine and action they were the very reverse of arbitrary innovators. It was not by a boldly snatched inspiration, or a sudden insight, or, as it were, a flick of the wrist that any of the Reformers—Melanchthon seems to come relatively the nearest—made the step from the exposition of Paul to the contemporary application, thus adopting his position and making his doctrine the lever for their own reforming enterprise.

And above all, in relation to this aspect of the matter, we can only maintain that the reaction of the Roman Church and theology to the doctrine of justification as presented by the Reformers in succession to Paul did allow that the Reformers were in the right at least to this extent, that in the opposition to them there is no sign of any understanding of the Paul of Galatians and Romans, or of the antithesis and exclusiveness of faith and works which he there develops in the question of justification.

Among the more notable Romanist theologians of the 16th century there were a few of whom it can be said that they did at least hear and understand the thesis of the Reformers and tried to treat it seriously. I will cite as an example Cardinal Caspar Contarini, who at the time of the colloquy of Ratisbon around 1541 wrote a treatise, *De iustificatione*, in which he tried to consider and present the matter, as it were, on two different levels : a first, on which to the great offence of his own party he described it in propositions which Luther himself might almost have written ; and a second on which his expositions moved along the usual lines of contemporary Romanist theology. As he saw it, the righteousness of the justified man is at one and the same time one which is imputed to him, the righteousness of Christ which can be apprehended only in faith, and an inherent righteousness which has to be put into effect in works of charity. His intention was that precedence should be expressly given to the first aspect over the second. It is not surprising that both parties accused him of temporising. And although he ought to be mentioned here, he did not found any school, and it was only perhaps his early death which saved him from ecclesiastical censure. The Church was not willing to learn anything in this matter but only to continue unaltered, and that is what it did.

The Roman Church adopted an official attitude to the Reformation teaching in the decree of the Council of Trent on justification (*Sess*. VI, 1547). And, unfortunately, we have to admit that in this decree it laid down its attitude for all time. The decree itself is theologically a clever and in many respects a not unsympathetic document which has caused superficial Protestant readers to ask whether there might not be something to say for it. But if we study it more closely it is impossible to conceal the fact that not even the remotest impression seems to have been made upon its exponents by what agitated the Reformers or, for that matter, Paul himself in this whole question of faith and works. Even more depressing is the reason for this lack of understanding : that what was not only to the Reformers but to Paul the climax of justification in its character as a divine work for man was to them a completely unknown quantity. Otherwise how could they possibly have described the death of Christ as the mere *causa meritoria* of justification (c. 7), transferring justification itself into the sphere of the Church which controls sacramental grace on the one hand, and of the believer who makes use of the Church's means of grace on the other ? How could they possibly have described it as a process in the man who enjoys the blessings of the Church's redemptive system and fulfils its demands ? What was this but the very idea which Paul had contested so vehemently, that there is a justification which can be attained in the sphere of the institution of the Law by the accomplishment of its provisions ? Does it sufficiently mark off the happening envisaged in the Tridentinum from that to which Paul so sharply opposed justification by faith that in the former it is set under the sign of the *meritum Christi* and the stipulation of infused grace ? Where in Paul—not only the Paul of Galatians but Paul generally—do we find anything like the *gratia praeveniens* in virtue of which even before a man believes and is baptised he is set in motion *ad convertendum se ad suam iustificationem*, that is, to the " disposing" (*c.* 5 and *can.* 4–5) of himself for grace as his own *liberum arbitrium*, which has only been weakened (c. 1), assenting to it and co-operating with it (*assentiendo et cooperando*) ? Does Paul know anything of a natural man who, by reason of this *gratia praeveniens*, is in a position to accept the revelations and promises of God, out of fear of Him to turn to His mercy, to trust in the goodness addressed to him *propter Christum*, to begin to love Him, to hate and despise his sins and to repent, and finally to ask for baptism and a new life and obedience (*c.* 6) ? And could Paul possibly have described baptism as the *causa instrumentalis* of what he called δικαιοσύνη, as the Council of Trent does (c. 7) ? Is there in Paul anything like a sacramentally infused and therefore inherent righteousness (*c.* 16) ? Could he have described true Christian faith as a mere *initium salutis* (*c.* 8) and therefore as something which needs to be filled out in relation to justification ? Could he have forbidden it to a Christian as a *vana et omni pietati remota fiducia*, the very words of the Tridentinum (*c.* 9), to cling in faith and to find comfort in the fact that his sins are forgiven ? Could he have regarded it as a " heretical and schismatic " opinion that Christian faith has an unconditional and not a conditional assurance of this, and that so far as it does not have this unconditional assurance it is not the true Christian faith which justifies a man ? Where did he ever say, and how could he possibly have said, that (*c.* 9) although the Christian ought not to doubt the mercy of God, the merits of Christ and the power of the sacraments, yet in view of his own *infirmitas* and *indispositio* even in faith there can be no absolute assurance *de sua gratia*, in the question whether there is grace for him ? Above all, where did he ever bring the sanctification of a Christian and his justification into the relationship which forms the substance of the positive teaching of the Tridentinum : that justification is only completed in sanctification, in the doing of the good and meritorious works provoked and made possible and accomplished by the grace of justification (*c.* 16)—a grace which only begins with the forgiveness of sins (*c.* 7) ? Where did he ever say, and how could he possibly say, that faith justifies a man in so far as it works by love ? How could he possibly speak of an *incrementum* or *augmentum* of the grace of justification by the practice of love, by the accomplishment of certain works, which carries with it an augmentation of the glory to be expected in eternity (*c.* 10 and *can.* 24 and 32) ? Or finally of a repetition of justification—the actual phrase is *rursus iustificari*—in view of the situation of a fall from grace which constantly arises in practice in the life of every Christian, a repetition which has to take place in the sacrament of penance by means of priestly absolution and the annexed satisfactions on the part of the one who is restored to grace (*c.* 14) ? Is not all this in effect a very exact parallel to the whole institution and enterprise in face of which, in the matter of man's justification, Paul gave to faith that isolated and exclusive position ? Does it not mean that in spite of Gal. 2¹⁶ there is " flesh " which is justified by " the works of the law " ? The decisive polemical sentence of the

Tridentinum is as follows : *Anathema sit,* whoever maintains, *fidem iustificantem nihil aliud esse quam fiduciam divinae misericordiae peccata remittentis propter Christum, vel eam fidem solam esse, qua iustificamur (can.* 12). Now Paul certainly spoke of love and hope as well as faith, and if our thinking is to be Pauline we must follow him in this. But in the matter of man's justification he spoke only of faith. And if faith undoubtedly has for him other dimensions than that in which in relation to man's justification it is *fiducia divinae misericordiae peccata remittentis propter Christum,* yet there can also be no doubt that in the contexts in which he connects δικαιοσύνη and πίστις faith is just this and nothing but this : the confidence of sinful man in the demonstration of the undeserved faithfulness of God as given in Jesus Christ, a demonstration in which he finds that his sins are forgiven. If there is any corresponding faithfulness of sinful man to the faithful God, it consists only in this confidence. As he gives God this confidence, he finds himself justified, but not otherwise. That was what the Reformers maintained.

They did not have the unequivocal backing of Paul for all their statements. But they undoubtedly had it for this statement. If the Roman Church of the time had been circumspect but open, it could have pointed to certain undeniable gaps in the Reformers' understanding of Paul and the Bible generally ; but for its own part it would have been ready to learn from this statement of Reformation theology, thus taking the initiative in the comprehensive reformation of the whole Church (and its better unification). But by placing this statement under anathema it placed itself under the ἀνάθεμα ἔστω with which Paul was ready to defend himself in Gal. 1[8f.] even against an angel from heaven, if he chanced to preach any other gospel than that which he himself championed against the Galatian errorists in this letter. It is difficult to see in the Tridentine doctrine of justification anything better than what Paul meant by another gospel. It has no light from above. It is admirably adapted to serve as a touchstone to show where we all stand in the matter. There are Protestant doctrines of justification—we will not enter into them now—which do not pass this test because they themselves are far too Tridentine. The aim of that Council was to be a reforming Council, and in many of its practical decisions this is what it actually was. But with its doctrine of justification the Roman Church closed the door to self-reformation and deprived itself of all possibility of seizing the initiative in uniting the divided Church. It was impossible for the Evangelical Churches to return to fellowship with Rome when the decisive point of dispute was handled in this way. They could not surrender truth to unity. This reaction of the Roman Church was convincing proof that the Reformation application of the Pauline (and not only the Pauline) texts to the contemporary situation was both meaningful and necessary here at the very heart of the tragic controversy, and that it will remain so—seeing that the Roman Church cannot very well go back on that decree. A Church which maintains that its official decisions are infallible can commit errors which are irreformable. It has more than once done so. [IV, 1, pp. 614–615 ; 617 ; 621–626]

7. RECONCILIATION

We will now turn to the parallel saying of Paul in 2 Cor. 5[19]: " God was in Christ reconciling the world unto himself, not imputing their trespasses unto them ; and hath committed unto us the word of reconciliation."

We are taking this sentence out of its context, and even out of its (in any case loose) syntactical connexion with the preceding verse. It is the main verse in the passage, enclosing and bringing together in a pregnant way all the decisive elements in the surrounding verses. It, too, speaks of that fulfilling of the covenant which is our concern here—its execution and its scope—and in doing so it makes express use of the concept of atonement (cf. for what follows the article καταλλάσσειν, etc., by F. Büchsel, in *THWB* 3.*N.T.*, I, p. 254 f.).

Again in the main part of the sentence a story is recounted. And it is obviously the same as that which we found in Jn. 3¹⁶. θεός is again the acting subject and κόσμος the object of His activity. The narrative serves as a basis for the preceding verse where Paul had said that his being as καινὴ κτίσις, a man for whom old things have passed away and all things have become new (v. 17), is the work of God (ἐκ τοῦ θεοῦ) who has reconciled him to Himself in Christ and committed to him the ministry of reconciliation. In verse 19 this is repeated with a wider reference, the particular being made universal and basic. Instead of the apostle being reconciled by God to Himself in Christ, it is now the world which is reconciled by God to Himself in Christ. The apostolic ἡμεῖς in v. 18 and the κόσμος in v. 19 are not contrasted, but in a remarkable way the apostolic " we " is a kind of particle of the world (almost the world *in nuce*, a microcosm) and the " world " is only the supreme form, the widest reference of the apostolic " we." In this way the saying about God's reconciling of the world can in fact be the basis of the preceding saying about His reconciling of the apostle. Naturally, this does not exclude the fact that for the apostle the knowledge of the reconciling of the world is grounded in the knowledge of his own reconciliation. The context makes it quite certain that the two cannot be separated.

We must insist at once that the initiative and the decisive action in the happening described as atonement are both with God (as in Jn. 3¹⁶). This is not to say that man's part is only passive ; we will see later that there is a proper place for his activity, and what this activity is. But atonement is not " mutual in the sense of both parties becoming friends instead of enemies. Rather, in every respect the transcendence of God over man is safeguarded in the atonement" (Büchsel). We must put this even more strongly. Atonement is altogether the work of God and not of man ; καταλλάσσειν is said only of God, and καταλλαγῆναι only of man. Compared with Jn. 3¹⁶, the statement of this divine reconciling is striking in its compactness. It does not say that God loved the world in what He did, but it simply describes the act itself. And nothing is said about the " giving of the Son " or the sending of Christ. All the more impressive, therefore, is the way in which the decisive point of Jn. 3¹⁶ is made in the participle construction, " God was in Christ reconciling . . ." : it is God Himself who intervened to act and work and reveal. The apostle and the world came to have dealings with God Himself. In Paul the concept "'world " is not so all-embracing but in most passages it has the same negative force as in John, and certainly in this context. Atonement takes place only where there has been strife. According to Rom. 5⁶ᶠ·, those who are reconciled with God are such as were formerly weak and godless, sinners and enemies. That is how Paul judged his own case, and it is in the light of this that he usually understands and uses the concept κόσμος. Neither here nor in Rom. 5 does he speak of an enmity of God against man which is removed by the atonement. According to Rom. 5¹, the peace established by the atonement is our peace, πρὸς τὸν θεόν, not the reverse. And his subject here is the reconciling of Paul and the world made by God with Himself, not the reconciling of God with Paul and the world. The hurt which has to be made good is on our side. Notice that in Rom 1¹⁸ the presentation of the ὀγρὴ θεοῦ consists solely in a description of the corruption of man to which God has given him up. God does not need reconciliation with men, but men need reconciliation with Him, and this verse tells us that God has made this reconciliation, and how He has made it. We are clearly taught the aim of His reconciling activity in Rom. 5⁵ : " The love of God is shed abroad in our hearts by the Holy Ghost which is given unto us." It is remarkable enough that if that is the goal there has to be a reconciling of the world, and this has already taken place. But that there is a reconciling activity of God in relation to the world may be read in Rom. 11¹⁵ and Col. 1²⁰. And the goal is undoubtedly this complete conversion of the world to Him. That is how Paul had clearly experienced and known it as God's activity in his own life. But he sees this activity in his own life in the context of God's activity in the world—according to the common denominator of the event of God's intervening in Christ to reconcile the world, and His actual reconciling of the world to Himself. We cannot overlook the scope of this thought in this verse any more (and even less) than we can in Jn. 3[16].

But what does " reconciling " mean ? How does God accomplish this conversion of the world to Himself ? Here Paul agrees with John : By His own active presence in Jesus Christ, by His special presence and activity under this name and in this form, as distinct from His being in Himself as God and within His activity as Creator and Lord of the world. With his ἦν καταλλάσσων he, too, recounts the concrete and unique story of Christ. What took place in this story ? I do not see how in this context we can avoid going back to the basic meaning of καταλλάσσειν. The conversion of the world to Himself took place in the form of an exchange, a substitution, which God has proposed between the world and Himself present and active in the person of Jesus Christ. That is what is expressly stated in the verse (21) with which the passage closes.

On the one side, the exchange : " He hath made him to be sin for us (in our place and for our sake), who knew no sin (God Himself being present and active in Him)." Here we have it in the simplest possible form. He has set Him there and revealed Him and caused Him to act and Himself acted as one who was weak and godless, a sinner and an enemy like ourselves. Here we see what is involved in that sending, that offering of the Son, that self-offering and self-hazarding of God for the sake of the world, of which we read in Jn. 3[16]. It means that in being present and active in the world in Christ, God takes part in its history. He does not affirm or participate in its culpable nature, its enmity against Himself, but He does take it upon Himself, making His own the situation into which it has fallen. Present and active in Christ, He enters into it. Indeed, it is His divine will—naturally without sinning Himself—to accept a complete solidarity with sinners, to be one with us.

And on the other side, the exchange : He does it, He takes our place in Christ, " that we (again in the simplest possible form) might be made the righteousness of God (δικαιοσύνη θεοῦ) in Him." It does not say simply that He was made sin and we the righteousness of God. The first is obviously the means or the way to the second. But here, too, the ἵνα is both final and consecutive. God willed the second with the first, and brought it about by means of it. There is an exchange on this side, too. In Christ we are made the righteousness of God as Christ was made sin for us. To be made the righteousness of God means (as the positive complement to Christ's being made sin) being put in a place or status in which we are right with God, in which we are pleasing and acceptable to Him, in which we have already been received by Him, in which we are no more and no less right than God Himself is right. And all this in utter contrast to our place and status as the enemies of God, in which we cannot possibly be right with Him, in which we break His covenant with us as far as in us lies. To be made the righteousness of God means to become covenant-partners with God who keep the covenant just as faithfully as He Himself does. To make us that, God made Christ sin. And because He made Christ sin, we have in fact become that. For because He in whom God was present and active, He who knew no sin took our place and status, caused our situation to be His, accepted solidarity with us sinners, in so doing He made our place and status as sinners quite impossible. For in so doing He has finally judged sin in our place and status (ἐν σαρκί, Rom. 8[3]), i.e., He has done away with it as our human possibility. Where are we as sinners when our sin has been done away in Him ? Where can we stand when our former place and status has been made impossible as such ? There is obviously no other place or status than that of the One who expatriated us by becoming ours : the place and status of the faithful covenant-partner who is pleasing and acceptable to God and who has been accepted by Him; the place and status of Christ Himself, yes, of the God present and active in Him. In that He took our place, and was made sin for us, we are made the righteousness of God in Him, because we are put in His place.

This exchange is what happened in Christ, according to v. 21. And of the happening in Christ understood in this way Paul says in v. 19 that it is the atonement, or reconciliation—we can now return to the more obvious meaning of the concept—of the world with God which has taken place in Him. The conversion of the world to God has therefore taken place in Christ with the making of this exchange. There, then, in Christ, the weakness and godlessness and sin and enmity of the world are shown to be a lie and objectively removed once and for all. And there, too, in Christ, the peace of the world with God, the turning of man to Him, his friendship with Him, is shown to be the truth and objectively confirmed once and for all. That is the history which Paul has to narrate. As such it is the history of God with Himself, as he has already said in v. 18. But now it is also the history of God with the world, as we are told in v. 19. And notice that in this respect too (and the two cannot be separated) it has taken place once and for all, the history of a decision which has been taken and which cannot be reversed or superseded. That is how He was in Christ—we might say with Jn. 3¹⁶ that is how He loved the world—and it is so, it is in force, and must and will be, whether there are few or many who know the fact, and whatever attitude the world may take to it. The world is God's. Whatever else we may have to say about it (e.g., that it perishes) we must also remember that it is God's—not merely because it is His creature, not merely because God has sworn to be faithful to man, but because God has kept His oath, because He has taken the world from a false position in relation to Himself, because He has put it in that place which belongs to it in relationship with Himself. The reconciliation of the world with God has taken place in Christ. And because it has taken place, and taken place in Christ, we cannot go back on it. The sphere behind it has, in a sense, become hollow and empty, a sphere which we cannot enter. The old has passed away, everything has become new. The new is conversion to God. In v. 18 Paul said that this had happened to him personally in Christ. In v. 19, and as the basis of the former verse, he says that it has happened to the world in Christ. It was a definitive and self-contained event.

Against this understanding of the statement we cannot appeal to v. 20 of the same passage, in which Paul singles out as the content of his activity in the " ministry of reconciliation " the entreaty : " Be ye reconciled to God." This does not refer to an extension of the atonement in the form of something which man himself can decide. We recall that in Jn. 3¹⁶ there is a corresponding mention of faith in the Son gifted, or offered up by God. The Pauline concept of faith is perhaps too narrow to permit us to equate the " Be ye reconciled to God " with a call for faith. But it does point in this direction. We can put it generally in this way. It is a request for the openness, the attention and the obedience which are needed to acknowledge that what has happened in Christ has really happened, to enter the only sphere which is now left to man, that of the new, that of the conversion to God which has taken place in Christ. The ministry of reconciliation which consists in this entreaty is not of itself self-contained, but it begins only with this self-contained and completed event. This ministry is its first concrete result. The world (the Jew first but also the Gentile) needs this ministry. The community in the world also needs it in order to be and to remain and continually to become a community. But reconciliation in itself and as such is not a process which has to be kept in motion towards some goal which is still far distant. It does not need to be repeated or extended or perfected. It is a unique history, but as such—because God in Christ was its subject—it is present in all its fulness in every age. It is also the immediate future in every age. And finally, it is the future which brings every age to an end. It rules and controls all the dimensions of time in whose limits the world and the human race exist. It is that turning from the lie to the truth, i.e., from the unfaithfulness of man to his faithfulness, and therefore from death to life, which is the basis of all world occurrence, and in a hidden but supremely true sense the purpose and measure of all contemporary occurrence, and also its goal, enclosing it on every side in order to direct it and set it right. As this completed and perfectly completed turning, reconciliation makes necessary the ministry of reconciliation, giving to it a weight and a power to arouse and edify which no other ministry and indeed no other human activity can ever emulate.

The second participle-clause in v. 19 is as follows : " not imputing their trespasses unto them " (i.e., to men in the world). It indicates the presupposition of this ministry. God took the trespasses of men quite seriously. But He did it, as we are told in v. 21, by accepting solidarity, oneness, with those who committed them. And by taking them seriously in this way, He did something total and definitive against human trespasses. He took them out of the world by removing in that exchange their very root, the man who commits them. They cannot continue, just as a plant or tree cannot live on without its root. They can still be committed, but they can no longer count, they can no longer be entered up—like items in a well-kept statement or account. What counts now, what is reckoned to men, is the righteousness of God which they are made in Jesus Christ. That and that alone is their true yesterday and to-day and to-morrow. It is on this basis that Paul takes himself and the world seriously. And it is on this basis that the world must take itself seriously, not on the basis of its trespasses which are written off in Jesus Christ, but on the basis of the righteousness of God which is reckoned to it in Jesus Christ. To call the world to the very different accounting which is only possible in Jesus Christ, that is the task and goal of the ministry of reconciliation, in which Paul finds himself placed as one who has experienced and known it.

This is what we are told in the third participle-clause in v. 19 : " and hath committed unto us (the person of the apostle) the word of reconciliation." Between the apostle and the rest of the world there is the decisive difference that he has eyes and ears for the atonement which has been made, and therefore for the conversion of the world to God, for the new thing which has come and therefore for the passing away of the old, whereas the world is still blind and deaf to it. The world still lives as though the old had not yet passed away and the new come. Not recognising the truth, it still regards the lie as the truth. It still believes that it can and must maintain itself in that sphere which is hollow and empty and in which we cannot live. It is still self-deceived. And Paul sees it dreadfully held by this deception and doomed to its consequences. But it is not this difference, and the tension of it, and the dynamic of this tension, which makes him an apostle. What moves him in this difference, what prevents him from evading the tension as a kind of private person reconciled with God, what forces him to make it his own, to bear it in his own person, is the fact that what has come about for him in Christ as his reconciliation with God has come about for him for the sake of the world. His conversion as such was his calling to be an apostle, his placing in this ministry of reconciliation, or, as it is expressed here, the committing of the " word of reconciliation " to the existence of his person. The " word of reconciliation " is the indicating and making known of reconciliation in the world to which it is still unknown and which is still in the grip of the most profound and tragic self-deception. As Paul is given by Christ eyes and ears for Christ, as the atonement made in Christ becomes his, the God to whom he owes this makes him a mouthpiece to speak of this atonement to those who are still blind and deaf, who are not yet aware of the valid and effective atonement which has been made for them, who therefore lived in opposition to this fact as those who are still unreconciled, as strangers to Christ and therefore to God, and for that reason in the most painful sense of the word, strangers also to the world and to themselves. As one who has been made to see and hear, Paul cannot be silent. Called to this office by God, he has to be the mouth-piece of reconciliation. And that is what makes him an apostle. That is what constrains him. And it is the concrete reach of the turning made in Christ that where it is experienced and known it evokes this movement, underlying the community and its ministry of attestation in the world and against the world and yet also for the world.

We concluded our consideration of Jn. 3¹⁶ with a reference to the ministry of those who, believing on the Son of God, do not perish but have everlasting life. It is not there explicitly in the text. We can only say that the verse can be logically understood only when we find in it this reference. But in 2 Cor. 5¹⁹ both the context and the wording make it the point of the whole verse. Where the atonement made in Jesus Christ is experienced and known, it necessarily evokes this witness. In this case, therefore, we have even better justification for concluding with the judgment that reconciliation manifests itself in the establishment and the actual bearing of a witness to it as the reconciliation of the world.   [IV, 1, pp. 73–78]

8. THE HISTORICITY OF THE RESURRECTION

In the first instance, it is essential to grasp that when the New Testament speaks of the event of Easter it really means the Easter history and Easter time. We are here in the sphere of history and time no less than in the case of the words and acts and even the death of Jesus. The event of Easter is as it were their prism through which the apostles and their communities saw the man Jesus in every aspect of His relation to them—as the One who " was, and is, and is to come " (Rev. 4⁸). But this prism itself is not just a timeless idea, a kind of *a priori*, hovering as it were above the relations between Jesus and His followers, above their memory of His life and death, above His presence in their midst or their expectation of His second coming and the final consummation. No, it happened " once upon a time " that He was among them as the Resurrected. This, too, was an event. And it was by this event that the prism was put into their hands. He, the man Jesus, was also in this time, this later time. Not only their faith in Him, or their preaching of Him, but the recollection which concretely created and fashioned this faith and preaching, embraced this time, the time of the forty days. It was by this specific memory, and not by a timeless and non-historical truth, that the apostles and the Churches they founded lived in all the relations between Jesus and them and them and Jesus.

This statement holds good whatever our personal attitude may be to this later history. Its truth does not depend on our own acceptance or rejection of the Easter story, or whether we prefer to accept it differently from the way in which the New Testament describes it, or to interpret it in a different sense. Nor, finally, does it depend on our recognition of its central importance for our own knowledge of Jesus Christ or faith in Him. We may relegate it to the periphery, or regard it as an incidental and dispensable feature in the story. But whatever our own personal attitude to the resurrection may be (and there are many alternatives to choose from), we can at least agree on one point. For the New Testament this later history is not just an appendix or afterthought to the main theme. It is not peripheral to the New Testament, but central ; not inessential or dispensable, but essential and indispensable. And it is all this, not in a different sense, but exactly in the sense in which the New Testament takes it. The Easter history is the starting-point for the Evangelists' portraits of the man Jesus. It is the real word with which they approached the outside world, whether Jewish or pagan, whenever they spoke of this man. It is the axiom which controls all their thinking about this man in His time. It is not just a mere reflection of their memory of Jesus or of their present life in communion with Him or of the hopes they set upon His person. It is the original object which is itself reflected in their entire relationship to this man, past, present and future. To put it sharply, while we could imagine a New Testament containing only the history of Easter and its message, we could not possibly imagine a New Testament without it. For the history and message of Easter contains everything else, while without it everything else would be left in the air as a mere abstraction. Everything else in the New Testament contains and presupposes the resurrection. It is the key to the whole. We can agree about this quite apart from our own personal attitude to the resurrection. And so we can agree finally that the acceptance or rejection of the Gospel of the New Testament, at any rate as understood by the New Testament itself, depends on our acceptance or rejection of the *evangelium quadraginta dierum*. Either we believe with the New Testament in the risen Jesus Christ, or we do not believe in Him at all. This is the statement which believers and non-believers alike can surely accept as a fair assessment of the sources.

R. Bultmann " demythologizes " the event of Easter by interpreting it as " the rise of faith in the risen Lord, since it was this faith which led to the apostolic preaching " (*Kerygma and Myth*, E.T., p. 42). This will not do. Faith in the risen Lord springs from His historical manifestation, and from this as such, not from the rise of faith in Him. But Bultmann evidently admits that the New Testament witnesses themselves took a different view. And we must at least give him credit for emphasising the central and indispensable function of the event of Easter for all that is thought and said in the New Testament. On the other hand, it is a matter for surprise that W. G. Kümmel never so much as mentions the resurrection in His otherwise excellent book. Can the subject of promise and fulfilment really be treated without mentioning the resurrection passages ? Can the general thesis be sustained—legitimate and important though it is in itself—that in the Synoptists the kingdom of God is at once present in the person of Jesus and yet still to come ? The same criticism applies to Cullmann's *Christ and Time*, where the resurrection comes in only at the end of the book (*op. cit.*, E.T., p. 231 ff.) and in a special connexion, without any real significance for the author's reconstruction of the New Testament conception of time and history.

We also join issue with Cullmann at another point. It is wrong to suppose that the New Testament authors started with a particular conception of time as an ascending line with a series of æons, and then inserted into this geometrical figure the event of Christ as the centre of this line. Surely it was a particular memory of particular time filled with a particular history, it was the constraint under which this laid their thinking, which formed and initiated their particular conception of time. What shaped and determined their conception of time was the fact that the God who was the Father of Jesus Christ stood before them as the βασιλεύς τῶν αἰώνων (1 Tim. 1¹⁷), not in the contemplation of a timeless truth, but in the recollection of this particular history. Jesus, revealed in the event of this particular time as the King of the æons, was the first and proper object upon which the gaze of the primitive community rested. It was from this vantage point that it looked upon the æons themselves. That is why it is hazardous to dogmatise about the early Christian conception of time, or to try and fit it into a nice geometrical pattern. Does it have such a pattern at all ? It may not be impossible to discover one, but it would be wrong to accept as the last word on the subject the picture of an ascending line from infinity to infinity.

But another delimitation which is even more important is demanded by Bultmann's proposed reinterpretation of the resurrection already mentioned.

(Cf. for what follows, Walter Claas, *Der moderne Mensch in der Theologie Rudolf Bultmanns*, 1947.) As we have seen, the event of Easter is for Bultmann " the rise of faith in the risen Lord "—this, and no more than this. " Can the resurrection," he asks, " . . . be understood simply as an attempt to convey the meaning of the cross ? Does the New Testament, in asserting that Jesus is risen from the dead, mean that His death is not just an ordinary human death, but the judgment and salvation of the world, depriving death of its power " (*ibid.*, p. 38). As the revelation of the meaning of the cross, it is certainly (with this last act of the Christ-event proper) the " act of God " on which the faith and preaching of the Church are founded. Indeed Bultmann can also speak of " the self-manifestation of the risen Lord " and therefore of " the eschatological event of redemption " (p. 42). But the meaning of the cross, as distinct from the cross itself, is not to be sought in time, but beyond it (p. 36). Apart from the cross and resurrection (understood in this sense) the eschatological event includes " the apostolic preaching which originated in the event of Easter Day " (p. 42), the Church " where the preaching of the word is continued and where believers gather as ' saints,' i.e., those who have been transferred to eschatological existence " (p. 43), and above all the " concrete achievements " of believers, their participation in the cross and resurrection of Christ, in which they die unto sin and the world with Him, and live with Him henceforth in " wrestling freedom " (p. 37 f., 40). All these events in time, says Bultmann, are supra-temporal in context and character, both objectively and also subjectively for faith. For by " eschatological " Bultmann means a verifiable event in history and time which also has a supra-temporal significance accessible only to faith. Thus the eschatological event includes the death of Jesus, the faith of the first disciples, their preaching, the Church, the sacraments and the Christian life. But the resurrection, understood as the allegedly objective fact of the restoration of the man Jesus who died on the cross, of His return to life in this world during the forty days (p. 39), is not a part of this eschatological event. It is a " nature-miracle" (p. 8), a " miraculous proof," and as such it must be " demythologized," like so much else in the New Testament. It is a mistaken objectifying of a concept of the Christian understanding of existence which needs be translated back into the reality (p. 10) because it cannot be accepted as an event in time and space and cannot therefore be recognised in its supra-temporal context and character. An " Easter event " in this sense can be regarded only as an objectifying of primitive Christian Easter faith in terms of the mythical world-view of the time, and it is no longer valid for those who have ceased to hold this view. The real Easter event, which belongs to that eschatological occurrence, is the rise of the Easter faith of the first disciples. This was not based on any event in time, but only on the supra-historical, supra-temporal act of God. For the Easter faith of the later Church and for our Easter faith, it has the significance of an " act of God in which the redemptive event of the cross is completed " (p. 42). Here Bultmann is aware that he himself is on the verge of relapsing into mythology, if indeed he has not already done so. But he reassures himself with the thought that this is not " mythology in the traditional sense," since the reference is not to a " miraculous, supernatural event," but to " an historical event wrought out in space and time " (p. 43).

Our first task is to try to see the implications of this view. If Bultmann is right, there are two ways of taking Jn. 1[14], and the even more explicit saying in 1 Jn. 1[1]. Either we must deny that these texts have anything whatever to do with the One who manifested His life during the forty days, or we must dismiss these statements (though both of them are fundamental in this context) from the sphere of the relevant content of primitive Christian faith and its preaching, explaining them as the mythological garb for the process in which the original disciples were brought by a direct divine influence to see the redemptive significance of the death of Jesus after it had taken place. On this view, the Easter history is merely the first chapter in the history of faith, and the Easter time the first period in the age of faith. The recollection of this time and history is a genuine memory of Jesus only to the extent that it was in this history and time that the disciples made up their minds about Him and about His death in particular. In so doing, they drew far too heavily on the mythical world-view of their age, and we cannot accept their particular way of expressing it as either obligatory or practical. The point is that Jesus Himself is at work during that history and time only in the faith of His disciples. The " self-declaration " of the " Resurrected " is staged in the minds of the disciples and nowhere else. Nothing happened between Him and them. There was no new, and in its novelty decisive and fundamental, encounter between Him and them to give rise to their faith. They alone were engaged in this history. He was not. They were quite alone. To be sure, they had their faith, which had come into being through an " act of God," whatever that may " signify." They had the insight into the mystery of the cross, which had suddenly become possible and actual. But they were alone. Their faith had no object distinct from itself, no antecedent basis on which to rest as faith. It stood majestically on its own feet. The " act of God " was identical with their faith. And the fact that it took place, that they believed, is the real content of the Easter history and the Easter time, the real burden of the Christian message, the basis of the existence of the Church and sacraments. Jesus Himself had not risen. In its simple and unqualified sense, this statement is quite untenable.

For our part, we maintain the direct opposite. The statement is valid in its simplest sense, and only in that sense is it the central affirmation of the whole of the New Testament. Jesus Himself did rise again and appear to His disciples. This is the content of the Easter history, the Easter time, the Christian faith and Christian proclamation, both then and at all times. This is the basis of the existence of the Church and its sacraments. This—if we may call it so—is the " eschatological event " in its manifest form which it acquired at Easter. This is the act of God—the act in which He appeared objectively in the glory of His incarnate Word, encountering first their unbelief and then, when this was overcome, their faith. Hence they were not alone with their faith. It was established, awakened and created by God in this objective encounter. Only in a secondary sense was their faith the imitation and reflection of the death and resurrection of Jesus in their lives. Primarily it meant that they were able to regard themselves as men for whom Jesus died and rose again. Jesus Himself for them ! Hence Jesus and His disciples were not identical in the Easter event. He Himself was with them in time, in this time, beyond the time of His earthly life between His birth and death, in this time of revelation. This is what really took place. In our view, we do violence to the texts of the New Testament if we take a different line, as Bultmann does. But having said that, we must try to explain briefly why we do not find Bultmann's argument convincing.

Bultmann is an exegete. But it is impossible to engage him in exegetical discussion. For he is also a systematic theologian of the type which handles texts in such a way that their exegesis is always controlled by a set of dogmatic presuppositions and is thus wholly dependent upon their validity. In what follows I shall try to come to grips with the most important of these dogmatic presuppositions.

1. Is it true that a theological statement is valid only when it can be proved to be a genuine element in the Christian understanding of human existence ? Bultmann rejects the claim that the resurrection of Jesus was an event in time and space on the ground that it does not fulfil this postulate. This, of course, is true enough. For in the resurrection God appears to act in a manner " inextricably involved in a nature-miracle " (p. 8). None of the major affirmations of the creed fulfils this postulate. True, they have a certain bearing on human existence. They provide the possibility and basis for a Christian understanding

of this existence, and suitably adjusted they can serve as definitions of human existence. But this is not what they are in the first instance. Primarily, they define the being and action of the God who is different from man and encounters man ; the Father, the Son and the Holy Ghost. For this reason alone they cannot be reduced to statements about the inner life of man. And for this reason, too, they are full of " nature," of cosmos. This applies equally to the claim that Jesus rose from the dead. The anthropological strait-jacket into which Bultmann forces his systematic theology, and unfortunately his exegetical theology as well, represents a tradition which goes back to W. Herrmann and even further to Ritschl and Schleiermacher. This tradition can just as easily be exploited in the opposite direction, so as to leave no genuine case against the resurrection of Jesus.

2. Is it true that an event alleged to have happened in time can be accepted as historical only if it can be proved to be a " ' historical ' fact " in Bultmann's sense ?—i.e., when it is open to verification by the methods, and above all the tacit assumption, of modern historical scholarship ? This is Bultmann's opinion. It is on this ground that he rejects the account of the forty days. He cannot include its content, in so far as this deals with the living Jesus, and not merely with the disciples who believed in him, among the " ' historical ' facts " in the restricted sense of the term. He is right enough in this, for it is quite impossible. But he jumps to a false conclusion when he insists that for this reason the facts reported could not have occurred. History of this kind may well have happened. We may well accept as history that which good taste prevents us from calling " ' historical ' fact," and which the modern historian will call " saga " or " legend " on the ground that it is beyond the reach of his methods, to say nothing of his unavowed assumptions. It belongs to the nature of the biblical material that although it forms a consecutive historical narrative it is full of this kind of history and contains comparatively little " history " in Bultmann's sense. The creation narratives in Gen. 1–2, for example, are history in this higher sense ; and so too is the Easter story, except for a tiny " historical " margin. Why should it not have happened ? It is sheer superstition to suppose that only things which are open to " historical " verification can have happened in time, There may have been events which happened far more really in time than the kind of things Bultmann's scientific historian can prove. There are good grounds for supposing that the history of the resurrection of Jesus is a pre-eminent instance of such an event. " It is not," he says, " just a pheno-menon of secular history, it is a phenomenon of significant history, in the sense that it realized itself in history." He is referring here to the Church (p. 43). And the same is true, *a fortiori*, of the resurrection of Jesus.

3. Is it true that the assertion of the historicity of an event which by its very nature is inaccessible to "historical" verification, of what we may agree to call the history of saga or legend, is merely a blind acceptance of a piece of mythology, an arbitrary act, a descent from faith to works, a dishonest *sacri-ficium intellectus* ? This is Bultmann's complaint (p. 4), and he expressly appeals to the shade of W. Herrmann against those who accept the resurrection of Jesus as an historical fact. Can we let this pass ? What grounds have we for accepting the view that the message of Christ's resurrection necessarily has the sinister aspect of a law of faith to which we can subject ourselves, if at all, only in a kind of intellectual contortion ? For the New Testament at any rate the resurrection is good news in which we may believe. And this faith, as those who accepted it were gratefully aware, was made possible only by the resurrection itself. They were not able to accept it because the prevailing mythical world-view made it easier to accept then than it is supposed to be to-day. Even in those days the Easter message seems to be utterly " incredible " (p. 9), not only to the educated Areopagites, but even to the original disciples. Hence there is no real reason why it should not be accepted freely and gladly even to-day. If it

is not presented as something to be accepted freely and gladly there is something wrong with the presentation. But this is no excuse for rejecting it as something which intellectual honesty forbids us to accept.

4. Is it true that modern thought is " shaped for good or ill by modern science " ? Is there a modern world-picture which is incompatible with the mythical world-view and superior to it ? Is this modern view so binding as to determine in advance and unconditionally our acceptance or rejection of the biblical message ? We are again up against the well-known Marburg tradition with its absolute lack of any sense of humour and its rigorous insistence on the honesty which does not allow any liberties in this respect. " It is impossible to use electric light and the wireless and to avail ourselves of modern medical and surgical discoveries, and at the same time to believe in the New Testament world of demons and spirits " (p. 5). Who can read this without a shudder ? But what if the modern world-view is not so final as all that ? What if modern thought is not so uniform as our Marburg Kantians would have us believe ? Is there any criticism of the New Testament which is inescapably posed by the " situation of modern man " ? And above all, what if our radio-listeners recognise a duty of honesty which, for all this respect for the discoveries of modern science, is even more compelling than that of accepting without question the promptings of common sense ? What if they felt themselves in a position to give a free and glad and quite factual assent not to a *fides implicita* in a world of spirits and demons but to faith in the resurrection of Jesus Christ from the dead ? What if they have no alternative but to do this ?

5. Is it true that we are compelled to reject a statement simply because this statement, or something like it, was compatible with the mythical world-view of the past ? Is this enough to make it untenable ? Is not Bultmann being a bit too heavy-handed in expecting us to reject this mythical world-view in its entirety ? After all, is it our job as Christians to accept or reject world-views ? Have not Christians always been eclectic in their world-views—and this for very good reasons ? There is absolutely no reason at all why we should really insist on this particular world-view. But we ought not to overlook the fact that this particular world-view contained a number of features which the primitive community used cautiously but quite rightly in its witness to Jesus Christ. But the world-view accepted nowadays has either lost these features, or regrettably allowed them to slip into the background. Consequently we have every reason to make use of " mythical " language in certain connexions. And there is no need for us to have a guilty conscience about it, for if we went to extremes in demythologising, it would be quite impossible to bear witness to Jesus Christ at all. When, for instance, Bultmann (p. 7 f.) dismisses the connexion between sin and death, or the concept of substitution, or the relation between death and resurrection, on the ground that they are particularly offensive and " obsolete " features in this mythical world-view, he is perhaps a warning example of what becomes of a theologian when he all-too-hastily jettisons the mythical world-view lock, stock and barrel. To speak of the " rise of the Easter faith " in the first disciples is a good thing. But we cannot pretend that this is an adequate substitute for what is now rejected as the " mythical " witness to the resurrection of Jesus Christ from the dead.

As I see it, these are the decisive reasons why, in spite of Bultmann, we must still accept the resurrection of Jesus, and His subsequent appearances to His disciples, as genuine history in its own particular time.

We misunderstand the whole matter, and fall into Docetism at the crucial point, if we refuse to see this and even to see it first. Apart from 1 Jn. 1[1], there are two specific texts in which the New Testament emphatically repudiates any docetic interpretation of the resurrection. The first is Lk. 24[36f.], where Jesus appears in the midst of the eleven just as they are about to listen to the story of the disciples on the road to Emmaus. Jesus says : " Why are ye troubled ?

and why do thoughts (διαλογισμοί) arise in your hearts ? Behold my hands and my feet : ὅτι ἐγώ εἰμι αὐτός : handle me, and see ; for a spirit hath not flesh and bones, as ye see me have." And the story continues : " And while they yet believed not for joy, and wondered, he said unto them, Have ye here any meat ? And they gave him a piece of a broiled fish. And he took it, and did eat before them." The second is Jn. 20²⁴f·, the story of " doubting " Thomas. Much injustice has been done to the latter through wrong exegesis. The fact that he wanted to touch Jesus before he came to believe shows only that he had no more doubts than the other disciples had according to the accounts. It is the fact that the risen Christ can be touched which puts it beyond all doubt that He is the man Jesus and no one else. He is not soul or spirit in the abstract, but soul of His body, and therefore body as well. To be an apostle of Jesus Christ means not only to have seen Him with one's eyes and to have heard Him with one's ears, but to have touched Him physically. This is what is meant by Ac. 1²², where we are told that what makes an apostle is the fact that he is a " witness of the resurrection." By beholding His glory, by seeing, hearing and touching the flesh in which this glory is made manifest, those who consorted with Jesus during this time were brought to believe in Him, and thus authorised and consecrated to proclaim the Gospel. " Blessed are they that have not seen, and yet have believed " (Jn. 20²⁹). This is not a criticism of Thomas, but (cf. 1 Pet. 1⁸) the blessing of all those who, though having no part in the seeing of this particular time, will " believe on me through their word," i.e., through the witness of those who did see (Jn. 17²⁰). It is impossible to erase the bodily character of the resurrection of Jesus and His existence as the Resurrected. Nor may we gloss over this element in the New Testament record of the forty days, as a false dualism between spirit and body has repeatedly tried to do. For unless Christ's resurrection was a resurrection of the body, we have no guarantee that it was the decisively acting Subject Jesus Himself, the *man* Jesus, who rose from the dead.

The fact of faith was created in this history. This faith did not consist in a reassessment and reinterpretation *in meliorem partem* of the picture of the Crucified, but in an objective encounter with the Crucified and Risen, who Himself not only made Himself credible to them, but manifested Himself as the ἀρχηγὸς τῆς σωτηρίας αὐτῶν (Heb. 2¹⁰) and therefore the ἀρχηγὸς καὶ τελειωτής of their πίστις (Heb. 12²). This being the case, He was among them as God Himself. " All power is given unto me in heaven and in earth " (Mt. 28¹⁸). The Jesus of the Easter history speaks not only with binding authority, but with effectiveness ; not only with validity, but with power. His declarations are able to overcome the fears, griefs, bewilderment, doubts and disbeliefs of His disciples. And the directions He gives them (especially the " missionary charge " of Mt. 28¹⁹) point to an enterprise which will neither depend on the resources or achievements of the disciples themselves nor be thwarted by their inadequacy. " (He) hath begotten us again . . . by the resurrection of Jesus Christ from the dead " (1 Pet. 1³). This is true quite apart from any inherent capacity of the disciples or any endowments of their own which they bring to the task. But it is also true quite apart from the obstacles which they might put in the way of this event. When the Bible says that He " hath begotten us again," it can only mean a mighty, creative act of God. That is what those who saw and heard this history remember. They remember it as an event which can never be reversed even when it is behind them as an event of their time and can be only an object of memory and retrospect. But it means something else as well. It means that what they look back upon is the presence of God Himself revealed among them. " God is present "—this is not just an intellectual notion of perception, but it is remembered as a real fact which has taken place before them and which cannot be confessed, but has given them their commission to preach the Gospel to all nations. They live by this recollection ; all their thinking and knowledge is grounded in it.

It is this memory which leads them to add the title *Kyrios* to the simple human name of Jesus. It is a token of their recognition that God was manifestly present in this man. Whether its origin is to be sought in the Hellenistic Emperor cult, or whether, as would seem more likely, it is a reproduction of the LXX rendering of Yahweh, it is the name which, according to Phil. 2[9], " is above every name," signifying absolute deity. This, and the transference of this name to the man Jesus, is borne out by the saying of Thomas in Jn. 20[28]. We do not have here merely an appraisal and interpretation of the existence of Jesus grounded in the depth and intensity of their contrition. Had it been that, it would have been open to question whether they had not exaggerated His status, and whether we for our part should not content ourselves with a more modest assessment. What we have here is a *Deus dixit* spoken in the existence of Jesus during these days. It is a decision which the apostolic Church cannot discuss or revise. For it is He who is responsible for it. He has appeared and acted as *Kyrios* among them. It is not they who have given Him this name, but God. And God has given it by exalting Him above all things (ὑπερύψωσεν, Phil. 2[9]) out of and after His death on the cross. Hence this name is inseparable from His person, and His person inseparable from this name. Although they had once known Him, as 2 Cor. 5[16] puts it, " after the flesh," i.e., otherwise than as *Kyrios*, they now know Him so no more, but henceforth, in retrospect of His resurrection, only as *Kyrios*. And in this way, as the only *Kyrios* they know, they thus proclaim Him—for how else could they have done so ?—and in the certainty given by these days that He was *Kyrios* they proceed to interpret and present His life and His words and acts prior to His death. In practice, therefore, the so-called Gospels, if they are taken and read as their authors intended, reveal from start to finish this decision (and therefore indirectly the resurrection of Jesus), and are to be read, understood and accepted or rejected only in face of this decision and therefore in recollection of the resurrection of Jesus. If we try to bypass this decision, concentrating our attention upon a human Jesus who is not the *Kyrios* because He is not risen, we simply show that we have failed to take note of what they really say, and intend to say.

Bultmann is splitting hairs when he calls the literal resurrection a " nature-miracle." Far from helping us to understand it, this is merely an attempt to discredit it. It is true enough, for in the appearance of God we necessarily have to do with the whole apprehensible existence of the man Jesus, and therefore nature, i.e., His body, has a part in this event. As a purely mental or psychological event, the appearance would not have been what it was, i.e., that of the Creator of the whole universe and therefore of the whole man. Yet it was not this circumstance, not the fact that the resurrection included nature, and took place as a physical resurrection, which made it what it was. No, it was because God Himself, the Creator, who was first hidden in the lowliness of this creature, in the death of this man, was now manifested in His resurrection, that it was absolutely necessary for this event genuinely and apprehensibly to include nature, and therefore to be physical. This was the mystery before which the apostolic community could adore. It was not interested in any resurrection or actuality of resurrection in general, but in the resurrection of this man, and the resurrection of all men inaugurated by it. In other words, it was interested in something which is beyond the reach of general polemics against the concept of a miracle which embraces nature, and indeed of general apologetics in favour of this concept. The concern of the New Testament was not with this concept but with the contingent fact to which reference is made in the hymn which probably belongs to the most primitive Christian tradition : ὅς ἐφανερώθη ἐν σαρκί, ἐδικαιώθη ἐν πνεύματι, ὤφθη ἀγγέλοις, ἐκηρύχθη ἐν ἔθνεσιν, ἐπιστεύθη ἐν κόσμῳ, ἀνελήμφθη ἐν δόξῃ (I Tim. 3[16]).

When we remember this, we can understand why the evidence for the resurrection can only be fragmentary and contradictory, as is actually the case in the New Testament. Compare, for instance, the Matthean and Lukan accounts, or the Synoptic accounts as a whole, with that of John ; or again, all the Gospel accounts with that in 1 Cor. 15. It is clearly impossible to extract from the various accounts a nucleus of genuine history, quite apart from the intelligibility or otherwise of the resurrection itself. The statement in Ac. 1[3] to the effect that the appearances extended over forty days is obviously connected with the forty days of the flood (Gen. 7[4] ; cf. also Ez. 4[6] ; Jonah 3[4]), and with the forty days of the temptation at the beginning of Jesus' ministry (Mt. 4[2] ; Lk. 4[2]). And they may also have some positive connexion with the forty days spent in Canaan by the spies when they went on ahead of the children of Israel (Num. 13[25]), and with the forty days and nights it took Elijah to get to Horeb, during which he went in the strength of the meat provided by the angel. These parallels are sufficient to show that the forty days are not to be taken literally but typically. They do not offer precise chronological information as to the duration of the appearances. The topography is just as vague. There is no clear dividing line between one scene and another, as a comparison of the various episodes will show. Nor have we any independent sources from which to check the evidence. Hence the harmonisations to which the older commentators resorted in an attempt to supply the deficiencies and clear up the obscurities, are almost amusingly incongruous. The narratives are not meant to be taken as " history " in our sense of the word. Even 1 Cor. 15[3-8] is treated in a strangely abstract way if it is regarded as a citation of witnesses for the purpose of historical proof. True, these accounts read very differently from myths. The Easter story is differentiated from myth, both formally and materially, by the fact that it is all about a real man of flesh and blood. But the stories are couched in the imaginative, poetic style of historical saga, and are therefore marked by the corresponding obscurity. For they are describing an event beyond the reach of historical research or depiction. Hence we have no right to try to analyse or harmonise them. This is to do violence to the whole character of the event in question. There can be no doubt that all these narratives are about the same event, and that they are agreed in substance, intention and interpretation. None of the authors ever even dreamed, for example, of reducing the event to " the rise of the Easter faith of the first disciples." On the other hand, each of the narratives must be read for its own sake just as it stands. Each is a specific witness to the decisive things God said and did in this event. And we can be glad that there is the possibility of adducing one in explanation of the others. Ἐγενόμην νεκρὸς καὶ ἰδοὺ ζῶν (Rev. 1[18])—it is here that all these very saga-like accounts have their common ground. This, and this alone, is what they have to tell us.

A few words may be said in conclusion about the empty tomb (Mk. 16[1-8] and par.) and the ascension (Lk. 24[50-53] ; Ac. 1[9-12]). These stories are indispensable if we are to understand what the New Testament seeks to proclaim as the Easter message. Taken together, they mark the limits of the Easter period, at one end the empty tomb, and at the other the ascension. (It is worth noting that the limits are drawn not only backwards and forwards, but also downwards and upwards.) In the later apostolic preaching both events, like the Virgin Birth at the beginning of the Gospel narrative, seem to be presupposed, and are certainly never questioned, but they are only hinted at occasionally here and there, and never referred to explicitly. Even in the Easter narratives the empty tomb and the ascension are alike in the fact that they are both indicated rather than described ; the one as an introduction, the other as a conclusion ; the one a little more definitely, though still in very general terms, the other much more vaguely. Indeed, in the strict sense the ascension occurs only in Ac. 1[9f.]. It is not mentioned at all in the genuine Marcan ending (though this is obviously incomplete). In Matthew it is merely implied in the reference of Jesus to the power given Him in heaven and on earth (Mt. 28¹⁸). Luke's Gospel, according to the more probable reading at 24⁵¹, is also very indefinite : διέστη ἀπ᾽ αὐτῶν, while in John it occurs only in the comprehensive terms ἀναβαίνειν and ὑπάγειν, ὑψωθῆναι and δοξασθῆναι, which are used to embrace the whole ascent to Jerusalem, the crucifixion, the resurrection and the reappearance, and do not refer to the ascension as a concrete event. There are reasons for this. The content of the Easter witness, the Easter event, was not that the disciples found the tomb empty or that they saw Him go up to heaven, but that when they had lost Him through death they were sought and found by Him as the Resurrected. The empty tomb and the ascension are merely signs of the Easter event, just as the Virgin Birth is merely the sign of the nativity, namely, of the human generation and birth of the eternal Son of God. Yet both signs are so important that we can hardly say that they might equally well be omitted.

The function of the empty tomb, with its backward, downward, earthward reference, is to show that the Jesus who died and was buried was delivered from death, and therefore from the grave, by the power of God ; that He, the Living, is not to be sought among the dead (Lk. 24⁵). " He is risen ; he is not here : behold the place where they laid him " (Mk. 16⁶). " He is not here ; for he is risen, even as he said " (Mt. 28⁶ ; Lk. 24⁶). He is not here ! But it is the angels who say this. Since the nativity and temptation the angels have not played any active part. But they now reappear at the tomb. And it is only the angels who say this ; who as it were draw the line behind which there can be no going back. They only point to the empty tomb. The empty tomb was obviously a very ambiguous and contestable fact (Mt. 27⁶²ᶠ. ; 28¹¹ᶠ.). And what has happened around this sepulchre is a warning against making it a primary focus of attention. The empty tomb is not the same thing as the resurrection. It is not the appearance of the Living ; it is only its presupposition. Hence it is only the sign, although an indispensable sign. Christians do not believe in the empty tomb, but in the living Christ. This does not mean, however, that we can believe in the living Christ without believing in the empty tomb. Is it just a " legend " ? What matter ? It still refers to the phenomenon ensuing the resurrection, to the presupposition of the appearance of Jesus. It is the sign which obviates all possible misunderstanding. It cannot, therefore, but demand our assent, even as a legend. Rejection of the legend of the empty tomb has always been accompanied by rejection of the saga of the living Jesus, and necessarily so. Far better, then, to admit that the empty tomb belongs to the Easter event as its sign.

The same considerations apply to the ascension. It is less directly attested in the New Testament, but unlike the empty tomb it has found a place in the creed, and has its own special feast in the Church Kalendar. In contrast to the first sign it points forwards and upwards, thus serving a positive function. Just as the discovery of the empty tomb by the women marks the beginning of the Easter time and history, its end is marked by the meeting of the disciples on the mountain, which in Mt. 28¹⁶ is located in Galilee, but which Ac. 1¹² identifies with the Mount of Olives. The end consists in their θεᾶσθαι αὐτὸν πορευόμενον εἰς τὸν οὐρανόν (Ac. 1¹¹). As the empty tomb looks downwards, the ascension looks upwards. But again the ascension—Jesus' disappearance into heaven— is the sign of the Resurrected, not the Resurrected Himself. " Heaven " in biblical language is the sum of the inaccessible and incomprehensible side of the created world, so that, although it is not God Himself, it is the throne of God, the creaturely correspondence to his glory, which is veiled from man, and cannot be disclosed except on His initiative. There is no sense in trying to visualise the ascension as a literal event, like going up in a balloon. The achievements of Christian art in this field are amongst its worst perpetrations. But of course this is no reason why they should be used to make the whole thing ridiculous. The point of the story is not that when Jesus left His disciples He visibly embarked upon a wonderful journey into space, but that when He left them He entered the side of the created world which was provisionally inaccessible and incomprehensible, that before their eyes He ceased to be before their eyes. This does not mean, however, that He ceased to be a creature, man. What it does mean is that He showed Himself quite unequivocally to be the creature, the man, who in provisional distinction from all other men lives on the God-ward side of the universe, sharing His throne, existing and acting in the mode of God, and therefore to be remembered as such, to be known once for all as this exalted creature, this exalted man, and henceforth to be accepted as the One who exists in this form to all eternity. The most important verse in the ascension story is the one which runs : " A cloud received him out of their sight " (Ac. 1[9]). In biblical language, the cloud does not signify merely the hiddenness of God, but His hidden presence, and the coming revelation which penetrates this hiddenness. It does not signify merely the heaven which is closed for us, but the heaven which from within, on God's side, will not always be closed. The words of the angels—note how they reappear at this point after playing no part in the Easter story proper—are a commentary on this : " Ye men of Galilee, why stand ye gazing up into heaven ? this same Jesus, which is taken up from you into heaven, shall so come in like manner as ye have seen him go into heaven " (Ac. 1[11]). Whatever it is, the cloud which takes Him out of their sight is not a cloud of sorrow. And the view that the ascension is Jesus' " farewell " to His disciples must be treated with caution. The mode of this leavetaking is what matters. He reveals Himself to them not only as the One who according to Mt. 28[20] will be with them in this heavenly mode of existence all the days, even to the consummation (συντέλεια) of the age, but also as the One who will come again to usher in this consummation. The ascension is the proleptic sign of the *parousia*, pointing to the Son of Man who will finally and visibly emerge from the concealment of His heavenly existence and come on the clouds of heaven (Mt. 24[30]). This conclusion to the Easter history gives to the whole retrospective memory of the Resurrected this joyous character. It shows that Jesus did not enter and is not to be sought after the Easter history and the Easter time in any kind of hiddenness, but in the hiddenness of God. And finally it describes the hiddenness of God in such a way as to suggest that it burgeons with the conclusive revelation still awaited in the future. As this sign, the ascension is indispensable, and it would be injudicious as well as ungrateful on any grounds to ignore or reject this upward and forward-looking sign.   [III, 2, pp. 442 ; 442–447 ; 448 ; 449–450 ; 451–454]

9. THE MEANING OF THE RESURRECTION

The New Testament proclaims the death of the Lord (1 Cor. 11[26]), the crucified Christ (1 Cor. 1[23]), the One who is dead ἀποθανών—μᾶλλον δὲ ἐγερθείς (Rom. 8[34]). But it proclaims this One who is crucified and dead (in and with whom the death of Christians and all men has taken place) as the One whom God has raised from the dead, as the One who is alive, as πάντοτε ζῶν εἰς τὸ ἐντυγχάνειν ὑπὲρ αὐτῶν (Heb. 7[25]). It proclaims His death (and in and with it the death of Christians and of all men, the judgment, the end of the world which has come upon us), but as the death of the One who has been called ἐκ τῶν νεκρῶν, from the ranks of the dead, the first of the dead to escape death (1 Cor. 15[20], Col. 1[18]), the raising of whom is to the men of the New Testament the guarantee of their own future resurrection and that of all men, in whose resurrection they have the basis of a life in this world which is assured of a future resurrection, which hastens towards it, which anticipates in hope their own future life out of death. It is to Him, the Resurrected, that their μνημονεύειν (2 Tim. 2[8]) and witness (Ac. 1[22], 4[33]) refer.

Their proclamation and the faith which it evokes are not "empty" or "vain" (κενὸν τὸ κήρυγμα ἡμῶν, κενὴ—ματαία—ἡ πίστις ὑμῶν) ; they are not still in their sins ; those who have fallen asleep in and with Him are not lost, because the One who died on the cross has been raised again from the dead (1 Cor. 15¹⁴, ¹⁷ᶠ.). To know Him is identical with knowing the power of His resurrection (Phil. 3¹⁰). The confession that He is the Lord is based on the faith that God has raised Him from the dead (Rom. 10⁹). Even the Christian's faith in God is itself and as such faith in the One who raised Him from the dead (1 Pet. 1²¹). It is because according to the Scriptures this took place on the "third day" that we can and must positively and thankfully confess what took place on the "first" day, the day of His cross : He died for our sins "according to the scriptures" (1 Cor. 15³ᶠ.). He, the risen One, opened up the Scriptures to them and opened their eyes to the Scriptures (Lk. 24²⁵ᶠ.).

In the concepts answer, confession and sentence, we gather together the distinctive thing which the New Testament sees in the resurrection of Jesus Christ as opposed to the event of His death. It is all summarised in the remarkable phrase used to describe the resurrection in the hymn quoted in 1 Tim. 3¹⁶ : ἐδικαιώθη ἐν πνεύματι. He Himself, Jesus Christ, the Son of God made man, was justified by God in His resurrection from the dead. He was justified as man, and in Him as the Representative of all men all were justified. Hence the continuation of the statement in Rom. 4²⁵ : ἠγέρθη διὰ τὴν δικαίωσιν ἡμῶν.

But what gives to the justification which took place there its true and decisive power is that in the unity of God with this man (and in and with Him in His fellowship with us all), in the resurrection of Jesus Christ, God Himself, His will and act in the death of Jesus Christ, was justified by God, by Himself and therefore definitively. Was this necessary ? Certainly not in the sense that at Golgotha everything had not taken place which had to take place for the reconciliation of the world with God, that the representation and sacrifice of Jesus Christ in His death were not wholly sufficient, that they were therefore referred back to some completion and continuation. Anything pointing in this direction, any limitations of the τετέλεσται are quite alien to the New Testament. But the direct continuation of the τετέλεσται in Jn. 19³⁰ is : καὶ κλίνας τὴν κεφαλὴν παρέδωκεν τὸ πνεῦμα. And the occurrence of Golgotha which is complete in itself consists ultimately in the fact that Jesus "bowed his head." What does this mean ? In obedience to the will of God ? Before God as Father ? His obedience consists in the fact that He commends or offers up His spirit, that is, Himself—He delivers up Himself. To whom ? To God His Father, to His decree and disposing ? Naturally, and this is emphasised in the saying handed down in Lk. 23⁴⁶ : "Father, into thy hands I commend my spirit," myself. But there, too, there is the continuation : τοῦτο δὲ εἰπὼν ἐξέπνευσεν. It is therefore to death that He bows His head and commits Himself. In and with the fulfilment there of the will of God it is nothingness which can triumph over Him—and in and with Him over the whole of the human race represented by Him. According to the disposition and in the service of God death and nothingness are brought in and used for the reconciliation of the world with God, as instruments in His conflict with the corruption of the world and the sin of man—but death and nothingness in all their evil and destructive power. It is also to the wrath of God which permits this force and judges evil by evil that Jesus commits Himself and in and with Himself the world and the individual sinner. The reconciliation of the world with God which took place in Jesus Christ had therefore the meaning that a radical end was made of Him and therefore of the world.

And that might have exhausted its meaning. The saying : "My God, my God, why hast thou forsaken me ? " (Mk. 15³⁴) shows how close was this frightful possibility. It might have been that God turned away His face finally from us. It might have been that by the same eternal Word by which as Creator He gave being to man and the world He now willed to take away that being from them, to let them perish with all their corruption and sin. The relationship between Himself and His creation might have been regularised by depriving it of its perverted actuality. He might have repented of having created it (Gen. 6[7]), and carried this repentance to its logical conclusion. Ruling as the Judge, He might have given death and nothingness the last word in relation to the creature. He would still have been in the right.

But He would have been in the right only in complete concealment, within Himself, and only by granting to death and nothingness as the instruments of His judgment a final right in relation to the creature. He would then have surrendered to them His own right in relation to the creature. He would then have renounced His own right, His own creature. And in so doing He would have recognised the power of death and nothingness over the creature, *de facto* if not *de iure*. He would not have confirmed His original choice between heaven and.earth on the one hand and chaos on the other, His decision for light and His rejection of darkness (Gen. 1[3]), Himself therefore as the Creator of the world and humanity which He made and found to be good. In short, He would not have justified Himself. But this is to say that He would have been in the right only in and for Himself. In His wrath He would have been content to maintain His right against the world, in its destruction. He would not have sustained or demonstrated or revealed His right to the world and in the world.

Did He need to do this ? Certainly not. On what ground can we postulate that He had to do it ? What reason is there to blame Him if He willed not to do so ? He did not owe it to anyone to justify Himself. It could only be His grace which bade Him do it. But in His grace He was, in fact, free to do it ; and therefore not to go back on His choice between chaos and the world which He created good, even in view of its corruption and in His righteous anger ; not to resign as Creator and Lord of the creature, but to act and confirm Himself as such ; to call in and use death and nothingness in His service, to fulfil His judgment on sinful man and a perverted world, but in grace not to surrender His own right, and His creature ; and therefore to be in the right without giving chaos the last word ànd supreme power over the creature ; to throw aside and trample underfoot these instruments when they have served their purpose ; to act and demonstrate and reveal Himself as God and Lord of the world after the fulfilment of His judgment on the world ; in relation to it not to be in the right in and for Himself in His wrath, bùt beyond that to maintain His right to it in an inconceivable love, which is again, to justify Himself ; and in so doing, when judgment has taken its course, when that which is worthy of death and nothingness has fallen a prey to death and nothingness, when that which is dust has returned to dust, to justify the creature, to justify man, to acknowledge Himself the Creator once again and this time in fulness, to create him afresh with a new : " Let there be light," to beget him and to cause him to be born again from the dead, freed from his sin and guilt, freed from the claim and power which death and nothingness and chaos necessarily had over him in his former corrupted state, freed for life for Him and with Him, and therefore for life everlasting. God was free to do this. He did not have to do it, but He was free to do it.

And this is what in His grace He actually has done in raising Jesus Christ from the dead when He had been delivered up to death for our trespasses, as our Representative, in fulfilment of the judgment which ought to have fallen on us. In so doing He answered the question which in Mark and Matthew forms the last words of the Crucified. But we can and must say that in so doing He has shown that as recorded in St. Luke's account Jesus commended His spirit into His hands, and that only in so doing did He subject Himself to death, that He bowed His head before Him, and only because He bowed before Him did He also bow before the claim and power of nothingness, that He was obedient even unto death only in this way and in this order (and to that extent as already the secret Lord of the death to which He subjected Himself). God abandoned Him to chaos, as had to happen because of our transgressions, only in order to save Him from it—the One whom chaos could only serve, in order to do despite to it and to make a show of it : " Death is swallowed up in victory. O death, where is thy victory ? O death, where is thy sting " (1 Cor. 15⁵⁴ᶠ·). He made Him the victor over death by letting death conquer Him, as He had to do in fulfilment of the judgment laid upon Him. He recognised and proclaimed not merely the innocence but the supreme righteousness and holiness, the incomparable and unsurpassable goodness, of the work of Him who gave Himself up to death in pure obedience—who was not a sinner in the very fact that He took upon Himself the sin of the world. According to the rendering of Ps. 16¹⁰ in Ac. 2²⁷, He did not suffer His Holy One to see corruption. And in that He did not suffer it, in that He reopened the doors of death which had necessarily closed behind Him, in that He caused Him to rise from the grave to life unto Himself (Rom. 6¹⁰), and therefore to eternal life, He confirmed the verdict which, according to Mk. 1¹¹, He had already pronounced at Jordan when He entered on the way which led Him to Golgotha : " Thou art my beloved Son, in whom I am well pleased." In raising Him from the dead, He justified Him (1 Tim. 3¹⁶).

And in and with Him He justified us (Rom. 4²⁵)—we shall be returning to this. But primarily He justified Himself. He did this first in the revelation of His faithfulness as the Creator and Lord of heaven and earth and all men, to whom in the person of this their Representative, after their destruction in their old and corrupted form of life, He has spoken a second Yes which creates and gives them new life : a Yes which He did not owe them, but which He willed to speak, and which was the gracious confirmation of His own original will to create and His act of creation. But then, and at an even higher level, He did it in the revelation of His faithfulness as the Father of this Son, in the revelation of the love with which He loved Him from all eternity and all along His way into the far country, at Jordan and in the wilderness and in Gethsemane, and never more than when the Son asked Him on the cross (Mk. 15³⁴) whether He had forsaken Him, and when He then cried with a loud voice and gave up the ghost. His whole eternal love would still have been His even if He had acquiesced in His death as the Judge who was judged, if His mission had concluded at that ninth hour of Good Friday, if it had been completed with His fulfilling and suffering in His own person the No of the divine wrath on the world. But then, like His right as Creator and Lord of the world, it would have been, and remained, a completely hidden love : without witnesses, without participants, because without proclamation, without outward confirmation and form, concealed in the mystery of the inner life and being of the Godhead. It pleased God, however, to justify Himself, that is, to reveal and give force and effect to His faithfulness and love in this supreme sense, by an ὁρίζειν (Rom. 1⁴) of His Son which the disciples of Jesus could see and hear and grasp, and which was ordained to be publicly proclaimed. He willed to give to His eternity with Him and therefore to Himself an earthly form. He willed to give to the inner and secret radiance of His glory an outward radiance in the sphere of creation and its history. He willed to give to His eternal life space and time. And that is what He did when He called Jesus Christ to life from the dead.

This helps us to understand an important characteristic in the New Testament view of the resurrection of Jesus Christ, that as a free work demonstrating and revealing the grace of the Father it took place by the Holy Spirit : ἐδικαιώθη ἐν πνεύματι is how we have it in 1 Tim. 3¹⁶, and in Rom. 1⁴ : ἐν δυνάμει κατὰ πνεῦμα ἁγιωσύνης. Similarly in 1 Pet. 3¹⁸ : ζωοποιηθεὶς πνεύματι. And surely this is the sense of Rom. 6⁴ : ἠγέρθη . . . διὰ τῆς δόξης τοῦ πατρός, of 2 Cor. 13⁴ : ζῇ ἐκ δυνάμεως θεοῦ, and Col. 2¹² : διὰ τῆς πίστεως τῆς ἐνεργείας τοῦ θεοῦ, as it clearly is of Rom. 8¹¹, which speaks of the Spirit indwelling the Christian as Him who raised Christ Jesus from the dead.

The Holy Spirit—who is also the κύριος according to 2 Cor. 3¹⁷—is within the Trinity : God Himself maintaining His unity as Father and Son, God in the love which unites Him as Father with the Son, and as Son with the Father; and outside the Trinity, in His work as Creator and Reconciler of the world : God Himself as the One who creates life in freedom, who gives life from the dead, thus making His glory active in the world : τὸ πνεῦμά ἐστιν τὸ ζωοποιοῦν, according to the definition of Jn. 6[63] ; τὸ πνεῦμα ζωοποιεῖ (2 Cor. 3[6])—and revealing it in this its characteristic activity : as πνεῦμα τῆς ἀληθείας (Jn. 14[17], 15[26], 16[13] ; I Jn. 4[6]), as the Spirit by whom God discloses Himself to man in all His profundity (1 Cor. 2[10], Eph. 3[5]), who helps our infirmities (Rom. 8[26]), who bears witness with our spirit with a divine incontrovertibility (Rom. 8[16]), by whom the love of God is shed abroad in our hearts (Rom. 5[5]).

In this context it is important that at least one group in the New Testament tradition understood the human existence of the Son of God, that is, the justification and sanctification of human nature in the person of the Virgin Mary which was indispensable to union with the Son of God, as the work of the Holy Spirit (Mt. 1[18, 20], Lk. 1[35]). It is also important that another series of passages—not 2 Cor. 3[17], but 1 Cor. 15[45] (" the second Adam was made a πνεῦμα ζωοποιοῦν "), Jn. 3[6] (" That which is born of the Spirit, is spirit ") and especially the accounts of His baptism in Jordan—understands His whole being as πνεῦμα, that is, as filled and controlled by the Spirit, so that in Heb. 9[14] it can already be said of His way to death that διὰ πνεύματος αἰωνίου He offered Himself without spot to God. If we were to try to speak of a necessity of His resurrection, then it is along these lines that we could and would have to do so, applying the question of Gal. 3[3] whether that which has begun and is continued in the Spirit can be made perfect in the flesh—which is here the destruction of the flesh. But it is better not to follow this track, remembering Jn. 3[8] : " The Spirit bloweth where it listeth, and thou hearest the sound thereof, but canst not tell whence it cometh, or whither it goeth," and also 2 Cor. 3[17] : " Where the Spirit of the Lord is, there is liberty ; " remembering, therefore, that when we speak of the Spirit, per definitionem we do not speak of a necessary but of a free being and activity of God. The fact that Jesus Christ was raised from the dead by the Holy Spirit and therefore justified confirms that it has pleased God to reveal and express Himself to the crucified and dead and buried Jesus Christ in the unity of the Father with the Son and therefore in the glory of the free love which is His essence : a revelation and expression which as such—and where the Spirit of God blows, where the Holy Spirit is at work, this does take place necessarily—must consist in the merciful work of creating the καινότης ζωῆς (Rom. 6[4]) of this One who is dead, in His presentation and exhibition as the One who is alive for evermore.   [IV, 1, pp. 299 ; 305-309]

10. BAPTISM : RESPONSE TO GOD'S GRACE

In the New Testament μυστήριον denotes an event in the world of time and space which is directly initiated and brought to pass by God alone, so that in distinction from all other events it is basically a mystery to human cognition in respect of its origin and possibility. If it discloses itself to man, this will be, not from without, but only from within, through itself, and therefore once again only through God's revelation. The appearance and development of certain demonic and ungodly powers, which in a puzzling way are tolerated for a while by God, though they hasten to their defeat and destruction, and hence to the revelation of their nothingness and of God's sovereignty, can be called a μυστήριον, cf. the great mystery of iniquity which precedes the final return of Jesus Christ (2 Thess. 2[7]), or the whore Babylon-Rome, which is drunk with the blood of the witnesses of Jesus (Rev. 17[5]). To be understood along the same lines is the partial hardening of Israel which for the time being is simply to be noted and bewailed as a fact (Rom. 11²⁵). As a rule, however, a μυστήριον is a form of the doing of God's positive will. Thus in Mk. 4¹¹ par. it is the divine seizure of power which takes place in the word and deed of Jesus, and which is hidden from the many but revealed to the few. Again, in 1 Cor. 2⁷ it is God's wisdom in relation to man's—a wisdom which in the cross of Jesus Christ is concealed from some and revealed to others. In Col. 2²ᶠ· it is simply Christ, in whom are hidden all the treasures of wisdom and knowledge. In Col. 1²⁷ it is again Christ in His presence ἐν ὑμῖν, in His community. In 1 Tim. 3¹⁶ it is the whole movement of His being, humiliation and exaltation. In Eph. 1⁹ and 3³, ⁹ it is the will and act of God in adding the Gentiles to Israel. In Eph. 5³² it is the relation of Christ to His community as the original of the relation of husband and wife. In 1 Cor. 15⁵¹ it is the changing of the living at the moment of the final *parousia*. Something of the same is in view when 1 Cor. 13² ascribes to Christian prophets a knowledge of (all) μυστήρια and 1 Cor. 14² says that those who speak with tongues utter mysteries (in a way that others cannot understand). One thing is clear. Whether in the singular or plural the New Testament uses the term exclusively with reference to God's work and revelation in history, not to the corresponding human reactions. The πίστις to whose μυστήριον 1 Tim. 3⁹ refers is obviously the *fides quae* and not the *fides qua creditur*, and the same may be said of the μυστήριον τῆς εὐσεβείας in 1 Tim. 3¹⁶. Faith as a human action is nowhere called a mystery, nor is Christian obedience, nor love, nor hope, nor the existence and function of the ἐκκλησία, nor its proclamation of the Gospel, nor its tradition as such, nor baptism, nor the Lord's Supper. Would this omission have been possible if the New Testament community had been aware that certain human attitudes, actions and institutions were freighted with the divine word and act, if it had ascribed to baptism in particular the quality of a bearer and mediator of grace, salvation, and its manifestation ?

There are mysteries of this kind in ancient Greece and then in the mystery religions of Hellenistic antiquity. Originally—and this is still discernible in all the meanings added later—the reference was to certain cultic rites which partly presuppose a special dedication of the participants and partly convey this. The details of these rites were shrouded in secrecy. In them the story of a (or the) godhead is set before the participants in specific acts which are designed to mediate to them a share in the history, and therewith salvation, namely, a life which conquers death. From the 2nd century onwards (plainly in Justin and Ignatius) the Church begins to use this concept, though it does not occur in the New Testament. Recollection of what the New Testament denotes by μυστήριον gradually fades. The new concept is applied to the action of the Church, and especially to what it does in baptism and the Lord's Supper. Pagan mysteries are naturally explained either as malicious imitations or (along the lines of the idea of the λόγος σπερματικός) as significant anticipations of the Christian mysteries. In fact, however, was not Christianity in the process of being given a new form which followed the dazzling pattern of these pagan mysteries but which was quite different from that found in the New Testament ? Baptism and the Lord's Supper now (for the first time) began to be regarded as cultic re-presentations of the act and revelation of God in the history of Jesus Christ, and consequently as the granting of a share in His grace. They thus began to be described and treated as mysteries.

The parallel translation of μυστήριον by *sacramentum* is a separate issue. As a term in Roman law a *sacramentum* is a deposit which litigants must leave at a holy place on the opening of a civil suit, and which is forfeited by the defeated party. In the military world it is the oath of loyalty accompanied by an act of religious devotion. One cannot say for certain whether the adoption of this word into the language of Christian theology is really to be explained by the fact—and again, therefore, by way of the mystery religions—that these legal and military pacts were in a sense dedicatory acts, while conversely the initiations of the mystery religions might be regarded also as quasi-legal or quasi-military acts. As Zwingli perspicaciously noted very much later (*Comm. de vera rel.*, 1525, at the beginning of the section *De sacramentis*), " sacrament " in the original twofold sense of the term could point in a very different direction when used of baptism. But the Church was hardly looking in this very different direction from the 2nd century onwards. In the vocabulary of Christian theology " sacrament " came to have irresistibly the sense of μυστήριον derived, not from the New Testament, but from the Greek and Hellenistic mystery religions. It came to be used for μυστήριον = re-presentation of the cultic deity = means of grace.

To come to grips with the matter, it is natural to begin with passages which are controlled by terms that correspond to the vivid realism of the action. Baptism is called a καθαρισμός at Jn. 3²⁵ in a context in which its technical character as water baptism plays a special role. Washing with water is obviously for the purpose of cleansing. In what sense does baptism cleanse ? " The blood of Jesus Christ cleanseth us from all sin " (1 Jn. 1⁷). Is it permissible or even mandatory to say this, with some modification, about baptism too ? This is the primary question.

" And now why tarriest thou ? (says Ananias to Saul in Damascus). Arise, and be baptised, and wash away thy sins, calling on his name (the name of Jesus) " (Ac. 22¹⁶). Nowhere else in the New Testament is baptism brought into such direct relation to cleansing from sin (without even the interposition of μετάνοια). Is the verse saying that Saul's washing with water is (causatively) the instrument of his cleansing from sin or at least the visible sign which he is given of this invisible grace ? If so, it refers (sacramentally) to a divine action which is at work in and with baptism or through its administration. A first glance at the wording shows that this interpretation cannot be ruled out altogether. Closer investigation, however, suggests that it is most unlikely. " Why tarriest thou ? " " Arise." This appeal, and the use of the middle βαπτίσαι, show that no wonderful experience of grace is held out to Saul. On the contrary, he has already experienced the grace, and he is not summoned to a resolute act, and this in the context of the disclosure (v. 15) that God has fore-ordained him to be a witness of Jesus Christ to all men. The basic act of baptism which he is commanded to perform at the beginning of the way that he must go is, however, that herewith, by having himself washed with water, he can and should call upon Him, Jesus (in v. 14 the Just One whom he has seen and heard), the One by whom his sins are already washed away, by whom he is cleansed from them, in whom he can know that he is truly clean, in whom he may thus find himself liberated to discharge that ministry. The guilty Saul, who is nevertheless ordained to be the witness of Jesus, will not pray in vain for the forgiveness of sins to Him, the Just One, who has called him to Himself. His water baptism will not effect this. It is, however, his prayer for it, not merely in words but in a concrete act. Its goal, then, is this ἀπολούεσθαι which is to be effected by the Lord upon whom he calls. This invocation or petition is thus the meaning of his baptism. All things considered, this non-sacramental exposition of the passage, though not incontestable, is to be regarded as decidedly the more probable.

The matter is much the same when we turn to Heb. 10²². The context here is that of exhortation to make undeviating use of the entry into the sanctuary of God which has been opened and assured by the blood of Jesus Christ (v. 19). Ii is the context of exhortation, then, to make an unwavering confession of hope (v. 23). The relevant verse runs : " Let us draw near (προσερχώμεθα) with a true heart in full assurance (ἐν πληροφορίᾳ) of faith, having our hearts sprinkled (ῥεραντισμένοι) from an evil conscience, and our bodies washed with pure water." It will be seen that there is no express reference to baptism. The final clause is so vivid, however, that one can hardly deny that there is actual allusion to water baptism. Washing of the body with pure water is exactly what takes place in the act of baptism. One thing which is not so clear in baptism, however, is that with the washing of the body there has also taken place the sprinkling of the hearts of the readers, so that in virtue of the washing of the body they are capable of drawing near with a true heart. Perhaps it might seem legitimate and even necessary to regard this statement as the purpose of what is done, and tacitly to supplement it thus. Hebrews, however, knows no entry into the sanctuary but that which was opened and assured once and for all by the blood of Jesus Christ, and quite obviously it also knows of no ῥαντισμός which is necessary for making use of this entry apart from that in which man participates again through the blood of Jesus Christ. Only in the power of what has taken place in the crucifixion of Jesus Christ, of the ῥαντισμὸς αἵματος Ἰησοῦ Χριστοῦ (1 Pet. 1²), only through the offering (προσφορά) of His body, are Christians sanctified (10¹⁰), or, according to the present verse, cleansed from an evil συνείδησις, from the continually disquieted knowing together (with God) which characterises the past with its constant sacrifices. They could not escape this disquietude without knowing the change brought about in Jesus Christ. But they are liberated from it, their hearts are liberated from it, by the coming of this change and its manifestation. They are liberated from dead works to serve the living God (9¹⁴). In the full assurance of the faith which knows, accepts and grasps this change and which is based upon it, with true hearts which are cleansed by the truth of this reality, they can and should dare to make this entry. Baptism does not effect this true and actual cleansing. It cannot be the object or basis of their faith. According to the whole tenor of Hebrews there are no cleansings apart from that which took place in the death of Jesus Christ : neither that of the old covenant nor any new ones which might replace it. But the baptism of Christians—this is perhaps the meaning of the final clause in the verse—can and may and should remind them of the cleansing which took place once and for all in the death of Jesus Christ. For they were the ones who, having themselves washed with pure water, committed themselves irrevocably to the ῥαντισμός of their hearts by the blood of Jesus Christ. In this connexion one should recall what is said in Heb. 6¹ᶠ· about the uniqueness of conversion to Jesus Christ which corresponds to the uniqueness of His being and work. If the baptismal action to which the readers once submitted could neither effect nor reveal their cleansing for entry into the sanctuary, they themselves, by submitting thereto, are witnesses to the fact that they are bound and pledged to Him who did in fact effect and reveal it, so that the drawing near to which they are summoned can only be a continuing on the way which they have already entered. Unless appearances deceive, one can hardly ascribe sacramental significance to baptism on the occasion of its mention in Heb. 10²².

The same cannot be said quite so definitely in respect of Eph. 5²⁶ᶠ·. Rather oddly, at a first glance, this says : " Christ loved the church, and gave himself for it, that he might sanctify and cleanse it with the washing of water by the word " (καθαρίσας τῷ λουτρῷ τοῦ ὕδατος ἐν ῥήματι). It must be conceded that when there is reference to washing with water neither author nor readers could avoid thinking of baptism too. The question is : In what sense did they recall it ? Do we have here—this is the decisive point—two different processes, a first in which Jesus Christ loved the community and gave Himself for it, and a second in which He sanctified it that He might present it without " spot, or wrinkle, or any such thing " (v. 27)—sanctified it by coming to it in His self-sacrifice, displaying His power, and cleansing it with the washing of water by the word ? If so, this sentence or clause undoubtedly ascribes a sacramental character to the cleansing and thus to the act of baptism. Christ Himself is at work, not merely in love and self-offering, but also in baptism, and the cleansing of the community does in fact take place, in and with its administration. On this view the rather disruptive ἐν ῥήματι (rendered " in conjunction with the word " in the Zürich Bible) is to be understood along the lines of Augustine's *accedit verbum ad elementum et fit sacramentum*, or Luther's water of baptism embraced in God's Word and command, or even as a reference to the magical formula which is part of the celebration of the Gnostic mystery of redemption. On this whole line of exposition the possibility that in Ephesians the mystery infiltrated into the New Testament certainly demands serious consideration. The exposition is by no means impossible, and if the statement does in fact contain two parts it is even to be described, perhaps, as necessary. Nevertheless, the whole saying can be construed and understood quite differently. The statement about the sanctification of the community does not have to be a second one standing over against that about the love and self-sacrifice of Jesus Christ. It, too, may refer to what took place for the community in the love and self-sacrifice of Jesus Christ, namely, its sanctification. It is undeniable that if this is so, then there is a plain reference to baptism as " washing with water." What is said is that the sanctification of the community which took place in the love and self-sacrifice of Jesus is the true cleansing of the community through the washing with water which it has truly undergone, which is the goal of water baptism, which is reflected in its technical administration, but which naturally does not take place in and with this. Its sanctification, effected in Jesus Christ on the cross of Golgotha, can be its true cleansing, and in fact it is. For it is not a remote or silent act. As the work of Jesus Christ, it is also a living and present word, and ἐν ῥήματι it is thus at work among and in them as the divine work which was spoken and which speaks to Christians. On this view we have a parallel here to Jn. 15³ : " Now ye are clean through the word which I have spoken unto you." Not last or least in view of this much more natural and fruitful interpretation of ἐν ῥήματι, a non-sacramental exposition of the passage is ultimately to be preferred.

A final verse which is relevant in this connexion is Tit. 3⁵, which has played a particularly eminent role in the history of the doctrine of baptism. In the immediate context (v. 4-7) the decisive saying is as follows : " After that the kindness and love of God our Saviour toward men appeared (ἐπεφάνη), not by works of righteousness which we had done, but according to his mercy he saved us, by the washing of regeneration, and renewing of the Holy Ghost, which he shed on us abundantly through Jesus Christ our Saviour ; that being justified by his grace, we should be made heirs according to the hope of eternal life." The more immediate passage is set in the broader framework of an admonition that Christians should as such be ready for every good work (v. 1) and that they should exercise themselves in good works (v. 8) (which are to be done in righteousness according to v. 5). The obvious point of the section is to make it clear that the admonition, directed to Christians, is not demanding the impossible but can and should be followed by them. They are no longer under the regime of ignorance, disobedience, error, unbridled desires and mutual hatred (v. 3). The epiphany of the Saviour God has taken place, and in and with it, not on the basis of works of righteousness which were expected, and which have been achieved by them, but on the basis of God's pure mercy, they have been saved, i.e., set in the position of men who are capable of such works. He did this διὰ λουτροῦ παλιγγενεσίας καὶ ἀνακαινώσεως τοῦ πνεύματος, the Spirit who was abundantly shed abroad on them in Jesus Christ. If this λουτρόν is identical with the act of baptism, then, since it can be taken only instrumentally and causatively, a sacramental meaning has incontestably to be ascribed to baptism. The baptism administered to them is the means by which men are set in this new standing, by which they become Christians, i.e., heirs of eternal hope who are justified through the grace of Jesus Christ. Now it is likely enough that the διὰ λουτροῦ is here an allusion to the act of baptism. But those who see more than an allusion, those who see a statement about its meaning, and consequently about its meaning as a means of renewing, as many have done in the history of exposition right up to that of the Reformers, those who take this course expose themselves to the following very considerable difficulties. (1) They must make the attempt—which is not a sound procedure exegetically—to expound this many-sided and materially heavily freighted passage solely in the light of the two words διὰ λουτροῦ, i.e., in the light of these two words as the point of the whole. (2) They have then to justify materially the orientation of the whole statement to this single point, showing that the aim of the epiphany of the Saviour God is to save, justify, and make into heirs of eternal life certain men, not by works required of them and performed by them, in virtue of His mercy alone, but through the fact that they have themselves baptised and are baptised. (3) They must assume that this thesis, in distinction from Tit. 2¹⁴, where it is said that Jesus Christ through His self-sacrifice has purified for Himself a people which is His possession and which is zealous for good works, refers to a second and different cleansing, which is in practice decisive, namely, that effected in baptism as that "washing." (4) They must give to παλιγγενεσίας, not the sense which it has in the only other instance in the New Testament (Mt. 19²⁸), namely, the universal restoration or new creation of the world, but a meaning which is abstracted from Jn. 3³ᶠ·, namely, that of the individual new birth of specific individuals. (5) They must assume that in this passage—in spite of what the Gospels say about the distinction between the baptism of the Spirit and the baptism of water, and in spite of what Acts presupposes in this respect—renewing with the Holy Spirit is identical or coincident with the act of baptism. Those who feel that these difficulties are too heavy must question whether διὰ λουτροῦ means "by baptism." Though these two words are reminiscent of baptism, they do not speak of it. In agreement with Tit. 2¹⁴ the cleansing bath in which Christians have their origin, described also at Tit. 3⁵ in the language of Ezek. 36²⁵ ; Is. 44³ ; Zech. 13¹, is the purifying and renewing outpouring of the Holy Spirit which has taken place on the basis of the new creation ushered in by the Saviour God in the history of Jesus Christ. Through this, not through baptism, men become Christians. This is the aim of the epiphany of the Saviour God. It is in this that Christians participate and, justified through the grace of Jesus Christ, become heirs of eternal hope as the people (Tit. 2¹⁴) which He has purified for His own possession and which is as such zealous of good works. In virtue of this, they can and may and must (πιστὸς ὁ λόγος, v. 8) be summoned and exhorted to the conduct which befits this new station of theirs. The probable allusion to baptism in the two words διὰ λουτροῦ consists once again, therefore, in a supplementary reminiscence. Having begun by submitting yourselves to the washing of baptism, you have recognised and confirmed for yourselves the renewal of the world which has taken place in Jesus Christ and which has led to your personal cleansing in the outpouring of the Holy Spirit.

It is thus legitimate and necessary to address you on the basis of this new position. One may thus venture to say that a sacramental interpretation of this passage to which appeal is most often made is ruled out almost completely.

We now turn to some of the most important verses in which baptism is referred directly to the relation or even the unity of Christians with Christ. What is its connexion with this unity or union which embraces all of man's salvation and founds the whole of the Christian life ?

Gal. 3²⁷ must be considered first. The saying which is decisive in this connexion is to be found in the narrower context of v. 26–29 : " For ye are all (πάντες) the children of God by faith ἐν Χριστῷ Ἰησοῦ (=that which you have in Him, i.e., by faith in Him). For all of you (ὅσοι) who have been baptised into Christ have put on Christ. There is neither Jew nor Greek, there is neither bond nor free, there is neither male nor female : for ye are all (πάντες) one in Christ Jesus. And if ye be Christ's, then are ye Abraham's seed, and heirs according to the promise." This narrower context stands for its part in the broader context of a demonstration that the Galatian Christians, by grasping in faith the promise fulfilled in Christ, are freed from the Mosaic Law which precedes this fulfilment, and especially rom the requirement of circumcision, so that they do not have to become Jews first in order to become Christians. In both the narrower and the broader context, then, we obviously do not have in v. 27 a mere allusion to baptism but a statement about its meaning : believers are addressed as the baptised. In the light of their baptism it is said to them that their freedom when, grasping the promise, they received baptism, was grounded not only in their faith, but ontically. On the basis of a specific happening they are the children of God, they are all one as those who belong to Christ —not Hellenes as distinct from Jews, under no obligation to become Jews first, just as slaves do not have to become free or men women or *vice versa*. As those they are, they are all Abraham's seed, heirs of the promise given to them and now fulfilled. They believe as people who are all these things. They are all these things because they are in Christ Jesus (v. 26, 28). They are in Him as they have put Him on, as in virtue of His intercession for them they have been set directly in the sphere of His dominion, of the dynamically advancing law of His life, of His Spirit, as they have become new and different men. This is what is said to them in the light of the fact that they have had themselves baptised. Does this mean that the act with which they all began was itself their putting on of Christ, their ontic renewing ? It may be conceded that, though v. 27 does not have to mean this, taken alone it could do so. It could thus lend support to a sacramental view of baptism. The narrower and broader context, and indeed the whole thesis of Galatians, makes it highly unlikely, however, that this is the real meaning. If it is, Paul is saying that the Mosaic Law with its demand for circumcision as initiation into salvation and the beginning of the new life no longer applies to you, and you are free from it, because you already have this initiation and beginning behind you in the event of baptism. The requirement of baptism thus replaces that of circumcision. In the light of its observance, of the fulfilment of this prerequisite, appeal can now be made to the new being of the Galatians as children of God. If this is what is meant, however, it is truly surprising that neither in the narrower or broader context nor in the rest of the epistle is there any explanation. Why is so decisive a statement made, or merely hinted at, in just a single sentence ? If this is the meaning of Gal. 3²⁷, how could Paul refrain from dealing plainly and explicitly with baptism in the basic passage Gal. 2¹¹ᶠᶠ. ? Instead, we find that in both passages the divine act and revelation in Jesus Christ, faith in Him, and the

work of the Holy Ghost are specified and described as that initiation and beginning, as the one great renewal of man's being, and hence as the effective abroga-
tion of the Mosaic Law. There is no more place in Galatians than there is in
Hebrews for any other alongside it or as the condition of its subjective actualisation. It is thus more natural to assume that Gal. 3²⁷ is looking back to the
divine change, to the putting on of Christ which in Jesus Christ Himself has been
effected objectively and subjectively for the recipients of the epistle by His
Holy Spirit, and that baptism is recalled as the concrete moment in their own
life in which they for their part confirmed, recognised and accepted their investing
with Christ from above, their ontic relationship to Him, not only in gratitude
and hope, but also in readiness and vigilance. They had themselves baptised into
Christ (εἰς Χριστόν) when, along with those who baptised them, they could see
and confess that they were men clothed upon with Christ, renewed and liberated
in Him. By this concrete moment in their own lives the apostle entreats and
charges them that, as those who have their origin in the divine change, but also
in the public human decision which responds and corresponds to it, they should
stand fast in freedom (Gal. 5¹). They themselves have affirmed the fact that
Christ has made them free. They have done this by having themselves baptised.
As viewed neither from above nor below, then, can they let themselves be brought
back under a yoke of bondage. They cannot link the entry into salvation and
the beginning of the new life with circumcision, with a prior conversion
to Judaism. If expounded in any other way, if expounded sacramentally,
the saying in Gal. 3²⁷ is a foreign body in its narrower and wider
context.

With respect to the unity of Christians with Christ, Rom. 6³⁻⁴ says of baptism :
" Know ye not, that so many of us as were baptised into Jesus Christ were
baptised into his death ? Therefore we are buried with him by baptism into
death : that like as Christ was raised up from the dead by the glory of the
Father, even so we also should walk in newness of life." A full exposition of
this passage would be possible only in the context of an analysis of the whole
complex Rom. 5–8. We can deal with it here only in the special light of the
meaning of baptism. It has been claimed again and again as the *locus classicus*
of the New Testament doctrine of baptism which is normative for its general
understanding. The attempt to treat it thus is not intrinsically impossible, but
it is undoubtedly difficult. If it is to turn out well, more care must be taken
than is usually the case to note what is actually said and not said. Especially
important is the thesis that what is said about baptism has here too, not an
independent or thematic character, but in the twofold sense of the word a subsidiary character. It is in the first instance a dramatic underlining of the statement which dominates the narrower context v. 2–10, namely, that Christians
are men who, as concerns the παλαιὸς ἄνθρωπος, the σῶμα ἁμαρτίας, are crucified
with Christ. They are dead to sin in Him. They have no future as sinners,
because they have no possibility of existence as such. Thus reduced to nullity,
dead with Christ, they may also live in Him, live to God. Also underlined
hereby is the point which Paul is making in the larger context v. 1–11. Not
even with the pious ulterior motive of v. 1 : " That grace may abound," can
Christians try to continue in sin. There can be no such continuance because
they are no longer in sin. Since they are dead with Christ, their existence as
sinners is irrevocably behind them. What is before them with and in Him can
only be a new and different life. This is the real thesis of the passage. It is thus
over-hasty exegesis to derive from v. 3–4 the secondary statement that in
baptism Christians have died with Christ and, if possible, been raised up with
Him also to a new life ; that in practice this radical change has taken place in

and through baptism ; that in baptism the old things have passed away and all things are made new (2 Cor. 5[17]). According to v. 3 they are certainly to remember that they were baptised into the death of Christ, in which their own dying as sinners took place, and from which, since it was followed by the resurrection of Jesus Christ from the dead, there is opened up the prospect of their own new life beyond this point of nullity. The verse does not say, however, that baptism was the change in which this dying (not to speak of their entry into new life) took place. What we do read is that they were buried with Him by their baptism into His death (in view of the reality of their own dying in His death). In this burial with Him they were not crucified and put to death with Him. When they had been crucified and put to death with Him, then, in view of His death in their place, which enclosed within it their own death, they were—in baptism—buried, laid to rest, interred with Him. This happened to Him too after His death. His body was laid aside in burial—the final confirmation that He truly died. This burial with Him, their baptism—this is the ultimate meaning of burial, and hence of the baptism which is behind them—is the regular confirmation of the fact that they have died with Him and in Him. It is not the actual conclusion of their existence as sinners, but the dramatic concluding line which denotes it. Nor is the line which denotes this conclusion a sad one. As participants in Christ's death they need experience no despair nor resignation in view of the resurrection from the dead which follows His death and burial. They can draw the line with the certain hope of a new life which follows their death with Him. This burial from which they come is a happy one —yet it is obviously a burial. Understood thus, the reference to baptism in v. 3–4 underscores the thesis of the whole context. As Christians are baptised with a view to the death of Christ in which they, too, died as sinners, they register the fact, and it is registered of them, that there is no going back on their way, but that there is for them a promised, permitted and commanded Forward beyond the point behind which they can never go back again. Done away once and for all in the death of Christ, their existence as sinners is behind them ; before them there is only a walk in newness of life corresponding to the raising of Jesus Christ from the dead. This is the great change in their situation which is graphically indicated, but not brought about, by their burial with Christ, and hence by their baptism. A subsidiary and incidental appeal can thus be made to this too. Subsidiary and incidental—for the burial of Christians with Christ to which v. 3–4 allude is one thing, their actual death and future resurrection with Him is quite another. Baptism cannot be—as though this were necessary—a repetition, extension, re-presentation or actualisation of the saving event which is the true theme of the argument in v. 2–10. It is a basic human Yes to God's grace and revelation, but not a " sacrament," not a means of grace and revelation.

The third passage in which baptism is mentioned in relation to the unity of Christians with Christ is Col. 2[12]. This saying, too, must be put in its context (2[9-12]) : " For in Him (Christ) dwelleth all the fulness of the Godhead bodily. And ye are complete in him, which is the head (sovereign) of all principality (ἀρχή) and power (ἐξουσία) : in whom also ye are circumcised with the circumcision made without hands, in putting off the body of the sins of the flesh by the circumcision of Christ : buried with him in baptism, wherein also ye are risen with him through the faith of the operation (ἐνέργεια) of God, who hath raised him from the dead." An obvious statement about baptism is made only in the parenthetical participial clause v. 12a (συνταφέντες . . .), and this agrees materially with the decisive statement in Rom. 6[4], so that it might suffice to refer to what was said about this. The possibility arises, however, that another and less obvious statement might be made about baptism—a statement which might be decisive for its meaning—in the context of this parenthesis. Because this is in fact maintained, we shall have to devote full attention to this verse. It should be noted first that, while Rom. 6 is directed against libertinism, Col. 2 is aimed at Judaistic Gnosticism. On the one side it is shown that in the light of the work of Christ which has been done for them, and which thus embraces their own history, Christians cannot possibly continue in sin ; on the other it is shown that in the light of the same work of Christ which was done for them, and which embraces their own history, they cannot possibly let themselves be controlled or influenced by other realities, truths and laws which are supposed to be necessary to salvation. First, then, the general statement is made that God's power, wisdom, holiness and mercy are present completely and perfectly and in all their plenitude in Christ, that the πλήρωμα τῆς θεότητος is present bodily (σωματικῶς) in a way which can be neither transcended nor supplemented. In Him who is the κεφαλή, who is sovereign over all actual or conceivable authorities and powers, Christians, too, have a share in this fulness (πεπληρωμένοι), so that they need no supposedly divine revelations, but are in fact sealed off in principle against them, since anything more is only less in comparison with this fulness. To what degree this is so is explained in the two statements in v. 11 : " Ye are circumcised in him," and v. 12 : " Ye are risen with him." Because this took place for Christians in the almighty being and work of Jesus Christ, we are told in v. 14 that He set aside the accusation against them and in v. 15 that He disarmed and subjected to Himself all competing ἀρχαί and ἐξουσίαι. Because they are not circumcised (ἀκροβυστία) in Him, because all their transgressions are forgiven through Him (v. 13), He sets aside and forbids all those things which certain teachers were trying to make plausible to the Colossian Christians, and to force on them as necessary to salvation, e.g., sacral dietary rules, feasts of the new moon and sabbaths, the worship of angels (v. 16f.), and obviously above all circumcision. Another circumcision which has already taken place for them in Christ withstands the temptation to meddle in such things, and so, too, does the awakening which they have already in Christ, in faith in the power of Him who first raised Him from the dead. With respect to this Paul will later challenge them (3¹ᶠ·) : " If ye then be risen with Christ (in Colossians and Ephesians, as distinct from Rom. 6⁴ᶠ·, the resurrection of Christians with Christ is an event which, like their dying with Him, is already behind them) seek those things which are above, where Christ sitteth on the right hand of God ... your life (which) is hid with Christ in God." The arbitrary worship (ἐθελοθρησκία, 2²³) which is commended to them by those false teachers is not a seeking of the things which are above. For this reason, too, they are forbidden to touch it. Decisive first of all, however, is the circumcision which has taken place for them already. This has not been done with human hands (but obviously with God's, v. 11). It is called a putting off of the " body of the flesh " (obviously the same as the " body of sin " in Rom. 6⁶ and the " body of death " in Rom. 7²⁴). It is the circumcision of Christ. Many expositors have tried to see in this circumcision Christian baptism, regarding this as the New Testament equivalent to the Old Testament rite called circumcision. If they are right, then in view of the lofty predicates ascribed to this circumcision in v. 11 it is clearly settled that we have in baptism a means, instrument, or channel of grace. There are serious objections, however, to the equation of this circumcision with baptism. Is not the statement : " You are baptised in Him " (along with : You are dead and you are raised again in Him), without any parallel in the New Testament ? Even with the strongest concentration on its deeper sense, can baptism, which is in any case a human act performed with water, be described so simply as a work not done with human hands ? In what tolerable sense can the statement in v. 11 : " You are baptised," be set in juxtaposition with that in v. 12 : " You are risen . . .," when in v. 12 the power which effects their resurrection is expressly said to be that of faith in the operation of God who raised Jesus from the dead, so that it cannot be described as baptism ? Finally, how odd it is if the whole attack on the rituals commended by the false teachers depends at the decisive point on the argument that they are not needed because in this respect Christians are best provided for in baptism ! Positively, when the clause in v. 12a, which undoubtedly refers to baptism, calls it a being buried with Christ, is it not pointing back to a preceding dying with Him ? All these difficulties disappear if one assumes that by the circumcision effected on Christians—described in an expression peculiar to Colossians but most appropriate to its thesis—there is denoted the crucifixion of Christ which took place for Christians and embraces their life. In this death of Christ which embraces them Christians receive a share in the fulness of the Godhead. This was the work done on them, not by human hands, but by God's hand. In it the body of the flesh in which they existed was put off and set aside like an old garment. If v. 11 speaks of the death of Christ which embraces Christians, its relation to the parallel v. 12, which speaks of their resurrection with Christ, is meaningful ; it is also one which is found else-where in Paul. The reference to Christ's death is a clear and cogent argument against the ἐθελοθρησκία by whose onset the Colossian community was threatened. To call the death of Christ which embraces Christians His circumcision, i.e., the circumcision effected by God in Him, is justifiable in a defence against Jewish-Gnostic ritualism, in which (cf. Col. 3[11]) the demand for circumcision probably played a prominent part. It is also justifiable on the ground that herein—in accordance with the meaning of Old Testament circum-cision (cf. Tit. 2[14])—God purified a people for His possession. On this view (but only on this view) one can also see why there is in v. 12a a reminiscence of baptism as the burial of Christians with Christ. This reminiscence is not an argument. As in Rom. 6[3-4] it gives emphasis to the real argument. It is to this effect : Even in your own lives as Christians you begin with the event in which your burial with Christ, and therewith your liberation from all autonomous attempts at deification or salvation, was concretely confirmed and registered by that which you yourselves desired and received from the community. Hold fast to this !

There is one New Testament saying in which baptism is related to what might be called individual regeneration as distinct from the universal παλιγγενεσία of Mt. 19[28] (and Tit. 3[5]). This is Jn. 3[5], where the second answer of Jesus to Nicodemus is : " Verily, verily, I say unto thee, Except a man be born of water and of the Spirit, he cannot enter into the kingdom of God." Champions of a sacramental understanding of baptism—Calvin is the only exception—have appealed with particular emphasis to this saying in support of their thesis. There is good reason for paying particular attention to it. " Born of water and of the Spirit " in v. 5 expounds the " born from above " (ἄνωθεν) in the first saying of Jesus in v. 3. The reference is to the unique event in a man's life which can be expected and effected only from above, from God, the event of his total transposition into one who may see (v. 3) the kingdom of God and who may thus enter it, receiving an active part in its establishment. How does this come about ? We note that the man born from above is later described in v. 6 and v. 8 as γεγεννημένος ἐκ τοῦ πνεύματος (with no ἐξ ὕδατος). The natural conjecture that ἐξ ὕδατος in v. 5 was added in an ecclesiastical redaction of the Gospel and should be excised has been advocated by several modern commentators, including R. Bultmann. This removes the difficulty, but it perhaps sets aside as well the true point of the verse. It has no textual support.

Hence it is as well to consider the meaning of the traditional text. What is meant by " of water and of the Spirit " ? Since the two terms could later be reduced to one, we do not seem to have here two different events. Since it is denoted first by the two terms, the one event obviously at issue could be the total renewal in which that which water does is identical with that which the Spirit does, or in which there is a secondary and instrumental operation of water and a primary operation of the Spirit, or in which the work of the Spirit is symbolically revealed in that of water. In the contemporary religious world Hellenism, Judaism and even the so-called disciples of John and related groups described in these or similar combinations the total renewal of man which they, too, preached in different terms. Jn. 3⁵ might have been influenced by these movements, and, if so, it might be speaking of a sacrament of baptism, to be interpreted more ontically or more noetically in detail. In this case the statement, made on ground common to the New Testament community and the world around it, would be an asserted, though not proved, commendation of Christian baptism : through this and this alone, not through the ordinary rites of initiation, does one enter the kingdom of God, for in this and this alone, in and with the operation of water, there is also—however one understands it—the operation of the Holy Spirit. In all its variations the dominant Christian theology of baptism has in fact taken this line. Jn. 3⁵ can be regarded as offering support for this. But Jn. 3⁵ does not have to be understood in terms of the theory and practice of the world around the New Testament community. It does not have to refer to a sacrament of baptism. That it speaks of baptism may be assumed from the fact that the story of Nicodemus is set in the context of the great contrast between John and his baptism on the one side and the person and work of Jesus on the other. This is the introduction to the Gospel which comes to an end only with 4¹. The question arises however : How is baptism treated here ? Might it not turn out that there is here a protest against the idea of a work or revelation of salvation in baptism and thus against the baptismal belief which was held in the surrounding world and which was perhaps widespread, or was just arising, in certain circles in the community itself ? If it is surely legitimate to consider the possibility of a non-sacramental interpretation of the ἐξ ὕδατος καὶ πνεύματος, it is natural to assume that we have in this formula one of the many pairs-in-tension which are characteristic of the thought and utterance of the Fourth Gospel, e.g., " the only true God, and him whom thou hast sent " (17³), " grace and truth " (1¹⁷), " spirit and truth " (4²³), " blood and water " (19³⁴), " resurrection and life " (11²⁵), " hear and learn " (6⁴⁵), " hear and believe " (5²⁴), " see and believe " (6³⁰), " believe and know " (6⁶⁹), etc. " Eat and drink " (6⁵³) might well belong to the same series. This Johannine form of speech cannot be regarded as simple parallelism. The second word, connected by a καί, certainly refers to the same thing as the first. Hence it does not set a second thing alongside that first mentioned. The accent, however, is always on the second, so that the order is not reversible. In this irreversible order a step is taken, a critical synthesis made, in which the second member totally explains the first, absorbs it, and thus completely replaces it. Knowledge of the true God shows itself to be such, not by being also knowledge of Him whom He has sent, but by being totally and exclusively knowledge of this One whom the true God has sent. Grace is true grace, Spirit true Spirit, not as they are also truth, but as grace can be no other than truth, and spirit no other than truth. What issues from the blood of the crucified Jesus is not blood and also water, but the blood which has power to heal because it is water which the thirsty drink. Jesus is not the resurrection and then also the life. He is the resurrection in the fact, and only in the fact, that He is the life. To see and hear Him are useless unless they take place wholly and utterly in faith in Him. Even faith in Him is useless alone ; it can consist concretely only in knowledge. It is surely strange, therefore, if the pair " water and Spirit " does not belong to this series of dynamically critical syntheses. What the " water " is by which a man is born from above is explained wholly and exclusively by " Spirit." In the function here ascribed to it there is no water at all outside or alongside the Spirit : not the water of Jacob's well ($4^{6f.}$), nor that of the pool of Bethesda ($5^{2f.}$), nor the water of Christian baptism which many were perhaps extolling in circles around the Evangelist ; not this water even as a representative, means or witness of the Spirit. In this function no water can supplement the Spirit, no water can mediate the Spirit even as a secondary cause, no water can reveal the Spirit. Water is to be defined in this function solely by Spirit. He who begets a man from above is He who moves where He wills, whose voice may be heard but not localised (v. 8). He, the Spirit alone, is the " living water " ($4^{10f.}$; 7^{38}). His baptism, the baptism of the Spirit, is the true and proper baptism, namely, that which begets a man from above, that which gives him the ability and power to see and enter the kingdom of God. Calvin (Comm. on Jn. 3^5, CR, 47, 55f.) understood the ἐξ ὕδατος καὶ πνεύματος thus : The copula καί is to be taken *exegetice, quum scilicet posterius membrum explicatio est prioris*. If this interpretation is correct, one can understand why ἐξ ὕδατος does not occur in v. 6 and v. 8 ; it has been rendered superfluous by the synthesis in v. 5. It is not denied, then, that water has another function which is also necessary. It is not denied that water baptism as such has its place and is necessary and mandatory. This is not the issue, however, in the present context. Nor is a sacramental understanding of water or baptism considered here if this interpretation is correct. Indeed, it seems to be called in question or even disputed.

Essentially much easier to answer is the problem posed by two verses in which a saving function is ascribed to baptism. The ἔσωσεν of Tit. 3^5 does not arise in this connexion, since baptism is not the theme of the verse. The two passages are first Mk. 16^{16} : " He that believeth and is baptised shall be saved," and then 1 Pet. 3^{21} (a verse which will have to be examined more closely in a later context) : " The like figure whereunto (sc. to the water through which Noah and his house were delivered) even baptism doth also now save us." With regard to these it is to be noted that σώζειν, σώζεσθαι, σωτηρία, unlike καταλλαγή and ἀπολύτρωσις, are ambiguous terms in the New Testament. For one thing, they usually refer to the liberation which Christians will experience in the future, in the consummation and final manifestation of the divine work of salvation, in the resurrection of the dead and the last judgment. They denote the liberation for which Christians are now hoping, the definitive preservation from the eternal death which is the consequence of sin. On the other hand, quite often and impressively there is denoted also the liberation and deliverance which, even as they hope for it, comes upon them and characterises them in the present, so that they can be, and can be called, " saved " even now. Again, and in connexion with this, salvation is usually an act or event whose subject is God or the Deliverer (σωτήρ), Jesus Christ, who has come from God and who acts and speaks in His name. Yet it can be also (and not infrequently) a work which is entrusted to men and enjoined upon them, obviously as and because they are "saved." It can be an action and mode of life in which they are to set forth and declare in practice, to work out (ἐργάζεσθαι, Phil. 2^{12}), the σωτηρία divinely promised and present to them, their salvation. In this secondary, indirect, but very serious sense the Philippian gaoler (Ac. 16^{30}) can ask in startled amazement : "What must I do to be saved ? ", while Mk. 8^{35} par. can speak of saving one's own ψυχή and Jas. 5^{20} of saving the soul of others. Paul, too, can refer to his work

among the Jews as a " saving " (Rom. 11¹⁴), and he can admonish Timothy
(1 Tim. 4¹⁶) to save himself and his hearers by taking heed to himself and the
doctrine. Again, in 1 Cor. 7¹⁶ the saving of a pagan partner is a problem for
married Christians, and in 1 Tim. 2¹⁵ it can be rather strangely said of Christian
wives that they will be saved διὰ τῆς τεκνογονίας " if they continue in faith
and charity and holiness with sobriety." Saving power can be ascribed to
preaching (1 Cor. 1²¹ : 1 Thess. 2¹⁶) and especially to faith (Lk. 7⁵⁰ ; 8¹² ; Rom.
10⁹). This can and may and should be done, not because the human work has the
δύναμις θεοῦ εἰς σωτηρίαν (Rom. 1¹⁶) within it, but because it is grounded in it,
because it is made possible by it, because it takes place in correspondence with it.
The two verses about the saving character of baptism obviously belong to this
context. In the case of 1 Pet. 3²¹ this is indisputable in view of the express
definition of baptism as an ἐπερώτημα εἰς θεόν, and in that of Mk. 16¹⁶ it is
highly probable in view of the juxtaposition with faith. Baptism saves because,
like faith and with it, it is an element in the action which God has entrusted to
and enjoined upon those who will be saved by God and who are saved already in
hope in Him. It is a human work which is, like faith, wholly appropriate and
indispensably proper to their position. A sacramental meaning of baptism can
hardly be deduced from either passage.

We conclude with a consideration of two Johannine verses in which baptism
is perhaps related to the most important New Testament concept of witness.
These are particularly interesting because they might seem to constitute a
biblical basis for the version of a sacramental understanding of baptism which
was advocated by Calvin, who in this respect followed very closely Augustine's
doctrine of the *signa visibilia gratiae invisibilis*. If in the New Testament
baptism does not effect man's renewing in unity with Christ, his baptism with the
Holy Ghost, his salvation, does it reveal these as a means of divine self-attestation ?

We turn first to 1 Jn. 5⁵⁻⁸ : " Who is he that overcometh the world, but he
that believeth that Jesus is the Son of God ? This is he that came by water and
blood ; not by water only, but by water and blood. And it is the Spirit that
beareth witness, because the Spirit is truth. For there are three that bear
witness, the Spirit, and the water, and the blood : and these three agree in one."
It is essential to take note of the first statement in v. 5, which controls the
whole passage : He who believes in Jesus as the Son of God overcomes the
world. As previously said in v. 4, the fact that Jesus is the Son of God is our
faith, the origin, basis and theme of our faith which has indeed overcome the
world already. But to what degree does Jesus prove to be worthy of faith as
God's Son, so that one can and must speak thus of faith in Him ? The answer
is : He is the One who has come, who comes, and who will come again. The
ἐλθών is best related to all the three tenses of His existence, but with emphasis
on the first. He comes and will come again as the One who has come. He is
and will be the One He was in His history. The δὲ ὕδατος καὶ αἵματος refers
to this history, to His having come in the flesh. We have here (cf. 1 Jn. 4², ³ ;
5²⁰ ; also 2 Jn. 7) the emphatically anti-docetic realism of the Christology of
the First Epistle of John. Jesus is the Son of God in His true and genuine
humanity, not in abstraction therefrom. To refer the two words ὕδωρ and αἷμα
to baptism is possible if they are taken alone, but once again we seem to have a
dynamically critical pair. Like the Spirit in Jn. 3⁵, the blood of Christ is now true
baptism. Less probable is a reference to baptism and the Lord's Supper, for it is
hard to see why the " matter " (water) should be mentioned in respect of baptism
when the eucharistic reference is to the *res sacramenti*, the blood of Christ (and why
not the body ?). In fact, the context suggests that it is erroneous to think of any
ecclesiastical action, whether baptism alone, or baptism and the Lord's Supper.

The reference is to the historical coming of Jesus as a demonstration of His divine sonship. It is to the fact that Christian faith overcomes the world specifically as faith in Him. When we read that He came δι' ὕδατος, we are undoubtedly to think of a baptism. This is not, however, the Church's baptism, but the event which is its basis, namely, the baptism of Jesus in the Jordan—and this in proleptic relation, not to the Lord's Supper, but to the crucifixion of Jesus, the shedding of His blood. He who came thus, beginning δι' ὕδατος in the Jordan, concluding δι' αἵματος at Golgotha, is Jesus Christ (v. 6a). The continuation in v. 6b underlines the fact that, while the reference is to both these events, it is decisively to the second, which is intimated in the first. He did not come "by water only," but by water and blood ; not in the event at the Jordan only, but in that at Golgotha too—which of the two was the more unpalatable to the Docetics. On the way from the one to the other, from that entry into service to its consummation, in this irreversible sequence, in this teleological determination, in this totality of His history, He has shown Himself to be the Son of God. But has He really done this ? Is this more than a (disputable) interpretation of His history ? Have not others been baptised and crucified ? Does not even that which took place between these pillars of the history of Jesus Christ find exact parallels in other histories ? The answer is given in v. 6c : The Spirit bore witness (and bears witness) that the One who was baptised in the Jordan and crucified at Golgotha was (and is) the Son of God. One might perhaps paraphrase it thus : The Spirit bore witness to this immediately after the baptism of Jesus when Jesus, as the One on whom He alighted, was manifestly approved by the voice from heaven : "This is my Son, on whom my good-pleasure rests." He also bore witness to it directly after the death of Jesus when Jesus (Rom. 1[4]) through the Spirit was raised up from the dead by the Father. The same Spirit, the Paraclete, Advocate and Comforter sent by the baptised and crucified Jesus, speaks in the community, and through it to the world, about Jesus as the Son of God. He who is the Spirit of truth (Jn. 15[26]), or who is here the truth itself, proclaims Him as such ; "our faith" hears His voice, and in so doing overcomes the world. At first, then, it sounds surprising that in v. 7–8—a theologoumenon peculiar to 1 John—the three concepts introduced in the course of the desired proof— the Spirit, water and blood—are associated as three witnesses. In their own way, however, the water and blood, the two pillars of the history of Jesus Christ, were already valid witnesses of His divine sonship. The Spirit was and is, of course, a very different witness who confirms the validity of the other two. He is mentioned first because He spoke and speaks the final and decisive word both then and now. But in their own tongues all three witnesses bear witness to the same thing with equal emphasis—the two historical facts on the one side, on the other the direct work of God which gives utterance to the first two as truth within, and which causes them to be heard as truth without : καὶ οἱ τρεῖς εἰς τὸ ἕν εἰσιν, they bear witness to the one thing. They all bear witness to the fact that He has come in the flesh, that He comes, and that He will come again, that He is not from below but from above, that He has come from God, that He is His Son. Inasmuch as "our faith" (v. 4), being faith in Him, is established in the mouth of two and even three witnesses, it overcomes the world. It is obviously a much less promising venture to try to seek in this saying about the three witnesses, even from afar, the distinctions which characterise the sacramental teaching of Augustine and Calvin, namely, between *signum* and *res*, visible temporal form and invisible eternal content, symbol and reality. This is impossible even if 1 Jn. 5[6f.] refers to baptism (ecclesiastical baptism), or to baptism and the Lord's Supper. Nowhere, not even in Hebrews, does the New Testament think in these (Platonising) categories.

We come finally to the crowning passage in the Johannine story of the Passion, Jn. 19 [33-37]. Just before, we have been told that the soldiers of Pilate broke the legs of those crucified with Jesus either to be sure that they were dead or to put an end to their lives. " But when they came to Jesus, and saw that he was dead already, they brake not his legs : but one of the soldiers with a spear pierced his side, and forthwith came there out blood and water. And he that saw it bare record, and his record is true ; and he knoweth that he saith true, that ye might believe. For these things were done, that the scripture should be fulfilled, A bone of him shall not be broken. And again another scripture saith, They shall look on him whom they pierced." According to the style of John, the passage is in all its constituent parts a distinctive blend of vivid, concrete pragmatism and symbolical significance. A twofold sense ? No, a single sense, but single in this very unity of history and salvation history. This certainly applies to the statement which now concerns us, i.e., that about the blood and water which flowed from the dead body of Jesus when it was pierced by the soldier's spear. Whether the stroke of the spear was a final attempt to make sure that Jesus was really dead as reported or a purely mischievous act, it was in any event the last deed of violence and shame perpetrated against Jesus by men. The point about it which interested the Evangelist may be incidentally (and anti-docetically) an insistence that Jesus really died physically, but obviously his main attention is focused on the effect of the spear-stroke, which was not part of the treatment accorded to the other two crucified with Jesus. This opened up the wound in the side which plays such a decisive, though not always felicitous, role in the later theology, preaching and poetry of Zinzendorf, and from which blood and water came out, ἐξῆλθεν. Does this note come from the Evangelist himself ? It is thought by some that the passage makes quite good sense without the statement about the coming out of blood and water. Yet on the one side, anti-docetically, it emphasises the reality of the death of Jesus, on the other the fact that final human violence was offered even to His dead body, and both with a reference back to the Old Testament prophecies which are mentioned in v. 36–37 and of which the second (" they shall look . . .") is to be understood as a threatening allusion to the last judgment. The suggestion has thus arisen, championed recently by R. Bultmann, that the saying about the blood and water (like the formula " water and the Spirit " in Jn. 3[5]) is the addition of a Church redaction. If, as expositors assume *magno consensu*, the blood and water denote the Lord's Supper and baptism, one can hardly deny that this critical conjecture has some probability. In this sense the statement is in fact a surprising intruder into the text. But the very order of the terms is against this interpretation, for why should the blood (the Lord's Supper) come first and the water (baptism) second ? Here too, as in 1 Jn. 5[6], one has to ask why the reference in the former is to the thing signified (and why not the whole body of Christ ?), whereas in the latter it is to the sign, water ? On the other hand, if there is critical emendation on the basis of the assumption that the saying refers to the Lord's Supper and baptism, one has to ask whether here too this does not perhaps rob the whole passage of its point. If this saying is left out, is not the rest a somewhat meagre statement for the climax of the whole story of the passion ? Since there is reason to question the assumption, we shall proceed on the basis of the traditional text including the saying. If we do this, then in respect of its context we may begin with the general affirmation that the verse speaks of the body of Jesus, the indisputably dead body, as a flowing source. What is it that flows out ? The ancient typological explanation, repeated in our own age in the encyclical *Mystici Corporis* of Pope Pius XII, may sound strange, but it does not have to be basically or totally distorted. It recalls the story of the creation of Eve from Adam's rib when he had been put in a deep sleep. Adam's sleep is the death of Jesus, the taking out of Adam's rib is the wound in the side of the dead Jesus, and Eve, who is associated with Adam and comes forth from him, is the Church. Now there can be no disputing the *tertium comparationis* in the decisive statements in both the New Testament story and the Old Testament story. The ἐξῆλθεν of the text undoubtedly refers to the springing or issuing forth of a new reality from Jesus, from Jesus crucified and slain. Nor can one dispute the fact that this new reality has something to do with the community of Jesus, and the issuing forth with the rise of this community. The only question is : What ? If blood and water really referred to the Lord's Supper and baptism, then the new reality (blood and water) which proceeds from the death of Jesus might be in the first instance the Church which exists in the administration of these two and perhaps other sacraments. It might even be the Church in its institutional character. This is naturally the opinion of the encyclical. But in view of the objections to the presupposed equation we can no more accept it than we can the modern proposal to eliminate the verse on the basis of the same equation. If, then, we must seek another interpretation of the two words blood and water, it is exegetically sound to look into the meaning and function of the terms elsewhere in John's Gospel. What power is in the first instance ascribed to the blood of Jesus here ? Rather surprisingly this is not in the Gospel a cleansing power, as it is in the First Epistle and elsewhere. According to the hard figure of speech in 6[60] the blood of Jesus is to be " drunk." His blood is here His life, which, unlike any other He has in Himself (6[53], cf. 5[26]), but which was in Him (1[4] ; 5[26]) ; His life, which as such is eternal life. He to whom He gives His life, he who, as it comes from Him and is dispensed from Him, drinks it, receives it into himself, he and he alone has it, " and I will raise him up at the last day " (6[54]). That He can give them His blood to drink, His life to share, presupposes that it is given, poured out ; it presupposes His death. Only the slain body of Jesus can be the source of His life, eternal life, for others. Only the community of the cross which receives its life from His death, only the Christian as an individual member of this community, can receive His life. But with the αἷμα, probably in critico-synthetic dynamic, not as a second added to the first, but as a second which interprets and defines the first, we find καὶ ὕδωρ. How can the blood which flows from the wound in His side, how can His life, eternal life, be " drunk " ? The great symbolical speech about water is relevant here. Jn. 7[37f.] : " In the last day, that great day of the feast (Tabernacles), Jesus stood and cried (as to Lazarus in 11[43]), saying, If any man thirst (at Tabernacles water was dispensed every morning), let him come unto me, and drink—as one that believeth in me ; the scripture hath said, out of his body shall flow rivers of living water." According to the unanimous view of modern commentators the body from which these rivers flow is not that of the believer but the body of Him in whom he believes, the body of Jesus Christ. Thus one reads also in 4[14] : " Whosoever drinketh of the water that I shall give him shall never thirst ; but the water that I shall give him shall be in him a well of water springing up into everlasting life." But what is this water which flows forth from Jesus, which is to be received from Him, which is, when received, to be drunk ? The Evangelist himself comments in 7[39] : " But this spake he of the Spirit, which they that believe on him should receive (later) : for the Holy Ghost was not yet given ; because that Jesus was not yet glorified." According to the Johannine view, the exalting and glorifying of Jesus took place in His crucifixion and death. Without this, before it, the water could not yet flow forth, the outpouring of the Spirit could not yet take place. " If I go not away, the Comforter will not come unto you ; but if I depart, I will send him into you " (16[7]). This happens. When there is no doubt as to His death, immediately (εὐθύς) the water begins to flow out, the Spirit comes forth from Him and begins His work. Jn. 19³⁴ tells of the fulfilment of the promise given in 7³⁷ᶠ· and 16⁷.   Consequently, as the thirst-quenching water of the Spirit proceeds from His slain body to be received and drunk by believers, so also does His blood, His life, the eternal life received from Him. This living water does not flow from His slain body without the blood, and especially—this is the emphasis here—His shed blood does not flow forth without the living water of the Spirit. The blood and the water, the eternal life and the Holy Spirit, the objective grace and its subjective appropriation—both flow from the same source. Hence the whole new reality of the Christian community and all its members does so too. What Zinzendorf said about this is right, though less so in the way he often said it. The community and all its members are " born " out of that wound in the side, and they live on that which flows there-from, the blood, i.e., the water which is the Spirit. It is a community of the cross or it is not the Christian community at all. The Christian is a member of this community or he is no Christian at all. The eye-witness of the death of Jesus to whom the Evangelist appeals (19³⁵) testifies that this is true " that ye might believe." Old Testament Scripture is also fulfilled in this event (19³⁶⁻³⁷). The thrust of the spear, or the blood and water which flowed from the wound caused by it, offered (both in history and salvation history) the decisive proof of the reality of His death, of the divine act which is fruitful in this event, of ζωοποίησις through the πνεῦμα. Because the breaking of His legs could not have offered a proof of this kind, this had not to take place in the case of Jesus as it did in that of the others. His dead body, and His alone, was the source of life and the Spirit. According to the second Old Testament saying, to look on Jesus as the One who was pierced, and therefore as the source of life and the Spirit, of life which goes forth and is to be received from Him as the Spirit—this and this alone (the Evangelist seems to have construed the saying as a promise rather than a threat) will be in every age the real seeing of the real Jesus (who was really slain). If this explanation of the passage, which we have taken from John's Gospel itself, is right, then one can understand all the elements in it : the importance of what is done specifically to the body of Jesus ; the indispensability of the saying about the blood and water ; the emphasis on the testimony of the eye-witness ; the point of the two allusions to the Old Testament. All these things are obscure if the blood and water denote the Lord's Supper and baptism. Even if they do denote these, one can hardly deduce from the passage the Augustinian and Calvinist doctrine of the significative force and hence the sacramental character of these two actions. If one can and should say that the passage speaks of the birth of the Church, it certainly does not lead us to think of the birth of the sacramental or institutional Church.

[IV, 4, pp. 108-109 ; 111-127]

CHAPTER VI

PENTECOST

1. RESURRECTION, ASCENSION AND PENTECOST

The sequence Easter-Pentecost is, therefore, irreversible. If there is an open witness of the Holy Spirit heard by men, if this is given to men and received by them, if there is a Christian community in the world enlightened and led by it, it is on the presupposition, and derives from the fact, that Jesus Christ is risen and ascended. It is in this character that He sends the Spirit, and the Spirit is the Holy Spirit as sent by Him in this character. In this character Jesus Christ is the heavenly Head of the community in which He has His body, the earthly-historical form of His existence. For in this character He is present to it by the witness of the Holy Spirit, giving Himself to be known by it, and through its ministry by the world.

As is well-known, the Evangelists conclude their record of the history of Jesus Christ—the first part of which described His way from Jordan to Galilee and Jerusalem, and the second His passion—with a much shorter third part, almost an appendix, in which they give some account of His existence in this character, and His appearance as such to His disciples after His death. Their record would obviously have been incomplete—indeed, even with reference to the first two parts they could either have given no account at all or only a very different one—if the decisive factor had not been before them, and therefore called for presentation in this third part. Later, on the basis of what happened in this third part, the second main division of the Lucan account can go on to speak of the outpouring of the Holy Spirit and its fruits in the " Acts of the Apostles." And the Epistles and Apocalypse look back to what happened here, to Jesus Christ in this character, as the One who appeared as such according to the concluding section of the narrative. There is nothing in any of them which directly or indirectly is not thought and said, and meant to be heard and understood, on this basis. And it is apparent that even the first two parts of the Gospels are actually conceived and thought out in the light of the content of this third part, this short sequel. It is only with the help of very doubtful procedures that we can separate out from the Gospels a genuinely pre-Easter tradition. Everything points to the fact that there never was such a tradition, and that the well-known saying of Bengel is true not only of the Gospels but of their conjectured literary precursors : *spirant resurrectionem*. It is always noticeably the case that the community looks back to that sequel, to that interspersed history, and therefore to Easter and the ascension. It expects Jesus to come again in the character in which He then appeared to the apostles. It expects to see Him again as such. It recognises its own origin and goal in this Jesus Christ. The New Testament tradition is naturally concerned with Jesus Christ in His being and words and acts and especially His crucifixion on Golgotha, but its concern is with the Jesus Christ who even in His crucifixion existed in the character in which He encountered His disciples according to this sequel, this interposed history. We may confidently say that if He were not this One, and not known to the community as such, there would never have been any tradition about Him. And then there would have been no giving and receiving of the witness of the Holy Spirit in execution of His self-witness. He would obviously not have attested Himself as the One He was—or His self-witness would not have been worth speaking about, let alone worth executing by the witness of the Holy Spirit.   [IV, 2, pp. 131–132]

2. THE HOLY SPIRIT : THE SPIRIT OF JESUS CHRIST

In what the New Testament thinks and says about the Spirit there is in this respect a clear and almost a direct line from Jesus Christ Himself to His community, to us Christians. We will begin with Jesus Christ, and here the simplest formula is that He is the Spirit of Jesus Christ (Phil. 1¹⁹ ; Rom. 8⁹), or the Spirit of His Son whom the Father has sent forth into our hearts (Gal. 4⁶). But this means primarily that He is *His* Spirit, the Spirit in whose power and operation He is who He is and does what He does. He is ἅγιον because He is κύριον, as He was later called in the *Nic. Constant.* He is the Spirit of the Lord Jesus, i.e., because by Him and in the power which He gave Him the man Jesus was a servant who was also Lord, and therefore became and is and will be wholly by Him. He does not, therefore, need to receive Him. He came into being as He became the One who receives and bears and brings Him. And He was this and continued to be and still is. As is said of Mary to Joseph (Mt. 1²⁰) : τὸ γὰρ ἐν αὐτῇ γεννηθὲν ἐκ πνεύματός ἐστιν ἁγίου. A good reason why the *conceptus de Spiritu Sancto, natus ex Maria virgine* should not be regarded as a theologically irrelevant legend is that if we do this we obscure the important basic connexion between Jesus Himself and the Spirit. Jesus is not a man who was subsequently gifted and impelled by the Spirit like others, like the prophets before Him by whom the Spirit also spoke (*qui loquutus est per prophetas, Nic. Constant.*), or His disciples after Him, or ourselves also as Christians. He has the Spirit at first hand and from the very first. The Word became flesh (Jn. 1¹⁴), and therefore a man like the prophets and apostles, like ourselves. But because as a man He was not conceived of the flesh, but of the Spirit (Jn. 3⁶), He at once became spirit in the flesh ; a man who in the lowliness of the flesh, as from the very first He was on the way to His abasement in death, lived also from the very first by the Spirit, Himself creating and giving life by the Spirit. It is in this sense that we have to understand both the pregnant saying about the last Adam who in contrast to the first was a πνεῦμά ζωοποιοῦν (1 Cor. 15⁴⁵), and also the pregnant equation in 2 Cor. 3¹⁷ : ὁ κύριος τὸ πνεῦμά ἐστιν. What John the Baptist " saw " by Jordan (and we have to remember that it is definitely a matter of vision according to the texts)—the heavens opened, and the descent of the Spirit like a dove upon Jesus as He came up from the waters of Jordan (Mt. 3¹⁶ and par.)—was not just the individual event of that particular moment, as though Jesus had only now come to participate in the Spirit whom He had hitherto lacked. The voice which the Baptist hears from heaven says that this " is " (not " has now become ") my beloved Son. In accordance with the function and position of the Baptist in all the Gospels it is a matter of the revelation and knowledge of the man Jesus by John as the man who stands at the threshold between the old covenant and the new and is therefore the first to receive it. What we have here, in anticipation of the Easter revelation, is the first proclamation of the reality of Jesus before the eyes and ears of this man. Jesus is the beloved Son of God, and as such He is from the very outset and throughout His existence the spiritual man, i.e., the true and exalted and royal man who lives by the descent of the Spirit of God and is therefore wholly filled and directed by Him. He is the man of the divine good-pleasure. And as this man, in order that the righteousness of God should be fulfilled and achieve its goal, He has subjected Himself to the baptism of repentance in solidarity with the whole people, so that He is concealed and wrapped in an incognito as this man. And He is to actualise and fulfil this sign of baptism in the even greater concealment of His death on the cross. " I saw the Spirit . . . abide upon him " is the phrase used in Jn. 1^{32}, and repeated in the following verse ; and according to the later witness of the Baptist (Jn. 3^{34}) God does not give the Spirit ἐκ μέτρου to the One whom He has sent (i.e., with the διαιρεῖν of 1 Cor. 12^{11}, as He gave and gives Him to the prophets and then to apostles and the community and Christians). He gives Him without reserve or limit—the fulness of the Spirit—so that His being as flesh is directly as such His being as Spirit also. It is as this man who is wholly sanctified, and therefore not in the form of an individual and sporadic inspiration but in accordance with the comprehensive necessity of His holy humanity, that the Spirit drives Him into the wilderness (Mk. 1^{12}), i.e., to His victorious conflict against Satan, in fulfilment of the penitence which He has accepted. And it is again as this wholly sanctified man that " through the eternal Spirit he offered himself without spot to God " in His death (Heb. 9^{14}). It is as this man that He was " put to death in the flesh " (σαρκί, according to the law to which He bowed when He became and was flesh), but was " quickened by the Spirit " (πνεύματι, according to the law of His being as life-giving and death-destroying Spirit, 1 Pet. 3^{18}). For as this man He is the Lord who is Himself Spirit. Or again, in terms of Rom. $1^{3f.}$, where Paul describes His two-fold historical descent, He is the Son of God who κατὰ σάρκα, as a man, derived from David and his seed ; but who at the same time—and it is in this that He was powerfully marked off (ὁρισθεὶς ἐν δυνάμει) and distinguished from all other men, and opposed to them, as the Son of God—κατὰ πνεῦμα ἁγιωσύνης, by the Spirit who sanctified Him as the Son of David and therefore as man, came from the place from which no other man has ever come, ἐξ ἀναστάσεως νεκρῶν. Or again, according to the remarkable hymn in 1 Tim. 3^{16}, He was revealed in the flesh (and therefore in concealment) and justified in the Spirit (as He who He was in the flesh). It is in this radical sense that the Holy Spirit is the Spirit of Jesus Himself. Because and as He is the Son of God, Jesus is the spiritual man. It is as such that He traverses the way which leads to the cross. But it is also as such that He is revealed and known when He is raised from the dead. The latter point is decisive in this context. The Spirit is holy as the power in which the man Jesus is present and alive even after death as the One who was crucified for the world's salvation, and in which He continually acts as the man He became and was and is, as the One who was crucified in the flesh.

The second point that now calls for emphasis is that He does this as the One who has suffered and conquered His death and therefore ours ; as the One who was humiliated and exalted in His humiliation ; as the One who was concealed in His majesty but who also reveals Himself in and from His concealment. He lives in this twofold and simple majesty of the Son of God, as the Subject of this twofold and simple occurrence. As the One who lives in this way He does not will to be alone, but to have fellow-participants and witnesses of this life : men in whom both His humiliation and exaltation, His death and resurrection, are reflected (although not repeated) ; in whose existence there is a correspondence to His life. And He does actually create this correspondence to His life in the existence of other men (His disciples, Christians, and even the prophets as the New Testament understands them). This is the event, the decision, which is described in the New Testament as His gift and sending and impartation of the Holy Spirit, as the outpouring of the Holy Spirit as proceeding from Him. We have to note that He is Himself the free active Subject in this event. But we have also to note that He is this as the Subject of that twofold and simple occurrence. Without Him, without His free and sovereign address to specific men, there is no Holy Spirit as a factor in the existence of other men. Nor is there any Holy Spirit except as the One whom He sends to them as the Crucified and Risen, who cannot deny that as a factor in their existence He comes from Him as the Crucified and Risen. The Spirit is holy in the New Testament because He is the Spirit of Jesus Christ. He shows Himself to be the Spirit of Jesus Christ by the fact that He is given to men by Him, i.e., by the Crucified and Risen, as the power of His death revealed in His resurrection. Both these points are brought out very clearly in the New Testament. To quote the Baptist again (Jn. 1³⁰), the One who comes after him is the One who baptises ἐν πνεύματι ἁγίῳ, in the power of the Holy Spirit and with the Holy Spirit, as the giver of the Holy Spirit. Or as He Himself puts it when He goes towards that twofold occurrence, He will send the Spirit from the Father (Jn. 15²⁶, 16⁷). Or as He tells the disciples : " I send the promise of my Father upon you " (Lk. 24⁴⁹). Or as we are told in Peter's sermon at Pentecost (Ac. 2³³), it is He who, exalted at the right hand of God, and as such the recipient and bearer of the promise, of the Holy Ghost, " hath shed forth this, which ye now see and hear." Or according to the abbreviated account in Jn. 20²² He breathes on His disciples as the Resurrected and says : " Receive ye the Holy Ghost." It is He Himself who does this, but He Himself on the far side and not on this side of that frontier ; He Himself as the One who has crossed it, who in His death has fulfilled both His humiliation and His exaltation, and in His resurrection proved Himself to be the " holy servant " (Ac. 4²⁷ᶠ·) and therefore the Lord. It is He, the One who is crowned in His death and revealed as the King in His resurrection, who achieves His presence and action in the existence of other men. If they have the Spirit, they have the Spirit from Him, from this One, and therefore as the Holy Spirit. Prior to this fulfilment, and otherwise than from it, there is no Holy Spirit, no empowered witnesses, no apostles, no Christians, no community. As we are told in Jn. 7³⁹, " the Holy Ghost was not yet (for others) ; because that Jesus was not yet glorified." " If I go not away, the παράκλητος will not come unto you " (Jn. 16⁷). The power of the reconciliation of the world with God as already accomplished and revealed, and therefore the power of the occurrence of Good Friday and Easter Day, is the presupposition which is made in the New Testament with reference to these other men. That this occurrence is reflected in their existence is the event of their reception and possession of the Holy Spirit, of their life by and with Him, of their government by Him. That they partake of the Spirit means that in distinction from all other men they are made witnesses to all other men. By Him they are to declare His being and action, His completed being and action. To live in the Holy Spirit is to live with and in and by and for this message.

But this brings us to the third point to which we are directed by the New Testament. The Spirit shows Himself to be holy, i.e., the Spirit of Jesus Christ Himself, by the fact that He testifies of Him. The men to whom He is given by Him are called to Him, reminded of Him, set in His presence and kept close to Him. They are brought to the place to which they belong according to the will of God revealed in Him. The Spirit reveals to them, not only Jesus Christ, but also their own being as it is included in Him and belongs to Him. He does this by causing them to see and hear Jesus Christ Himself, as the One who has power over them, as the One to whom they are engaged and bound, as the One whom they have to thank for everything and to whom they are indebted for everything, as the Lord and salvation of the whole world whom they are called to proclaim. The Gospel of John is particularly explicit and impressive on this point. The Spirit is τὸ πνεῦμα τῆς ἀληθείας, " the Spirit of truth " (Jn. 14¹⁷), the power which does not work arbitrarily or independently, but simply declares Jesus, accomplishing again and again the disclosure and revelation of His reality. ὁδηγήσει ὑμᾶς εἰς τὴν ἀλήθειαν πᾶσαν, He will lead them to the fulness of the revelation of this reality, and finally to its last and perfect form (Jn. 16¹³). " He shall glorify me : for he shall receive of mine, and shall shew it unto you " (Jn. 16¹⁴). " He shall teach you all things, and bring all things to your remembrance, whatsoever I have said unto you." (Jn. 14²⁶). "He shall testify of me" (Jn. 15²⁶). Μαρτυρία in the New Testament is a supremely active and aggressive impartation which makes neutrality quite impossible for its recipients. It consists in a παρακαλεῖν, i.e., a calling and summoning and inviting and demanding and admonishing and encouraging, an address which at one and the same time asks and corrects and comforts. The Spirit will thus be for the community and the individual Christian the great παράκλητος. As applied to the Spirit in the Fourth Gospel (14¹⁶, ²⁶, 15²⁶, 16⁷) this term describes Him as the Mediator and Advocate and Spokesman of Jesus Christ to His own. He speaks both of Him and for Him, as the representative of His cause, and with the aim of bringing them to see that it is their own cause, and leading them to make it their own. He sets them before Him as the One who is Himself (the same word is actually used of Him in 1 Jn. 2¹) their Mediator and Advocate and Spokesman with God. He sees to it that He is not forgotten or misunderstood as such, but always recognised and confessed as the One He is. He sees to it that He does not meet with disobedience but obedience ; that His truth, i.e., His revelation is not halted among them ; that His light is not set under the bushel, but remains on the candlestick on which it belongs, and gives light to all that are in the house (Mt. 5¹⁴ᶠ.). He will be the ἄλλος παράκλητος (Jn. 14¹⁶) to the extent that His work will begin on the far side of the dying and rising again of the man Jesus, consisting in, and deriving from, the self-revelation of this man in His fulfilment. That as this man the Son of God was once revealed, in His own time and place, in the world, flesh of our flesh, as the reconciliation of the world with God in His death and the Reconciler in His resurrection, is not a fact which is confined to that one time and place, nor should it ever be regarded as such by Christians. What was then, and took place then, is the living promise given to the world to the men of all times and places, that it was and took place, not just once but once for all, and for them all. But this promise is a living promise because He Himself, raised again from the dead, lives within it, making Himself present in it. This is where the Spirit comes in as His Mediator, Advocate and Representative. "I will not leave you comfortless : I will come to you" (Jn. 14¹⁸). That is to say, world history, having attained its goal in this man and the death of this man, cannot continue as though nothing had happened. His community, Christians, are now present in the world as His witnesses. But these cannot and must not be left to their own devices. They cannot be without Him in the world. He Himself will be with them, even to the συντέλεια of the world, i.e., to the time when it is generally revealed that they and all men did actually attain their goal then and there (Mt. 28²⁰). The fulfilment of the promise of His coming in time before His final revelation is the presence and action of the Holy Spirit. He proves Himself to be the Spirit of the Son of God who was and is among us men by the fact that He continually makes the life of Jesus fulfilled in His death and revealed in His resurrection an object of the knowledge of the community and Christians, impressing it upon them, revealing it even in their own bodies and persons (2 Cor. 4⁶), causing it to be the decisive factor in their own human existence. It is in this way that He shows Himself to be the Holy Spirit.

But when we say this, we say already the fourth and final thing which the New Testament tells us concerning the Spirit on this line from above downwards. His presence and action may be unequivocally known by the fact that the men in whom He works know Jesus Christ, the Son of God in the flesh, the man Jesus, as their living Lord, as the living Head of His community, as the living Saviour of the world, but that in so doing they also know themselves as His own, as those who are bound and committed to Him. They stand in the light of His life bursting forth from His death, of the revelation of the atonement achieved in His death. They see and hear Him. And as those who see and hear Him, they think of Him and also of themselves. And in accordance with this thinking of Him and of themselves they may now live, starting each day from this beginning. On this final point we have to state and develop once again all that we have said already, in outline and by way of illustration, concerning the power of the Holy Spirit in the effecting of that joyous light, that liberation, that knowledge, that peace, that life. We shall have to treat of this more explicitly when we come to speak of the sanctification of man as such. For the moment, we note only the basic and comprehensive truth that the work of the Spirit in those to whom He is given consists in the fact that the being and life and presence and action of Jesus Christ as Reconciler, Mediator, Lord, Head, and Saviour—and all in the form of the royal man Jesus—is to them the decisive and controlling factor in their own existence. In the light of the miracle of Pentecost, Acts is bold to end the address of Peter with the proclamation (2³⁶) : "Therefore let all the house of Israel know assuredly (ἀσφαλῶς), that God hath made that same Jesus, whom ye have crucified, both Lord and Christ." This ἀσφάλεια is *in nuce* the alteration of their existence as it is effected by the Holy Spirit. "All the house of Israel" is assembled in this sure knowledge of Jesus as it is to be received and fulfilled by the Holy Spirit. By this knowledge it is marked off from the nations and enters on its mission to them. By this knowledge men are divided, not into the good and bad, the elect and reprobate, the saved and lost, but into Christians and non-Christians. They are divided, we may add, in the relative and provisional way in which they can be divided in the relative and provisional state of human history, where sin and death are still powerful, this side of this æon. They are divided, we may add further, subject to the judgment of Jesus Christ on those who are divided in this way, on the relative and provisional genuineness of their division, and therefore on whether or not they are really Christians or non-Christians. And we must also add that this division has to be made continually. Each new day we are all asked whether we are Christians or non-Christians. Each new day we must cease to be non-Christians and begin to be Christians. Each new day we need the Holy Spirit for this purpose. Yet it is still the case that there is a division at this point. As we are told in 1 Cor. 12³ : "No man speaking by the Spirit of God says : ἀνάθεμα 'Ιησοῦς (which is only a sharpened form of the confession of those who think that they can be neutral in relation to Him) : and no man can say : κύριος 'Ιησοῦς but by the Holy Ghost." Or again in 1 Jn. 4²ᶠ· : "Hereby know ye the Spirit of God : Every spirit that confesseth that Jesus Christ is come in the flesh is of God : and every spirit that confesseth not that Jesus Christ is come in the flesh is not of God." And the right to assert this criterion is underlined in 1 Jn. 4⁶ with the statements : "He that knoweth God heareth us (i.e., will acknowledge this criterion) ; he that is not of God heareth not us (i.e., does not acknowledge it). Hereby know we the spirit of truth, and the spirit of error." It should be noted how brief and general are the formulæ used in these passages. Neither in the λέγειν of 1 Corinthians nor the ὁμολογεῖν of 1 John is there any question of the acceptance or rejection of theological propositions. The attitudes described can, of course, be given the sharper and summarised form of propositions. But both Paul and the author of 1 John recognise that it is not the assent to propositions of this kind which divides the Christian (who does not withhold his assent) from the non-Christian. They and their readers must have known well enough the dominical saying about those who say "Lord, Lord" (Mt. 7²¹) but do not do the will of their Father in heaven. The First Epistle of John speaks elsewhere against an incipient dead orthodoxy, and its language is quite unmistakeable, being much sharper than that of any other New Testament writings. In the attitudes indicated by these short formulæ we have to do with man himself, the whole man—1 Jn. 4²ᶠ· speaks of a πνεῦμα which confesses or does not confess. We have to do with an orientation of man's existence as such. But for all their brevity the formulæ are quite explicit that we have to do with his attitude to the man Jesus, with His κυριότης, with Jesus Christ as the One who has come in the flesh. It is the rejection of this which makes a non-Christian.

And it is the acceptance of this—seriously possible only in the Holy Spirit, in a decision that effectively determines his existence—which makes a Christian.

Paul hazarded the strongest expressions about the unity with Christ into which Christians enter with their acceptance as evoked by the Holy Spirit. Ἡμεῖς δὲ νοῦν Χριστοῦ ἔχομεν, he can say in 1 Cor. 2¹⁶, and in 1 Cor. 6¹⁷ (capping even the συμμαρτυρεῖν of the Holy Spirit with ours of Rom. 8¹⁶) : " But he that is joined unto the Lord is one Spirit (ἓν πνεῦμα) with him." The whole context of Rom. 8¹⁴⁻¹⁷ (cf. Gal. 4⁶⁻⁷) refers to the relationship of the Christian to Christ as created by the Holy Ghost, and here the Spirit is described as πνεῦμα υἱοθεσίας, and therefore as the power in which the Christian is granted a part in the filial being and authority of Christ. In virtue of this πνεῦμα they can be sons of God here and now, and therefore free from the servile fear for which they would have good reason of themselves. Here and now de profundis, but in the depths in which they still dwell, they can cry with the one Son of God : " Abba, Father." Here and now they can already say of themselves: ὅτι ἐσμὲν τέκνα θεοῦ, and, because sons, heirs of the inheritance which this Father alone, God Himself, controls—joint-heirs with Christ. They can bear their suffering as a subsequent suffering with Him, and with Him, following the One who has gone before them, they can move toward the glory, their own glorification in the light of God. In short, in and with their " Jesus is Lord," their confession of the majesty and kingdom of this man, Christians find their own εἶναι ἐν Χριστῷ, themselves as the brothers and fellows of the royal man Jesus, who in Him and with Him are elected and beloved by God. " The love of God (in itself and from our own standpoint as much hidden from us as from other men) is shed abroad in our hearts by the Holy Spirit which is given unto us " (Rom. 5⁵). What makes them Christians and divides them from non-Christians is that they can find themselves at the side of the One on whom there rests the good-pleasure of God, and that they can live by this discovery. It is impossible to say whether the first consequence of this outpouring is their free acceptance of Jesus as the Lord or their free acceptance of themselves as those who belong to Him and share His prerogatives. For how can the second be lacking if they accept the first ? Or how can the first not be included in the second ? The love of God is directed to them, but it is directed to them in Christ (Rom. 8³⁹). There can be no pragmatising at this point. The love of God which is in Christ and directed to them is one event as it is gathered together in the " by the Holy Ghost." The only thing is that it is marked and characterised in its totality by the " in Christ," being clearly distinguished from all other happenings, even of a spiritual type, by the fact that it is the work of the Holy Ghost shedding abroad the love of God in our hearts. But to understand this we have to take into account the three passages which succeed Rom. 8¹⁴⁻¹⁷.

In Rom. 8¹⁸⁻²² we look back from the glory to which Christians already move forward in Christ to the παθήματα τοῦ νῦν καιροῦ which they still bear with Him. We are first told that these are not worthy to be compared with the glory which is to be revealed in them. They are so immeasurably small in relation to it. But, in the light of the fact that they have actually to be borne here and now in the following of the sufferings of Christ, we are then reminded that their Christian existence as those who suffer and hope is not something isolated and particular—an end in itself. They are surrounded by the ἀποκαραδοκία, the earnest expectation, of all creation, of the whole non-Christian world which does not yet know of the atonement accomplished for it in Jesus Christ, a world which as Paul saw it seems to have included all creatures, even the non-human. What is the existence of men, and other creatures, who are not participant in the Holy Spirit, and therefore in the knowledge of Jesus Christ, and therefore in the knowledge of themselves, and therefore in the new determination of their being ? Seeing that they too have to bear the παθήματα τοῦ νῦν καιροῦ, is it not in fact (and Christians know this as those who partake of the Spirit of Christ and live with Him) one in which they also groan and travail together with Christians, because they are subjected with them to vanity (ματαιοτης), contrary to what they intend and seek and desire as the creatures of God, but with no possibility of effective resistance ? And is it not in fact an existence ἐφ᾿ ἐλπίδι, in the hope of another form of being which can only be for them, as for Christians, a hope, because it is not yet seen ? Is this hope in vain ? No, says Paul. It can be positively asserted of them : " The creature itself also shall be delivered (ἐλευθερωθ-ήσεται) from the bondage of φθορά into the glorious liberty of the children of God." Thus, although Christians are genuinely divided from them by their " Jesus is Lord," they are not really divided from them, but bound up with them in the twofold solidarity of suffering with them, bearing the burdens of the whole fellowship of time (as those who in the light of Jesus know why), and of hoping with them (as those who in the light of Jesus know for whom and what). For all its peculiarity, therefore, their existence is not a particular one, but that of a universal mission. In all the singularity of their existence they are the advance-guard of the crucified and risen Jesus Christ in a world which does not yet know Him and its atonement as it has been achieved in Him.

In Rom. 8²³⁻²⁵ the form of Christian existence as established and fashioned by the Holy Ghost is expressly described as provisional, and the world of the Holy Ghost as that which now determines it as the gift of a beginning (ἀπαρχή). In the words of Lk. 24⁴⁹ and Ac. 2³³ He is the promise which is given them. His work is to put men in possession of a hope which is certain, because it is already fulfilled in Jesus Christ, but even in its fulfilment not yet revealed and visible to them, to these men, to Christians. The man who partakes of the Spirit of Christ and is united with Him knows this. " Ourselves also, which have the ἀπαρχή of the Spirit (whose existence is already determined by the knowledge of the κυριότης of the man Jesus and our membership in Him), even we ourselves groan within ourselves, waiting for the adoption (the direct experi-ence of what is bound up with the fact that in Christ we also are the children of God), to wit, the redemption of our σῶμα (the completed form of our persons, removed from φθορά, in which God already sees us, which belongs to us, and is already prepared for us, as those who are elect in and with Christ, but in which we do not yet live)." We are saved (ἐσώθημεν), but we are saved as we continue to hope that, although we do not yet see it, we are on the way to seeing it, so that even in the night in which we do not see it we are summoned to wait (ἀπεκδέχεσθαι) and to be patient. The only thing is that Paul does not put this in the form of an imperative, but of an indicative. It is a statement of fact : As those who do not see, but hope, δι᾿ ὑπομονῆς ἀπεκδεχόμεθα. This is the present situation. This is what we do.

Finally, Rom. 8²⁶⁻²⁷ tells us that the fact that Christians live in and with the ἀπαρχὴ τοῦ πνεύματος is proved by the fact that they are in a position to hope, and to hope without wavering, even though they do not see ; that they can actually wait with patience. They can do this because He, the Spirit, helps their infirmities, i.e., strengthens them in the weakness to which they are exposed by the fact that they do not yet see what they are. And He does this (and the man who partakes of the Spirit of Christ knows that everything depends on this and that this is where help is to be found) by making prayer both a possibility and a reality : a possibility because He puts them in a union and relationship with God in which they can really speak with Him as they could not do of them-selves, so that by His mediation, in virtue of His ὑπερεντυγχάνειν, they do actually talk with Him ; and a reality because in virtue of His mediation their own stam-mering (the στεναγμοὶ ἀλάλητοι), their own attempts to speak with God, are heard and understood by Him. As they speak with God and are heard and understood by Him, they endure the long night through, looking for the morning. And all this as the Spirit is the power in which the love of God, electing and acting in Jesus Christ, is shed abroad in their hearts. He makes them Christians. He divides them from non-Christians. But He also unites them with non-Christians. He is the promise which is given them, and He sets them in the position of hope. He gives them the power to wait daily for the revelation of what they already are, of what they became on the day of Golgotha. He is the power of the prayer which makes this expectation their own powerful action. And as He does all this, showing Himself in all this to be the Spirit of Jesus Christ, He is the Holy Spirit.   [IV, 2, pp. 323-330]

3. NEW CREATION

We read of this whole alteration in the remarkably central verse 2 Cor. 5[17] : " If any man be in Christ, he is a new creation : old things are passed away ; behold, all things are become new." Alongside this we have to place Rom. 8[10] : " And if Christ be in you, the body (you yourself in virtue of what has taken place for you in the death of Jesus Christ) is dead because of sin (judged there in His body as your Representative) ; but the Spirit (you yourself in virtue of what is promised and has already taken place for you in the resurrection of this your Representative) is life because of righteousness (proclaimed and put into effect there)." Alongside it, too, we must put Rev. 21[4f.] : " And God shall wipe away all tears from their eyes ; and there shall be no more death, neither sorrow, nor crying, neither shall there be any more pain : for the former things are passed away. And he that sat upon the throne said, Behold, I make all things new." All these can and should be read (according to the meaning of the New Testament writers) as a commentary on Is. 43[18f.] : " Remember ye not the former things, neither consider the things of old. Behold, I will do a new thing ; shall ye not know it ? I will even make a way in the wilderness, and rivers in the desert." Or on Is. 65[17f.] : " For, behold, I create new heavens, and a new earth : and the former shall not be remembered, nor come into mind. But be ye glad and rejoice for ever in that which I create : for, behold, I create Jerusalem a rejoicing, and her people a joy." The New Testament community knows what is meant by this. It stands at the heart of the event which is proclaimed here, face to face with the Jerusalem which comes. Again, the prophetic word is for it a commentary on that which confronts it as its basic text. It is the witness of it. The old, the former thing, has passed away : the new has come, has grown, has been created. It is " in Christ "—the Crucified and Risen —and Christ is in it. In His death its own death and that of the world is, in fact, already past, and in His life its own life and that of the future world is before it. It has turned away from the one, it has turned to the other. It has put off the one, it has put on the other. Its existence looks back to the Crucified and forward to the Risen. It is an existence in the presence of the One who was and will be. He is its *terminus a quo* and its *terminus ad quem*. It is an existence in that alteration, that is, in that differentiated relationship between the death and the resurrection of Christ. When a man is in Christ, there is a new creation. The old has passed, everything has become new. This means that the event of the end of the world which took place once and for all in Jesus Christ is the presupposition of an old man, and the event of the beginning of the new world which took place once and for all in Jesus Christ is the goal of a new man, and because the goal, therefore the truth and power of the sequence of human existence as it moves towards this goal. The world and every man exist in this alteration.

Note that it is not dependent upon whether it is proclaimed well or badly or even at all. It is not dependent upon the way in which it is regarded, upon whether it is realised and fulfilled in faith or unbelief. The coming of the kingdom of God has its truth in itself, not in that which does or does not correspond to it on earth.

By way of illustration, let us suppose that the kingdom of heaven is like a king whom it has pleased to confer on someone an order. Now normally the man will be in the happy position of being able to receive the distinction. But there may be the abnormal case when because of pressing or tragic circumstances, or because he is hindered by outside forces, he is not in a position to do this. Is it not clear that in both cases the will and act of the king form a complete action, and all is well and good for the recipient even in the second and abnormal case ? Has he failed to receive the order because he could not do so in person ?

The men of the New Testament are the normal case, those who not only receive that which has taken place in Jesus Christ, but do so in person, those who with open eyes and ears and hearts, in faith and in the knowledge of faith, hold to the fact that they can and must, not only exist, but walk (περιπατεῖν, στοιχεῖν, πολιτεύεσθαι) from this presupposition to this goal and in this sequence, who are therefore summoned and empowered and enabled to proclaim this alteration and therefore the death and resurrection of Jesus Christ, or rather the crucified and risen Jesus Christ Himself. The divine verdict pronounced in the resurrection of Jesus Christ has been heard by them. The " blowing " (Jn. 3⁸) of the Holy Spirit which creates life and leads into all truth is received by them. They are " baptised " (Mk. 1⁸) by Jesus Christ Himself, or they have " drunk " of Him (1 Cor. 12¹³). As they pray for Him, He is to them the One who is " given " by their Father in heaven (Lk. 11¹³). He " dwells " in them (Rom. 8¹¹). They are " led " by Him (Gal. 4⁶, 5¹⁸ ; Rom. 8¹⁴). They walk in conformity with Him (κατὰ πνεῦμα, Rom. 8⁴) or in Him (πνεύματι, Gal. 5¹⁶, 2 Cor. 12¹⁸), not as blind and deaf participants in this alteration of the human situation, but as those who see and hear.   [IV, 1, pp. 311–312]

4. THE BODY OF CHRIST

We must now explain briefly the remarkable New Testament expression σῶμα Χριστοῦ. And first it will be as well to try to survey together the different meanings within which the word σῶμα oscillates. To understand the New Testament usage we must not forget that in the first instance it means a dead body, a corpse. But in relation to the human body it also means the living body, either as contrasted with the soul, or with its individual parts, the members, or even with the blood in which it has its life (as in the texts relating to the Lord's Supper). From this we may conclude that σῶμα is the seat of the earthly-historical life, so that being in it can indicate the time of man's being on earth, and the σῶμα in which he lives the limitation of that time. But σῶμα is also the medium of man's experience and suffering, the organ or instrument of his activity. We must also not forget that (in Rev. 18¹³) it can indicate the bodily possession, or slave, and (in Col. 2¹⁷) the body which throws a shadow in distinction from the shadow. In the sequence Χριστός-σῶμα-ἐκκλησία the word σῶμα can have all these different meanings with greater or lesser pregnancy.

We will start with the main passage, 1 Cor. 12¹². Here primarily we have to note that in the first instance it is not the community which is called a body, or compared to it, but Christ Himself. He is a body. By nature He is not simply one (for a body is the unity of many members), but one in many. It is not that σῶμα is a good image for the community as such, but that Jesus Christ is by nature σῶμα. Hence the force of Paul's argument in 1 Cor. 12⁴⁻³¹ for the necessity of the unity and plurality of gifts in the community (which, although they differ from another, are all gifts of the one Spirit). It is in the " bodily nature," in the simplicity and plurality of Jesus Christ Himself, that the Corinthians are able to recognise the necessary order, the relatedness and the freedom of their life as His community. From Him they are one as ἐκκλησία, that is to say, they are His body, and members of this body in the reception of the different gifts of the one Spirit granted to them : ὑμεῖς δέ ἐστε σῶμα Χριστοῦ καὶ μέλη ἐκ μέρους (1 Cor. 12²⁷). The community is not σῶμα because it is a social grouping which as such has something of the nature of an organism, which reminds us of an organism, which, *ceteris imparibus*, can therefore quite suitably be compared with it, which can be called a σῶμα. It is σῶμα because it actually derives from Jesus Christ, because of Him it exists as His body. The relationship to Him, or rather from Him, is everywhere evident: οἱ πολλοὶ ἓν σῶμά ἐσμεν ἐν Χριστῷ (Rom. 12⁵). He is the "Head" of this body, the centre which constitutes its unity, organises its plurality, and guarantees both (Col. 1¹⁸, Eph. 5²³). "From Him (ἐξ οὗ) all the body by joints and bands supported, and knit together, increaseth with the increase of God" (αὔξει τὴν αὔξησιν τοῦ θεοῦ, Col. 2¹⁹, Eph. 4¹⁶). The work of the ministry of the saints is for the edification of His body (Eph. 4¹²). "We are members of his body" (Eph. 5³⁰), and He is its Saviour (Eph. 5²³). Apart from Jesus Christ there is no other principle or *telos* to constitute and organise and guarantee this body. Even the *kerygma*, baptism, the Lord's Supper, the faith and love and hope of Christians, the work and word of the apostle, cannot have this function. It is the function of Jesus Christ alone. As the Head He is Himself and primarily the body, and He constitutes and organises and guarantees the community as His body.

He does this as the One who was crucified on Golgotha. Of course as the One crucified there He was raised again on the third day and is therefore able to act. All the same, to understand who it is that acts, we must first think of the meaning of σῶμα as a dead body or corpse, as in Rom. 7⁴: "Ye also are become dead to the law by the body of Christ," or, again, Col. 3¹⁵: "Ye are called to peace in one body" (His), or Col. 1²²: "He hath reconciled us in the body of his flesh through death," "by the cross" (Eph. 2¹⁶), or 1 Pet. 2²⁴: "He bare our sins in his own body on the tree," or Heb. 10¹⁰: "We are sanctified through the offering of the body of Jesus Christ once for all." He lives and acts as the One who was put to death in the body, who offered up His earthly-historical existence, who was deprived of it, who in His body delivered up to death, bore and bore away "the body of sin" (Rom. 6⁶), the "body of the flesh" (Col. 2¹¹), the "body of this death" (Rom. 7²⁴). In Him it was all humanity in its corruption and lostness, its earthly-historical existence under the determination of the fall, which was judged and executed and destroyed, and in that way liberated for a new determination, for its being as a new humanity. It was the body of everyman which became a corpse in Him and was buried as a corpse with Him. All men, "Jew and Greek, bond and free, male and female," as they are now representatively gathered in the community, were one in God's election (Eph. 1⁴), were and are one in the fulfilment of it on Golgotha, are one in the power of His resurrection, one in Jesus Christ (εἷς, Gal. 3²⁸), His body together in their unity and totality.

This is revealed in His resurrection from the dead, in the light of which it can and must be said to the community : "Ye are the body of Christ" (1 Cor. 12²⁷). In His risen body the sinful, fleshly humanity which had fallen a prey to death and had been destroyed in Him is awakened to being in a new right and life. "The body without the spirit is dead" (Jas. 2²⁶). Without the Holy Spirit the body of Jesus Christ and in it all humanity can only be dead. But the body of Jesus Christ was not a body abandoned by the Holy Spirit. The Holy Spirit has shown Himself to it as the life-giving Spirit. The body of this One who was slain has become a body which is alive by the Spirit : σῶμα πνευματικόν, 1 Cor. 15⁴⁴). During the forty days He appeared to His disciples in this body. He, the one man Jesus of Nazareth, who had been raised from the dead—that is the concrete history of the forty days. But not He alone, abstractly as this one man, just as He had not died alone, abstractly as this one man. But the one man who as their Representative and the Representative of all men, the bearer of their sin and flesh and death, had delivered all this up to the past in His death, dying on the cross—this one man now appeared to His disciples (in their own person first and then of all humanity) as the bearer of their new right and life, and as such the Revealer of their future, Himself in His person, in His body, the promised πνεῦμα ζωοποιοῦν, which is His remarkable title as the "last Adam" (1 Cor. 15⁴⁵). The content of Easter Day and the Easter season consisted in this, not in an "attesting miracle," not merely in a parthenogenesis of the Christian faith, but in the appearance of the body of Jesus Christ, which embraced their death in its death, their life in its life, their past and their future in itself, thus including them all in itself. As He encountered them in this corporeity, the disciples heard addressed to themselves as such, to the ἐκκλησία which arose in virtue of it, the call which is the disclosure of the secret of His earthly-historical existence : " Ye are the body of Christ."

Therefore the mystery of the community is not in the first instance its own. In the first instance it is His mystery : the mystery of His death in which He was this Victor ; the mystery of His resurrection in which He was this Revealer. In His body He is elected, called and instituted from all eternity as this Victor and Revealer. It is His body which includes them all to their salvation and the salvation of the world. Because it includes them, it is their body and they are His body. In Him they themselves have turned away from sin and flesh and death as their past and have turned to the right and life as their future. His mystery is theirs. Having been given life by the Spirit, and Himself a life-giving Spirit, He has made it known to them—His election and birth and calling and institution as their Head and the Head of all men, His earthly-historical existence as that of their Representative and Substitute and Advocate, and therefore as the truth of their own earthly-historical existence. He is always the Head of this body. He is the giver and they are the recipients. He is the Master and they are the brethren (Mt. 23⁸). He is the vine and they are the branches (Jn. 15⁵). "Without me ye can do nothing "—you cannot be my body, you cannot be a body at all. For only He, Jesus Christ, the "last Adam," is the unity in plurality of humanity which the first Adam could only prefigure. He alone can be the Head of a body which includes them all—so that if they are to be a body, they can only be His body.

The mystery of the community is not in the first instance its own mystery in the further sense that its Head Jesus Christ was elected the Head of all humanity (as the last and true Adam, 1 Cor. 15⁴⁵ᶠ·), that He was made the one Mediator between God and all men (1 Tim. 2⁵), that He died for the sins of the whole world (1 Jn. 2²), and that He rose again as the Revealer of the right and life of all men (1 Cor. 15²¹ᶠ·). The New Testament never expressly uses the term body of humanity as a whole, of the totality of Jews and Greeks, slaves and free men, males and females. It uses it only of the Christian community. For only in this community is there a dispensing and eating of the bread which is broken in common. Only in it is there the visible fellowship (κοινωνία) of this body, the perceiving and attesting of His real presence, the recognisable and recognised union of a concrete human fellowship with Him (1 Cor. 10¹⁶). ὅτι εἷς ἄρτος : " Because it is the one bread which the many break and eat (together) "—ἓν σῶμα οἱ πολλοί ἐσμεν : " we, the many, are one body "—οἱ γὰρ πάντες ἐκ τοῦ ἑνὸς ἄρτου μετέχομεν : " for we are all partakers of the one bread " (1 Cor. 10¹⁷). Their communion with one another, their common action in remembrance of Him, their common proclamation of the death of the Lord until He comes (1 Cor. 11²⁶), as it takes place in this action, does not create and put into effect their union with Jesus Christ Himself—which is unnecessary ; it reveals and publishes and documents that union, it is that union *in concreto*, as the earthly-historical activity and experience of these particular men. Where there is not this communion, we cannot speak with the New Testament of a union of men with Jesus Christ and therefore of a real presence of His body. To that extent the expression σῶμα Χριστοῦ is in the New Testament an esoteric expression. The reality indicated by it is to be seen only in the concrete life of the community. A saying like 1 Cor. 12²⁷ (" Ye are the body of Christ, and members in particular ") is obviously not a part of missionary preaching. It is clearly a kind of repetition of the call which in the forty days was not directly addressed to humanity as a whole but to the few whom the risen One encountered. But it is open to question whether the same can be true of the saying in 1 Cor. 12¹² in which Jesus Christ Himself is called a body. For how can we proclaim His death and resurrection to Jews and Gentiles as their own death and the promise of their right and life without proclaiming Him as the Head and Representative and Mediator of all men, the " last Adam " ? And how can we do that without approximating very closely to the concept of the body of Christ including and uniting all men ? That logic drives us in this direction is something we have to remember for an understanding of the being and mission of the community. As σῶμα Χριστοῦ it is not an end in itself. In the first instance and originally Jesus Christ as the Head is the one body visible in the bread, and the community only because He is this one body and calls it to be and makes it a unity. Similarly, the community itself, participating in the bread, is only the arrow which points to that unity of the many which is grounded and—although hidden— actual in the fact that He is the Mediator and Substitute and Representative of all men. How can it be the body of this Head if it tries to be a house with closed doors and windows, if it tries to exist like a ghetto, if as the body of Christ it wants to be defined by its own limits ? If it has a right understanding of itself in its common breaking and eating of the one bread and therefore in its concrete life as a community, then as the body of Christ it has to understand itself as a promise of the emergence of the unity in which not only Christians but all men are already comprehended in Jesus Christ. The great truth of Eph. 1²³ can never be forgotten but must always shine out in it. As His body it is " the fulness of him that filleth all in all." And the same is true of Eph. 1⁹ᶠ·: God has " made known unto us the mystery of his will, according to his free resolve purposed in himself and to be accomplished in the fulness of times ἀνακεφαλαιώσασθαι τὰ πάντα : to give to all things their head in Christ—to all things, both which are in heaven, and which are on earth, in him, in whom also we have obtained an inheritance, being predestinated according to the purpose of him who worketh all things after the counsel of his own will, that we should be to the praise of his glory, who already have our hope in him " (προηλπικότες, lit. those who have hoped before in Him).

This is the Magna Carta of the being of the community in Him. We do not decrease but bring out its true glory if we understand the exclusiveness in which it is called and is His body in the world as an exclusiveness which is relative, provisional and teleological. Sayings like Col. 1¹⁸, ²⁴: " The church is his body," or, conversely, Eph. 1²³ : " His body is the church," or Rom. 12⁵, in which the many are one body in Him, or the direct statement in Eph. 5³⁰ that " we are members of his body," speak of the glory of the being of the community in so far as they speak properly of the glory of Jesus Christ Himself and therefore of the σωτὴρ τοῦ κόσμου (Jn. 4⁴²; 1 Jn. 4¹⁴), of His being and work for the whole of humanity which is both one and many. In the first instance they are christological and therefore teleological statements, and only as such ecclesiological.

For that reason they do not provide any basis for the idea of a Church which exists ipsa quasi altera Christi persona, as fully proclaimed in the encyclical "Mystici corporis" (p. 54). There are not two or possibly three bodies of Christ : the historical, in which He died and rose again ; the mystical which is His community ; and that in which He is really present in the Lord's Supper. For there are not three Christs. There is only one Christ, and therefore there is only one body of Christ.

For the same reason there is no need to take the statements symbolically or metaphorically. As His earthly-historical form of existence, the community is His body, His body is the community. Why, and to what extent ? Because the community and those who belong to it have received the " manifestation of the Spirit" (1 Cor. 12⁷) in the unity and diversity of His gifts (Rom. 12⁶), because they have " drunk " with Him (1 Cor. 12¹³) and therefore are free to confess Jesus as *Kyrios* (1 Cor. 12³). To put the same thing in another way, because the Gospel once and still proclaimed to them has shown itself powerful and effective and fruitful to and in and among them, as described in the thanksgivings with which Paul opens a whole series of his letters. The equating of the body of Christ and the community is valid only with reference to this divine action, but it is unconditionally and actually valid with this reference. With this reference these sayings can be uttered with no less definiteness than the great christological statements concerning the death of Jesus Christ implying our death as it has already taken place in Him, and the resurrection of Jesus Christ implying our future resurrection. Here we have the invisible being of the community, the being which is visible only to faith. This is what permits and enjoins us to celebrate " thanksgiving " (εὐχαριστία) within it, to give thanks as Paul does for its existence. For in the community the truth of these christological statements, the justification of man as it has taken place in Jesus Christ, is known, in as much as Jesus Christ has shown His power and revealed and asserted Himself within it. For in Him " ye heard the word of truth, the gospel of your salvation ; in whom also after that ye believed, ye were sealed with that holy Spirit of promise, which is the earnest of our inheritance, until the redemption of the purchased possession, unto the praise of his glory " (Eph. 1¹³ᶠ·). With the foundation and preservation of the community this event actually takes place in the space and time of these men, in the sphere of their experience and activity, although it is an event which, according to 1 Cor. 2⁹, ¹⁴, cannot be brought about by any human experience or activity. In the light of this event, as the Spirit who raised up Jesus from the dead dwells within them (Rom. 8¹¹), the community can be referred to as the body of Christ, and its members as members of this body. In the light of this event its earthly-historical existence can be known as the earthly historical existence of Jesus Christ Himself (who, as its Head, is in heaven at the right hand of the Father), so that He can concretely ask the persecutor of the community (Ac. 9⁴) : " Saul, Saul, why persecutest thou me ? ", and He can say no less definitely of that which is done (or not done) to the least of His brethren (Mt. 25⁴⁰, ⁴⁵) : " Ye have done it (or not done it) unto me." With reference to this event the equation of the body of Christ and the community has itself to be described as a very secondary christological statement, but one which is of decisive practical importance for the time of the community in the world.

We must be clear that the community is not made the body of Christ or its members members of this body by this event, by the Spirit of Pentecost, by the fulness of His gifts, by the faith awakened by Him, by the visible, audible and tangible results of the preaching and receiving of the Gospel, let alone by baptism and the Lord's Supper (as so-called " sacraments "). It is the body, and its members are members of this body, in Jesus Christ, in His election from all eternity (Rom. 8²⁹, Eph. 1⁴). And it became His body, they became its members, in the fulfilment of their eternal election in His death on the cross of Golgotha, proclaimed in His resurrection from the dead. In this respect the insight of patristic tradition cited in " *Mystici Corporis* " (and combining Jn. 19⁴⁰ and Gen. 3²⁰) is not only ingenious but substantially correct : *in cruce ecclesiam e latere salvatoris esse natam instar novae Evae matris omnium viventium* (p. 28). The only thing is that we at once have the usual encroachment when this " new " Eve is equated with the infallible teaching and ruling ecclesiastical institution (p. 32) which is focused on the papacy as the visible head of this Church in place of the invisible Christ (p. 40). There can be no doubt that the work of the Holy Spirit is merely to " realise subjectively " the election of Jesus Christ and His work as done and proclaimed in time, to reveal and bring it to men and women. By the work of the Holy Spirit the body of Christ, as it is by God's decree from all eternity and as it has become in virtue of His act in time, acquires in all its hiddenness historical dimensions. The Holy Spirit awakens the " poor praise on earth" appropriate to that eternal-temporal occurrence, the answer to the Easter message in the hearts and on the lips of individual men, faith and the one and varied recognition of obedience to the Son of God as the Head of all men. " Thou worthy Light, shine here below / Teach us our Saviour Christ to know / That we in Him alone may stand / Who brought us to our fatherland. *Kyrie eleis.*" It is the work of the Holy Spirit that the Lord does do this in His mercy, that He shines on men to give them this knowledge of Jesus Christ and themselves. And in this knowledge, in and with Jesus Christ, His body is known as His community, His community as His body. It is known because this union has already been created in that eternal and temporal happening. It is known in such a way that its being precedes the knowledge of it, and the knowledge of it can only follow its being.

Where the knowledge of it does follow its being, there the men who share this knowledge are necessarily called to it and claimed by it. The mystery of Jesus Christ is then in fact the mystery of their own existence. The Corinthians are necessarily summoned (1 Cor. 12$^{4-31}$) not only to the preservation of their unity but also to the freedom of varied movements in the sphere of the one and manifold Spirit and His gift and gifts given to them : " God hath tempered the body together" (v. 24) ; " But now hath God set members every one of them in the body, as it hath pleased him " (v. 18) ; " But it is the same God which worketh all in all." If they confess Jesus Christ as Lord, which can only be by the Holy Spirit (v. 3), they confess themselves as His body, and therefore the necessity not to deny either the unity of the community or the diversity of its membership, not to suppress either but to maintain both. How they would misunderstand themselves as the community and its members, how they would misunderstand the one Spirit and His many gifts, if they were ever in danger of doing this, if they were ever tempted to do it, if it became to them a source of self-will and arrogance and division ! God does not tempt anyone (Jas. 1^{13}) and neither does His Holy Spirit. Such dangers cannot derive from their being as the community of Jesus Christ. When they are awakened by the Holy Spirit, when they know Jesus Christ and in this knowledge are really in Him as He is in them, " in the midst " (Mt. 18^{20}), then they are in the one bread which they break and eat together and in that way represent and attest both Him and themselves—His body as it was crucified on Good Friday and raised on Easter Day ; then they are representatives and precursors of all the Jews and Greeks, the slaves and the free men, the males and the females who are many in Him and who are also one in Him. Their unity cannot jeopardise their plurality, nor their plurality their unity.

We are again reminded of the temporary, provisional and teleological character of this special being of the community as the body of Christ when we think of Jas. 1^{18} : " Of his own will begat he us with the word of truth, that we should be a kind of first-fruits ($\dot{a}\pi a\rho\chi\dot{\eta}$ $\tau\iota s$) of his creatures ; " or of 1 Pet. 2^9 : " Ye are a chosen generation, a royal priesthood, an holy nation, a people of possession ; that ye should proclaim the manifestations of power ($\dot{a}\rho\epsilon\tau a\dot{\iota}$) of him who hath called you out of darkness into his marvellous light ; " or finally of Mt. 5^{14} : " Ye are the light of the world," which stands in a similar relationship of apparent contradiction and real agreement to Jn. 8^{12} : " I am the light of the world," as does Paul's reference to the body which is the body of Christ and as such His community.   [IV, 1, pp. 662–668]

5. THE MANNER OF LOVE

We have been describing the background and context of 1 Cor. 13. This short chapter interrupts the two sections of instruction given concerning the right way to deal with the different *charisma* in which the Corinthian community seems to have been particularly rich but in the expression and application of which it was correspondingly endangered. Paul does not question for a moment that they were genuine gifts. But in the light of the fact that they are genuine, and therefore that they derive from the Holy Spirit, the community is (1) admonished in chapter 12 to remember the unity of the derivation of that which is entrusted to it and therefore the fellowship of those who as members of the one body of Christ are counted worthy of one or other of these gifts ; and it is later (2) reminded in chapter 14 that their importance is only relative and therefore greater or less. This second note is sounded already in 12^{31} : " But covet earnestly the best ($\mu\epsilon i\zeta o\nu a$) gifts." In 14^{1} and the whole of chapter 14 we learn that what Paul had particularly in mind was the precedence of prophecy over the speaking with tongues which was obviously so rampant and so greatly overestimated in Corinth. Among the higher gifts he clearly counts the $\gamma\nu\hat{\omega}\sigma\iota s$ and $\pi i\sigma\tau\iota s$ of 13^{2} and the readiness for poverty and martyrdom of 13^{3}, while those of secondary importance seem to include ($12^{28f.}$) miracles ($\delta\upsilon\nu\acute{a}\mu\epsilon\iota s$), gifts of healing, helps, governments and the interpretation of tongues, which are not mentioned again. Bengel has described as *theologia comparativa* the process indicated in 12^{31} and carried through in 14. But before Paul goes on to the second part of his presentation with its clear differentiation, he cuts right across his own thinking and that of his readers with a threefold statement in which he brackets and leaves behind him for a moment the whole problem of *charisma* and questions concerning their distinction, their unity and their greater or less importance, and turns expressly to the factor which forms in some sense the key to the exposition which both precedes and follows : " And yet beyond this (beyond all spiritual gifts, beyond all that has to be said concerning the right way to handle them) I will shew you the way " (12^{31b}). He refers to the way which Christians have always to tread whether or not they are endowed by the Holy Spirit or however they may be endowed. He refers to the human action which has as its basis, not a special liberation and endowment of the Spirit, but the one liberation and endowment which precedes every special liberation and endowment. He refers to the action whose occurrence is the criterion of a right handling of all the others. This way, this action, which is necessary " beyond all this " ($\kappa a\tau'$ $\dot{\upsilon}\pi\epsilon\rho\beta o\lambda\acute{\eta}\nu$), which is the *unum necessarium*, is the distinctive reality concerning which the Christian is asked before and in and after the reception of all particular *charisma* if he is to use them as gifts of the grace of the Holy Spirit.

The way or action to which Paul refers is love. There can be no doubt that he is speaking of the love which is grounded in the love of God ; of the love whose primary human subject is Jesus Christ ; of the love which takes place in His fellowship with man and His discipleship ; of the $\dot{a}\gamma\acute{a}\pi\eta$ $\tauο\hat{\upsilon}$ $\pi\nu\epsilon\acute{\upsilon}\mu a\tauο s$ (Rom. 15^{30}). There is this in common between love and the *charisma* to which it is opposed. The freedom for it too is the freedom of the children of God. It too is the freedom originally realised in Jesus Christ and then awakened in man by the Holy Spirit. It is no mere rhetoric that in the verses which follow Paul describes love almost hypostatically as a person coming and acting independently. If we read vv. 4–7 (and especially 7) we shall soon realise which person he has seriously and ultimately before him. And except with reference to this original, love could not be described in vv. 8–13 as the unceasing and never-failing element in Christian existence. To this extent it was quite in order that at an earlier point (*C.D.*, I, 2, p. 330) I stated that we best understand the concept of love in 1 Cor. 13 if we simply insert the name Jesus Christ in place of it. All the same, we must not allow this to obliterate the fact that Paul describes love as a way, obviously meaning that his readers must tread it, that they can and should do something for themselves, and that in the transition to chapter 14 (v. 1a) he could ask them to " follow after " love. Man does not merge at this point into God or Jesus Christ, but lives in and with Him as a new man in the human freedom given him by the Holy Spirit. It is to be noted that the word θεός, and even the name Jesus, does not occur in the whole chapter. The reference of the text is obviously to what is to be done by Christians in the freedom given them by God in Jesus Christ through the Holy Spirit. The idea of A. Nygren that love is to be understood only as an " effluence from God's own life " flowing through man (*op. cit.*, Vol. I, p. 120) is quite impossible in an exposition of 1 Cor. 13. How could Paul oppose love to the practical exercise of the *charisma* at Corinth if he was not thinking of it as itself a practice, as the true practice of the Christian, as the *via maxime vialis* (Bengel) ? On the other hand, it is certainly a matter of Christian love as grounded in the love of God. Thus in regard to the debate forty years ago between A. v. Harnack and R. Reitzenstein whether what is meant is love for the neighbour or love for God (cf. Nygren, *op. cit.*, p. 114 f. and Harbsmeier, *op. cit.*, p. 33 f.), we must say quite definitely that in relation to 1 Cor. 13 this is a false alternative. It is as well to avoid both abstractions and look constantly at both the dimensions in which Christian love takes place. On the basis of God's self-giving to man, it is man's self-giving to God and therefore also his self-giving to his neighbour.

V. 1 : " Though I speak with the tongues of men and of angels, and have not love, I am become as sounding brass, or a tinkling cymbal." Paul begins by contrasting love with the exercise of one of the endowments which he will later describe quite clearly as of the second rank. In the eyes of his readers, however, it is of primary importance. He does not question that it is genuine, nor does he desire to suppress it : " I would that ye all spake with tongues " (14[5]). Indeed, he knows and exercises it himself : " I thank my God, I speak with tongues more than ye all " (14[18]). He has no wish to " quench " the Spirit in this respect (1 Thess. 5[19]). Speaking with tongues lies on the extreme limit of Christian speaking as such. It is an attempt to express the inexpressible in which the tongue rushes past, as it were, the notions and concepts necessary to ordinary speech and utters what can be received only as a groan or sigh, thus needing at once interpretation or exposition (14[7f.]). The fact that this is possible seems to show that we are not to think of it as a wholly inarticulate, inhuman and bizarre stuttering and stammering. Certainly there can be no question of purely " emotional eruptions " (Harbsmeier, *op. cit.*, p. 14), otherwise Paul could hardly have described the capacity for them as pneumatic. On the other hand, it is a speech which in its decisive utterances leaves any clear coherence behind, necessarily falling apart unexpectedly in its elements, or recombining in equally unexpected equations, and finally consisting only of hints or indications with very forcible marks of interrogation and exclamation. In the last resort, it may well be asked whether there is any Christian speech, any utterance of the evangelical *kerygma*, which does not finally become speaking with tongues, overleaping ordinary notions and concepts in its decisive statements, and then, of course, having to return by way of exposition to ordinary speech. In any case, however, this point cannot be reached artificially. It is not open to all and sundry to advance to it. Such advance presupposes a gift, a permission and a freedom, or it is simply a movement to absurdity. Human speech may reach here the limit in which it becomes the hymn, but even as Christian speech it is held within this limit. The Corinthian community enjoyed in its gatherings a superfluity in respect of the advance to this limit of Christian speech. Paul does not try to dissuade them from it. He knows that there are points where a choice has to be made between speaking with tongues—even at the risk that some will not understand—and illegitimate silence. He tries to curb their over-estimation of this advance, but not to dissuade them from it. He presupposes in 1 Cor. 13 that it may be lawful and right. He maintains, however, that it is possible to speak with tongues (as enabled to do so by the Holy Ghost) and yet not to have love but to omit all self-giving to God and one's neighbour. The capacity for the highly pregnant statement in which it is a matter of expressing the inexpressible, the *esprit* needed for it, cannot make good this lack. And where there is this lack, speaking with tongues—Paul takes his own case as an example —is an instrument which is not really a musical instrument because, although it is sound, it has only the one note and is therefore hollow and empty and inexpressive and wholly unmusical. The sound of a bell or a gong is not music. It is simply a noise. And so, too, is speaking with tongues without love—no matter how significant and arresting it may sound, or how seriously it may have God and Jesus Christ and the Holy Spirit in intention. If it is without love, its good intention is of no more value than the spiritual wealth which seeks expression in it. What sounds in it is only the exalted self-enjoyment and the forceful self-expression of the one who speaks with tongues, and it is something which is monotonous, tedious, uninspiring and finally irksome and annoying. No *Kyrie* or *Gloria* can help a performance of this nature. Even if the one who speaks with tongues were miraculously placed already among the 144,000 of Rev. 14²ᶠ·, and therefore able to learn and sing the new song of the angels before the throne of the Lamb—a song which is undoubtedly of an all-surpassing wealth —it would be of no avail if he is without love. Even in this exalted company he would still be " as sounding brass, or a tinkling cymbal." It is love alone that counts—and not speaking with tongues, not even statements which are full of content and spoken or sung enthusiastically in the best sense of the term.

V. 2 : " And though I have the gift of prophecy, and understand all mysteries, and all knowledge ; and though I have all faith, so that I could remove mountains, and have not love, I am nothing." It is now a matter of the gifts which according to 12³¹ and chapter 14 are higher and most to be desired. By προφητεία we have to understand a definite, important form of Christian speech, not given to all or to any in the same way, which differs from speaking with tongues—with which it is contrasted in 14³—in the fact that it makes use of distinct notions and concepts. In 12²⁹ (and Eph. 4¹¹) the Christian prophet ranks immediately after the apostle. The foretelling of the future is not the essential thing which constitutes the prophet. We are to think, perhaps, of the demonstration of the divine revelation in the *hic et nunc* as it takes place in consequence of the apostolic *kerygma*, of the " intelligible call to the obedience here and to-day " (Harbsmeier, *op. cit.*, p. 27), which may, of course, also and not least of all include the opening up of certain vistas into the future. Understanding of μυστήρια and γνῶσις is the not at all self-evident presupposition of all Christian speech : the apprehension of the message and its theoretical and practical implications ; the consideration of its different dimensions ; the reflection in the union and confrontation of God and man, in the context of the old and the new, which according to Mt. 13⁵² constitutes a " scribe instructed unto the kingdom of heaven." At its noblest this means " theology "—and we must remember that in current usage as heard and used by the Corinthians γνῶσις did not mean *intellectus* in a banal but in the highest sense of the word and therefore " an intelligent participation of the whole man in the redemptive deity " (Harbsmeier, *op. cit.*, p. 17). Finally, πίστις is used in the sense of the faith which works miracles. In this sphere, too, Paul does not raise any doubts or questions. He thinks of the extreme possibilities which may become realities—all mysteries, all knowledge, all faith, the faith which according to Mt. 17²⁰ moves mountains. And he again speaks in the first person and therefore of possibilities known to himself. But he again maintains that he may be enabled to do all these things, and actually do them, and yet be without love. And in this case, no matter how perfect they may be, his prophesying is only idle words, his knowledge a mystico-rational game and his wonder-working faith a higher magic or a massive but sterile orthodoxy. In spite of all his prophetic, theological or hierurgical brilliance, he is οὐθέν, nothing, a string of noughts before which there is unfortunately no " one." We are reminded of Mt. 7²²ᶠ· which tells us that we may speak as prophets, or cast out demons, or do many mighty works in the name of Jesus, and yet do that which is against God and therefore belong to those whom He has never known. It is love alone that counts—and not this brilliance, however great it may be within this limit.

V. 3 : " And though I bestow all my goods to feed the poor, and though I give my body to be burned, and have not love, it profiteth me nothing." Paul now works back to willingness for poverty on behalf of needy fellow-men, or for martyrdom at the specific awakening and in the particular enabling of the Holy Spirit, and he is again thinking of possibilities not unknown to himself. It is to be noted—and this verse is obviously the climax of this first section— how close he now comes to love itself in the description of Christian action. Is it not love for the neighbour when a man gives all that he has as alms ? Is it not love for God when he willingly offers himself up to death for the faith (Paul seems to have had in mind the LXX version of Dan. 3²⁵ᶠ·) ? Does he not expressly speak of a παραδοῦναι in the second part of the sentence ? But this is the whole point. There is in fact a love which is without love, a self-giving which is no self-giving, a paroxysm of self-love which has the form of a genuine and extreme love for God and one's brother and yet in which it is not really a question of God or one's brother at all, but only of the delight which can be found in oneself, in the unlimited nature of one's heroism, when all things, even life itself, are offered. And in these circumstances the action is of no avail. It does not in any sense qualify a man as a Christian. It has nothing whatever to do with the occurrence of the history of salvation in his life. It is love alone that counts —not acts of love as such, however great. The latter may be done without love, and if so they are without significance—indeed they are done in opposition to God and one's brother.

V. 4a : " Love suffereth long, and is kind." This is a kind of heading for all that is to be considered in this section. If we were right to describe Christian love as free self-giving, we may now expound as follows. Just because it is self-giving it is longsuffering, it has that staying power, it is that bright and never-failing light, it stands on that solid ground. Where the wind is short, and the light necessary to the life of man flickers and fades, and the ground is uncertain under his feet, it is finally because he tries to live otherwise than in self-giving ; because he is not ready to be free for God and the brother and therefore himself ; because he wants always to be free for himself. In love he gives himself up. He has God and the brother always before him—and only in this way, in them, himself. And because love is self-giving it is also " kind " or friendly. The word is not to be understood in a weak sense. In the sense of the New Testament χρηστότης it is literally " fitness " and therefore the very opposite of anything weak or soft. A man is " kind " when he has the freedom, the ability, to be spontaneously good to another—a voluntary friend of God and therefore of men. As such he does not do anything alien or accidental. He is not " friendly " amongst other things—casually—when he gives himself to God and his brother. He does that which is most proper to him. He loves in doing it. It is this which makes him *a priori* superior. As, therefore, love is longsuffering and kind, it conquers and triumphs and is victorious, no power being able to match it.

VV. 4b–5b : " Love envieth not ; vaunteth not itself, is not puffed up, doth not behave itself unseemly, seeketh not her own." It is to be noted that its superiority is not easy ; that there is genuinely something to overcome. The many negations in this first list, which are increased in the second, have always demanded the attention of the exegete. In the light of these many negations it seems appropriate to regard the whole of this central part of the chapter from the standpoint of a conflict triumphantly waged by the Christian against hostile forces. The words quoted refer first to sinister powers which he encounters in himself—for he is only a man. All his other activities, even though they derive directly from the Holy Spirit, do not exclude the manifestations of these forces in his own thinking and volition. But love does. Even as one who speaks with tongues, or as a prophet, or as a theologian, or as a miracle-worker, or as an ascetic or martyr, he can still " envy," still covet rights and honour and the recognition he deserves and the clear-cut success of his action. But if he loves, there is no place for envy, and in the fact that this is so love conquers. Again, in all these activities he can " vaunt himself," displaying himself and his spirit-wrought accomplishments and achievements (perhaps set off against his weakness and cares and concern for the world) for the admiration of God and the world and himself. But if he loves, there is no place for boasting, and in the fact that this is so love conquers. Again, he can " puff himself up " like a bubble or a balloon. In defiance of the Holy Ghost to whom he owes it all, he can try to make of himself, perhaps as a pneumatic or gnostic (1 Cor. 8[1]) or in an unnatural estimation of his particular interests and efforts, his particular " cause," a gigantic figure whose proportions bear no relationship to what he really is and has to offer and represent. If he loves, there is no place for this exaggeration. Again, in an obvious confusion of the freedom he is given with one arbitrarily fixed and extended by himself, he may think that he should ignore and transgress the bounds of what is proper, of decorum, of custom, of *civilitas* (Bengel), making himself of interest to himself and others as a kind of bohemian genius. If he loves, there is certainly no place for this. Love cannot in any way—the final phrase sums up all the rest—seek " her own " ; which means that the man who may love cannot seek " his own." The whole threat to his endowment which would at once poison its exercise at the root, the whole danger of a headlong fall from genuine spirituality into unspirituality, consists in the temptation to use the Holy Ghost for the self-assertion and self-preservation and self-embellishment of the man endowed by Him. If he loves, he gives himself (with the by-product that he is no longer of interest to himself), and thus overcomes this temptation. The fact that he is a man means that at any moment he may seek " his own." But the fact that he loves means that there is no place for the envy and boasting and exaggeration and affectation of genius in which he seeks " his own." For if he loves, then *per definitionem* he cannot seek " his own," himself. Thus far concerning the sinister forces which love has to conquer in the man who loves, and which in virtue of its power it does in fact really conquer.

VV. 5c–6 : " It is not easily provoked, thinketh no evil, rejoiceth not in iniquity, but rejoiceth in the truth." In this second list we have to do with the sinister forces which the Christian encounters not only in himself but also very definitely in the being and action of his neighbour. It is to be noted that the list is shorter than the previous one, and that at the end there is for the first time a positive definition of love. The neighbour, the fellow-Christian (more perhaps than one's fellow-man generally, in whom much may be overlooked), is also a serious problem to the one who has noted that he is himself the most serious problem of all. It may be gathered from this passage that even those who were spiritually gifted in Corinth did not strike one another at once as pure angels. The neighbour can get dreadfully on my nerves even in the exercise of what he regards as, and what may well be, his particular gifts. And he can then provoke and embitter and in some degree enrage me. Love cannot alter the fact that he gets on my nerves, but as self-giving (and this perhaps with salutary counter-effects on my poor nerves) it can rule out *a limine* my allowing myself to be " provoked " by him, i.e., forced into the position and role of an antagonist. The Christian cannot become an antagonist of his neighbour. Love neither has nor cherishes nor tolerates any " anti "-complexes. This is one of the secrets of its superiority, its victory. But it may find itself even more seriously blocked by the neighbour. The fact cannot be altered that in his person, even if it is that of the most outstanding Christian brother, I will encounter at some point and in some form the " evil " in which he (like myself) unfortunately has a part. Shall I then reckon it to him ($\lambda o \gamma i \zeta \epsilon \sigma \theta a\iota$) ? Shall I take it down in writing against him ? Shall I always hold it against him ? Shall I nail him to it so that in part at least I always interpret him in the light of it, shaping my attitude accordingly and always regarding him as in some degree a bad man ? I can do this, and there is no little inclination to do so. But love cannot and does not do it, not only because it is self-giving, but because as such it is a reflection of the love of God, which has to do with men who are wholly bad but according to 2 Cor. 5[19] does not impute or reckon their trespasses to them. The man who loves does not compile a dossier about his neighbour. There is, however, a third possibility—the most dreadful of all. This consists in the blatant perversity of actually " rejoicing " that even the most upright of our neighbours continually put themselves in the wrong in relation to us and others, not to speak of God. There is a refined satisfaction which I can procure for myself by making perhaps a show of the deepest sympathy, by actually experiencing it in the guise and feeling of the greatest readiness to forgive, but by seeing that I am set by contrast in a much better light myself, that I am equipped and incited to a much more worthy representation of that which is good, and that I am thus confirmed and strengthened and exalted and assured in my own excellence. Is it not easy to come to the point of waiting expectantly for others continually to do something culpable, to put themselves in the wrong, in order that we may be nourished in this way ? How much of the impulse of private and common Christian action would fail at once if deprived of its basis and nourishment in this " rejoicing ! " But love finds no nourishment here. It does not live by this " rejoicing." How can it be self-giving if it rejoices because it stands out against the dark background of the wickedness and folly and confusion of others ? It does indeed rejoice, but with a very different joy. And this leads us to the first positive definition—what we are to do in face of the wrong of others. We might have expected to be told that instead of rejoicing in the wrong of others love rejoices in the right that we always find in them as well. But this is not the case. The verse tells us rather (with the same antithesis to $\dot{a}\delta\iota\kappa\iota a$ as is found in 2 Thess. 2[10, 12] and Rom. 2[8]) that it rejoices in the truth. It is worth noting perhaps that the verse uses the compound $\sigma\upsilon\gamma\chi a\iota\rho\epsilon\iota$, thus signifying that love rejoices together or in union with the truth which triumphs objectively over all human wrong. It is certainly a matter of the truth in whose service love itself may stand as an attestation of the divine covenant of grace, and therefore for the Christian of $\dot{a}\lambda\eta\theta\epsilon\dot{\upsilon}\epsilon\iota\nu$ $\dot{\epsilon}\nu$ $\dot{a}\gamma\dot{a}\pi\eta$ (Eph. 4[15]). As love for the neighbour, love is self-giving to the attestation of the truth that according to 1 Jn. 3[20] God is " greater than our heart " ; to the guaranteeing of that which is greater than all the corruption in which we may stand the one to the other. Love rejoices as it participates in this thing which is greater, and in its superiority. In this joy it will certainly not weaken in relation to the wrong of others. It will not call wrong right. For in and with the truth it undoubtedly has to bear witness to supreme right. But it will bear witness to this right with gladness, as the grace which avails for others too, and as the freedom for which they too are ordained. It will thus give them the desire to rejoice in this right as well, and in this rejoicing to recognise their wrong as wrong and cease to do it. This is its superiority in face of sinister forces in the being and action of others. In this superiority it is victorious from the very first in its encounter with them.

V. 7 : " It beareth all things, believeth all things, hopeth all things, endureth all things." On this aspect, too, it acts as love for the neighbour, overcoming the evil which we all meet in others and especially in ourselves. But the terms now used indicate that love for the neighbour, its conflict and conquest, and the most serious problem which the Christian meets in himself, are now seen as taken up into the love of God, and into the defeating of the forces deployed against this love. There are so many things between man and God : the many painful burdens of life which love has to bear ; the distressing invisibility of God in face of which love can only believe ; the darkness of the present world-order within which love can only hope ; the seemingly never-ending and purpose-less trials which love can only outlast and endure (ὑπομένειν). In all these respects we may waver in relation to God, tiring of our love for Him and therefore ceasing to love Him. And in all these respects there may be fellow-men and even Christian brothers in relation to whom we are tempted to this kind of doubt, weariness and suspension. On this wide and complicated front there is no certain victory apart from that to which Paul points—the victory which takes place in and with the fact that love cannot waver, tire or cease in relation either to God or the neighbour, because and as it does as such the only thing that there is left to do in face of all these perplexities, but the thing which certainly does not give way to these perplexities. It bears and believes and hopes and endures. It does do this. And note that in the two central phrases it is the subject of faith and hope : of the faith which according to 1 Jn. 5[4] is the victory that overcomes the world ; and of the hope which according to Rom. 5[5] does not make us ashamed. For this reason it is also the subject of a strong and victorious στέγειν and ὑπομένειν. And note especially the fourfold πάντα. At this point we catch an unmistakeable glimpse of the pattern of Christian existence. And this pattern, the royal man Jesus, is not only the pattern but also the living Head of His community and all its members, in whose life and therefore in whose victory they may participate as such, not just passively but actively, as active subjects. When they love, they become and are this. When they love, they withstand the whole world of hostile forces and defeat it. If in all activities wrought by the Spirit Christians are in undecided conflict with this world, when they love this world is already under and behind them. We may recall Rom. 8[37] : " In all these things we are more than conquerors." How ? " Through him that loved us." The cry " Jesus is Victor " (J. C. Blumhardt) is more than the applause of spectators. It is the cry of those who are his followers and triumph with Him. The final statement in the series—that love endures (ὑπομένει) all things—forms a transition to the third part of the chapter.

V. 8a : "'Love never faileth." There is a particular emphasis on the " never " (best brought out in German by Luther's rendering : *Die Liebe höret nimmer auf*). Οὐδέποτε πίπτει means that it is the one form of Christian action which does not require and is not subject to transformation or absorption into another, higher and future form, and to this extent to destruction. In virtue of love there is already in the temporal existence of the community and Christians a ὑπομένειν (v. 7) ; a persistence in face of hostile forces. In what follows there is no further reference to threats to Christian existence, but to a relativisation in the light of its glorious future, of the eternal light which is still hidden but will one day shine ; a relativisation to which it is already secretly but genuinely subject. But this relativisation will not overtake love, nor the whole life-act of the Christian to the extent that it is done in love. Love, therefore, is not subject to it. Love is the connecting link between now and then, between here and hereafter. In the famous sentence of Troeltsch, it is " the power of this world which already as such is the power of the world to come."

V. 8b : " But whether there be prophecies, they shall fail ; whether there be tongues, they shall cease ; whether there be knowledge, it shall vanish away." The futures are references to the goal and end of the present age ; of the inter-vening time which is the time of the community. Prophecy, tongues and know-ledge will then and there be subject to the relativisation to which they are already subject as determined and seen from this standpoint. Relativisation is the right word to use. To translate καταργηθήσονται by " set aside " (Harbsmeier) or even " destroyed " (Lietzmann) is a mistake. " We shall all be changed " (ἀλλαγησόμεθα, 1 Cor. 15⁵¹ᶠ·)—this and not destruction is what will there and then overtake our existence, even our existence and action as Christians. This is the future which already determines its present. We may begin by quoting a saying of J. C. Blumhardt : " The Saviour is not a destroyer." In the eternal light to which we move prophecy, tongues and knowledge will be taken up into a new and higher form. Their present form will certainly be destroyed. Prophets will have done their work, and those who speak with tongues will no longer need to deliver their ecstatic utterance because the extreme case will once and for all have become normal. And Paul definitely says of knowledge in v. 12 that it will not be set aside or abolished but will take place in a new and more perfect form : ἐπιγνώσομαι. It can certainly be said that it will " vanish away " (καταργηθήσεται), for there will be an end of the *theologia viatorum* as such and of its whole character, and its transformation and assumption wholly and utterly into the *theologia patriae*. Theological research and instruction will then be outmoded. Demythologisation will no longer be required. There will be no further scope for the investigation of a correct hermeneutics and debates concerning Law and Gospel, etc. No more volumes of *Church Dogmatics* will be written. There will be no further need for the *furor theologicus*. Not because all these things are vain and futile, not because they are ashes or wind, but because they will all be genuinely real only in their *telos* and perfection, which includes the fact that their worth and worthlessness will be weighed on the eternal balances, that the wheat will be separated from the chaff, that they will all pass through the refining fire of 1 Cor. 3¹²ᶠ· in which it will be shown whether the building is of gold, silver and precious stones or wood, hay and stubble, and there will be surprises in both respects for all theologians, both small and great, both regular and irregular, both orthodox and heterodox. This wholly salutary relativisation is the πίπτειν to which love is never, never exposed even there and then. And when the Christian loves, he already does something here and now which is not exposed to this relativisation but abides absolutely. Even in the best of cases the same cannot be said of his prophecy, tongues and theology in themselves and as such.

VV. 9–10 : " For we know in part, and prophesy in part. But when that which is perfect is come, then that which is in part shall be done away." The reason for the " ceasing " of v. 8 is not the fact that what Christians now do and should do in the power of the Holy Spirit is only " in part " (so Lietzmann). The reason for it is to be found in the coming of what is perfect, by which the time of the community and all that it contains is bounded. Measured by this great light the little lights by which we now live show themselves to be necessary and useful but in the last resort only a very feeble means of illumination. Their poverty, in which love does not share, is indicated by the ἐκ μέρους. The reference is no longer to tongues but to the endowments and activities which Paul obviously regards as of the first order. Tongues, too, are obviously shown to be impoverished in the light of the coming perfection. But the unmistakeable weakness even of prophecy and knowledge in this light consists in the fact that they are possible only " in part." Is this expression a reminder that the statements and arguments of Christian prophets and theologians are at best only approximations to their theme, or better perhaps the final remnants of its revelation as this has already taken place in the resurrection of Jesus Christ ? Or does it recall the discursive and therefore the disparate character of even their most learned and assured pronouncements ? Does it keep before us the fact that even the greatest prophet or the most cautious and penetrating theologian can speak only in the form of distinct *loci*, chapters and sections which have always to be completed the one by the other, and can never express the one whole truth as such in a single word or statement ? Are we referred to the distinctions and divisions and contradictions and antitheses which burden even genuinely

Christian prophecy and theology because in the succession and conjunction of periods they are represented by so many different witnesses whose theses can never be reduced to a common denominator ? Are we to think of the differentiation of stages on life's way, i.e., of the aspects of the one truth which one and the same prophet or theologian may successively glimpse in the course of a lifetime ? Paul may well have had something of all this in mind. But at all events the partial character of prophecy and knowledge is their poverty. It is the form in which, although they do not become " worthless " (so Lietzmann), they cannot persist or continue when the perfect comes. It is the form in which they have to be taken seriously in gratitude and obedience, but also in their relativity, so that they cannot be confused with the true reality, but are asked only concerning their content as love (vv. 2–3).

V. 11 : " When I was a child, I spake as a child, I understood as a child, I thought as a child : but when I became a man, I put away childish things." This is a first comparison in elucidation of what is said in vv. 8b–10. As the comparison shows, Paul was not thinking of any suppression of the identity of the acting Christian in his transition from now to then, or of any extinction of his present being and activity in favour of the very different being and activity which will be his in the future. Even in the enjoyment and exercise of supreme gifts of the Spirit, the Christian is now a child from whom we can expect and require only childish thoughts and words. The same Christian will then be a man, and as such he will think and speak *totaliter aliter*. But even in this total transition he will not become another person, nor will he basically think and speak anything different. The statement in v. 11b is made rather too stark with the rendering of $\tau\grave{a}$ $\tau o\hat{v}$ $\nu\eta\pi\acute{\iota}o\upsilon$ as " childish things " and of $\kappa a\tau\acute{\eta}\rho\gamma\eta\kappa a$ as " done away." It is a matter of the thinking and speaking which are appropriate to the child and do not disqualify it as such (i.e., the childlike rather than the childish). And it is a matter of the taking up of these things into a new and higher form rather than their abolition. Is not the child the father to the man ? And does not the child still persist in the man, even though he be seventy or eighty years old ? Man certainly goes through a radical change of form when he becomes an adult. And the same will be true of the prophecy and knowledge now living in the community with the coming of that which is perfect. And the fact that this will be so limits and determines its fulfilment in the present. In this connexion Bengel has made the acute observation that it does not say : *quum abolevi puerilia, factus sum vir*—which would mean that that which is perfect comes in and with the progress and maturity of the Christian and his activity. But as it is not winter that brings spring, but spring that banishes winter, so it is in and with the coming of that which is perfect that there comes about the transformation of the present form of childlike thought and speech, of Christian prophecy and knowledge in their present form, into the new form which awaits them, or rather which already comes to meet Christians, and with which they and their prophecy and knowledge have to let themselves be clothed upon (2 Cor. 5[2f.]) ; the form in which they will no longer take place in part, and therefore very differently from the way in which we see them now.

V. 12 : " For now we see through a glass, darkly ; but then face to face : now I know in part ; but then shall I know even as also I am known." A second comparison is offered in elucidation of vv. 8b–10. But first we must note the climax with which we have to do in this third section too. In v. 8 the reference was to prophecy, tongues and knowledge, in vv. 9–10 only to prophecy and knowledge and now in v. 12, corresponding to an obvious concentration of interest in Paul's own thinking, only to sight and knowledge as the presupposition of all that he wished to set against the true, the coming and eternal light as the epitome of " the best gifts " (12[31]). The continuity between now and then is, if possible, even clearer in this case than it was before, for both now and then it is a matter of sight and knowledge. Seeing in a mirror is already seeing, and seeing face to face is still seeing. Knowing in part is already knowing, and knowing " as also I am known " is still knowing. Nor can there be any material break because the present object of seeing and knowing is the same as the future, and the future will be the same as the present : God in His revelation, in His self-presentation ; and in the light of God man, the world, time and what takes place in time. To be sure, the change in the form of the same happening will be most radical between now and then. At the moment we see in a mirror. This has the general meaning that we see in an element and medium foreign to the object itself ; in the form of human perceptions and concepts ; in an earthly history visible in earthly terms ; in a consideration of the external aspect of the works of God, the life of the people Israel and even the life of the man Jesus. It also has the particular meaning that we see in a way which corresponds to the nature of a mirror : the interchanging of right and left ; God in His disclosure in which He conceals Himself and His concealment in which He discloses Himself. Thus even at best our life is an indirect seeing, a seeing *in contrario*, and to this extent an improper seeing. Even at best there is only a seeing ἐν αἰνίγματι ; a seeing which awaits its true fulfilment. Similarly there is only a knowing in part in the manifold sense of the expression already indicated in relation to vv. 9–10. This seeing and knowing is the presupposition of all Christian speech to-day both within the community and through the community to the world. But then there will be a seeing face to face. The revelation of God in Jesus Christ will mean that we " see him as he is " (1 Jn. 3²), directly, unparadoxically and undialectically. Paul was perhaps thinking of what was said of Moses in Num. 12⁸ : " With him will I speak mouth to mouth, even apparently, and not in dark speeches." And then there will be a knowing " as also I am known." As God understands me, I will understand Him, and through Him all things ; the whole context of providence. My present knowing in faith will then be taken out of its isolation and taken up into a knowing in sight (2 Cor. 5⁷). This is the change of form between now and then, and for all its continuity it is the most radical change. But in what does its continuity consist ? What is it that persists, that " abides ? " It is certainly not the present form of Christian activity, even though this derives from the quickening power of the Holy Spirit, and has thus to be rated very highly and is to be gratefully fulfilled with all zeal and fidelity. Its present form perishes in and with the perishing of the form (the σχῆμα) of this world. What does not perish, however, is the true reality in this activity, that which makes it Christian, that which counts in it, that in which it is already a triumphant activity. The true reality of Christian activity participates already in its future form which is still hidden from us but is carried toward it as its new clothing with the coming of that which is perfect.

  V. 13 speaks of this true reality of the life-act of the Christian (in full agreement with v. 8a) : " And now abideth faith, hope, love, these three ; but the greatest of these is love." It is to be noted that faith also abides, even though in the coming great change it is taken up into sight. It is to be noted that hope abides, for how can it fail to do so when it is specifically the orientation of the life-act of the Christian on that which is perfect, whose coming will be its fulfilment ? But faith and hope abide only as and because love abides. It is in love that faith and hope are active, and that there takes place that which is specifically Christian in the life-act of the Christian. Thus love is the " greatest of these." It is the future eternal light shining in the present. It therefore needs no change of form. It is that which continues. For whatever else may be revealed in and with the coming of that which is perfect, in whatever new form Christian activity and the life of the community may attain its goal with everything that now is and happens, one thing is certain and that is that love will never cease, that even then the love which is self-giving to God and the brother, the same love for which the Christian is free already, will be the source of the future eternal life, its form unaltered. Already, then, love is the eternal activity of the Christian. This is the reason why love abides. This is the reason why to say this is to say the final and supreme thing about it. This is the reason why we had to say previously that it is love alone that counts and love alone that conquers. This is the reason why it is *the* way (12³¹).

[IV, 2, pp. 826–828 ; 829–831 ; 832–835 ; 837–840]

6. THE PAROUSIA OF JESUS CHRIST

The word παρουσία (cf. for what follows the article by A. Oepke in Kittel) derives from Hellenistic sources and originally means quite simply " effective presence." A *parousia* might be a military invasion, or the visitation of a city or district by a high dignitary who, as in the case of the emperor, might some-times be treated so seriously that the local calendar would be dated afresh from the occasion. The term was also applied sometimes to the helpful intervention of such divine figures as Dionysius or Aesculapius Soter. What is signified by the term, if not the term itself, is familiar and important in the thinking of the Old Testament. From His place, whether Sinai, Sion or heaven, Yahweh comes in the storm, or enthroned over the ark of the covenant, or in His Word or Spirit, or in dreams or visions, or simply and especially in the events of the history of Israel. To the men of His people He comes finally as universal King in the unfolding of His power and glory. The coming of " one like the Son of man with the clouds of heaven " (Dan. 7¹³) ; the coming of the righteous and victorious Messiah-King abolishing war and establishing peace (cf. Zech. 9⁹ᶠ·) ; above all the recurrent Old Testament picture of the coming God of the covenant Himself manifesting Himself in movement from there to here—all these constitute materially the preparatory form of what in the New Testament is called παρουσία in the pregnant technical sense, namely, the effective presence of Jesus Christ.

What is formally meant by the word is best seen from the fact that in the later New Testament (especially the Pastorals, yet also as early as 2 Thess. 2⁸) it is found in close proximity to, and sometimes replaced by, the term ἐπιφάνεια. In its Hellenistic origin at least ἐπιφάνεια denotes the making visible of concealed divinity. In 2 Thess. 2⁸ both terms appear in a way which is not just plerophoric (so W. Bauer) but materially instructive. With the breath of His mouth the Lord Jesus will slay a hidden but one day manifested ἄνομος, destroying him τῇ ἐπιφανείᾳ τῆς παρουσίας αὐτοῦ. What else can this genitive conjunction mean but that the epiphany of Jesus Christ is the manifestation of His *parousia* or effective presence, or conversely that His *parousia* takes place in His epiphany and therefore His manifestation ?

As far as I can see, there are no passages (not even 2 Tim. 1¹⁰) where either term refers abstractly to the first coming of Jesus Christ as such, i.e., to His history and existence within the limits of His birth and death, of Bethlehem and Golgotha. In relation to these there would be no point in speaking either of ἐπιφάνεια (manifestation) or of παρουσία (effective presence). In them He is not even " manifest in the flesh " (1 Tim. 3¹⁶), and none of the other references in this passage can really apply to His pre-Easter existence as such. To be sure, the Word then became flesh, and His whole work was done in all its dimensions. But the incarnate Word was not yet revealed and seen in His glory (Jn. 1¹⁴). This took place in the event of Easter. In this event we certainly have the coming of the One who came before in that sphere. But it is now His coming in effective presence, because in visible manifestation in the world. It is now His coming in glory as the active and dominant factor within it. It is thus His new coming as the One who came before. It is now His " coming again," and in spite of Oepke I do not see how we can avoid this expression as we have provisionally and generally explained it.

If we allow the New Testament to say what it has to say, we shall be led in this matter to a thinking which is differentiated even in its incontestable unity, formally corresponding to that which is required for an understanding of the three modes of being of God in relation to His one essence in triunity : *una substantia in tribus personis, tres personae in una substantia.*

When the matter is usually spoken of in the New Testament under the terms *parousia* or epiphany, the reference is usually or chiefly to the third and final form, to the eschatological form in the narrower traditional sense, of the return of Jesus Christ, i.e., to His manifestation and effective presence beyond history, the community, the world and the individual human life, and as their absolute future. But reference to this climax of His coming dominates New Testament thought and utterance even where it is materially concerned with the subject without using these particular terms. We can hardly deny or explain this away in such typical passages as the *parousia* passages in the Synoptists, or the Thessalonian Epistles of Paul, or 1 Cor. 15, or the Apocalypse with its final ἔρχου κύριε ᾿Ιησοῦ (22²⁰). Even the Gospel of John, which seems particularly to invite us to do this with its placing of both the gift of eternal life and the judgment in the present, resists it inasmuch as it is rather strangely the only book in the whole of the New Testament to speak of the last day (ἐσχάτη ἡμέρα) when Jesus will awaken the dead (6³⁹, ⁴⁰, ⁴⁴, ⁵⁴) and His Word spoken to men will judge them (12⁴⁸) ; and it is advisable not to solve the implied difficulty of interpretation by critical amputation. According to the New Testament, the return of Jesus Christ in the Easter event is not yet as such His return in the Holy Ghost and certainly not His return at the end of the days. Similarly, His return in the Easter event and at the end of the days cannot be dissolved into His return in the Holy Ghost, nor the Easter event and the outpouring of the Holy Spirit into His last coming. In all these we have to do with the one new coming of Him who came before. But if we are to be true to the New Testament, none of these three forms of His new coming, including the Easter event, may be regarded as its only form. The most that we can say is that a particular glory attaches to the Easter event because here it begins, the Easter event being the primal and basic form in which it comes to be seen and grasped in its totality.

Oepke is surely right when he says of the so-called last discourses in John that in them the " coming of the Resurrected, the coming in the Spirit and the coming at the end of the days merge into one another," and when he also says of the Synoptic Jesus that it is impossible to decide to what extent He made a clear distinction between His resurrection and His *parousia* in its final form. Yet may it not be that we can very definitely decide that He, or the Synoptic and also the Johannine tradition concerning Him, did not in fact make any absolute distinction between them at all in respect of either matter or form ? What do we learn from the well-known passages (considered in detail in *C.D.*, III, 2, pp. 499 ff.) in which Jesus unmistakeably prophesies the manifestation of the kingdom of God ἐν δυνάμει (Mk. 9¹ᶠ·), the coming of the Son of Man (Mt. 10²³, 26⁶⁴), or at least the sign which directly precedes (Mk. 13³⁰ and *par.*) within the lifetime of those around Him ? If we may eliminate in advance what is in its way the greatest triviality of any age, what are we to make of the assumption which underlay a particular school of Neo-Liberal theology, and which is unfortunately encountered only too often outside the narrow circle of this school, namely, that Jesus was deluded ? If we find in the coming of the Resurrected, His coming in the Holy Spirit and His coming at the end of the age three forms of His one new coming for all their significant differences, there need be no artificiality in explaining that these passages refer to the first and immediate form in which His coming did really begin in that generation as the Easter event and in which the two remaining forms are plainly delineated and intimated. We are then forced to accept the statement of W. Michaelis which Oepke contests : " The resurrection . . . is the *parousia*," or again the statement of R. Bultmann (with particular reference to John's Gospel) : " The *parousia* has already taken place," although we must be careful to make the proviso that these statements are not to be taken exclusively but need to be amplified by the recollection that this is not the whole story. The outpouring of the Holy Spirit is also the *parousia*. In this it has not only taken place but is still taking place to-day. And as it has taken place in the resurrection and is taking place to-day in the outpouring of the Holy Spirit, it is also true that it will take place at the end of the days in the conclusion of the self-revelation of Jesus Christ.

When we treat of the unity of the three forms or stages of the one event of the return of Jesus Christ, it is perhaps worth considering and exegetically helpful, again in analogy to the doctrine of the Trinity, to think of their mutual relationship as a kind of perichoresis (cf. *C.D.*, I, 1, p. 425). It is not merely that these three forms are interconnected in the totality of the action presented in them all, or in each of them in its unity and totality, but that they are mutually related as the forms of this one action by the fact that each of them also contains the other two by way of anticipation or recapitulation, so that, without losing their individuality or destroying that of the others, they participate and are active and revealed in them. As the Resurrected from the dead Jesus Christ is virtually engaged already in the outpouring of the Holy Spirit, and in the outpouring of the Holy Spirit He is engaged in the resurrection of all the dead and the execution of the last judgment. The outpouring of the Holy Spirit obviously takes place in the power of His resurrection from the dead, yet it is already His knocking as the One who comes finally and definitively, and it is active and perceptible as such. Similarly His final coming to resurrection and judgment is only the completion of what He has begun in His own resurrection and continued in the outpouring of the Holy Spirit.

To be sure, this is a view which is never systematised in the New Testament or presented in the form of instruction. But this does not mean that we are false to the Bible, or obscure its statements concerning the *parousia*, by adopting this view. Are we not more likely to throw light on them if we advance it with the necessary prudence yet also boldness? Are there not many passages in the New Testament which with their apparent contradictions cannot be satisfactorily explained except on the assumption of such a view? This is not a key to open every lock. But it is one which we do well not to despise.

[IV, 3, pp. 292–293 ; 294 ; 294–295 ; 296]

7. THE COMING OF THE LORD AT THE END OF TIME

If we are to understand the New Testament consciousness of time in this third component, it is perhaps best to start with the fact that the apostles and their communities always had before them the witness of the Old Testament to Christ, and therefore the coming Jesus, promised and prefigured, but only prefigured, and according to the Word of God to be expected in the near and certain future. According to the Gospel records before them, however, He had already come, and with Him the kingdom. And on the basis of the climax and crown of these records, of the Easter message, they were privileged to live in His presence. Hence their hope was a hope already fulfilled. It was thus radically distinguished from the ordinary hope or longing in which they might well have been disappointed. Yet they still went on waiting, or began to wait as never before, together with the fathers of the old covenant, hoping and living wholly and utterly in Advent. Clearly, there was a genuine tension in their consciousness of time, a tension between the preliminary glory of the resurrection and its consummation in the future *parousia*. It was in this tension that they believed in Him and proclaimed Him as the Deliverer of those " who through fear of death were all their lifetime subject to bondage " (Heb. 2¹⁵). This, though already accomplished, was not yet realised and experienced even in themselves, let alone in creation as a whole. They walked by faith and not by sight (2 Cor. 5⁷). They were indeed saved, but only in hope (Rom. 8²⁴). They had indeed received the Holy Spirit, but only as an ἀπαρχή (2 Cor. 1²², 5⁵; Eph. 1¹⁴), i.e., as a first instalment of the final gift. The instalment was of a piece with the final gift and a pledge and guarantee of it, yet it was no more than the deposit on an account, an ἀπαρχή (Rom. 8²³), i.e., the first fruits consecrated to the Deity, but not yet the full harvest distributed among all the people. They knew of their hidden life with Christ in God, but only when Christ their life was made manifest would they be manifested with Him in glory (Col. 3³ᶠ·). " Behold, what manner of love the Father hath bestowed upon us, that we should be called (and be) the sons of God . . . Beloved, now are we the sons of God, and it doth not yet appear what we shall be : but we know that, when he shall appear, we shall be like him : for we shall see him as he is " (1 Jn. 3¹ᶠ·). What has still to be realised, as Paul sees it, is the manifestation of the life of Jesus in ·His body (2 Cor. 4¹⁰), the general " manifestation of the sons of God " (Rom. 8¹⁹), the making of their " body of humiliation " conformable to His " body of glory " (Phil. 3²¹), and the liberation of all creatures from the bondage of corruption to the glorious liberty of the children of God (Rom. 8²¹). When Jesus had been obedient even to the death of the cross, He was exalted by God to be the Bearer of the name which as the name of the Lord is above every other name. This was clear to the proclaimers and recipients of the Easter message, and they believed and responded with their confession and a life of love for Him and for the brethren. But they did not yet see the knees of all things in heaven and earth bow to Him as the only Lord, nor did they yet hear the song of praise with which every tongue must willingly or unwillingly confess Him as the Lord (Phil. 2⁹ᶠ·). This was the supremely visible and real tension in their consciousness of time between the times. But it must be seen and understood that this tension—with the need and yearning and sighing inevitably entailed—could not have a negative accent, because they saw themselves set in fellowship with the Old Testament fathers, in the time, not to be evaluated negatively, of their expectation of the coming Lord and His salvation ; because they were privileged to stand with these ancient witnesses of truth in Advent.

2 Pet. 1¹⁶⁻²¹ is particularly noteworthy in this connexion. The author is talking about his proclamation of the " power and coming of our Lord Jesus Christ." He maintains that it is different from any " cunningly devised fables " (σεσοφισμένοις μύθοις). To begin with, he points out that he had been an eye-witness (ἐπόπτης) of the transfiguration. He then continues in v. 19 : " Hence we have the word of prophecy the more surely (βεβαιότερον) ; whereunto ye do well that ye take heed, as unto light that shineth in a dark place, until the day dawn, and the day star arise in your hearts." According to the Gospel record, Moses and Elijah had actually stood by the side of Jesus when He was transfigured before their eyes, and had spoken with Him. This prophetic word was not therefore outmoded, but acquired genuine relevance for those who had their origin in the appearance of Jesus. It was confirmed in its character as a prophetic word pointing to the future and became an indispensable light on their path. The disciples did not come down from the mount alone, or as eschatological innovators, but in company with the ancient witnesses, accredited by the fulfilment of the long-prepared history of the covenant and salvation. It was in this company that they moved afresh to meet the coming Lord. The visible and palpable unity of prophecy and fulfilment, of fulfilment and prophecy, is what factually distinguishes their proclamation of the " power and coming of our Lord Jesus Christ " from all " cunningly devised fables."

The same line is taken in Peter's second speech in Ac. 3¹⁹ᶠ·. He summons men to repentance and conversion and the remission of sins on the ground that " seasons of refreshing " are coming ; the sending of Jesus, Israel's destined Messiah, " whom the heaven must receive until the times of restoration of all things (ἀποκατάστασις πάντων), which God hath spoken by the mouth of all his holy prophets since the world began." The implication is that the prophets foretold not only the first advent of Christ, but implicitly His second advent as well, to which the Church now looks and the whole world actually moves. Far from being obsolete, the witness of the prophets has acquired a vital relevance and admonitory significance for the people of Israel to whom the apostles in the first instance addressed their message. Whatever happens, Israel must not miss a second time, and to its final judgment, the chance to experience the fulfilment of this message, as it did the first time to its detriment.

Even more illuminating is 1 Pet. 1[10-12], which merits particularly close attention. In 1[5] the author had stated that those who had been begotten again unto a living hope by the resurrection of Jesus Christ from the dead were being kept by the power of God through faith unto salvation ready to be revealed at the last time. In vv. 6–9 he had spoken of the " joy unspeakable and full of glory " awaiting those who were now suffering persecution. Although these had not seen Jesus they loved Him, and believed on Him without beholding Him. That joy would be theirs in His final revelation. He now continues in v. 10 f. : " Of which salvation the prophets have inquired and searched diligently, who prophesied of the grace that should come unto you : searching what, or what manner of time the Spirit of Christ which was in them did signify, when it testified beforehand the sufferings of Christ, and the glory that should follow. Unto whom it was revealed, that not unto themselves, but unto us they did minister the things, which are now reported unto you by them that have preached the gospel unto you with the Holy Ghost sent down from heaven, which things the angels desire to look into." The meaning of this is that they have been translated into the state of faith, hope and love by the fact that the prophets, taught by the Spirit of Christ, have done and are still doing them the same service as the messengers of the Gospel now do them as they are sent by the same Holy Spirit. The prophets preached and still preach to them the sufferings and glory of Jesus Christ, and in so doing they preach their salvation already accomplished in Jesus Christ but still to be revealed to them. The fulfilment of Old Testament prophecy has become a reality among them, and they have thus come to participate in the resurrection of Christ. They are born again to a living hope. Therefore, in spite of the sufferings of the present time, they have been translated into the state of love and faith in One whom nevertheless they cannot see or behold. We may note in particular that the enquiries and declarations of the prophets belong formally and subjectively to their own time and history. But in this historical particularity they were materially and objectively inspired and moved and impelled by the Spirit of Christ, by the truth of His coming person and history, by His sufferings and glory. What makes their enquiries and declarations prophetic is that objectively and materially they are witnesses of Him who was still to come, i.e., of the grace now vouchsafed to Christians. It is for their sake that Jesus Christ suffered, and for their sake that He is glorified. Thus the prophets can be of service to Christians because they are prophets, and their testimony is a προμαρτύρεσθαι (v. 11). They too, like the messengers of the Gospel (v. 12), are wholly dependent on the Holy Spirit of Jesus Christ. Like them, they are unable to make the object of their proclamation visible or perceptible to their hearers. For them too the salvation wrought in Jesus Christ is a hidden mystery, only to be revealed later. Hence in a way they really minister to Christians " the things which are now reported unto you." But because their testimony takes the form of a προμαρτύρεσθαι, and their existence that of prophets, unlike the evangelists, and perhaps to their advantage, they are witnesses to the truth that what they attest with the evangelists is not just an ordinary event in the flux of history, and that the God proclaimed by the evangelists as the Father of Jesus Christ is not a new God. *Certitudinem salutis confirmat ab ipsius vetustate : quoniam ab initio mundi legitimum a Spiritu sancto testimonium habuerit* (Calvin). Unlike the evangelists, however, and perhaps to their disadvantage, the prophets are witnesses of the Jesus Christ whom they do not yet know as come, and can attest therefore only as One who is still to come. " What or what manner of time " will be His, is all that they can investigate. They cannot bear witness to His actual manifestation. The sufferings and glory of Jesus may form the object of their message objectively and materially, but they cannot be its content subjectively and formally. Since they think and speak only of their own time, the actual occurrence of the event which they foretell can only be for them a matter of research and investigation. Yet this is no fortuitous limitation. Indeed, it is not really a limitation at all. It makes no difference to their testimony or status. As the sufferings and glory of Christ are revealed to the prophets by His Spirit, it is also revealed to them that with the later evangelists, the heralds of the accomplished event of salvation, even in this apparently disadvantageous distinction they have a very real and special service to render to Christians instructed by the latter. The rigorously future orientation of the prophetic message only becomes vital in Christianity. For Christians living in time the enacted salvation has become past. But in its general revelation it is still future. And in this futurity it is the event which leads Christians forward in time, urging them ahead, drawing them on like a magnet, out of the sufferings of the present time, out of the darkness of the present and into the light. The present status of Christians, with its tribulation, is related to that of the future deliverance to which they move as the sufferings of Christ are related to His subsequent glory. The two together, and in this order, are the Messianic reality : the first being subordinate and transitory, the second real and permanent ; the first being the way and the other the goal. In virtue of this order and structure of the one event commonly attested by the prophets and evangelists, the evangelical and apostolic message can be no less prophetic, no less a message of Advent, than that of the prophets. It proclaims not only the Crucified, but also the Resurrected ; not only the faith and love which Christians are to maintain in their present tribulation as they look back to the completed Messianic event, but, as in vv. 3–9, and in agreement with the structure of this event, the future revelation of the deliverance of those who believe and love (corresponding to the glory of Christ), and therefore Christian hope. Christians could not really come from this event if they were not moving towards it again. Thus it is Christianity which first does justice to prophecy even in its particularity, even in the strict futurity of its message. In fact, this passage seems almost to reduce the apostles and evangelists to the level of subordinates. All that they have to do is to take up the Old Testament message of the future and give it the honour which it could not enjoy prior to the events, in its distinctive character as prophecy. The message of the Messiah already come gives a new edge to the message of the coming Messiah, of the salvation which is not only future, but demonstrated to be future. Now that grace and salvation have become present and future and not just future, the ministry of the prophets really begins, as by the word of the apostles and evangelists the Holy Spirit speaks to Christians in this twofold way, making them Christians, and translating them into the state of living hope in which even in the sufferings of time they move towards the glory of the future revelation. Only here, within the Christian community, does the prophetic word come into its own. Christians have to see themselves standing as it were between two choirs singing antiphonally— the apostles on one side and the prophets on the other. And the passage closes at v. 12 with the statement that even the angels are amongst those who look forward to the future revelation of the salvation already accomplished. They, too, desire to see and look into the mystery of the things, the grace and salvation, in the proclamation of which the prophets and apostles have ministered to them and do so still. Like the apostles and prophets, like Christians themselves, the angels wait for the consummation of the process inaugurated by the resurrection—a consummation which according to 1 Pet. 4[7] will also be " the end of all things." The word used to denote the "looking into" of the angels (παρακύψαι) is the same as that which in Jn. 20[5] is used of Peter when he looks into the empty tomb. Thus Christians are surrounded by a cloud of witnesses, some eloquent and others silent, some on earth and others in heaven, but all looking into the future. This is sufficient to warn them to hold fast to the state of salvation to which they have been called. "Wherefore gird up the loins of your mind, be sober, and hope to the end for the grace that is to be brought unto you at the revelation of Jesus Christ " (v. 13).

Remarkably enough therefore, but also instructively, it was primarily the Old Testament background to the New Testament message which gave to the first Christian consciousness of time its forward direction and eschatological orientation, and to Christian life the form of a " looking for and hasting unto the coming of the day of God " (2 Pet. 3[12]). The Gospels would be very different from what they are, i.e., accounts of the historical existence, fulfilled in His crucifixion and revealed in His resurrection, of the man Jesus who was the Lord, Messiah and Saviour, if in telling of Him who was, they were not everywhere full of Advent, of the One who comes and will be in His revelation.

As is well known, the Fourth Gospel takes its own particular line in this matter. In fulfilment of the promise : " I will not leave you comfortless ; I will come to you " (Jn. 14[18]), Easter, Ascension, Pentecost and *parousia* are here seen as a single event, with much the same foreshortening of perspective as when we view the whole range of the Alps from the Jura. This perspective is legitimate and necessary side by side with the other. The Fourth Gospel shows us that it is necessary to understand the event of Easter and that of the *parousia*, with the intervening history of the community under the present power of the Holy Spirit, as different moments of one and the same act. The theses of those who advocate a thoroughgoing eschatology are quite superfluous once this has been realised. There is no need to suppose that there was unforeseen delay in the *parousia*, or that hope in the *parousia* was repeatedly deferred, or that the primitive Church and even Jesus Himself were disillusioned or mistaken on the subject in consequence of an exaggerated enthusiasm—a view which is so clumsy that it is surely condemned from the very outset.

For there is a unity of eschatological outlook even behind and above the different approach which we find in the Synoptists. As we have seen already, the latter start with the initial assumption that the kingdom of God promised in the Old Testament has already entered history as an effective reality in the person and words and acts of the man Jesus. The time is fulfilled as He is present, embarking on a way which will end in His death as the decisive event of salvation, but which is from the very first this way, on the higher stages of which this end is already the meaning not only of the being of Jesus as such, but of all His words and acts. The Synoptists would agree with the view which the Evangelist attributes to John the Baptist in 1[29]—that from the very outset Jesus is " the Lamb of God, which taketh away the sin of the world." But He is still concealed as the One He is and shows Himself to be in His words and acts. At first, it is only the demons who recognise Him with any certainty in this way : " What have we to do with thee, thou Jesus of Nazareth ? art thou come to destroy us ? We know thee who thou art, the Holy One of God " (Mk. 1[24]). The crowds are amazed and dumbfounded, but they only call Him a great prophet (Lk. 7[16]). Their spiritual leaders are offended at His claim to be the coming One, and dismiss it as a piece of arrogant self-assertion. But this only shows how blind and deaf they are, how far they have abandoned the hope of Israel, whose first and most discerning and willing advocates they ought to have been in face of this fulfilment. John the Baptist surmises His true status, but according to Mt. 11[2] he is not sure whether Jesus is He that should come or whether they should look for another. Indeed, He is hidden even from His disciples apart from preliminary illuminations like Peter's confession and the transfiguration. They will forsake Him and flee when He stands at the end of His way. Peter will even deny Him, and Judas will be the first and decisive agent in Israel's last act of unfaithfulness and disobedience to its promise, initiating the handing over of its Messiah to the Gentiles. As the One He is Jesus is thus both present and not present. The kingdom of God is real but not operative. It has come, but not come. It has still to be prayed for. It is present in reality, but not in revelation. To the extent that the New Testament contains good news, but not yet Easter news, the prophetic history of the Old Testament is continued in the New. The New Testament witness to the Messianic " now " is unmistakeable, yet it is shot through with the " not yet,' with more expectation, as though the Messiah were still only promised. In the very centre of the picture Jesus Himself waits, looking forward to things to come, to His own future.

This is the second reason—the Advent witness of the Old Testament was the first—why the apostolic community would not concentrate exclusively on the past or present, but when it thought of Jesus had to look forward to this future. Throughout the tradition—in the New Testament even more clearly than in the Old—we see at the heart of the actuality of salvation a people always blind and deaf, obstinate and determined enemies of God, a Church which always runs away and denies and even betrays Him, and above all Jesus Himself still waiting and looking forward to His own future. How could anyone who remembered this Jesus do other than follow Him, looking with His eyes and according to His express command to the future, His future ? But to look to His future is to look to the revelation of His actuality, to the irresistible, invincible and triumphant visibility of His kingdom as it has already come.

The reader of the Gospels is bound to look to the future, if only because the Jesus attested by them was not waiting for nothing but positively living and speaking and acting towards His future revelation. For His goal is not just death, although this is the saving event to which His whole life was in the first instance directed. His goal is the subsequent revelation of the meaning of His death, and therefore the putting into effect of the salvation won in Him for men, for the community, for the whole world, for which He had come as the Fulfiller of time. It is the kingdom with the veil removed, manifest, and visible in glory. Everything Jesus said revolved implicitly, and in the parables explicitly, around the coming kingdom in this sense. And the acts of Jesus, His signs and wonders, are in this sense effective anticipations and therefore real indications of the coming kingdom to which Jesus moves through His provisional concealment and finally His passion, crucifixion, death and burial : not of the reality of the kingdom, for the kingdom was already a reality in His person from the very outset and could not be more real than in His self-offering to death, in which the saving event of His whole existence, His Messianic reality is perfected ; but certainly of its revelation, by which the kingdom acquires form and becomes saving and effective for men, for the community, and for the world.

This also explains why New Testament expectation is always characterised as imminent expectation. It is primarily the expectation of the man Jesus Himself (in the subjective sense) : the expectation in which He Himself lived and went to His death ; the expectation of what He saw before Him as the goal of His life and death. It is the expectation of His own resurrection from the dead. All three predictions of the passion in the Synoptics expressly mention this expectation : " On the third day he will rise again." Yet the Gospels obviously rule out the imminent expectation which is expectation of a definite date. Jesus Himself admitted that He shared the human uncertainty understandable in this respect : " That day and that hour knoweth no man, no, not the angels which are in heaven, neither the Son, but the Father " (Mk. 13[32]).

Even after the resurrection He can still say : "It is not for you to know the times or the seasons, which the Father hath set in his own power," i.e., which He has appointed for the manifestation of His kingdom (Ac. 1[7]). The revelation of the kingdom is linked with the consummation of the life of Jesus in His death. It is its revelation. And this fulfilment of His life in His death, which will be followed by His revelation, is accomplished by the incarnate Son in obedience to the will of His Father and therefore in acceptance of the right point of time appointed not by Himself but by the Father. What He does know and teach, because His disciples are always to know it too, is that the kingdom of God, the revelation of its hidden reality, will come soon and suddenly like a thief in the night, as He Himself puts it (Mt. 24[43]), in a simile repeated in 1 Thess. 5[2] ; 2 Pet. 3[10] ; Rev. 16[15]. Its coming will be soon because it is the goal of the limited life in time of Jesus of Nazareth and will follow hard on His death and therefore in the foreseeable future. And it will come suddenly because it is foreordained and foreknown by God alone, and will occur when men are least expecting it, beneficially if terrifyingly upsetting all their expectations and plans, and thus their anxieties and hopes, as actually happened in the first instance with the resurrection of Jesus.

These considerations throw light on Mk. 9[1] : "Verily I say unto you, that there be some of them that stand here, which shall not taste of death, till they have seen (ἕως ἂν ἴδωσιν) the kingdom of God come with power (ἐληλυθυῖαν ἐν δυνάμει)." This passage assumes that the kingdom of God has already come. What has still to happen is that it should be seen. Some of those standing around Jesus are to see it. It follows, therefore, that this "coming of the king- dom," this revelation of the fact that it has come, must occur within the fore- seeable future. The context in which the three Synoptists placed the saying shows that they connected it with the transfiguration, which is its immediate sequel. The indefinite τίνες, which is used to indicate those who are to see the kingdom in their lifetime, is probably meant to confirm this. Only "some" (Peter, James and John) witness the transfiguration. But this event is only a proleptic anticipation of the resurrection, as the latter is only a proleptic antici- pation of the *parousia*. This being the case, it is best to see the fulfilment of Mk. 9[1] in all three events, transfiguration, resurrection *and parousia*. In the transfiguration they see and know Him already, though only transitively, as the Resurrected. And in His resurrection they finally see the kingdom come with power, and therefore, *in parte pro toto*, as ἀρραβών and ἀπαρχή that which in the *parousia*, as His general revelation, will be comprehensively and con- clusively knowable and known as His glory. Not all, but only a few even of His disciples at the transfiguration, and only the disciples at the resurrection, will in their own lifetime see the kingdom of God come in the person of Jesus, and therefore the end of all time. This is the meaning of Mk. 9[1]. Calvin's comment is thus correct : *Antequam vobis moriendum sit, regnum illud Dei, a cuius spe vos pendere iubeo, conspicuum erit oculis vestris. . . . Adventum vero regni Dei intellige gloriae coelestis manifestationem, quam a resurrectione auspicatus est Christus et plenius deinde spiritum sanctum mittendo et mirificas edendo virtutes exhibuit ; nam in illis primitiis gustandum suis praebuit coelestis vitae novitatem, quam veris et certis experimentis ipsum ad patris dexteram sedere agnoscerent* (C.R. 45, 483).

In similar vein Jesus says in Mt. 10[23] : "Ye shall not have gone over the cities of Israel, till the Son of man be come." The disciples' mission to Israel will be overtaken by the coming of the Son of Man ; their proclamation of the Messiah among the Messianic people will be forestalled by His own revelation. This saying, which is peculiar to Matthew, occurs in the missionary charge, where it is placed just after the prediction of persecution and sufferings for the disciples in the course of their mission. There are, of course, more encouraging and consoling features in the charge. When the disciples are brought to trial they are not to be anxious what answer to make because the Spirit of the Father will speak in them (v. 19 f.). And then " he that endureth to the end shall be saved " (v. 22). This encouragement and consolation is not relative but absolute. A new and wonderful source of help will become available. God will intervene and rescue them from their tribulation. And then we come to v. 23, which obviously takes up the catchword τέλος (v. 22). Their own τελειοῦν of their task in the cities of Israel, where all that they can really do is to flee from one city to another, will be suddenly cut short by God's τέλος. The Son of Man will come and put a stop to the activities of their persecutors. But it will also mean the end of their own mission. Clearly, this is the supreme form of the promise of help which Jesus gave to His disciples. This is how the special Matthean source means us to take it. He will come in person and judge between them and their persecutors, between the new Israel and the old. The great transition of Jesus Himself, accomplished in His death and according to Mt. 28[16f.] manifested in His resurrection, from His mission to His own people to His mission to the world ; the exaltation of His office as the Christ of Israel to His office as the σωτὴρ κόσμου, is reflected in this saying to the disciples and offers the real clue to its meaning. In the words which immediately follow (vv. 24–25), Jesus predicts the same fate for His disciples as for Himself. It is in this transition, in this exaltation, that the Son of Man " comes " and reveals Himself, but also changes completely the mission and office of His disciples. " Go ye therefore, and make disciples of all nations " (Mt. 28[19]). This mission will be both possible and necessary even before they have finished with the cities of Israel. These cities are only the starting-point of the apostolic mission. They are this still. But the apostles cannot wait any longer for their conversion. " Your blood be upon your own heads ; I am clean : from henceforth I will go unto the Gentiles " (Ac. 18[6]). This is what is in store for the disciples according to this saying. They will witness the resurrection of Jesus, which will not only mark the transition and exaltation of Jesus Himself, but their own transition and exaltation to a new and, according to Mt. 24[14], eschatological ministry of proclaiming the Gospel to the ends of the earth. The coming of Jesus is again spoken of as imminent and the saying had the advantage, the practical significance of showing what the promise must have meant for the " little flock " at the pre-Easter period.

There is another saying of Jesus in Mk. 13[30] and *par.* : " Verily I say unto you that this generation shall not pass, until all these things be done." In this case the exegetical situation differs from that of Mk. 9 and Mt. 10. The things which are so imminent that the existing generation will experience them are not identified directly with the coming of the Son of God as the Gospels see it. For they agree in placing it immediately before the parable of the fig tree. When the sap rises, the branches sprout and the leaves grow, it is a sign that summer is nigh at hand. " So, in like manner, when ye shall see these things coming to pass, know that he is nigh, even at the doors." He is at the doors, not yet present, but near, very near. Since the second half of v. 29 asserts this, the ταῦτα of the first half cannot be referred to the days *after* that tribulation, or to the coming of the Son of Man (vv. 25–26), but only to the immediate prelude. And the ταῦτα πάντα of v. 30 must have a similar reference, at any rate as understood by the Evangelists. The present generation will witness the immediate prelude to the coming of the Son of Man. This clearly means that they will actually witness His coming. But the emphasis here is on the fact that they will be witnesses of the three groups of events described in vv. 7–20 as the immediate prelude to His coming : of world-wide disasters (vv.7–8) ; of the tribulation of the Church (vv. 9–12) ; and as a climax, the fall of Jerusalem, which the surviving elect must escape by headlong flight (vv. 14–20). The complex in vv. 7–20 is enframed at either end by warnings against the seductions of false messiahs and prophets with their fictitious claim : Ἐγώ εἰμι (vv. 5–6 and 21–23). But the point of the whole discourse emerges in vv. 24–27 and 33–37. The light of the sun, moon and stars will be extinguished, i.e., the light of the bodies by which, according to Gen. 1[14], created time is measured. And then (v. 26) God will send forth His angels to gather in the elect from the four winds. But, because the tribulation immediately precedes the final event which is also the end of time, it follows that the Church contemporary with the events of the tribulation—perhaps the Church of to-day!—must (vv. 33 f.) watch. Although it does not know—nobody knows according to v. 32—when the καιρός of the great καὶ τότε of vv. 26 and 27 will occur, yet the Lord of the house will suddenly come at an hour chosen by Himself during the night which begins with these events. The whole point and purpose of the existence of the Church in this night is to watch. This is the point and purpose of the existence of the whole generation which will be overtaken by this night : " And what I say unto you I say unto all, Watch " (v. 37). Be ready for the Messiah, who cannot possibly be mistaken for any other. He will come when all this has taken place. While it is taking place, He is " at the doors " (v. 29)—just as summer is nigh when the sap rises in the fig tree and the branches begin to put forth their leaves. The discourse of Mk. 13 is a repetition of the three prophecies of the passion and resurrection of Jesus elevated to a cosmic scale. It must be remembered that the whole discourse is occasioned by the question of the disciples when Jesus predicted the destruction of the temple (v. 2) : " Tell us, when shall these things be ? and what shall be the sign when all these things shall be fulfilled ? " As Mk. 14[58] suggests, the Synoptists too know something of a saying of Jesus about the rebuilding of the temple after three days, and they are clearly aware that this whole complex is susceptible of various interpretations. Jn. 2[19-22] is illuminative in this respect. The destruction of the temple is a reflection of the death of Jesus Himself, and its rebuilding a reflection of His resurrection. The prophecy of what the present generation will experience supremely in the destruction of the temple will begin to be fulfilled at once with the story of the passion (Mk. 14[1ff.]) with which the life story of Jesus reaches its climax. All the disasters of world history, all the persecutions and trials of the community, and above all the judgment on Israel which culminates in the destruction of Jerusalem, are only the great shadow of the cross falling on the cosmos, the Messianic woes which not even the cosmos can evade, the participation in the divine judgment, effected in the death of Jesus, to which even the cosmos is subject, though this judgment is to its salvation, to the salvation of Israel, the salvation of the community, the salvation of all men, and indeed of the whole cosmos. In the cosmos in which and for which Jesus will and must be crucified, things can only turn out as predicted in vv. 7–20. Hence Jesus is primarily foretelling His own impending death when He speaks of these imminent events, and His resurrection when to the comprehensive picture of man tormented by war, division, earthquake and famine, of the persecuted and tormented community, of Jerusalem standing under moral threat, He opposes the imminent end of time, the great καὶ τότε, the coming of the Son of Man to gather His elect, and therefore His triumphant life as the Lord of His community. The disciples can and should look vigilantly to this future in the deep shadows lying across the world, in the afflictions by which it is threatened, in the judgments which must fall on it, and primarily in face of the judgment of which all the other judgments are only the accompaniment, the judgment of His passion, now about to commence. When all this has taken place He will come, He who now goes to destruction. He will then be revealed, He who is now shrouded in the deepest obscurity. He will triumph in judgment upon the cosmos, He who is now vanquished by the cosmos. " Heaven and earth shall pass away : but my words shall not pass away " (v. 31). And according to v. 30 even the present generation shall not " pass away " either until all this has come to pass. Even now, as it begins to experience the passion of Jesus, it is about to take part in the opening of the series of events which will be immediately followed by the coming of the Son of Man. Hence the urgency of the demand that it should look forwards, watching and waiting for Him, and not waiting for any other, nor confounding His coming with that of any other. It thus receives the law which will be normative for every subsequent generation which in its own time and in its own way will witness these events ; the law of hope in the One who has already come and will come again in His glory.

A further case in point is the eschatological saying at the Last Supper recorded by all three Synoptists (Cf. Markus Barth, *Das Abendmahl*, 1945). The clearest version of this is to be found in Mt. 26²⁹ : " But I say unto you, I will not drink henceforth of this fruit of the vine, until that day when I drink it new with you in my Father's kingdom." The negative form in which this saying is couched recalls the Nazarite vow. Jesus is consecrating Himself to be the sacrificial victim. How he kept this oath will be recorded in Mt. 27³⁴. But more important than the negative aspect is the positive—that His next meal, which is the *terminus ad quem* of the oath, will take place in the kingdom of God, and will therefore be the Messianic banquet. This saying is another expression of urgent expectation. In the brief interval in which a man can go without food and drink Jesus will be with His disciples in the kingdom of God. Next time He sits at meat with them they will see and know that the kingdom of God has come. This is exactly what happened according to Lk. 24³¹⁻³⁵. There is also emphatic mention of a meal of the Resurrected with His disciples in Jn. 21⁵, ¹², ¹⁵. Jesus' intercourse with His disciples during the forty days is comprehensively described as a συναλίζεσθαι (" to take salt with ") in Ac. 1⁴. And it is said of the apostles in Peter's speech in Ac. 10⁴¹ : " (We) did eat and drink with him after he rose from the dead." This not only proves the reality of the resurrection (Lk. 24⁴¹ᶠ·), but also its tremendous import and far-reaching consequence. No longer, as at the Last Supper, will they sit at meat with Him in anticipation of His sacrifice, but in retrospect of its completion ; not in a re-presentation and repetition, as in the Romanist doctrine of the Mass, but in a simple and full enjoyment of its benefits, of the eternal life won for us in Him, within the revelation of the completion and benefits of this sacrifice, and therefore with open eyes and ears, and even open mouths, within the kingdom of God. For this reason the κυριακὸν δεῖπνον of the primitive Church, formally celebrated in repetition of the pre-Easter passover in " remembrance " of the Lord (1 Cor. 11²⁰), is materially a continuation of these festive meals in the personal presence of the Resurrected. While in the Lord's Supper the Church looks back upon the " night in which he was betrayed," it cannot confine the memory to this night. On the contrary, " the death of the Lord " is " proclaimed " (1 Cor. 11²⁶) through the action of the community. It is continually made known to the community and the world, on the basis of His self-revelation at Easter as a saving event. Thus the passover meal becomes an Easter meal : not kept in sorrow but in joy (ἐν ἀγαλλιάσει) ; not with complicated arguments as to the precise nature of the bread and wine, but in "singleness of heart " (καὶ ἀφελότητι καρδίας, Ac. 2⁴⁶). Each occasion is the Messianic banquet of the revealed kingdom of God. Each is the most pregnant form of the fellowship of Christians with the Lord now revealed to them. Each is an anticipation of His final and general revelation, inaugurated, but no more, in His resurrection. The resurrection was the ἀρραβών and ἀπαρχή of this final revelation, but the totality is still to come, so that every celebration of the Lord's Supper can only look forward to it. For that reason and to that extent it is celebrated " till he come " (1 Cor. 11²⁶)—and His own general and visible presence renders the Church's human proclamation of His death superfluous. For that reason and to that extent it is particularly appropriate at the Lord's Supper to use the grace : " Come, Lord Jesus, be our Guest." Hence the Gospel accounts of the Last Supper and the institution of the Lord's Supper are to be numbered with the many passages which in the first instance point to the resurrection, which find in the resurrection their initial yet very real fulfilment, but which in the light of this fulfilment point all ages in imminent expectation to the *parousia* as the last event consummating that of Easter.

Our final example is Jesus' reply to the Sanhedrin when He was asked whether He was the Christ, the Son of God. According to Mt. 26⁶⁴ this is as follows: " Thou hast said : nevertheless I say unto you, Henceforth ye shall see the Son of man sitting on the right hand of power, and coming in the clouds of heaven." The Markan version has (14⁶²) : " I am " (’Εγώ εἰμι), but lacks the pregnant " henceforth." The Lukan version (22⁶⁷f.) puts the question with greater reserve : " Art thou the Christ ? tell us," and Jesus first answers : " If I tell you, ye will not believe : and if I ask you, ye will not answer me," and only then adds : " Hereafter shall the Son of man sit on the right hand of the power of God,"—with no mention of the coming on the clouds. Only then is the direct question put by the Sanhedrin : " Art thou then the Son of God ? " and the reply is a combination of the Markan and Matthean versions : " Ye say that I am." All three Gospels agree that Jesus makes a public declaration of His Messiahship just before the end of His life on earth. It is this admission, together with the prediction of His impending exaltation and second coming, that seals His fate in the eyes of His enemies. The high priest rends his clothes. There is no need of further evidence against Him, for this is blasphemy. The death sentence is pronounced forthwith, and the mocking and scourging follow. We will now confine ourselves to the Matthean version. It is at this point that the passion story proper begins. The Messiah is arraigned by the supreme authority on earth—the high court of the Messianic people. For centuries they have been without a king. Political power has been in the hands of the priestly caste. Now their promised King stands before them, accused before the bar of the priestly aristocracy. Until now He has never publicly claimed to be this King. Indeed, He has prevented His disciples from spreading it abroad. According to Jn. 6¹⁵, He withdrew to the mountains when the crowd wanted to make Him a King by force. He deliberately staged His entry into Jerusalem in such a way as to make it clear that, as far as He is concerned, there is no question of any royal claim. True, He is their King, but He must keep this a secret. Now, however, the whole position has changed at a single stroke. He now stands before a body which can rightfully claim to be " anointed." It has a right to ask whether He is the Christ. There is no telling what happy results might flow from the question. Here is Israel's great opportunity. Never before has it had such a chance to affirm and accept its King through the mouth of its supreme representatives. At last the covenant, so faithfully kept on God's side since the days of the patriarchs and now fulfilled, must be ratified by a practical decision on the part of His people. If it is, the kingdom of God will come on earth in all its glory. Thus Jesus' answer : " Thou sayest it," is not to be regarded as ironical. We should remember that Jn. 11⁵¹ expressly ascribes to the high priest in his official capacity the power to speak as a prophet. Jesus nails him to his own saying : σὺ εἶ ὁ Χριστὸς ὁ υἱὸς τοῦ θεοῦ, which is identical with Peter's confession at Cæsarea Philippi : (Mt. 16¹⁶), and which might be taken as indicative, and might even have been meant as such. He is, as it were, making a last offer through the high priest to the whole people of Israel : You say yourself who and what I am. What follows—the *sessio ad dexteram* and the *parousia*—can and must in the first instance be seen in connexion with this final offer. The King of Israel who stands before them will " henceforth," i.e., now that Israel has decided its attitude to Him, disclose and reveal Himself. It will now see Him as the One He is, the Son of Man enthroned in the glory of God and coming from His glory. But what will He see in His people when He comes ? Will He find it obedient, ready and willing ? And what will His coming mean for it ? Redemption as a reward for its proven loyalty ? We

are at the supreme crisis in salvation history, and world history. Did the high
priest really mean what He said ? Jesus at any rate took him at his word, and
affirmed in all seriousness that he had spoken the truth. And by way of confirmation He elaborates it further. He promises to the high priest, to the Sanhedrin, and through them to the whole people, what hitherto He has confined
to His disciples. The kingdom will come immediately, and in the full glory of
its revelation. " Ye shall see . . ." No conditions are attached to this offer.
It holds good even if the high priest has not really meant what he said, even
if Israel, at the supreme moment of its destiny, has not decided for Him but
against Him. Jesus is still Israel's King whatever happens, even if it rejects
Him. He is who He is and will manifest Himself as such. And the very next
moment, of course, they do reject Him. Is. 29¹³ is repeated once more. " This
people draw near me with their mouths, and with their lips do honour me, but
have removed their heart far from me." It is made clear at once that the high
priest's words were not uttered in knowledge, and therefore as a confession of
faith. He was the one who was really guilty of blasphemy. For he spoke in
blackest unbelief, in malice and guile. The opportunity is there, but it is scorned
and thrown away. The decision is still awaited, but it has already been given
in malam partem. So things take their inevitable course. The high priest rends
his garments and accuses Jesus of blasphemy. The trial is broken off when it
has hardly begun, and the death sentence is pronounced. This means, however, that Israel denies and rejects its king, the King of the last times, who now
stands before it as its King, who has confessed and declared Himself as such,
and who is the Accuser rather than the accused in virtue of His rejection. For
He is who He is, and will manifest Himself as such. They will see Him sitting
on the right hand of power and coming on the clouds of heaven—the self-same
Jesus whom they have rejected and delivered to death. Against their will He
will be victorious, overcoming the death of which they make themselves guilty.
They will see Him in this state of the fulfilment of all the promises as the Revealer
of God's faithfulness in the teeth of all the faithlessness of His people (Jesus
Himself excepted) ; as the righteous Judge, announcing the merited condemnation which would fall on it were it not that He was on the point of taking it
upon Himself and suffering in its place what it ought to suffer, were it not that
His righteousness is therefore righteousness of His grace. But since this is the
meaning of the sessio ad dexteram, since His coming on the clouds of heaven will
be the coming of this righteous Judge, it is clear that everything had to happen
as it did. It was foreseen and determined, not only in the counsels of wicked
man in time, but in the eternal counsel of the righteous God, that the decision
made at this point had to be made, that Jesus' last offer had to be rejected,
that He " must suffer many things of the elders and chief priests and scribes,
and be killed " (Mt. 16²¹). It is not He who is in their hands, but they in His.
But what interests us here is that this last offer (destined from all eternity to
be rejected, as we have seen) also includes the promise of the irresistibly approaching revelation of the glory of the One who is already and immutably the Lord,
and that this promise is actually addressed to His accusers, who themselves
stand at this point under the gravest accusation. The passion of Jesus, and
therefore the last and decisive act of Israel's unfaithfulness, cannot begin before
it has been declared that henceforth—behind the decision first made by God
and then by them, and executed in His actual death on the cross—He will
be seen only in glory. His resurrection, the outpouring of the Holy Spirit on
His community, and His parousia as His final appearance to every creature as
the Judge, are all to be understood as a unity, as a single fulfilment of this last
prediction of His future destiny.

    We learn from these illustrative passages (selected as such from the theology
of the Synoptists) that when our retrospect of the life and death of Jesus is
related to the imminent expectation commanded in the Synoptic Gospels, it

cannot possibly remain retrospective, because in these Gospels Jesus Himself continually looks and moves forward to the revelation of His glory which, inaugurated in the resurrection, will be consummated in the *parousia*.

In conclusion, again adopting the position of the community schooled by the Old Testament and the Gospel accounts of the words and acts of the man Jesus, we maintain as the third ground of its hope the simple fact that it is the community which, after the life and death of Jesus, and the commencement of the final revelation in the forty days, exhibits and experiences the lordship of Jesus in the form of the lordship of His Spirit. We refer to the lordship of Jesus in the time between the resurrection and the *parousia* and therefore between the commencement and the completion of His final revelation. That it has the form of the Spirit means that the community not only derives temporally from this commencement and moves towards this consummation, but that it is effectively established and gathered by the One who was and who comes, being not only ruled but continually nourished and quickened by Him. That is why it lives always in expectation, and even in imminent expectation. That is why its prayer is *Maranatha* (1 Cor. 16^{22} ; Rev. 22^{20}). That is why it finds its consolation in His promise : " Behold, I come quickly " (Rev. 22$^{7, 20}$). That is why it receives the encouragement : " Behold, I stand at the door, and knock " (Rev. 3^{20}). That is why it is given the consolation : " The Lord is at hand " (Phil. 4^{5} ; Jas. 5^{8}). That is why it also receives the daily admonition : " And that, knowing the time, that now it is high time to awake out of sleep : for now is our salvation nearer than when we believed " (Rom. 13^{11}).

In this respect Mt. 25 is of particular relevance for the present existence of the community, for it is asked in this chapter whether it understands and takes seriously and turns to good account its present existence under the lordship of Jesus in the form of the Spirit as considered in relation to the future. Does it realise that the end before it is the consummating coming of the Lord, the glory, the liberation, but also the judgment of the final revelation to which it now moves, so that its present life and action is weighed in the balances of His future ?

This is the challenge of the parable of the ten virgins. (Mt. 25$^{1-13}$). It asks the community whether it is active in relation to the new coming of the Lord, or whether it is merely passive. The ten virgins are supposed to go out and meet the bridegroom. This is the meaning of ὑπάντησις (v. 1), or ἀπάντησις (v. 6), and it is implied by the description in v. 10 of their going out to escort the bridegroom and accompany him to the marriage feast with their lamps alight. Exactly the same picture is given in 1 Thess. 4$^{13-18}$, where Paul states that the community, both living and departed, will be " caught up . . . in the clouds, to meet the Lord in the air " (εἰς ἀπάντησιν κυρίου). With Jesus Himself, His community as such, in His service, will come and be revealed in the world in glory, and will even assist its Lord in the judgment of Israel (Mt. 19^{28}), in the judgment of the world and angels (1 Cor. 6$^{2f.}$), and in His kingly rule (1 Tim. 2^{12}, 1 Cor. 4^{8}, Rev. 5^{10}), so that it can be called a " royal priesthood " (1 Pet. 2^{9}), and it can be said that the whole creation is waiting for this revelation of the sons of God (Rom. 8^{19}). The picture of the virgins escorting the bridegroom with their lamps in Mt. 25 is reminiscent of a similar eschatological saying in Dan 12^{3} : " And they that be wise shall shine as the brightness of the firmament ; and they that turn many to righteousness as the stars for ever and ever " —to which allusion is also made in Mt. 13^{43}. When Jesus is finally revealed, the Church of the interim will stand at His side, with its testimony to the whole world. This is the promise of the parable. But it also contains a challenge. Five virgins are wise and five foolish. The wise ones, having kept their lamps alight for a long time, and apparently to no purpose, had themselves fallen asleep from weariness (v. 5). Fortunately, however, they had replenished their lamps with oil and could thus fulfil their function at the decisive moment. The foolish virgins were also to hand with their lamps burning and shining, but unfortunately they had no reserves of oil and could not therefore meet and escort the bridegroom. The available oil could not be divided, and their rush to the shops to buy some could only seal the fact that their lamps were not burning and shining at the decisive moment, and therefore that they would have no share in the entry of the bridegroom. The parable is thus controlled by the question whether oil is available to replenish the lamps at the critical moment. If the lamps stand for the witness of the community, with which it can and should stand at the side of the returning Lord at the end of time, the oil represents something which makes this witness vital and strong not only now but then, something which is essential if it is to render this supreme service in the final revelation, because, if it does not have it, it cannot acquire it, and it will be unable to render this supreme service. The parable asks the community of the interim between the resurrection and the *parousia*, which might stand at any moment before the goal of creation which is the goal of its very existence, whether it will have this absolutely indispensable something. It is a matter of that which will make its witness equal to the revelation of its Lord in this decisive test, even though it may have failed a thousand times in the interval. It is a matter of the harmony in which it must find itself with Him for all its human frailty and perversity if it is to stand at His side in face of the world. What is meant is clearly the self-witness of Jesus by the Holy Spirit apprehended in faith and love. This is what founded the community of the intervening time. That is the content of its witness. This alone can give its witness vitality and strength. That is the only pledge of its hope, constant in all its inconstancy. That is the vital element in virtue of which the community can be equal to its returning Lord for all its lowliness, associating itself with Him and having a place at its side in His final revelation. The parable does not ask the community concerning its witness as such. It presupposes that it will finally be there with its lamps burning and shining. And it asks concerning the oil to furnish these lamps of witness at the decisive moment when its mission reaches its goal ; and therefore, since the goal may be reached any moment, concerning that which makes its witness possible here and now, in the interim period. What is its attitude to the source which alone can preserve it ? What is its attitude to the self-witness of Jesus now given to it by the Holy Spirit ? How about its faith in Him and love to Him ? If it lacks that which is necessary enough now but absolutely indispensable at the end, its hope will prove to be its judgment, its witness will be lacking at the very moment when its hope is on the brink of fulfilment, and it will be incapacitated at the very moment of its supreme service. Let the community see to it that it is wise and not foolish. Let it see to it that its relation to the Jesus Christ who was yesterday and is to-day is such that it can only encounter and serve as His community the One who will live and reign for ever.

The parable of the talents (Mt. 25^{14-30}) deals with the same theme, though from rather a different angle. The question is now directed more definitely to the community's present action, for the meaning and results of which it will have to account when the Lord returns. Its Lord has " (gone) into a far country " (v. 14). This is how the interim period is now described. Before His departure, however, He has given His community the care and control of His goods. In this case one is given more and another less : " to every man according to his several ability " (v. 15). But however small or great the amount entrusted, each represents the Lord in the handling of what is no less genuinely His own property and no less valuable. In all its manifold tasks, the Church has the duty of turning this property to profitable use. What is entrusted is His Gospel, and His Spirit. The interval between the resurrection and the *parousia* is the time of Jesus because it is the time of the community and its service. His final revelation will therefore be critical for His community because it will reveal that, entrusted with His Gospel and Spirit, it has really served Him. It will be admitted to the marriage feast only if it has increased in good and loyal service the comparatively few goods entrusted to it. The Word which belongs to it seeks new hearers ; it must not cease to pass it on to others. The Spirit given to it seeks new dwelling-places and new witnesses ; it must so obey the Spirit that its witness makes new dwelling-places and evolves new witnesses. This is the whole purpose of the witnessing time, the time of the Church. It is not a time when it can be content to guard and keep what it has received. Naturally it must do this too. It can hardly render its service if it fritters away its heritage. The New Testament speaks very plainly at other points about the duty of maintaining what is given in relation to the last time : " I come quickly : hold that fast which thou hast, that no man take thy crown " (Rev. 3[11]). But the parable of the talents shows us that this cannot be an end in itself. The servant who buried his talent made it safe, but did not put it to use. His conduct was not merely unprofitable, but positively lazy and wicked. It was not merely a refusal of service, but rebellion against the Lord. Thus the community which in the interim period is not a missionary community, winning others by its witness according to the measure of its power, will be banished, at the return and final revelation of the Lord, into outer darkness, where there can be only weeping and gnashing of teeth instead of the promised banquet. At the end of the time between the community will be justified before the Lord, and will stand and have a share in His glory, only if in the time between it has understood and realised that all its faith and love, all its confession and works, are nothing at all without daring and aggression, without sowing in hope, only if it has understood and practised its witness as a commission. For the time between is not the time of an empty absence of the Lord, nor is it the time of a bewildering delay in His return, in which it is enough for the community to maintain and help itself as best it can. On the contrary, it is the time of God's patience and purpose, and it is the business of the community to recognise the character of this time, and therefore never to think that it has plenty of time in this time, but to " buy up " this time in relation to those who are " without " (Col. 4[5] ; Eph. 5[16]). It can never have enough time here and now for the fulfilment of its task. For it knows what the world does not know, and it owes it to its Lord to make it known to the world. It has the light which cannot be placed under a bushel (Mt. 5[15]) but must be put in a candlestick. Note that in the series of historical signs listed in Mt. 24[6-14], the last and culminating sign is the work of the community : " And this gospel of the kingdom shall be preached in all the world for a witness unto all nations ; and then shall the end come." Whether this sign is set up or not, is the question of its present existence, addressed to it in this parable in relation to the end of time which will decide concerning it too.

The discourse on the last judgment (Mt. 25[31-46]) presses home the same question in a third form. It is the Son of Man, the Messianic King, who according to v. 31 f. will come in glory with His angels, take His seat upon His throne, gather the nations around Him, and divide them as a shepherd divides the sheep from the goats. In the centre of the picture, among all the nations, stands the community. It is asked concerning its being and conduct in this present age, again in the light of the approaching end. This community hopes for this Judge, and rightly so. As surely as it is His community, and has received His Word and His Spirit, and bears witness to Him, it expects to be identical with the flock on the right hand, and to be invited to enter the kingdom prepared for it from the foundation of the world (v. 34). How else can the community live but in this expectation ? Who but the community can do so ? But what is the community that it may enjoy this expectation ? This has not yet been decided. It will be decided when Jesus comes again : " We must *all* be made manifest before the judgment seat of Christ " (2 Cor. 5[10]). And it is from this future that the parable looks back so strikingly to the present time when Jesus is still hidden. The issue will be decided by the attitude and conduct of

the community to Him while He is still hidden. Then it will be known what
the community will be which will stand at His right hand in this future. But
where is He hidden now ? With God, at the right hand of the Father ? in His
Word and sacraments ? in the mystery of His Spirit, which bloweth where it
listeth ? All this is true enough, but it is presupposed in this parable, and the
further point is made, on which everything depends, that He is no less present,
though hidden, in all who are now hungry, thirsty, strangers, naked, sick and
in prison. Wherever in this present time between the resurrection and the
parousia one of these is waiting for help (for food, drink, lodging, clothes, a visit,
assistance), Jesus Himself is waiting. Wherever help is granted or denied, it
is granted or denied to Jesus Himself. For these are the least of His brethren.
They represent the world for which He died and rose again, with which He has
made Himself supremely one, and declared Himself in solidarity. It is for them
that He sits at the right hand of the Father, so that no one can know Him in
His majesty, or honour and love Him as the Son of God, unless he shows concern for these least of His brethren. No one can call God his Father in Christ's
name unless he treats these least as his brethren. This is the test which at the
last judgment will decide concerning the true community which will inherit
the kingdom : whether in this time of God's mercy and patience, this time of
its mission, it has been the community which has succoured its Lord by giving
unqualified succour to them in this needy world. It will be well with it if it
has obviously done this, if it has been affected by the concrete miseries of the
world, not passing by on the other side with haughty disdain, but being simply
and directly human, with no excuses for the contrary. It will then be shown
to be the community devoted to God in the person of Jesus. It will then be
found righteous at the last judgment and be able stand on the right hand as the
community which participates in the work of its Master. It is to be noted,
however, that the righteous and therefore the justified at the last judgment do
not know with whom they really have to do when they act with simple humanity
(v. 37 f.) : " When saw we thee an hungred, and fed thee . . . ? " They had
helped the least of His brethren, they had helped the world in its misery for its
own sake. They had no ulterior motive. As the true community of Jesus,
they saw the need and did what they could without any further design or
after-thoughts. They could not do their duty or fulfil their mission without
realising their solidarity with those in affliction and standing at their side.
They found themselves referred quite simply to their neighbours in the world
and that wholly " secular " affliction. They had no spiritual strategy. They
obeyed without explanations. They thus carried their lamps like the wise
virgins or the faithful stewards of the other parables. They were not occupied
with metaphysical considerations. They were simply concerned with men as
men, and therefore treated them as brothers. If they had not done so, they
could not have claimed Jesus as their Brother or God as their Father. It is
because they knew Jesus as their Brother and God as their Father that they
fed the needy, gave them drink, clothed and visited them. But did they do
this ? This is what will be revealed when Jesus returns. So will everything
they have left undone. The false community will also be revealed and rejected
and condemned for its inhumanity. Such is the question addressed to the community of the present by the approaching *parousia*. It is posed to all its members,
to its orders and cultus and preaching and theology. What has all this had to
do with the afflicted who as such are Jesus' brethren ? Has the community
been first and foremost human in all that it has done ? The question may be
comforting or disconcerting, but there can be no doubt that it is crucial, and
where it is heard it can hardly fail to be incisive and therefore admonitory.
This is the *Magna Carta* of Christian humanitarianism and Christian politics,
established not only as a promise but as a warning in view of the approaching
end—not so much because it will be the end of all things, but because it bears

the name of Jesus, who has come, and will come again.

The situation of the community in the time between, as presented in Mt. 25, may be summed up by saying that it is really the community of the last time. That is to say, it has the completion inaugurated with the resurrection of Jesus as a driving force behind it and the consummation in His *parousia* as a drawing force before it. It comes from the revelation of the man ᵗesus as it moves towards it, and it moves towards it as it comes from it. " This same Jesus, which is taken up from you into heaven, shall so come in like manner as ye have seen him go into heaven " (Ac. 1¹¹). This is what determines the whole logic and ethic of the community of the end. If we are to understand what is meant by ἄγεσθαι πνεύματι (Gal. 5¹⁸ ; Rom. 8¹⁴), by περιπατευεῖν or στοιχεῖν πνεύματι (2 Cor. 12¹⁸ ; Gal. 5¹⁶, ²⁵), it is essential that we keep in mind this double motivation of Christian existence in this intervening time. The Christ who comes again in glory is as near to His community as the Christ of the resurrection. As the risen Christ cannot fall behind it and become merely historical, so the Christ of the *parousia* cannot yield before it, so that it has only a profane and empty future not determined by Him, and its situation between the two comings can only repeat and renew itself at every moment of the continuing interim. The community lives under the lordship of Jesus in the form of the Spirit. In the Spirit that double proximity is actual presence. In the Spirit Jesus at every moment of the interim is not only at the right hand of the Father, but also here on earth. Hence the community at every moment is really His and under His lordship. " Lo, I am with you alway, even unto the completion of time " (ἕως τῆς συντελείας τοῦ αἰῶνος, Mt. 28²⁰). Two opposite but closely connected errors must be noted at this point and avoided.

The first consists in an underestimation of the majesty of Jesus in this intervening time in consequence of an underestimation of the origin of the community in His resurrection, or, as we may also say, of a failure to recognise the consolation of the Holy Spirit in whose work the community may find full satisfaction at every moment in its time of waiting. If this is not perceived, the imminent expectation in which it lives is bound to be an enigma and the " delay," the constant " non-arrival," of the *parousia* an offence. The view is thus adopted that early hopes quickly gave way to disappointment and disillusion ; that a lofty but impractical expectation was replaced by a clever adaptation to realities ; that a new and more subtle interpretation was given of the original attitude. This movement is thought to be the true secret of the New Testament consciousness of the present. And it may be recalled that there were some who thought along these lines even in the New Testament itself : " Where is the promise of his coming ? for since the fathers fell asleep, all things continue as they were from the beginning of the creation " (2 Pet. 3⁴). But the adoption of this conclusion entails the hazardous assumption that this opinion, naturally repudiated in 2 Peter, expresses the painful, laboriously suppressed, but clear and objective truth of the witness of the New Testament. If this is so, the whole of the New Testament must be expounded accordingly, as though it were really wrestling at every point with this opinion, or occupied rather feebly with this objective truth. The real witness of the Evangelists and apostles, and in the last resort Jesus Himself, is to the delay of the *parousia*, though they will not admit it. Any exposition of the New Testament running counter to this opinion (or objective truth), from the days of the apostolic fathers right down to the present, must be denounced as a dishonest and unsuccessful evasion. The one question to be asked of New Testament and theological research is whether and how far it has voluntarily or involuntarily helped to support this opinion and further exposed the insincerity of all attempts to deal with the question which are not consistently eschatological. A kind of monomania develops. Everything thought and said and written is demagogic. Pride is found in being to the whole cosmos a great and maliciously ignored source of unsettlement, and the tedium thereby caused to more usefully employed angels, men and animals is not perceived. The mistake in all this is to be found in its failure to take account of the Holy Spirit as the driving and drawing force behind the community in the time between the resurrection and the *parousia.* For through the Spirit the lordship of Jesus is never merely past or merely future. It is always present, but in such a way that we must expect His coming, indeed, His imminent coming, and yet may wait for it with patience. If this eager expectation of the *parousia* is a genuine problem in the New Testament, of crucial importance for the present, the same cannot be said of anxiety over its supposed delay or non-occurence. Regarded in the light of the New Testament teaching about the situation of the community in the last time, this anxiety bears all the marks of a pseudo-problem. The answer given in 2 Pet. 3 is just as true to-day as it was then. It is that the question comes from "mockers with mockery" (ἐν ἐμπαιγμονῇ ἐμπαῖκται v. 3). There will be plenty of them in the "last days." But they are people who do not realise (vv. 5–7) that the created world as we know it is only temporary, as the story of the flood once proved. It is moving, indeed, towards total dissolution—"reserved unto fire." The question is that of those who, for all that they are so critical when it would be better to be uncritical, are far too uncritical about their own existence and existentialist philosophy. And when Christians hear their question, they are not ignorant (v. 8) that "one day is with the Lord as a thousand years, and a thousand years as one day" (Ps. 90⁴). In God's sight—and after all they live in His sight—not only is nearness distance, but distance nearness. What are thousands and thousands of years when it is a matter of the longsuffering of God, giving us time right up to the end of time (v. 9), "not willing that any should perish, but that all should come to repentance"? It is to be noted in passing that in 1 Tim. 2⁴ the existence of the state is attributed to the same divine purpose. For Christians who remember this, can even a single day be wasted in thousands and thousands of years? Is there any cause to complain, then, at the delay of the final denouement? Have they time to worry their fellow creatures with a theology of self-satisfied complacency? No, the objective truth is very different from this theory: "The Lord is not slack concerning his promise, as some count slackness" (v. 9). The theory has to be read *into* the New Testament, for the New Testament itself contradicts it both implicitly and explicitly. Only if it is read in can it have any importance for an understanding of the New Testament awareness of the present. And it needs only little experience of the consolation of the Holy Spirit to make this understanding completely impossible.

The opposite error consists in an exaggerated estimate of the greatness of the community in consequence of an equally exaggerated estimate of its present existence in relation to the *parousia*, or, as we may also say, of a failure to recognise the criticism of the Holy Spirit, whose work keeps the community moving towards its Lord in dissatisfaction with its present condition, preventing it from regarding its condition as absolute. When this is not perceived, the community—or the "Church" as it loves to call itself—forgets that it is on the march, and that though the inauguration of Jesus' revelation of His glory is behind it, the consummation is still to come. It secretly anticipates the change of front foretold in Mt. 25 and 1 Thess., when at the end of time it will stand at the side of its Lord before the world. It is not content to be a handmaid like the virgins at the marriage feast, but obviously behaves as if the *causa Dei* were in its own hands. Instead of bearing witness to the authority of Jesus, it invests itself with His authority, attributing absolute perfection to its order and ministry and cultus and dogma, and interpreting historical evolution as the automatic development of the divine truth incarnate in itself. Thus at each successive stage of its development it acts and speaks as if it were itself permitted and commanded to blow the last trumpet now. Its doctrine at any given moment is the normative voice of Jesus and His apostles. Its tradition perpetuates the original apostolic witness, claiming equal dignity and attention. Its particular interpretation of the original witness is the authentic interpretation. Its divine commission is the basis of a claim made in its own favour. But in these circumstances, what place is there for Christian hope ? In what sense are we still in an intervening time, still waiting for the consummated revelation ? Has it not been realised already in the being and activity of the Church ? Is there any need for the risen Lord to come again ? Is there any more embracing form of His presence and power than that taken already by the Church itself ? In 1944 the Congregation of the Sacred Office passed a remarkable resolution to the effect that belief in a visible second coming could " not be taught as a certainty "—the very thing which for the New Testament is the greatest certainty of all on the basis of the resurrection. On this view, all we have left to hope for is the golden lining of a future heavenly glory. And even this is under the control and apparently belongs to the sphere of the Church on earth, with its indulgences, its merited assurances and guarantees, its purchased rights, its express beatifications and canonisations. Certainly there can be no place for a Judge who will confront the Church itself in sovereignty and whom it is bound to fear. If He comes at all, it will be to judge the world for persecuting and oppressing the poor Church in time, for resisting and ignoring it. The Church itself will stand triumphant at His right hand, self-evidently before the judgments have even begun. The future at the end of time will simply be the confirmation of its own present and distinctive perfection. The true and divine safeguard against the real threat of Christian arrogance and pride and sloth and obstinacy has been abandoned. The Church on earth, with its power to change bread and wine into the body of Christ, and to effect this in daily sacrifice, with its infallible teaching office, its Virgin Mary already ascended into heaven, is itself already on the throne with the returning Lord. What need is there then for His return ? And how can it take place in this time that judgment begins at the house of God (1 Pet. 4[17]) ? It is obviously treason even to contemplate the mere possibility. The Church has completely forgotten Mt. 25, and the Seven Letters of the Apocalypse. Yet in these Letters it is not just fallible Christian men but the very angels of the churches who are summoned to judgment at the *parousia.* And what about the prophetic word of the Old Testament, which as such, in its reference to the Lord coming to judgment, is addressed with unparalleled severity, not to the world but typically to the elect people of God with its temples and priests and authorised sacrifices ? This is the " de-eschatologising " of Christianity with a vengeance ! This is real obstinacy in face of the critical power of the lordship of Jesus Christ in the form of the Holy Spirit. The Church of Rome is the typical form of this de-eschatologised Christianity. But there are also Protestant, Anglican and other versions. Wherever the Church entertains an exaggerated estimate of itself, the same error is at work in its opposite form. For in both cases it is Jesus Himself who is absent, the Lord of the Church who as such is the Lord of time. In the first case He is absent because there is no recognition of the consoling power of His resurrection for the present life of the community. In the second He is absent because no serious account is taken of His future and its critical power for the present life of the community. And as His future is also denied in the one, His presence is also missed in the other, being identified with that of the community. The one error leads to the other. If the community of the last time is already seated on the throne of Christ, it is high time to say that His return is not to be expected. And if that is not to be expected, it is quite in order to look for a self-sufficient community which can dispense with this expectation. But if we are to follow the New Testament, we must resist both errors with the same determination. [III, 2, pp. 493-511]